EMPIRICAL FOUNDATIONS OF INFORMATION AND SOFTWARE SCIENCE IV

Empirical Methods of Evaluation of Man-Machine Interfaces

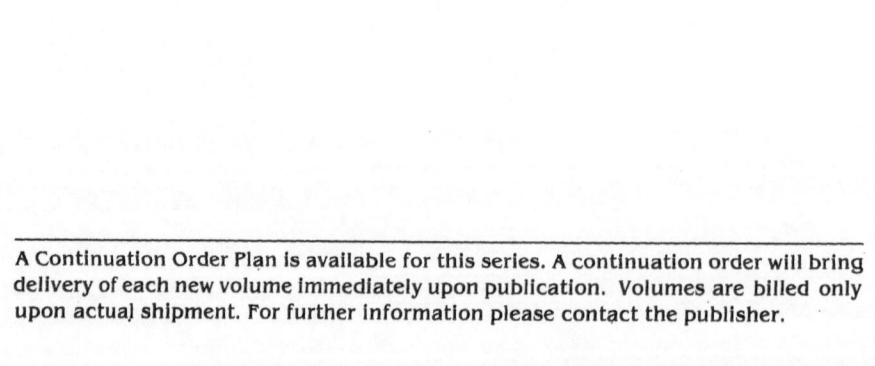

EMPIRICAL FOUNDATIONS OF INFORMATION AND SOFTWARE SCIENCE IV

Empirical Methods of Evaluation of Man–Machine Interfaces

Edited by
Pranas Zunde
School of Information and Computer Science
Georgia Institute of Technology
Atlanta, Georgia

and
Jagdish C. Agrawal
Embry-Riddle Aeronautical University
Daytona, Florida

PLENUM PRESS • NEW YORK AND LONDON

Library of Congress Cataloging in Publication Data

Symposium on Empirical Foundations of Information and Software Science (4th: 1986:
Atlanta, Ga.)
    Empirical foundations of information and software science IV.

    "Proceedings of the Fourth Symposium on Empirical Foundations of Information and
Software Science, held October 22–24, 1986 in Atlanta, Georgia"—T.p. verso.
    Bibliography: p.
    Includes indexes.
    1. Electronic data processing—Congresses. 2. Computer software—Congresses. 3.
Man–machine systems—Congresses. I. Zunde, Pranas, 1923-   . II. Agrawal, Jagdish C.
III. Title.
QA75.5.S956   1986   005.3   87-36060
ISBN-13: 978-1-4684-5474-1   e-ISBN-13: 978-1-4684-5472-7
DOI: 10.1007/978-1-4684-5472-7

Proceedings of the Fourth Symposium on Empirical Foundations
of Information and Software Science,
held October 22-24, 1986, in Atlanta, Georgia

© 1987 Plenum Press, New York
Softcover reprint of the hardcover 1st edition 1987

A Division of Plenum Publishing Corporation
233 Spring Street, New York, N.Y. 10013

SYMPOSIUM ADVISORY COMMITTEE

Dr. Harold Bamford, National Science Foundation; Joseph P. Cavano, Rome Air Development Center; Dr. William Curtis, Microelectronics and Computer Technology Corporation; Dr. James W. Gault, U. S. Army European Research Office; Dr. John J. O'Hare, Office of Naval Research; John R. Mitchell, U. S. Army Institute for Research in Management Information, Communications, and Computer Sciences; Dr. Edward C. Weiss, Essex Corporation.

SYMPOSIUM ORGANIZING COMMITTEE

Dr. Jagdish C. Agrawal, Embry-Riddle Aeronautical University, Daytona, Florida; Jens Rasmussen, Riso National Laboratory, Roskilde, Denmark; Dr. William B. Rouse, Dr. Valdimir Slamecka, and Dr. Pranas Zunde (chairman), all from Georgia Institute of Technology, Atlanta, Georgia.

The organizers gratefully acknowledge partial funding of the symposium by the U. S. Army Institute for Research in Management Information, Communications, and Computer Sciences, Atlanta, Georgia.

v

CONTENTS

3. USER-SYSTEM INTERFACE EVALUATION

4. USER-SYSTEM INTERACTION

5. INFORMATION SYSTEM DESIGN AND DEVELOPMENT

6. SOFTWARE ENGINEERING

7. SOFTWARE AND SYSTEM PERFORMANCE EVALUATION

8. SOFTWARE TRANSITION TOOLS AND TECHNIQUES

9. INFORMATION, KNOWLEDGE, AND VALUE

10. WORKSHOPS

INTRODUCTION

The purpose of the symposia on Empirical Foundations of Information and Software Sciences (EFISS) is to explore subjects and methods of scientific inquiry which are of common interest to these two disciplines, and to identify directions of inquiry that will benefit from their mutual interaction. Authors contributing papers to the symposia are at liberty to address any aspect of the empirical foundations such as measurement theory and techniques in information and software sciences, methods of experimental design, empirical laws and theories, validation and verification of empirical laws, requirements for data bases to support experimentation, and evaluation of software properties. But over and above that, each symposium has a main theme to focus on. The main theme of this Fourth Symposium of Empirical Foundations of Information and Software Sciences was Empirical Methods of Evaluation of Human-Machine Interfaces.

A total of 36 papers were presented at the 4th EFISS Symposium, of which 18 papers, including six of the seven invited papers, were on the subject of the main theme. The invited presentations dealt with the following: balancing efficiency and effectiveness in interactive design and evaluation of human-machine interfaces (William B. Rouse); research priorities for the psychology of human-computer interaction (John M. Carroll and Robert L. Campbell); design and evaluation of human-machine interfaces based on models of the task domain and the actual requirements of the user-task interaction (Annelise Mark Pejtersen and Jens Rasmussen); development of a theory of human-machine interaction in the process of design of interface systems (Gerhard Fischer, paper not included in the Proceedings); optimization of human-machine interfaces and the role of concurrent computation for machines that are intended to provide their operators with decision-support and other capabilities that are normally believed to require intelligence (Howard L. Resnikoff); and an overview of issues in the evaluation of natural language interfaces to expert systems (Ralph M. Weischedel).

Significant contributions to the state-of-the-art of the evaluation of human-machine interfaces were made also by contributed papers exploring topics such as evaluation of formal specifications for user interfaces; application of operation research models to the study of complex human-machine interfaces; analysis of interface specifications using software complexity measures; evaluation of psychological consistency of interface models; evaluation of design decisions for human-machine interfaces using a design tool for interactive programs (DIADES); empirical results of field studies of human-machine interaction in natural language with English and German interface systems; evaluation of adaptive user interfaces for information systems; criteria and techniques for objective measurement of user's reactions in the evaluation of human-machine interfaces; and methodologies and techniques for human-machine interface evaluation.

1

Other contributed papers addressed various empirical aspects of information system design and development, software engineering, software and system performance evaluation, software transitioning tools and techniques as well as certain foundational problems associated with information, knowledge, and value.

An essential component of the program of the Symposium were two Workshops on Research Directions and Opportunities in Information and Software Sciences. In the first of the two workshops, current research support programs and research opportunities were described and discussed by representatives of granting agencies participating in the Symposium, i.e., the National Science Foundation (NSF), the Air Force Office of Scientific Research (AFOSR), the Army Research Institute (ARI), the Army Institute for Research in Management Information, Communications, and Computer Sciences (AIRMICS).

In the second workshop, promising research directions and open research problems were discussed in a panel session, members of which were the invited speakers. There was also a very active participation of other participants and attendees in the open floor discussions which followed both workshops.

The last event of the Symposium was a panel discussion on the main theme of the Fifth EFISS Symposium to be held November 23-25, 1987, at the Riso National Laboratory in Roskilde, Denmark. The theme selected for that symposium was From Data to Models: Modelling Advanced Information Processing Systems.

We conclude this introduction with the same observation, which we made in earlier symposia of this series: the contributions of many -- invited speakers, authors of papers, session chairs, workshop panelists, members of the Organizing and Advisory Committees, sponsoring organizations -- made the Fourth Symposium on Empirical Foundations of Information and Software Sciences another great success. There was a common agreement that such interdisciplinary conferences are essential for a vigorous and healthy development of these two disciplines.

Last, but not least, our special thanks to two key persons, without whose assistance the job of the editors would have been much more difficult: Mrs. Angela R. DuBose of Georgia Institute of Technology, who word-processed the entire manuscript of the proceedings, and Mr. John Matzka of the Plenum Publishing Corporation, who assisted in getting the figures and tables in a form ready for publication and also advised us on many other technical matters of editing.

Pranas Zunde

Jagdish C. Agrawal

SYMPOSIUM OPENING ADDRESSES

WELCOMING ADDRESS BY DR. LES A. KARLOVITZ, DEAN, COLLEGE OF
SCIENCE AND LIBERAL STUDIES, GEORGIA INSTITUTE OF TECHNOLOGY

It is my pleasure to welcome all of you to the fourth Symposium on the
Empirical Foundations of Information and Software Sciences. It is a particular pleasure because the symposium is being co-sponsored by Georgia
Tech and the U.S. Army Institute for Research in Management Information,
Communications, and Computer Sciences, because a number of colleagues from
the campus have put a large effort into the symposium, and, finally, because
as a mathematician who represents the <u>analytical</u> side of science, I feel
honored to be part of a symposium dedicated to the <u>empirical</u> side. I admire
your field of endeavor. You research the human-technology interface in
areas wherein man is engaged in some of his most esoteric cognitive and
creative functions and wherein the capabilities of the machines are evolving
at a staggering rate. You are, indeed, taking on a very great challenge.

In perusing the titles of the papers and sessions of this symposium
and some of the papers from past symposia, I find an impressive range of
topics from the speculative to the applied. I also noted that the participants represent a very desirable mixture of industry, academia, and
government. I congratulate the organizers for their work.

Like you who are participating in the symposium, Georgia Tech strives
to be at the leading edge of information and software sciences, both in
research and application. Thus, we welcome you as kinsmen and have high
expectations for your contributions.

Finally, I note that this is the third time that the symposium has
been held at Georgia Tech. In fact, this makes three times out of four. I
hope that you will return many more times in the future.

My best wishes for a productive symposium and pleasant stay in Atlanta.

Thank you.

WELCOMING ADDRESS BY JOHN R. MITCHELL, DIRECTOR, THE U.S.
ARMY INSTITUTE FOR RESEARCH IN MANAGEMENT INFORMATION,
COMMUNICATIONS, AND COMPUTER SCIENCES

It is my pleasure to welcome you on behalf of the Army Institute for
Research in Management Information, Communications, and Computer Sciences
(AIRMICS). AIRMICS and Georgia Tech co- sponsored the first and second
EFISS symposia and I am pleased that we can co-sponsor this fourth symposium.

There is a real need for the development of theories and models of information processing that can only be validated through the collection and
analysis of experimental data. By bringing together a variety of disciplines
and emphasizing empirical foundations, this symposium helps fulfill that
need and promotes the sharing of research results and data.

The Army has undergone considerable change during the past two years.
In 1984, the Army Communications Command and the Army Computer Systems
Command merged to form the Army Information Systems Command with the mission
to merge technologies in communications, data processing, office automation,
printing and publications, and audiovisual areas. The Information Systems
Command engineers, designs, installs, operates, and maintains these systems
and is responsible for world wide information management and transfer.

To accomplish this mission, the Information Systems Command (ISC) has
about 40,000 people in 14 countries with 1,500 facilities worldwide and a $2
Billion plus annual budget. AIRMICS is part of the Information Systems
Engineering Command, a major subcommand of ISC, with research responsibilities supporting all ISC elements.

The Army has realized the value of information and the need to manage
and provide information to decision makers at all levels, not as a by-product
of information systems, but as their primary goal.

From the success of the first three symposia, the quality of the papers
and workshop sessions, your participation and the support of participating
organizations, it is very easy to predict that this symposium will make
significant contributions in the information and software sciences.

Thank you.

WELCOMING ADDRESS BY DR. RAYMOND E. MILLER
DIRECTOR OF THE SCHOOL OF INFORMATION AND COMPUTER SCIENCE
GEORGIA INSTITUTE OF TECHNOLOGY

On behalf of the School of Information and Computer Science and Georgia Tech I am happy to welcome you to this Fourth Symposium on Empirical Foundations of Information and Software Sciences. We are very pleased to be able to host the symposium here at Georgia Tech, and I am particularly pleased with the leading organizational role that Dr. Pranas Zunde, of our faculty, has been taking in these conferences.

The particular topic of this conference, the interface between the computer and the human, is a major area requiring further study and development. Computers have found their way into all parts of our society. Even though great improvements have been made in how an individual can effectively interact with the computing and information processing technology to better perform the desired tasks, much remains to be accomplished. I like to use the term "transparency" in what is often desired for the man-machine interface. By this, I mean that individuals should be able to do their jobs in much the same way as before, but, yet have the assistance of the computing technology to more effectively perform the job, without diverting attention to the computing task rather than the primary job to be performed. Admittedly, it is often advantageous to use the technology in a way that requires a different form of user interaction, but, this should be so only if there are distinct advantages in doing so. A favorite example of mine concerning "transparency" is the driving of a new car. Almost all new cars have computing devices incorporated into them to provide a more efficient utilization of the engine, and to measure, control, and display various parameters. Yet, the driver is essentially unaware of the use of this technology. The method of driving the car is basically the same as before, and, thus, the embedded computer hardware and software is "transparent" to the driver. A major challenge is to extend such ease of interaction, or "transparency of use", to an ever increasing complexity of environments and systems. I would hope that this Symposium would provide a stepping stone to furthering the understanding of the problems and potential approaches for improved man-machine interfaces.

In closing, let me welcome you again, especially all of our international participants. We hope you enjoy the symposium and that you will have some extra time while here to enjoy Atlanta and other parts of Georgia before you leave.

1. USER-SYSTEM INTERFACES: KEY ISSUES

SOFTENING UP HARD SCIENCE: REPLY TO NEWELL AND CARD

John M. Carroll and Robert L. Campbell

User Interface Institute
IBM Thomas J. Watson Research Center
P.O. Box 218
Yorktown Heights, New York 10598

Abstract: A source of intellectual overhead periodically encountered by
scientists is the call to be "hard", to insure good science by imposing
severe methodological strictures. Newell and Card (1985) have undertaken to
impose such strictures on the psychology of human-computer interaction.
Although their discussion contributes to theoretical debate in human-computer interaction by setting a reference point, their specific argument
fails. Their program is unmotivated, is severely limited, and suffers from
these limitations in principle. A top priority for the psychology of
human-computer interaction should be the articulation of an alternative
explanatory program, one that takes as its starting point the need to understand the real problems involved in providing better computer tools for
people to use.

1. NEWELL AND CARD ON BEING HARD

Newell and Card (1985) have presented a program for psychological
research in human-computer interaction couched as an analysis of how psychology can avoid being "driven out" of human-computer interaction. Their
touchstone is an analog to Gresham's Law: "Hard science drives out the
soft.". They argue that only by hardening up the psychology of human-
computer interaction can psychology avoid being driven out by "harder"
disciplines in computer science. Newell and Card define their program in
terms of three key features: task analysis, calculation, and approximation
(Newell and Card, 1985, p. 215). Their objective is to provide fine-grained
analyses of user tasks in terms of numerical parameters so as to afford the
calculation of specific predictions. Because of the complexity of real
human thought and action, these calculations must be approximate.

In this reply, we press the invocation of the original Gresham's Law:
"Bad money drives out the good.". Or more strictly: Overvalued money
drives out undervalued money. The appropriate response, of course, is not
to learn to live with overvalued money but to see to it that undervalued
money is valued at its true worth--or to change the system that produces
these distortions of value in the first place. Newell and Card may be
correct in worrying that hard science could drive out soft science, examining
that approximative calculation could undermine conceptual and explanatory

---

*Reprinted with permission from Journal of Human Computer Interactions,
Vol. 2, No. 3, 1986, pp. 227-249.

science. The appropriate course of action, we argue, is to redress distortions in value, not to accommodate them; to protect and develop conceptually deep science, not to abandon it.

For the sake of this discussion, we need to address two potential confusions. The first pertains to the use of the term "hard science". This is a loaded term. In adopting it, Newell and Card place alternative programs in the position of advocating "soft science". Not only do we find Newell and Card's conception of "hard science" problematic, their use of the term clouds questions about theory and method with irrelevant value connotations. The second confusion derives from the contrast between Newell and Card's program and the earlier research monograph of Card, Moran, and Newell (1983). Where the Newell and Card paper is a broadly couched program for psychology in human-computer interaction, the Card et al. monograph is a tightly focused research project. Where Newell and Card focus on implications for interface design. Card et al. focused on research and approached design cautiously and peripherally. Finally, the Newell and Card essay is situated in the mid-1980s where the Card et al. work was undertaken in the mid-1970's.

We are uncomfortable with the "hard science" terminology, but we feel that we have inherited it from Newell and Card (1985) in this debate. We are also uncomfortable making too sharp a distinction between Newell and Card (1985) and Card et al. (1983). Both approaches use a simplified information processing box diagram of human cognition, called the Model Human Processor, and a family of models for approximative calculation of human performance times, called GOMS (an acronym for the key components of the models: goals, operators, methods and selection rules.) Yet it seems to us very different to speak of GOMS as a specific technical innovation in the human factors of computing systems (circa 1976), and GOMS as a prescriptive program for what can count as scientific psychology in human-computer interaction (circa 1985). The former we recognize as a foundational contribution to human-computer interaction; the latter we see as limiting and mistaken. Moreover, specific features of Card et al.'s research approach are eliminated from Newell and Card's program; chief among these is the detailed, qualitative analysis of behavioral and thinking-aloud protocols. We have respected this contrast by limiting our own use of Card et al.'s terminology (such as GOMS) when discussing Newell and Card.

Our argument takes the following course. First, we examine the motivation for Newell and Card's hard science program. We try to show how they misrepresent the current role of human factors in system design, the nature of theory in computer science, and the design process itself. Against a background of progress in human-computer interaction, they dismiss current human factors practice as a failure, without identifying its genuine strengths and weaknesses. They portray computer science theory as hard, when virtually no aspect of computer science theory involves calculation or approximation in their sense. They present no design-scale success stories of their approach, but merely invoke the term "design" and a limited view of what design is like and how it really works. The conclusion we draw is that the need Newell and Card imagine for their hard science simply does not exist.

Second, we examine their responses to existing criticisms of their approach. We show how these responses fail to answer the criticisms and how they are mutually contradictory. Their reply to the charge that their hard science it too low-level to redefine "psychology", so that it will perfectly coextend with their enterprise, leaving critics to attack psychology itself and not them. Their reply to the charge that their hard science is too limited in scope is to assimilate a variety of current work (much of it not so low-level) to their enterprise merely by saying "it fills out our 'vision'". (These two replies contradict each other.) Their reply to the charge that hard science is chronically too late to help in the development of new technology is to argue that interface technology is elaborated far more slowly than is commonly thought. Finally, their reply to the criticism that their hard science is too difficult to apply is merely to suggest that we look for better opportunities to apply it. The conclusion we draw is that these criticisms identify true limitations on Newell and Card's approach.

Finally, we examine Newell and Card's research program in terms of its underlying methodological and theoretical commitments. The lack of adequate motivation for their proposals and the serious limitations on their scope and applicability suggest an underlying scientific agenda that goes beyond their official program of task analysis, calculation, and approximation: a view of task analysis as pure description; a conception of tasks as analyzable into highly isolable subtasks; and a conception of hard science as working with interval measurable quantities only. These underlying views are problematic in their own right (even as an understanding of hard science), and would require us to discard most of the information that psychology can render. The stereotype of hard science that underlies their program (a form of positivism) imposes limits on the scope of psychology needlessly and without basis. If adopted, this program would produce a sterile discipline of human-computer interaction that would satisfy neither psychologists nor system designers.

2. NEWELL AND CARD MISREPRESENT THE STATUS QUO

2.1 Misrepresenting Human Factors

Newell and Card claim that the available roles for human factors professionals are few and unsatisfying: in human factors, one can offer human factors guidelines or maxims, or one can build calculational performance models. Newell and Card dismiss human factors guidelines as vacuous and imply that computer scientists will ignore them. They regard their style of hard science as highly informative and imply that computer scientists will be eager to use it. These are debatable claims. To begin with, there are other roles that human factors professionals can fill. In particular, they can be members of a design team (practicing iterative behavioral testing in context of rapid prototyping). Newell and Card do not acknowledge published case studies of how the iterative measurement approach, in the context of prototyping, has guided the design of usable interfaces (e.g., Kelley, 1984; Good, Whiteside, Wixon, and Jones, 1984; Boies, Gould, Levy, Richards, and Schoonard, 1985). A view of human factors work that overlooks such roles, and the degree of cooperation between psychology and computer science inherent in them, is seriously incomplete.

Newell and Card portray usability guidelines as vacuous, common sense maxims like "Communicate with metaphors" (Newell and Card, 1985, p. 213). This maxim, like many others, however, has falsifiable empirical content. The designers of Apple Lisa followed this maxim. Specifically, they used the metaphor of a desktop. It turns out, however, that professionals learning to use the Lisa are sometimes confused about the referent of "top of the desktop" (The screen after all is flat). Users are also confused by the fine distinction the metaphor makes between "stationery pads" and "stationery paper", and about the function of "folders" (Carroll and Mazur, 1985). The guideline that Newell and Card cite has empirical content, and our examples show that the guideline needs to be revised and made more specific. We are accordingly skeptical of Newell and Card's unqualified claim that guidelines derive "from a little common sense, plus placing value on serving the user well" (Newell and Card, 1985, p. 214). It would be useful to see this claim argued in more detail against a comprehensive corpus of guidelines like Smith and Mosier (1984).

As Newell and Card have underestimated the potential importance of iterative measurement in the context of prototyping and of guidelines, they may have overestimated the potential role of calculational performance models. The considerable human factors tradition of predictive models of human performance on control tasks (such as the optimal control model; Pew and Baron,1978) has been most successful in analyzing tasks that afford little user discretion (e.g., continuous response as opposed to decision), and experience with these models has shown that aggregated predictions at higher levels of behavior organization, in fact, depend little on low-level modeling structures (Pew & Baron, 1983). Newell and Card are concerned with modeling task environments that incorporate decision making and explicitly assume that low-level modeling can fix aggregated predictions at higher levels (Newell and Card, 1985, p. 227). In summary, neither the history of human factors nor the nature of current progress in it supports the mono-lithic program of Newell and Card.

2.2 Misrepresenting Computer Science

Newell and Card portray computer science as hard, and, therefore, unreceptive to a psychology that is not also hard. In some sense this is true: systems work in computer science is a design domain; its results are codified in designs and implementations, and to that extent it produces hard results. Psychology is part natural science and part social science, but it is not a design science. Psychologists study minds; they don't build minds (of course Artificial Intelligence tries to be a design science in just this sense). However, Newell and Card do not primarily intend the contrast between hard and soft as a stand-in for the design science/natural science contrast (as they make clear in their remarks about rapid proto-typing) (Newell and Card, 1985, p. 213). There are two other senses of "hard" to consider: (1) science that seeks to provide formal descriptions whose properties can thereby be analyzed further, and (2) science that seeks to provide tools for approximative calculation. Plainly, these need not be the same.

Newell and Card list examples in making the claim that computer science is hard: "compiler construction, parsing, program specification, correctness proofs, denotational semantics..." (Newell and Card, 1985, p. 213). This work is hard science in the first sense, but not in the second. Indeed, mathematical modeling in computer science rarely traffics in numbers or in interval measurements: it works with other abstract structures in mathe-matics. Parsing theory, theories of compiler construction, and semantics for programming languages are hard in the ordinary sense, but not in Newell and Card's restricted sense. Algebraic semantics for programming languages do not generate quantitative predictions; the activity that goes on in this area consists of proving theorems and exploring properties of formal systems (Guessarian, 1981). Newell and Card do not produce a single example of computer science research that is hard in their restricted sense, (2) above.

Other areas of computer science that Newell and Card cite, such as structured programming and artificial intelligence (Newell and Card, 1985, pp. 213-214) are not hard in any sense. They are conceptual, in fact, psychologically conceptual. Structured programming, as well as recent de-velopments in object-oriented languages (e.g., Smalltalk), knowledge engi-neering languages (e.g., Prolog) and interface toolkits, have emerged in response to usability issues in programming itself. Psychological concerns (at least implicit ones) under the current concern in computer science is with making programs easier to inspect, more modular, and more reusable. All of these demands stem from what programmers need in order to do their work better. They are not pure computer science, because they are not strictly necessary for programs to get the job done: automata theory guarantees that if a program can be written at all, a flat, unstructured program (without subroutines!) will always get the job done.

The interdisciplinary thrust of some of these new areas of computer science is problematic for Newell and Card's "hard science" thesis. For example, they allude to work on intelligent interfaces in a strangely exaggerated manner: "if the interface is intelligent, then it is not necessary to know anything about the user, because the interface will be able to interact with the user intelligently" (Newell and Card, 1985, p. 214). Clearly, the limited, and often toy-scale, examples of intelligence now available in demonstration systems have not eliminated the need for us to know how users think. And much current thinking in AI holds that the interface will not be able to "interact with the user intelligently" unless it also has means of finding out what the user really knows; this endeavor will rely on psychological theories of knowledge (Carroll and McKendree, 1986; Goldstein, 1982). In another example, they characterize rapid prototyping as a "panacea" that "bypasses the need to know anything about the human" (Newell and Card, 1985, p. 213). However, one of the chief impacts of rapid prototyping is that it affords iterative measurement of usability within the software development process (e.g., Richards, Boies, and Gould, 1986). It thus belongs to the same family of usability motivated developments in computer science as structured programming and object-oriented languages.

We suspect that it is a fundamental mistake to analyze the differences between psychology and computer science in terms of their methodological credentials, in terms of "hard" and "soft". Psychology and computer science are both broad and fragmented disciplines, and simple bases for global comparisons between them should be treated with skepticism.

2.3 Misrepresenting System Design

Newell and Card argue that the psychology of human-computer interaction must become harder in order to establish and maintain a role for itself in interface design. However, they provide almost no analysis of either the specific nature of current barriers to psychology in interface design work or of specific benefits that would accrue from adopting their program. To establish that problems exist they cite one newsletter (Human Factors Society Bulletin) article complaining that things should be better. They fail to discuss any of several analytical case studies of new roles and new successes for psychological applications in interface design (e.g., Good, et al., 1984; Boies et al., 1985). They also fail to show how their hard science approach could guide the development of advanced workstations and new applications.

In fact, Newell and Card's optimism about the utility of hard science for system design seems based on an oversimplified model of the system design process. They model design as a process with fixed, antecedently clear goals, a process consisting of top-down refinement only. "The designer searches (the design) space by successive refinements of the initial partial representation" (Newell and Card, 1985, p. 223). Their diagram (Newell and Card, 1985, p. 224) does not provide for iteration, although it is a defining characteristic of design; it completely ignores the redefinition or discovery of goals that often occurs in the design process (Carroll and Rosson, 1985; Dreyfus, 1953). Even Jeffries, Turner, Polson, and Atwood (1981), working with Simon's (1973) top-down approach, found extensive trial-and-error activity in the design process. Newell and Card have abandoned the caution displayed by Card et al. (1983, p. 406), who stated that "design is an open process, in the sense that the design problem is constantly being redefined".

A specific assumption that Newell and Card make is that design trade-offs can be computed. They assert that only when design trade-offs can be computed will usability trade-offs be considered in system design, giving as an example the trade-off "between the effort to learn a complex interface and the power of having it" (Newell and Card, 1985, p. 222). Unfortunately, they give no indication of how such a trade-off would be calculated, and, indeed, it would appear to lie beyond the purview of performance time models (requiring models of the process of problem-solving, and of learning and motivation, as well as longitudinal studies of learning and performance patterns in a naturalistic setting). Even if Newell and Card could provide a real worked-out example, they would still need to show why it is important to quantify given trade-offs: these are frequently not quantified in branches of engineering like civil engineering that draw on hard science bases far more well-developed than those of either psychology or computer science.

A key limitation on an approach that focuses on quantitative trade-offs are the many discontinuities in usability effects. Small differences in interfaces often cause large differences in usability. For example, altering semantic and structural relations between command names may have no impact whatsoever on keystrokes or other quantitative measurements of errorless expert performance, but may cause specific and recurrent errors (in one case of this type, Carroll (1982) reported 7-fold differences in error rate, persisting through repeated learning trials; see Buxton (1986) for discussion of related phenomena pertaining to input devices). Also, in the many case studies Newell and Card do not cite, discuss, or show how details matter (Boies et al., 1985; Good et al., 1984).

In criticizing Newell and Card's representation of the status quo in human factors, computer science, and system design, we do not wish to imply that there are no problems. We agree with Newell and Card that systems designers do not always pay enough attention to usability issues. However, as we have noted above, Newell and Card have not demonstrated that the reason for this lies in presenting concepts and qualitative relations rather than numbers or that the remedy lies in approximative calculations of expert performance times. In fact, Newell and Card themselves raise and discuss four important criticisms of their program.

3. NEWELL AND CARD FAIL TO ANSWER THEIR CRITICS

Newell and Card devote more than half their paper to defending their program against four fundamental criticisms, namely that it is too low-level, too limited in scope, too late, and too difficult to apply to provide any real science base or leverage in system design. We claim they fail to answer any of the four criticisms in a satisfactory manner. Indeed, the very manner in which they try to address these criticisms shows how well founded they are.

3.1 Being Too Low-Level

Newell and Card respond to the criticism that their approach is too low-level (concerned only with keystrokes and unit tasks) by claiming that psychology itself is very low-level. Indeed, they seek to redefine psychology so that it becomes coextensive with the range of phenomena that their approach is able to handle. The basis for this redefinition can be found at the beginning of the article: "the hard science will tend to be used and the soft science ignored, regardless of whether all of the important issues are within the scope of the hard science" (Newell and Card 1985, p. 211). The problem with their response is not only that many important issues in psychology lie outside the scope of their hard science, but that the way that they have chosen to define the scope of hard science is not coherent.

Newell and Card (1985, p. 225) propose a classification of mental processes in terms of time bands or time scales of human action. From short duration to long, these are: the domain of natural law, the domain of psychology, the domain of bounded rationality, and the social/organizational domain. (Historically, this scheme seems derived from Newell and Simon's (1972) notion of "cycle time", a notion that succeeding work in cognitive psychology has made little use of.) Newell and Card define "psychology" in terms of the temporal durations of the events that it studies. (We will call their low-level psychology "psychology*" so as not to presume any connection with the scientific domain of psychology as normally understood.) The scope of psychology* is processes ranging from 1/10 second to 10 seconds (Newell and Card, 1985, p. 225). This happens to be the same range of low-level processes as those Newell and Card seek to account for: the basic operators of GOMS vary from 1/2 to 2 seconds in duration (Newell and Card, 1985, p. 217).

Newell and Card's redefinition of psychology raises many new questions. To begin with, duration seems to be an incoherent basis for individuating mental processes into natural kinds. Learning, for instance, may happen quickly or slowly. If we are to understand learning, we had better examine longer- as well as shorter-term examples of it. In Newell and Card's time band of bounded rationality "human activity is described by the goals or ends being attempted" (Newell and Card, 1985, p. 225). This conflates goals, which on many analyses are an inherent part of all cognitive processes, with conscious deliberation, which their examples of bounded rationality all seem to involve. Indeed, most of the processes studied by cognitive psychologists lie outside of psychology* in the bounded rationality and social/organizational time bands. The larger tasks that people do with computers (tasks that they define for themselves, or plan in terms of, like writing letters) cover much longer spans of time than psychology*. Learning and exploring a computing system or an application, and developing serious expertise, can take weeks or months. Perception is also important to human-computer interaction, but much of it lies outside psychology* too, in the natural law time band.

After redefining the scope of psychology to suit the narrow horizons of their style of modeling, Newell and Card have little to say about the consequences of rethinking the scope of the science. They cast aspersions on the quality of all undertakings outside of psychology*: "scientific psychology seems to traffic heavily at the low end of things" (Newell and Card, 1985, p. 225), whereas everything else is "pop psychology" and unfounded speculation. In a single dictum, they implicitly dismiss organizational, social, and developmental psychology along with a substantial part of cognitive psychology, ignoring the genuine research successes in all of those areas. The only argument they raise for confining attention to psychology* is a reductionist one:

"New psychological laws of information processing do not arise at longer durations. There are, instead, the accumulated effects of long-term memory and skill acquisition.... New psychological phenomena occur as time increases, but their theoretical explanation is to be found in the interplay of the limited processing mechanisms of the psychological band (that is, psychology*) and the

19

user's intendedly rational endeavors." (Newell and Card, 1985, p. 227).

As a programmatic claim, this is highly dubious (indeed, see Section 2.1 above and Pew and Baron, 1982). Even if true, it is virtually irrelevant to applied work. If the derived phenomena are important for understanding human-computer interaction, then modeling efforts will have to focus on them and not on the supposedly basic phenomena studied by psychology*.

Newell and Card's redefinition of psychology is irrelevant to the question of whether the range of phenomena they address are too low-level to help analyze the interesting problems of human-computer interaction that motivated the enterprise in the first place. Changing the name of the domain of endeavor cannot save it from being too low-level. What we need instead is a demonstration that the reductionist analysis can be carried out.

3.2 Being Too Limited

Newell and Card's approach has often been criticized for having too limited a scope (Shneiderman, 1984). Its prime application has been to predict the performance times of highly skilled users on line editors (Card et al., 1983). Providing a conceptual account of the structure and genesis of user error (i.e., beyond error times and frequencies) is beyond its capabilities (e.g., Robertson, 1983). Providing an analysis of people's problem solving activities is beyond its capabilities (Card et al., 1983; Polson, 1986). Newell and Card's response to this criticism is to claim that a vast amount of current research in cognitive science -- none of it explicitly related to their program -- is in fact filling out their "vision". For example, Newell and Card assimilate Anderson's (1983) ACT* model as filling out their vision in the areas of problem-solving and memory. Newell and Card's vision is so expandable that any area in cognitive psychology can be annexed by fiat (Newell and Card, 1985, p. 230). Whereas elsewhere they implicitly dismiss most psychology as soft, and insist that models must be constructed to meet their criteria of hardness, to bolster the vision they appropriate theories that have never yielded calculational models, that have no apparent prospect of doing so, and that lie outside of psychology*.

What exactly is Newell and Card's vision and how is it related to their main program? They do not provide specific criteria and arguments for the assimilation of a variety of work into their vision. This makes it impossible to assess the claim that such work, in fact, plays a role in the vision, or indeed to discriminate the vision from an arbitrary and vacuous device masking an equivocation about what the program advocated actually encompasses. Further, it must be noted that Newell and Card's replies to the first two criticisms contradict each other. They defend against the charge that their approach is too low-level by saying that this focus is appropriate because it is coextensive with that of psychology*. They defend against the charge that their approach is too limited in scope by claiming that research in areas like learning and mental models that lie outside of psychology* are in fact filling out their vision. On grounds of consistency alone, at least one of the two criticisms is true.

Perhaps sensing these problem with their notion of vision, Newell and Card present a second response to the criticism of limited scope in assertin that many psychological issues just don't come up in the area of interface design.

"Our topic is the psychology of the human-computer interface, not all of psychology. This distinction is important, because the

20

proposal is not to make all of psychology better. The human-computer interface is, in fact, a psychologically limited micro-world. Many issues of the wider world of psychology do not arise." (Newell and Card, 1985, p. 222).

This is an untenable claim, made without argument. The user interface, after all, can be used to present "microworlds" in many different task domains. Although there are many human activities not encompassed by the user interface, the range of problems that get solved, or could be solved, using the interface is far broader than the range of problems actually studied in the laboratory by academic cognitive psychology (Carroll, 1986; Norman, 1986). It is hard to name an area of a psychology that is not involved in understanding the cognitive interface: perceptual personality, educational, developmental, social, organizational, etc.

3.3 Being Too Late

Newell and Card respond to the criticism that their approach is too late in application to make a difference in system design by arguing that computer technology develops far more slowly than commonly thought. They represent interface technology development as a process in which a canonical interface design is introduced every 5 years, then quickly stabilizes for a 15-20 year life cycle. This pacing, they suggest, can provide the time for a psychology of human-computer interaction to have impact (Newell and Card, 1985, p. 235). This seems gravely over-optimistic. Indeed, the view of interface development as the stately progress of canonical technologies is just irrelevant to the problem of being too late. Whether a canonical interface lasts 15 years or one year, the place to have real influence on its design is at the birth of the new technology. After that, constraints are imposed by the initial choices that were made, wise or unwise, as Newell and Card themselves acknowledge: "throughout the life cycle ... the gestalt of the interface does not change" (Newell and Card, 185, p. 234). If Newell and Card need, even one year after the technology is introduced, to calculate the right design, they will be one year too late.

A secondary problem with the appeal to canonical interface technology is exposed by the depiction of the development process in a bar chart with unlabeled axes (Newell and Card, 1985, Figure 7, p. 235). What purports to be a taxonomy of interfaces merely classifies visual display devices, listing as "correlated features" such aspects as amount of intelligence and rates of interaction. These features may be indeed correlated, because the chart provides a scale of historical time. Such correlations are only interesting if they point to causal reactions or relations of constraint between different aspects of the interface. But it is clear that they do not (progress in knowledge engineering has been independent of display devices, and interaction rates, at least early on, _slowed_ as character-based CRTs were replaced by bitmapped displays). Mere correlations between features give us no insight into the evolutionary development of interfaces.

3.4 On Being Too Difficult to Apply

Newell and Card respond to the charge that their approach is difficult to apply by suggesting that "ripe application domains" (Newell and Card, 1985, p. 236) be sought. They recommend that their approach be extended to intelligent tutoring systems. Clearly, this is an important area, and one in which models of human knowledge and skill play a central role. (This suggestion also enables them to assimilate the work of Anderson once again -- in this case, the research on LISP tutoring -- Anderson and Reiser (1985)). However, it is clear that Newell and Card are again being inconsistent here. Intelligent tutoring, as they acknowledge (1985, p. 225) is not in the purview of psychology*: tutoring is a "high-level task" in the bounded rationality time band. Moreover, intelligent tutoring is an extremely soft area in which foundational questions are still being addressed: theories of knowledge domains and knowledge construction have not been developed or applied in this area (Carroll and McKendree, 1986). None of the work in this area seems suited to approximative calculational modeling, and Newell and Card do not indicate how such modeling could be carried out.

Beyond the problem of identifying domains to which Newell and Card's approach might be extended, we need to ask about the applications that have already been made (the approach, after all, has been around for nearly 10 years). Newell and Card are disappointingly cursory: they present a list of "studies that have applied, tested, improved, or extended the approximative models" (Newell and Card, 1985, p. 236). Demonstrating how these examples worked would have been much more valuable than just listing them. In particular, it would have been valuable to show which of these studies, if any, applied calculational models in design rather than strict research settings. Newell and Card themselves insist that "design is where the action is, not evaluation" (Newell and Card, 1985, p. 214) and that "the payoff for design must be demonstrated" (Newell and Card, 1985, p. 223). Yet they provide no evidence that their calculational models have been used in any real designs, much less that they were useful.

Given the dearth of successful applications of Newell and Card's approach, we might well ask what has impeded its application. An approach can be difficult to apply because it introduces unfamiliar concepts whose implications are hard to work out, or because it requires the construction of auxiliary theories before it can be tested empirically or used practically. On the other hand, an approach can be difficult to apply because its content is too thin, not too rich. It is difficult to generalize a conceptually impoverished program beyond the narrowly conceived set of problems that it was originally designed to address. We will argue that the limitations that Newell and Card have imposed on themselves in the name of hard science intrinsically prevent the approach from being extended beyond predicting ideal expert performance items on line editors.

4. NEWELL AND CARD'S PROGRAM IS INADEQUATE

To this point in our discussion, we have argued that the motivation for hard science, as cited by Newell and Card, is grounded in misunderstanding of the status quo (Section 2) and that their replies to specific criticisms of their approach are unsuccessful (Section 3). It is possible that these deficiencies apply only to current implementations of their research program, and not the program itself. The way to resolve this question is to examine the underlying program, to isolate its presuppositions, its methodological and theoretical commitments, and the constraints they impose on the program (Campbell and Bickhard, 1986). The other reason for examining the program, of course, is to better understand just what Newell and Card mean by "hard science", in order to determine whether a cognitive psychology of the interface is either possible or desirable.

We have referred many times to Newell and Card's focus on calculation and approximation, and to their view of task analysis. Each of these requires further explication, however, if we are to understand how the program has been applied and how Newell and Card respond to the alternatives to it. For instance, is the task analysis that they advocate descriptive or explanatory? What kinds of values will be calculated? What will be retained in the approximations they urge and what will be left out? Is there any causal connection between tenets of the program for hard science and the fact that the particular research projects do not address the conceptual nature of user errors? These questions can be answered, but only if certain

icit features of the program are brought to light. Newell and Card's
oach rests on three important commitments: their program of task-
ysis is <u>descriptive instead of explanatory</u>, their task analyses are
istic; tasks are built up out of independent low-level units; their
oximative calculations produce predictions of <u>interval measurements</u> only.

Descriptivism

The distinction between <u>descriptive</u> and <u>explanatory</u> models is funda-
al (Campbell and Bickhard, 1986). An explanatory psychological model
mpts to account for the mental processes by which the user does a task.
scriptive psychological model attempts to account for the mental pro-
es by which the user does a task. A descriptive model predicts perfor-
e on tasks, but without modeling the actual means by which the user
the tasks. Newell and Card clearly distinguish between tasks as
rstood by people performing them and tasks as objectively analyzed
ell and Card, 1985, p. 227). Their concern is with the latter, which
do not view as being a psychological endeavor: "the cognitive psychol-
t has no unique capabilities for ... investigations of specific task
ins" (Newell and Card, 1985, p. 227; Card, Moran, and Newell, 1983,
0). Thus, when Newell and Card envision the extension of their approach
ntelligent tutoring systems (Newell and Card, 1985, p. 237), they aim
objective calculation and task analysis". By contrast, those who tried
uild such systems have been interested in the nature of learning and
constraints on teaching systems (Brown and Burton, 1978), and in making
iled investigations of learner goals and learning paths (Goldstein,
). But which task analysis, the learner's or the observer's, actually
cts the learner's behavior, helps to account for what is learned, makes
learner enthusiastic or inattentive? Newell and Card use task descrip-
s to predict selected measures of user performance; an explanatory
oach would model the user's mental processes and representations in
r to account for skills, learning, and motivation.

Newell and Card's commitment to descriptivism is not limited to task
ysis (which belongs to the time band of bounded rationality) or to
ined extensions of the model to new domains, like intelligent tutoring.
s evident in their discussion of psychology* itself. They denigrate "the
ry game" in psychology -- the interest in generating and contrasting
anations of phenomena. They explicitly attach the view that theories
for explaining, not predicting (Newell and Card, 1985, p. 219).
anatory psychology "will never beat Gresham's Law" (Newell and Card,1985,
19). The attack on the theory game by Card, Moran, and Newell (1983)
be understood as a reaction to academic cognitive psychology in the
1970's, which often consisted of trivial information-processing models
., the models of sentence verification that prevailed at the time), and
oliferation of experimental paradigms and measurements specialized for
inguishing one small-scale model from another. Against this background
desire for an alternative that could address practical questions, even
t was only descriptive, is understandable. Serious explanatory psychol-
however, has always been concerned about more fundamental issues and a
der range of phenomena than the miniature, paradigm-bound approaches that
et al. (1983) seem to have reacted against. Insofar as foundational
tions about perception, learning, and communication are raised by the
y of human-computer interaction, we can ill afford to dispense with the
urces and concerns of explanatory psychology.

Once the descriptivism that underlies Newell and Card's project has been
gnized, other aspects of the project become more understandable. The
of attention to understanding errors in their program can be derived
the fact that task descriptions tend to be a priori models of perfect
ormance. Descriptive task models usually derive from a formal theory of

23

the task domain. Thus, if they model knowledge of that domain, they model perfect knowledge. Newell and Card allow that their analysis is easier to apply to experts than to novice users (Newell and Card, 1985, p. 233). But this is not the real point. Their model is a model of ideal experts, not of real experts or real novices. Real experts make errors, use non-optimal methods, and don't bother to learn or use some aspects of system function (Draper, 1985; Rosson, 1983).

Errors have no place in Newell and Card's predictive models of ideally skilled performance. Newell and Card's suggestion that errors be split off, and that their "GOMS-like" regularity be captured in theories of error (Newell and Card, 1985, p. 230), underscores their descriptivism. In explanatory psychology, errors are of interest because they test boundary conditions of knowledge and skill and, thereby, provide valuable insights into the underlying structure of knowledge and skill. The analysis and interpretation of errors is a crucial part of approaches to cognition and development from Piaget to Anderson. Of course, using errors for this purpose presupposes that one is interested in understanding how human beings act and the purposes for which they act, and not merely in describing the distribution of behavior tokens in the stream of events. The limitations of descriptivism may explain why Newell and Card appeal to a vision, as a device for saving their approach from being too limited.

4.2 Atomism

Accompanying the predilection for descriptive task analysis, though not entailed by it, is the commitment to analyzing performance into isolable units or atoms. This has led to extreme disregard for context effects or interactions. For example, the simplified instantiation of the GOMS model known as the Keystroke-Level Model (Card et al., 1983) assumes only one operator at a time and the independent execution of contiguous plans and actions. These assumptions are incorrect empirically as shown by coarticulation phenomena in speech (Denes and Pinson, 1973), and nonindependent components of human movement (Smith and Smith, 1962). Proposals now being made to model the full range of cognition in terms of massively parallel processing (Rumelhart and McClelland, 1986) suggest that atomistic analyses are unacceptable in general.

Although the Keystroke-Level Model is readily understandable as an instance of atomism. Newell and Card seek to justify it in terms of approximation. Just what sense of approximation do Newell and Card have in mind? They claim that approximation is characteristic of engineering; this suggests selective and simplified applications of a hard basic science, as in the applications of Newtonian mechanics made in civil engineering. Such applications are virtually impossible in human-computer interaction. How could a "hard" applied psychology be built out of a basic psychology that is mostly "soft"? Newell and Card specifically claim that they want to reform the psychology of human-computer interaction without reforming all of psychology (Newell and Card, 1985, p. 222). This suggests that they will not be applying basic psychology, approximately or otherwise.

More generally in science, approximation is carried out against a background of surveying the problems of interest, and the complexity of their solution. A model is not to be called an approximation simply because it is incomplete and imprecise; all models are incomplete and imprecise. Approximation is also not the same as arbitrary simplification, or idealizations adopted for expediency. Some thought has to go into the real nature of the problem, what is left out by the approximation, whether anything essential to the problem has been left out, and how much of a practical difference it makes. Newell and Card neither carry out nor draw on any such survey of the important problems in human-computer interaction, and the means available to solve them. They never consider what the relevant trade-offs are; they do not show, for instance, that in return for specific simplifying assumptions, it becomes easier to make a useful prediction. Without these details, we cannot distinguish Newell and Card's advocacy of approximation from a commitment to atomism.

The commitment to atomism entails a reductionist ontology, which Newell and Card clearly accept in their argument that higher level psychological time bands of human behavior and experience can be reduced to atomic mechanisms that live within the psychology* time band. Their consideration of goals is limited to very low-level goals, which function in their analysis as unanalyzed atoms. Newell and Card's cursory discussion of error amounts to the assertion that error be split off into a separate atomic theory. The kind of theory that they want for dealing with errors is a general theory of error (or at least, of error-recovery times), not tied to skill or understanding in any specific domain. They want "a way of accumulating data on errors that has cross-situational validity" (Newell and Card, 1985, p. 231). We interpret this as a call for a general theory of errors, not dependent on the knowledge or learning that are being assessed. Indeed, Newell and Card reinterpret (1985, p. 230) Norman's (1981) account of action slips, which was intended as part of a model of skilled action, as a general-purpose theory of error. Do errors ever have context-free information value?

4.3 Interval Measurements

Newell and Card advocate calculation as a touchstone of hard science. Their discussion of partly linear models (Newell and Card, 1985, pp. 232-233) illustrates what they mean by calculation. The linear part of a model is "linear in time, errors, solution opportunities, or whatever" (Newell and Card, 1985, p. 233): it requires something that is continuously measurable or countable. The nonlinear part or "difficulty component" is to be estimated and plugged into the equation so predicted times, etc., can be obtained -- its qualitative features or underlying explanation are not of interest. Performance can thus be resolved into number of operations performed, number of chunks learned, and so on, with a non-linear, grab-bag difficulty component tacked on, in order to facilitate the generation of quantitative predictions. Not only do partly linear models waste qualitative information, such models are inherently unsuited to situations in which small changes in the interface, which have a major influence on understanding or motivation, lead to big changes in performance. Partly linear models presuppose that small changes in the interface will produce small increments or decrements in performance, but this is wrong (Carroll, 1982; see, also, design case studies like Boies et al., 1985, and Good et al., 1984).

All of the examples Newell and Card cite are consistent with this bias for interval measurement. They dismiss "qualitative factors" as soft (Newell and Card, 1985, p. 211). The GOMS technical work, that their program rests on, predicts performance times. The best-known extensions of the GOMS model (Roberts and Moran, 1983; Polson, 1986) predict learning times. Newell and Card seek "a simplified model of the human in terms of memories, processors, and <u>a few quantitative parameters of each</u>" (Newell and Card, 1985, p. 215, our emphasis).

This orientation leads them to place higher priority on identifying" a few quantitative parameters" than on developing analyses that fit the target phenomena. It deprives the hard science approach of most of what psychology has to offer. Outside of psychophysics and motor control, there are few interval measurements available in psychology: performance times and percent correct are the most widespread. Since nominal categories and ordinal measurements are not hard, they can play no role in this program (at most, they can be included in the vision, or packed into a nonlinear model component) -- regardless of the information they provide. Errors, interview and protocol statements, explanations, etc., do not provide the right kinds of data and so are to be banished from the study of human-computer interaction. In psychology, we labor under the restriction of not being able to observe mental processes, and having only a few kinds of behavioral data to provide empirical constraints on our accounts of process. Under these circumstances, we had better use all of the information that we can get. Newell and Card's approach is not low-level and limited in scope by accident, rather it has these limitations as a consequence of its commitment to interval measurement.

Perhaps in recognition of these problems, Newell and Card state that, "The prominence of performance-time measurements ... occurred because of the locus of the initial research successes" (Newell and Card, 1985, p. 228) -- implying an interest in a wider range of phenomena. This may have been true of the original GOMS research program (Card et al., 1983). However, Newell and Card have sought to turn the limitations of that research into prescriptions for hard science. They have moved from selecting performance times for one program of research, to promulgating norms of calculation and approximation that compel the use of measures like performance times in all research. Performance times (along with learning times and error-recovery times) are among the few things in cognitive psychology that can be measured on an interval scale. Errors are essentially qualitative. Indeed, the non-role of errors in Newell and Card's hard science is over determined by its three underlying commitments: errors as a means of exposing boundary conditions belong to explanatory and not descriptive psychology; errors, because they derive their meaning from the contexts in which they occur, cannot be usefully examined atomistically; errors are qualitative and so cannot be measured as interval quantities.

5.   PROSPECTS FOR THE NEW POSITIVISM

Although Newell and Card's discussion contributes to theoretical debate in human-computer interaction by setting a reference point, their specific argument fails. As we have seen, the program is unmotivated (Section 2); suffers from serious limitations (Section 3); and in fact, suffers from these limitations in principle (Section 4). Newell and Card's program does not proceed from a consideration of the problems to be solved in the domain of human-computer interaction and the methods that might be useful to address those problems. It races ahead of fundamental questions like "what is our science about?" and "what should our science do?" What Newell and Card have focused on is the _form_ of their theory rather than the _content_. They have in effect undertaken a scare campaign, arguing that unless our science takes a particular _form,_ computer scientists will disdain and ignore us. Although Newell and Card claim to be concerned about what will produce good design (Newell and Card, 1985, p. 210-211), their arguments appeal much more strongly to the demand for scientific credentials than to any benefits for interface design. This emphasis on scientific credentials recalls positions that have prevailed in the past --for instance, the doctrine that talk of mental states is unscientific.

In the history of science, soft conceptual science lays the necessary groundwork for hard quantitative science. The appropriate ontology, the right problems and the right ways of looking at them, and the mathematical techniques appropriate to the subject matter, have to be in place for hard science to develop. In the past, philosophy of science tended to ignore the actual reasoning of scientists, in favor of legislating methodological criteria a priori (Shapere, 1977; Laudan, 1977). A particularly disruptive instance of this approach was logical positivism, a philosophy of science founded on doubts about the legitimacy of inferred entities in scientific explanation (Carnap, 1928; Hempel, 1965). Theoretical entities were to be tolerated only as part of a deductive system for yielding empirical predictions (metaphysical claims were forbidden) and strict rules of correspondence between theoretical and observational statements were to be followed. Logical positivism did considerable and lasting damage to the social sciences which, unlike the natural sciences, have been chronically vulnerable to worries about appearing "scientific" enough. Social scientists have often rushed to adopt the trappings of hard science without the substance, for instance, by using mathematical modeling techniques inappropriate to their subject matter (ranging from structural models of cognitive operations, (Campbell and Bickhard, 1986) to models of static equilibrium in economics (von Mises, 1966) to frankly bizarre applications of mathematics in sociology (Andreski, 1973)).

The worst distortion of all was the ascendancy of behaviorism, which was accepted because it imposed extrinsic requirements on what could count as scientific, not because it could answer many of the questions understood as psychological (e.g., Chomsky, 1959). The effect was to detour psychology from asking or dealing with most of the interesting questions in its domain for 40 years. Eventually these questions were addressed anyway, but at the price of starting over almost from scratch (e.g., Miller, Galanter and Pribram, 1960). Although the behaviorist prohibition against mental entities is no longer accepted, the view of science that underlay behaviorism -- logical positivism -- still exerts a strong influence on thought and method in psychology 20 years after philosophers of science rejected it (Bickhard, Cooper, and Mace, 1985). Clearly, Newell and Card are not behaviorists, but in other respects they are renewing the methodological strictures of logical positivism. Their view of theory as predicting instead of explaining, and of quantification as the hallmark of good science, are vintage positivism (Suppe, 1977; Campbell and Bickhard, 1986). The legacy of behaviorism and positivism should make psychologists deeply suspicious of any attempt to restrict the range of their science to suit an extrinsic criterion of correct method. Methodology should fit the subject matter, not the other way around.

History suggests how Newell and Card's approach might develop. Newell and Card have clearly articulated their position: they will ignore many of the most important empirical problems in the area, to obtain analyses with the correct form. They will not seriously address perception, problem-solving, or learning, although they may blur this by conflating their approach with its limitless "vision" and by invoking a grab-bag of nonlinear model components. They will probably not impress computer scientists as they hope to. Computer scientists already have a richer view of theory (as evidenced by their current practice) and, in any case, look to psychologists for answers to important problems, not limited, low-level, late and inapplicable theories that are methodologically pure. Positivist strictures are easier to impose on pure laboratory research than on applied design work, precisely because the insignia of methodological purity matter less in applied areas. In the meantime, the institutional barriers to human factors influence on the design process (the ones that motivated Newell and Card in the first place) will not be affected at all.

History suggests some possible reactions against the new positivism in human-computer interaction. Behaviorism strengthened the appeal of phenomenology and hermeneutics by showing that "science" was incapable of dealing with meaning in human thought and action. Should Newell and Card's approach become an establishment view in human-computer interaction, it will stimulate a backlash in the form of approaches that reject all information processing analysis, not just Newell and Card's overconstrained analysis. The elimination of meaning, even in the context of simple problem-solving, makes Newell and Card's approach a natural target for advocates of hermeneutics.

Whiteside and Wixon (1986) have urged the rejection of information processing cognitive models; they recommend a hermeneutic approach which aims at interpretation of particular cases rather than generalization or explanatory theory (Winograd and Flores, 1986).

We are concerned with distinguishing the baby from the bath water. We favor an explanatory psychology of human-computer interaction; one that starts from an understanding of the real problems that have to be solved in order to provide better computer tools for people to use. Indeed, such work is going on in many places right now, and could only seem extraordinary in the context of Newell and Card's revival of positivism. What this work lacks is a clearly articulated statement of its program, and we suggest this as a top priority work item for the psychology of human-computer interaction.

Newell and Card have supposed that the problems facing psychology in human-computer interaction are due to a conflict between hard computer science and soft psychology. We see the problem more simply; interfaces can be built without the contributions of psychologists, but, they cannot be built without the contributions of programmers. We also see the solution more simply; psychologists need to make the case for usability by providing concepts, methods and demonstrations of impact. An alternative to Newell and Card's monolithic view of conflict between hard computer science and soft psychology is the view that an interdisciplinary field of human-computer interaction is taking form, and that psychology and computer science must work together to develop research areas like artificial intelligence and rapid prototyping. This interactive relationship will thrive if psychologists can play an effective role within the design loop for new interface technology. To do this they will have to address the questions that designers really need answered, at a useful grain of analysis, and at the pace of the design process.

Real interface design problems arise when real users use real applications to achieve their real goals. Psychologists working in human-computer interaction need to examine rich slices of behavior in realistic settings. Laboratory studies of undergraduates performing simple and repetitive tasks with toy-scale mock-ups will often be irrelevant. Users make many errors, so explanatory prototheories of error must be developed that will guide the re-design of interfaces to minimize errors and support error recovery. Analyzing only errorless performances, or merely timing error recovery, may not be useful. Understanding difficult areas like sustained motivation and long-term learning (including perceptual learning), in which the psychological theory base is deficient, is critical; human-computer interaction may have to drive explanatory theory development in these areas. Psychologists in human-computer interaction will have to pursue these issues if they are to be effective.

Human-computer interaction is a frontier science: it is at a frontier of method and theory in psychology and of technology and application in computer science. It is evolving faster perhaps than any area in psychology ever has. As such, it will probably be impervious to monolithic and methodologically narrow paradigms. Rather, it will favor interdisciplinary cooperation between psychology and computer science. It will require of its participants a thorough appreciation of what system design is really like. It will not sustain approaches that are too low-level, too limited in scope, too late, and too difficult to apply in real design. Technological change will continually impose new problems on the area, and methods will have to be developed to address and resolve these problems whether some limited view deems them scientifically legitimate or not. It is our hope that good science cannot be driven out by science that merely tries to look good.

ACKNOWLEDGEMENTS

    This article is fully collaborative. We would like to thank Mark
Bickhard, Stu Card, Don Foss, Wendy Kellogg, Clayton Lewis, Tom Moran, Dick
Pew, Peter Polson, Michael Rosenbloom, Eric Wagner, and John Whiteside for
comments, criticisms, and discussion.

REFERENCES

Anderson, J. R., 1983, The Architecture of Cognition, Harvard University
    Press, Cambridge.

Anderson, J. R., and Reiser, B. J., 1985, "The LISP Tutor", Byte, 10, (4),
    pp. 159-175.

Andreski, S., 1973, Social Sciences as Sorcery, St. Martin's, New York.

Bickhard, M. H., Cooper, R. G., Jr., and Mace, P. G., 1985, "Vestiges of
    Logical Positivism: Critiques of Stage Explanations", Human Develop-
    ment, 28, pp. 240-258.

Boies, S. J., Gould, J. D., Levy, S., Richards, J. T., and Schoonard, J.,
    1985, The 1984 Olympic Message System -- A Case Study in System Design,
    IBM Research Report RC 11138.

Brown, J. S., and Burton, R. R., 1978, "Diagnostic Models for Procedural
    Bugs in Basic Mathematical Skills", Cognitive Science, 2, pp. 155-192.

Buxton, W., 1986, "There's More to Interaction Than Meets the Eye: Some
    Issues in Manual Input", User-Centered System Design, Norman, D. A., and
    Draper, S. W., eds., Lawrence Erlbaum Associates, Hillsdale, NJ, pp.
    319-337.

Campbell, R. L., and Bickhard, M. H., 1986, Knowing Levels and Development
    Stages, S. Karger, Basel.

Card, S. K., Moran, T. P., and Newell, A., 1983, The Psychology of Human-
    Computer Interaction, Erlbaum, Hillsdale, NJ.

Carnap, R., 1974, The Logical Construction of the World and Pseudoproblems
    of Philosophy, University of California Press (Originally Published in
    1928), Berkeley, CA.

Carroll, J. M., 1982, "Learning, Using, and Designing Command Paradigms",
    Human Learning, 1, pp. 31-62.

Carroll, J. M., ed., 1986, Interfacing Thought: Cognitive Aspects of
    Human-Computer Interaction, Bradford/MIT Press, Cambridge.

Carroll, J. M., and Mazur, S. A., 1985, Lisa Learning, IBM Research Report
    RC 11427, In press, IEEE Computer.

Carroll, J. M., and McKendree, J. E., 1986, Interface Design Issues for
    Advice-Giving Expert Systems, IBM Research Report.

Carroll, J. M., and Rosson, M. B., 1985, "Usability Specifications as a
    Tool in Iterative Development", Advances in Human-Computer Interaction,
    1, Hartson, H. R., ed., Ablex, Norwood, NJ, pp. 1-28.

Chomsky, N. A., 1959, "Review of B. F. Skinner's 'Verbal Behavior'",

Language, 35, pp. 26-58.

Denes, P., and Pinson, E. N., 1973, The Speech Chain, Anchor Books, Garden City, NY.

Draper, S. W., 1985, "The Nature of Expertise in UNIX", Human-Computer Interaction - Interact '84, Schackel, ed., North Holland, New York, pp. 465-472.

Dreyfus, H., 1953, Designing for People, Simon and Schuster, New York.

Goldstein, I. P., 1982, "The Genetic Graph: A Representation for the Evolution of Procedural Knowledge", Intelligent Tutoring Systems, Sleeman, D., and Brown, J. S., eds., Academic Press, New York, pp. 51-77.

Good, M. D., Whiteside, J. A., Wixon, D. R., and Jones, S. A., 1984,"Building a User-Derived Interface", Communications of the ACM, 27, pp. 1032-1043.

Guessarian, I., 1981, Algebraic Semantics, Springer-Verlag, New York.

Hempel, C. G., 1965, Aspects of Scientific Explanation, Free Press, New York.

Jeffries, R., Turner, A., Polson, P., and Atwood, M., 1981, "The Processes Involved in Designing Software", Cognitive Skills and Their Acquisition, Anderson, J., ed., Lawrence Erlbaum Associates, Hillsdale, NJ.

Kelley, J. F., 1984, "An Iterative Design Methodology for User-Friendly Natural Language Office Information Applications", ACM Transactions on Office Information Systems, 2, pp. 26-41.

Laudan, L., 1977, Progress and Its Problems, University of California Press, Berkeley.

Miller, G. A., Galanter, E., and Pribram, K. H., 1960, Plans and the Structure Behavior, Holt, Rinehart, and Winston, New York.

Newell, A., and Card, S. K., 1985, "The Prospects for Psychological Science in Human-Computer Interaction", Human-Computer Interaction, 1, pp. 209-242.

Newell, A., and Simon, H., 1972, Human Problem Solving, Prentice-Hall, Englewood Cliffs, NJ.

Norman, D. A., 1981, "Categorization of Action Slips", Psychological Review, 88, pp. 1-15.

Norman, D. A., 1986, "Cognitive Science -- Cognitive Engineering", Interfacing Thought: Cognitive Aspects of Human-Computer Interaction, Carroll, J. M., ed., MIT Press, Bradford.

Pew, R. W., and Baron, S., 1978, "The Components of an Information Processing Theory of Skilled Performance Based on an Optimal Control Perspective", Information Processing in Motor Control and Learning, Stelmach, G. E., ed., Academic Press, New York, pp. 71-78.

Pew, R. W., and Baron, S., 1983, "Perspectives on Human Performance Modeling", Automatica, 19, pp. 663-676.

Polson, P., 1986, "A Quantitative Theory of Human-Computer Interaction", Interfacing Thought: Cognitive Aspects of Human-Computer Interaction,

Carroll, J. M., ed., MIT Press, Bradford.

Richards, J. T., Boies, S. J., and Gould, J. D., 1986, "Rapid Prototyping and System Design: Examination of a Toolkit for Voice and Telephony Applications", <u>Proceedings of CHI '86 Conference on Human Factors of Computer Systems</u>, ACM, New York, pp. 216-220.

Roberts, T. L., and Moran, T. P., 1983, "The Evaluation of Text Editors: Methodology and Empirical Results", <u>Communications of the ACM</u>, <u>26</u>, pp. 265-283.

Robertson, S. P., 1983, <u>Goal, Plan, and Outcome Tracking in Computer Text-Editing Performance</u>, Cognitive Science Technical Report 25, Yale University Ph.D. Dissertation.

Rosson, M. B., 1983, "Patterns of Experience in Text Editing", <u>Proceedings of CHI '83 Conference on Human Factors of Computer Systems</u>, pp. 171-175.

Rumelhart, D. E., and McClelland, J. L., 1986, <u>Parallel Distributed Processing: Explorations in the Microstructure of Cognition, Volume 1: Foundations</u>, MIT Press, Cambridge, MA.

Shapere, D., 1977, "Scientific Theories and Their Domains", <u>The Structure of Scientific Theories</u>, Suppe, F., ed., 2nd ed., University of Illinois Press, Urbana, pp. 518-565.

Shneiderman, B., 1984, "Review: The Psychology of Human-Computer Interaction", <u>Datamation</u>, <u>30</u>, January 1984, pp. 236-237.

Simon, H. A., 1973, "The Structure of Ill-Structured Problems", <u>Artificial Intelligence</u>, <u>4</u>, pp. 181-201.

Smith, K. U., and Smith, W. M., 1962, <u>Perception and Motion: An Analysis of Space Structured Behavior</u>, W. B. Saunders Company, Philadelphia.

Smith, S. L., and Mosier, J. W., 1984, <u>Design Guidelines for User-System Interface Software</u>, Technical Report No. MTR-9420, MITRE Corporation, Bedford, MA.

Suppe, F., 1977, "The Search for Philosophic Understanding of Scientific Theories", <u>The Structure of Scientific Theories</u>, 2nd ed., University of Illinois Press, Urbana, ILL, pp. 3-254.

von Mises, L., 1966, <u>Human Action</u>, 3rd ed., Regnery, Chicago, ILL.

Whiteside, J. A., and Eixon, D. R., 1986, "Improving Human-Computer Interaction: A Quest for Cognitive Science", <u>Interfacing Thought: Cognitive Aspects of Human-Computer Interaction</u>, Carroll, J. M., ed., Bradford/MIT Press, Cambridge.

Winograd, T., and Flores, F., 1986, <u>Understanding Computers and Cognition: A New Foundation for Design</u>, Ablex, Norwood, NJ.

DESIGN AND EVALUATION OF USER-SYSTEM INTERFACES OR OF USER-TASK INTERACTION:
A DISCUSSION OF INTERFACE DESIGN APPROACH IN DIFFERENT DOMAINS FOR APPLICA-
TION OF MODERN INFORMATION TECHNOLOGY

Annelise Mark Pejtersen and Jens Rasmussen

Risø National Laboratory
D-4000 Roskilde
Denmark

Abstract: The application of modern information technology is now considered
for man-machine systems design in a wide variety of application domains. In
general, two aspects of the impact of this new technology are considered
separately. One is the potential for new user interfaces, another is the
transfer of human activities to "intelligent" computer functions, for instance in "expert systems". There is, however, a need for a more integrated
system design considering the basic user-task interaction in advanced systems. In this paper, the approaches taken to models of the work content and
user performance in different professional domains are discussed, such as
industrial process control, emergency management, office systems, and library
systems.

   It is concluded that design and evaluation of user interfaces should be
explicitly based on models of the task domain and the actual requirements of
the user-task interaction, not only on the interface communication language.
It is also concluded that development of a common framework for design and
evaluation of interfaces in different work domains will be feasible, in
spite of the great differences in the characteristics of the application
domains.

INTRODUCTION

   The rapidly increasing use of modern information technology in the
interface between humans and their work leads to a significant change in the
content and methods of the disciplines of 'human factors' and 'ergonomics'.

   Traditionally, tools for professional workers were specialized and,
therefore, often designed to support one separate function. Consequently,
the coordination of the individual functions of a task was the concern of
the worker, and was not reflected in the design of tools, only in the selection of tools to use. This has also been the case for the early computerized
tools, and the concern of the human factors studies have been the user-tool
interface, i.e., to match the design of the individual tools to the interface
manipulation, not the influence of work semantics.

   This situation is now changing in many work settings when advanced computerized tools are introduced. More integrated tools are designed in terms

of work stations for particular jobs; many trivial routines are automated, and the role of the worker or user will, in a rapidly increasing degree, be to control the cofunction of advanced tools and their effective adaptation to variance in the work condition. Advanced tools are frequently introduced in order to achieve effective change of work content in order to match the increasing dynamic requirements of the environment. For example, the requirements of a user in a supervisory role for simultaneous access to different sources of data; the use of numerically controlled equipment for 'flexible manufacturing'; the rapidly and individually changing demands from library users caused by increased educational level, growth of information, and the influence from the mass media of the electronic age.

These examples have the same requirements for integrated tools and for flexibility to adapt to a dynamic work environment. In this situation it is necessary to consider not only the user-tool interface, but the user-task interaction in human factors studies. Human factors considerations cannot be added separately as a front-end system to the finished functional design of the system in order to achieve a good user-system match. The analysis of user-task interaction in interface design will be the basic problem of the design of integrated work stations. In addition, in a dynamic environment, the user in a way will have to continue the activities of the designer when trying to adapt to changing requirements. For instance, the task of a user in a supervisory role, process operators as well as intermediaries in a library, will be to find work procedures to meet new requirements. In both cases in a context similar to that of the initial system designer. And in both cases the user will have to modify and supplement the designer's conception of the work content and its requirements along with use and experience with the system.

Several distinct phases in the general development of human work can be formulated. The mechanization period was typical for the early industrialization and was, in particular, led by the mechanical manufacturing plants. The next phase, the cybernetic period (Hirshhorn, 1986) brought the automation of industrial installations, and was, in particular, led by the petrochemical process industries. This brought the plant operators into the role of supervisory controllers, and the rapidly increasing size and, therefore, potential risk from their operation early led to extensive studies of man-machine cooperation and modeling of human decision-making in real-life settings, in addition to the classical interface studies (see, for instance, Rasmussen, 1969). The rapidly increasing centralization, also, of information systems, with the increasing consequences of mistakes made by decision makers, programmers, and end-users cause this problem to spread to many other areas of human work, even office systems.

In the library context the second stage of automation of work routines and a large number of bibliographical databases are accessible with powerful technological capabilities added to the traditional tools, no conceptual development of task analysis, interface and system design has actually taken place. Real life studies have been very scarce and usually not subject to operational analysis in relation to automated functions in libraries. Automation has mainly focused on the implementation of card catalogues to on-line facilities. But, recently, the attention has also been drawn towards user modeling, task performance, decision making, and user-system communications as a must within this area for a conceptually improved system design. In conclusion, two major tendencies will influence the design and evaluation of advanced information systems; 1) it will be for an efficient user-work interaction, and 2) the trend toward integrated work stations brings with it the need to consider a much wider work domain in one integrated design. It will, therefore, be important to develop a domain independent frame of reference for conceptual design.

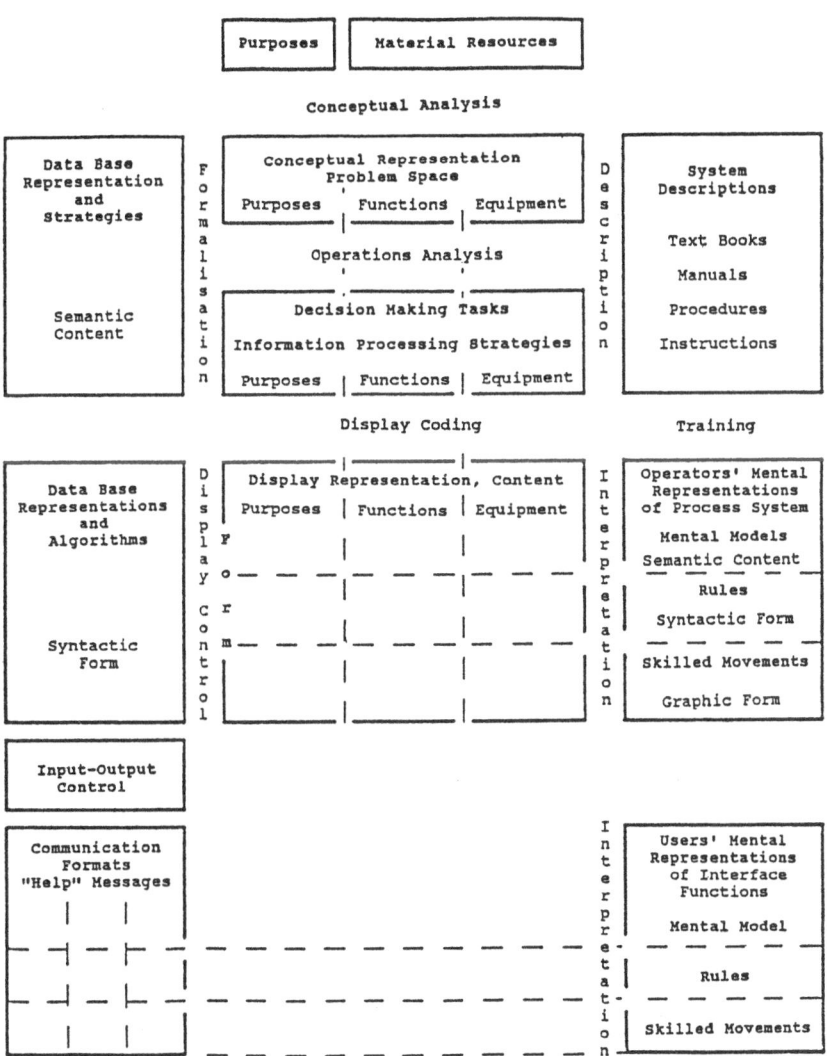

Figure 1. Overview of Conceptual Representations in Design.

A schematic map of the different representations of a process system which are relevant for a cognitive task analysis is shown in Figure 1. The aim of such an analysis is an integrated consideration of these representations and their mutual compatibility. During design, analysis along the path represented by the center column should ensure proper content of the displayed information. The form will depend on the level of cognitive control aimed at. This will also depend on the communication through the right hand training path. If a proper system design results, the interface will be transparent, i.e., the task is directly manipulated through the interface. If this is not the case, an interface manipulation and information retrieval task represented in the bottom of the figure will be added. The representations of the left hand column are related to the formalization necessary for software development.

For such a framework, different points of view upon the system properties should be considered. The _information content_ of the system will
depend on the particular work domain and, since the information system should
be able to support improvisation and adaptation to new requirements, the
work domain should be analyzed and represented in task independent terms.
However, to plan the interface communication and to _select and format infor-
mation_ to make available on user request, the decision task which is faced
by the user and the mental strategies preferred should be studied. Finally,
to be able to design the proper _form of displays_, cognitive mechanisms
brought to use of the user, depending on background and level of training
should be taken into consideration. Such considerations lead to a framework
for interaction in process industries. This framework is discussed in the
following sections. In addition, the present state of affairs in a number
of specific applications areas are reviewed to judge the general applicability of a general model framework.

Problem Space

In this domain of analysis, an explicit task and transaction independent
description of the work content is established in the terms of means-end
and part-whole relationships. These relations are important for analysis
of the state of affairs, for setting priorities, and for planning in any
work situation involving resource management and adaptation to changing
conditions. Decisions, in general, are not based on primary data about the
state of affairs and consideration of the ultimate goal. Goals have to be
interpreted and concreted to be operational, and primary data must be integrated and generalized before they can be related to goals. For effective
support of decision processes, therefore, the substance matter of a work
domain should be represented at several levels of abstraction, representing
goals and requirements, general functions, physical processes and activities,
as well as material resources. That decisions are called upon at all,
depend on a many-to-many mapping between these levels. Any work function
(_what_ should be used) can be seen both as a goal (_why_ it is relevant) for a
function at a lower level, and as a means for a function at a higher level
(_how_ it is realized). It is a basic feature that any work content can be
described in very different terms, related to different levels of abstraction
and decomposition, and any element can be described in terms of 'what' it
is, 'why' and 'when' it can be useful, and 'how' it can be implemented. An
explicit formulation of the problem or work space is necessary for support
of any improvised solution of new demands.

This explicit representation of the means-ends relational network is
necessary for problem solving and resource management in unfamiliar situations. In highly familiar situations, the relevant net of relations may be
activated at a more subconscious and intuitive level like a 'frame' or
'script', since there will be no need for repeating the analytical evaluation
that was necessary the first time, the problem was met. However, the explicit representation of the problem space will still be useful to identify the
information needs, also during the more routinized situations.

Two important conclusions for interface design can immediately be recognized from the problem space perspective:

- System design cannot only be focused on familiar tasks with
  procedural support. Also problem solving and improvisation
  in higher level functions should be supported effectively.
  Means-end relations, therefore, should be explicitly represented, not only implicitly in terms of general practice.

- For such decision support, it is important that the information of the substance matter of work can be retrieved from different points of view, defined by the mapping in the means-end space, i.e., seen as means, ends, or function. System design, therefore, is not a question of designing a proper interface to a selected set of existing databases. The representation and retrieval attributes of the information itself depend on the actual users' needs.

- Furthermore, this information has two different sources. Information on functional resources and the actual state of affairs can be collected and represented by means of rational analysis of the work domain, and information will propagate upward through the means-end mapping. On the other hand, information on goals, ends, and intent, propagating top-down through the means-end map will have to include, in addition to institutional goals and constraints, the subjective goals and preferences of individuals and will, consequently, be extremely difficult to collect and to formalize. Generally, such value information is propagated through social contacts in all kinds of meetings and get-togethers; a mechanism which is very difficult to replace by computer based communication and which is typically studied as a separate social science topic. It is, however, very important to consider the system as one integrated whole, even if it cannot as such be implemented by a computer system, but, requires social face-to-face contact of some kind.

The Decision Task

It follows, from the approach taken, that the problem space and the decision task have to be considered separately in order to be able to design systems which also support unforeseen problem solving scenarios. It, also, follows that particular decision processes cannot be modelled explicitly since they will be very situation and person dependent. In advanced systems, the user will have to coordinate at a high level of decision making the interaction with complex tools dedicated to a variety of functions serving a broad repertoire of information processing functions. For the design of an interface to support proper user-task interaction, it is important to be able to structure the decision task at this coordination level in task independent terms, since coping with a specific situation will depend on the combination of a wide variety of computer supported functions.

In complex tasks, mental economy can be achieved by partitioning subroutines connected by more or less standardized key nodes representing different states of knowledge in terms of the actual state of affairs, goals to pursue, target states, and work procedures. Such key nodes are very useful for linking different processes, for bringing specialized tools or results from previously successful cases into use in new situations, and for communicating with colleagues, advisors or computers. This is also important, since a complex decision task may be shared by a number of cooperating decision makers, procedure designers and, in modern systems, systems programmers and computers. Such key nodes, therefore, are also well suited to separate the decision task elements which should be considered for design of decision support systems. The different decision subtasks connecting the key nodes are dependent on basically different decision functions, such as analysis, state identification and classification, prediction of responses to hypothetical acts, value judgment and choice, resource evaluation and planning, and execution. Therefore, these different subtasks depend on different reasoning processes, are based on different kinds of "mental" models, and use different kinds of data, and standardized "states of knowledge" must be selected and expressed in terms suited to connect the different subtasks. The system designer, the user, and the computer have very different resource profiles for the various functions, and different information processes will be selected for/by them for the same decision function. It is, therefore, important that the key-nodes for communication are chosen carefully in order to ensure mutual understanding during cooperative decision making.

Analysis in the domain of the decision task is necessary for resolution of important interface issues related to the user-system interaction:

- Which is the set of decision sub-functions which are needed to serve the overall task content of the user? How will the appropriate role allocation between designer, user, and computer be, considering the different resource profiles with respect to basic knowledge, state data, and processing capacity?

- Proper selection and grouping of the information to be available in the various display formats depends on a careful analysis in this domain.

- When should messages communicated between partners be interpreted as neutral messages, as a piece of advice, as a recommendation, or as a direct order? In systems with drastic consequences of mistakes, this raises some questions regarding responsibility of ethical as well as legal kind.

- What is required from this communication in order to assure the understanding and acceptance by the user? Such understanding is not only needed for the user to be motivated to use the system, but is a prerequisite for the ability of a user to detect his/her own errors, erroneous messages caused by cooperators mistakes, as well as violations of the basic conditions of the system operation.

The fact that information will be available in several different formats corresponding to different task situations invariably will lead to a more complex information retrieval task which should be considered explicitly during design. In consequence, the information retrieval methods and tools for support of the approach to information and library science become generally applicable for design of advanced information systems in any domain. In a way, integrated design of systems for effective user-task interaction depend on a 'cognitive task analysis' for proper representation of work content, while interface design for easy access to the information will depend on special tools for navigation and search in databases, including approaches like 'intelligent systems' building a model of users and their strategies, effective means for designing close mapping from display formats to work content for 'direct manipulation', as well as more traditional tools like menus, windows, thesauri, etc.

Mental Information Processing Strategies

For each of the generic decision tasks, a set of different mental strategies can be formulated that can be used to solve the task. In the present context, strategies are defined as higher level categories of information processes. The information processes which can be used for a particular strategy are characterized by being dependent on the same kind of mental model, on the same type of data, and by similar resource requirements with respect to information processing capacity.

It is immediately clear that novices and experts will use different mental strategies. Novices - and experts facing new situations - will have to use more or less rational analysis involving consideration of the means-end relationships as well as causal arguments. Routine performance by skilled experts, however, will be based on know-how in terms of associations directly from signs representing familiar situations to stereotypical patterns of actions. For an analytical approach to a problem, different strategies will be available. These strategies will typically require different resource profiles and, consequently, shift in strategy may be used to avoid violation of capacity limits. It is generally found that skilled persons, having a repertoire of effective work strategies, follow a rule of 'least effort', which means that every time difficulties are met in a running strategy because of, for instance, inadequate mental models, high cost of observation, etc., there is a good chance, a shift will occur to another strategy which has less requirements in that particular dimension of the resource envelope. Such shifts result in a very varied course of a particular decision process depending on very subjective and situation-dependent details. Thus, to control the users' choice of strategy, the content and form of information displays should be carefully matched to the relevant strategies, not to a particular path to solution.

It is generally found that a given cognitive task can be solved by several different strategies varying widely in their requirements as to the kind of mental model and the type or amount of observation required (see, for instance, for concept formation: Bruner et al., 1956; for trouble shooting: Rasmussen et al., 1974; and for bibliographic search: Pejtersen, 1979). An analysis of the task is, therefore, important in order to identify the different strategies which may serve the different phases of the decision sequence, and to identify the subjective process criteria for choice of strategy, such as cognitive strain, load on short-term memory, time available, data and resource limitations in general, cost of mistakes, etc. (Bruner et al., 1956; Rasmussen and Jensen, 1974).

This analysis, which is related to operations research rather than psychology, identifies the information processes required in implementation-independent terms as a basis for a subsequent human-computer task allocation based on demand/resource matching. It may be difficult to identify the useful, possible strategies by rational analysis, but, since users are very inventive when searching for clever tricks, the strategies may be identified by empirical studies of user behavior. This, of course, requires psychological as well as domain expertise.

An important part of the analysis is an identification of the general resource requirements of the strategies in terms of data describing the actual system state, the basic functional relations, the processing capacity needed, etc., and of the consequences of errors. The results will be the basis for matching these requirements with the resource characteristics of the designer, the computer, and the operating staff for planning of their roles in the interactive decision task.

In addition, guides can be obtained for selection of a suitable support of the mental models required in terms of information content of suitable display formats and of the data integration required. The design objective is to match the displays to a mental model which will be effective for the task and to choose interface design, operator selection and total job content in a way which will guide operators' subjective preferences in that direction. It should be noted that different strategies will have very specific needs with respect to type of useful data, to support of the mental model, etc. In "intelligent" decision support systems it should be possible to let a computer analyze the user queries in order to identify the strategy a user is trying to apply and then to supply the required support by displays and messages of the proper form.

The requirement, that the interface design should lead operators to form effective mental models and adopt proper strategies, presupposes that it is possible to characterize the different strategies with respect to features related to the users' subjective criteria for choosing a given strategy in the actual situation.

Analysis of the users' repertoire of strategies is important for the following interface design issues:

- Each effective strategy has a particular requirement with respect to support in terms of level of generalization of data, and the mental model as reflected in the structure of display formats, timing of the selection among displays to match strategies, etc.

- It is important to support novices without frustrating the expert. Therefore, different display formats may be needed for different users.

- This may result in a great repertoire of display formats, and support of the user's easy retrieval of information in her/his preferred form should be considered. In 'intelligent' support systems, it should be possible to have the computer recognizing the user's 'cognitive style', given the relevant strategies and their communication terms have been identified.

The User's Cognitive Style and Level of Interpretation

For the proper interface design, it is important to have a conceptual model of the different ways in which a user may interpret the information presented, depending on his skill in the particular task. A useful distinction is the distinction between skill-, rule, and knowledge-based behavior.

Skill-Based Behavior represents sensorimotor performance during acts or activities that, after a statement of an intention, take place without conscious control as smooth, automated, and highly integrated patterns of behavior. At this cognitive level, performance is based on a direct time-space manipulation of the appearance of the configuration of the environment, in the case of computer-interaction, of the elements of the surface of the system in terms of display elements and control keys.

In general, human activities can be considered as a sequence of such skilled acts or activities composed for the actual occasion. The flexibility of skilled performance is due to the ability to compose from a large repertoire of automated subroutines the sets suited for specific purposes.

At the next level of rule-based behavior, the composition of such a sequence of subroutines in a familiar work situation is typically consciously controlled by a stored rule or procedure that may have been derived empirically during previous occasions, communicated from other persons' know-how as an instruction or cookbook recipe, or it will be prepared on occasion by conscious problem solving and planning. The point is, here, that performance is goal-oriented, but structured by "feed-forward control" through a stored rule. Very often, the goal is not even explicitly formulated, but is found implicitly in the situation releasing the stored rules. The control is teleologic in the sense that the rule or control is selected from previous successful experiences. The control evolves by "survival of the fittest" rule.

40

During unfamiliar situations, faced with an environment for which no know-how or rules for control are available from previous encounters, the control of performance must move to a higher conceptual level, in which performance is goal-controlled and <u>knowledge-based</u>. Knowledge is, here, taken as possession of a conceptual, structural model and the level might be called model-based. In this situation, the goal is explicitly formulated, based on an analysis of the environment and the overall aims of the person. Then a useful plan is developed - by selection, such that different plans are considered and their effect tested against the goal, by trial and error, or by means of understanding of the functional properties of the environment and prediction of the effects of the plan considered. At this level of functional reasoning, the internal structure of the system is explicitly represented by a "mental model" that may take several different forms.

This domain of analysis of the users' cognitive style is important for consideration in the interface design:

- The configuration of a display is generally designed to support the structure of the mental activity. This means that the configuration in familiar tasks should be related to the rules of users' know-how. For support in problem solving situations, the configuration should reflect the structure of the problem domain.

- The information given will be interpreted as stereotype signs during familiar situations. The display surface will be manipulated according to empirical rules. When problems arise, information is to be interpreted symbolically with reference to a mental model. This switch should be supported explicitly in system design.

- 'Direct manipulation' is typically discussed with reference to manipulation of computer functions directly from the display surface, i.e., a proper mapping between the configuration of display onto computer functions is aimed at. Direct manipulation of the task content should be considered by proper 'externalization' of the proper mental model for direct manipulation from the display configuration.

APPLICATION DOMAINS

The approach toward design of integrated 'work stations' at present is taken in several domains, each starting from a perspective depending on the specific tradition for work organization and tools within their trade and, therefore, with their particular emphasis on the different design problems. To be generally useful in the attempts to create a common ground, a design framework should be compatible with the aims and concepts developed within these trades. It is the aim of the present section to review the state of the art of modelling and design within a number of fields for which decision support and information systems are presently considered in order to judge the general applicability of the framework presented in the previous section. The application domains are selected, also, because they focus on different aspects of the framework and, consequently, will be well suited to serve as the experimental test beds for the individual aspects. In the following sections, the approaches taken to analysis in the different domains are discussed. The discussion is not intended to be exhaustive, but those aspects which are typical for the different domains, are mentioned for sake of the evaluation of the usefulness of the framework.

Supervisory Process Control

Information systems for support of operators in control of industrial
process systems such as large chemical plants and nuclear power plants
have been discussed intensively since the major accidents which have occurred
during the recent decade. Emphasis in this development has been on support
of a control room operator faced with a plant disturbance for which no
formal operating procedure has been devised. Design emphasis, therefore,
has been on support of the problem solving required by a decision maker
faced with a well structured technical system obeying causal physical laws.

In modern process plants, the normal operation and many of the routine
state changes such as start-up and shutdown are typically automated and the
role of the operating staff will be disturbance analysis and control.
The staff will be thoroughly familiar with the plant which will appear
as a well structured work environment. Due to the large production units
and the potentially risky processes, concern of designers will be the
ability of the operating staff to cope with rare but risky courses of
events.

The supervisory control task during disturbances involves a demand/re-
source management task which cannot be preplanned in detail. During disturbances, a complex many-to-many mapping between goals and purposes, functions,
processes, and physical equipment should be considered. In any situation,
several goals and constraints related to production and safety are important.
Each of these will be affected by changes in several plant functions which,
in turn, can be implemented by the processes of different pieces of equipment. Without this complex mapping there would be no means for control,
and no decision task. Consequently, access to a representation of the
plant in terms of a means-end, part-whole problem space is a prerequisite
for decision making. In this problem space, causes for changes in the
actual state of affairs is propagating bottom-up, and inference depends on
knowledge about functional properties at the various levels. Reasons for
proper changes in operating conditions, however, will propagate top-down
and depend on knowledge about the intentions behind plant design. Both
kinds of knowledge are necessary for decision making (Rasmussen, 1984).

The functional information, i.e., descriptions of the functional mapping
upward in the hierarchy, in general, will be immediately accessible in engineering manuals and system descriptions. Such information can be generated
by established and well documented methods for engineering analysis. This
is not the case for information describing the downward mapping which represents the design decisions, i.e., the reasons behind the chosen implementations. This information is typically implicit in company or engineering
practice or is based on the designer's personal preferences and seldom
finds its way to operators. This can be crucial for control decisions when
overruling of a design requirement, e.g., an interlock protection has to be
considered during critical situations. Traditionally, much effort is spend
on presenting operators with analytical, bottom-up information about the
system. Only little attention has been paid to the need for top-down,
intentional information on reasons for the implementations chosen during
the design. The information can be difficult to collect, once the design
has been completed, since there may be a long time span between the design
choice and the situation creating a need for information about the underlying
intention. It is a frequent experience for operating organizations that
questions to system suppliers concerning their design basis are hard to
have answered; typically, minutes from project meetings have to be retrieved
since the man having the knowledge has moved to another position. The
problem space in terms of a means-end representation will serve to identify
the information which should be recorded during design and operations
planning.

In the decision task for disturbance analysis to consider during design, different typical subtasks can be identified, such as diagnosis, setting goal priority, and planning of control sequences. In a well structured system like a process plant, the resources are well-known, and for most categories of situations, the control sequences to bring resources into operations can be preplanned and instructions prepared. The difficult part will be to predict the decision task related to diagnosis and goal setting. However, some general characteristics of the appropriate strategies can be stated. The diagnostic task implied in supervisory systems control is a search to identify a change from normal or planned system operation in terms that can refer the controller to the appropriate control actions. Such a diagnostic search can be performed in a number of different ways. It is, however, possible to categorize the potential strategies, and to specify the information needed in terms of kinds of mental models and of the nature and amount of measured data.

In advanced systems for support of supervisory process control, the information retrieval aspects of the decision task are becoming important. To support decision making during plant disturbances, easy access is necessary to databases including large amount of information in addition to the factual information about plant state. As discussed above, information on design intentions, operational specifications from safety authorities, preplanned procedures, etc., may be needed by the operating staff for advice, and effective retrieval tools are needed as an integral part of the interface.

Also, the mental strategies used by operators should be studied in detail. Generalizations from analyses of verbal protocols from real life work situations clearly show that, in a mental task, a satisfactory result can be reached by very different information processes. As an example, a review of the different diagnostic strategies applicable for trouble shooting in technical systems will be given here, for details reference is made to Rasmussen and Jensen (1974).

In general, the diagnostic task implied in supervisory systems control is a search to identify a change from normal or planned system operation in terms that can refer the controller to the appropriate control actions. Such a diagnostic search can be performed in two basically different ways.

A set of observations representing the abnormal state of the system - a set of symptoms - can be used as a search template to find a matching set in a library of symptoms related to different abnormal system conditions. This kind of search is called symptomatic search. On the other hand, the search can be performed in the actual, maloperating system with reference to a template representing normal or planned operation. The change will then be found as a mismatch and identified by its location in the system. Consequently, this kind of search strategy can be called topographic search.

The topographic search is performed by a good/bad mapping of the system through which the extent of the potentially "bad" field is gradually narrowed down until the location of the change is determined with sufficient resolution to allow selection of an appropriate action. The topographic search is performed as a good/bad mapping of the system, which results in a stepwise limitation of the field of attention within which further search is to be considered. The information available in observations is used rather uneconomically by topographic strategies, because they depend only upon good/bad judgments. Furthermore, they do not take into account previously experienced faults and disturbances. Therefore, switching to other strategies may be necessary to reach an acceptable resolution of the search or to acquire good tactical guidance during the search.

MEANS-ENDS LEVELS	*	WHOLE-PART DECOMPOSITION
	*	
	*	(FUNCTIONAL DECOMPOSITION AT EACH LEVEL INDEPENDENTLY)
	*	
GOALS AND VALUES CONSTRAINTS	*	Customer and Market Relations; Competitors; Production Volume Requirements; Legal Requirements for Financial Relations and Environmental Protection; Work Safety Legislation; Agreements with Worker's Unions
FLOW, DISTRIBUTION, AND ACCUMULATION OF MATERIAL, ENERGY, MONETARY VALUES, AND MANPOWER	*	Topology of Product Flow and of Major Mass, Energy, and Information Flows; Major Mass, and Energy Balance Systems, their Properties and Limitations; Flow of Monetary Values; Manpower Turnover; etc.
GENERAL FUNCTIONS AND ACTIVITIES	*	Production Functions; Cooling, Heating, Purification Functions; Control Functions and Feed-back Loops, etc.
SPECIFIC WORK PROCESSES. PHYSICAL PROCESSES OF EQUIPMENT	*	Technical Characteristics of Equipment, Machinery, and Components; Their Capabilities and Limitations, Control Characteristics; Content of Manuals and Technical Specifications; Maintenance Properties;
APPEARENCE, LOCATION, AND CONFIGURATION OF MATERIAL RESOURCES	*	Material Characteristics, Sizes, Weight, Appearance, and Location; Anatomy and Configuration of Equipment and Installations; Building Layout; Drawings; Access Roads and Site Topography;

Figure 2. Problem Space of Supervisory Process Control.

Symptomatic search strategies are based on the internal relationship in data sets and not from the topological structure of system properties. In principle, a search is made through a library of abnormal data sets, "symptoms", to find the set that matches the actual observed pattern of system behavior. The symptomatic search can be a parallel, data-driven pattern based on reference patterns generated on-line by modification of a functional model in correspondence with a hypothetical disturbance, the strategy can be called "search by hypothesis and test". Symptomatic search is advantageous from the point of view of information economy, and a precise identification can frequently be obtained in a one-shot decision.

The point to make here is that different possible strategies for the same task may have very different resource requirements, for instance in terms of data, knowledge of basic system functions, processing and memory capacity. Shifts in strategy, therefore, will be very effective for obtaining a suitable resource/demand match. In general, choice of strategy to use depends on subjective process criteria, rather than consideration of goal or product criteria.

Finally, the cognitive style of the operators are to be considered. The characteristic feature of the work situation of industrial plant operators is that they are faced with a physical system, the operational feature of which they become intimately familiar during normal operation as well as a large repertoire of more or less frequent disturbances. The characteristics of the interface system for such situations are, due to the stable and well structured nature of the system, accessible to empirical studies. The key problem to consider for advanced support systems, is to design a system that will support decisions during unforeseen situations, i.e., during stringent requirements for effective shift from skill- and rule-based to knowledge based performance.

The problem space in supervisory process control (Figure 2) has two principle dimensions. One is the part-whole dimension representing the span of attention of the operator, the part of the system he is considering. The other is the means-end dimension representing the level of abstraction in the decision process. Note that the highest level of goals includes goal specification and constraint satisfaction. Considering the means-end space as a many-to-many mapping space enables initial "top-down" design, by considering constraints as part of the initial goal specification.

Emergency Management

A similar area, where the application of modern information technology is presently considered for decision support, is the general emergency management related to protection of the public against effects from events like major fires, flooding, chemical accidents, etc. (Rasmussen et al., 1986). In particular, after a number of serious chemical and nuclear plant accidents, the need for advanced information systems to support emergency and accident control has been discussed together with the requirements for a formal risk analysis of all major installations. The requirements can be seen as an extension of the decision support systems needed for control of disturbances, once they have run out of the control of the operating staff.

Problem Space. Compared to process plant control, the task domain of general accident and emergency management has a very unstructured nature. The domain does not exist until an accident has happened and, consequently, can only be described in terms of sets of unrelated elements that will be activated and structured during an accident and the following efforts for control. In fact, two domains can be identified and represented in separate means-end/part-whole domains.

One domain will represent the risk potential in terms of the properties of the potential sources of accidents together with the environments through which they may propagate: at the lowest level is found information on geographic and topographic features of potential risk sources and their environment in terms of maps of installations, likely routes of propagation and of access, etc. At functional levels are specified the physical processes involved in normal and accidental chains of events, and in the propagation of consequences as well as the consequences of such events on the general public, in more general terms comparable with the acceptable limits specified in laws and regulations which are represented at the highest level.

Another domain represents the properties of resources available for counteraction in terms of fire brigades, hospitals, transport facilities, etc. in terms of geography, anatomy, and physical functioning at the lower levels, through more general functions to the policies and general goals of society at the highest.

Until an accident has occurred, these domains appear as sets of separate elements. Consequently, the information is of a very varied nature: geographical, and meteorological data, information on road planning and repair, on functional properties of equipment in plants and emergency equipment, results of risk analysis, requirements in laws and instructions, etc. Furthermore, it is coming from a wide variety of sources with very different

RISK DOMAIN	RESOURCE DOMAIN
GOALS, VALUES, AND CONSTRAINTS; LAWS, REGULATIONS AND PUBLIC OPPINION	
CRITERIA FOR SETTING PRIORITY: RISK, ECONOMIC AND SOCIAL EFFECTS	CRITERIA FOR SETTING PRIORITY: FLOW OF MONETARY VALUES, AND MANPOWER
GENERAL ACCIDENT CATEGORIES: FIRE, FLOODING, EXPLOSIONS, ETC.	GENERAL RESOURCES: MEDICAL CARE, EVACUATION, FIREFIGHTING, ETC.
PHYSICAL PROCESSES IN POTENTIAL ACCIDENTS AS SPECI-FIED BY ANALYSIS OR PRIOR EVENTS	PHYSICAL FUNCTIONING OF TOOLS AND EQUIPMENT; INTERACTION WITH TARGET
TOPOGRAPHICAL, DEMOGRAPHICAL CHARACTERISTICS OF POTENTIAL DANGER SOURCES AND LOCALITIES	APPEARANCE, LOCATION, AND CONFIGURATION OF MATERIAL TOOLS AND RESOURCES

Figure 3. Problem Domain in Emergency Management.

professional and institutional routines. A recent review (Rasmussen, Pedersen, and Grinberg, 1986) has shown that the means-end/part-whole framework is well suited to specify data formats for decision support systems.

<u>Decision Task</u>

As is the case in process control, diagnosis, goal evaluation and planning are important decision tasks. In general, great effort is spent on the planning of formal procedures for the activities of emergency services such as fire brigades, civil defense corps, hospital teams, etc. Such procedures have to be at a general level and adaptation to the specifics of an accident will be necessary. This implies the communication between the acting commander needing procedural advice, and the subject matter experts mainly in possession of basic technical knowledge. Several attempts have been made to establish expert-system-like advice services, but with limited success, and more empirical research on decision strategies in actual cases is needed, based on a framework like the present, able to model in categories rather than particular scenarios.

The <u>information retrieval</u> aspect of the decision task appears to be particularly important for systems to support emergency management. Large amounts of information about very different aspects such as geographical features, meteorological data, road conditions, and traffic data, physical and chemical properties of plants and substances, resources of medical centers, may be needed in advance by an accident manager. This information

will be supplied by many different sources and, typically, not in formats
suited for a stressed decision maker needing procedural advice on short
notice. Database formats and retrieval tools, therefore, become a central
issue of the interface design.

Mental Strategies

No detailed studies of the mental strategies of decision makers during
emergency management are available. Empirical evidence, however, suggests
that great difficulties are experienced in the communication between subject
matter experts serving as advisors from their basic 'deep' knowledge and
the actual emergency controllers needing procedural information (Rasmussen
et al., 1986).

In conclusion, for emergency management important topics for research
for which the present framework seems to be well suited are the study of
diagnostic and planning strategies in an unfamiliar problem space, and
information retrieval and advice given in a context which is very similar
to the library context described in a later section.

The problem space of emergency management will not be defined until an
emergency is present. For a general description serving system design,
therefore, it will be useful to consider a representation of the potential
risk and the resources for accident control separately. Figure 3 shows a
common goal representation for the two aspects, because political and public
attitudes are the basis for requirements to industry as well as for the
resources made available for control of emergencies.

Engineering Design

Engineering design is yet another area for which information technology is introduced in the work interface in the form of systems for computer-
aided design (CAD) and computer integrated manufacturing (CIM). Since
design and planning of manufacturing basically depend on means-end considerations in order to find the practical means to meet a given goal, it should
be expected that the present framework immediately applies.

Problem Space. It also appears that the problem space description is
similar to concepts adopted in design. For the planning of databases,
abstraction hierarchies are well known forms of representations in design
(Alexander, 1964; Eastman, 1978); in particular in architectural design.
The major differences in these approaches, compared to the problem space in
the present approach has been that means-end and part-whole relations were
not kept separate in the concept of abstraction.

Furthermore, the process of design and manufacturing are frequently
treated in separation. Interviews of designers of electronic equipment
show (Hovde, 1986) that an important feature of the decision process is an
iteration between consideration of two different problem spaces; one representing the part being designed in its functional context of the final
application, another representing the part in the manufacturing context.

The first problem domain is a means-end hierarchy representing the
many-to-many mapping between the various levels of descriptions bridging
the space between the purpose and constraints the final system should meet,
and the physical resources of the technology considered for the system
implementation. Another domain will be considered for manufacturing,
representing the means-end relations of the available manufacturing resources
in terms of processes and machinery. Both of these problem spaces will
represent properties of technical systems and, consequently, will be similar
to the problem space of supervisory process control. In addition, since

components designed previously for other applications may be available on stock and useful for the new design, access will be needed to information about such items in a database with retrieval attributes related to the various levels of the design hierarchy.

Traditionally, design and manufacturing have been considered rather separate activities in formal modeling approaches, involving different professional groups of an organization. This is no longer the case, and tools for 'computer integrated manufacturing' are being widely considered. In this case, the design of supporting tools will have to include the three domains discussed above. The design process will imply an iteration between the levels in the functional hierarchy in order to identify the acceptable functional properties of a component, but at the same time, iteration across the manufacturing hierarchy together with consultation of the properties of the designs already in stock should be supported. For easy shifts between these hierarchies during the design process, consistent search attributes should be used for the different databases.

This approach to a consistent design of the user-task interface for computer-aided design and manufacturing is in good accordance with recent developments in the field. Alting (1978) has proposed a morphological process model to support an integrated planning of design and manufacturing, which is a multi-level model with basic features similar to the means-end hierarchy considered in the present approach. Alting bases his description on a taxonomy derived from consideration of mass, energy, and information flows at the highest level, general manufacturing functions like casting, forging, welding, etc. at the next lower level and, finally, particular processes like sand-, die-, and centrifugal-casting.

He concludes his description: "--all manufacturing processes can be described by a morphological model made up of a material flow and information flow, and an energy flow.-- In practice it can be used in the generation of alternative production methods for a given component and it can be used in process development. Both the design and manufacturing engineer have, in this approach, a new and powerful tool. If one considers the rapid increase in the application of computers in design and in manufacturing, the new systematic approach fulfills the long existing need for a coherent and systematic 'theory of manufacturing'." And he adds, that the principles are valid for all types of manufacturing methods, including processes in mechanical, civil, electrical, and chemical engineering. Thus, the development within engineering design is well compatible with the present concept of problem space description.

Decision task and mental strategies of designers in real life work situations need some detailed field studies. Most work on design strategies are theoretic schemes describing a 'vertical' top-down process deriving implementations from goals. This is a feasible description for design of new implements based on new technology. This is, however, the exception in most design tasks, change or updating of an old design, 'horizontally' or bottom-up, plays an important role, which will have influence on the design of databases and information retrieval systems.

Since an integrated work station for engineering design will have to include a number of different databases representing technical standards, calculation and simulation tools, production equipment characteristics, laws and regulations, raw material characteristics, etc., each designed with search attributes matching the way a user will express his needs, proper information retrieval tools will be an important requirement for the interface design.

The conclusion in the present context will be that the framework

MANUFACTURING ENVIRONMENT		FUNCTIONAL SYSTEM ENVIRONMENT	ATTRIBUTES OF COMPONENTS ON STOCK
MANUFACTORING GOALS AND CONSTRAINTS		FUNCTIONAL SYSTEM GOALS AND CONSTRAINTS	FUNCTIONAL GOALS AND CONSTRAINTS OF PREVIOUS APPLICATIONS
MANUFACTURER'S PRIORITY SETTING; FLOW OF ENERGY, MATERIAL, AND MONETARY VALUES, MANPOWER, ETC.		CUSTOMER'S PRIORITY SETTING; FLOW OF ENERGY' MATERIAL, AND MONETARY VALUES, MANPOWER, ETC.	PRICE, RELIABILITY AND OTHER HIGHER ORDER SPEC'S
GENERAL MANUFACTURING SYSTEMS AVAILABLE: CASTING, FORGING, ASSEMBLING, CUTTING, ETC.		GENERAL FUNCTION TO BE PERFORMED IN TARGET SYSTEM: BEARING; SUPPORT; CONDUCT;TRANSFER;	INTENDED FUNCTIONAL CONTEXT OF INITIAL DESIGN
PHYSICAL FORMING PROCESSES AVAILABLE		ACCEPTABLE PHYSICAL FUNCTIONS OF SEPARATE PART	PHYSICAL FUNCTIONING SPEC'S
AVAILABLE TOOLS AND MACHINERY	PART TO BE MANUFACTURED.	RELATED FUNCTIONAL COMPONENTS	SHAPE, SIZE MATERIAL
GEOMETRICAL FORM, MATERIAL, SURFACE FINISH.			

Figure 4. Problem Domain in Computer Aided Design.

proposed here for the systematic and integrated design of user-task interfaces, appears to be immediately compatible with the morphological model
framework for design and manufacturing developed from technical engineering
considerations. The domain of formal design may be a vehicle very well
suited to study the information system problems related to a user's navigation and interaction with a work domain structured in several levels of
means-end representations, as used in the present framework.

Figure 4 illustrates the different problem domains relevant for design:
the manufacturing environment, the ultimate functional context; and the stock
of available previous solutions to similar design problems.

Administration and Executive Management

Information systems for support of administrative and management tasks
have been a major field of study for several decades. The particular feature
of this domain is the involvement of a social organization. The design
problems are, therefore, different from the domains discussed so far, which
have been characteristic of the technical, causal dominance in the system
behavior. Administrative systems or 'office systems' are typically considered as 'intentional' rather than causal systems. Consequently, a dominant feature in one line of approach has been the social science approach
to 'decision support systems' which have focused on the quality of work

features. Unfortunately, such social or value features are unsuited as design guides even though they are important for choosing among the possible functional designs.

The functional approach to design has typically been based on procedural models of the activities, for the higher level functions on rational decision models based on normative, economic theories. Recently, however, other approaches have been taken which appear compatible with the present framework.

The approach to office information systems is generally important since the trend toward integrated systems will require an integration of the information systems related to work in the different domains and the administrative tasks. It is, therefore, important to judge the compatibility of the present approach the general development within studies of office systems.

Problem Space. For a typical office like, for instance, the administration of a manufacturing company, the problem domain can theoretically be described in terms of a means/end - part/whole hierarchy, similar to that discussed in the previous section. There are, however, important differences since a team of decision makers, 'the organization', have allocated roles individually and each are coping with only part of the problem domain.

For each of the decision makers, the system considered will have a significantly 'intentional' character (Rasmussen, 1986), since the response of the system to the act of any one of the decision makers will depend on the reactions of the other actors of the organization. If the system response is not in accordance with their aims, they will tend to make compensatory actions. An intentional system will be highly homeostatic and seek to maintain its states stable. This aspect is, however, very well covered by the means-end hierarchy, because intentional reasoning is depending on the top-down propagation of reasons.

In office systems, many tasks are formally proceduralized and, consequently, one of the traditional approaches to the modeling of office activities has been in terms of task procedures and transaction sequences. The actual work procedures, however, 'the tricks of the trade', will form a much more diversified network of cues and heuristics in which detailed branching takes care of the familiar nuances of the work conditions.

In reality, office work is a very open-ended sequence of occurrences. Work procedures have many degrees of freedom and the actual work process will depend on the performer's subjective preferences, minor variations in work content, work load on the performer and the immediate cooperators, etc. The set of potentially possible work sequences form a network in which the performer navigates subject to the law of least effort; like water draining off a landscape after rain. The most effective description will a generic description of the features of the landscape of work, together with the most relevant modulating factors, as well as a characteristic of the features relating to performance criteria like 'least effort'.

A suitable representation of the landscape through which work flows appears to be a multi-level representation in terms of the means-end hierarchy, identifying available resources and specifying constraints at several levels of generality. Representation of the actual state of affairs in close relation to the means-end topology will support judgment of the actual 'modulations' of the landscape.

The use of the means-end/part-whole space to model the problem space of office work does not necessarily mean adoption of a 'hard system model' in Checkland's (1981) terms. The problem space will represent the world of possible means-end relations, i.e., of the available resources. The actual choice in a particular situation will depend on the performance criterion of the acting person which is a totally subjective matter. As discussed previously, there is a many-to-many mapping between the levels in any real-life problem space or else there would be no room for decisions, and the appropriate model should represent the potential for choice by the individual. A model should not, a priori, determine what will be the 'rational' choice and become a normative model (a 'hard system' model). Consequently, to have an 'office model' satisfying the requirement for 'soft system' models, the means-end description should be complemented by a model of the social organization of the office workers and a model of office workers' subjective criteria for choice in the means-end space.

The line of arguments presented here is in good agreement with a general trend in the current approaches to models of office systems. Typically, present system development rely on task analysis expressed in terms of the overt task activities in the existing office environments, and models have been expressed in terms of procedures. 'Generally they (i.e., the available descriptions) contain information about the surface phenomenon in offices such as communication characteristics, document flow characteristics, or authority relations' (Barber, 1984).

Typically, the focus on proceduralized descriptions is maintained, partly because of the general human preferences for procedural accounts when asked for information about work content; partly because the proceduralized formalism of computer science is familiar to those specialists who are arguing for the introduction of computers in office environments (Hammer, 1984).

There are, however, now arguments for a shift in the fundamental research focus. Suchman (1982) of Xerox Parc argues that in contrast to the traditional aim of office analysts to optimize the procedural models to the point where they can be automated, research should be focused on 'the problematic relationship between organizational specifications of procedure and the work of 'carrying them out'.' Office work should be considered as 'trouble management'. 'The arguments for a fundamental shift in research focus, accordingly, is that the work of the office is organized by the practical problems of accomplishing action according to procedure, rather than by the procedural specifications themselves.' The point is later elaborated in a study where the topic is 'finding the 'definite meaning' of office procedures as a constituent feature of the work of getting them done.' This relates to the intentional structure represented in the means-end problem space.

In a sequence of papers, Barber (Barber, 1983; Barber, 1984) of MIT argues along similar lines. Office work is considered a problem solving activity and an abstract characterization is sought under the name of 'office semantics' which is concerned with 'the intent behind the act'. The world of organizational knowledge is not closed, and a complete set of actions relevant to the organizational world is unknown and unknowable because unforeseen situations are a common occurrence.

A procedural characterization is considered to be problematic for several reasons. Even routine tasks in offices encounter unexpected obstacles and all alternatives cannot be determined in advance. 'As a result, a procedural approach is not a very useful style of work description because it needs to be augmented by the procedures' goal structure.' A description of office work in terms of goals and actions is considered a more direct way of characterizing office work.'

An explicit representation of goals and actions provides the resources to cope with unexpected contingencies. Office workers are able to handle unexpected contingencies in their daily work only when they know the goals of the office work and what actions are needed to achieve these goals. 'These goals and actions are often implicit in the work and in the office worker's knowledge of their work.'

Barber (Barber et al., 1983) reviews current office models and concludes that 'Information-action models are an active research area today for computerization of organizational work. They focus on the information used in office work and the actions performed on the information.' None of the models reviewed explicitly describes the goals of the office work and how each action is related to the accomplishment of the overall goal of the work. 'These systems do not deal well with the unanticipated conditions.'

They continue 'the goals of the organizational work provide a basis for dealing with work that does not fit within the information action models. A goal presents a problem to be solved and can be decomposed into subgoals. The problem decomposition process is repeated until subgoals are reached that may easily be attained by the workers.

Seen in the light of this trend in modeling office work, the approach in the present paper is a further step away from the modeling of proceduralized action. The focus here is on a representation of the means-end domain, the repertoire of <u>potential actions or action alternatives</u> and criteria for choice.

Also, for this application domain, the means-end problem space appears to be an effective tool for design of support systems.

Explicit models of the <u>decision tasks and mental strategies</u> in executive management are scarce, except for normative models. Sutherland (1983) on the basis of a general description discusses the different needs for support 'instruments' at the various levels of an organization which, implicitly, characterizes the kinds of strategies relevant for the levels.

Four levels of decision types are identified by Sutherland and correlated with decision processes and support models:

- Goal programming and long range planning at the highest level of an organization are related to sequential state models for heuristic problem solving procedures or structured decision making procedures. Support in this function is essential for executives who are responsible for development of the firm over the long run. At this level, development of a plan serves to define the trajectory an organization will be expected to take from some current position to an assumedly more favorable position in the future.

- Strategic analysis at the next lower level includes contingency planning related to stochastic-state techniques to provide for deductive techniques for problems the 'state' outcomes of which are variable, such as game-theoretic models or logical analysis programs. This technique underlies most classic military contingency planning.

- The tactical programming, one level further down includes 'equilibrium maintenance' mainly based on statistics-based decision and control instruments for dealing with probabilistic problems, such as econometric methods, parametric

MEANS-ENDS LEVELS		WHOLE-PART DECOMPOSITION
	*	(FUNCTIONAL DECOMPOSITION INDEPENDENTLY AT EACH LEVEL)
GOALS AND VALUES; CONSTRAINTS	*	Market Conditions, Competitors, Economic Relations Industrial Branch Policies, Legal Constraints,
FLOW, DISTRIBUTION, AND ACCUMULATION OF MATERIAL, ENERGY, MONETARY VALUES, AND MANPOWER	*	Flow of Monetary Values, Material and Products Through Organization, Effectiveness and Loss Representations, Manpower Allocations and Turnover Salary and Employment Characteristics
GENERAL FUNCTIONS AND ACTIVITIES	*	Production, Marketing, Design, Accounting, Personnel Management, Maintenance, etc.
SPECIFIC WORK PROCESSES; PHYSICAL PROCESSES OF EQUIPMENT	*	Specific Production Equipment and Processes, Activities of Particular Groups and Offices: Typing, Filing, Mail Expedition, Invoice Form Execution
APPEARANCE, LOCATION, AND CONFIGURATION OF MATERIAL RESOURCES	*	Maps of Premises, Buildings, Furniture Arrangements, Inventory Lists, Identifiers of Personnel and Equipment

Figure 5.   Problem Space of Office Environment.

decision theory, etc. Instruments of this form dominate
at the tactical level of most organizations, where the am-
bition is to try to keep the parameters of the organization
in some sort of equilibrium position with the near term
properties of the immediate operating environment by means
of functions such as forecasting, logistical programming,
budgeting, and financial control.

The lowest level is concerned with operations management,
based on discrete-state instruments which are primarily
algorithmic and analytical methods that allow optimal solutions of deterministic problems. This is the domain of
methods of industrial engineering and operations research.

Considering the amount of documents, economic information, inventory
list, etc., involved in administrative systems, it is immediately clear
that the information retrieval aspects are very important. One present
approach is the desk top metaphor used to mimic the traditional work place
by the new technology. In a longer perspective, transparency should not be
sought to a material analogue, but to the work content directly. However,
even if a good mapping from the display surface to the work content can be
found, special tools for easy retrieval will be necessary, not only in
terms of windows and menus, but, also, in terms of 'query by example',
search by analogy, etc.

Cognitive Style. The office system domain is different from the previous examples, not being predominantly related to problem solving in coping with unique new situations, but to resource management in a more familiar work context. The domain, therefore, will be well suited to study the requirements for tools for performance in a work based on skill and know-how, and the interaction in an organization among different decision makers operating in different cognitive styles on different levels in the means-end domain. This is immediately reflected in the typical forms of displays. In office systems, displays are frequently based on stereotypical signs, or icons related to objects, states, and actions, the desk-top metaphor, whereas displays related to problem solving, as, for instance, in design and process control are related to symbols representing functional system properties.

In conclusion, the framework appears to be in line with the recent development in modeling activities in an office environment. This appears to be important since the administrative tasks and executive management will be an important ingredient in any integrated information system, whether this is related to an industrial plant, a manufacturing company, or a library system.

The problem space of executive decision making in the means-ends and parts-whole dimensions with indication of the relationships which are the subject matter content of analytical, knowledge based reasoning. The problem space represents the available means for meeting multiple ends in a decision task (Figure 5). A decision task depends on a many-to-many relationship between levels, and a representation for the criteria of choice in addition to the functional properties represented by the problem space will be needed.

Information Retrieval in Libraries

Library systems are interesting in the present context, not only because the framework for cognitive task analysis appear to be relevant for design of information retrieval support in libraries, but, in particular, because the information retrieval task is generally becoming increasingly important in the user-system interaction of decision tasks in many other domains: from decisions aided by computer based systems follows necessarily that the user can identify, retrieve and comprehend information embedded in the database. Database design and information retrieval is the core feature of library and information science. There is a long tradition in this domain for developing linguistic and classificatory methods for analysis, organization, representation, display, and retrieval of information across different knowledge domains - all facilities of relevance to interface design in any integrated work station. Information retrieval systems in libraries are not causal, technical systems, but they are intentional systems like office systems. Similar to office systems both the social and cultural value features of the whole organization of a library unit as well as the administrative tasks are of relevance for interface design of integrated decision support systems in libraries. However, in the library domain the approach to integrated support systems has generally been automation of procedural, administrative routine tasks like on-line performance of locating and reservation to different libraries of a reference retrieved in the database. (Like the OCLC tool, for instance.) Since the nature and comprehension of decision support systems are much more advanced in the office context, the reader is referred to the office discussion in the previous chapter. The following discussion, therefore, deals with the information retrieval task in libraries.

The Problem Space. The problem of information search for data or bibliographical items in libraries has been empirically investigated in a limited number of projects (Belkin et al., 1986; Ingwersen, 1981; Ingwersen,

54

1986; Morehead, Pejtersen, and Rouse, 1984; Rouse, 1984). Field studies by
Pejtersen (1980) have led to a formulation of a search space which has
features similar to the problem space discussed in this study. Analyses of
end-user - intermediary searches in public libraries have shown that users
express their reading needs in a way which can best be represented in a
multifaceted or multidimensional classification system.

The content of the various facets were:

1. Author's intention with the book, such as to give the
   user emotional experience, information, education, etc.
   or to promote ideas, e.g., social criticism, philosoph-
   ical attitudes, etc.

2. Frame or setting of the subject matter content in terms
   of time and place, i.e., the geographical, historical,
   social, or professional environment, etc.

3. Subject matter of a book, in terms of action and course
   of events ('plot'), psychological development/description,
   social relationships.

4. Accessibility, the physical characteristics of a book or
   document, readability, printing, book format, publisher,
   etc.

In order to support user access to literature in a database system, it
should be possible to identify and locate items by search terms in any of
these facets of the user demand or in combinations of them. In consequence,
the information retrieval task in libraries will involve a mapping between
two separate multi-level problem spaces, the user need, and the contents of
available bibliographical references.

In general, these problem spaces are not formulated in compatible
terms. The user needs are frequently intuitive and only implicitly present
in the search situation, and the references in a database are classified in
bibliographical terms, keywords and short abstracts. Since these characteristics are not necessarily compatible with a user's need, a search
is frequently supported by an intermediary, a librarian, with extensive
knowledge about the database and the information contents of its knowledge
domains as well as skill in interviewing users.

Thus, design of computer supported retrieval systems requires development of a classification system and a database in terms compatible with
facets of users needs (Pejtersen, 1984; Pejtersen, 1986). This involves
database requirements similar to those of engineering design and emergency
management. The facets of the library classification system can be arranged
similarly to the means-end hierarchy discussed previously for design. The
decision tasks of librarians searching for references to match a user's
need and of a designer looking for already available components to match
higher level functional requirements seem to involve the same kind of multifaceted classification taxonomies.

The 'problem space' of the retrieval task, therefore, can be described
as a multi-level representation of the user needs on one hand, and a similar
representation of the contents of the available documents on the other. As
mentioned earlier, in addition to this problem space, a representation of
the problem space related to the general administration of the library
(including the policy of management, the organization of work, the practical
features of acquisition of books, of tools and of equipment for location of
physical volumes, etc.). All these are aspects of the problem domain and

relevant for interface design, since they will influence the user's perception and performance of the decision task.

The Decision Task. Two decision makers are typically involved in the task, the user who may only know the reading needs in implicit terms, and an intermediary who may know only part of the content of the individual databases and of their knowledge domain. The joint decision task during a search then will be to analyze/determine a user's need in terms compatible with the database structure, select documents, and compare their match with the need. Or, the decision task is performed by the end-user himself/herself. Finally, in intelligent retrieval systems the decision task during a search may be shared between the end-user and the computer. When degrees of freedom are left in the need-document match they may be used by an intermediary to promote cultural or other values according to institutional policies.

Mental Strategies. By analysis of actual user-librarian conversations in public libraries, several different strategies for identification of books to match user needs have been identified (Pejtersen, 1979):

- Bibliographic Search. The user is in control and explores the documents and compares by himself needs and book contents. The documents are identified by author and title. The intermediary acts as an assistant, provides bibliographical information, explains arrangement of books, equipment, and the use of auxiliary tools. The intermediary may also assist in verification of match with a selected book by communicating its contents and thus support the user's judgment of its relevance to his need.

- Analytical Search. The intermediary is in control, explores systematically the dimensions of the user's needs, retrieves documents, compares aspects of needs with aspects of documents, suggests titles for the user's consideration and approval. This strategy is the rational, problem solving strategy.

- Search by Analogy. The intermediary is in control and explores the user's need by asking for information about the user's previous reading, to be able to find 'something similar'. Prototypes thus identified are then analyzed to identify search terms for new documents.

- Empirical Strategy. This strategy represents the shortcuts of the skilled intermediary. It is based on a prototypical classification of users and documents by the intermediary. Titles to suggest are selected from correlation experienced between user categories and typical reading habits. Users are classified according to a number of informal features such as visual appearance, verbal style, dress, age, etc., in addition to their expressed wishes, and books are classified in simple genre classes.

- Browsing Strategy. Finally, an information seeker in a library may have a need which is so ambiguous that specification of a search template is evaded and, instead, the content of a shelf or a database is scanned to explore a match with the intuitively present need and the available items. Comparing with the mental strategies discussed for supervisory process control, it will be seen that these strategies are formulated at the same level of generality and can be used to specify the mental model and the categories of information which should be considered for the design of support systems and their interfaces.

The User's Cognitive Style. In the strategies described above, an information seeker will interpret the information available in different ways, depending on his/her skill in the performance of a task. An analogy can be seen in the levels of interpretation mentioned in the introduction. The bibliographical search strategy is predominantly a skill-based behavior, where the intermediary's familiarity with the information systems and the bibliographical tools of a given library often makes bibliographical searches to pure routine tasks performed by automatic responses. The empirical strategy and the search by analogy is typically a search characteristic of a set of rules developed through repeated experience of certain patterns of user behavior. The knowledge-based behavior is typical for the analytical search strategy and this behavior puts the heaviest requirements on the designer of a computer interface that supports a searcher on this level of interpretation. A browsing strategy may take the route of any of the levels described above.

For a proper interface design it is also important to consider the different demands of information seekers to the selectivity and precision of a search. This is a typical cognitive style consideration in a library context, where searchers' perception of need-document match may leave several degrees of freedom open, since a user's need is rarely defined within all the aspects of a document (Pejtersen, 1981), and since searchers may have individual and varied perception of the "match" concept (David, 1979). In a library context, this gives the intermediary the opportunity to promote cultural values and draw the user's attention to alternative options of materials in accordance with a library policy, with political issues, and with different professional, value criteria of the literature. Different strategies for this mediation of values can be identified (Pejtersen, 1981), and is an important role of intermediaries especially in public libraries.

Conclusion. Library systems are interesting in the present context, not only because the framework for cognitive task analysis appear to be relevant for design of information retrieval support in libraries, but, in particular, because the information retrieval task is becoming increasingly important in the user-system interaction, as it has been indicated in the previous sections. For system design, careful consideration of the tools and methods developed within the information and library sciences should be considered.

Figure 6 illustrates the levels of representation implied in the analysis of features of a book and of a user's needs for library information retrieval. In addition, the general problem space for library administration, use of auxiliary tools, and book manipulation, is sketched.

CONCLUSION

The aim of the present report is an initial evaluation of the applicability of the cognitive engineering framework developed for supervisory process control for systems analysis and design in other work contexts. The result is judged to be promising. The framework appears to match very well the need for systems analysis in a wider area of application when supervisory control framework is supplemented by an analysis of decision making in a distributed organization of decision makers. In addition, the approach taken will facilitate a further development of system modeling in a direction for which the need has been identified in the recent literature from various domains such as, for instance, office systems,

DOCUMENT CONTENT	USER NEEDS	LIBRARY SYSTEM
AUTHOR INTENTION; INFORMATION; EDUCATION; ENJOYABLE EXPERIENCE.	READERS ULTIMATE GOAL	POLICIES, GOALS CULTURAL ENVIRONMENT LAWS AND CONSTRAINTS
LITERARY OR PROFESSIONAL QUALITY; PARADIGM, STYLE, OR SCHOOL.	VALUE CRITERIA RELATED TO READING PROCESS AND PRODUCT	FLOW OF MONEY, FUNDING SOURCES AND DRAINS. BOOK AND USER STATISTICS
GENERAL FRAME OF CONTENT; CULTURAL ENVIRONMENT, HISTORICAL PERIODE, PROFESSIONAL CONTEXT.	GENERAL TOPICAL INTEREST OF HISTORICAL OR SOCIAL SETTING	BOOK ACQUISITION, INDEXING CATALOGING, RETRIVAL,
SPECIFIC, FACTUAL CONTENT. EPISODIC COURSE OF EVENTS; FACTUAL DESCRIPTIONS.	TOPICAL INTEREST IN SPECIFIC CONTENT	USE OF SPECIFIC TOOLS, CARD CATALOGS, FILES; DESK EXPEDITION OF USER, SHELVING OF BOOKS, ANSWERING REQUEST ON PHONE
PHYSICAL CHARACTER-ISTICS OF DOCUMENT. FORM, SIZE, COLOR, TYPOGRAPHY, SOURCE, YEAR OF PRINT.	READING ABILITY	PHYSICAL CHARACTERISTICS OF BOOKS, SHELVES, EQUIP-MENT, OFFICES, BUILDINGS

Figure 6. Problem Domain of Library Systems.

library systems, and CAD/CAM.

This is, at present, a change in the basic requirements for systems design. In classical engineering design, the analysis and implementation of a system is based on the choice of normative functional properties, except for advanced self-organizing and adaptive systems. The appropriate functioning of a system is judged by mathematical analysis or computer simulation of the intended functional course of events. Similarly, analysis of organizations and decision support systems has frequently been based on the assumption of normative, rational work procedures.

The arguments in the present approach to cognitive engineering, i.e., the design of integrated cognitive systems, have been that design should not be based on the establishment of normative functionality, but on the creation of a multidimensional envelope spanned by the resource boundaries of a system. A successful design, then, will be one in which the user is able to improvise and to choose a procedure according to situational as well as purely subjective criteria, without having the trajectories of his performance violate the limits of this multidimensional space of possible and acceptable performance.

The basic difference in the present approach and the normative models based on economic utility theories is not a difference in 'rational' basis, but is related to the traditional a priori selection of the proper way of doing things compared to the present models' repertoire of possible solutions leaving the end-user the freedom to determine the proper way.

In summary, the roles of the different model dimensions are the following:

The work content is represented by a <u>means-end space</u>. This problem space can be identified by a rational analysis of the work context. The description is, however, neutral rather than normative, since it offers several alternatives for action in representing the total domain of potential resources. In fact, this representation will only directly serve as the problem space for rational, knowledge-based problem solving, but it can also be used as a map to structure descriptions of the implicit 'frame' representations of skilled actors.

For operations in this neutral problem space, the <u>decision task</u> can be described separately, and the <u>strategies</u> which <u>can</u> be applied for the different parts of the task can be identified by analysis and by study of actual performance in present systems. Again, this model will not be normative, but represent the <u>possible ways</u> to cope with the task which should be within boundaries of the design envelope. Once the possible strategies have been identified, their requirements, in terms of processing and memory capacity, knowledge, etc., can be found and used for function allocation with reference to humans' and computers' resource profiles.

If a designer wants to restrict his design to a selected subset of the possible user strategies, or he wants to predict which will be used in a particular situation, he needs a complex psychological model making it possible to identify the situational and subjective performance criteria of an individual user.

Note, there is a basic difference in the requirements for psychological models for design of an acceptable system envelope and for prediction of the actual performance of a particular population of users. Design can be based on a kind of smallest common denominator model, whereas prediction requires knowledge of the factors actually present.

Another feature of the present approach is that it goes beyond the actual discussion of syntactic features of the communication across <u>user-system interface</u>, dealing mainly with the content of the <u>user-task interaction</u> at the semantic, symbolic level.

The models for analysis of the interface at the syntactic level are important, and an extensive literature is available as well as human factors guidelines for design of an appropriate interface, once the user/computer task allocation has been resolved and the user-task interaction planned. It is worth noticing that the analysis for system design has to proceed top-down since there is no need to analyze user-system interface formats before the communication content has been properly established. For empirical design evaluation, the opposite is the case. Such evaluation has to be performed bottom-up; there is no sense in planning complex experimental scenarios to test compatibility with user strategies, if users cannot read and understand the basic messages (Rouse, 1984).

Figure 7 illustrates several levels of human-machine interaction to be considered in systems design and evaluation. The focus of the present work is the <u>user-task interaction</u> at the semantic, symbolic information processing level. During analysis for system design, the features of user-system interaction are to be considered top-down, i.e., the user-task interaction should be planned as an integrated system before the syntactic user-system <u>interface</u> is considered.

LEVELS OF HUMAN FUNCTIONS	DESIGN CONSIDERATIONS
SUBJECTIVE VALUE FORMATION	MOTIVATING WORK CONTEXT
SYMBOLIC INFORMATION PROCESSING	PROPER INFORMATION CONTENT
PSYCHOLOGICAL MECHANISMSM	UNDERSTANDABLE COMMUNICATION LANGUAGE AND FORMATS
PHYSIOLOGICAL MECHANISMS	COMPATIBILITY WITH SENSORY MECHANISMS; ACCEPTABLE WORK PHYSICAL CONDITIONS
ANATOMICAL PROPERTIES	COMPATIBLE WITH ANTROPOMETRIC FEATURES

Figure 7. Levels of Human System Interaction.

REFERENCES

Alexander, C., 1964, Notes on the Synthesis of Form, Harvard University Press, Cambridge, MA.

Alting, L., 1978, "A Systematic Theory of Manufacturing", Environment and Planning B, 5, pp. 131-156.

Barber, G. R., 1983, "Supporting Organizational Problem Solving with a Work Station", ACM Transactions on Office Information Systems, 1, (1), pp. 45-67.

Barber, G. R., 1984, "An Office Study: Its Implications on the Understanding of Organizations", SIGOA Newsletter, 5, (1-2).

Barber, G. R., DeJong, P., and Hewitt, C., 1983, "Semantic Support for Work in Organizations", Information Processing 83, Mason, R. E. A., ed., Elsevier Science Publishers, Mason, New York.

Bruner, J. S., Goodnow, J. J., and Austin, G. A., 1956, A Study of Thinking, John Wiley & Sons, New York.

Checkland, P. B., 1981, Systems Thinking. Systems Practice, Wiley & Sons, Chichester.

Cyert, R. M., and March, J. G., 1963, A Behavioral Theory of the Firm, Prentice-Hall, Englewood Cliffs, NJ.

Eastman, C. M., 1978, "The Representation of Design Problems and Maintenance of Their Structure", Artificial Intelligence and Pattern Recognition in Computer-Aided Design, Latombe, J.-C., ed., North-Holland, New York.

Hammer, M., 1984, "The OA Mirage", Datamation, 30, (2), pp. 36-46.

Morehead, D. R., Pejtersen, A. M., and Rouse, W. B., 1984, "The Value of Information and Computer-Aided Information Seeking: Problem Formulation and Application to Fiction Retrieval", Information Processing and Management, 20, (5/6), pp. 583-601.

Pejtersen, A. M., 1979, "Investigation of Search Strategies Based on an Analysis of 134 User-Librarian Conversations", Third International Research Forum in Information Science, Henriksen, T., ed., Oslo.

Pejtersen, A. M., 1980, "Design of a Classification Scheme for Fiction Based on an Analysis of Actual User-Librarian Communications; and Use of the Scheme for Control of Librarians' Search Strategies", Theory and Application of Information Research, Harboe, O., and Kajberg, L., eds., Mansell, London, pp. 146-159.

Pejtersen, A. M., 1981, "The Librarian's Role as a Mediator in Fictional Literature", The 4th International Research Forum in Information Science, Friberg, I., ed., Bibliotekshogskolan, Boras, pp. 178-207.

Pejtersen, A. M., 1984, "Design of Computer-Aided User-System Dialogue Based on an Analysis Users' Search Behavior", Social Science Information Studies, 4, pp. 167-183.

Pejtersen, A. M., 1986, "Design and Test of a Database for Fiction Based on an Analysis of Children's Search Behavior", Information Technology and Information Use, Ingwersen, Kajberg, and Pejtersen, eds., Taylor Graham, London.

Rasmussen, J., 1984, "Strategies for State Identification and Diagnosis", Advances in Man-Machine Systems Research, Rouse, W. B., ed., J. A. I. Press, Greenwich, CT.

Rasmussen, J., 1985, "The Role of Hierarchical Knowledge Representation in Decision Making and Systems Management", IEEE Transaction on Systems, Man, and Cybernetics, SMC-15, (2), pp. 234-243.

Rasmussen, J., 1985, A Framework for Cognitive Task Analysis, Riso-M-2519. Also in, Intelligent Decision Support Systems in Process Environment, Hollnagel, E., Mancini, G., and Woods, D., eds., Springer Verlag, Berlin, in press.

Rasmussen, J., 1986, Development and Testing of a Model for Simulation of Process Operators' Responses During Emergencies in Nuclear Power Plants, ANE/ENS Topical Meeting on Human Factors in Nuclear Power, April 1986, Knoxville, USA.

Rasmussen, J., and Jensen, A., 1974, "Mental Procedures in Real Life Tasks: A Case Study of Electronic Trouble Shooting", Ergonomics, 17, (3), pp. 293-307.

Rasmussen, J., Pedersen, O. N., and Grinberg, C., 1986, Evaluation of the Use of Advanced Information Technology (Expert Systems) for Data Base System Development and Emergency Management in Non-Nuclear Industries, to be published.

Rouse, W. B., 1984, <u>Computer-Generated Display System Guidelines: Volume 2, Developing an Evaluation Plan</u>, NP-3701, Search Technology, Atlanta under ORNL Contract No. W-7405-eng-26 for Electrical Power Research Institute, Palo Alto, CA.

Rouse, W. B., Frey, P. R., and Rouse, S. H., 1984, <u>Classification and Evaluation of Decision Aids for Nuclear Power Plant Operators</u>, Report No. 8303-1, Search Technology, Atlanta under ORNL Contract No. 62X-43185V for Nuclear Regulatory Commission, Washington, D.C.

Suchman, L. A., 1982, <u>Systematics of Office Work: Office Studies for Knowledge-Based Systems</u>, Office Automation Conference, Moscone Center, San Francisco, April 5-7.

Suchman, L. A., 1983, "Office Procedures as Practical Action: Models of Work and Systems Design", <u>ACM Transactions on Office Information Systems</u>, <u>1</u>, (4), pp. 320-328.

Sutherland, J. W., 1983, "Normative Predicates of Next Generation Management Support Systems", <u>IEEE Trans. Syst. Man. Cybern.</u>, <u>SMC-13</u>, (3), pp. 279-297.

CONCURRENT COMPUTER AND HUMAN INFORMATION PROCESSING

H. L. Resnikoff

Aware, Inc.
University Place, Suite 200
Cambridge, MA 02138

Abstract: The category of machines is generalized to include living systems
as well as conventional mechanical and electrical systems. The man-machine
interface is treated as a special case of the interaction of two subsystems
of a complex machine. The problem of optimizing the man-machine interface
can be considered as a special case of the problem of matching the impedance
of interacting systems. The role of concurrent computation is discussed
for machines that are intended to provide their operators with decision-support and other capabilities that are normally believed to require intelligence.

1. INTRODUCTION

    The problem of optimizing the man-machine interface is a particular
case of the more general problem of matching the impedance between subsystems
of a complex system. Implicit in this point of view, however, is a philo-
sophical assumption of far-reaching significance: that human beings and
other living systems are nothing more than biological machines that can be
completely analyzed in terms of universal categories that apply to machines
in general. Thus, machines have two concrete realizations, as "hardware"
and as "wetware", whose differences are fundamentally without significance.
Perhaps the term "software" describes something else, something more malleable and indefinite, compounded in part of genetic experience ("product
improvement engineering") and in part of environmental experience -- the
experience of the individual, which is the carrier of those quantities that
embody what some people think of as characteristic differences between man
and machine, such as self awareness, aesthetic sensibility, and a sense of
humor. Whether these "characteristic differences" are merely another human
vanity remains an open question.

    Recent advances in information science, particularly in the theory of
computation and the cognitive disciplines, have provided increasing evidence
for the hypothesis that living systems are machines, albeit machines of
incredible complexity that incorporate the ability for self-organization,
which even the simplest organism possesses, and are capable of self-awareness, which appears to be restricted to the hither life forms. But the
issue is as complicated and ravelled up with self-reference as time-travel
-- if not more so -- and the few superficial experiences that have thus far

been conducted to test the difference between man and machine have hardly been sufficient to decide the question. Nor are future experiments, made with the aid of incomparably more powerful computing equipment, likely to entirely free us from doubt about this question, for no matter how exactly a suitably programmed machine may simulate a finite collection of responses of a living system, there will still be room to wonder whether it has indeed captured "everything". Some researchers are inclined to believe that practical and effective demonstrations of machine simulation of the gamut of performance of living systems, including pattern categorization, reasoning, a sense of ethical and moral behavior, and even self-awareness, are quite likely in the foreseeable future. Even such remarkable capabilities can, in the end, prove nothing about a hypothesized equivalence of man and machine. They should, however, act as a powerful goad to theoreticians, who must have the final say on the subject. The situation is reminiscent of the study of prime numbers, where _experiments_ on any conceivable practical scale suggests conclusions that the _theory_ of prime numbers shows to be false.

In these brief ruminations about the ultimate nature of life as we believe we know it, we must not ignore the role of quantum phenomena and the uncertainty principle which, perhaps, provides room for rational explanations of free will and the creative impulse in a world otherwise (if man is a type of machine) determined. But then machines too must experience a kind of "free will" and "creativity" (which we, with a kind of tired anthropocentrism, identify with wear and breakdowns) that differs in magnitude rather than in quality from our own.

The previous remarks suggest that a complete theory of the man-machine interface would be possible in principle if the hypothesis that life is a certain type of machine is correct. Such a theory could guide the optimal design of complex systems of which men and machines are parts, thereby insuring that "human error" in their operation and interpretation would be brought to the absolute minimum that is possible given the intended design constraints of cost and time. If a complete theory is not possible, then the intellectual underpinning for a comprehensive theory of the man-machine interface may be impossible, although the prospects for an incomplete but satisfying theory (using the term introduced by Herbert Simon) remain good. Since complex systems normally consist of parts that need only minimize impedance for certain transfers of energy and entropy, but not necessarily for all, the way is opened for building an approximate theory of interface impedance whose applications could include most situations of practical significance, just as the classical theories of physics still suffice for most purposes that do not involve space-time volumes that are too small (the realm of quantum physics) or too large (the realm of reality).

Historically, the task of adapting people to the machines they use can be decomposed into three conceptually distinct problems that coincide, roughly, with the three different stages in the development of machine terminology. (Hereafter we will mean "man-made machine" when we use the word "machine".)

The first machines provided direct extensions of human muscle power. The level is among the elementary machines, the Archimedean screw, the water wheel, and the windmill are among the more complex ones and, later, prime movers including the internal combustion engine and the electric motor, are examples that come readily to mind of machines of this kind, which we will call Class I machines. Although human interaction with these machines usually involves some degree of control or modulation, in earlier times the man-machine interface was primarily concerned with mediating power transfers from one to the other. The necessity to adapt human energy-intensive activities to machine energy-intensive activities lies at the heart of the traditional time and motion studies that form the foundation for early human factors research and its application to assembly-line manufacturing.

Telecommunication technology ushered in the second stage in the development of machines through its focus on machines and machine subsystems, whose primary function is to transmit information rather than power, precursors such as clocks, navigational instruments, and the Jacquard "programming" system for weaving patterns notwithstanding. The distinction between power-intensive Class I machines and communication-intensive Class II machines was institutionalized by the electrical engineers who partitioned their discipline to correspond to these two great branches. Class II machines interact with the sensory systems of their operators: the role of the human is information-intensive rather than energy- or power-intensive. It follows that the scientific knowledge required to optimize the man-machine interface belongs to the province of sensory psychology rather than to physiology. The corresponding human factors issues have largely dominated the field since World War II. Many of the current major military human factors programs can be best understood as specific efforts to attack the problem of reducing the impedance between the sensor- and communication-subsystems of weapon systems and the visual-, auditory-, and speech-communication subsystems of their operators. Problems that call for matching man to machine information systems are legion. Particularly interesting and important ones include monitoring and controlling the activity of complex and potentially dangerous process control systems, where the ability of the operator to monitor communication from the machine is the essence of his job. The combat or commercial aircraft pilot and the nuclear power plant control room operator come to mind at once. A different example is provided by the communication interface between the sonar or radar operator and the machine, which is the only link that binds the two subsystems into an integrated whole, for in these cases the output of the combination is information used indirectly to stimulate another system, rather than directly to implement an action.

The invention of the computer marks the third stage in the development of machines. Whereas power-intensive machines perform "work" as that term is understood in physics, and communication-intensive machines re-organize and transmit information, computing machines provide the opportunity to perform analytical and evaluative information processing, including reasoning and decision-support. The latter implicitly involves learning and pattern categorization and is fundamentally depend on them. These tasks transcend the capabilities of the earlier and simpler classes of machines. The interaction of these Class III machines with their human counterparts occurs on the level of manipulating (that may not be the best word!) abstractions of abstractions. Their performance is intended to be similar to, and perhaps the same as, the behavior that is normally thought of as demanding intelligence, although lower animals, including insects, appear to be able to perform some activities of this kind with much simpler "wetware" and "software" than the author or readers of this paper appear to require. Thus, it may be the better part of wisdom to refrain from committing oneself to the belief that categorization, learning, and decision-making are characteristic of intelligent behavior, although it is likely that they are necessary for it. In this regard, the reader will profit from a study of the research of Herrnstein (1982) and his co-workers on the categorization capabilities evidenced by lower animals.

The problems of designing an interface for Class III machines are of entirely novel character. Their solution will depend upon deep results, present and future, from the cognitive sciences, and the theory of computation. They may require contributions from the mathematicians who are, after all, the current experts in the study of structures and relationships of abstractions of abstractions. Whereas physical measures of time and power formed the quantitative foundation for the study of the interface with Class I machines, and the measure of channel capacity and of information, or entropy, associated with a communication provides a foundation for the study of the interface with Class II machines, an analytical theory and a quantitative measure of pattern categorization and recognition, and of the effectiveness of decision-making in the face of uncertainty, have yet to be developed. The creation of this theory will be a landmark in the annals of science.

2. BIOLOGICAL AND ELECTRONIC INFORMATION PROCESSING

Let us turn from these relatively abstract issues to the more concrete ones that govern whether, and how, a method for improving the interface with machines that are intended to support pattern classification and decision-making might be accomplished. The typical practical questions of this type fall into two categories, according to whether the desired decision must be made in real-time or nearly so, or whether timeliness is not critical to utility. In the latter case, the computing power needed to perform the necessary calculations will not be the most important issue. Most realistic situations belong to the other category, where the process of decision-making is conducted in an interactive environment and the timeliness of the decision weighs heavily in its utility. Air traffic control, target evaluation, tactical combat decision support systems, speech language translation systems, image interpretation systems, and others that the reader will easily bring to mind call for prompt conclusions. This leads to consideration of the computational requirements for various types of interface systems.

The microelectronic hardware constituents of computer machines are much more reliable and operate much faster than the neurons of living systems. Neurons switching in a few milliseconds whereas the circuits in common personal microelectronic switches are faster than biological switches by a factor of 10,000. But, biological computing machines currently occupy much smaller volumes and dissipate less heat than their microelectronic counterparts. Thus, each type of computing machine is particularly cost-effective in an application environment that is matched to its capabilities. Because biological computing mechanisms are very slow, their real-time application is most effective for problems that have an inherently high fraction of concurrency, for in these cases the large number of neurons that constitute, e.g., the human brain (which may contain as many as 10^{12}), can be brought to bear on the problem simultaneously in order to provide a response within a sufficiently brief time (Resnikoff, 1986). But not every problem possesses a high degree of latent concurrency and, as is well known, the "speed up" that can be provided by a "parallel" computer is bounded from above by the reciprocal of the fraction of instructions in the program that must be executed serially. This simple, but fundamental, fact implies that parallel computers, and a fortiori, the computers that living systems use, must necessarily be ill-adapted to the solution of problems that do not have a high degree of latent concurrency. This constraint limits the performance of living systems and shows, that in practice, a living system cannot do everything that a computing machine can do because of the slow switching speed of its neurons. (This does not imply that in practice a computing machine can do everything that can be done by a living system.) This is the reason that hand-held calculators are commonplace but hand-held pattern recognition machines do not exist: the algorithms of arithmetic possess relatively little latent concurrency, whereas the algorithms of image processing and pattern recognition have a relatively large fraction of latent concurrency. This difference also limits the ability of a human to interact with a machine in an efficient manner if the machine is performing tasks that are embodied in highly serial algorithms. Thus, we should expect to encounter special problems in designing man-machine interfaces for these situations.

The component elements of biological computer systems cannot be rapidly improved; they will remain slow and unreliable and have, even in terms of evolutionary epochs, remained essentially unchanged. They have probably approached their performance limits. On the other hand, information technology continues its rapid pace of development (Dare we say "evolution"?) and one can be assured that future microelectronic devices will be even faster and more reliable and more compact and less energy consuming than they presently are. This offers the possibility that computing machines consisting of large numbers of concurrently active processors may become competitive with traditional serial computers in the near future. In this event, the computing machine and the living system would share a functional mode of operation and might be capable of comparable levels of performance for highly concurrent problems such as image processing.

At this point one should recall that a parallel computer can never be more cost-effective than a serial computer if the measure of cost-effectiveness is restricted to include only the performance and cost of the processor constituents of the computing system (Adelson and Burt, 1981). This implies that in order to be cost-effective, concurrent computers (such as those employed by living systems) must be applied to problems that are memory-intensive and the computing system must include a large memory unit. This may be the principal reason that knowledge plays such a great role in the performance of living systems, whereas algorithms play the greater role in most serial computations.

These are points that should be considered when one attempts to design an efficient man-machine interface. In normal circumstances, the human component of the system will be most effective in performing information-integrative tasks that employ pattern recognition and evaluative analysis of alternatives that are imprecisely defined or for which decisions must be made based upon incomplete information, but, relying on prior experience, i.e., knowledge. The computing machine constituent will be most effective for those tasks that employ well-specified algorithms and require high speed and accuracy of intermediate results. But the boundaries between these alternatives continue to fade as increased speed and memory capacity allow computing machines to reproduce the results of human reasoning processes, if not the procedures themselves, and even relatively low degrees of parallelism in computer architectures can enable a machine to match human response time for massively parallel applications such as image processing and speech signal processing if adequate memory for storage of intermediate results and a large inventory of prior experience expressed in the form of domain knowledge is available. Thus, the way is open to design complex systems that can interact with humans in each of the sensory modalities with near-minimal impedance. But these interfaces are likely to require distinct computer architectures tailored to both the application class and the sensory modality: processors specialized for auditory, for vision, and for tactile information can be combined with general purpose processors for numerical computation and intrinsically serial algorithms. However, the architecture best suited to pattern recognition and decision-making has not yet been discovered.

One may imagine a man-machine interface specified by an analysis of the information flow intrinsic to the problem which identifies the latent concurrency inherent in the application and also partitions the information flow into its essentially independent segments. These properties of the application can be represented by a precedence graph, a directed acyclic graph whose nodes correspond to executable primitive "instructions", i.e., changes of state, and whose edges represent the ordering induced by sufficiency of information for executing the state change that corresponds to a node in the graph. The nodes of a precedence graph can be partially ordered accordingly to an increasing positive real parameter that can be thought of as "time". Precedence graphs are acyclic, for otherwise some of the information that is needed in order to execute a state change at one time would only be available at a later time, that is, after the change of state. The nodes in this partial ordering that do not have successors are said to be "terminal"; the terminal nodes represent the final states -- the "solution" to the problem.

We can employ the precedence graph to decompose an application (more precisely, the algorithms that represents an application) into its essentially independent components. The distinct maximal independent components of a precedence graph correspond to subalgorithms of possibly different types that combine to solve the application problem. Each component will be adapted to a particular computational architecture; some may possess a high degree of latent concurrency, whereas others may correspond to a largely serial algorithm which is best adapted to a traditional von Neumann computer architecture. In any event, an analysis of the components of the precedence graph will provide, in principle, means for assessing the cost-effectiveness of various computer architectures and combinations of architectures in minimizing the impedance of the man-machine interface for the problem. In this regard the quantity of computation that must be performed for each of the components as well as the time that is available for completing the computation must be taken into account in order to determine the most cost-effective architectural combination for the solution of the problem: a component that has a relatively high degree of latent concurrency, but involves relatively few computation cycles, is not likely to justify the deployment of a special purpose parallel processor.

Thus, we arrive at the notion of a man-machine interface for decision-support problems that consists of a collection of special purpose computing subsystems, some concerned with the communications aspects of the problem, others with the component subgraphs of the precedence graph that represents the decision support algorithms. Each computing subsystem should be designed to minimize the impedance between it and the other component subsystems, including the human operator(s) of the system.

3. SOME RELEVANT COMPUTER ARCHITECTURES

The simplest precedence graph is the directed linear graph of N nodes. In this case the partial ordering is an ordering. The node that precedes all others in the ordering represents the initial state and the terminal node represents the final state. Execution of the state change represented by the node (n-1) provides necessary and sufficient information for execution of the state change represented by node n. There is no latent concurrency in an algorithm represented by a linear precedence graph, so the corresponding optimal computer architecture is fully serial. Although few applications will correspond to linear precedence graphs, most applications will correspond to graphs which contain linear subgraphs of significant length. This is equivalent to the assertion that most applications will have a significant fraction of serial applications.

Hierarchical algorithms of the "divide and conquer" type correspond to (binary) tree precedence graphs. If the value of the parameter that denotes the depth of a node in the tree is increased by 1, the number of changes of state that can be executed concurrently doubles. Thus, the latent concurrency inherent in the algorithm increases exponentially with the depth of the graph. If the component of the system that corresponds to the tree precedence graph is relatively deep and, if it is frequently executed in the course of the application, then a special purpose computer architecture devoted to the "divide and conquer" component is likely to be cost-effective. If the graph of the tree consists of N nodes, then the time required for an optimal execution that takes full advantage of the latent concurrency will require a time proportional to log N. If the number of nodes is very large, then an implementation of the application on a serial computer may not be able to keep pace with a human operator, whereas a parallel implementation will speed up machine processing by a quantity proportional to the large factor N/log N.

Man-machine systems frequently involve image processing and pattern recognition functions. The human normal daylight vision system accepts 8 bit light intensity data as input from the approximately 6 million retinal photoreceptors in each eye This information is refreshed at a frequency of about 60 Hz. It follows that the input bandwidth of the human vision system is approximately $6x10^9$ bits per second. A color video signal requires a bandwidth of only 125 million bits per second. Processing of image data by even the fastest serial computer cannot keep pace with human image processing rates.

As a first approximation, we may assume that image data is arranged in a rectangular (or hexagonal) array of pixels, and that the earliest stages of processing involve application of a fixed algorithm to all pixels in a neighborhood (of fixed geometry) of each pixel. It follows that calculations that refer to distinct base pixels are independent of one another and can be concurrently executed. Concurrent execution will provide a speed-up equal to the number of pixels in the image. We have previously remarked that microelectronic circuits are at least 10,000 times faster than circuits built from neurons; hence, for images that contain about 10,000 pixels, serial processing of a single instruction sequence applied to all pixels and processing by the human retina will require about the same time. For images that are larger or have higher resolution, the serial computer will generally be unable to keep pace with the human.

Since image data is naturally arranged in a 2-dimensional array, an apparently natural architecture for an image processing computer (at least for the early stages of image processing, which are likely to employ convolution operators and other linear operators associated with Fourier transforms) would be a 2-dimensional lattice of processors with local memory and nearest neighbor communication. This arrangement provides for computational analogues of lateral inhibition and excitation. If the early stages of image signal processing employ a single algorithm indexed solely by pixel location and the initial conditions that correspond to pixels in a neighborhood (of fixed geometry) of each pixel, as convolution and lateral inhibition do, then a single-instruction-multiple-data (SIMD) control strategy will be appropriate.

Several types of parallel computers having a 2-dimensional grid architecture with local memory and an SIMD control structure have been built and applied to low level image processing tasks. In 1983, Goodyear Aerospace Corporation delivered the Massively Parallel Processor (MPP) for the NASA Goddard Space Center. This machine was designed for processing satellite pictures. It consists of 16,384 bit-serial processors with local memory and an SIMD control structure to provide a claimed peak processing rate of 6,500 MIPS (1 MIP = 1 million instructions per second.) The Connection Machine, with as many as 65,536 bit-serial processors, is organized in a hypercube communication architecture as well as a 2-dimensional grid and also employs an SIMD control structure; it yields a comparable level of performance for low level image processings. The WARP computer designed at Carnegie-Mellon University is based on a so-called "systolic array" 2-dimensional architecture and achieves high performance by pipelining data through processor arrays that are optimized to the particular algorithms that constitute the application.

Recent research in image understanding suggests that the human vision system analyzes images at several scales of representation. This idea was championed by David Marr (1982) and has led to the development of so-called "pyramid" theories of image processing by Adelson and Burt (1981), Ahuja and Swamy (1984), Burt (1984), Dyer and Rosenfeld (1977), and Tanimoto (1983; 1984), among others. An image pyramid is a data structure that is derived from an image. Let an image be identified with an NxN array of pixels and a (vector valued) function representing the (color) intensity as a function of pixel position. We will assume that N is a power of 2. We inductively associate with each MxM array in the image pyramid an (M/2)x(M/2) array and a (vector valued) "intensity" function defined on it whose values are the averages of the intensity function on the 2x2 blocks of the MxM array. If "log" denotes the base 2 logarithm, then an image pyramid constructed from an NxN image array consists of a total of (1 + log N) arrays which we may label from 'level 0', corresponding to the 1x1 array, to level log N, corresponding to the original image. The value of the scale intensity function on the single element of level 0 is equal to the average value of the intensity function over the original image. Values of the scale intensity function for intermediate levels are local averages (or differences of local averages for corresponding positions in successive levels: the so-called "Laplacian" pyramid construction) of the intensity function at corresponding scales. The information contained in the lowest log N levels requires 1 pixel less than half as much storage as the original image; the original image data cannot be constructed from the data contained in the other levels of the pyramid.

Image processing computers that employ a pyramid architecture provide an efficient means for performing many low level image signal processing and early pattern recognition tasks because they realize the minimum number of inherently serial steps in many algorithms, thereby making it possible to obtain maximum speed up. For instance, calculation of average image intensity (which is important for determining the neutral level for many feature detection algorithms and for presenting images to viewers) requires serial addition of the image intensity values unless provision for additional intermediate data storage is provided. Utilization of a dynamic pyramid structure makes possible the concurrent calculation of local averages over 2x2 pixel blocks and, after log N recursive steps corresponding to ascent of the pyramid, the global intensity average emerges. Image segmentation also benefits from algorithms that employ a pyramid representation (Grosky and Jain, 1986).

One can assert in general that, when they are applicable, pyramid based algorithms reduce computational complexity from O(n) to O1(log n), where n denotes the number of pixels in the image. This implies a remarkable reduction in processing time compared with serial computation and offers one of the most promising avenues for the exploitation of computational concurrency and parallel computers in the context of the man-machine interface.

The reader should observe that, in order to make effective use of the concurrency latent in the application, it is essential to have adequate memory resources. The deployment of many processors in parallel is not in general sufficient for cost-effective exploitation of parallel processing nor even for maximizing performance, i.e., speed up, although special purpose architectures that are application-specific can sometimes substitute communication topology for memory resources (Resnikoff, to appear).

4. VISUAL ATTENTION AND PARALLEL PROCESSING

Vision has the greatest bandwidth of all human sensory systems. For this reason it plays a privileged role in the man-machine interface. In this section we will discuss some of the implications of the neurophysiological and psychological mechanisms that are employed by the human vision system to accomplish its contribution to pattern categorization and classification with respect to their implications for the design of impedance-minimizing interfaces.

The high degree of concurrent processing performed by the human retina and higher level sites in processing images, particularly the lateral geniculate nucleus, have been used by parallel computer architects as canonical illustrations of the advantages of parallel computation. The human vision system certainly does employ concurrency in a way that is crucial to its effectiveness, but, recent research has revealed certain limits to concurrent computation for cognitive image analysis tasks that are typical of the problems that arise in the man-machine interface.

Consider, for example, the problem of visual attention, which underlies every use of display interfaces for control applications. As part of his study of the perception of texture, Julesz (1981) has shown that the human vision system is capable of detecting and locating within the image domain a unique image atom (a "texton") embedded within a set of identical atoms. The time required to perform this task (between 50 and 200 milliseconds) is essentially independent of the number of elements in the set. This demonstrates that the process of detection is performed concurrently throughout the retina, although the algorithms that underlie this capability are unknown. These results suggest that it would be possible to design an image interface that would signal anomalous states of a controlled system by encoding them as unique visual signals embedded in a set of uniform visual signals that correspond to the 'normal' system states (a blinking cursor is an example of this type of coding scheme). From this standpoint, and taking into account both the great bandwidth of the vision system and its high recognition speed (reaction times on the order of a few hundred milliseconds independent of the number of elements in the target set), the way would appear to be open for the design of interfaces enabling timely, reliable, sensitive, and positive control of complex systems. Unfortunately, this objective has not been achieved in practice. The work of Treisman (1986(a); 1986(b)) suggests one important reason for this failure. She has shown that visual attention must have significant serial processing components. Her work indicates that the higher the level of abstraction that is involved in decision-making, the greater the fraction of serial calculation that may be required. If true, this would deal a blow to the hope that the great increases in power that are anticipated from parallel computers will provide the key that unlocks the secrets of thought: more particularly, of the kind of thought that goes into decision-making, planning, learning, and the creative process. These abilities may not fall out automatically, as some believe they will, merely from a sufficient increase in computing power.

Treisman considered visual attention tasks that call for the identification of a visual target atom that is embedded in a set of atoms characterized by multiple parameters, including the number of elements in the set. Consider the following typical example. Let a collection of congruent rectangles of a given color, say 'red', be distributed throughout an image. Suppose that the length of a rectangle is noticeably greater than its width and that the rectangles are all arranged so that the longer sides are horizontal, with the exception of one rectangle oriented so that its longer sides are vertical. The visual attention task of locating the exceptionally oriented rectangle requires a time that is essentially independent of the number of rectangles in the image. Now suppose that the uniquely oriented rectangle is removed and that a number of vertically oriented 'green' rectangles, congruent, and approximately equal in number, to the horizontally oriented rectangles are added to the image. Let one additional rectangle be added to the image which is colored 'red' but oriented vertically. It turns out to be much more difficult to locate the vertical red rectangle in this 2-parameter discrimination task: the time required is the sum of a constant (which is approximately equal to the time required to locate the target in a 1-parameter task) and a term proportional to the total number of rectangles displayed in the image. In this case it is evident that the recognition task has a serial component. It is as if the various local sets of rectangles of fixed orientation and color are searched sequentially in order to find the singleton whose color and orientation constitute a unique combination.

This result is of special significance for those who design man-machine interfaces because it exhibits an information processing mode which appears to distinguish machine computational algorithms from natural computational algorithms. It is easy to design a concurrent computer architecture that can solve the two parameter visual attention tasks described by Treisman in a time that is independent of the number of targets. In particular, searching a visual field to locate all instances of the presence of a target depending on a (binary) parameter, such as 'color alternation' can be done concurrently for all targets; simultaneously, targets depending on a second (binary) parameters, say 'orientation alternation', can be located concurrently. The presence of any of the four possible combinations of the pair of binary parameter values can be ascertained concurrently along with their locations, and, if a particular combination of parameters corresponds to a single target, then the potential problem of serialization of the readout will not occur. Thus, in these circumstances, the entire process can be carried out in a time that is independent of the number of targets. In this sense we see that there are problems that admit concurrent solution in principle, although the human brain does not appear to be capable of solving them by fully exploiting the latent concurrency inherent in them. It remains to be determined whether there is an advantage to the employment of serial computation which makes it a survival characteristic and, therefore, preferable for some biological information processing purposes, to a more fully parallel solution. These questions require further research into human information processing and its relationship to concurrent computation.

We have argued that the problem of optimizing the man-machine interface can be interpreted as a problem of minimizing the impedance between a machine and its user. Thus, optimization of the man-machine interface implies matching the information transfer rates as well as adapting the algorithms and architecture of the machine to be compatible with those employed by the human. We have seen that contemporary computing systems are characterized by high speed and high reliability delivered through serial control architectures, whereas some of the more accessible human information processing functions, such as early vision, are characterized by unreliable low speed computation components that make up for their performance limitations by using a dedicated massively parallel processing architecture. These applications are typically characterized by large quantities of data that are all processed in a similar manner. But, we have also seen indications that as one proceeds from the sensory input apparatus to the cortical centers that implement higher functions, such as decision-making, pattern recognition, and categorization, there appears to be an increasing degree of serial processing, and there may be a decreasing degree of concurrency latent in the algorithms that underlie the higher thought processes. Thus, an ideal interface, capable of supporting communication-intensive sensory information as well as abstraction and decision-making, will likely involve hybrid architectures that dedicate highly concurrent subsystems to certain subtasks, and serial computational subsystems to others. The surprise may be that the highest mental functions turn out to correspond to largely serial algorithmic procedures for processing information.

REFERENCES

Adelson, E. H., and Burt, P., 1981, "Image Data Compression with the Laplacian Pyramid", Proc. Conf. Pattern Recognition, Dallas, TX, pp. 218-223.

Ahuja, N., and Swamy, S., 1984, "Multiprocessor Pyramid Architectures for Bottom-Up Image Analysis", IEEE Trans. Pattern Analysis and Machine Intelligence PAMI-6, pp. 463-475.

Burt, P. J., 1984, "The Pyramid as a Structure for Efficient Computation", Multiresolution Image Processing and Analysis, Rosenfeld, A., ed., Springer-Verlag, Berlin, pp. 6-35.

Dyer, C. R., and Rosenfeld, A., 1977, Cellular Pyramids for Image Analysis, Dept. Comput. Sci., University of Maryland, Part I: Technical Report TR-544, May 1977, Part 2: Technical Report TR-596, November 1977.

Grosky, I., and Jain, R., 1986, "A Pyramid-Based Approach to Segmentation Applied to Region Matching", IEEE Trans. Pattern Analysis and Machine Intelligence PAMI-8, pp. 639-650.

Herrnstein, R. J., 1982, "Stimuli and the Texture of Experience", Neuroscience and Biobehavioral Review, 6, pp. 105-117.

Julesz, B., 1981, "Textons, the Elements of Texture Perception", Nature, 290, pp. 91-97.

Marr, D., 1982, Vision, W. H. Freeman, San Francisco.

Resnikoff, H. L., 1986, "Concurrent Computation and Models of Biological Information Processing", Advances in Cognitive Science, Kochen, Manfred, ed., Westview Press, to appear as Chapter 8.

Resnikoff, H. L., to appear, "Cost-Effectiveness of Concurrent Super-Computers".

Tanimoto, S. L., 1983, "A Pyramidal Approach to Parallel Processing", Proc. Tenth Int. Symp. Comput. Architecture, Stockholm, June 1983, pp. 372-378.

Tanimoto, S. L., 1984, "Sorting, Histogramming, and Other Statistical Operations on a Pyramid Machine", Multiresolution Image Processing and Analysis, Rosenfeld, A., ed., Springer-Verlag, pp. 136-145.

Treisman, A., 1986(a), "Properties, Parts and Objects", Handbook of Perception and Performance: Volume 2, Boff, K., Kauffman, L., and Thomas, J., eds., John Wiley & Sons, Inc.

Treisman, A., 1986(b), "Features and Objects in Visual Processing", Scientific American, 225, pp. 114B-125.

ON MEANINGFUL MENUS FOR MEASUREMENT: DISENTANGLING EVALUATIVE ISSUES IN

SYSTEM DESIGN*

William B. Rouse**

Search Technology, Inc.
Technology Park/Summit
Norcross, Georgia 30092

Abstract: This essay argues that system evaluation should be viewed in the broader context of measurement. Seven measurement issues are discussed including testing, verification, demonstration, evaluation, validation, acceptance, and viability. These issues are discussed from the perspectives of both system designers and users. It is proposed that a comprehensive approach to measurement should invoke planning and execution of four phases of measurement including naturalist, marketing, engineering, and sales and service phases. The prerequisites to the success of this approach are discussed.

INTRODUCTION

For almost two decades, I have been concerned with designing and evaluating human-machine systems. For much of this time, I have viewed evaluation as mainly involving experimental issues of methods, measures, analysis, and interpretation. In the past few years, however, I have come to realize that such a perspective is much too narrow.

This realization was prompted by several experiences. First, I was, and continue to be, involved in a variety of efforts that started with system conceptualization and continued all the way to implementation and ongoing system use. A second catalyst has been the increasing importance of evaluating "intelligent" support systems for operations, maintenance, management, and design. The inherent nature of this type of support system has caused me to reconsider various fundamental evaluative issues. Finally, my increasing participation in multidisciplinary design efforts has resulted in an emerging perception that different disciplines and types of organizations view evaluation in quite different ways.

As I organized my thinking in preparation to write this essay, it

_____

*Presented as the keynote address at the Fourth Symposium on Empirical Foundations of Information and Software Science, Atlanta, October 1986.
**Also with the Center for Man-Machine Systems Research, Georgia Institute of Technology, Atlanta, Georgia 30332.

TESTING ⟶ Does the System Run, Compute, Etc?

VERIFICATION ⟶ Is the System Put Together as Planned?

DEMONSTRATION ⟶ How Do Observers React to System?

EVALUATION ⟶ Does the System Meet Requirements?

VALIDATION ⟶ Does the System Solve the Problem?

ACCEPTANCE ⟶ Do Organizations/Individuals Use the System?

VIABILITY ⟶ Are the Benefits of System Use Sufficiently Greater than its Costs?

Figure 1. Measurement Issues.

occurred to me that terminology is a primary hindrance to disentangling evaluative issues in system design. In discussing this observation with colleagues, the notion emerged that the general issue is one of _measurement_ which is much broader than the problem of evaluation. This idea provided the caption for Figure 1, as well as the general theme of this essay.

To an extent, Figure 1 is self-explanatory -- the seven terms on the left side of this figure are commonly, but, often not consistently, used by many of the individuals involved in system design efforts. Several types of individuals are involved with planning for and resolving the issues shown in Figure 1. System _producers_, which includes management, design, development, fabrication, marketing, sales, and service, are concerned with all of these issues at different points in the product life cycle. System _users_, which may include operators, maintainers, managers, and consumers, in general, are at least implicitly concerned with many of the measurement issues.

This essay is concerned with balancing and integrating the measurement issues in Figure 1, from the perspectives of both producers and users, and outlining a comprehensive approach to measurement. This requires disentangling evaluative issues in system design by both clarifying terminology and providing guidelines for planning and executing measurements across the range of issues in Figure 1. The need for clearer terminology and practical guidelines motivated my choice of a title for this essay -- on meaningful menus for measurement.

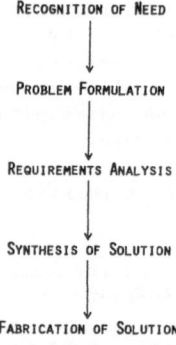

RECOGNITION OF NEED

PROBLEM FORMULATION

REQUIREMENTS ANALYSIS

SYNTHESIS OF SOLUTION

FABRICATION OF SOLUTION

Figure 2. Simplified System Design Process.

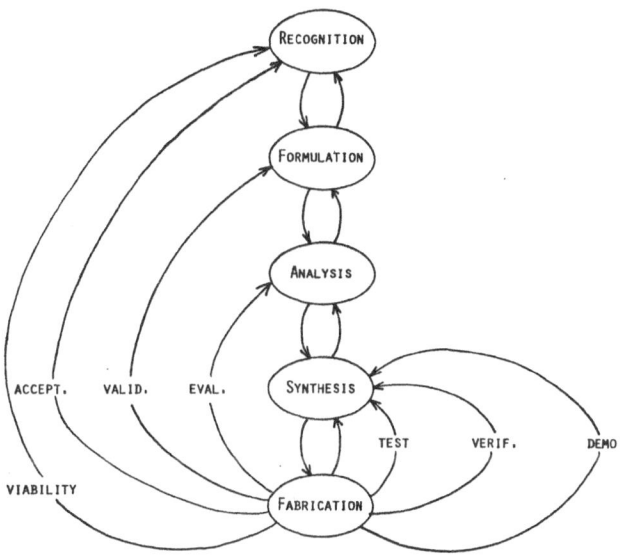

Figure 3. Integration of Measurement Issues and System Design.

MEASUREMENT AND SYSTEM DESIGN

The recognition that there are at least seven distinct measurement issues is an important first step. However, this recognition is only of intellectual interest unless we can be fairly specific about when and how these issues should be resolved in the process of system design. Figure 2 presents a very simplified view of the system design process. It is simplified in the sense that the process is depicted as much too linear and too orderly. In fact, reality involves much iteration and a great amount of parallelism. Nevertheless, the general sequence from needs to solutions provides the necessary structure for the line of reasoning that follows.

Figure 3 illustrates how the issues from Figure 1 tend to be integrated within the process of Figure 2. This illustration depicts measurement in terms of feedback loops from products to needs, problem formulation, requirements, and solution concepts. This type of representation provides a useful means for differentiating the planning and execution of measurements.

The planning of measurements should proceed from the outer to inner loops of Figure 3. (In other words, planning should start at the bottom of the list in Figure 1.) Thus, one should determine very early in the design process how viability, acceptance, and validity will be assessed. More specifically, what methods and measures will be used to make these assessments long before product sales, or equivalent, provide an indication of the success or failure of the product?

The execution of measurements should, and often must, proceed from the inner to outer loops of Figure 3 or, equivalently, start at the top of the list in Figure 1. Once a product or prototype emerges from fabrication, one can then execute the plans formulated earlier. In the absence of plans, measurement issues may be pursued in an inappropriate manner or, more unfortunately, not pursued at all.

The distinction between planning and execution provides a useful means of identifying potential measurement problems. There are two general classes of problems that are readily apparent from Figure 3. The first class is

NEEDS ─────→ Do Users Understand Their Needs?

REQUESTS ─────→ Can They Communicate These Needs?

RESPONSES ─────→ Are Substantive Responses Possible?

USABILITY ─────→ Can These Responses Be Utilized?

IMPACT ─────→ Does Usage Help Satisfy Needs?

VALUE ─────→ Is This Help Worth the Price?

Figure 4.   System Usage Concerns.

outer loop planning too late where, for example, failure to plan for assessing acceptance can preclude measurement prior to putting a product into
use. The second class of problem is inner loop execution too early where,
for example, demonstrations are executed prior to resolving test and verification, and potentially lead to negative initial impressions of a product.

The conclusions drawn from Figure 3 provide important elements of the
comprehensive approach to measurement that is presented later in this essay.
These conclusions are not particularly elaborate or subtle -- one might
reach similar conclusions from a careful analysis of planning and executing
a vacation or a gourmet meal. However, these conclusions, when combined with
a few observations regarding system users, suggest very substantial changes
of traditional ways of viewing system design.

MEASUREMENT AND SYSTEM USAGE

It seems to me that all of the issues in Figure 1 are inevitably addressed. If producers do not address some of the measurement issues, then
users eventually will, sometimes with unfortunate results. Of course, the
primary concerns of system users do not include measurements per se, but
rather involve performing tasks of interest. Nevertheless, system usage is
likely to eventually uncover prior inadequate or inappropriate resolutions
of the seven measurement issues.

System usage concerns are summarized in Figure 4. The wording in this
figure was chosen to illustrate usage of information systems. Different task
contexts might require rewording the questions, but the nature of the questions would remain the same.

A comparison of Figures 1 and 4 provides an interesting contrast in
"tones". While the designer is asking (in Figure 1) whether or not his (or
her) solution is appropriate, adequate, etc., the user is asking (in Figure
4) whether or not the system is appropriately and adequately supportive.
In other words, Figure 1 reflects the concerns of the provider of a service,
while Figure 4 summarizes the concerns of the consumer of a service.

It strikes me that a comprehensive approach to measurement requires
that the designer ask all of the questions in both Figures 1 and 4. Obviously, there is a significant (but not complete) overlap between these
two sets of concerns. Figure 5 illustrates this overlap by integrating

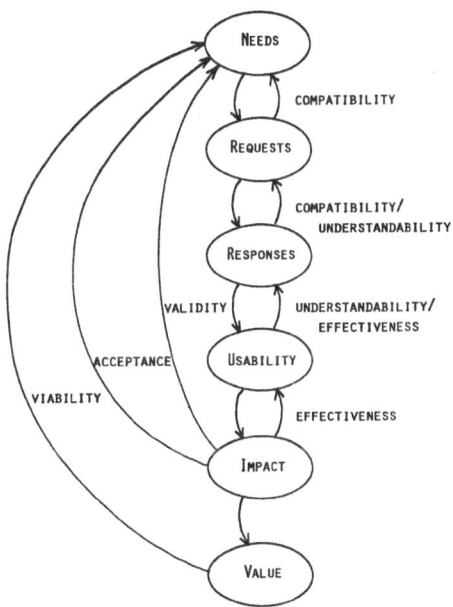

Figure 5. Integration of Measurement Issues and System Usage.

a subset of the measurement issues and the system usage concerns.

In this figure, the concept of evaluation (as defined in Figure 1) has
been decomposed into three finer-grained issues. Compatibility is the extent
to which the nature of physical presentations to the user and the responses
expected from the user are compatible with human input-output abilities and
limitations. Understandability is the extent to which the structure, format, and content of the user-system dialogue results in meaningful communication. Finally, effectiveness is the extent to which use of the system leads
to improved performance, makes a difficult task less difficult, or enables
accomplishing a task that could not otherwise be accomplished.

Elsewhere, I have argued that successful evaluation depends on assuring compatibility and understandability and effectiveness (Rouse, 1984).
For example, in order for an information system to meet requirements (as
defined in Figure 1), the user must be able to read the display and reach
the keyboard (compatibility), express queries and comprehend responses
(understandability), and utilize the resulting information to satisfy the
needs motivating the queries (effectiveness). By decomposing a broad concept
such as evaluation into more specific and potentially measurable attributes,
and also specifying a logical relationship among these attributes, it is
possible to gain substantial methodological leverage in terms of usefulness
and efficiency. I will later discuss an example of this type of leverage.

It is important to note that Figure 5 includes only a subset of the
issues in Figure 1. Testing, verification, and demonstration are, hopefully,
not part of system usage although, as noted earlier, users will inevitably
make these measurements if designers avoid them. It is also useful to
emphasize that users seldom plan measurements -- they simply experience the
measurement process and, implicitly or explicitly, make inferences that
relate to measurement issues. To assure that the resulting inferences are
desirable, producers should plan users' experiences in the sense of an-
ticipating users' reactions and choosing system functionality and features
accordingly. The following section provides a framework within which this
type of planning can be pursued.

The discussion thus far has served to emphasize the diversity of measurement issues from the perspectives of both producers and users. If each of these issues were pursued independently, as if they were ends in themselves, the costs of measurement would be untenable. Yet, each issue is important and should not be neglected.

What is needed, therefore, is an overall approach to measurement that balances the resources devoted to each issue at each stage of design, while also integrating intermediate measurement results in a way that provides maximal benefit to the evolution of the design product. I suggest that this can be accomplished by viewing measurement as a process involving four phases: 1) naturalist, 2) marketing, 3) engineering, and 4) sales and service. Producers should develop a measurement plan that explicitly recognizes these four phases, anticipates the specific methods and measures that will be used to address each issue in each phase, and consider the decision making criteria that will be used to judge the outcomes of each measurement effort.

Naturalist Phase

This phase involves understanding the domain and tasks of users from the perspectives of individuals, the organization, and the environment. This understanding not only includes users' activities but also the prevalent values and attitudes relative to productivity, technology, and change in general. Evaluative assessment of interest includes identification of difficult and easy aspects of tasks, barriers to and potential avenues of improvement, and the relative leverage of the various stakeholders in the organization.

The results of this phase include a characterization of users' tasks and needs, as well as users' perceptions of how these needs might be met. To an extent, this characterization may involve a formal taxonomy of, for example, component tasks of situation assessment, planning and commitment, and execution and monitoring (Rouse, Kisner, Frey, and Rouse, 1984; Rouse, 1986). Use of such a task taxonomy allows a fairly direct mapping to alternative concepts for supporting users' activities.

However, general characterizations of this type are not sufficient. They must be augmented by very context-specific assessments of the abilities, limitations, and preferences of individuals and their organizations relative to why activities are pursued in particular ways, who is involved at various levels, and what avenues of change are likely to be valued. Some of the answers to these questions will be generalizable across all organizations in a particular domain; other answers will be more organization-specific.

This leads to the question of identifying users and assuring that their answers to the types of question posed above are representative of the total user population of interest. Since any single user or group of users will obviously reflect their own organizations, it will usually be necessary to sample multiple organizations to understand the overall population of interest. An exception to this guideline occurs when the total population of users resides in a single organization. At an extreme, I can recall a design effort where we only queried and studied a single user because that individual was the only potential user of the design product.

The suggestion that it is very important to characterize users' activities and needs is far from novel -- the important point is that this characterization should be formalized and documented. The usual case is that designers think, perhaps only tacitly, that they understand the users and, therefore, attempt to act as users' surrogates as well as designers. To the extent that designers are former users, this approach has some value. However, it is inherently limited from capturing the abilities, attitudes, and aspirations of current or potential users and the current or potential impact of their organizations.

It is often argued that the eventual users of the system of interest do not yet exist -- there are no incumbent users. This is very seldom true because there are actually extremely few systems that are designed "from scratch". Even, for example, when designing the initial spacecraft much was drawn from previous experiences in aircraft and submarines. For those very rare cases where a truly new system is being designed, one still should know the population from which users will be drawn and attempt to characterize their abilities, limitations, and preferences. For example, regardless of what systems the military envisions, they know that the population from which they can recruit users over the next 18 years is already born; the population available over the next 5 years is defined even more crisply in terms of the extent and nature of their education, attitudes toward work and the military, and likely aspirations. Thus, the argument that we are inherently limited from identifying and understanding the likely users of our systems is a fairly weak argument.

Marketing Phase

Once we understand the domain and tasks of current and potential users, we are in a position to conceptualize alternative products to support these users. There are three sources of product ideas. First, the formal task characterizations briefly discussed earlier can lead, in a fairly "top-down" manner, to general product concepts (Rouse, Kisner, Frey, and Rouse, 1984; Rouse, 1986). A second source of ideas is one's "bottom-up" reactions to the experiences of the naturalist phase. Finally, and of most importance, users are a rich source of product ideas.

Each of these ideas can be pursued using the process of Figure 3 at a fairly cursory level. As a result, several product mockups and usage scenarios can be fabricated. These "products" can then be used for initial marketing in the sense of determining how users react to the concepts. Users' reactions are needed relative to validity, acceptability, and viability. In other words, one wants to determine whether or not users perceive a product concept as solving an important problem, solving it in an acceptable way, and solving it at a reasonable cost.

More specifically, questions related to validity are concerned with the accuracy of the conclusions drawn from the naturalist phase. User acceptance may, at first glance, seem quite simple, but one quickly realizes that acceptance is multi-dimensional and subtle. Therefore, a fairly structured approach to measurement may be helpful (Rouse and Morris, 1986). Viability concerns how much one would be willing to pay for the product, who would make the ultimate purchase decision, and what process is used to recommend and justify product purchases.

While one cannot resolve all of the validity, acceptability, and viability questions during the marketing phase, one can test and elaborate the plans for eventual resolution of these issues. Thus, this phase produces both an assessment of the relative merits of the multiple product concepts that have emerged up to this point, as well as a preview of any particular difficulties that are likely when one later tries to assure that users perceive the resulting product as valid, acceptable, and viable. .

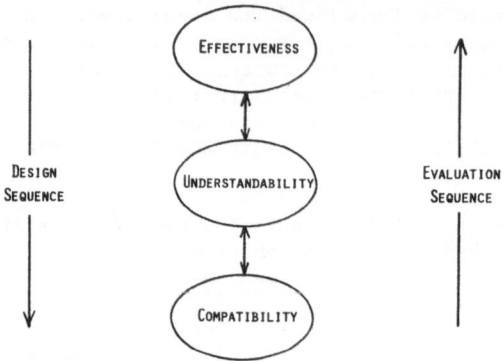

Figure 6.   Top-Down Design Vs Bottom-Up Evaluation.

Engineering Phase

One now is in a position to begin tradeoffs between desired conceptual functionality and technological reality. Technology development will, of course, have been pursued prior to and in parallel with the naturalist and marketing phases. This will have at least partially assured that the product concepts tested in the marketing phase were not technologically or econom-ically ridiculous. However, one now must be very specific about how desired functionality is to be provided, what performance is possible, and the time and dollars necessary to provide it.

Most of the effort in this phase is associated with using various design methodologies to transform conceptual designs to detailed designs. For example, within the area of computer-generated display systems, method-ologies developed and applied by Frey, Hunt, and this author (Rouse, Kisner, Frey, and Rouse, 1984; Frey, Sides, Hunt, and Rouse, 1984) provide a struc-tured approach for determining information requirements and, subsequently choosing display elements, integrating these elements into display pages, and developing the associated human-computer dialogue. While such method-ologies are and should be the central theme in the engineering phase of product development, this topic is not central to this essay -- our primary concern is with how measurement should proceed in parallel with design.

Figure 6 illustrates a fundamental conflict between design and measure-ment during the engineering phase. Design necessarily tends to proceed top-down from the results of the naturalist and marketing phases. The focus is on providing effective solutions to the requirements identified earlier, consideration of understandability and compatibility is usually delayed until one or more potentially effective solutions emerge.

In contrast, measurement will tend to proceed bottom-up. Testing and verification must occur early if an operational prototype is to be available. Approaches to testing and verification include "talk-throughs", analytical methods for products that are not too complex, and empirical methods for more complicated products.

Early demonstrations to users can be very important and contribute to continued marketing of the product concepts. However, unless the user population is very sophisticated and technically oriented, it is quite pos-sible to create a lasting negative impression by premature demonstrations. This is particularly likely if users stumble on incompatibilities and mis-understands and, as a result, never fully appreciate the approach to effec-tiveness being proposed.

METHOD OF MEASUREMENT	EVALUATION ISSUE		
	COMPATIBILITY	UNDERSTANDABILITY	EFFECTIVENESS
STATIC PAPER EVALUATION	USEFUL AND EFFICIENT	SOMEWHAT USEFUL BUT INEFFICIENT	NOT USEFUL
DYNAMIC PAPER EVALUATION	USEFUL AND EFFICIENT	SOMEWHAT USEFUL BUT INEFFICIENT	NOT USEFUL
DATA-DRIVEN PART-TASK SIMULATION	USEFUL BUT INEFFICIENT	USEFUL AND EFFICIENT	MARTGINALLY USEFUL BUT EFFICIENT
MODEL-DRIVEN PART-TASK SIMULATION	USEFUL BUT INEFFICIENT	USEFUL AND EFFICIENT	SOMEWHAT USEFUL BUT EFFICIENT
FULL-SCOPE SIMULATION	USEFUL BUT VERY INEFFICIENT	USEFUL BUT INEFFICIENT	USEFUL, BUT SOMEWHAT INEFFICIENT
IN-USE EVALUATION	USEFUL BUT EXTREMELY INEFFICIENT	USEFUL BUT VERY INEFFICIENT	USEFUL, BUT INEFFICIENT

Figure 7.   Usefulness and Efficiency of Alternative Measurement Methods.

Users, as well as evaluators, tend to view a product initially in terms of the physical presentations they observe and the types of response they initiate. If they cannot read the display and reach the keyboard, it is impossible for them to comment on, for example, the structure of the human-computer dialogue. Similarly, if compatibility is not a problem, but the menus, prompts, and computer messages are not meaningful, they cannot provide their perceptions of the likely effectiveness of the product relative to their needs.

Thus, users and evaluators inevitably approach a product from a bottom-up perspective, while designers quite naturally think of their product in the top-down manner that it emerged. As a result, when resources are scarce there is an inherent competition between those whose initial goal is assuring compatibility and understandability (i.e., users and evaluators) and those who would like to enhance the product's effectiveness (i.e., designers). The "winner" in this competition is usually dictated by the orientation of the decision makers involved -- for example, a market-oriented management appears to be more likely to take the user's perspective.

It may be possible to decrease the extent of this inherent conflict by providing means for efficiently and inexpensively resolving compatibility and understandability issues. Figure 7 summarizes an approach to achieving this goal that has been applied in a variety of design efforts (Rouse, 1984). As can be seen from this figure, compatibility issues often can be resolved with paper evaluations. This type of evaluation usually involves a trained analyst using guidelines such as developed and applied by Frey and his colleagues (Frey, Sides, Hunt, Rouse, 1984). The compatibility of the interface is usually assessed both statically and dynamically, with the emphasis in the latter case being on the readability of time-varying parameters, response time requirements, and so on.

Evaluation involving simulations or actual systems are incrementally more expensive, involving much more equipment and many people. Use of guidelines for planning and documenting such efforts can maintain a reasonable level of efficiency (Rouse, 1984). Of particular importance is choosing methods and measures that maximize the opportunity for definitive results. In a recent evaluation of almost 200 previous experimental studies of complex man-machine systems, we found that one is more likely to obtain definitive experimental results if the method chosen allows a reasonable degree of control and the measures chosen allow fine-grained analyses of performance (Rouse and Rouse, 1984). This conclusion was based on comparisons of the methods shown in Figure 7 as a function of the particular measures employed and the domain of study.

While the usefulness vs efficiency guidelines in Figure 7 are concerned with the components of evaluation, this tradeoff is obviously important for measurement issues other than evaluation. It is not possible to elaborate these tradeoffs within the scope of this paper. It is worth noting, however, that rapid prototyping (vs analytical methods) has precipitated many concerns that too much emphasis is being placed on efficiency (time) and too little on well-reasoned usefulness (validity).

Sales and Service Phase

As this phase begins, the product should have successfully been tested, verified, demonstrated, and evaluated. From a measurement point of view, the focus is now on validity, acceptability, and viability. If the earlier naturalist and marketing phases were well done, the sales and service phase should not be calamitous. Nevertheless, the final marketing, sales, installation, and ongoing service of a product are the activities that should provide the validation, acceptance, and viability measurements planned earlier. To an extent, sales volume (e.g., number of units bought) can be viewed as a measure of these three attributes. However, the single measure of sales volume is very much inadequate, and usually much too late, to serve as a means for diagnosing and remediating problems. The aforementioned approach to user acceptance (Rouse and Morris, 1986) is an example of directly addressing a measurement issue rather than inferring its resolution by sales or equivalent.

The sales and service phase of measurement is important even if the product is "pre-sold" -- for example, delivered as the result of a contracted R&D effort. If the goal is for the product to be accepted and used as intended, then marketing in one form or another has to continue throughout the product life cycle. During installation and service, one can maintain, enhance, and extend the relationships with users developed during earlier phases. This will provide both formal and informal means for assessing validity, acceptability, and viability during ongoing use of the product. This will also substantially lessen the investments necessary for subsequent naturalist and marketing phases for new products.

Summary

In this section, I have argued that the measurements associated with developing a product can be viewed as occurring in four phases: 1) naturalist, 2) marketing, 3) engineering, and 4) sales and service. The earlier phases emphasize planning of measurement, while the later phases emphasize execution of measurements, with the balance between planning and execution depending on which "loops" of Figures 3 and 5 are involved. Each of the four phases has a rather different orientation, but the overriding measurement philosophy is continual assessment and refinement of whether or not the product is on target.

DISCUSSION AND CONCLUSION

Reflecting upon the line of reasoning that I have advanced in this essay, it seems to me that many of the points are quite simple and obvious. However, there are alternative points of view. Predominant among these

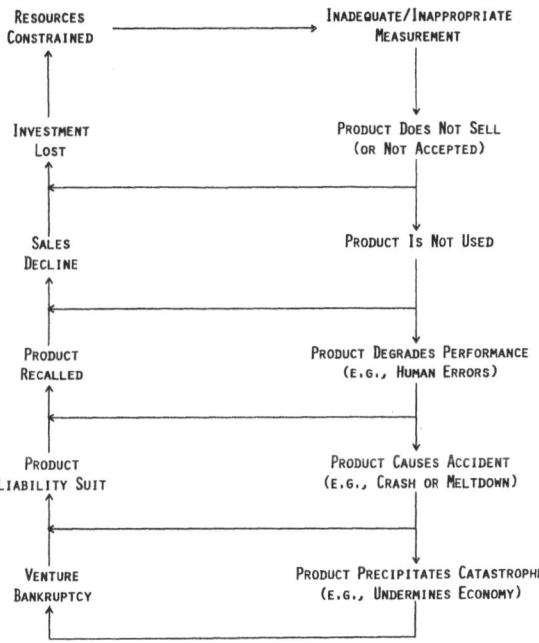

Figure 8.   The Causes and Costs of Inadequate/Inappropriate Measurement.

alternatives is the view that technology issues must be addressed first, from which products will "emerge".

This point of view is not inherently wrong, but it tends to consume many resources and often precludes adequate and appropriate measurement. As shown in Figure 8, the results of inadequate/inappropriate measurement range from lost investments to failed ventures as users inevitably make the measurements that producers neglected to make. Further, as shown in Figure 8, a cycle can result whereby inadequate/inappropriate measurement yields poor products that cause decreased sales and depleted resources, which precipitates inadequate/inappropriate measurement and so on.

It seems to me that planned measurement, perhaps in the matter advocated in this essay, is the most economical way to proceed. Such planning should enable producing viable, acceptable, and valid products within reasonable schedule and budget constraints, and with relatively few unfortunate surprises. While this conclusion does not seem particularly astounding, product development often does not proceed in this manner. In fact, there appear to be several prerequisites to successful planning of measurement.

1.   A long-term perspective is needed to balance and integrate measurement issues -- a lack of this perspective often results in measurement being a victim of resource constraints.

2.   A sense of accountability, both ethical and legal, is needed throughout the product development process -- otherwise, individuals pursuing one phase of design tend to feel that issues associated with later phases of design are "not their problems".

3.   Since product developers are rarely clairvoyant, it is necessary to have a flexible design process that enables feedback of measurement into design refinements prior to

production -- if feedback is not possible, the motivation for measurement may be limited to satisfying contractual requirements.

4. Cooperative user-producer relationships are the key elements in providing the requisite flexibility -- the adversarial nature of these relationships in many domains provides a strong disincentive to planned measurement.

This essay has attempted to foster a consistent and comprehensive view of the role of measurement in system design. I have proposed an overall approach and suggested how we might proceed. While this approach makes great sense to me, I am also realistic and recognize that many people and perspectives are involved. Thus, for example, the prerequisites listed above may not be universally endorsed by all of the parties involved. However, at this point, it would be quite useful if everyone at least agreed on goals and terminology. Hopefully, the meaningful menus for measurement offered in this essay will contribute to this agreement.

ACKNOWLEDGEMENT

The preparation of this essay was supported in part by the U.S. Air Force Armstrong Aerospace Medical Research Laboratory under Contract No. F33615-86-C-0542, "Automated Data Management for Designers: A Designer's Associate". Dr. Kenneth R. Boff of AAMRL is the technical monitor for this contract.

REFERENCES

Frey, P. R., Sides, W. H., Hunt, R. M., and Rouse, W. B., 1984, Computer-Generated Display System Guidelines: Volume 1, Display Design, Technical Report NP37091, Volume 1, March 1984, Electric Power Research Institute, Palo Alto, CA.

Rouse, W. B., 1984, Computer-Generated Display System Guidelines: Volume 2, Developing an Evaluation Plan, Technical Report NP3701, Volume 2, March 1984, Electric Power Research Institute, Palo Alto, CA.

Rouse, W. B., 1986, "Design and Evaluation of Computer-Based Decision Support-Systems", Microcomputer Decision Support Systems: Design, Implementation, and Evaluation, Andriole, S. J., ed., QED Information Sciences, Wellesley, MA.

Rouse, W. B., Kisner, R. A., Frey, P. R., and Rouse, S. H., 1984, A Method for Analytical Evaluation of Computer-Based Decision Aids, Technical Report NUREG/CR-3655; ORNL/TM-9068, July 1984, Oak Ridge National Laboratory, Oak Ridge, TN.

Rouse, W. B., and Morris, N. M., 1986, "Understanding and Enhancing User Acceptance of Computer Technology, IEEE Transactions on Systems, Man, and Cybernetics, SMC-16.

Rouse, W. B., and Rouse, S. H., 1984, "A Note on Evaluation of Complex Man-Machine Systems", IEEE Transactions on System, Man, and Cybernetics, SMC-14.

ISSUES AND RED HERRINGS IN EVALUATING NATURAL LANGUAGE INTERFACES*

Ralph M. Weischedel

BBN Laboratories Inc.
Cambridge, MA

Abstract: Due to growing interest in using natural language interfaces, it is appropriate to begin discussing their evaluation. This position paper presents the point of view that natural language interfaces offer special problems for evaluation, compared to problems encountered with other computer software. If ignored, such problems will make evaluation ineffectual. First, the paper describes the purposes and dimensions of problems in such an evaluation; differing purposes dictate differing approaches to evaluating natural language interfaces. Then, the paper points out some issues that turn out to be red herrings, and suggests a modest proposal that covers much of the broad spectrum of difficult issues involved. Since some of the issues and problems are common to both expert systems and natural language interfaces, comparisons of issues in evaluation of expert systems is also provided.

This position paper offers the point of view of one in research and development of natural language processors to those not involved in developing natural language interfaces. Consequently, it is an overview of issues, rather than a case study of an existing system or an argument for a particular mathematical evaluation technique.

1. INTRODUCTION

There is a growing need for a methodology of evaluating natural language interfaces (NLI), as evident from several relatively recent developments:

- Commercial availability of a natural language interface (INTELLECT from AI Corp.) for data bases on mainframes.

- Natural language interfaces to data bases on personal computers, e.g., Q&A from Symantec Corp.

- Explicit goals in requests for proposals for NLIs to various expert systems under DARPA's Strategic Computing Program.

---

*Part of this paper appeared earlier. 1986 IEEE. Reprinted, with permission, from 1986 IEEE INTERNATIONAL CONFERENCE ON SYSTEMS, MAN AND CYBERNETICS, Atlanta, GA, October 14-17, 1986.

In addition to expert systems and data base management systems, it is likely that other software systems will soon become candidates for natural language interfaces. Of course, this is a pleasant situation, since it signifies the maturing of a research and development technology to the point of application and commercialization.

In light of this, there is significant need for an evaluation methodology. Other papers in this Symposium deal with detailed models of human-machine interface evaluation. Since there is a large literature on evaluating software and on evaluating interfaces, the goals in this paper are to review the issues that are peculiar to natural language interfaces, to offer the beginnings of answers regarding the issues, and to provide pointers to what literature there is that addresses the topics. As a consequence, this position paper, of necessity, is more of an overview than a detailed proposal.

Section 2 states my assumptions in writing this paper. Section 3 lists various purposes for which one would conduct evaluation of natural language interfaces and various dimensions that must be considered in evaluating natural language systems. Section 4 lists some issues that are red herrings and justifies them being classified as such. In Section 5, the issues that arise in expert system evaluation are compared with those of NLI's. A modest proposal of a flexible approach to natural language interface evaluation is provided in Section 6.

2. ASSUMPTIONS

First, by <u>natural language interfaces</u> we mean a processor that accepts as input human communication forms that occur in nature, such as English, French, Chinese, and Swahili, and that acts upon them in a way consistent with the intent of the user, furthermore, an NLI may generate natural language as output as well. The user may generate expressions freely to convey his/her intent. The natural expression need not consist solely of words, but could include pointing and special forms such as chemical formulas or mathematical expressions. The interface should not require expressions to be perfectly well-formed nor complete in themselves. For instance, the following examples are appropriate natural language expressions to a navy information system.

    User: "Are any carriers in the West Pacific M1 on AAW"
    System: ...
    User: "There overall readiness"

Those expressions include a symbol that is not a word ("M1"), jargon ("AAW"), spelling mistakes ("there" for "their"), and cryptic expressions ("their overall readiness" for "list the overall readiness of the carriers that you just mentioned in West Pacific having an M1 rating on AAW").

There are many systems for which an NLI seems inappropriate, for example, systems where an individual uses highly constrained, highly repetitious requests as in airline check-in.* For such systems, interfaces that can reduce the number of keystrokes can be far more natural.

---

*Highly repetitious, highly constrained activities, such as airline reservation clerks perform, seem inappropriate for <u>typed</u> natural language input; were continuous speech input possible, some of those tasks may in fact be very appropriate candidates for an NLI. Furthermore, if the task involves heavy use of the hands of the individual, as in a pilot of a fighter aircraft, speech natural language input may be the only alternative.

There are several kinds of applications of NLIs, including document retrieval, decision support, text processing, and answer/explanation generation. We confine ourselves here to applications that require an <u>understanding</u> of the input. Though some may argue that document retrieval should involve understanding, we will not assume that and will consider only the other application areas.

3. PURPOSES AND DIMENSIONS OF EVALUATION

There are many differing goals one could have in evaluating an NLI or natural language technology; since the differing goals will dictate differing evaluation techniques, it is important to clearly identify the purposes from the start. Similarly, there are many different dimensions to the evaluation techniques and to the facets of an NLI, therefore, we also describe those dimensions briefly.

3.1 <u>Purposes</u>

There are at least the following differing purposes.

1. <u>Specification Verification</u>. Particularly in the context of government contracts and in the context of custom-designed NLIs, a paramount purpose of evaluation is determining whether the specification for the NLI, mutually agreed upon by contractor and contractee, has been met. A particular problem in this context is writing the specification in a flexible, yet concrete way in light of the fact of the heuristic nature of natural language processing techniques. For instance, it seems that any NLI must include processing of conjunctions, e.g., and, or, etc. Nevertheless, the full range of the use of conjunctions in natural language is well beyond the state-of-the-art, and it seems unlikely that a comprehensive solution is possible within the foreseeable future. Therefore, the specification must indicate some class of expressions involving conjunction that a user should expect to be processable by the system; using conjunction outside of that class of expressions may be correctly understood by the NLI, but is not guaranteed.

2. <u>System/Technology Selection</u>. When an organization is considering whether a proposed application would be appropriate for an NLI, it is necessary to identify the important characteristics of the application and target user community so that evaluation of the appropriateness of the possible technologies and systems can proceed. An overview of the critical characteristics of the application and user community, as well as insight into the advantages and disadvantages of the current alternatives in the state-of-the-art of NLI is available (Bates and Bobrow, 1984).

3. <u>Single System/Technology Evaluation</u>. Suppose the need is to assess the state-of-the-art of a given technology, for instance, as illustrated in a given NLI. This can be the need of a funding agency, or can be the purpose of an internal corporate review of an R&D effort. This itself divides into multiple purposes. The goal might be to determine how much to fund the effort in the future, if at all. Alternatively, the primary goal might be to provide the scientists and engineers with concrete feedback regarding the heuristics and aspects of the system or technology that most need further work, as evidenced by the needs or use of one or more concrete user communities. One of the implicit goals of DARPA's Strategic Computer Program is such feedback to the scientific community.

3.2 Dimensions

One class of dimensions for evaluation involves around the language coverage of the NLI system or technology. For any given underlying system or set of underlying systems to which the natural language process is an interface, there is some set of basic, underlying functional capabilities available to the user community. These include data items, tables of data, numerical calculations on the data, graphics capabilities, diagnosis of a problem situation, situation assessment, ranked alternative recommendations, and explanation, to name a few. The degree of <u>domain coverage</u> is the degree to which the NLI provides access to those underlying system capabilities. It is not necessarily the case that free form natural language input is the most appropriate means of communication for each underlying system capability. For instance, if access to statistical packages is part of the underlying system, much of the information the user must supply could be selection among options and specification of parameters. Presentation of the options via menus and presentation of requests to type a numerical parameter would be useful aspects of a natural language interface.

One could use the term <u>fluency</u> to represent the degree to which the user can express his/her need or request in their own way. For instance, the list below identifies some of the many ways one could request the overall combat readiness rating of the USS Enterprise.

'What is the overall combat readiness of Enterprise?'
'What is the CROVL of Enterprise?'
'What is the overall readiness of Enterprise?'
'What is Enterprise's combat rating?'
'List Enterprise's readiness.'
'What is its readiness?'
'What readiness does Enterprise have?'
'Enterprise has what readiness?'
'Show me Enterprise's readiness.'
'Show Enterprise's readiness.'
'Print the current readiness of Enterprise.'
'CROVL Enterprise.'
'Readiness Enterprise.'

There is no known way to numerically quantify the degree of fluency of an NLI. However, there have been some initial attempts to characterize the linguistic competence of an NLI by providing (partial) checklists of linguistic capabilities (Bates and Bobrow, 1984; Pollack, Hirschberg, and Webber, 1982; Tennant, 1980). Work that would provide a more comprehensive checklist is still needed.

Another class of dimensions involves principles of computer-human interface design. Certainly, the natural language capabilities provided in an NLI are of paramount importance, nevertheless, the computer-human interface issues are fundamental to a successful NLI. Poor management of the screen, an editor oriented to programmers rather than users, or any other failure to take into account the user of the NLI will cause frustration. A report on an interesting case study that addresses some of these issues is available (Koile and Walker, 1986).

3.3 Collecting Data

There are several ways one can collect data for evaluation purposes. One is a checklist of features. One approach (Tennant, 1980) to such a checklist is in terms of language expressions; though at first glance the classification given there may appear exclusively syntactic in nature, it in fact touches on many of the critical issues in semantics of natural language since the semantic issues tend to have a correlate in syntactic expression. For instance, quantification is clearly a semantic issue, for the quantifiers in a logical expression are a critical part of meaning; nevertheless, it has a syntactic correlate in terms of how certain meanings may be expressed in English noun phrases, prepositional phrases, and clauses. Contrast the meanings of "Did any carrier remain C1 through 1985?" with "Did every carrier remain C1 through 1985?" Another checklist (Pollack, Hirschberg, and Webber, 1982) includes many communication functions that a question answering system should perform, e.g., verifying understanding and eliciting further information. There are additional phenomena that belong on a complete checklist, e.g., anaphora (expressions, such as pronouns, that refer to something previously evoked in the context), idiomatic expression, figures of speech, input that appears ill-formed, and ellipsis (fragmentary forms that in context express a complete thought); however, a more complete list is still needed.

A second technique is measuring user evaluation. Of course, there are well-known techniques for surveying opinion and evaluation that are both statistically reliable within a given desired range of error and are also quantitatively useful. The care necessary in designing such a questionnaire so that the opinion is meaningfully solicited about important issues and so that the user sample is reflective of the user community at large is also well known. The analytic hierarchy process, employed to evaluate an expert system (Liebowitz, 1986), may be a useful supplement to questionnaires, for it offers the potential of helping a user explain why he/she has chosen one alternative of a binary choice, even though many dimensions may enter into the decision.

Third, techniques for formal studies of computer-human interface issues are well known. Nevertheless, it goes without saying that early prototyping of the visual displays and interaction media for informal evaluation by experts during the design phase can influence what the end user sees so successfully that more expensive formal studies may not be necessary.

Fourth, careful empirical studies evaluating various aspects of the linguistic competence of the system can be devised. Unfortunately, a clear methodology here has not yet emerged, and there have been relatively few such studies thus far. They may be summarized as follows:

- One study by Malhotra (1975) was designed for assessing adequacy of existing state-of-the-art techniques prior to building an NLI. The approach involved giving the potential end users a typical problem to solve, providing them a computer terminal, and instructing them to solve the problem using a "new" decision support system. The user's input was intercepted by scientists and converted by hand to appropriate code for existing underlying systems which provided answers to the user's requests. The transcripts of those sessions provided a corpus representing typical use <u>before an NLI was built for the application</u>. Then the transcripts of those sessions were analyzed for inputs that were processable within the state-of-the-art, were diagnosed regarding any problem which would prevent processing by state-of-the-art techniques, were statistically analyzed, and were examined for patterns of problems requiring research.

- Evaluation of an existing system, REL, was conducted by giving college students representative problems for which the system was designed. Unfortunately, the problems (loading cargo on a vessel) were not highly familiar to students, so, the corpus may not have been fully reflective of the target user community. This study (Thompson, 1980) involved detailed analysis of each input, regarding the frequency of occurrence of particular classes of phenomena, e.g., conjunction, and regarding the cause of any failure to interpret the input correctly.

- One of the most realistic approaches for detailed evaluation of the state-of-the-art involves collecting a corpus by introducing a prototype system into the daily working environment of representatives of the end user community. Such a study has been conduced and reported for the TQA system (Damerau, 1981). A bevy of statistics on the performance of the system over a period of several months of installation in the working environment was performed.

I wish to emphasize the _means_ of collecting the corpus of input, rather than its subsequent analysis. Placing a prototype in the hands of real users solving their everyday problems as part of their normal function is most desirable because of the realism in reflecting the user community's environment. If this cannot be performed, then to collect a body of input prior to availability of even a prototype, the mock situation created in Malhotra's experiment is quite useful.

A corpus of input representative of the user community has several uses:

- It can help focus discussion of the NLI specification. If certain features show up in the corpus, are deemed essential, and are beyond the state-of-the-art, infeasibility will be evident early. Less drastically, for each linguistic phenomenon present, a discussion and agreement on realistic expectations regarding the NLI system can be achieved.

- It provides direction to the technical staff regarding customization of the NLI to the needs of the user community. For instance, it might suggest improving the heuristics for treating fragmentary input.

- It provides frequencies for constructing a benchmark set of inputs for testing and evaluating the system.

- It provides realistic examples for the research community, outside of the project.

4.   RED HERRINGS

A number of suggestions that have arisen in the past regarding evaluation criteria appear to be red herrings. One such is _the percentage of input correctly understood by a system._

- While it is alluring to think in terms of a single critereon for evaluating an NLI's effectiveness, it is too simplistic. The quality of responses to an unprocessable input, the number of requests to get to an understandable one, indications that the request may not be answerable by the underlying system, online aids to help the individual identify what can be understood, etc., are factors that contribute in a way making the percentage of interpretability less important than the users' sense of the system's utility.

- It is also too simplistic, in that it does not adequately credit the natural, unconscious adaptation of a user to the peculiarities of language in another individual. Many people have had personal experience in communicating with someone who speaks broken English. At first it is difficult to understand that individual or to be understood by that individual; however, one learns about the language that is actually understood and used by the individual. In the same way, users can naturally, unconsciously adapt to the idiosyncrasies of an NLI. Experiences with ROBOT, the predecessor to INTELLECT, a commercially available NLI product from AI Corporation, showed that consistent users of the system rapidly adjusted to the subset of language the NLI understood (Harris, 1977).

- Furthermore, the purposes of the evaluation must be taken in-account. If the purpose is to evaluate the state-of-the-art for a given system or technology, and if the evaluation is of a research and development system rather than a product, then the overall percentage of inputs correctly interpreted is far less important than a more detailed study of the kinds of input for which the system performs correctly and even more importantly the kinds of input and the cause in each example when it does not perform correctly. Careful analysis when the system fails is important because an NLI is a very complex integration of a large collection of interdependent heuristics to cover a wide variety of language phenomena. For any given input it is quite possible that dozens of heuristics come into play; failure of just one causes misinterpretation of the input. For instance, failing to state that a verb such as break can be both transitive and intransitive would mean that some sentences including that verb would fail to be understood correctly. Such an omission is not necessarily a failure of the technology, but may be a trivial software bug that can be corrected in a matter of seconds. On the other hand, if the heuristics for understanding anaphora are weak, even though those heuristics are just a small part of the complete picture, the degree of success in anaphora treatment can have a big impact on user acceptance.

A corollary of this is that one should not expect natural language interfaces to understand every input. Even people do not understand everything; when misunderstanding arises, people engage in dialogue to facilitate understanding.

A second red herring is computation time. If the underlying system is an expert system or a data base management system, in all likelihood typical requests written in an artificial language would require dozens of seconds or even minutes to be fulfilled by today's underlying systems. If one adds a few seconds to that for the processing of a natural language input, that is little to pay to have the extra capability provided by the natural language interface.*

---

*Perhaps the practical implication of the possibility of as much as an order of magnitude or more difference in the time to fulfill a request versus the short time to understand a request is that the last action of the natural language interface in understanding a request should be to emblazon on the output screen that it has done its processing and it is now the expert system's turn or to announce it with fanfare if speech output is possible.

A third red herring is <u>estimates of productivity changes or estimates of the expense of using a natural language interface</u>. Of course the issue cannot be ignored at some level; however, a very simple evaluation technique will suffice, whereas complex analytical techniques are difficult to apply relevantly. The availability of a natural language interface literally could change the nature of work by the individuals involved. For instance, consider the environment for which BBN has experimentally provided a natural language interface (IRUS (Bates, Stallard, and Moser, 1985; Koile and Walker, 1986)). The target users are navy officers involved in decision making at the Pacific Fleet Command Center; these are top-level executives whose energy is best spent on navy problems and decision making rather than on the details of which of four underlying systems offers a given information capability, on how to divide a problem into the various information capabilities required, and how to synthesize the results into the desired answer. They have not accessed the data base or OSGP applications programs themselves; rather, on a round-the-clock basis, two operators are available as intermediaries between commander and computer. Consequently, the need for a natural language interface is paramount.

Similarly, the cost of obtaining or using a natural language interface to an expert system or other decision support system may pale in comparison to the potential cost of not using one. Suppose that the availability of the natural language interface makes the expert system or decision support system accessible to top-level decision makers who, otherwise, would be very remote from such systems. Suppose further that the availability of those systems helps them manage their resources in a more effective way than they would otherwise. If as a result of command staff accessing such systems, an aircraft carrier and its entourage of vessels is more effectively used even five or ten days per year, the impact on proper use of limited, highly expensive resources is worth the comparatively small cost of artificial intelligence systems. In a parallel way, suppose that the decision makers are using medical experts systems, one cannot measure the value of lives saved. Since these things really cannot be meaningfully quantized, the real issue is whether the people who would be provided access to the decision support tools want that access and are willing to pay for it.

Yet another red herring is <u>to equate evaluation with a single number rating an NLI</u>. We agree with the point of view quoted below, which arose in "Evaluation of Expert Systems: Issues and Case Studies" (Gaschnig, Klahr, Pople, Shortliffe, and Terry, 1983, p. 248), in the context of evaluating expert systems.

Principle 1. Complex objects or processes cannot be evaluated by a single criterion or number.

Principle 2. The larger the number of distinct criteria evaluated or measurements taken, the more information will be available on which to base an overall evaluation.

Complex decisions in government and industry are not made by simplistic measures; evaluating complex software systems should not be either.*

---

*In Liebowitz (1986), the analytic hierarchy process is suggested as an expert system evaluation techniques satisfying those principles (Liebowitz, 1986). However, that process still tries to reduce the result of evaluation to a single number, though it does so by weights on choice points on potentially many dimensions. Rather, what it could be useful for is helping an individual make a binary choice of recommendation, pro or con, and understand what dimensions he/she ranks importantly in doing so.

5. COMPARISON WITH EXPERT SYSTEMS

Several issues make evaluation of expert systems extremely difficult. Since natural language interfaces are certainly knowledge based systems, the difficulties in evaluating expert systems may carry over to natural language interfaces. The purpose of this section is to compare how those issues arise in natural language interfaces.*

5.1 Correctness

For a given problem-solving domain is there a sense of absolute correctness, as in mathematics? Alternatively, is the best one can hope for is that one somehow replicates the answer of a typical expert? Can one go even further to replicate the kinds of reasoning that experts would use on given cases?

In expert systems, there is often no clearly correct answer. For instance, if a military vessel's readiness is degraded such that a substitute in its scheduled activities should be found, the advantages and drawbacks of each alternative may mean there is no correct answer regarding replacement. Furthermore, if the highest ranked alternative replaces the given vessel, it will also need to be replaced for its scheduled activities, resulting in the possibility that there is no global optimal distribution of the fleet's resources.

The problem of correctness can become so complex that one needs to survey experts about the goodness of a recommendation. It is reported that in evaluating MYCIN, for 75% of the case studies analyzed, a majority of experts consulted approved of the system's recommendation (Buchanan and Shortliffe, 1984). Though this seemed disappointing, when faculty members specializing in the subject area were similarly rated, their performance was also at best in the 70% to 80% range. To factor out issues of differing standards in evaluating computer performance compared to evaluating human performance, the evaluation may be performed blind (Buchanan and Shortliffe, 1984), where the evaluators do not know whether the case was handled by human or by machine.

For natural language interfaces, the situation is simpler. Inputs that are ambiguous, involve unclear references (e.g., pronouns where more than one interpretation is possible), cryptic forms, vague or otherwise incomplete expressions whose specifics may be completed in more than one way, and ill-formed input, all provide examples where more than one interpretation is possible, though not all are equally likely. One cannot eliminate all such cases from an evaluation, since such input is common in natural communication. Instead, performing the evaluation in a dialogue setting rather than in a setting of isolated sentential input, a large class of forms that would otherwise appear ambiguous, vague, or unclear will be clear to human evaluators. Care in constructing the test cases must still be taken, however, since some expressions will still remain unclear. An example, is "which ships are ...." The set of ships that form the background for such a question can always be unclear between the set of all the ships known to the underlying system and the set of ships most recently referred to in dialogue context.

---

*A natural language interface is not an expert system in our view, for much of the knowledge and processing occurs below our level of consciousness. Therefore, though there are many naturally occurring experts in the use of natural language, their expertise is largely inaccessible.

We conclude, therefore, that careful control of the test set by 1) including sufficient context so that the meaning of an input is clear and by 2) eliminating inputs that could not be made clear, will make correctness less of an issue for natural language interfaces than it is for expert systems.

5.2 Explanation

It is generally agreed that a major function of expert systems is to provide not only advice, but, also an explanation of why a certain recommendation was made, why certain alternatives were rejected, why a certain path was followed, etc. Furthermore, a good explanation should be tailored to the user so that information that he/she already knows is not repeated and so that the explanation reflects the level of the user.

A correlate problem for natural language interfaces is providing explanations that are clear, unambiguous, and not vague. If the English output is likely to be misunderstood, the explanation capabilities of the expert system will be judged a failure due to ineffective communication. Therefore, natural language generation capabilities must focus on clear textual output.

If the explanation is several sentences long, the prose must read well, as well as being well-organized. To illustrate this, consider selection of phrases to refer to an entity after it has been originally introduced in the output. Subsequent references must contain enough information so that the user can identify that the same entity is being referred to again, but, should not include extraneous information, for such information makes phrases unclear as well as difficult to read (Koile and Walker, 1986).

The natural language interface must, furthermore, provide for questions, so that the user may respond to an explanation with

- further questions regarding details in the explanation and

- questions clarifying anything the user did not understand in the English output.

As others have indicated regarding expert systems (Buchanan and Shortliffe, 1984), it is important in evaluating natural language interfaces that evaluation be ongoing during the interface's development. We are engaged in such a project now under the sponsorship of DARPA's Strategic Computing Program. In developing a natural language interface for Navy decision making, interaction between representatives of the artificial intelligence community and representatives of the user community has been ongoing so that the resulting interface better reflects the needs and desires of the user community. Evaluation at this point has been informal, involving frequent demonstrations and hands-on use.

5.3 Acceptable Performance

The question of what level of performance qualifies as "expert" is an important issue. A correlate in natural language interfaces is what performance qualifies as acceptable or desirable to the user community. As stated earlier in the paper, such evaluation is best left to the user community.

5.4 Characteristics

The characteristics to be evaluated in expert systems are still a matter of debate. There are at least the following criteria (Gaschnig, Klahr, Pople, Shortliffe, and Terry, 1983; Liebowitz, 1986):

- <u>Quality of systems decisions and advice</u>. This is the issue of correctness of expert systems. As argued above, the issue though difficult for natural language interfaces as well, seems more manageable for NLI evaluation.

- <u>System efficiency</u>. As argued earlier in the paper, run time efficiency of natural language interfaces tends to be relatively unimportant, since the natural language interface tends to add a very small amount of processing time to the performance of the underlying system.

- <u>Cost effectiveness</u>. Cost effectiveness for an expert system tends to be emphasized; perhaps because the expert system is competing against some existing technique for applying and using the expertise, such as human experts. The question of utility is critical: a system may offer so much added utility that cost is a secondary factor. Natural language interfaces could make information systems available to users who simply would not have direct access to those systems otherwise, therefore, cost may be a less important issue.

- <u>Quality of human-computer interaction</u>. This is of course one of the most fundamental issues in comparing one natural language interface against another. As pointed out earlier, the issue divides among several dimensions: a checklist of the classes of language phenomena handled by the interface, issues in computer-human interface design, and extensibility both for broadening the domain that the interface applies to and for incorporating new technology such as speech input.

- <u>User design time</u>. The time alluded to here is that for the user to set-up the problem of concern for the expert system to solve. The correlate for natural language interfaces is the time required to successfully specify user needs and requests. This must include all online aids to help the user formulate requests within the total system capability and to reformulate those requests if they are not fully understood the first time.

- <u>System maintainability</u>. This is the same for both expert systems and natural language interfaces. Namely, how easy is it to incorporate new knowledge into the system, modify and maintain the existing knowledge bases, and incorporate new technical advances? Of course, this is a dimension that is extremely difficult to measure formally; rather evaluation informally by specialists in expert systems or in natural language interfaces is requisite.

6. CONCLUSION: A MODEST PROPOSAL

Let us revisit the various purposes for evaluation and comment on appropriate techniques to apply given those purposes. For a specification verification, the critical issues are:

- defining a mutually agreed upon specification for the NLI, and

- defining an adequate set of inputs for verifying that the specification is met.

The set of sentences may be derived fairly straightforwardly from an adequate specification; however, to be certain that the set of sentences is representative of user behavior, two things are highly advisable:

- to collect them via a mock situation as Malhotra (1975) did for the purposes of collecting a representative corpus of user input, and

- to include examples in any test, based on frequency of classes occurrence of linguistic phenomena. (See Thompson (1980) for an example study and frequency tabulation.)

For the purposes of system/technology comparison, it is essential to identify the nature of the application and the nature of the user community based on several critical dimensions, for instance, as compiled by Bates (Bates and Bobrow, 1984). Without that, one lacks a sound basis for matching technology to needs. Furthermore, it may be critical to collect a corpus of the kinds of user interactions that should be anticipated using the kind of collection technique by Malhotra mentioned earlier. As in the case of specification verification, collection of that corpus is the main issue, however. It may not be necessary to perform the detailed analytical study such as Malhotra did after the corpus is collected.

If the purpose is the evaluation of a single system or technology, so that the state-of-the-art as represented in that system or technology is evaluated, then many approaches are possible. Providing the system to users in their daily work environment, even if it is only a testbed system, is highly desirable because of the high degree of reality to the context of data collection. No matter how brilliant the scientists or engineers, it is far too easy for significant surprises to arise in the working environment. User surveys are definitely valuable, though the most telling test of all, of course, is the marketplace itself.

For detailed feedback to the scientists and engineers, a careful analysis of transcripts of representatives using the system in their daily work, such as performed in other case studies (Damerau, 1981; Thompson, 1980), is highly valuable. For those managing research and development efforts, such case studies provide a detailed assessment of the state-of-the-art and of the aspects needing further work; analyses by scientists of fundamental limitations to a technology are also of critical importance.

For evaluations serving the user community, some overall assessment of utility is most critical, for that can outweigh all other issues, such as cost, runtime efficiency, and linguistic capability. Consequently, making early prototypes available to representatives of the user community is highly desirable.

ACKNOWLEDGEMENTS

The work presented here was supported under DARPA Contract #N00014-85-C-0016. The views and conclusions contained in this document are those of the authors and should not be interpreted as necessarily representing the official policies, either expressed or implied,.of the Defense Advanced Research Projects Agency or of the United States Government.

REFERENCES

Bates, M., and Bobrow, R. J., 1984, "Natural Language Interfaces: What's Here, What's Coming, and Who Needs It", Artificial Intelligence Applications for Business, Reitman, W., ed., Ablex Publishing Corp., New York.

Bates, M., Stallard, D., and Moser, M., 1985, "The IRUS Transportable Natural Language Database Interface", Expert Database Systems, Cummings Publishing Company, Menlo Park, CA.

Buchanan, B. G., and Shortliffe, E. H., 1984, "The Problem of Evaluation", Rule-Based Expert Systems, Addison-Wesley, Reading, MA, Chapter 30, pp. 571-588.

Damerau, F. J., 1981, "Operating Statistics for the Transformational Question Answering System", American Journal of Computational Linguistics, 7, (1), pp. 30-42.

Gaschnig, J., Klahr, P., Pople, P., Shortliffe, E., and Terry, A., 1983, "Evaluation of Expert Systems: Issues and Case Studies", Building Expert Systems, Hayes-Roth, F., Waterman, D. A., and Lenat, D. B., eds., Addison-Wesley, Reading, MA, Chapter 8, pp. 241-282.

Goodman, G., to appear, "Reference Identification and Reference Identification Failures", Computational Linguistics, to appear.

Harris, R., 1977, "User Oriented Data Base Query with the ROBOT Natural Language Query System", International Journal of Man-Machine Studies, 9, pp. 697-713.

Koile, K., and Walker, E., 1986, An IRUS Interface, Technical Report 6261, BBN Laboratories Inc., Cambridge, MA, May 1986.

Liebowitz, L., 1986, "Useful Approach for Evaluating Expert Systems", Expert Systems, 3, (2), pp. 86-96, April 1986.

Malhotra, A., 1975, "Design Criteria for a Knowledge-Based English Language System for Management: An Experimental Analysis", MAC 146, Massachusetts Institute of Technology, February, 1975, Cambridge, Mass.

Pollack, M. E., Hirschberg, J., and Webber, B., 1982, User Participation in the Reasoning Processes of Expert Systems, Technical Report, University of Pennsylvania, July 1982.

Tennant, H., 1981, Evaluation of Natural Language Processors, Technical Report T-103, Coordinated Science Laboratory, University of Illinois, Urbana, Illinois, November 1980.

Thompson, B. H., 1980, "Linguistic Analysis of Natural Language Communication with Computers", Proceedings of the Eighth International Conference on Computational Linguistics, International Committee on Computational Linguistics, October 1980, pp. 190-201.

2. USER-SYSTEM INTERFACE ANALYSIS

CRITERIA AND TECHNIQUES FOR THE OBJECTIVE MEASUREMENT OF HUMAN-COMPUTER

PERFORMANCE

Peter Jagodzinski* and David D. Clarke**

   *Department of Computing
    Plymouth Polytechnic
    Drake Circus
    Plymouth PL4 8AA
  **Department of Experimental Psychology
    University of Oxford
    South Parks Road
    Oxford

Abstract: The experiments described in this paper compare four prototype
versions of a user interface, each of which had a different design of screen
dialogue. Test procedures included are the selection and stratification of
groups of test subjects, the design of transaction sets, the pre-training
and pre-testing of subjects, the conduction of test runs, and the post-
testing of subjects' comprehension, attitudes, and perceptions.

   The analysis of test results was carried out mainly with univariate
statistics and Analysis of Variance (ANOVA). These techniques are relatively
simple to apply and revealed some clear distinctions between alternative
versions of the interface with degrees of significance. They also showed
relationships between effects; some of which supported the original hypothesis that dialogue, task, and job elements are closely interconnected. For
example, there was significant positive correlation between perceived ease
of use and expectation of improved job prospects.

   The conclusions of the research were that techniques of this sort
provide a valuable means of interface evaluation. They are, also, for the
most part, sufficiently easy to use to be cost-effective and practical for
medium and large scale computer systems analysis, design, and implementation
projects in which their cost would be a relatively small fraction of the
total cost.

1.   THE COMPONENTS OF INTERACTION

   The research literature in HCI frequently contains descriptions of the
results of the evaluation of user interfaces, for example, to compare the
relative effectiveness of different styles of terminal dialogue. For the
most part, these evaluations have been based on the well-proven methods of
experimental psychology and their related statistical techniques. However,

the techniques of evaluation are usually incidental to some other objective of the research.

The focus of this paper is on the evaluation of user interfaces as an end in itself. It is directed particularly towards the needs of the computer systems analyst who, in a commercial system implementation, is responsible for testing the effectiveness of the interface before the system is turned loose on the users. The aim is to present a coherent strategy for user interface evaluation which can be applied by the systems analyst as a normal part of his implementation procedures. The proposals are derived from a 3 year research project based on a live on-line system implementation in a university library.

Discussion of the interface between computers and their users is often restricted to merely the elements of the terminal dialogue. However, there are additional important interactions through the medium of task effects and job effects which must also be considered. For example, the users' perceptions of the deskilling effect of the computer system on a task can seriously hamper their acceptance of the system. Similarly, users' perceptions of the effects of computerization on job security or job status can also seriously hinder the implementation process. (Mumford and Weir, 1979).

The quality of terminal dialogue depends on the match between the technical elements of the computer system and the cognitive characteristics of the user. Some of the more important facets of system and user are summarized in Figure 1.

They are shown in the context of task which drives and defines the man-computer system.

Figure 2 adds the job effects, those elements of organization and larger world in which the task and system are set.

The users' attitudes, beliefs, and personal objects are in complex interaction with the host organization's objectives and norms, its task structures and with the general information and misinformation about computers that exists in the world in general. These affect the broader acceptability of the computer system to the user and cover such problems as deskilling, loss of status, job security and so on (Jagodzinski, 1985). A complicating factor is that the three aspects of interaction, that is job effects, task effects, and terminal dialogue, can often be inextricably linked in their effect on users' attitudes. There are explanations for this, for example the principle of cognitive consistency which describes how individuals who perceive some disadvantage in a situation then find it hard to recognize or acknowledge its possible advantages (Jagodzinski and Clarke, 1986).

Clearly, the terminal dialogue provides the most direct and concentrated medium of interface, but the more diffuse, amorphous channels of interaction can be at least as significant for the acceptance of a computer system by its users. Thus, task and job should probably be seen as providing the

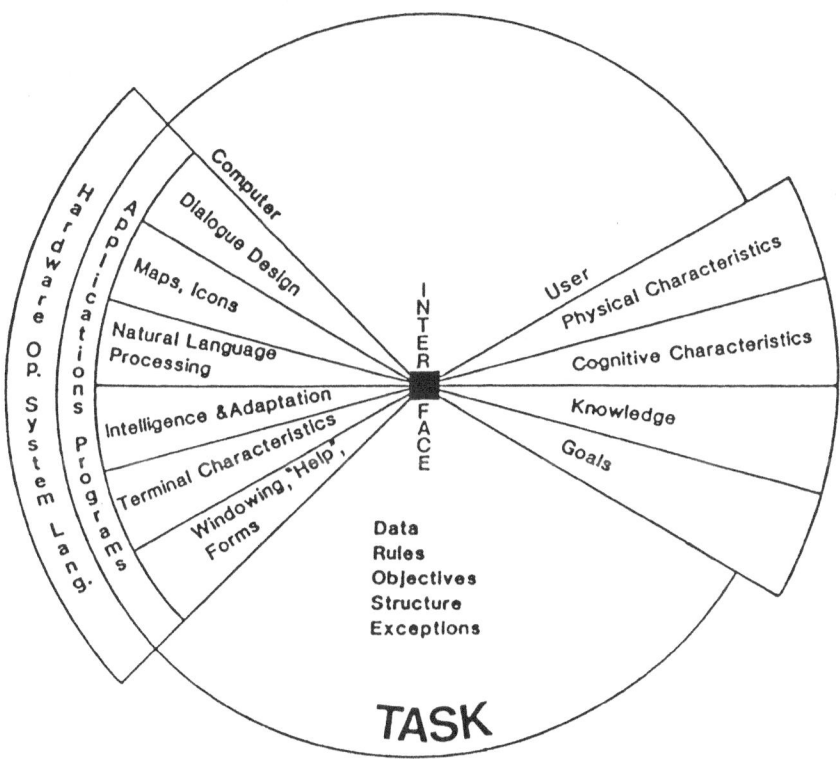

Figure 1. Facets of System and User
in Interface Evaluation.

1.1   Technical Performance

This includes factors such as response time, screen refresh rate,
ambient lighting, and anthropometric details. There is already a considerable amount of guidance for design and evaluation of these factors which
were among the first to be identified by ergonomists. It is undoubtedly
important to get this part of the design right, but the techniques can be
found elsewhere and were not included within this research (De Greene, 1970).

1.2   Transaction Processing Performance

In traditional approaches to systems analysis and design, for example
Thierauf (1986), the rate and accuracy of operators processing a representative cross-section of transaction types is generally considered to be the
best test of the system's effectiveness. Such measures can obviously be
linked to the ease of use of the system and possibly to its value as an aid
to productivity. For this reason they were included, but interpreted in
the light of the more penetrating analyses which follow, rather than taken
simply at face value.

1.3   Ease of Use

This was inferred partly from performance measures as in (2) above,
partly from tests of the users' perceptions of how easy the system was to
use and partly from tests of users' comprehension, that is the accuracy of
their mental models of the system, and by observation of their navigation
from one task to the next.

Figure 2. A Broader Perspective of Human-
Computer Interaction.

1.4 Perceived Effect on Task and 1.5 Perceived Effect on Job

These elements of performance are probably best interpreted in terms of
users' perceptions of effects, rather than, for example, by some external
yardstick of task size or job status which may not equate with the users'
criteria. Users' perceptions of task and job effects were assessed by the
use of attitude questionnaires. Factors tested included task size, both
vertical and horizontal, deskilling, job security, job status, and job
prospects.

Details of how these performance measures were applied are described
in Section 3.

2. THE TEST SYSTEM

The performance measures described above may be applied in a variety
of ways. The examples which follow are from a journals control system in a
University library. Four prototype interfaces were created, performing
functionally identical tasks, but with distinctly different dialogue designs.
The basic functions of the system were as follows:

1. Registration: recording the arrival of a new issue
   of a journal.

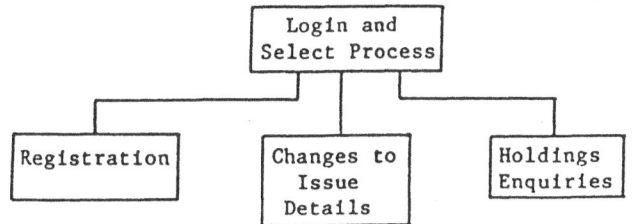

Figure 3. The Functions of the Journals Control System.

2. Holdings Enquiries: finding out whether or not a
particular issue is held by the system.

3. Changes to Issue Details: modifying details of issues
already on file.

Routes between these functions are shown in Figure 3.

The four versions of the system had the following interface features:

Version 1.   Standard, menu-driven dialogue; continuous
scrolling.

Version 2.   "Chunked Processes" - also menu drive, but
with dialogue divided up into functional
groupings separated by page breaks.

Version 3.   "Ancillary Maps" - in addition to the standard
interface, a second screen showing pictorial
maps of the various stages of processing, for
example see Figure 4.

Version 4.   "Chunked Processes" and "Ancillary Maps" -
pictorial maps as in Version 3 with functional
grouping of processes, as in Version 2.

3. TEST PROCEDURES

3.1 Test Design

The purpose of the evaluation was to measure the effect of enhancing
the system with "chunked processes", "ancillary maps", and a combination of
both features. In addition, a control test (Version 1) with neither enhancement was needed for comparison. Thus the experiment was set up as a 2 x 2
matrix of tests as shown in Figure 5.

3.2 Arrangement of Subjects

Volunteers were enlisted from the population of potential users of the
system.

With two hours available per subject and a test consisting of nine
separate stages it was necessary to expose each subject to only one version
of the system.

This design prevented the study of transfer effects between different
versions of the system. However, it also avoided the possibility of subjects

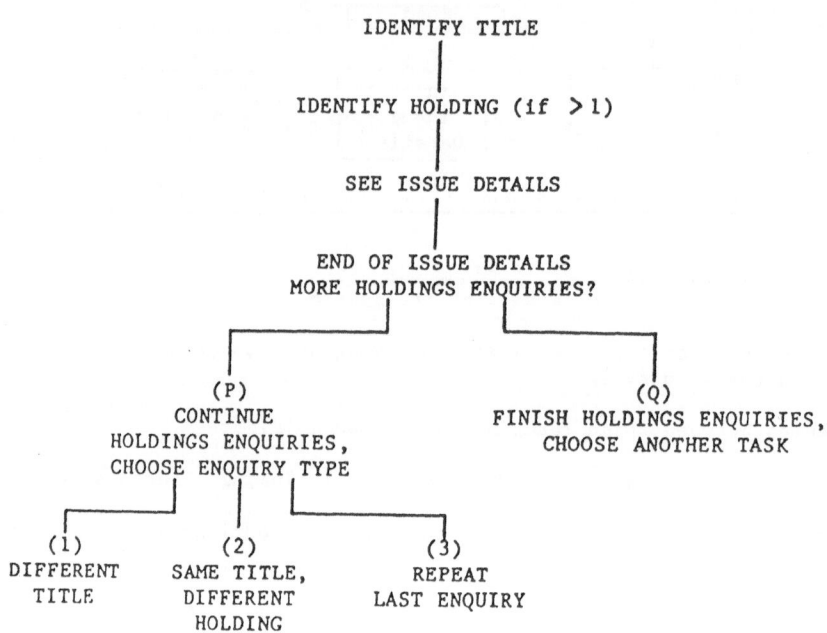

Figure 4. Ancillary Map Showing the Holdings Enquiries Function.

becoming confused by exposure to the different versions, with the ensuing difficulties in measuring attitudes.

Volunteers' job grades and approximate ages were known before they were assigned to test groups. Eight subjects were assigned to each of the four test groups. Extra subjects were also tested for groups A, B, and D; these permitted a small amount of adjustment of group membership so that the groups' mean ages could be almost equalized (age proved to be a significant covariant with some aspects of subjects' performance).

Job grades were assigned equally to groups and as closely as possible to the proportions occurring in the whole population of the staff of the Library.

Job Grades Per Group.

Secretarial staff	1
Library assistants	3
Principal/Senior Library assistants	3
Academic related staff	1

Thus, as far as possible, the composition of test groups was equalized by stratification. The only aspect remaining which could not be assumed to be equally distributed was the subjects' previous experience on serials control work. This was taken into account by step 4 of the tests (see Section 3.4). In practice, there was no significant correlation between this measure and any other aspect of performance.

	PRESENT	ABSENT
PRESENT	GROUP A	GROUP C
ABSENT	GROUP D	GROUP B

CHUNKED
PROCESSES

Figure 5.   The Set-up of the Test Groups.

3.3   Physical Layout of Tests

The stages of the test involving the use of the computer were conducted using the room layout shown in Figure 6. The observer was able to see the actions of the subjects and read the screen dialogues, but could not easily be seen by the subject. A separate version of the updated file was used for each subject so that the effect of their updates was permanently recorded and could be examined later to check their scores.

The tests were scheduled in conjunction with the co-users of the CTL 8046 computer to run at pre-arranged periods of low demand for service so that response times would be consistent between tests.

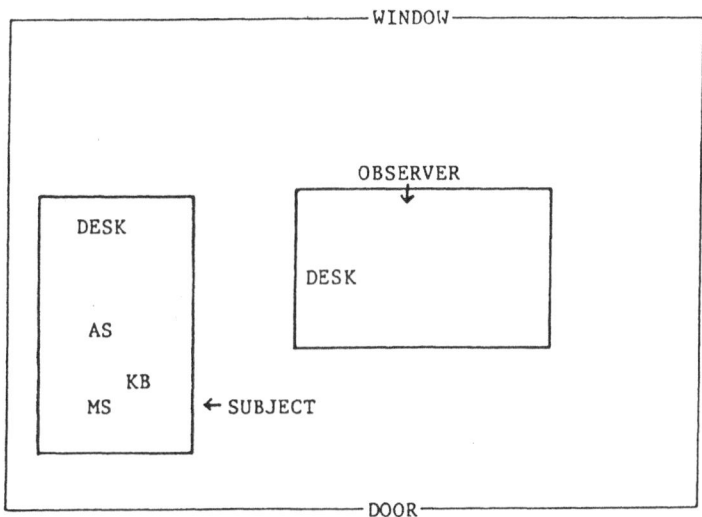

Figure 6.   The Layout of Test Equipment, Subject, and Observer.

3.4   Contents of Tests

All subjects received identical instructions and performed functionally identical tasks. Each subject's test lasted about 2 hours and comprised the following stages:

109

```
18.  Register volume 4 of "Medicine and Sport:.  It is
     damaged.  Search-key is MEDSZZ.

19.  Check the status of "Medical School Admission Require-
     ments" 1969.  If it is not "binding" or "on loan"
     change it to "lost".  Search-key is MEDSAR.

20.  Record the arrival of parts 1, 2, and 3 of "Medicines
     Act 1968 Information Leaflets".  They are not com-
     bined.  Search-key is MEDAIL.

21.  Register volume 73 part 432 of "Medicina Espanola".
     Search-key is MEDEZZ.

22.  One privileged reader has asked to borrow part 17 of
     "Medicine in Ireland" and another has asked to borrow
     part 18.  Can both requests be satisfied simul-
     taneously?  Search-key is MEDIZZ.

23.  The 1965 "Members handbook" has been lost.  Change
     its status accordingly and add the note "photocopy
     requested from BL".  Search-key is MEMHZZ.
```

Figure 7. Some Examples of Tasks in Serials Control. Up to 70 Such
          Tasks Were Included in Manual and Computer System Tests.

1. An introduction to the exercise.

2. An introduction to the general principles of serials
    control.

3. A set of guided exercises in manual serials control.

4. A timed set of exercises in manual serials control.
    (This was included to measure previous experience in
    serials registration in case this was a covariate
    with performance on the computerized registration
    system.) (10 minutes.)

5. A set of guided exercises in serials control with
    the computer system.

6. A timed set of exercises in computerized serials
    control. (30 minutes.)

(Examples of tasks in manual and computerized serials control are given
in Figure 7.)

7. A test of comprehension of the system. (Based on the
    principles laid down by Bloom (1956). See Figure 8 for
    examples.

8. A questionnaire to elicit the users' attitudes following
    their use of the system. See Figure 9 for examples.

9. A questionnaire on subjects' personal details, included
    to ensure that ages and job grades of subjects were
    equally distributed between groups.

2. When Registering an issue it may be the next-expected part in the sequence. What are the other four possibilities for its sequence?

    (1) _____

    (2) _____

    (3) _____

    (4) _____

3. When you have identified the sequence of an issue during Registration, what do you do next? Tick <u>one</u> of the following lists:

    (1)   Record the details of the issue.

    (2)   Examine the issue to see if it is damaged.

    (3)   Register the next issue.

4. If you are Registering an issue but there is no indication of its sequence, is it possible to use the system to record its details? Tick one:

                 YES

                 NO

Figure 8. Some Examples of Comprehension Questions. All Subjects Were Required to Perform 10 of These.

This test design enabled the subject to carry out the required operations with little reference to or help from the experimenter, thereby reducing the risk of bias being introduced.

An observer was on hand throughout each test to give help to the subject if required. An experimental design in which no help would be given to the subjects was considered. This would have made scoring somewhat easier, as it is difficult to equate one form of help with another. However, as the subjects were real members of the library staff and as the tests represented their introduction to the use of computers it was thought to be highly undesirable to risk alienating them by offering no help when they became stuck.

4. SCORING

Score sheets were kept for each subject. For example, the scoring for the computer system exercise is shown in Figure 10.

The "RESULT" column was coded 1 for a correctly completed transaction or 0 for an error or incomplete transaction. The "HELP" column was filled

variable LOST
1. After using the system for half-an-hour or so did you still feel
   lost at any time?

All of the time						Never
1	2	3	4	5	6	7

variable MOVE
3. Do you understand how to move from one task, e.g., Registration, to another, e.g., Holdings Enquiries?

Not at all						Very well
1	2	3	4	5	6	7

variable COMP
7. Do you think that the system is difficult or easy to understand?

Very easy						Very difficult
7	6	5	4	3	2	1

variable SKIL
10. How do you think that the use of the computer in your work
    would affect the use of your skills and knowledge?

I'd worry that they would be less well used with a computer			I wouldn't expect it to have any effect on me			I'd look forward to their being used used with a computer
1	2	3	4	5	6	7

variable DEVL
11. How do you view the effect of a computer system at the Library
    on your opportunities to develop your skills and knowledge?

I'd look forward to better opportun- ities			I wouldn't expect any change to be signi- ficant			I'd worry that oppor- tunities would be worse
7	6	5	4	3	2	1

Figure 9. Some examples from the questionnaire on users' attitudes.
           Each subject completed 34 such questions.

SESSION 2 SCORESHEET

NAME: TIME:
GROUP: VERSION: DATE:

---(1)--- QUESTION NUMBER	---(2)--- RESULT	-(3)- HELP	-(4)---------- NET RESULT (2)-(3)	----(5)--- NO. OF DETOURS	----(6)------- NAVIGATION RESULT 3-(5)	------------
...1.....	....	.....	....	....	....	....
...2.....	....	.....	....	....	....	....
...3.....	....	.....	....	....	....	....
...4.....	....	.....	....	....	....	....

Figure 10.   The Score Sheet for the Computer System Tests.

in with the number of separate requests for help in any one transaction.
In practice this never exceeded 1.

The "NET RESULT" column was coded 1 for each transaction completed
correctly without help.

The "NO. OF DETOURS" column was coded with the number of sub-optimal
branches chosen by the operator for each transaction. For example, at the
end of question 9 the screen prompts the operator as follows:

"This enquiry is now completed.
    Please input EITHER "P" if you wish to make another enquiry,
                OR "Q" if you wish to finish:-"

If the operator responds with "Q" he is given 1 point for a detour as
the next transaction is another enquiry.

The "NAVIGATION RESULT" column was not used in practice, but was intended for calculation of the proportion of detours to possible detours.

Comprehension, stage 7 of the test, was simply scored on the number of
correct answers, with a possible maximum of 1 point per question, 1 being
deducted for each missing or wrong response.

The attitude questionnaire was designed according to the principles
suggested by Oppenheim (1966), with a bipolar scale divided into 7 equal
intervals each of which is subsequently given a numeric score. The subject
rates each item by assigning to it the position on the continuum which his
perception of the item merits.

5.   ANALYSIS OF SUBJECTS' PERFORMANCE SCORES

5.1 Correlations Between Variables

Prior to the tests being carried out it was suspected that there may
be important covariance between scores on performance with the computer
systems and scores on the manual registration task, a measure of previous
experience with the manual system. In practice there was none. Consequently, no analysis of covariance with scores on manual registration was carried
out.

Correlations between other aspects of performance in processing

Table 1. Significant Correlations Between Performance
Scores (All Groups).

Variable 1	Variable 2	Pearson r	P
Age	Help given	.4089	0.020
Age	Comprehension	−0.3755	0.034
Age	Net score	−0.4687	0.007
Comprehension	Net score	0.5963	0.001
Comprehension	Errors on 1st 10 questions	−0.4187	0.017
Comprehension	Reported ease of understanding	−0.2137	0.240
Errors on 1st 10 questions	Navigation detours on 1st 10 questions	0.3661	0.039
Ease of use	Reported ease of understanding	0.6058	0.001
Ease of use	Reported ease of relating system to task	0.3630	0.041

transactions were investigated using two-tailed tests of significance and the PEARSON CORR option of the SPSS package (Nie, et al., 1970).

There were interesting significant negative correlations between some variables across all subjects. These are shown in Table 1.

There were significant negative correlations between several aspects of performance and the subjects' ages. However, groups were stratified to ensure that ages and grades were balanced so that the effect of age as a covariate may be ignored. The group means for age are shown in Table 2.

Comprehension scores from stage 7 of the tests seem to reflect closely the subjects' performance scores, as might be expected. However, subjects' reported ease of understanding had an insignificant, but, negative correlation with comprehension scores, suggesting that subjects were generally not able to judge how well they understood the system.

The significant positive correlation between navigation detours and errors on the first 10 questions in stage 6 of the tests shows that these two aspects of performance are related, although not necessarily causally.

Predictably, subjects' reported ease of use of the system correlated positively with their reported ease of understanding and reported ease of relating the system to the task. These three correlations of variables from the attitude questionnaire are included with the performance variables because they reveal the disparity between actual and reported ease of use, even though reported ease of use is consistent with reported ease of relating the system to the task and understanding. No other correlations between

Table 2. Group Means for Subjects' Ages.

ANCILLARY MAPS

		PRESENT	ABSENT
CHUNKED PROCESSES	PRESENT	GROUP A 32.5	GROUP C 32.5
	ABSENT	GROUP D 31.1	GROUP B 32.875

Table 3. Group Totals of Help Given
During First 10 Transactions.

Ancillary maps

		Present	Absent
Chunked Processes	Present	Group A 4	Group C 6
	Absent	Group D 11	Group B 12

attitude variables were considered, these being examined by means of discriminant function analysis and analyses of variance in Section 6.

5.2 Analyses of Variance

Two-way unrelated ANOVA calculations were used to see if there was any significant variance between the results of the 4 groups of subjects on the performance variables.

Initially, it was thought that a simple comparison of total numbers of correctly processed transactions might be all that was needed. However, the large within-group variances of such a gross score effectively obscured inter-group differences.

It was also realized that this result would have been distorted by the fact that subjects were given help by the observer when they could make no further progress on their own (these occasions were recorded too).

Assuming that subjects' abilities are distributed equally between the groups, for a given set of tasks the best indicator of the differences between the user interfaces was judged to be the number of occasions on which help had to be given by the observer.

Accordingly, the number of requests for help during the first 10 transactions in stage 6 of the tests was used as the score for the first ANOVA. The group totals are shown in Table 3.

Groups A and C clearly required far less help than groups B and D.

The significance of this finding is shown by the results of the ANOVA in Table 4.

This result shows that an interface with chunked processes enables the user to process transactions with significantly less help than otherwise. Presumably process chunking makes the operation easier to grasp (as was predicted by Rasmussen (1980) and Jagodzinski (1983(a)) so that less external help is necessary.

In practical terms this improvement would have important benefits for installations with naive users. If, as would be the case in the library system, the users never got the chance to develop fluency with the system, the benefit might turn out to be a significantly reduced error rate. The second aspect of performance which was chosen as having potential for distinguishing between groups was the number of navigational detours (i.e., sub-optimal choices at branch-points) made in the first 10 transactions.

Table 4. ANOVA of Help Given on First 10 Transactions.

Sources of variance	Sums of squares	Degrees of freedom	Mean Squares	F ratios	Significance
Variable A (Ancillary maps)	0.0313	1	0.0313	0.0279	-
Variable B (chunked processes)	5.2813	1	5.2813	4.7154	< 5%
A x B Interaction	0.28	1	0.28	0.25	-
Error	31.3763	28	1.12		
TOTAL	36.9689				

Navigation performance can probably be taken as an indicator of the quality of the subjects' overall view of the system and the routes available to them.

The group totals are shown in Table 5.

Both ancillary maps and chunked processes appear to have a beneficial effect on the subjects' navigation. The exact nature and significance of this effect is shown by the ANOVA results in Table 6.

This result shows clearly the value of the combination of chunked processes and ancillary maps in assisting the users' navigation through the system. The two facilities were designed to be complementary, with matched headings indicating the relationship between current process and overall position in the function. It appeared that this aspect of the interface design was successful.

In practical terms fewer navigational detours show that these subjects are finding the optimum routes through the system more quickly and may ultimately perform faster and with greater confidence.

However, it is interesting to note that this enhanced version of the system was less popular than some of the others (see Section 6, Analysis of Attitudes.).

ANOVAs were also carried out on other aspects of subjects' performance and, although these generally showed better results with the enhanced

Table 5. Group Totals of Detours Made on The
          First 10 Transactions.

Ancillary maps

		Present	Absent
Chunked Processes	Present	Group A 7	Group C 12
	Absent	Group D 11	Group B 24

Table 6. ANOVA of Navigational Detours on the First 10 Questions.

Sources of variance	Sums of squares	Degrees of freedom	Mean Squares	F ratios	Significance
Variable A (Ancillary maps)	0.0625	1	0.0625	0.0016	-
Variable B (chunked processes)	0.5	1	0.5	0.0126	-
A x B interaction	19.5625	1	19.5625	13.7803	$<0.1\%$
Error	39.75	28	1.4196		
TOTAL	59.875				

versions of the system, the advantages were not significant at less than 10%. These results are summarized in Table 7.

6. ANALYSIS OF SUBJECTS' ATTITUDES

Stage 8 of the tests, described in Section 3.4, was an attitude questionnaire designed to elicit the perceptions of subjects to a range of issues affecting the quality of the dialogue, the tasks they were asked to perform, and the larger context of their jobs.

Discriminant Function Analysis (Nie, et al., 1970) was used in an attempt to identify functions which would effectively discriminate between the groups. Wilk's Lambda was used as the criterion of discriminating power on which variables were to be selected for the analysis. With 32 subjects and 34 variables, there was a danger that an uninterpretable solution, tending towards one variable per case, could have been reached. Consequently, the maximum number of steps in the selection of variables was set to nine so that only the nine variables with the most discriminating power would be selected.

The results from the Discriminant Function Analysis were not particularly revealing. Briefly, the most strongly defined variable emerged as question 11, "How do you view the effect of a computer system at the Library on your opportunities to develop your skills and knowledge" (variable DEVL).

Table 7. Comparison of Group Means for Tests Which Showed No Significant Benefit From the System Enhancements.

Description of score	Group Means			
	Maps & chunks	Chunks only	Maps only	No maps No chunks
Comprehension test scores	8.5	7.5	8.1	7.25
Errors on first 10 transactions	0.625	0.75	0.625	0.875
Total transactions attempted	16.5	13.9	12.4	14.25
Total correct transactions excluding those where help was given	16	12.6	10.9	12.5

Table 8. Group Means for Variable DEVL.

Ancillary maps

		Present	Absent
Chunked processes	Present	Group A 6.125	Group C 5.75
	Absent	Group D 5.25	Group B 4.375

Group A and Group C, both of which had the "chunked processes" feature, appeared to be most popular in this respect. However, the nine variables identified as having the most discriminating power were then examined in more detail using Analysis of Variance, as described in Section 5.2.. The selected variables are those obtained from the questions shown in Figure 9. Some caution must be used in evaluating the significance of the results of such a wholesale approach. At a significance level of 10% one would expect 1 in 10 tests to appear significant by chance. The results which follow include only those with results significant at the 5% level of probability or less. They do appear to be consistent with each other and with the results of the discriminant function analysis.

The results for variable DEVL are shown in full below, followed by a summary of the other variables which were regarded as significant.

Table 8 shows the group means for this variable.

Groups A and C clearly have more optimistic expectations for their opportunities following computerization than groups D and B. The significance of the finding is shown in Table 9.

The high degree of significance of this result, coupled with the fact that this variable was the most significant in the discriminant function analysis, shows it to be highly important. An explanation of the effect could be that subjects felt better able to cope with the system when it was provided with chunked processes and, therefore, view their development under computerization more optimistically than those who did not have the

Table 9. ANOVA of DEVL.

Sources of variance	Sums of squares	Degrees of freedom	Mean squares	F ratios	Significance
Ancillary maps	3.125	1	3.125	2.5925	
Chunked processes	10.125	1	10.125	8.3997	< 1%
Interaction	0.5	1	0.5	0.4148	
Error	33.75	28	1.2054		
TOTAL	47.5				

Table 10. Results of ANOVA for Question 15
(Effect on Job Security).

Ancillary Maps	Chunked Processes	Interaction
F ratios 3.00	16.5	2.8
Significance <10%	<0.1%	<10%

benefit of the enhancement.

The results for questions 15 and 33 are summarized below in Tables 10 and 11. The perception of subjects for job security and job employment are significantly more optimistic using the version of the system with chunked processes. Again, the interpretation of these results was that subjects felt better able to cope with the computer system.

Table 12 summarizes the results for question 27.

The group means for this variable (Table 13) reveal 2 effects.

First, group C with chunked processes, but no ancillary maps, stands out as expecting more use of judgement and decision-making than any of the other three groups. (Use of judgement and decision-making were identified in an earlier survey (Jagodzinski, 1983(b)) as desirable characteristics of a computer system.)

Secondly, this expectation is absent in group A, which had ancillary maps as well as chunked processes. Thus it seems that the presence of a second screen generates pessimistic expectations which cancel out the advantages of chunked processes.

The low scores of group A obscure the high scores of group C, so that, overall, chunked processes do not appear to have a significant effect. The presence of ancillary maps appears to have the overall effect of reducing scores, although a look at Table 13 shows that this is only the case between groups C and A, and not between groups B and D.

This undesirable interaction effect between the two system enhancements was not expected. Section 5.2 shows that there is a significant improvement in users' performance in navigation when both enhancements are present, but perhaps this is gained at the cost of the user feeling spoon-fed by the interface and not being able to exercise his own judgement. Alternatively, it may be a reaction against having two screens to look at with a

Table 11. Results of ANOVA for Question 33
(Enjoyment of Job).

Ancillary Maps	Chunked Processes	Interaction
F ratios 0.9	4.2	0.4
Significance >5%	<5%	>5%

Table 12.   Results of ANOVA for Question 27
(Use of Judgement and Decision-Making).

	Ancillary Maps	Chunked Processes	Interaction
F ratios	4.8	3.3	10.1
Significance	<5%	<10%	<0.5%

possible feeling of pressure from having to operate in the data domain and functional domain simultaneously.

Rasmussen (1980, p. 85) explains:

"...no mental task should be forced into a level of consciousness higher than the task itself justifies (due to some inappropriate coding of information or choice of strategy in the computer). If this principle is not followed, the operator may have to time-share the main task with the extra irrelevant task of data recording."

Table 13.   Group Means for Question 27
(Use of Judgement and Decision Making).

Ancillary maps

		Present	Absent
Chunked processes	Present	Group A 2.875	Group C 4.75
	Absent	Group D 3.375	Group B 3.00

7.   CONCLUSIONS

The method of evaluation described here was proven to be capable of distinguishing clearly between the quality of the four alternative styles of user-interface.

Of the two enhancements to the system's interface, the chunking of processes was clearly the more successful. On the measures of transaction-processing performance it significantly reduced the amount of help required by the users, and, on the measures of attitudes, it was found to improve significantly several aspects of the users' expectations of the effects of computerization.

The most plausible explanation of this outcome is the effect predicted by Rasmussen (1980), that is, an improvement in the users' capacity to grasp the processes of the system, has occurred. This manifests itself directly in that the users require less help in operating the system, and indirectly in that their confidence as computer users, and, thus, their optimism about their future under computerization, increases.

Ancillary maps appeared to improve navigation performance, but, at the same time reduce the optimism of users' expectations. This effect was not expected by the systems designers (although, maybe, it should have been in the light of Rasmussen's work).

An important characteristic of the method was that the distinctions it revealed were empirically derived from analysis of transaction processing performance and ease of use (Section 5) in combination with users' perceptions of the likely effect of the computer systems on their tasks and jobs (Section 6). Because of this, the results were able to strongly support the view that the quality of the man-machine dialogue has a significant effect, not just on transaction rates, but, also in interaction on the much wider issues of task and job factors.

Most of the costs incurred by this example of evaluation arose from time spent in reviewing the techniques of experimental psychology and statistics required for the design of tests, questionnaires, and analyses. The cost of implementing similar tests for a different system would, therefore, be considerably lower. It is estimated that two man-months for a systems analyst would be sufficient to set up the tests, run them, and analyze the results, with about 2 hours per subject in addition. The total labor costs of this project, including systems analysis, design, and programming, were of the order of 50 man-months.

In this academic library, as in many other organizations, the staff, with their thousands of man-years of combined experience and expertise, represent the institution's most valuable asset. In such circumstances, it is probably important to pay attention to the acceptability of any computer system which they may be required to use. The approach adopted should recognize the priority of user-acceptability at all stages of the computerization project from systems analysis and design through to implementation. System evaluation using methods, such as those described here, can provide a valuable indication of acceptability both relatively between alternative designs and to some extent, as an absolute measure of users' perceptions of how it will affect their working lives.

REFERENCES

Bloom, B. S., 1956, Taxonomy of Educational Objectives, Longmans, New York.

De Greene, K. B., 1970, "Systems and Psychology", Systems Psychology, De Greene, K. B., ed., McGraw-Hill, pp. 3-50.

Jagodzinski, A. P., 1983(a), "A Theoretical Basis for the Representation of an On-Line Computer System to Naive Users", International Journal of Man-Machine Studies, 18, pp. 215-252.

Jagodzinski, A. P., 1983(b), Some Applications of Cognitive Science in the Analysis, Design, and Implementation of Interactive Computer Systems: D.Phil. Thesis, Oxford.

Jagodzinski, A. P., 1985, "The Interaction Between Electronic Storage Systems and Their Users", Proceedings of the 11th Meeting of IATUL, Gotenborg, pp. 133-138.

Jagodzinski, A. P., and Clarke, D. D., 1986, "A Review of Methods for Measuring and Describing Users' Attitudes as an Essential Constituent of Systems Analysis and Design", The Computer Journal, 29, (2), pp. 97-102.

Mumford, E., and Weir, M., 1979, _Computer Systems in Work-Design - the ETHICS Method_, Associated Business Press, London.

Nie, N. H., Hull, C. H., Jenkins, J. G., Steinbrenner, K., and Bent, D. H., 1970, _Statistical Package for the Social Sciences_, 2nd Edition, McGraw-Hill, New York.

Oppenheim, A. N., 1966, _Questionnaire Design and Attitude Measurement_, Heinemann, London.

Rasmussen, J., 1980, "The Human As a Systems Component", _Human Interaction with Computers_, Academic Press, London, pp. 67-96.

Thierauf, R. J., 1986, _Systems Analysis and Design_, Merril Publishing Company, Columbus.

HUMAN-TO-MACHINE INTERACTION IN NATURAL LANGUAGE: EMPIRICAL RESULTS

OF FIELD STUDIES WITH AN ENGLISH AND A GERMAN INTERFACE

J. Krause

IBM Scientific Center   and   Linguistic Information Science
Heidelberg   University of Regensburg
West Germany   West Germany

Abstract: Questions of feasibility and desirability of natural langauge
interfaces for human-machine interactions gain more and more interest in
empirical research. There is growing consensus that field studies provide
valuable leads with respect to design decisions.

One of the most important aspects of user friendly interfaces are the
restriction rules. The problem is how to restrict the diversity of com-
municative use of the human native language without losing the advantage of
this form of communication with computers.

The paper tries to answer this question on the basis of several empirical studies which investigate the same domain-independent natural langauge
query system, using various applications in two different natural languages -
- English and German. The studies were performed in cooperation with the IBM
Heidelberg Scientific Center (West Germany), the New York University (Advanced Language Project), and the Department of Linguistic Information
Science at the University of Regensburg (West Germany). Altogether, these
experiments involved about 100 subjects and over 12,000 queries, constituting
the bulk of empirical evaluations of natural query language systems reported
to date. Results of these experiments are presented and one of the most
recent successful software packages Q&A is discussed with respect to the
selected restriction rules.

1.   INTRODUCTION

At the moment interesting developments can be observed in two areas
which influence each other, namely in natural language processing and in
the field of graphical interfaces. Both are part of the concept of fifth-
generation computers, the culture of which is intended to be "user natural
in its human factors" (Gaines and Shaw, 1986; Hirose and Fuchi, 1984).
Both are in the headlines these days, but the reasons for it are different.

a)   Natural Language Interfaces to Databases (NLI).

In the 1970's and early 1980's NLI's were the undisputed
favorite application for computational natural language
research. But this broadly accepted consensus no longer

exists. At COLING 1984, Karen Sparck-Jones invited the
members of a panel "Natural Language and Databases" to
"speak to the proposition ... that database query is no
longer a good, let alone the best, test environment for
language processing research, because it is insuffi-
ciently demanding in its linguistic facts and too idio-
syncratically demanding in its non-linguistic ones."
(Sparck-Jones, 1984, p. 182). The comments given at
the panel clearly showed that there was a shift in
research interest in the last years. Sparck-Jones
(1984, p. 183) claimed "that the database application
is an inadequate test environment for natural language
understanding systems." Others (McKeown, 1984;
Flickinger, 1984; Carbonell, 1984) supported a more
balanced view.

"the database query task was an excellent para-
digmatic problem for computational linguistics ...
it is now time for the field to abandon its pro-
tective cocoon and progress beyond this rather
limiting task."

At this time increasing public interest in NLI comes
from another area; people are fascinated in a series of
commercially available NLI. In 1985 three new NLI's
appeared on the market: NLMenu, Language Craft, and
Question and Answer (Q&A). The latter was supplemented
by a German version in 1986. People are giving much
attention to Q&A, which is cheap ($299 list price) and
runs on a PC with 512K RAM.

b) The second area mentioned before concerns the domain of
graphical interfaces, that is icons, mouse, and direct
manipulation (DM).

The fascination of interacting with the computer in the
DM mode did not lose its attraction both for expert and
novice users, as it can be detected for instance in
Shneidermann (1983) and Hutchins (Hutchins et al.,
1986). With tools like MS-WINDOWS these positive feel-
ings will also reach the mass of PC-users in the near
future. The fascination with DM reminds one of the
enthusiasm with which the first attempts at natural
language communication were caught up.

Both NLI and DM are today of special interest, because they now can be
realized on PC's. Both claim to substantially improve human computer interaction (HCI), and both have the image of being so convincingly better than
formal query languages. But this is not enough. Can we validate the superiority of NLI against alternatives like formal query languages or DM, or
of DM against NLI? And can we decide between design alternatives of NLI?

In this paper I want to demonstrate which design criteria of an NLI
are validated by empirical testing, and I want to take a first glance at a
differentiation of areas where DM will be preferred to NLI and vice versa.

2. NLI FOR THE REQUEST OF FACTS, ORGANIZED IN TABLES.

Those NLI's which are now commercially available have much in common
with those which produced significant empirical results from field studies,

e.g., INTELLECT, Q&A, or the experimental natural language query system (NLQS) described in Lehmann (1978), Krause and Lehmann (1980), Ott and Zoeppritz (1979), Zoeppritz (1984) and Lehmann, Ott, and Zoeppritz (1985). They use different algorithms and strategies for analyzing the queries and are different in the scope of the grammar and additional features, but the general base is comparable. NLI's of this kind (and I will restrict myself to this type of NLI in the paper) allow the user to question facts which are organized in tables (e.g., an employee database). There is only minor deduction (mainly mathematical functions) on the base of the facts in the database and the user-dependent vocabulary (unlike expert systems). Users ask directly (e.g., with <u>Where</u>, <u>Who</u>, <u>What is</u>, <u>List</u>, <u>How much</u> (not with <u>Why</u>). The conceptual difference between the facts in question and the facts stored in the database is small. The examples given by the authors of the systems are similar and give an intuitive impression of the type of HCI aimed at:

INTELLECT:	How many clerical people work for the company?
	Count the clerical people.
	Who lives in Boston and Buffalo?
Q&A:	Show me the departments and salaries.
	What is John's salary plus bonus?
	List the departments and salaries of people with bonus over $1000.
NLQS:	How many accounting graduates are there?
	Which alumni live in the city of Boston?
	Is there a donor who gave more than 5000 dollars?

The algorithm of a NLI must find a way from the syntactic structure and the vocabulary of the questions to the columns and rows of the fact tables. In NLQS each adjective, adverb, verb, or noun is interpreted as the name of a relation in the database (a special type of table). The aim is to select the appropriate rows and columns and join relations if necessary (Lehmann, 1978; Ott and Zoeppritz, 1979).

Systems like Q&A are even more restricted: Q&A cannot organize the facts in different tables (no join).

A lot of questions arise when we judge the sense or nonsense of an NLI of this type. It is not enough that their functionality is correct. The more interesting point is whether the subset of human natural language communication they allow is sufficient and general enough to support a practical application (and all systems - even the most sophisticated ones - use subsets (Krause, 1984)) or are there better solutions for the user, e.g., with formal query languages or with DM. And how to decide between design alternatives at a lower level? Is it, for instance, necessary to have a big lexicon in the background because it is too demanding for the user to define his own vocabulary? Do we need an extensive syntactic analysis or can we start with semantics, using only small syntactic fragments for disambiguation?

There is growing consensus that all these questions can only be decided by empirical testing including field studies in real-life situations. It would be nice if valid insights could be gained without empirical testing, which is time consuming and troublesome, but, unfortunately, this is not the way to improve HCI.

3. EMPIRICAL FINDINGS

In spite of the large number of developed NLI's (Lehmann and Blaser, 1979; Krause, 1982; Bundy, 1983), evaluation studies are rather rare. Only

a few experimental systems like NLQS have reached a degree of maturity
where they can be subjected to rigorous empirical testing. There are no
substantial results from real world field studies with respect to more
sophisticated systems (e.g., integrating the handling of fuzzy expressions,
user-specific dialogue strategies, why- questions, dialogue-orientation
instead of query-orientation).

An overview of evaluation studies is given in Lehmann and Blaser (1979)
Krause (1982), and Jarke, Krause and Vassiliou (1986). The papers show that
the bulk of empirical evaluations of natural query language systems reported
to date comes from tests with NLQS. There were two large studies, the
KFG-Study with a German version (IBM Heidelberg and Linguistic Information
Science of the University of Regensburg), and the "Advanced Language Project'
of the New York University (ALP) with an English version, and some smaller
studies. Taken together, these experiments involved about 100 subjects and
over 12,000 queries. Therefore, most of the empirical facts we know today
about NLI can be derived from the NLQS tests.

The results gained until 1985 are summarized in Jarke and Krause (1985),
Zoeppritz (1983), and Jarke, Krause, and Vassiliou (1986).

As a concluding activity, a mainly qualitative reinterpretation of the
materials of the ALP-project was performed in cooperation between the ALP-
group of the New York University, the Scientific Center of the IBM in Heidelberg, and the Linguistics Information Science Department of the University
of Regensburg. The starting point of these activities was the materials of
ALP, especially the protocols of the ALP-field study and laboratory experiments. The main focus concentrates on combining the results of the KFG- and
ALP-study and on formulating some empirically validated thesis on the use
of the user-dependent vocabulary, on strategies of handing the tasks/requests
and on error situations.

In this paper I will give an example of this kind of work concerning
the definition of the user-dependent vocabulary after describing shortly the
empirical materials we could start from.

3.1   The KFG- and ALP-Study

Both evaluation studies can be regarded as parts of an extended evaluation scheme. They started with real applications to be analyzed in real
world field studies coupled with controlled laboratory experiments (paper
and pencil tests) to answer special questions of system design and to compare
user performance in the NLQS against formal query languages.

The KFG-Study was performed at the IBM Scientific Center at Heidelberg
and at the University of Regensburg. The main field study of KFG was carried
out by three teachers, supported by the system development team. For instance, the teachers wanted to know whether low grades in mathematics in
earlier years have predictive power on grades at graduation. The database
contained 41,250 grades for 430 students and further information about
social background and class repetition. 7,278 questions were asked in 46
sessions. At the heart of KFG was the long term observation (16 months) of
a single user (6,603 questions). Detailed qualitative analyses were performed, and the original field study was complemented by another field
study and several minor laboratory experiments (Krause, 1982). The overall
evaluation plan of these studies is shown in Figure 1.

For the ALP evaluation study the NLQS was transferred to a different
natural language (English), and to a site where little linguistic or technical support by the development team was available. A quantitatively
oriented evaluation strategy was chosen for comparing the NLQS to the formal

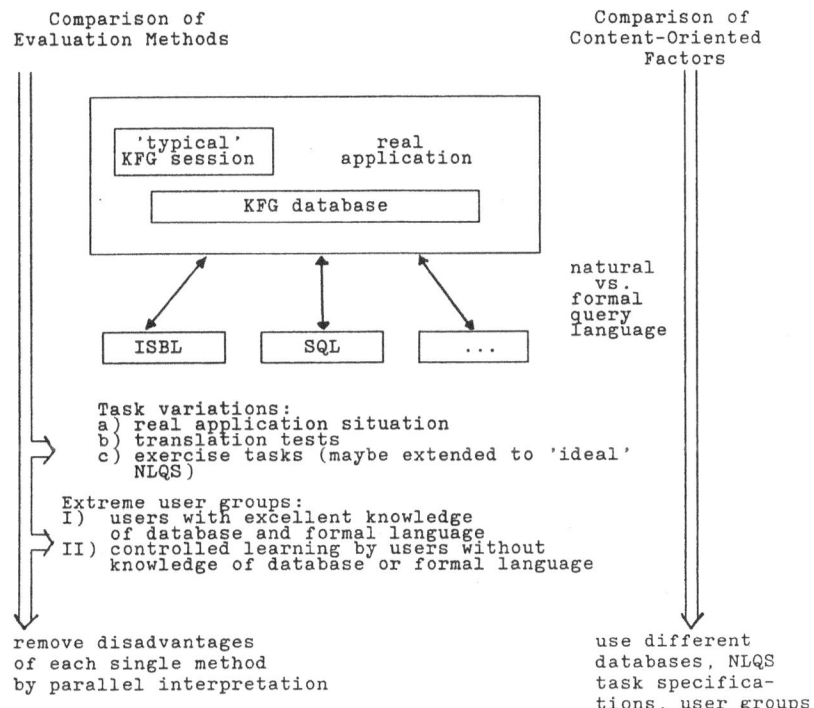

Figure 1. Overall Evaluation Plan – KFG Studies
(Partially Realized).

database query language SQL in a partially controlled field study and two
controlled laboratory experiments (Figure 2).

The application, a database about alumni of the Graduate School for
Business Administration at New York University, maintained demographic data
and donation histories of school alumni, foundations, other organizations,
and individuals. The school has over 40,000 graduates as well as some 5,000
non-graduates, who have given money to the school over the past 20 years.
The ALP database contained four base relations with approximately 100,000
tuples. Data retrieved from this database usually serve as a basis for
decision making in fund raising drives (Jarke et al., 1985; Vassiliou et
al., 1983).

Concerning the reinterpretation of the ALP-materials with respect to
the natural language components, the most interesting fact is that there
are different comparable natural language formulations of the same theme in
different parts of the study.

a) The ALP-field study used students as paid intermediaries
serving as information users or clients. The intermediaries spoke with the alumni department about the
tasks necessary to be solved and wrote the tasks down
in their own words. With their notes they went to the
NLQS to get an answer to their problem.

b) The computer protocols of the field studies show how the
eight intermediaries tried to reformulate the content
of their note in a way so that the NLQS could answer
their question.

127

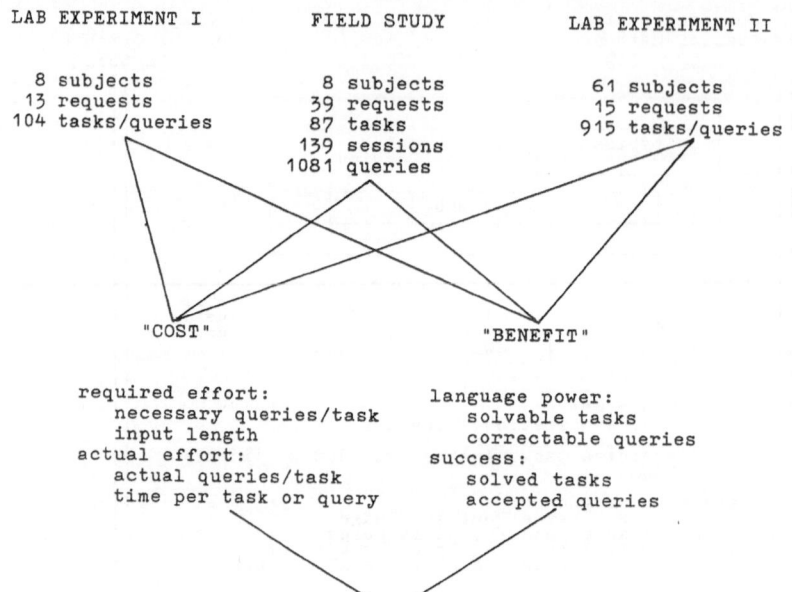

LAB EXPERIMENT I   FIELD STUDY   LAB EXPERIMENT II

```
   8 subjects            8 subjects            61 subjects
  13 requests           39 requests            15 requests
 104 tasks/queries      87 tasks              915 tasks/queries
                       139 sessions
                      1081 queries
```

                    "COST"   "BENEFIT"

```
required effort:                     language power:
  necessary queries/task               solvable tasks
  input length                         correctable queries
actual effort:                       success:
  actual queries/task                  solved tasks
  time per task or query               accepted queries
```

                        PROBLEM ANALYSIS

```
      task and query complexity
      problem sources
      user perceptions
      technical problems
```

Figure 2.   Evaluation Plan and Descriptive Statistics - ALP
            Studies (from Jarke and Krause (1985, p. 156)).

c)   On the basis of experience with the field study, the
     ALP-group formulated 15 test questions which described
     problem situations of the alumni department.

     Example Q1:   The dean of GBA is going to Pittsburgh.
                   He has requested a list of names and ad-
                   dresses of all alumni in this city.

d)   All students of the laboratory experiments II were
     first given a two hour tutorial about the application
     description. One group of 16 students was additionally
     taught for three and a-half hours how to query using
     the NLQS (examples, restriction rules) (= the group
     with NLQS training); 10 students received no addi-
     tional training (= the group without NLQS training).

After the training, both groups were asked to express a query (or a
series of queries) to answer the 15 test questions (paper and pencil test).
The group without NLQS training were asked to imagine that they could use a
natural language interface and to employ English queries.

As a result we have formulations of three different types:

-   the starting questions, formulated as typical tasks
    of the alumni department,

-   the reformulations using the background of some
    knowledge of NLQS, and

- the reformulations without any special knowledge about
a NLI (only: I have to ask a computer in natural
language)

    Example Group with NLQS Training:

        List the names and the addresses of the alumni
        in Pittsburgh.

    Example Group without NLQS Training:

        Find the name of any alumni whose city of resi-
        dence is Pittsburgh and make a listing of those
        alumni.

Concerning natural language formulations in ALP we thus have 25 different formulation types from 25 students and the ALP-researchers. Grouping
the formulation types with respect to their distance from the NLQS questions
of the field study results in the following list:

a)   Questions of the field study (1,063),

b)   Questions of the laboratory experiment II of the group
      with NLQS training (17 students solving 15 requests
      with 502 questions),

c)   Questions from the laboratory experiment II of the
      group without NLQS training (10 students solving 15
      requests with 337 questions),

d)   Notes of the 8 participants of the field study, and

e)   15 exam requests formulated from the ALP-researchers as
      being typical for the problems in an alumni department.

When I want to combine the ALP-materials with those of the KFG-Study,
there are only formulations of type a), the questions to the NLQS of the
field study (three teachers, 7,278 questions). Besides the differences in
languages (German vs. English), users (real users (teachers) vs. paid intermediaries), and application areas (school database vs. alumni database),
there is another important variation: the questions of the KFG-Study were
successfully answered (error rate less than 7%); the result of the ALP-
queries was rather discouraging (only 22.3% successful questions). Therefore, the ALP intermediaries tried very hard to reformulate their questions
so as to have a further chance to get the desired answer.

3.2 Example: Definition of the User Dependent Vocabulary

Before working with the NLQS, the user had to define the application
vocabulary, including the roles (arguments) attached to the verbs, nouns,
and adjectives, and their prepositions possible at the surface structure of
a query. If different users need a different vocabulary (including the use
of the roles) or if there are changes over time, NLQS will not work well.
Therefore, it is important for the practical feasibility of NLQS whether or
not there are major differences in vocabulary among users or over time.
Systems like the NLQS, INTELLECT, Q&A or others differ with respect to the
way they define the application-oriented vocabulary. It is possible to add
only the word class or to expand word definition to world knowledge information. The more information a NLI requests from the user, the more critical
is the amount of words a user has to define. Thus it is an important question for the design of a NLI, what is the maximum size of the user-dependent

Table 1.   Results of the KFG Study.

1	2	3
Defined relations	Not defined before starting the study	discrepancies: - roles (argum.) - prepositions
121	10	14

vocabulary and whether there are changes over time and with respect to different users. The antithesis will be: There is never an end to defining words. New users will need new words and new questions over time will need them as well. Therefore, learning a formal query language could be easier than the continuous interruptions of the HCI to define missing words.

To argue against the antithesis is difficult, because we would need several long term field studies with many users, which do not exist. Therefore, the idea was to construct an evaluation environment which favors the antithesis. All variations of formulations of the KFG- and ALP-study were brought into consideration. We asked how much and what kinds of completion and changes in the definition of the vocabulary of both studies would have been necessary to analyze all formulations made. It is evident that a lot of the variations of the ALP field study derived from the fact that the error rate was too high for an acceptable dialogue: therefore, the users experimented with words and structures they would never use in a normal NLI-dialogue. It is also evident that the notes of the users of the ALP field study were not intended for a NLI and also the students of the laboratory experiment without NLQS training chose formulations they never would use after looking at some example dialogues with NLQS.

But, if the necessary changes and completions of the vocabulary defined for the applications will be small after adding all these formulation types, the plausibility will be high for our starting hypothesis.

3.2.1 KFG-Changes and Completion. Krause (1982) showed that the vocabulary of the KFG-Study was rather stable. It was possible to define the user dependent vocabulary in such a way that the amount of necessary changes and completions did not question the success of the NLI (Table 1). But there are two weak points in this argumentation:

a)   The users were teachers (mainly one teacher). Perhaps teachers have fewer difficulties in adapting to a restricted vocabulary than other users (like secretaries).

b)   The first phase of the KFG-Study, the preparation of the application, could not be observed. The suspicion has been voiced that the training phase of the teachers was untypically intensive.

3.2.2 ALP-Study. The basis of the following table is a vocabulary of the ALP field study after about two months of usage (Table 2). The situation cannot be strictly compared with the KFG-Study, as the alumni application never became stable; the error rate was always too high to produce acceptable results. Therefore, for example, some words used in the query were not defined and, in spite of this defect, it was not analyzed why the NLQS could not answer adequately.

Table 2. Results of the ALP Study.

	Defined relations necessary	Additional view definitions necessary	Discrepancies - roles (arguments) - prepositions
a) Questions of the field study	127	5	9
b) Questions of lab. exp. with NLQS training	132	4	12
c) Questions of lab. exp. without NLQS training	136	3	6
d) Notes of the field study	139	2	3
e) Formulations of the exam requests	141	0	1

The table shows that the necessary completion rate and the changes with respect to the roles (arguments) and the prepositions of the surface structures are surprisingly low; also the formulation types d) and e), which are rather far from a real dialogue of a NLI, only slightly expand the vocabulary definitions necessary. Therefore, we can conclude that the plausibility of our starting thesis is high. The vocabulary definitions are rather stable with respect to different user groups, to different languages (German, English), to different training conditions, and to different frameworks of methodology (laboratory or field experiments). The design decision of a NLI to work with a user dependent vocabulary which has to be defined by the user before starting the application, therefore, seems also reasonable if the amount of information requested from the defining user is more extensive than in NLQS. Small vocabulary subsets are sufficient for restricted application areas. In the NLQS applications from 49 to 313 words became necessary (Zoeppritz, 1983). This result may not be transferred to any of the knowledge-based systems, where additionally the values appearing in the database (e.g., names like Müller, Smith) must be defined.

3.3 Further Results of the KFG- and ALP-Study

There are further statements which seem to have a similar strong empirical backing. I will only summarize the findings which were validated by both studies (Jarke, Krause, and Vassiliou, 1986; Zoeppritz, 1985):

a) Users do not communicate with a NLI in the way they do with a human being. In particular, they are very careful in typing input, as evidenced by a low percentage of typographical errors. It is an open question how this would change with widespread availability of automatic spelling correction for NLI.

b) Neither study confirmed the fear that natural language queries grow more and more complex over time.

c) Natural language is more concise than formal query languages. In particular, SQL requires substantially longer input even for rather simple queries.

d) Formal query languages cannot be rejected on reasons

that a substantial effort is needed to learn them. In laboratory experiments, subjects achieved comparable success in formulating formal language queries as in formulating formal language queries as in formulating NLQS queries after the same short period of training.

The statement d) leads to the question whether there exists an empirical confirmation of the intuitive feeling of many persons that NLI is a better solution for HCI than formal query languages.

4.   NLI VS. ALTERNATIVES

Attempts to evaluate the potential superiority of NLI vs. formal queries languages did not succeed in either the KFG- or in the ALP-Study. It could only be shown in a long term study (16 months, 7,278 questions) that it is possible for real users (not paid students) to solve a real-world problem with an error rate less than 7%. It could not be validated empirically that the natural language HCI was the better alternative.

As far as I know, the situation is similar with respect to DM, the second HCI-alternative, which also seems to have the image of being convincingly better than formal query languages that further argumentation or empirical examination for many people seems unnecessary. With respect to DM, one has to remember the tests of Whiteside (Whiteside et al., 1985) who included commercially available command-driven, menu- and icon-oriented (with extensive use of the mouse) interfaces. Whiteside (Whiteside et al., 1985, p. 190) came to the conclusion that:

"Style as manifested in real systems is simply not an important factor for human factors ... New interface styles do not in themselves solve old human factor problems ... the care with which an interface is crafted is more important than style."

Both HCI techniques have a plausible theoretical background in cognitive psychology and linguistics. But this is not enough. There are a lot of design decisions with many alternatives, which we do not know how to solve and where progress can only be expected from empirical testing in real-world field studies and laboratory experiments.

On the other side it seems obvious that the development of DM-systems will change the landscape for NLI's. Shneidermann (1986) gives an intuitively convincing example for the superiority of a DM-solution in certain areas. He contrasts a natural language dialogue for the reservation of a flight with Boswash airlines with a graphical solution where the user can choose the departure and destination city with the help of a landscape and the date and time of departure by menu selection.

We do not know where the frontiers are, but, I think, that the simpler the application structure is, the lower will be the chances of NLI's to dominate. I do not believe, that one HCI-type (formal language, natural language or DM) will be the better solution in all cases. We have to find out which type of HCI will be the best for which application area and user group. To investigate this question empirically should be seen as being equally as important as the construction of algorithms.

REFERENCES

Bundy, A., ed., 1983, Proceedings of the 8th IJCAI, Karlsruhe.

Carbonell, J. G., 1984, "Is There Natural Language After Databases?", Proceedings of COLING 1984, Stanford, pp. 186-187.

Flickinger, D., 1984, "Panel on Natural Language and Databases", Proceedings of COLING 1984, Stanford, pp. 188-189.

Gaines, B. R., and Shaw, M. L. G., 1986, "From Time-Sharing to the Sixth Generation: The Development of Human-Computer-Interaction. Part I.," Intl. J. Man-Machine Studies, 24, pp. 1-27.

Hirose, K., and Fuchi, K., 1984, The Culture of the Fifth Generation Computer, Tokyo.

Hutchins, E. L., et al., 1986, "Direct Manipulation Interfaces", User Centered System Design, Norman, D. A., and Draper, S. W., eds., Hillsdale-London, pp. 87-124.

Jarke, M., and Krause, J., 1985, "New Empirical Results of User Studies with a Domain-Independent Natural Language Query System", Artificial Intelligence Methodology Systems Applications, Bibel, W., and Pettkoff, B., eds., North-Holland, pp. 153-159.

Jarke, M., Krause, J., and Vassiliou, Y., 1986, "Studies in the Evaluation of a Domain-Independent Natural Language Query System", Cooperative Interactive Information Systems, Bolc, L., and Jarke, M., eds., Berlin et al., pp. 101-130.

Jarke, M., et al., 1985, "A Field Evaluation of Natural Language for Data Retrieval", IEEE Transactions on Software Engineering, SE-11, (1), pp. 97-114.

Krause, J., 1982, "Mensch-Maschine-Interaktion in natürlicher Sprache", Evaluierungsstudien zu praxisorientierten Frage-Antwort-Systemen und ihre Methodik, Tübingen.

Krause, J., 1984, "Praxisorientierte natürlichsprachliche Frage-Antwort-Systems: Zur Entwicklung vor allem in der Bundesrepublik Deutschland", Nachrichten für Dokumentation, 34, (4/5), pp. 188-194.

Krause, J., and Lehmann, H., 1980, "User Specialty Languages. A Natural Language Based Information System and Its Evaluation", Dialogsysteme und Textverarbeitung, Krallmann, D., ed., Essen, pp. 127-146.

Lehmann, H., 1978, "Interpretation of Natural Language in an Information System", IBM-Journal of Research and Development, 5, pp. 560-572.

Lehmann, H., and Blaser, A., 1979, Query Languages in Database Systems, IBM Heidelberg Scientific Center Technical Report 79.07.004.

Lehmann, H., Ott, N., and Zoeppritz, M., 1985, "A Multilingual Interface to Databases", IEEE Database Engineering Bulletin 8.3, September 1985.

McKeown, K. R., 1984, "Natural Language for Expert Systems: Comparison with Database Systems", Proceedings of COLING 1984, Stanford, pp. 190-193.

Ott, N., and Zoeppritz, M., 1979, "USL - An Experimental Information System Based on Natural Language", Natural Communication with Computers, Bolc, L., ed., Munchen et al., pp. 3-32.

Shneidermann, B., 1983, "Direct Manipulation: A Step Beyond Programming Languages", IEEE, 8, pp. 57-69.

Sparck-Jones, K., 1984, "Natural Language and Databases, Again", <u>Proceedings of COLING 1984</u>, Stanford, pp. 182-183.

Vassiliou, Y., et al., 1983, "Natural Language for Database Queries: A Laboratory Study" , <u>MIS Quarterly</u>, <u>7</u>, (4), pp. 47-61.

Whiteside, J., et al., 1985, "User Performance with Command, Menu, and Iconic Interfaces", <u>Human Factors in Computer Systems-II. Proceedings of the CHI'85 Conference</u>, Bormann, L., and Curtis, B., eds., Amsterdam, et al., pp. 185-192.

Zoeppritz, M., 1983, "Human Factors of a 'Natural Language End User System'", <u>End User Systems and Their Human Factors</u>, Blaser, A., Zoeppritz, M., eds., Berlin et al., pp. 62-93.

Zoeppritz, M., 1984, <u>Syntax for German in the User Specialty Languages System</u>, Tübingen.

Zoeppritz, M., 1985, "Computer Talk?", <u>IBM Heidelberg Scientific Center Technical Note 85.05</u>.

APPLYING OPERATIONS RESEARCH MODELS TO THE STUDY OF COMPLEX MAN-MACHINE

INTERFACES

Ronald J. Reiner and Ashok K. Tandon

Essex Corporation
333 N. Fairfax Street
Alexandria, Virginia 22314

Abstract: The research reported here is one phase of a programmatic effort at the Essex Corporation to expand the system designer's ability to assess the efficiency of complex man-machine interfaces. The first effort was development of the Computer-Aided Performance and Reliability Assessment (CAPRA) model which predicts time-on-task (TOT) and probability of success (P_s) for relatively simple interfaces. This paper describes the extension of the earlier research into the domain of multiple operators working with concurrent interfaces. Under this effort, the Multiple Operator/Parallel System Interface Evaluation (MOPSIE) model was developed. It utilizes conventional operations research techniques to better quantify task complexity and assess the importance of operator skill and intelligence.

MOPSIE equates the skill of the operator to the efficiency with which he can process his workload using the proposed interface. By assessing the importance of efficiency on productivity, the model is projecting the importance of operator skill on productivity. The model enumerates the multitude of paths which an operator can follow in order to process a given workload in the context of a concurrent interface. Every possible path represents a certain level of efficiency which can be quantified in terms of overall productivity. By comparing the best cases to the worst within the path set, the model can demonstrate the importance of operator skill and intelligence.

1. INTRODUCTION

The research reported here is one phase of a programmatic effort at the Essex Corporation to expand the system designer's ability to assess and predict the efficiency of complex man-machine interfaces during the conceptual design phases. The first effort was development of the CAPRA (Computer Aided Probabilistic Risk Assessment) (Reiner, 1986) model which predicts time-on-task (TOT) and probability of success (P_s) for relatively simple interfaces. CAPRA utilizes a state-space approach to predict these metrics and allows the formal integration of hardware and operator reliability.

A recent new thrust is into the area of information intensive interfaces where TOT must be considered in the context of the "quality" of the results. Quality considerations apply to software interfaces like word pro-

cessing, bibliographic retrieval, and graphics drawing programs. The methodology developed to describe such interfaces was generated under a contract
to the Air Force and is called the Iterative Control Assessment Methodology
(ICAM) (Reiner and Weiss, 1986). Like the work described in this paper,
the ICAM concept is based on the application of operations research techniques to the study of man-machine interface issues.

This paper describes the extension of the earlier research into the
domain of multiple operators working with concurrent interfaces. Interfaces
are considered "concurrent", if they allow two or more operators to work
concurrently or, if the system itself can perform many of its tasks concurrent with the human operator's tasks. Examples of this may include many
large scale reprographic devices on the market. While the copier is busy
producing copies, the operator can be preprogramming for the next job,
unloading copies, filling paper trays or binding off-line. A potential
application of concurrency modeling in the copier context is the ability to
compare the productivity of a single large copier to that of two smaller
ones. This comparison can be made assuming any number of operators.

Copier designers have been taking advantage of the microcomputer revo-
lution by designing increasing amounts of sophistication and power into the
copiers targeted for the commercial marketplace. Of special interest to
the copier manufacturer is the so-called high volume market which is generally serviced by high capacity machines operating in centralized repro-
duction centers and run by specially trained operations staff. The major
concern in such an environment is productivity, and productivity is determined by the capacity of the copier (e.g., number of copies per minute
produced), downtime due to maintenance (preventive and corrective), and the
effectiveness of the operator.

Someone who is acquainted with only the mid and low-volume copier
lines might find it difficult to imagine a trained operator as limiting the
productivity of the system. However, the high volume lines include functions
and capabilities not found in models from the lower volume lines. These
capabilities have been added in order to increase productivity and include
features such as:

Program Ahead:	The ability to program one job while another is in the copy mode.
Multiple Paper Trays:	The ability to prefill paper trays while the copier is running in anticipation of upcoming jobs.
Preprogramming:	This allows the operator to change the default settings for programming parameters such as amount of reduction, image placement, etc.
Job Interrupt:	This allows the operator to interrupt a long running copying job in order to process a small higher priority job. The interrupted job can be continued exactly where it left off.

These features already exist on commercial copiers. There are, however, numerous other features which represent quantum leaps in function
which are planned for future models.

While looking through the list of advanced features, one question immediately springs to mind: Will the operator be able to utilize these cap-

136

abilities to their fullest extent or will he only utilize the simpler functions and ignore the rest? It is extremely important to answer this question prior to building and fielding a copier. It must be addressed during the conceptual design phases in order to decide whether to incorporate the advanced features at all.

The answers to such questions are not easy to generate; especially during the early design phase when mock-ups and prototypes are not yet available for operability testing. Instead of trying to answer this question directly, Essex took a backdoor approach and developed a modeling concept which answers a different question: given the expected workload and capabilities of the system, will the system require highly skilled operators in order to work at peak efficiency?

If the answer to this question is "no" then there is no point in pursuing the original question. The advanced features will work effectively because they do not place any additional burden on the operator. If the answer is "yes", on the other hand, then the original question deserves further consideration. In this case, the model will shed some light on the important underlying issues and help determine how the operator's burden can be alleviated. The options for lowering the operator's burden usually include adding more operators, improving the training, simplifying some of the system interfaces, adding a skilled job manager or including some automated "intelligent" job planning aids.

2. THE BASIC CONCEPTS

The model which was alluded to in the previous paragraph is called the Multiple Operator/Parallel System Interface Evaluation (MOPSIE) methodology. The basic concept behind MOPSIE is to use standard operations research techniques to characterize complex man-machine interfaces. The purpose of the operations research approach is not to try to predict how well (e.g., time-on-task and error rate) the operator will perform. Instead, the purpose is to investigate how efficient the operator must be in order to perform effectively. MOPSIE analyzes an interface by assessing the operating efficiency of the interface using the inherent constraints of the operator.

A prime example of this approach is a sophisticated office copier. The copier offers a number of individual interfaces that the operator must learn how to use including the input hopper, the programming console, the paper tray, and the output hopper. Each one of these separate interfaces can be modeled with some form of task-flow model in order to estimate how long it takes to perform simple functions such as loading 20 original sheets or programming for 10 copies on legal size paper. Indeed, it would be impossible to analyze the copier interface without some knowledge of the operator's performance on these subsets of the interface.

However, these individual analyses do not go far in evaluating the true usefulness of the copier as a whole. The designer of the copier and the prospective user really want to know how "productive" the device will be in its projected operating environment. In order to estimate the eventual productivity, it is necessary to know the characteristics of the equipment's operator(s) and the type of workload that will be processed. It is relatively easy to specify a workload for a copier. Workload can be expressed in terms of a list of copy jobs. For each job on the list, the number of originals, the number of copies and any special requirements such as binding, double-sided copying, or special imaging (e.g., reduction) must be specified. Choosing a set of jobs to serve as the "typical" workload for evaluation purposes requires some careful thought.

Describing the operator is seemingly a far more difficult task. The operator possesses physical dexterity and mental astuteness which must be considered in any estimation of potential system productivity. Quantifying and scaling these multidimensional human traits is a difficult task laden with many pitfalls and should be avoided if at all possible. However, the operator's performance is critical to the understanding of the system's eventual performance.

The MOPSIE approach circumvents these complex issues by formulating the analysis in terms of an optimization problem in which the operator's skills are treated as constraints. The less skilled the operator is, the more constraining he is on overall system productivity. The perfect operator will allow the system to process its workload at a rate limited only by the hardware constraints of the system. These observations are best understood in terms of a simple example.

Suppose that a copier operator is presented with two copy jobs and that each job consists of two individual steps: prepare for the job (load blank paper, program number of copies, etc.) and allow the machine to perform the copying. The times for performing the four subtasks are shown in Table 1 below.

Assume, also, that the copier being used allows all preparation for one job to be done while another is in the process of being copied. Thus, while Job 1 is copying, the operator can be loading paper, programming ahead and making ready the next job. The sort of copier which allows this is clearly more sophisticated than one which does not offer "program ahead" features or multiple paper trays.

If the hypothetical operator is not aware of these features (poor training) or is too lazy to use them (poor motivation) or not intelligent enough to comprehend them (poor selection), then he will perform very little of his work in parallel with the copier and the workload will require about 105 seconds to process. A properly trained and well motivated operator will take advantage of parallelism and overlap the preparation for Job 2 with the copy time of Job 1. This operator will process his workload in about 90 seconds. That represents almost a 15% improvement in overall productivity.

If the operator is truly on the ball he will notice that he can save even more time by doing Job 2 first. This strategy will allow him to overlap 30 seconds of job preparation time with 40 seconds of copy time. This realization works in a workload processing time of 75 seconds. The use of such tricks does not necessarily require great intelligence on the part of the operator. Automated job planning aids or a specially trained job dispatcher could help the copier operator realize and implement improved strategies.

What conclusions can be drawn from this simple, hypothetical example? One important conclusion is that the capability to overlap operator time and copy time on a copier can provide significant improvements in productivity.

Table 1.
TASK PERFORMANCE TIMES
(SECS)

	JOB 1	JOB 2
PREPARE	30	20
COPY	15	40

This result is derivable from standard operations research considerations. However, if the operator does not take advantage of the indicated capabilities, then these sophisticated features will not pay off. These are very obvious pronouncements based on a trivial example. However, the examples become complicated very quickly and the conclusions far less obvious. If the workload consisted of 50 jobs to be processed by two operators on two copiers (each with different capacities and capabilities), then the analysis would become effectively intractable. Some of these complexities are described in Section 5 of this paper.

3. CONSIDERATION OF OPERATOR SKILL

MOPSIE allows consideration of operator skill in sensitivity studies (Rasmussen, 1980). This was illustrated in the original two-job example. A poorly prepared operator will not utilize any aspects of concurrent processing (between man and machine) allowed in the interface. A better trained operator will benefit from concurrency as he processes the jobs one by one. The ideal operator will not only utilize concurrency, but he will also plan out the execution of his workload in order to best take advantage of it. MOPSIE accounts for operator limitations by evaluating the improvements to productivity which result when various degrees of workload planning are exercised. In the case of a copier workload, this is easily quantified by assuming that the operator can plan ahead n jobs at a time.

If n is assumed to be one, then the modeler is saying that the operator simply takes and processes the jobs in the order they are presented to him. If n is two, then the operator takes jobs in pairs and plans out the individual tasks for each pair so as to minimize the overall time for processing each pair. If n is set to three, then the operator is presumed to optimize task performance for sets of three jobs. Due to computational limitations, the model presented in this study was limited to four jobs at a time.

4. APPLICATION OF THE MOPSIE CONCEPTS

The preceding section described the rationale for applying operations research techniques (Wagner, 1975) to problems which possess a human factors flavor. Traditionally, the study of man-machine interfaces has been the purview of the human factors community (Newell and Card, 1985). A concept such as MOPSIE is not intended to supplant the human factors engineer; it is only intended to provide him with an additional tool for performing studies. In addition, MOPSIE requires human factors input in order to operate. In the example above, it was not glibly stated that job preparation times are 30 seconds and 20 seconds. Where did these estimates come from? Estimates of task performance times are generally provided by human factors models such as Essex's CAPRA (Computer Aided Probabilities Risk Assessment) model.

The task performance times given in the two-job example depend on many things. They depend on the skill and experience of the operator. They depend on the complexity and structure of the workload. They also depend on the design of the equipment and the physical layout of the working environment. The time to load blank paper depends on the accessibility of the paper tray, the ease of inserting paper, and the proximity of the paper supply to the copier. MOPSIE depends on independent methods for combining these factors and producing a time-on-task figure-of-merit. Once such values are derived, MOPSIE provides a framework for integrating piece part interface studies into a full-fledged productivity evaluation.

MOPSIE is a productivity analysis tool. It permits the analyst to

assess the importance of equipment design, working environment, projected
workload and operator skill and training on the productivity of a complex
man-machine system. This does not mean that MOPSIE is intended to be a
high precision productivity prediction tool. Most people would be hard
pressed to justify a MOPSIE prediction that two operators can utilize three
copiers to process a hypothetical workload comprised of 50 jobs (involving
possibly 300 individual tasks) in exactly 2 hours, 15 minutes, and 32
seconds. It would be presumptuous of any model to claim it could predict a
human being's performance to this degree of precision.

Suppose, however, that this questionable estimate of 2 hours and 15
minutes drops by 50% when a third operator is introduced into the picture.
MOPSIE has offered something which is perhaps believable and justifiable.
The methodology has indicated that a major constraint on productivity was
the number of operators. This is certainly a feasible condition. If the
MOPSIE model demonstrates its point with details of how man/machine processing episodes overlap in the two instances, then the analyst can assess by
veracity of the MOPSIE result and draw his own conclusions.

This example illustrates the overall purpose of a methodology like
MOPSIE. It is a decision support system which allows the man-machine interface analyst to play "what-if" games with his design and environment in
order to identify the important factors and considerations. Instead of
adding another operator, the analyst could have postulated a workload where
there are fewer jobs, but the jobs are larger on the average. This modified
workload could represent the same overall copy output, but the restructuring
may result in more efficient performance by two operators. The MOPSIE methodology can compare these alternatives and detail the reasons for any significant changes.

5.   MODEL IMPLEMENTATION

The MOPSIE model was initially applied to a reprographic machine still
undergoing design. The machine was selected because it incorporated multiple
man-machine interfaces and some powerful new operational constructs. Another
reason for choosing this copier was that the number of operators to be employed and their skill levels were still under determination. Alternative
designs were evaluated on the basis of an average job workload. Various
component combinations were tried and the sensitivities of the generated
metrics to the above-mentioned factors were noted in order to arrive at a
reasonable design.

5.1 MOPSIE Algorithm

The model's algorithm consist of the following steps:

- Each copying job is broken into tasks. Some of the examples
  of tasks are loading a job, loading the paper, programming
  the job, unloading the job, etc.

- Resources required by each task are assigned to it. Examples
  of limited resources include human operator and machine components such as paper trays, input hopper and the copying
  engine itself.

- Tasks that can be accomplished concurrently, e.g., loading
  paper, loading originals, and programming, etc., are flagged
  as such.

- Tasks are then grouped at various levels based on the obvious task sequencing requirements and the allowable parallel tasks. Level 1 tasks must be completed before level 2 tasks can be initiated; level 2 tasks must be completed before level 3 tasks can be initiated; and so on. The levels have significance for the same job only. For multiple job workloads, the levels lose some of the significance because level 2 tasks of one job can be accomplished before level 1 tasks of another job.

- Once the job breakdown and task groupings are accomplished, the model estimates total workload processing time under different assumptions. The worst case assumption is that the operator utilizes no parallelism. The next worst case is that the operator (or operators) are capable of planning ahead one job at a time. The next case is two-job preplanning and so forth on up to four jobs at a time. In each case, MOPSIE isolates that particular ordering of tasks which consumes the least amount of time assuming the stated amount of look-ahead. Determination of this sequence of tasks, or path, is performed via the "Best Path" algorithm.

5.2 Best Path Algorithm

Given the workload, the machine constraints, the number and the skill level of the operators, and the environmental conditions, the best path is defined as that sequencing of tasks which processes all the jobs in the least amount of time. The search for a best path is typical of optimization problems often encountered in operations research studies.

The derivation of the best path algorithm was quite laborious. A number of established approaches were tried and rejected. A state-space approach using Markov Chains (Gaver and Thompson, 1983) was too cumbersome as the total number of states was determined to be astronomical. Generalized Shortest Path Technique (Wagner, 1975) was infeasible, because it does not account for complex resource constraints. Machine Sequencing and Scheduling algorithms (Baker, 1974) were also inappropriate. They require a fixed, preset task sequence. They cannot incorporate sequences where any of a number of tasks can be the starting tasks or the ending tasks. Simple Monte-Carlo simulation was rejected because the number of possible paths implied a prohibitive number of trials for any acceptable accuracy.

The final choice of method is a modified form of "exhaustive enumeration". It has been modified with some look-ahead and pruning in order to reduce the state-space to manageable proportions. The selected algorithm evaluates each path (checks for path validity, performs resource allocation, measures idle time, if any, and accumulates the task times for each job and for the entire workload) and selects the one which requires minimum time to do the workload. Let us look at the simplified example presented in the previous section to explain the best path concept in more detail.

Table 2 depicts a list of all tasks sorted by jobs. There are a total of 4 tasks in this workload. Figure 1 shows the total number of paths after the tasks have been categorized into levels, i.e., obvious sequencing constraints have been incorporated. Obvious sequencing constraints, for the copier example, underscore the fact that job preparation (loading the paper, loading the job, programming the job, etc.) has to be accomplished before copying can begin for that job. Without these constraints, the number of paths would have been even greater (12, in our example). The task numbering scheme shown includes leveling so the tasks have to be done in ascending order for the same job.

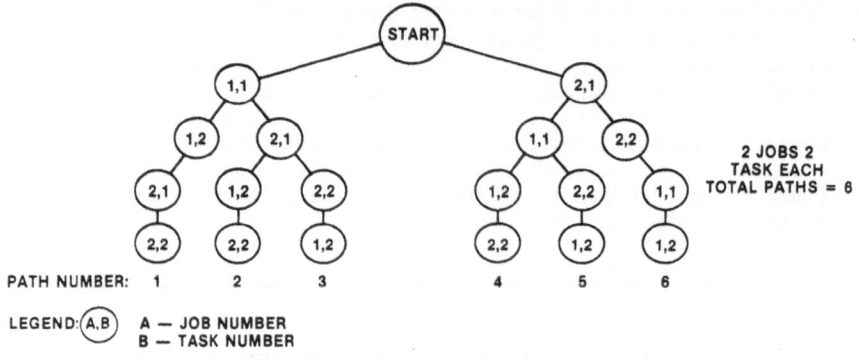

Figure 1. Task Parallelisms.

One point needs clarification here. The branches of the tree in Figure 1 show tasks strung together in a sequence. The reader should not get the impression that all tasks have to be done in those sequences. If this were so, all paths would consume the same amount of time, which is 105 seconds. The path consists of the sequence of task initiation, not task completion. For example, in path 1 {1,1 - 1,2 - 2,1 - 2,2}, task 2,1 does not have to wait for task 1,2 to finish. Task 2,1 can be initiated anytime after 1,2 has been initiated as long as resources required by it are available. The model traverses each path and initiates tasks in the sequence in which they occur. It accumulates various statistics, primarily the total time consumed. The flowchart shown in Figure 2 depicts the simple algorithm. The path with the smallest total time is selected as the best path.

In our example, it is clear that concurrent task execution is possible because both resources are not required for all 4 tasks. The Gantt chart presented in Figure 3 shows how the workload will be accomplished along paths 1 and 6. Paths 2, 3, 4 or 5 will be traversed in serial requiring the full 105 seconds and have not been shown. Path 6 requiring the least amount of time (75 secs) is selected as the best path. It is interesting to note that the best path also has idle time (dotted line) for the operator.

The true power of the MOPSIE concept comes from its extensive report generation capabilities. The concern of the MOPSIE user is not the exact amount of time it takes to process the workload, but where the processing bottlenecks occur and how they can be rectified. MOPSIE is fully capable of showing how long the operator was idle and how his idle time was distributed as waiting time for other resources such as the copying engine and committed paper trays. MOPSIE can also show the time the machine components spent waiting for a busy operator to get to them.

Table 2. Job Breakdown By Tasks.

JOB NO.	TASK NO.	TASK DESCRIPTION	TASK TIMES (SECS)	RESOURCES REQUIRED
1	1	PREPARE FOR COPY	30	OPER
1	2	COPY	15	OPER,MACH
2	1	PREPARE FOR COPY	20	OPER
2	2	COPY	40	OPER,MACH

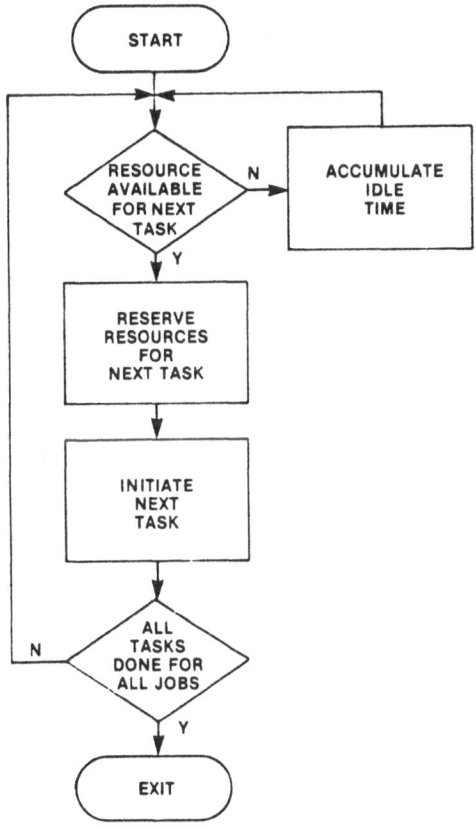

Figure 2.   Task Flow Algorithm.

5.3   Computational Complexity

The example presented in this paper is overly simplified. In reality,
the average workload consists of tens of jobs, each job consisting of 10 to
15 tasks. Also, the machine resource is a combination of resources, e.g.,
programming screen, input station, output station, etc., to be represented
separately. The escalation of all these tasks and resources takes the total
number of paths into the trillions and would require days of execution on a
supercomputer if enumerated exhaustively. For example, the addition of 1
more task yields a total of 20 paths; the addition of 1 more job with 3 tasks
yields 1,680 paths; the addition of 2 more jobs yields 369,600 paths; and so
on.

MOPSIE utilizes various techniques, specific to the reprographic machine
environment, to reduce the problem to manageable proportions. With these
techniques in place, the best path algorithm can be executed on a VAX 11/780
in a reasonable amount of time. The technique that aided the most was based
on empirical observations of the machine operators. It was observed that
operators have a preset way of approaching a copying task, e.g., some would
always program first; some would always load the paper first; some would
always load the job in the input hopper first, etc. Incorporation of these
operator strategies into the model algorithm reduced the number of total
paths tremendously. Copying machine constraints (in addition to the resource
constraints mentioned previously) also helps reduce the universe of total
paths. These techniques do not guarantee an optimal path, but the best path

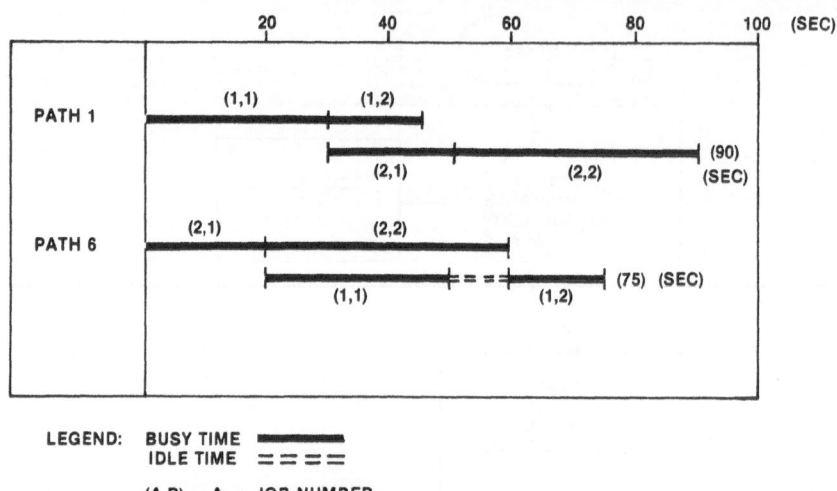

Figure 3. Workload Timeline.

isolated is close enough to be acceptable.

5.4 Multiple Machines

MOPSIE was also applied to a reprographic environment consisting of more than one machine. In order to determine the advantage, if any, of utilizing two smaller machines in lieu of one large machine, both situations were modeled with the same workload. Modeling multiple machines made the problem far more complex as various combinations of the job workload were tried on the two machines to determine the best combination. The process of "exhaustive enumeration" was continued for the case of multiple machines too.

6.   SUMMARY AND CONCLUSIONS

The concept behind MOPSIE is really quite straightforward. Equipment productivity is assessed in terms of the workload the subject equipment will have to process in its working environment. This workload consists of numerous jobs which can be further refined into individual tasks. It is up to the operator to perform the required list of tasks in the most efficient manner he can dream up. Improvements in efficiency can only be realized by taking advantage of the equipment's ability to process some of the tasks independently of the operator and by properly allocating tasks to multiple operators. If there is no potential for concurrency of operation, then all tasks must be performed serially and efficiency can never be improved by planning ahead. MOPSIE is only appropriate to an environment which is postulated to allow concurrent operations.

MOPSIE, itself, is an operations research optimization model. It compares the hypothetical workload to the equipment's capabilities and finds the order of tasks which leads to the most efficient processing of the workload. The model is said to be searching for the "best path" of the myriad of possible paths for processing the workload. When performing this optimization, the model does not look at tasks associated with the entire workload. Instead, it looks at the task lists formed by taking jobs in smaller chunks (1,2,... or n at a time). This leads to a suboptimal

144

situation which is more representative of the operator's ability to plan and perform jobs.

REFERENCES

Baker, K. R., 1974, Introduction to Sequencing and Scheduling, John Wiley & Sons, New York.

Gaver, P., and Thompson, G. L., 1973, Programming and Probability Models in Operations Research, Brooks/Cole Publishing Co., Monterey, California.

Newell, A., and Card, S. K., 1985, The Prospects for Psychological Science in Human Computer Interaction, 1, (3), 1985.

Rasmussen, J., 1980, "The Human as a Systems Component", Human Interaction with Computers, Smith, H. T., and Green, T. R. G., eds., Academic Press, London.

Reiner, R., 1986, Maintainability Prediction Using Sophisticated Task Simulation, Paper presented at the 13'th International Reliability Availability and Maintainability Conference for the Electric Power Industry, June 1986, Syracuse, NY.

Reiner, R., and Weiss, E. C., 1986, Quantitative Techniques for Assessing Complex Man-Machine Interfaces, Final Report submitted to Air Force Human Resources Laboratory, Wright Patterson AFB, Ohio, Contract No. F33615-85-C0016.

Wagner, H. M., 1975, Principles of Operations Research, Prentice-Hall, Inc., Englewood Cliffs, New Jersey.

3. USER-SYSTEM INTERFACE EVALUATION

ADAPTIVE USER INTERFACES FOR INFORMATION SYSTEMS: AN EVALUATION

A. T. Hockley

R19.2.3 Tutoring Systems Group
British Telecom Research Laboratories
Martlesham Heath
IPSWICH
Suffolk IP5 7RE
England

Abstract: This paper discusses the implications for evaluation procedures
of adaptive systems, and describes the results of applying the suggested
approach to an adaptive front-end to an electronic mail system. The results
are discussed and interpreted, and as a result, suggestions are made on how
the system may be improved.

1.   INTRODUCTION

The trouble with most systems is that they take no account of the fact
that every user is different. They force all users into one way of working,
which inevitably results in a large number of users using systems which are
not ideally suited to them. Users also change over time; they get more
experienced, have off days, or simply forget how to use the system. Most
systems do not take this fact into account. There are, therefore, good
reasons to suppose that there would be distinct advantages for a system which
could adapt both to individual users, and changes in those users over time.

While, almost by definition, it must be an advantage for systems to
adapt to individual users, there are obvious pitfalls. One of the most
widely accepted tenets of good MMI is that of consistency, and an interface
that adapts is obviously not consistent in a superficial sense. Given that
sufficient care is taken in building adaptive systems, it should be possible
to ensure that they appear consistent at a fundamental level. In other
words, they should be consistent in the way that they adapt. If this requirement is not met, there is a real possibility that such an interface
may be harder to use than a non-adaptive one.

The Alvey Programme (1982) is a collaborative research program into
advanced information technology for the UK. The Alvey Adaptive Intelligent
Dialogues (AID) project is a four year program of research into the issues
and practicalities surrounding adaptive systems. This paper describes the
design and the construction of an exemplar system built during the first
phase of the project, and its subsequent evaluation.

2. HOW ADAPTIVE SYSTEMS WORK

All adaptive interfaces are fundamentally similar in the way that they operate. They collect some information about the user, and then use that information in order to produce some internal change, which results in a corresponding change in the system's response to a given user input. This change in the system's response is the adaption. Differences between adaptive systems may, therefore, be expressed in terms of the information that they referred to for reviews of the issues involved in user-modeling (Sleeman and Brown, 1982; Rich, 1979). To summarize, the information stored may range from simple descriptive statistics of error rates, and frequency of command usage, to the complicated focus tracking involved in natural language understanding. The nature of the corresponding adaptions is as varied as the information stored, ranging from shifting of menu items in a hierarchy (Witten et al., 1984), to the tailoring of output to a level of concept that the user will understand (User Modeling Front End (UMFE), Sleeman, 1985).

3. DESIGN OF AN EXEMPLAR SYSTEM

3.1 Aims of Building the System

As a first step in the project, an adaptive system was produced. The aims of building this system were to discover something of the practicalities of providing adaption in a real application, while at the same time developing expertise in the technical issues involved. The design of the exemplar represents a practical attempt at providing adaption to an existing application.

The exemplar functions as a front end to a remote electronic mail system (Telecom Gold). It translates the user's requests into commands valid for the application, and translates responses from the application into a form suitable for display.

3.2 System Architecture

The system runs on a SUN workstation, and is composed of four separate but communicating UNIX processes (Figure 1). Overall control of the system is performed by a dialogue controller which runs under Rapid/USE (Wasserman, 1984). This process switches control between the various component processes, and supports the delivery dialogue. The User Model is written in Prolog and POP11, and runs under Poplog (Hardy, 1984). The Application expert also runs under Poplog, and is written in POP11. The communications process links the system to Telecom Gold via a modem, and is written in C.

3.3 Functioning of the System

3.3.1 Overview. On the basis of its knowledge of the application domain, and of likely sequences of user actions, the system infers whether the user is having difficulties or not, and triggers an adaption as a result. If the system 'thinks' the user is performing well, the level of guidance given by the system is reduced. If the system thinks the user is having difficulties, the level of guidance is increased. Other dimensions of adaption allow the user to return to a task he has not yet completed, and use commands from UNIX mail.

3.3.2 Knowledge About the User. Knowledge about the user is stored in the user-model, which tracks the user's task, and infers his level of skill with that task, as represented by a count of the number of errors and help requests for the task. The user model contains a database of sequences of

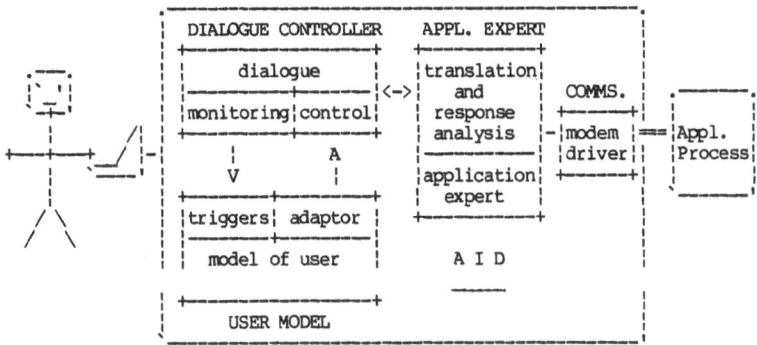

Figure 1.   System Architecture.

actions which together may be used to achieve a task.   Each of these sequences of actions is termed a plan.   Individual users are represented as a
collection of frames.   A general frame stores user specified information,
such as whether they have used mail systems before, whether they find the
system too verbose, etc.   Plan frames store a record of usage of a particular
plan, and plan errors, determined as departures from sequences of actions
stored in the plan recognizer's database.   Action frames store information
on the use of particular actions, broken down into frequency of errors and
help requests.   Action errors are identified from the application expert's
knowledge of legitimate commands within the application domain.   A separate
frame, termed the output frame, is used by the plan recognizer to post its
assessment of the user's current context.   Thus the user model contains
general information about users, maintains a record of user expertise at
both a plan and action level, and tracks the context in which the user is
working.

   3.3.3 Adaptions to the User.   The system adapts to users along three orthogonal dimensions.   The dimensions are:

1)   Guidance dimension

     This is the primary dimension of adaption.   For every task,
     there are six levels of guidance available.   The levels differ
     in the amount of feedback given to users, and the amount of
     prompting the system gives.   The level of guidance for a par-
     ticular task is determined by the user model output frame.

2)   Context dimension

     The system maintains a focus of the user's particular task.
     If at any time it notes a user entry which does not corres-
     pond to an expected action, as stored in its database of
     valid user plans, a change in the user's task is logged.
     When the user finishes his next task, the system will offer
     him the opportunity to return to what he was doing previously.

3)   Familiarity with UNIX mail

     If the user is familiar with UNIX, as noted from an intro-
     ductory logon questionnaire, the system will attempt to
     parse UNIX commands, if they have a logical equivalent in
     the application.

These dimensions were selected because they operate at a syntactic level, which reduces implementation problems. Totterdell and Cooper (1986) contains a fuller description of the operation of the system, together with examples of its operation.

4. ADAPTIVE SYSTEMS AND EVALUATION

Static systems may be effectively evaluated by defining a dimension of performance, and then measuring this dimension under controlled conditions. Moran (1981) gives as examples: the range of tasks which may be undertaken on a system, the time taken to learn a number of tasks, the time taken to perform a set task, the number and nature of errors, the quality of the user's output, the 'robustness' of a user's performance, and user acceptability.

In the case of adaptive systems, such measures are still valid. However, given that adaptive systems are a recent innovation, a measure of the performance of the processes supporting adaption is also desirable. The overall performance of the system is not the main interest. Instead, it is of interest to determine what is the most appropriate way of building adaption into systems. The first step is, therefore, to define and delineate the processes supporting adaption. In general, all adaptive systems make inferences or track information about the user, and then use these to perform some internal change. In addition to measures of overall performance, there are, therefore, two additional points at which an adaptive system may be evaluated; its collection of information about the user, and the suitability of the changes made in response.

4.1 Evaluating the Collection of Information on the User

The first step is to assess whether the collection of information about the user is simply a logging process (i.e., is totally deterministic), or whether any degree of inference takes place. Clearly, an experimental evaluation would be inappropriate in the case of a simple logging process. In the case of the system described here, user actions are logged and compared with a fixed representation of likely sequences of actions and tasks. Deviations from the system's expectations, in combination with a log of simple action errors derived from the application expert, are then taken as evidence of a lack of user expertise. The system, therefore, makes inferences about users in the form of whether they are having difficulty or not. It was, therefore, decided to measure the correctness of these inferences of user difficulty. This was achieved by comparing system inferences of user difficulties directly with the user's own statements of their difficulties. The assessment metrics were the percentage of user difficulties successfully inferred by the system, and the number of false positive inferences of difficulties.

4.2 Assessing the Value of Adaptions

The first point that should be made about assessing the adaptions made by the exemplar is that they embody a theory, albeit a crude one, of human performance. The theory is that experienced users need little guidance, and are actively hindered by too much, while inexperienced users need more guidance and support.

Adaptions in the exemplar are made on the basis of a rolling average of errors made for the task concerned. If an error has recently been made for the fragment, the level is increased. If no errors are made, the rolling average decreases until it is below a threshold, when an adaption down is made. To assess whether an adaption has taken place it is, therefore, necessary to compare the levels called on the last occasion that the command was used. It was decided to use expert ratings to assess the value of adaptions, to avoid the need for directly questioning the user, as it was felt that this would draw the attention of the subject to the system's adaptivity rather than the task in hand. It was proposed, therefore, to rate each adaption as either useful or not useful, depending on the user's declared or apparent difficulties and what the user was trying to do.

4.3 Assessing the Overall Performance of the System

While an adaptive system may make correct inferences about users, and produce suitable adaptions based on these inferences, this is clearly not sufficient. The adaptions produced may result in a trivial increase in satisfaction and performance when considering the overhead incurred in extra processing and development time. Alternatively, users might genuinely dislike adaptive systems, preferring something static and predictable. Therefore, in common with the evaluation of static systems, a measure must be taken of the performance of the overall performance of the system. The basic requirements for this are an experimental task, a control, and some definition of what is meant by performance.

4.3.1 Experimental Task.
Given that the exemplar is a system for processing mail, some type of office activity was the most logical task. It was decided the subjects would play the role of a manager in a company, and would have as a task the job of processing a set number of letters. By adjusting the contents of the letters, it was possible to ensure that users covered a wide range of the system's commands.

4.3.2 Control.
A control is necessary as a comparison, so that regardless of what it is decided to measure, some reference is available with respect to which it is possible to interpret the results. It proved difficult to decide on a control. Initially, it was proposed to use the static system to which the exemplar was a front end. This proved impossible, as it was not practical to implement an adaptive system using a broadly equivalent MMI to the static system. Therefore, a second system was built, identical in all respects to the exemplar adaptive system, except that all dimensions of adaption were switched off.

4.3.3 Measures of Overall Performance.
There are many different levels at which the overall performance can be addressed, ranging from the lowest syntactic level (inter-character timings), to the highest task level (business cost effectiveness). It is important that any evaluation should aim to cover a spread of these different levels, because without information from lower levels, the causes for differences in performance at the highest levels may be impossible to determine. (The higher the level, the greater the importance of the measure; the use of measures at lower levels is primarily to aid the interpretation of measures at higher levels). It was decided to concentrate on three levels of measurement.

Command entry rate is a low level measure of performance, which takes no account of the accuracy or value of user entries. It is simply a measure of the quantity of input that the user achieves.

Task completion rate is a higher level of performance. By task completion is meant any discrete, categorizable success in the application domain. Some examples are reading a letter, writing a letter, posting a letter, deleting a letter, forwarding a letter, and creating a new folder.

Goal achievement rate is a still higher level of measurement. This is a measure of the user's effectiveness in terms of the task he has been set. For the exemplar system, this was defined as letter processing rate.

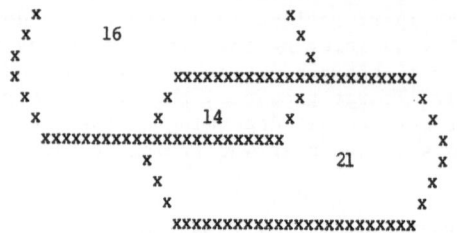

Number of difficulties stated by users

Figure 2.   System Inferences and User Statements of Difficulty.

4.4   Assessing User Reactions

In addition to testing the performance of the system/user combination, a measure of user's opinions is desirable. There is no point in producing powerful systems if they are not pleasant to use. A two section questionnaire was, therefore, devised. The first section assess the user's opinions of the ease of use of the system on a variety of functions. The second part of the questionnaire assesses whether users like the system or not. In this part of the questionnaire, users selected from a list of adjectives those that they thought applied to the system. An equal number of positive and negative descriptions were in the list, and they varied in the kinds of qualities that they assessed. By this spread of descriptions it was hoped that every user would be able to find at least some that he felt applied to the system. From the ratio of positive to negative comments, an overall measure of the perceived quality of the system was produced.

5.   EXPERIMENTAL DESIGN AND PROCEDURE

The experiment was designed to allow the comparison of the phase one exemplar with adaption, against a control of the same system with all adaptions inactive, and fixed at the default level of guidance. There were nine subjects. Subjects were of mixed levels of experience with computers. Six were computer experienced, three computer naive. Subjects used either the adaptive or non-adaptive system. Six subjects used the adaptive condition, three used the non-adaptive condition, balanced by previous experience across the conditions. One experienced subject in the non-adaptive condition had to be eliminated due to technical difficulties with the system.

Each subject used the system for three sessions, performing a different scenario in each session. Each session was separated by three days, and the order of scenario was randomized for each subject. Each session lasted for half an hour, timed from the first user entry after receiving

	Correct Direction	Incorrect Direction	Number Useful	Number not Useful
More Guidance	23	4	5	22
Less Guidance	26	15	0	41
Sub Totals	49	19	5	63
Total	68		68	

Figure 3.   Adaptions Classified by Direction, Usefulness, and Correctness.

the main system prompt. The subject's task during the session was to answer nine letters contained in their intray. Each session involved working on a different set of nine letters. Answering the letters involved performing a range of supporting tasks such as filing, deleting, forwarding, etc.

At the start of each session, subjects were given a one page guide to the system, a description of their task, and a list of users to which mail could be sent. Subjects were allowed to read the instructions until they were ready to start, and were asked to provide a running commentary to their actions. The experimenter was permitted to answer simple operational questions during the session, such as how to move the cursor, where various keys on the keyboard were. If the subject's commentary dried up, they were prompted to continue with the question 'What are you doing now?'.

After each session, subjects had a ten minute coffee break. They were then replayed a video of their session without their commentary. They were asked to explain, on every occasion that they typed something, what they were trying to achieve, and what problems they were having. Finally, subjects completed the two part questionnaire.

A log was kept of both system and user activity. This consisted of a time stamped:

Record of changes in the user model and application expert.

Log of individual keystrokes.

Log of carriage returns.

A recording of the screen, with the subject's commentary on one audio channel, and subsequent debriefing on the other was also made.

6.   RESULTS

A random sample of 180 user entries which could have resulted in adaptions was taken from the 24 sessions. For these 180 calls, Figure 2 illustrates the overlap between difficulties inferred by the system and those stated by users. The remaining calls (129) had neither user difficulties, nor system inferences of user difficulties associated with them.

The results show the system detected 40% of difficulties stated by users, at the expense of a false positive rate of 53%.

Figure 3 shows the 68 adaptions resulting from the 180 calls, broken down by direction, usefulness, and correctness of direction. Adaptions were counted as useful if they either helped a user overcome a difficulty, or helped the user achieve his immediate aim. Adaptions which did not help to overcome a difficulty or achieve an immediate aim were counted as not being useful. The direction of an adaption was assessed as being correct if it matched the user's statements of his difficulties or lack of difficulties, and in conflict if it was in the opposite direction.

Figures 4-6 show for each session, the number of commands entered, the number of tasks completed, and the number of letters processed for each experimental system.

To assess the relative effectiveness of users in the two conditions, the number of commands required for each letter processed are plotted in Figure 7. The lower the number of commands required for each letter, the greater the effectiveness of user operation.

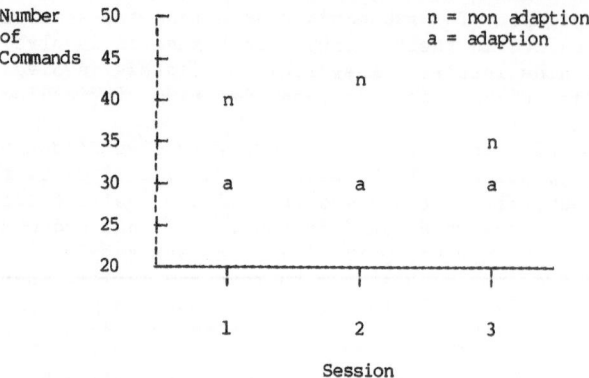

Figure 4. Plot of The Number of Commands
Entered in Each Session.

User ratings of the quality of operation of the two systems, and of
their acceptance of the systems are plotted in Figures 8 and 9. In Figure
8, the range of possible ratings is from 0 to 135.

7.   SUMMARY AND INTERPRETATION

The figures show a general performance advantage for the non-adaptive
condition, coupled with what appears to be faster learning. This is visible
from the lowest level of performance, commands entered, to the highest level,
letters processed. Examination of expert judgments of the usefulness of the
adaptions made throws some light on this; only 18% of adaptions to user
difficulties were counted as useful in overcoming the difficulty; none of
the adaptions to inferred user expertise were judged as useful. Overall
only 7% of adaptions were counted as useful. This is in contrast to the
hit rate for the system's inference of user difficulties, which was 40%.
It, therefore, appears that the system's ability to infer user difficulties
is rather higher than its ability to use this information.

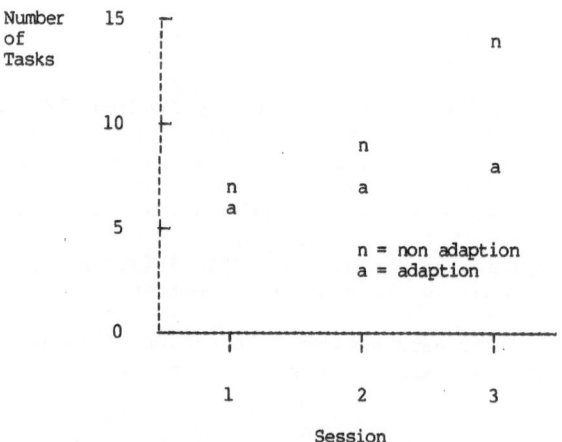

Figure 5. Plot of The Number of Tasks
Completed in Each Session.

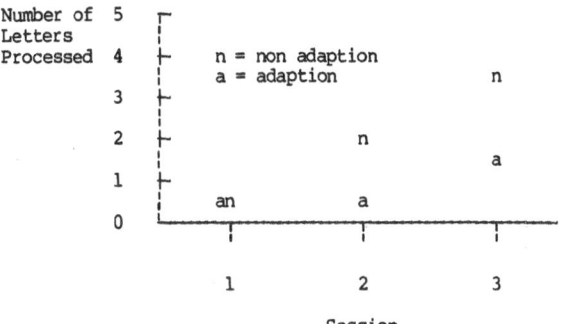

Figure 6. Plot of the Number of Letters
Processed in Each Session.

From the graphs of user reactions to the system, it appears that users
rate the quality of operation of both adaptive and non-adaptive systems
more highly as their experience increases, and suggest that users rate the
adaption condition more highly than the non-adaption condition, at least
for the first few sessions. However, user acceptance of the adaption condition appears to polarize against the system over the three sessions.

Overall, the results indicate that adaption as implemented was not
entirely successful. More important than differences between the two systems, however, is the low level of performance with both adaption and non-
adaption conditions. This suggests very strongly that there are important
factors at work which are unconnected with adaption.

8.   EXPLANATION OF RESULTS FROM OBSERVATION

8.1 MMI

As a result of the emphasis on adaption, the MMI of both adaption and
non-adaption conditions was poorer than was desirable. Additionally, design

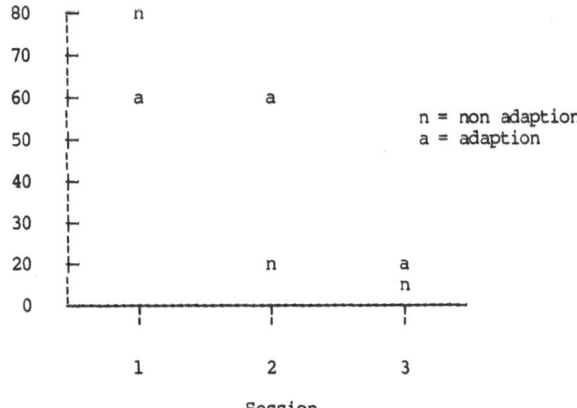

Figure 7. Plot of The Number of Commands/
Letter in Each Session.

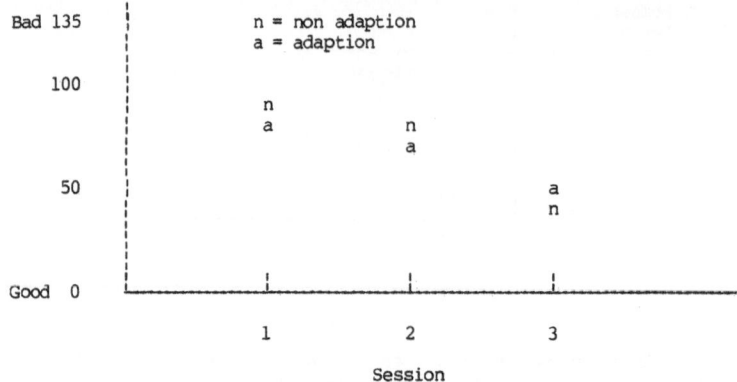

Figure 8. User Ratings of Quality of Operation.

constraints were imposed early on in the project which affected the quality of the interface. The performance of subjects in both conditions has suffered as a result.

More problems were caused in the adaptive condition than the non-adaptive condition, because in the former, the system was actively changing itself to suit the user's level of difficulty on the basis of its understanding of what the user was trying to do. Because users were confused, their actions were often somewhat random, making it hard for the system to do this. When considering building any adaptive front end, it is, therefore, important to consider the requirements that adaption places on the MMI.

8.2 Problems with Adaption Strategy

Several ways were noted of improving the system's strategy for adaption. The level of guidance is set individually for each dialogue fragment. Thus a user making mistakes with one command may be given high levels of guidance for that command, but not for another with which he has more experience. In the long term, this has the advantage of giving the system the flexibility to represent different levels of expertise with different

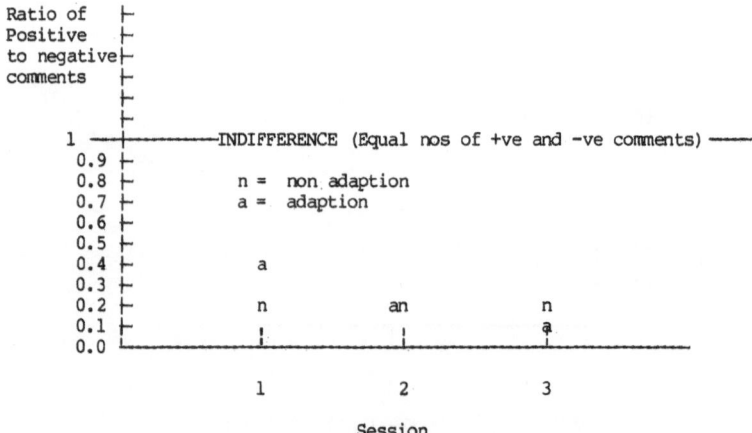

Figure 9. Ration of Positive to Negative Comments by Session.

parts of the system. In the shorter term, it may be unnecessarily conservative. This is because initially, the inexperience of a user in one part of a system may be taken as good evidence of a user's inexperience with all parts of a system. A simple approach to making the system more responsive would be to have an initial strategy of allowing adaptions to propagate to all dialogue fragments. Thus for a novice user, difficulties with one part of the system would be taken as evidence of low abilities with all parts of the system. (Inexperience is, of itself, sufficient grounds upon which to infer lack of ability.) As users gained in experience, then use could be made of the likely structure of knowledge in the domain to increase the scope of the systems inferences. For example, knowing that users have expertise in identifying letters to read may be taken as good evidence that they also have expertise with reading the letters. This is one of the strategies adopted by Sleeman (1984), in his User Modeling Front End. A refinement of this approach would be to cease propagating inferences to other areas of the domain as user's expertise increased. This would give added accuracy at the expense of power.

8.3 User's Model of Adaption

A further difficulty is that the way the system adapts is at odds with many people's expectations. Users expect the system to respond in a broadly consistent way to successive commands. However, because the system adapts to individual commands, it sometimes happens that the responses of the system can change markedly over a very short space of time. This happens when the user enters successive commands, each having a different level of associated expertise.

In addition, the 'grain' of adaptions is often at odds with user's model of the task. This became apparent from analysis of users statements of their difficulties. Rarely did such statements refer to difficulties at the level at which the system attempted to perform adaptions. Instead, users referred to difficulties associated with larger compound tasks, such as reading a letter, forwarding a letter, etc. There is clearly a great need for either a dimension of adaption which is not dependent on the user's level of task representation, or for the system to infer the level of representation at which the user is operating. Use could be made of timing information to do this.

8.4 Difficulties with Adaption Dimensions

At a more specific level, the prime dimensions of adaption, the guidance dimension, provided unsuitable. In fact, the whole approach of adaption through different levels of guidance is open to question. While it seems reasonable to assume that if users are in difficulty, more guidance would be useful, the other side of the coin, that we should take information away from users who are doing well seems less reasonable. It seems more likely that the content of the information should be changed as a result. Simply tailoring the amount of guidance given seems an insufficient response to user difficulty. Instead it might be hoped that on a richer understanding of the user, a more specific systems response aimed at the particular difficulty, or ability could be provided.

The context dimension also caused problems. The system maintains a track of user actions. If at any time a user entry does not match its list of expected user entries, a context switch is registered. On the next occasion that the user finishes something, the user is offered the option of returning to the command they abandoned. However, users were unfamiliar and unhappy with the idea of returning to a half completed command, and were often plainly baffled by the switch when it was offered to them. Many users accepted a context switch because they were confused, and did not want to run the risk of losing something important. The way in which returns were offered to users was confusing. The system offers to return to all of the options available from the point which had been reached, rather than in terms of the command entered to get there.

Even on theoretical grounds, the context-dimension seems a poor choice for an adaption dimension. First, users don't usually stop what they are doing. Users normally finish one task and then do another. If they do break off a command, it is usually for a good reason. Second, the facility places a great strain on the quality of the plan representations that the system contains. Any omission in the plan database will lead to unwanted offers of context switches. More importantly, differences in the grain of conceptualization of users and system are likely to have unpredictable, but negative, effects.

9. CONCLUSIONS

It is argued that adaptive systems can be evaluated by a simple extension of the methodologies used for non-adaptive systems. The crucial extension is the need to measure the abilities of the system at collecting information about the user, and the value of the adaptions that it produces as a result. A simple adaptive system has been evaluated using such a methodology. Given that adaptive systems are still at an early stage of development, the results presented give grounds for optimism. On purely common sense grounds, adaptive systems should be better than non-adaptive systems, and the question that is of real interest is, therefore, how best to build adaptive systems. The crucial requirement for this is a methodology that enables an adaptive system to be evaluated. This paper has shown how existing techniques may be applied, and the importance of combining simple measurement with observational studies in order to enable measured differences to be interpreted.

Although this first exemplar has not proved totally successful in terms of overall performance measures, it has succeeded in demonstrating that systems can be built which can identify user characteristics and problems, and change the interface accordingly. On the basis of evaluations like the one reported here, such early systems can be improved and developed to exploit the potential offered by truly adaptive systems. The next step in the project is to produce further demonstrator systems which make use of what has been learned from this phase of the project.

ACKNOWLEDGEMENT

I would like to thank the members of the Adaptive Intelligent Dialogues team at STC Technology Limited, Data Logic, Heriot-Watt University, the University of Strathclyde, the University of Essex, and British Telecom Research Laboratories for their contributions to the project. The AID project is partly funded by the UK's Alvey Programme for Advanced Information Technology and the Science and Engineering Research Council.

Acknowledgement is made to the Director of Research, British Telecom Research Laboratories, for permission to publish this paper.

Rapid/USE was developed jointly by the University of California and the Vrije Universitaet, Amsterdam, Netherlands.

REFERENCES

Alvey Committee, 1982, <u>A Programme for Advanced Information Technology</u>, HMSO ref ISBN 0 11 5136533.

Hardy, S., 1984, "Poplog: A New Software Environment for List Processing and Logic Programming", <u>Artificial Intelligence</u>, Harper and Row, pp. 110-136.

Moran, T. P., 1981, "An Applied Psychology of the User", <u>Computer Surveys</u>, <u>13</u>.

Rich, E., 1979, <u>Building and Exploiting User Models</u>, Building and Exploiting User Models, Ph.D. Thesis, Carnegie Mellon University.

Sleeman, D., and Brown, J. S., 1982, <u>Intelligent Tutoring Systems</u>, Academic Press.

DIADES: A DESIGN TOOL FOR INTERACTIVE PROGRAMS WITH PROVISIONS TO ASSESS

DESIGN DECISIONS ABOUT THE MAN-MACHINE INTERFACE

Hans-Juergen Hoffmann

Fachgebiet Programmiersprachen und Uebersetzer
Fachbereich Informatik, Department of Computer Science
Technische Hochschule Darmstadt, FB Informatik
Darmstadt Institute of Technology
Alexanderstr. 24
D-6100 Darmstadt, Germany

Abstract: A design tool for interactive programs, DIADES, presently under
development will be described. In the paper, the approach for design assessment employing an expert system will be highlighted. The concept "menu"
is used as an example.

INTRODUCTION

The DIADES project (Hoffmann, 1984) covers ongoing research work in
design methodology for interactive programs <u>and in</u> development of tools
<u>supporting the methodology</u>.

We see a lack of tools for designing interactive programs that, by
best expectations, will achieve a certain level of <u>user-friendliness</u> when
used. Thus, an essential aspect of DIADES is that it integrates an <u>expert
system for design assessment</u>.* Other important components of DIADES are a
<u>specification editor</u> (based on an adequate visualization of design concepts
and able to act as an interaction simulator) and a <u>program generator</u>.

The specification editor, the expert system for design assessment, and
the generator access a <u>common design data base</u>. It is organized following
well developed techniques of knowledge representation in a <u>semantic net-
work/frame net</u>. Here all design decisions as provided by a programmer in

---

*Earlier we used the term "evaluation" instead of "assessment". We changed
the terminology for three reasons:

- The main goal of the "assessment" is not a (score) value but
  an identification of weak design decisions.

- Overlapping terminology with "attribute evaluation" in the
  design data base.

- (Hopefully) better adherence to English terminology.

his work with the specification editor are instantiated from conceptual knowledge covering (a wide segment of) the universe of features relevant both for generation of interactive programs (in a scope as traditionally provided by design tools like template generators, interaction sequence generators and the like) and for assessment (the challenging goal to be achieved under the DIADES project). Thus, the design decisions will become factual knowledge structured according to conceptual relations expressed in the conceptual knowledge mentioned above.

As it is a problem in itself to build up an adequate universe of conceptual knowledge (a problem that will not be addressed under a general view in the paper at hand) this approach is flexible enough to start with even a small segment of the universe and to investigate the implications of those features covered (implications both for generation and for the assessment of design decisions). One such segment covers menu handling, an important and characterizing aspect of work with an interactive program (the segment that will give the examples to be discussed in the paper at hand).

Psychology, cognitive science, and ergonomics have intensively studied menu handling. There are comprehensive collections of what is called design guidelines for menu handling. One can not expect that the designer of an interactive program will correctly follow all the guidelines (to take for granted that the guidelines are well established); the designer of an interactive program will be 'ham-handed' or even will make errors in deciding how the program will handle menus, too. Here, we think that an assessment of design decisions gains its motivation (as it does in other programming areas, e.g., by strong typing in designing non-interactive programs with respect to their algorithmic correctness).

DIADES provides an expert system to do such as assessment. It understands the conceptual knowledge in the design data base (the requirements of design assessment, of course, will influence -- and have influenced -- the amount and the interrelations of conceptual knowledge contained in the data base); it accesses the factual knowledge derived from the design decisions of the programmer; and it has inferential knowledge build-up (by the designers of DIADES) from guidelines in order to allow the design assessment intended.

In the paper at hand this approach will be discussed. First, an architectural overview will be given. The scope of conceptualization required will be worked out next. Conceptual knowledge on menu handling will be considered as an example. Then, relevant guidelines will be identified and the methodological build-up of inferential knowledge representing them will be discussed.

ARCHITECTURAL OVERVIEW OF DIADES

A DIADES-built interactive program is understood to be roughly structured as shown in Figure 1. A reader should compare this architectural structure with that of similar developments (Olsen et al., 1984; Hartson et al., 1983; Hartson and Johnson, 1984; Kamran and Feldman, 1984) which certainly have influenced our thinking.

There is a set of program modules called application modules that (are programmed in a traditional way, e.g., as a set of MODULA 2-modules) perform when activated application oriented tasks (like calculations, like tasks investigating and editing data structures representing application data, like tasks controlling other equipment in a control room, etc). The modules are not closed in themselves; they have an open interface under which

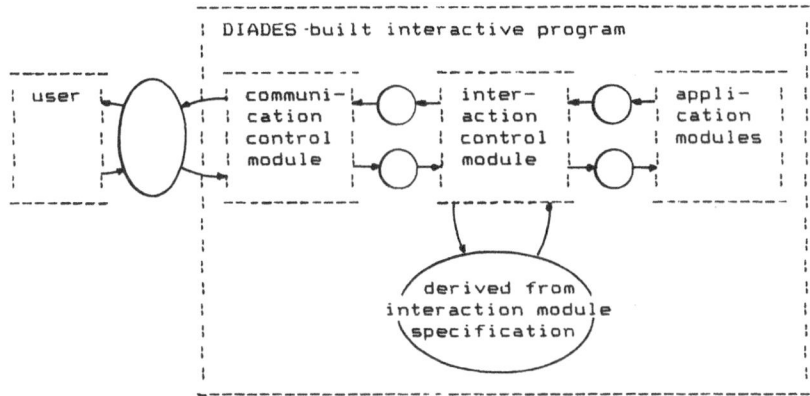

Figure 1. Architecture of DIADES-Built
Interactive Programs.

parameterizing and controlling data is supplied, through which additional
data is requested from the outside, if required, and to which data describing
their state is transmitted. In case the interface would be connected to a
controlling program module (a "main"-module) a complete, closed application
program would be available. And, the expectations of the application modules
on the behavior of the main module could be specified in the usual way in
what we call application-interface specification. No user interaction would
take place.

In an interactive situation the behavior of the main-module (which is
not present in such a system) has to be simulated by activities originating
from user manipulation (Hoffmann, 1983). User activities can not be programmed; in order that a user acts as expected according to the application-
interface specifications more information should be made available to him
permanently or upon request; all information presented to him has to be
communicated as data in a way so that he easily can conceive it; his activities may be erroneous (i.e., not in correspondence with the application-
interface specifications -- formal errors -- and/or not appropriate to
achieve a goal that the user has set for himself in communication with the
application modules -- intentional errors --). In other words, there has
to be an interaction control module which, on one side, guarantees to support
the application-interface specifications and, on the other side, inserts
data representing additional information as required for the user and ex-
tracts data to be directed to the application modules also from erroneous
user input -- may be as the result of a "dialogue excursion" demanding
corrections by the user --. Here, we have an interaction-module specification. User interaction and its treatment are the main areas to be covered
in the specification.

In communicating data to and from the user device characteristics
(i.e., mainly of screens, of key boards, of pick devices) play a certain
role. However, we want them not influencing the interaction-module specification. This has two implications:

● The interaction-module specification is "task-oriented"
  (to explain this by an example, an interaction situation
  where a user should make a decision and should communicate the outcome of his decision through the interaction
  control module to the application modules is considered
  as a task that, according to the designer's decision in
  in the interaction-module specification, is realized by

165

a menu selection), not "device-oriented" (stating -- to continue the example -- that menu markers like "*" should be put by user manipulations into column position, say, i; something that definitely is not adequate for a pop-up menu under mouse manipulation).

- There has to be a <u>communication control module</u> in the communication channel between the user and the interaction control module. It takes care of device characteristics translating data flow from the task-oriented form to the device-oriented form and vice versa. And, that communication control module is not derived from any design specification; it is inherent to the device considered and -- idealistically -- implemented by the supplier of the device*).

Of course, all communication control modules have to be able to handle all communication tasks eventually occurring under control of any interaction-module specification.

Up to now we have considered <u>run-time</u> only, i.e., an interactive application program as it works and services provided to have user interactions supported. So far user-friendliness aspects are not discussed. We only could consider what a communication control module contributes (or does not contribute) to a general, device dependent quality measure. However, this is not the topic of the paper at hand (and would have to be discussed for every module separately).

User-friendliness and provisions to achieve it are <u>design-time</u> considerations. So, we understand that the DIADES approach is directed also (and mainly!) towards the design process for an interactive program. And, we understand that the interaction-module specifications play the most important role as there are (device independent, task-oriented) design decisions for how interactions are handled and concentrated.

Again, we will start the discussion by presenting an architectural diagram, Figure 2. The design assessment component identified here will not be found in more traditionally developed design tools for interactive programs. It is the contribution of the DIADES project.

To prepare the discussion of implications of the decision to include a design assessment component in the design tool, we briefly have to cover the other components (although they are not a main topic of the paper at hand).

The central component of the tool is the <u>design data base</u>. It is the component that handles the representation of the interaction-module specification. Insofar, we understand the specification more to be an internal description than to be a traditional, textual design specification in some kind of a formal language. Therefore, the structure of the contents of a specification, i.e., the description of the complex interdependencies under concept instantiations derived from task-oriented design decisions, is of higher importance than formal, analytical structure.** Definitely, the

---

* As developers of DIADES we plan to provide communication control modules just for those devices that are used in our installation. They are integrated (linked) into any DIADES built program when a user logs in through a supported device.

**This does not mean that a specification could be (and has to be formulated for external purposes in a formal language style where an analytical structure is impressed upon the language constructs.

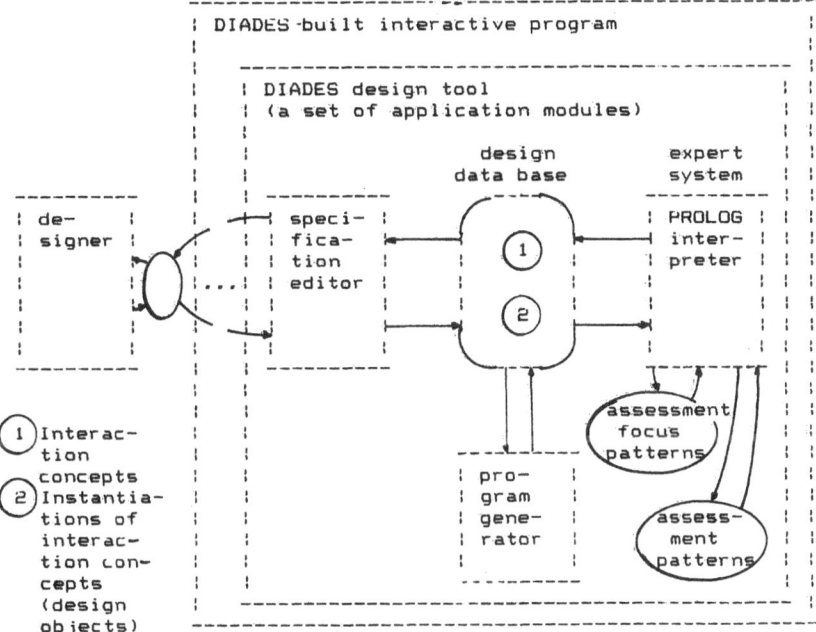

Figure 2.   Structure of The DIADES Design Tool.

traditionally utilized textual string or tree-like structure of programs/spe-
cifications in programming environments is too weak to represent what we
want to be represented in a specification. We have chosen a representation
derived from methods of knowledge representation in artificial intelligence
research, viz., a semantic network/frame net as proposed, e.g., in papers
by Brachman (1977; 1978), Minsky (1975), and Hayes (1979)*. This approach
allows us to represent also the <u>conceptual knowledge</u> about the design universe in the design data base. An interaction module specification consists
of appropriate instantiations of (task-oriented) design concepts as <u>factual</u>
<u>knowledge</u> with all necessary links established under the network nodes
(i.e., slots in the frame net terminology). This approach offers the advantage that the components accessing the data base do not have to have any
embedded structural knowledge about details of the design universe. They
access the conceptual knowledge to control their operation; and they access
the factual knowledge as data to be manipulated by the operations.

We will recur to the approach of knowledge representation chosen in
another section below. There an example will be given (covering the concept
"menu") also. The <u>specification editor</u> specification editor is a structure-oriented editor; it is the component that makes the design data base
accessible for and accessible by the designer to inform him about design
concepts, to inform him about details of his design already instantiated,
and to collect his design decisions in order to continue the instantiation.
Conceptual knowledge accessible in the design data base controls its operation. Already instantiated design decisions and design decisions to be
newly instantiated, i.e., factual knowledge, are the data manipulated by
the operations.

We have some ideas how the interface to the designer as realized by

_____

*The entity-relationship approach of data base research is rather
 similar to what we intend to do.

the specification editor should look like. We call it <u>specification by example</u>. It employs visual aids as far as possible. Detailed discussion of this approach, again, is not the topic of the paper at hand (Hoffmann, 1986(a)). (Meta-)conceptual knowledge contained in the design data base has to provide factual knowledge about the designer's interface (VISUALIZE_AS-slot of concepts).*

Similarly, the <u>program generator</u> is a structure-oriented generator. Again, (meta-)conceptual knowledge accessible in the design data base controls its operation (GENERATE_AS-slot).**

The <u>design assessment component</u> is, in the same sense, structure-oriented too. The (meta-)conceptual knowledge controlling its operation is provided in the ASSESS_AS-slots. So far, this is a statement on implementation techniques. It is more important to discuss how the assessment is achieved.

The quality standard of man-machine interfaces is nothing that can be postulated or defined per se. Thus, a yes/no, deterministic assessment is not possible, makes no sense. It is a complex field of criteria derived from research and practical experience in areas like psychology, cognitive science, and ergonomics, that constitute knowledge about what man-machine interface can be attributed to be of a high quality standard. It is a changing field of criteria influenced by technology evolution, even by sociological movement. There is no chance to have the knowledge about quality standards stated in a set of logic formulas. Nevertheless, a method for assessment has to be found, interactive programs are in daily use and their user-friendliness have to be improved. Dzida et al., (1979) proposed to have an assessment by human experts when a design effort is terminated. The initiative to start the DIADES project came from reading this proposal, yet the human experts replaced by an <u>expert system for design assessment</u>.

As we do not intend to perform basic research in expert system development, our approach for implementing the design assessment component of DIADES as an expert system is to code it in PROLOG. Later in this paper, we discuss the structure of the assessment program. Here, it only has to be mentioned that the constituents of the assessment program are found in the ASSESS_AS-slot as (meta-)conceptual knowledge in the design data base.

The design assessment component is activated by the designer whenever he has completed a substantial part of the design of an interactive program***, certainly whenever he thinks that the design effort is carried through. Then, the expert system has to assess the design decisions in their totality, giving evidence of the quality level of user-friendliness

---

*Meta-conceptual knowledge is conceptual knowledge of the design process describing how conceptual and factual knowledge about the design universe has to be handled by components of the design tool. Its representation is not distinguished from the representation of conceptual knowledge, its instantiation, however, is factual knowledge linked through, here, the VISUALIZE_AS-slot to concept nodes.

**It is not of much interest whether the generation process tends more to get a compiled program text (that implies that the interaction control module is a program module like the others -- an approach to which we give preference --) or more to get interpretable code (that implies that a general interaction control module, working interpretatively, has to be at disposal).

***At the moment it is an open research topic what "substantial" has to mean here.

achieved as well as -- even more important! -- explaining the assessment process, identifying unfavorable design decisions.

One should notice that all components accessing the design data base have some specific needs in conceptualization. This is especially true for the design assessment component: in order to be able to perform an assessment the designer has to provide more than only a technical specification (useful for the generation process); there are additional specification requirements, e.g., on the intention of interactions, on interrelations between data elements communicated in a single unit, on timing etc., that have to be conceptualized in the design data base and that have to be handled by the specification editor.

We can summarize the architectural overview. DIADES (essentially) consists of:

- A run-time module -- the module that we call interaction control module -- operating according to what has been generated from a specific interaction-module specification, linked with the set of application modules.

- A set of communication control modules, one for each device supported.

- The design data base initialized by conceptual (and meta-conceptual) knowledge.

- The specification editor, controlled by VISUALIZE_AS-knowledge.

- The program generator, controlled by GENERATE_AS-knowledge.

And, last, but definitely not least:

- The design assessment component (expert system), controlled by ASSESS_AS-knowledge.

CONCEPTUAL KNOWLEDGE IN THE DESIGN DATA BASE

The design tool components accessing the design data base are structure oriented. The structuralization of the knowledge accessed is not only of a uniform manner.* Therefore, a (meta-)structuralization has to be employed that allows flexibility in expressing the structure of concepts and of instantiations. Semantic networks/frame nets as introduced by Brachman, Minsky, and Hayes serve that purpose. We prefer a notation derived from Brachman's approach.

To remind the reader we list below the set of so-called epistemological (i.e., meta-structural, non-taxonomical) links** as introduced by Brachman (1977). We characterize the links (slots) by their signature:

- DATTR;   concept_node -> role_description_node

- ROLE: role_description_node ->
                SET_OF_INSTANTIATIONS_OF (Functional_roles)

---

*As it is in a compiler for a programming language where almost all structurization of programs is in tree-form.
**We will not list the link types for concept creation.

note: This is the most important link type that
that allows introducing the different "roles"
of a concept,* roles that may be used to
attach values (see below) and/or to establish the application dependent links between
design notions and their instantiations as
design objects, resp.

- V/R: role_description_node -> concept_node
                   (V/R stands for "value restriction".)

- NUMBER: role_description_node -> PREDICATE

- MODALITY: role_description_node ->
                       SET_OF_INSTANTIATIONS_OF (System_roles)

- DEFAULT: role_description_node -> V/R (self))

- INSTANCE_OF: instance_node -> concept_node

- ATTR: instance_node -> role_instance_node

- INSTANTIATES: role_instance_node -> role_description_node

- VALUE: role_instance_node -> value_node

- S/C: concept_node ->
                       union (PREDICATE,
                           SET_OF_INSTANTIATIONS_OF (Concept))
                   (S/C stands for "structural condition")

- E/R: concept_node -> FORMULA
                   (E/R stands for "evaluation rule")**

Note that the S/C- and E/R-links are not instantiated (i.e., there is
no counterpart that serves as a link between design objects).

For our purposes, i.e., to provide the information controlling the
components of the design tool we add further link types, the so-called
control links, also not to be instantiated in design objects.

- VISUALIZE_AT: concept_node ->
                 SET_OF_INSTANTIATIONS_OF (Design_dialogue)

- ASSESS_AS: concept_node ->
                 SET_OF_INSTANTIATIONS_OF
                     (Assessment_focus_and_assessment pattern)

---

*Roughly, roles correspond to slots as identified in frames.
**The E/R-link is not identified in Brachman (1977). We think
  that, at least in the application to design data bases that
  have to be able to represent interaction module specifications
  such a link type is useful and is required (Hoffman, 1986(b)).
***To use a very popular term, this can be considered an "object
  oriented" representation of knowledge; design objects (i.e.,
  design concepts from which design objects are instantiated)
  know how they are to be visualized for design, how they are
  to be generated, and how they are to be mapped under the
  generation process.

- GENERATE_AS: concept_node ->
                 SET_OF_INSTANTIATIONS_OF (Generation_pattern)

Their meaning, especially that of the ASSESS_AS-slot, will be discussed
below.

To be able to formulate the control links, appropriate concepts have
to be available. In the scope of a tool for design of interactive programs
this is easy for the VISUALIZE_AS-slots: Conceptism, may be somehow specialized*, that are already included in the design universe, viz., "design
dialogues", are employed. For GENERATE_AS-slots, in general, structural
mappings from instantiations of design concepts into program text fragments
are employed; this is a standard technique of compiler design. Concepts
required for the ASSESS_AS-slot will be discussed in the section on assessment strategy.

In Figure 3, we exemplify the conceptualization by describing the
concept "menu". Note, that it is easy to change details of the conceptualization. The notation used should be self-explanatory. We are not
much interested in syntactical details as long as an analytical structure
is maintained that allows us to derive the internal representation in the
semantic net/frame net that we want to use automatically. Certainly, the
wording used in the example is too clumsy; consider this somehow as comments.

DESIGN GUIDELINES

Of course, by stating that we try to solve the problem of assessing
user-friendliness of interactive programs by replacing human experts with an
expert system we state only half of the truth. The knowledge of human
experts has to be available and has to be acquainted (manually) by the
expert system. It has to be knowledge about what the characteristics of a
good design are _and_ knowledge about the assessment process itself. As
computer scientists, here, we cannot provide this knowledge. What we can
provide is a methodology to structure the knowledge, to represent it in the
computer, and to develop tools for its accessing. The knowledge itself has
to be collected by scientists working in the relevant disciplines** and has
to be prepared for acquisition by the design data base, to be concise,
in the form of (meta-)conceptual knowledge filling the ASSESS_AS-slots.

We want to exemplify this process. From one of the available collections of "Design Guidelines for User-System Interface Software" (Smith and
Mosier, 1984) we take the first guideline on menu selection (guideline
3.1.3-1):

    Consider menu selection for tasks that involve choice among a
    relatively constrained set of alternative actions, that require
    little entry of arbitrary data, where users may have relatively
    little training, and where computer response is relatively fast.

Typically -- and just as good for our purpose --, it is task-oriented,
describing a situation that may occur in an interaction sequence. Therefore,
we will include the knowledge expressed in this guideline in the design data
base under the ASSESS_AS-slot of the concept "step in an interaction

---

*Specialization is handled by one of the link types for concept
 creation not treated here.
**We are in cooperation with colleagues working there.

```
CONCEPT Menu WITH
    ROLES #_of_entries: V/R = {n|n>1}, NR = 1, required, DFLT = 2;
        #_of_hidden_entries: V/R = {m|m≥0}, NR = 1, optional;
        markings_for_selection: V/R = Marker_combination,
            NR = S/C#1 ( VALUE ( #_of_entries ) ), required,
            DFLT = {(x,-), (-,x)};
        accessed_from: V/R = Path_in_decision_network, NR ≥ 1,
            required, DFLT = Empty_path
                    AS_AN_INSTANTIATION_OF Path_in_decision_network;
        level: V/R = Length_of_path, NR = 1, (required, derived),
            DFLT = 0;
        menu_identification: V/R = TEXT, NR = 1,
            (optional, defaulted), DFLT = 'Main menu';
        explanation: V/R = TEXT, NR = 1, optional;
        prompt: V/R = TEXT, NR = 1, (optional, defaulted),
            DFLT = 'Select one item';
        task: V/R = Tasks, NR ≥ 1, optional;
        bypass: V/R = Commands, NR ≥ 1, optional;
        #_of_defaulted_entries: V/R = S/C#2 (
                VALUE (#_of_entries), VALUE (#_of_hidden_entries) ),
            NR = 1, (optional, defaulted), DFLT = 0;
        identification_of_defaulted_entry:
            V/R = Pair_entry_identification_and_entry_marker,
            NR = S/C#3 ( VALUE ( #_of_defaulted_entries ) ),
            required;
        reconfirmation: V/R = BOOLEAN, NR = 1,
            (optional, defaulted), DFLT = true;
        entries: V/R = Menu_entry, NR = S/C#4 (
                VALUE (#_of_entries), VALUE (#_of_hidden_entries) ),
            (required, ordered), DFLT#1 = Uninitialized_menu_entry
                            AS_AN_INSTANTIATION_OF Menu_entry,
            DFLT#2 = Uninitialized_menu_entry
                            AS_AN_INSTANTIATION_OF Menu_entry;
    S/C#1: ( Lambda x: {p|p≥x} );
    S/C#2: ( Lambda x, y: {p|0≤p≤x+y} );
    S/C#3: ( Lambda x: {p|p=x} );                fig._3
    S/C#4: ( Lambda x, y: {p|p=x+y} );           (part of) a semantic
    E/R#1: VALUE (level) := ... ;                net/frame net for the
    VISUALIZE_AS: ... .                          design notion "menu"
    ASSESS_AS. ... .
    GENERATE_AS: ... .
CONCEPT Marker_combination WITH ... .
CONCEPT Menu_choice WITH ... .
CONCEPT Path_in_decision_network WITH ... .
CONCEPT Length_of_path WITH ... .
CONCEPT Tasks WITH ... .
CONCEPT Commands WITH ... .
CONCEPT Pair_entry_identification_and_entry_marker WITH ... .
CONCEPT Menu_entry WITH ... .
```

Figure 3. Conceptualization by Concept "Menu".

sequence"*. Based upon the structural links, INSTANCE_OF and INSTANTIATES,
of design objects "menu choice" instantiated from the concept considered, as
well as based upon structural links to nodes of concepts and design objects,
somehow "in the neighborhood" achieve what we call the "assessment focus
patterns". They identify the "cut" in the design data base that has to be
considered when the relevance of a guideline for the assessment process has
to be determined**. At the moment we do not see a way different from that
to code the assessment focus patterns individually for all concept nodes in
the PROLOG language taking into account where the cut has to be made.***
In Hoffmann (1985), some typical situations are described.

---

*To be more concise; in that specialization of the concept "step in
 an interaction sequence" which is a "menu choice".
**Note that also the non-occurrence of a cut, i.e., a situation that
 is not covered by an assessment focus pattern, may be important
 for the assessment process.

As a comment added to the guideline, formatting of lengthy menus in the form of separate menu displays is mentioned by Smith and Mosier (1984). We have to conceptualize a "network" of menu displays,* where the "menu"-concept may be instantiated as often as decided by the designer. The gateway to the network is through the "menu choice"-concept mentioned above. In our conceptualization of "menu" given above, the accessed_from- and the level-role is a sketchy indication of the consideration of menu networks.**

From the viewpoint of PROLOG-programming, what we have established by inclusion of the assessment focus patterns are access-paths to factual knowledge.

BUILD-UP OF INFERENTIAL KNOWLEDGE FOR DESIGN ASSESSMENT

Now, the assessment of an instantiation of a "menu choice" has to quantify the term "lengthy" and has to relate it to the menu network structure found in the design data base (following the "accessed_by"-links in the instantiations of menus). It has to quantify the term "little entry of arbitrary data". Typically, we have found here a situation where "technical" decisions for the interface-module specification have to be assessed. Another example of the same kind could be derived from the condition "constrainted set of alternative actions".***

Also, one has to quantify the amount of training that can be attributed to the user. A designer should have a conception of what user group the interactive program he is designing is intended, whether it is a user group with "relatively little training" or not. This is a situation where additional specification requirements have to be met by the designer making a statement on the training level as a (quasi-)design decision. A similar argument can be used with respect to the condition "computer response is relatively fast" although it looks somewhat more technical (and probably it would be good if statements on timing also would influence the generation process or would be taken into account at run-time depending on the actual machine timings observed.**** We can record that also non-technical design decisions covered by additional specification requirements have to be assessed.

Together with the assessment focus patterns already introduced we provide what we call "assessment patterns". They control, based upon the outcome of the execution of the assessment focus patterns involved, the assessment process. They combine the contribution of all design decisions (as represented in the design objects instantiated in the design data base) to the overall quality measures on user-friendliness which the expert system makes evident for the designer. And, by observing the inference process, they help to explain how the combined quality measure has been achieved

---

*In fact, they are even not included in the design data base but are stored separately -- see Figure 2 --.
**Instead of "menu display" we use the term "menu" in the sequel, the section on conceptualization.
***We do not restrict the consideration to menu trees.
****Note that our approach of conceptualization of design notions and of structure-orientation of the tool components deriving the structural knowledge from conceptual descriptions that can easily be modified gives here much flexibility. We as developers of the DIADES design tool have not fixed a lot of those concepts; they can be adapted to the imagination of the people preparing DIADES for use by designers in a specific area. Insofar, we consider DIADES to be a "system development shell" (Hoffmann, 1986(c)).

(identifying unfavorable design decisions). Again, at the moment we do not see a different way to code the assessment patterns individually in PROLOG. Typical situations again are described in Hoffmann (1985).

CONCLUDING REMARKS

The conceptualization of design notions relevant in the design of <u>and</u> in the design assessment for interactive programs is a huge task. We can only cover some areas. Menu design is one such area where we already have done some conceptualization. This allows us to test and, hopefully, to demonstrate the feasibility of the approach taken in the DIADES development for assessment of design decisions about the man-machine interface. At the moment, we push the implementation of the design tool with the components described.

ACKNOWLEDGEMENT

The DIADES project covers, as already mentioned, ongoing research work. There are contributions by J. Bergmann, D. Keyer, B. Kostka, T. Milbredt and others. Discussions with colleagues leading to an outside project proposal are gratefully acknowledged.

REFERENCES

Brachman, R. J., 1977, "What's in a Concept, Structural Foundations for Semantic Networks", <u>Intl. J. Man-Machine Studies</u>, <u>9</u>, pp. 127-152.

Brachman, R. J., 1978, <u>On the Epistemological Status of Semantic Networks</u>, BBN Report No. 3807, Bolt Beranek and Newman Inc., April 1978.

Dzida, W., et al., 1979, "A Multidimensional Approach Towards User-Oriented Definitions of Reliability", <u>Workshop on Reliable Software</u>, Raulefs, P., ed., C. Hanser, München Wien, 1979, pp. 247-255.

Hartson, D. R., et al., 1983, <u>The Management of Dialogue for Human-Computer Interfaces</u>, Virginia Polytechnic Institute and State University, Blacksburg, Virginia.

Hartson, D. R., and Johnson, D. H., 1984, <u>Dialogue Management, New Concepts in Human-Computer Interface Development</u>, Virginia Polytechnic Institute and State University, Blacksburg, Virginia.

Hayes, P. J., 1979, "The Logic of Frames", <u>Frame Conceptions and Text Understanding</u>, Metzing, ed., deGruyter, Berlin, New York.

Hoffman, H.-J., 1983, "Anwendung von Spezifikationstechniken auf die Komponente >> Bediener << eines interaktiven Systems", <u>Psychologie des Programmierens</u>, Schauer, H., and Tauber, M., eds., R. Oldenbourg, Wien München, pp. 211-251.

Hoffmann, H.-J., 1984, <u>DIADES -- Ein Entwurfssystem für die Mensch-Maschine-Schnittstelle interaktionsfähiger Systeme; Notizen zu Interaktiven Systemen</u>, <u>Heft 12</u>, März 1984, pp. 59-69.

Hoffmann, H.-J., 1985, <u>Research Work in Design Methodology for Interactive Programs -- On the Methodology to Code, in a Knowledge Bank, Rules Phrased in Natural Language, Discussed by an Example</u>, in press.

Hoffmann, H.-J., 1986(a), <u>On the Visualization of Design Notions, of Notion Instantiations, and of Structural Relationships in a Design Data Base Realized as a Semantic Net</u>, in press.

Hoffmann, H.-J, 1986(b), <u>On Context Conditions and Attribute Evaluation in Tree-Structured and Network-Structured Design Data Bases</u>, in press.

Hoffmann, H.-J., 1986(c), <u>DIADES as an Example of a System Development Shell</u>, in preparation.

Kamran, A., and Feldman, M. B., 1984, "Graphics Programming Independent of Interaction Techniques and Styles", <u>ACM Computer Graphics</u>, <u>17</u>, (1), pp. 58-66.

Minsky, M., 1975, "A Framework for Representing Knowledge", <u>The Psychology of Computer Vision</u>, Winston, P., ed., McGraw-Hill, pp. 211-277.

Olsen, D. R., et al., 1984, "A Context for User Interface Management; Computer Graphics & Applications", <u>IEEE</u>, <u>4</u>, (12).

Smith, S. L., and Mosier, J. N., 1984, <u>Design Guidelines for User-System Interface Software</u>, Report MTR-9420, The MITRE Corp., Bedford, Mass., September 1984.

AN OUTLINE OF TECHNIQUES FOR EVALUATING THE HUMAN-COMPUTER INTERFACE

Stephen Howard* and Dianne M. Murray**

*National Physical Laboratory
Teddington, Middlesex
United Kingdom
**Ergonomics Unit
University College
London
United Kingdom

Abstract: Although evaluation is seen as a crucial stage in the development of computer systems, a number of problems beset the evaluator of a human-computer interface. Firstly, there is a poor understanding of the theoretical underpinnings of many techniques developed by the behavioral sciences. Secondly, the way in which the utility of each possible technique will vary with differing evaluation environments is not well understood. Thirdly, there is little advice available to aid the evaluator in the selection of an evaluation package.

A recent wide-ranging literature review is summarized from which five different forms of evaluation can be identified and a variety of currently used techniques categorized. Two possible taxonomies, one based upon criteria such as validity and reliability and one based upon a proposed evaluation environment, are discussed. Neither of the taxonomies alone are adequate in aiding in the selection of an evaluation package; however, aspects of both may prove useful in the future.

INTRODUCTION

Why And When to Evaluate?

The proliferation of computing systems in the public domain, available to both naive and occasional users, has meant that there is now a greater requirement for computer systems which are fully functional while still being easy to use and quick to learn.

It is often suggested that, in order to achieve this state, a specific evaluation stage should be included in the design cycle of all computer systems. Without such an evaluation stage, the valid and reliable data required to supplement the designer's model of the user (based on general knowledge derived from past experience of similar situations, intuition, and hearsay) remains absent (Norman, 1986).

Moreover, if evaluation takes place incrementally, throughout the whole of the system design process, then a number of advantages are evident. A way of evaluating a chosen design solution, and also data upon which present and future design decisions can be based, is provided. Information can be made available sufficiently early (preferably at the conceptual stage of design) to avoid major and costly design changes and thus increase the likelihood that any required changes will actually be implemented.

What Is Evaluation?

Evaluation is an activity which provides information on some aspect of a system for the purpose of designing or assessing the system and which is conducted in a specific context. The generality of this definition allows for market success and long term system use (or non-use) to also be considered valid and useful, if informal, sources of data.

Any evaluation method should provide at the very least a means of collecting and organizing the data. There may, in some circumstances, also be a requirement for suitable ways of interpreting the data in line with certain principles.

Present Deficiencies of The Evaluation Process

Three main deficiencies can be identified:

- Firstly, there is a poor understanding of the theoretical underpinnings of the many techniques derived from other disciplines.

- Secondly, the way in which the utility of each technique will vary with differing evaluation environments is not well understood.

- Finally, while the consequences of using an inappropriate evaluation technique may range from unnecessary expenditure of resources to the collection of data irrelevant to the evaluation questions posed (and the making of specific recommendations on the basis of this information), there is little advice available to aid an evaluator in the selection of an evaluation package.

Rather, evaluation techniques are chosen haphazardly, either because they are the only ones known or because they have worked in the past in other evaluation environments. The selection of evaluation techniques appears to be conducted independently of the specification of the evaluation objectives (and, therefore, the information necessary to achieve those objectives).

In order to avoid collecting useless or unnecessarily large amounts of data, the following evaluation procedure is proposed:

- Specify evaluation objectives/problems.

- Decide on information necessary to achieve those objectives.

- Choose techniques capable of providing that information.

- Collect and analyze data.

- Make recommendations.

178

The choice of the evaluation technique is thus made contingent upon the specification of the evaluation objectives.

PREVIOUS WORK: INVESTIGATION OF EVALUATION TECHNIQUES

Identified Main Types of Evaluation

We draw the distinction between formal and informal evaluation. Formal evaluation involves the evaluator in the systematic collection and analysis of data whereas informal evaluation involves the evaluator (often the designer) in subjective assessment during interface design. We are concerned here with formal evaluation, although we acknowledge the fact that, not only does informal evaluation occur, but in many circumstances this may be the only form of evaluation conducted.

A wide-ranging literature search produced some forty references involving various aspects of interface evaluation. From these it was possible to identify five main types of formal evaluation:

Expert-Based	Commonly called human factors walk-through, where an ergonomics expert may employ expert knowledge, scientific principles, and intuition to evaluate the interface (Maclean et al, 1985(a); Martin, Carlisle, and Treu, 1973).
Theory-Based	Where the mapping relationships between formal representations of the user and the device are examined with a view to identifying any mismatch (Kieras and Poulson, 1985).
Subject-Based	Consists of four main components - metric, task, user and system.
	Data collection may involve running naive or practiced subjects under laboratory conditions.
	Data collection techniques range from traditional reaction time type experiments to multi-user attitude surveys.
	Data on a user may be collected at four different levels - affective, cognitive, behavioral, and physiological.
	Data from one level of the user alone is likely to be insufficient. For example, it is possible to maintain performance with respect to some criteria by varying the amount of effort invested in the task, measures of primary task performance alone would not be sensitive to this. Data should be collected from at least two, if not three, levels of the user.
	Table 1 lists the subject-based techniques presently discernible from the literature.
	(Barrett, Thornton, and Cabe, 1968; Hammond et al.,1984; (Penniman and Dominick, 1980; Meister and Sullivan, 1967; Maclean et al., 1985(b); Meister and Sullivan, 1967; Levine,

179

1978; Anders-Ericsson and Simon, 1984; O'Malley,
Draper, and Riley, 1984; Rushinek and Rushinek,
1984; Peach and Easterby, 1973; Monk, 1986)

User-Based   relates to personal evaluation by the user
               reflected in terms of patterns of system use.

Market-Based   relates to the final evaluation conducted by
               the market place.

Table 1
Currently Reported Subject Based Evaluation Techniques
(Number of Times Employed in Currently Available
Literature Follows in Brackets)

	Type of measure	
	Performance Measures	Attitude/Knowledge Elicitation
Data	Response Time Error rates System use patterns	Attitudes/Opinions Knowledge System use patterns

Data Collection	Observation (5)
	
	On-line logs (9)
		Questionnaire (12)
		
		Interview (6)
		
		Protocol Analysis (5)
		- Constructive
		   Interaction (1)
		
		Factor Analytic (3)
		
		Repertory Grids (1)
		
		Predictability
		   Analysis (1)

Data Analysis and Display	Parametric and Non-parametric Statistics "Eyeball" methods Graphical methods	Parametric, non-parametric and multi-variate statistics "Eyeball" methods Graphical Methods

Table 1 illustrates the subject based evaluation techniques currently
reported in the available literature. It can be seen that on-line logs and
questionnaires have been applied most and that some possible techniques such
as critical incident techniques (Flanagan, 1954) and multi-dimensional
scaling are absent. It is also interesting to note that the available
applications of protocol analysis are recent and seem likely to grow in
number.

The section on data analysis lists some of the techniques used for
illustrating the data that are collected by the data collection techniques.
Examples of the application of each of the above techniques are listed in the
reference section. Some of the references are due to a previous review by

Penniman and Dominick (1980).

There are a number of advantages and disadvantages which apply to these general categories:

- While expert-based evaluation can, if necessary, be conducted quickly, it requires the evaluator to have extensive knowledge of the user, is open to possible unchecked bias, and is, therefore, likely to remain the province of the Human Factors expert.

- The formal representation of the system provided by theory-based evaluation can be used as a basis for simulation, allowing predictions to be made about system performance.

  Theory-based evaluation is also capable of fine grain analysis. It does, however, require considerable expertise and may need extensive tailoring from one system to the next, which brings its applicability into question.

- Subject-based techniques are those which have been most extensively employed. In general they present less constraints on the data that can be collected than the previous two approaches and are less open to bias. This, however, may not be true of some questionnaires, structured interviews and the like.

  The great variety of techniques - and the limited advice available regarding selection of a technique - can result in an inappropriate application and can affect the worth of the data collected. The extensive application of these techniques seems to reflect the fact that they can be easy and quick to use, requiring less expertise than do others.

- The data yielded by the first three techniques are a direct result of the evaluation enterprise. With user and market evaluation, however, the data are a by-product of system use and, as such, open to influence by a large variety of other variables (e.g., organizational policy and the state of the market).

CRITERIA FOR TECHNIQUE ASSESSMENT

There have been a number of such criteria proposed for the assessment of many behavioral techniques.

Each technique mentioned above is, in fact, a collection of techniques whose performance on a selected set of criteria will depend not only on the particular technique itself, but also on the context in which the data are collected and the purpose to which the data are put. When a particular technique has been fairly well specified it will be necessary to examine it in relation to these criteria.

Kak (1981) proposed reliability, validity, freedom from artefacts, standardization, representativeness, invasiveness, and practicability as criteria by which to assess physiological indices of stress. Aside from reliability and validity, representativeness (the degree to which the technique is sensitive to a variety of salient variables) seems useful with respect to the economy of an evaluation package.

Wickens (1984) proposed diagnosticity, sensitivity, selectivity, reliability, and practicability, as criteria for the assessment of mental
workload indices. Diagnosticity seems particularly important for interface
evaluation, especially with respect to design-change recommendations.

Finally, Ainsworth (1986) reported accuracy, amount of detail and
necessary resources as important criteria in evaluating process control
rooms.

EVALUATION ENVIRONMENT

As a framework in which to consider evaluation techniques an evaluation
environment is proposed. The environment is considered to consist of all
of those variables which can reasonably be expected to affect the utility
of a particular technique or package of techniques.

Figure 1 lists the more important aspects of the environment.

Evaluation techniques are required that consider the multi-dimensional
nature of the human-computer dialogue in the context of both task and user
variables. There is also a requirement for suitable ways of classifying
techniques and understanding the way in which the utility of each technique
will vary across stage, resource, situation, and evaluation objective.

THE EVALUATION ENVIRONMENT AS A TAXONOMY

Nelson and Marshall (1986) propose a taxonomy which can be used to
categorize evaluation techniques in terms of their characteristics (e.g.,
type of data collected and whether collected in the field or laboratory)
and the aspect of the interface to which they are sensitive (e.g., screen
or dialogue). A number of problems are evident, mostly due to the ill-de-
fined nature of the environment and the techniques, when using the current
evaluation environment as an aid in selecting an evaluation package. Some
of the following problems also apply to the taxonomy of Nelson and Marshall.

- To use the taxonomy both the components of the taxonomy
  and the techniques to be classified need to be precisely
  defined. Thus, only when the particular technique has
  been developed can the taxonomy inform as to its application. Only in special cases when any form of the
  technique will be inappropriate is the taxonomy useful.

- There is little data available to assess how the utility
  of the techniques will vary across the human-computer
  system.

- As previously mentioned, most techniques are in fact
  groups of techniques and, as such, inclusion or omission
  from a particular cell requires qualifying.

- The component elements in the evaluation environment may
  require tailoring (e.g., in an application such as video
  conferencing it may be appropriate to consider users in
  terms of personality as well as cognitive variables).

FUTURE WORK

On the basis of this analysis an experiment has been designed to collect

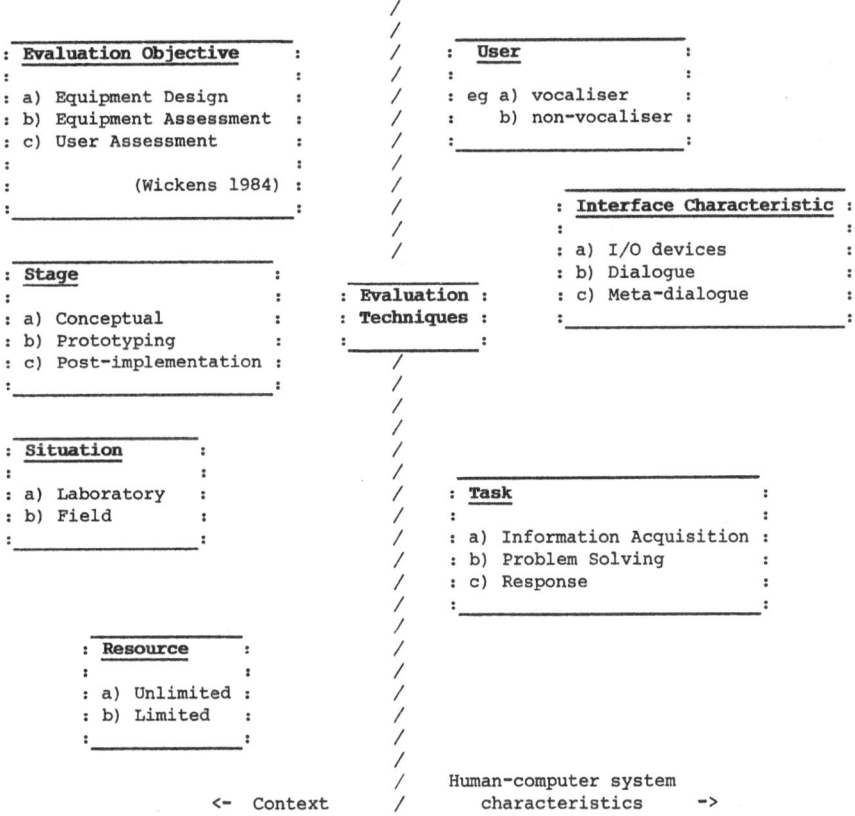

Figure 1. The Evaluation Environment.

data using a variety of techniques (protocol analysis, questionnaires, on-line logs, video recordings) from the affective, cognitive and behavioral levels of the user. The physiological level was not included because it was considered to be too many conceptual steps away from the kinds of inferences the designer wishes to make (but see Powers, et al., 1973).

Data analysis will be conducted separately for each technique and a cost benefit analysis conducted, based on the resources required and the information acquired assessed on a variety of criteria (e.g., amount of detail and diagnosticity). The results will provide experimental data upon which to develop a tool to aid in the choice of a technique or package of techniques given certain knowables in the evaluation environment.

REFERENCES

Ainsworth, L., 1986, A Comparison of Control Room Evaluation Techniques, Presented at the American Nuclear Society Conference held in Knoxville during 1986.

Anders-Ericsson, K., and Simon, H. E., 1984, Protocol Analysis: Verbal Reports as Data, MIT Press, Cambridge, Mass., London, England.

Barrett, G. V., Thornton, C. L., and Cabe, P. A., 1968, "Human Factors Evaluation of a Computer Based Information Storage and Retrieval System",

Human Factors, 10, (4), pp. 431-436.

Flanagan, J. C., 1954, "The Critical Incident Technique", Psychological Bulletin, 51, (4), pp. 327-358.

Hammond, N., Long, J., Clark, I., Morton, J., and Barnard, P., 1984, Documenting User Difficulties - Annotated Protocols, Hursley Human Factors File No. HF024, IBM, Hursley Park, Hampshire, SO21 2JN.

Kak, A., 1981, "Stress: An Analysis of Physiological Assessment Devices", Machine Pacing and Occupational Stress, Salvendy, G., and Smith, M. J., eds., Taylor Francis, London.

Kieras, D., and Poulson, P. G., 1985, "An Approach to the Formal Analysis of User Complexity", IJMMS, 22, pp. 365-394.

Levine, D. H., 1978, "A Generalized Methodology for Determining the Correlation of User Requirements to the Information System", Proc. of the 7th Mid-Year Meeting of the American Society for Information Science, May 1978.

Maclean, A., et al., 1985(a), Recall as an Indicant of Performance in Interactive Systems, Hursley Human Factors File No. HF088, IBM, Hursley Park, Hampshire, SO21 2JN.

Maclean, A., et al., 1985(b), Evaluating the Interface of a Document Processor: A Comparison of Expert Judgement and User Observation, Hursley Human Factors File No. HF089, IBM, Hursley Park, Hampshire, SO21 2JN.

Martin, T. H., Carlisle, J., and Treu, S., 1973, The User Interface for Interactive Bibliographic Searching: An Analysis of the Attitudes of Nineteen Information Scientists, Hursley Human Factors File No. HF089, IBM, Hursley Park, Hampshire, SO21 2JN.

Meister, D., and Sullivan, D. J., 1967, "Evaluation of User Reactions to a Prototype On-line Information Retrieval System", Report to NASA by the Bunker-Ramo Corporation under Contract No. NASA-1369, Rep. No. NASA CR-918.

Monk, A., 1986, "Personal Communication on Predictability Analysis".

Nelson, C., and Marshall, C., 1986, "Human Computer Interaction Evaluation", Presented at the Working with Display Units Conference, Stockholm, May 1986.

Norman, D. A., 1986, "Cognitive Engineering, Chapter 3", User Centered System Design, Norman, D. A., and Draper, S. W., eds.

O'Malley, C., Draper, S. W., and Riley, M. S., 1984, "Constructive Interaction: A Method for Studying User-Computer-User Interaction", Interact '84, Shakel, B., Elsevier Science Publishers B.V.

Peace, D. M. S., and Easterby, R. S., 1973, "The Evaluation of User Interaction with Computer Based Management Information Systems", Human Factors, 15, (2), pp. 163-177.

Penniman, W. D., and Dominick, W. D., 1980, "Monitoring and Evaluation of On-Line Information System Usage", On-Line Information System Usage, 16, (1).

Powers, W. G., Cummings, H. W., and Talbott, R., 1973, "The Effects of Prior

Computer Exposure on Man-Machine Computer Anxiety", Presented at Int. Commun. Assoc. Ann. Meeting, 25-28 April 1973, Montreal, Canada.

Rushinek, A., and Rushinek, S. F., 1984, "A User Evaluation of Information Characteristics Related to Demand Deposit System: An Empirical Analysis", Information and Management, 7, pp. 69-72.

Wickens, C. D., 1984, Engineering Psychology and Human Performance, Charles E. Merrill Publishing Company, London.

SOFTWARE COMPLEXITY ASSESSMENT AND HUMAN-MACHINE INTERFACE EVALUATION

Leslie J. Waguespack, Jr.

Computer Information Systems Department
Bentley College
Waltham, MA 02254

Abstract: Man-machine interfaces may be complex in two ways: 1) they may be complex in their construction, and 2) they may be complex for a user to manipulate. A human-machine interface model is presented which focuses on these two forms of complexity which we term intrinsic and extrinsic complexity, respectively. In terms of their construction we may wish to evaluate their complexity based on metrics defined for computer programs in software science, control structure complexity, or logical complexity. In terms of their manipulation, each interface may be viewed as a language composed of abstractions representing objects and/or actions that the interface embodies. We relate various software metrics to the different aspects of the model and attempt to identify aspects for which measures don't currently exist. Finally, we discuss implications this model may have on interface design decisions.

INTRODUCTION

Man-machine interfaces may be complex in two ways: 1) they may be complex in their construction, and 2) they may be complex for a user to manipulate. In terms of their construction we may wish to evaluate their complexity based on metrics defined for computer programs in software science, control structure complexity, or logical complexity. In terms of their manipulation, each interface may be viewed as a language composed of abstractions representing objects and/or actions that the interface embodies. It may be seen as a linguistic model of interaction regardless of its actual control/feedback instrumentation. Contemporary examples of such characterizations are command-language grammars (Moranda, 1981) and graphical interactive dialog specifications for user interface management systems (Reisner, 1981; Rosenthal and Yen, 1983).

Our human-machine interface model focuses on these two forms of complexity which we term intrinsic and extrinsic complexity, respectively. Our model identifies the various conceptual transforms that occur as a human interacts with a machine (program, language, software tool, etc.). Evaluation of an interface requires the separate assessment of both the intrinsic and extrinsic complexity of the interface. We relate software metrics to aspects of the model that they may be used to measure. We discuss aspects for which measures don't currently exist.

Software complexity literature depicts four basic categories of program feature measurement based on 1) information theory, 2) control graph theory, 3) data flow analysis, and 4) cognitive psychology. We briefly review these areas of study to form the backdrop for evaluating the complexity of user interfaces. We present the human-machine interaction model. We define intrinsic and extrinsic complexity factors that effect the effort necessary to accomplish the human-machine interaction. We conclude by discussing the implications this approach of interface evaluation may have on interface design.

SOFTWARE COMPLEXITY ASSESSMENT

There are four basic categories of software complexity study found in the literature. They vary, primarily, in the characteristics on which they focus in evaluating the difficulty of developing, comprehending, modifying, or reproducing programming specified in some formal programming language. The categories are software science, control structure complexity, logical complexity, and psychological complexity.

Software science was proposed by Halstead as an integrated and comprehensive system of formulae based on counts of tokens in the software text (Halstead, 1977). Based on these counts of operators and operands, Halstead axiomatically explained relationships between program length, volume, difficulty, and language level that could be experimentally studied by applying these formulae to both production software and academic algorithm specimen. The roots of Halstead's system of relationships was the message transmission function that the program text performed in conveying the programmers' sentiments to the compiler. He drew numerous parallels to Shannon's information theory (Shannon, 1948). Because of its empirical nature, Halstead's work depended on the credibility lent by numerous early studies of software inventories (Bulut and Bayer, 1974; Fitzsimmons and Love, 1978; Love, 1977; Gordon, 1979(a); Gordon, 1979(b); Gould and Drongowski, 1974; Gould, 1975; Sheppard, Kruesi, and Curtis, 1981). Later work (Elshoff, 1978; Fitsos, 1979; Moranda, 1981; Shen, Conte, and Dunsmore, 1983) pointed up anomalies in his system of formula and questioned the fidelity of software science to actual experience across a variety of software types. Control structure complexity is most closely identified with McCabe (McCabe, 1976), who focused attention on programs represented as control graphs. Drawing from graph theory for parallels with network complexity, McCabe's metric was generally consistent with software science measurements in ranking programs, but, could not be experimentally calibrated with it. The initial metric was amended by Myers (Myers, 1977) to compensate for ambiguities caused by rewriting nested predicates as compound Boolean expressions. McCabe's metric has been variously adjusted or incorporated in other work (Baker and Zweben, 1980; Hansen, 1978; Harrison, 1981; Harrison et al., 1981,; Harrison, and Magel, 1981; Hennell, Woodward, and Hedley, 1976; Negrini and Sami, 1983; Piwowarski, 1982; Woodward, Hennell, and Hedley, 1979; Zweben, 1977).

In both software science and control structure complexity the interrelationships between data objects are ignored. In software science the order or arrangement of statements is ignored. In the case of McCabe's metric, there is no difference discerned between a simple assignment and a long involved algebraic expression. Logical complexity addresses these issues by drawing on data flow analysis, the analysis of the computational dependencies between procedural and data objects in the program text (Cater, Iyengar, and Fuller, 1982; Cater, Iyengar, and Fuller, 1984; Iyengar, 1982; Iyengar and Bruno, 1983; Iyengar, Bastani, and Fuller, 1984). The metric considers the span of dependency of computations and the proximity of expressions dealing with the same data objects. Unlike McCabe's metric, logical complexity also addresses the relative difficulty of various control constructs (e.g., IF-THEN-ELSE vs FOR loop) by comparing the computational complexity of their underlying definitions in propositional calculus (Hamilton, 1978). This path of study is relatively new compared to Halstead or McCabe's work, but, there is growing interest in this approach (Bastani, 1983; Hou and Iyengar, 1983; Parameswaran and Iyengar, 1983; Parameswaran, Iyengar, and Ramesh, 1983; Oviedo, 1980; Rama Rao and Iyengar, 1984).

Where the previous focus of complexity addressed the program text primarily, psychological complexity focuses more directly on human subjects in an attempt to distinguish behavioral and methodological symptoms of complexity. Shneiderman's work is perhaps the most well known in this area (Shneiderman, 1976; Shneiderman, 1977; Shneiderman, 1979; Shneiderman, and Mayer, 1979; Shneiderman, 1980). Based on experimental models often used in psychology or sociology researchers study a variety of program charac-teristics (structure, indentation, choice of variable names, documentation) and their effects on comprehension, learning, and recollection of program text (Atwood and Ramsey, 1978; Brooks, 1977; Brooks, 1983; Curtis, Sheppard, and Milliman, 1979; Curtis, Sheppard, Milliman, Borst, and Love, 1979; Curtis, Forman, Brooks, Soloway, and Ehrlich, 1982; Fitter and Green, 1979; Mayer, 1979; Mayer, 1981; Ramsey, Atwood, and Van Doren, 1978; Sheppard, Kruesi, and Curtis, 1981; Weiser, 1982; Woodfield, Dunsmore, and Shen, 1981; Woodfield, Shen, and Dunsmore, 1981). The most exciting facet of this path of research has been the attempt to model human cognition of programs and program structures. This area of research has produced the largest number of prescriptions for "good software" and the most controversy concerning the credibility of its results.

Although none of the areas abstracted above offer (or professes to offer) a comprehensive method for measuring program complexity, each high-lights a different aspect of program manipulation requiring human perception and focus. Each illuminates some aspect of cognitive process. It is against this kaleidoscope of feature foci that we propose yet another perspective on human-machine interaction that may be used to study interface complexity.

A HUMAN-MACHINE INTERFACE MODEL

The interaction between human and machine in the process of accomplish-ing some task may be described as a system composed of various models and the transformations required to exchange information between these models (to allow the models to communicate). This characterization provides a framework in which to assess the relative complexities of such interaction systems and to develop theories and methodologies to manage the various complexities particularly as these systems relate to human-computer inter-actions.

PARTITIONING REALITY

A human-machine interaction is composed of user, interface/tool, and the problem space. The interaction system is composed of three instances of reality. An instance of reality here is meant to comprise a set of axioms and procedures that are correct - correct at least in the sense of internal consistency. (Brookes alludes to partitioning when describing "mappings between domains" in his work characterizing the comprehension of computer programs (Brooks, 1983)).

The first instance is the problem space. This is the set of real world entities and relationships that the human wishes to manipulate either

189

for the purpose of changing its state or for the purpose of modeling it to develop knowledge about it. The problem space exists outside the mind of the human. (In our modeling system, we are assuming that the problem space is somehow material and that even problems of information that are generally considered abstract are represented materially through data storage or physical inventory of some kind. In this latter case the problem space has been "created" by a human.) The task of the human in manipulating the problem space is to first internalize that subset of the problem space relevant to the manipulation, develop a strategy of manipulation, and, finally, to direct and monitor that manipulation.

The second instance of reality is the mind of the human. This comprises the mechanisms for perceiving and internalizing problem space state information, selecting or devising a model of the problem state to which to apply the data, developing a manipulation strategy, and articulating that strategy to the machine's interface. This instance of reality is the least well defined and is studied in the disciplines of psychology and sociology. Perception involves noticing problem space data, classifying and correlating that data with respect to some internal model, a mental model. A mental model is a system of axioms and procedures. The extent to which this model corresponds to the problem space is sometimes referred to as truth. The process of finding an appropriate model with which to correlate problem space data is recognition. The process of merging existing internal models or of devising new models to deal with problem space data is learning (Brooks, 1977; Newell and Simon, 1972; Soloway, Ehrlich, and Bonar, 1982). The manipulation strategy is based on the functionality of the chosen internal model. That models offers alternative transformations that may effect the eventual problem space manipulation desired. The act of manipulation is achieved via articulation with the machine. Articulation is the translation of the manipulation strategy based on the mental model into the machine interface model provided with the machine. The third instance is the machine (often referred to as the tool). The machine is connected to the problem space physically; as a bulldozer can move earth, as a steering wheel directs tires and, thus, the automobile, and as a computer that inputs data and outputs data. The machine is composed of two main parts: the problem space interface and a user interface. In the example of the bulldozer, the problem space interface is the blade, the treads, the winch, etc., while the human interacts with an interface of controls, switches, dials and meters. The machine interface is a model of the machine's connection to the problem space. (It is an abstraction for solving the problem.) The activation of a control causes some manipulation. Each manipulation is perceived through human senses or through dials and meters. The interface is usually designed to somehow maximize the efficient use of the machine to manipulate the problem space. The essence of a tool is the mechanical or psychological advantage that it may bring to bear on the user problem. In the case where a machine is designed as a constituent part of a larger mechanism its interface design is usually chosen for its "mechanical" efficiency. When that interface is designed for human interface, it has a characteristic of psychological efficiency as well. To leverage the mechanical or psychological advantage, machines are placed "on top of" machines and so on forming a multi-layered architecture. Only the simplest of machines are atomic - composed of one and only one mechanism. Most machines are systems of constituent mechanisms, each a machine in its own right. The relationship among these constituent mechanisms is called the composite machine's architecture. Depending on the circumstance, we may prefer to think of the architecture as a collection of distinct mechanisms or as a monolithic whole. In the latter case, the interface replaces the inner architecture as the user's view of the machine. The interface, the user's view, is a virtual machine.

The foregoing description is represented in Figure 1.

190

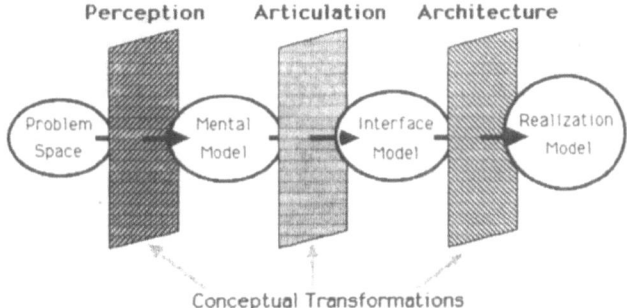

Perception   Articulation   Architecture

Problem Space   Mental Model   Interface Model   Realization Model

Conceptual Transformations

Figure 1. The Composite Machine's Architecture.

MODELS OF REALITY

Our physical perception of reality is embodied largely in the sciences,
physics, chemistry, biology, etc. (We choose not to consider metaphysical
perceptions.) These, in turn, are usually modeled through mathematics.
Mathematics becomes the lowest common denominator of models. There are a
variety of models used in computer science; predicate calculus, the general
systems model, petri-nets, and the entity-relationship model are a few.
Because the system of interaction we describe here is primarily a behavioral
one, the models we describe are finite state automata. (This is convenient
since we're attempting to work our way through to computing at some point.)

Problem Space

The problem space contains the material objects which are the ultimate
target of our manipulations. The other models are related to it in that
they all attempt to capture relevant characteristics of the problem space
to facilitate manipulating it. (Often in computing, the problem space is
the creation of humans, a database for example. In this case, the structure
of the problem space has been specifically chosen to facilitate manipulation.
We shall see later how this directly effects interface design.)

Mental Model

The mental model is selected or devised based on the data perceived
about the problem space. The process of recognition is not sequential.
One doesn't take in data and in a second discrete step select an internal
model. Experiments have shown that the predisposition to certain internal
models is very strong, even to the extent that known patterns are sometimes
misrecognized because of partial correlation with strong preconceptions.
(An example is "hidden pictures" in silhouettes.) It is often necessary to
review the data repeatedly before recognition is achieved. In the case
where recognition is not achieved learning is necessary. Learning is the
process of constructing a new internal model either by merging or adapting
resident models. The expense involved depends on the similarity of the new
model with prior ones and the facility the human has with combining or
permuting resident models. The form of the mental model varies greatly
among humans. Language based and pictorial based seem to be two very general
categories. Language based can be further divided into written language
and auditory language categories. Humans display varied facility to recognize and learn via these various perception media. The ability to apply
structure in mental models also distinguishes humans. It has been suggested
that chunking rather than intelligence is what explains the superior

performance of experienced chess players over novices in recalling board situations. Chunking appears to play a prominent role in programming as well (Adelson, 1981; Atwood and Ramsey, 1978; McKeithen, Reitman, Rueter, and Hirtle, 1981; Shneiderman, 1982). This would suggest that the ability to incorporate structure in a mental model increases the correlational potential between problem space and mental model.

Interface Model

The interface model is a communication language between human and machine. As a finite state automation it provides a set of objects and transformations that may be applied to those objects to change the state of the machine. Most interfaces also provide instrumentation which provides artificial indications of the machines internal state. The interface model spans the conceptual gap between mental model and machine. It is common to refer to these conceptual bridges as abstractions.

Realization Model

The realization model is the machine itself. This is the component in the system that actually does something in the physical sense. It may be monolithic or composed of various subcomponents. Knowledge of its structural nature, its architecture, may or may not be visible through the machine interface. This is an interface design decision.

When the construction of the machine is invisible, because the interface completely obscures it, we might forget that the machine is distinct from the interface. It is distinct. This distinction allows us to consider different interface models for the same machine or different machine implementations for the same interface model.

COMPLEXITY

Intrinsic Complexity

Each of the models described above has a complexity: the number of parts, the interrelationship of those parts, etc. If we accept that each of the models described above is a finite state automation then each has an intrinsic complexity based on the computational difficulty of realizing the model in mathematical form (Zeigler and Rada, 1982).

The complexity of the problem space is inherent in the problem. It changes as it is manipulated or as it evolves, but, the complexity of any problem space situation is fixed. It is somewhat like mass in physics. Although we sense the mass of an object differently depending on where we are in the universe, its mass is constant.

The intrinsic complexity of the other three models is not fixed. That is to say that functionally equivalent models may be found for any of the three. Each might have different intrinsic complexity. For example, if the realization model is a station wagon in which we attempt to deliver produce it could be replaced by a truck, a bicycle, a scooter, an airplane, etc. Each would be theoretically capable of accomplishing the delivery task, but, each would have a distinct intrinsic complexity. To the extent that we have a choice among models, we have some control over the complexity of the entire system.

Extrinsic Complexity

The intrinsic complexity of each of the models in the human-machine

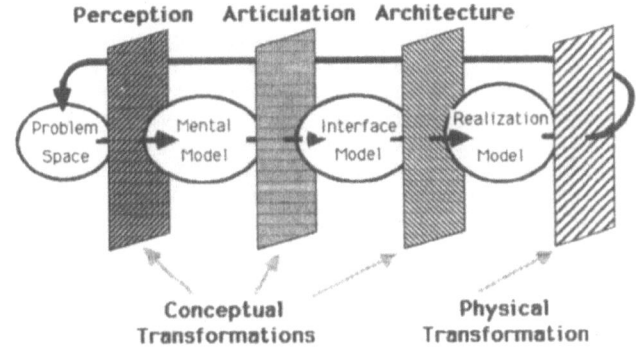

Figure 2. Composite Machine's Architecture Imbedded in
the Closed-Loop Model of the Overall System.

interaction system contributes to the overall complexity. Additional complexity is introduced at the points where these models must be articulated
(Curtis, 1980). Between each adjacent pair of models there is a connection
path. Each path transmits information between models. To the degree that
the models differ in their modeling and structuring of information, the
connection path must transform the information to make it useful. In general, the degree of difference is proportionate to the degree of transformation required. If we model this transformation as a language translation,
we may define each transformation's complexity based on the complexity of
the automation required to translate it. This complexity is extrinsic in
the interaction system.

If we close the loop in the interaction system to show the connection
between the machine and the problem space (as shown in Figure 2), we can see
each of the models in the interaction and each of the transformations between
them.

The physical transformation between the realization model, the machine, and the problem space is usually evaluated on the physical efficiency
of the machine. We consider physical relationships such as leverage. Each
of the conceptual transformations has a time/space efficiency as well, but
that is different from complexity. In many instances of physics, for example, the simpler the mechanism, the more time required to complete the
task (as in comparing a shovel with a tractor for digging canals).

There is one instance when transformation efficiency and extrinsic
complexity correspond. That is when the connecting models are completely
consistent. In such a case the complexity of the transformation would be
zero, since no translation is required and the efficiency would be one. In
an idealized example, this might be accomplished by a mind-reading automobile
where the machine interface simply responded to the thoughts of the driver
and there was no "articulation" required between human and machine interface.
Even in this case, however, one should expect that the mental model would
require additional "discipline" of thought over and above what we're normally
used to (controlling day dreaming for instance).

USING COMPLEXITY TO EVALUATE INTERFACES

Software complexity research analyzes cost/effort and reliability
aspects of computer programs. The software metrics measure static features

of program text. The human-machine interaction model defines a basis for partitioning interfaces into static and dynamic components. The static components exhibit intrinsic complexity. The dynamic components exhibit extrinsic complexity. The following section discusses how intrinsic complexity may be assessed using software metrics and what these measures can contribute to an overall interface evaluation. We explain why dynamic interface components can not be adequately measured with software metrics alone. The succeeding section proposes a combination of software metrics and application environment analysis that provides an environment specific evaluation.

Assessing Complexity

The model of interaction described above may be used to characterize machine interface scenarios from two separate perspectives. One perspective is the construction and maintenance of the tool itself. The second is the use of the machine as a tool to accomplish some task. Each of these perspectives focus on time/space efficiencies for the tool builder and for the user, respectively. A variety of disciplines may be brought to bear on the scenarios in order to evaluate the system's complexity. The natural sciences may be applied to the problem space. The social sciences may be applied to the perception, mental model, and articulation components. And software metrics may be applied to the interface, the architecture, and the realization models.

Software metrics have been devised to measure the artifacts of tool building. Software science, cyclomatic complexity and logical complexity measure features of the text of programmed tools (Cater, Iyengar, and Fuller, 1984; Fitzsimmons and Love, 1978; Halstead, 1977; McCabe, 1976). They all attempt to affix a metric to the tool specification in some programming language. If we apply these to the formal specification of the interface as a program we can measure aspects of intrinsic complexity. To the extent that these metrics reflect the complexity of the task that the programs are attempting to accomplish, they have been useful in explaining and, sometimes, predicting the social expense of working with them. Explaining and predicting cost have been central to the development of complexity metrics (Zunde, 1982).

Measuring extrinsic complexity (involving the mental model) has been less successful in producing numeric valuations. Cognitive psychology has been effective in ranking some features in terms of relative difficulty. Halstead purported to be able to count mental discriminations necessary to compose program text (Halstead, 1977). It was later effectively argued that he had so badly incorporated cognitive psychology theory in his formulations such as Stroud's number in his "time to code" metric that many of his explanations for the empirical results were highly suspect (Coulter, 1983).

For the most part, extrinsic complexity study has been feature oriented. Most experiments attempt to place relative merit on methods, style, form, or some other feature of tool use relative to variations on that feature by observing the rate of errors, the time to reproduce, or the ability to translate specifications in some text (Atwood and Ramsey, 1978; Shneiderman, 1982). These studies address psychological aspects of interaction - specifically, the mental model interaction with the program (machine) interface.

Attempts to measure complexity are sometimes confused by the difficulty of distinguishing experimental results due to either intrinsic or extrinsic factors independently. In the case of programs, one cannot separate the characteristics of the programming language as an interface from the program as an interface. For example, software metrics unanimously ignore the presence of documentation in program text. Yet, it is an obvious fact that the presence of documentation materially effects the cost of use, development, and maintenance of software. Documentation's primary purpose is to ameliorate extrinsic complexity. Intrinsic complexity is not a clear indicator of extrinsic complexity in non-trivial experiments (Coulter, 1983; Shen, Conte, and Dunsmore, 1983). It is clearly the case that "good" documentation addresses the articulation of the mental model with the interface by providing the reader with references to the particular mental model that the interface was intended to accommodate. Indeed, documentation's primary purpose is to communicate mental models.

Software metrics are best applied to the measure of intrinsic complexity features. Controlling extrinsic complexity must be guided by psychological complexity results which basically offer alternative specification and construction methods to tool builders along with indications of the method's relative merits.

Measuring Interface Complexity

Our assessment of interface complexity has two distinct facets: 1) the complexity of using the interface, and 2) the complexity of the interface itself. These amount to extrinsic and intrinsic complexity, respectively. To the extent that an interface may be described by a finite state automation and, therefore, may be implemented as a computer program, we can leave the assessment of the intrinsic complexity of the interface to the methods and metrics used for measuring program complexity (Halstead, 1977; McCabe, 1976; etc.). Measuring the extrinsic complexity of an interface is more difficult because the interface's complexity is relative to the model with which it must be articulated - the mental model.

McLennan's metric for programming languages can be applied here to measure the complexity of the interface as a language (MacLennan, 1982). It can give us a metric with which to compare interfaces as to their static, linguistic complexity. The difficulty that the human experiences trying to use the interface, however, will be effected by other less static factors. First, the task that the user is attempting will require a subset of the interface's whole linguistic power. Indeed, most interactions deal with a very small subset of the interface (e.g., pocket calculators, word processors, ANSI COBOL, spreadsheets) particularly if the interfaces are extensible (offer features to extend the expressive power of the base language such as macros in Lotus-1-2-3 or object classes in Smalltalk-80 (Goldberg and Robson, 1983). The practical complexity of using an interface is more appropriately tied to the relevant subset of the interface required to accomplish specific user tasks.

We can measure one part of an interface's extrinsic complexity as a weighted average where each term is the product of the probability of the task times the (MacLennan's) linguistic complexity of the subset required to accomplish it. This measure is sensitive to the mix of tasks to which the tool will be employed. A second part of the extrinsic complexity is the effort required to adopt a mental model that can be accommodated by the interface. This includes the consumption of documentation. In an ideal case, the documentation would exactly describe the process to solve the specific task the user has in mind. More often the user must abstract a solution from existing solutions. Stated differently, this second part of extrinsic complexity is the training cost involved in preparing and sustaining a user of an interface.

INTERFACE DESIGN IMPLICATIONS

Choosing Models

Ultimately the cost of using an interface is based on compatibility between the user's mental model and the interface model. The cost will be exacted in training, interaction errors, and time/space efficiency. Training and interaction errors can be controlled by choosing interface models consistent with existing user mental models. The latter depends on effective systems analysis and user/designer interaction during model development. Re-using existing mental models is the basis for application interface design on the Apple Macintosh as described in the user interface guidelines (Apple, 1985). Under the guidelines, visual metaphors and mouse movement metaphors are established for a variety of interactions which would be common across virtually all Macintosh applications. Subscribers to these guidelines are relieved from significant interface documentation concerning these metaphors and users benefit from the transport of training from one application to the next. The use of interface standards and tangible interface support (Macintosh ToolBox) is a guiding force in user interface Management System development (Olsen, 1983; Olsen and Dempsey, 1983; Rosenthal and Yen, 1983). (By the same token, similarities in interface metaphors should be avoided when the similarities would mislead the user. This form of interactive mistake tends to be the most vexing.)

Time/space costs can be controlled by providing a modularized interface. A modularized interface is one which allows the user to deal with subsets of the interface as is appropriate to the task. This narrows the scope of interface features needed and allows the user to learn the interface in steps. Interface subsetting offers the user the option of dealing with the interface by stepwise abstraction as in learning attachments one at a time (Zeigler and Rada, 1982). Extensible interfaces provide this capability by allowing "mentor users" to provide abstraction through interface extensions that simplify certain aspects of the interface while the novice user is adapting. It is this concept of novice user "bootstrapping" on experienced user that is the basis for "end user programmable tools". (A pitfall, in such a case, is the fact that both intrinsic and extrinsic complexity may be introduced by extending the interface - software engineering concerns for which the user community is not prepared.)

The concept of modularization is very strong in programming language interfaces. The introduction and popularization of high level block structured languages is motivated by the desire to facilitate chunking and information hiding. The thrust toward modularization is based on the notion that systematizing module relationships decreases design, control, and maintenance complexity (Gannon, 1976; Shneiderman, 1982; Weiser, 1982). Abstract data types and object oriented language constructs provide material to build conceptual bridges between modules minimizing the visible instrumentation between system components (Cox, 1984; Ledbetter and Cox, 1985).

Building Models

Interface design and development is model building. As a model the interface will present the user with abstractions, objects that will be manipulated. As the scope of functionality required of the interface increases the interface will order a system of abstractions. It may offer extensibility, a means of stepwise abstraction, as a means for simplifying the delivery of the system and adapting the system once installed. To the extent that the interface is programmable, we must consider its complexity as that of a programming language and the extension that is programmed as a new layer, a new virtual machine possessing its own complexity independent of the supporting layers.

There seem to be at least two themes for interface design prevalent today. One is to make the interface model as close to the mental model as possible. To some extent this is the effect gained by developing applications facilitated by 4th generation language where data objects and transactions are gleaned from the user's environment to become database fields and data entry screens in the application. Another theme is to bring the mental model closer to the interface model. The Apple Macintosh's icon studded desktop and "pull-down" menus represent this approach. By designing a metaphorically driven world of icons the user is preconditioned to a variety of interactions with virtually no training required beyond the initial familiarization with the icon-world. In either case, the task is drawing the mental model and interface model together into _psychological synchronization_.

Which interfaces are best? It is unclear that we shall ever be able to discern _best_. We must strive to devise metrics for discerning _better_ to start with.

CONCLUSION

A human-machine interaction takes place in a system of models of the real world. Each model (except the problem space) abstracts the features of the problem space appropriate to manipulation. The models themselves can be described as finite state automata with a corresponding computational complexity. This complexity is intrinsic to each model. The interaction between the models involves the transformation of internal model objects for correlation with the adjacent model's abstractions. This transformation (translation of information) has a complexity based on the degree of translation required. This complexity is extrinsic to the models of the interaction.

The measure of the intrinsic complexity of an interface (that is the software science, control graph, or logical complexity of the interface's implementation) provides an indication of the cost of developing and sustaining the interface from the tool builder's perspective. These measures do not clearly indicate the effort required to use the interface to accomplish a user task. That effort is best characterized by the extrinsic complexity and is affected by the linguistic complexity of the interface, the scope of the interface required per user task, and the training effort the user will expend to internalize the interface model in order to interact with it. Extrinsic complexity measure is heavily dependent on the environment in which the interface will be employed.

The overall complexity of an interaction system depends on the continuity of abstraction from one model to the next. This continuity is based on comprehensive analysis of the problem space to be modeled and thorough familiarity with existing mental models in the user community.

ACKNOWLEDGEMENTS

The author would like to thank David Haas and Donald Chand for their careful reading and insightful comments on prior versions of this paper.

REFERENCES

Adelson, B., 1981, "Problem Solving and the Development of Abstract Categories in Programming Languages", _Memory Cognition_, _9_, (4), pp. 422-433.

Apple Computer, Inc., 1985, Inside Macintosh: The Macintosh User Interface Guidelines, Addeson-Wesley, Reading, MA, pp. 23-70.

Atwood, M. A., and Ramsey, H. R., 1978, Cognitive Structures in the Comprehension and Memory of Computer Programs: An Investigation of Computer Program Debugging, ARI Technical Report TR-78-A21, Science Applications, Inc.

Baker, A. L., and Zweben, S. H., 1980, "A Comparison of Measures of Control Flow Complexity", IEEE Transactions on Software Engineering, SE-6, pp. 506-512.

Bastani, F. B., 1983, "An Approach to Measuring Program Complexity", Proceedings of COMPSAC '83, Chicago, IL, pp. 1-8.

Brooks, R., 1977, "Toward a Theory of Cognitive Processes in Computer Programming", International Journal of Man-Machine Studies, 9, pp. 465-478.

Brooks, R., 1983, "Towards a Theory of the Comprehension of Computer Programs", International Journal of Man-Machine Studies, 18, (6), pp. 543-555.

Bulut, N., Halstead, M. H., and Bayer, R., 1974, "Experimental Validation of a Structural Property of Fortran Algorithms", Proceedings of the ACM National Conference, pp. 207-211, San Diego.

Cater, S., Iyengar, S. S., and Fuller, J. W., 1982, Algorithms to Compute Logical Effort in Programs, Technical Report, Department of Computer Science, Louisiana State University.

Cater, S., Iyengar, S. S., and Fuller, J. W. 1984, "Computation of Logical Effort in High Level Languages", Journal of Computer Languages, 9, (3/4), pp. 133-148.

Coulter, N. S., 1983, "Software Science and Cognitive Psychology", IEEE Transactions on Software Engineering, SE-9, (3), pp. 166-171.

Cox, B. J., 1984, "Message/Object Programming: An Evolutionary Change in Programming Technology", IEEE Software, 0740-7459/84/0100/0050, January 1984.

Curtis, B., Sheppard, S. B., Milliman, P., 1979, "Third Time Charm: Stronger Replication of the Ability of Software Complexity Metrics to Predict Programmer Performance", Proceedings of the 4th International Conference on Software Engineering, September 1979, pp. 356-360.

Curtis, B., Sheppard, S. B., Milliman, P. M., Borst, M. A., Love, T., 1979, "Measuring the Psychological Complexity of Software Maintenance Tasks with Halstead and McCabe Metrics", IEEE Transactions on Software Engineering, SE-5, pp. 95-104.

Curtis, B., 1980, "In Search of Software Complexity", IEEE Workshop on Quantitative Software Models, pp. 95-106.

Curtis, B., Forman, I., Brooks, R., Soloway, E., and Ehrlich, D., 1982, "Psychological Perspectives for Software Science", Empirical Foundations of Information and Software Science, Proceedings of the First Symposium, Atlanta, GA, November 1982, pp. 119-128.

Elshoff, J. L. 1978, "An Investigation Into the Effects of the Counting Method Used on Software Science Measurements", ACM SIGPLAN Notices, 13,

(2), February, pp. 30-45.

Fitsos, G. P., 1979, Software Science Counting Rules and Tuning Methodology, IBM Technical Report TR 03.075.

Fitter, M., and Green, T. R. G., 1979, "When do Diagrams Make Good Computer Languages", International Journal of Man-Machine Studies, 11, pp. 235-261.

Fitzsimmons, A., and Love, T., 1978, "A Review and Evaluation of Software Science", Computing Surveys, 10, (1), pp. 3-18.

Gannon, J. D., and Horning, J. J., 1975, "Language Design for Programming Reliability, IEEE Transactions on Software Engineering, SE-1, (2), pp. 179-191.

Gannon, J. D., 1976, "An Experiment for the Evaluation of Language Features", International Journal of Man-Machine Studies, 8, pp. 61-73.

Gannon, J. D., 1977, "An Experimental Evaluation of Data Type Conventions", Communications of the ACM, 20, (2), pp. 584-595.

Goldberg, A., and Robson, D., 1983, Smalltalk-80: The Language and Its Implementation, Addison-Wesley, Reading, MA.

Gordon, R. D., 1979(a), "Measuring Improvements in Program Clarity", IEEE Transactions on Software Engineering, SE-5, pp. 79-90, March, 1979.

Gordon, R. G., 1979(b), "A Qualitative Justification for a Measure of Program Clarity", IEEE Transactions on Software Engineering, SE-5, pp. 177-128.

Gould, J. D., and Drongowski, P., 1974, "An Exploratory Study of Computer Program Debugging", Human Factors, 1, (6), pp. 258-277, June 1974.

Gould, J. D., 1975, "Some Psychological Evidence on How People Debug Computer Programs", International Journal of Man-Machine Studies, 7, (1), pp. 151-182, January 1975.

Halstead, M. H., 1977, Elements of Software Science, Elsevier, New York.

Hamilton, A. G., 1978, Logic for Mathematicians, Cambridge University Press.

Hansen, W., 1978, "Measurement of Program Complexity by the Pair (Cyclomatic Number, Operators Count)", ACM SIGPLAN Notices, 13, pp. 19-33.

Harrison, W., 1981, A Hybrid Metric to Measure Software Complexity, Master's Thesis, University of Missouri-Rolla, Department of Computer Science.

Harrison, W., et al., 1981, "A Topilogical Analysis of the Complexity of Computer Programs with less than Three Binary Branches", ACM SIGPLAN Notices, 16, pp. 51-63.

Harrison, W. A., and Magel, K. I., 1981, "A Complexity Measure Based on Nesting Level", ACM SIGPLAN Notices, 16, (3), pp. 63-74 March 1981.

Hennell, M. A., Woodward, M. R., and Hedley, D., 1976, "On Program Analysis", Information Processing Letters, 5, pp. 136-140.

Hou, T., and Iyengar, S. S., 1983, The Logical Complexity of Data Flow Programs, Technical Report TR 83-018, Department of Computer Science, Louisiana State University.

Iyengar, S. S., Parameswaran, N., and Fuller, J. W., 1982, "A Measure of Logical Complexity of Programs, Journal of Computer Languages, 7, pp. 147-160.

Iyengar, S. S., and Bruno, G., 1983, Formalization of Logical Complexity of Programs, Technical Report TR 83-013, Department of Computer Science, Louisiana State University.

Iyengar, S. S., Bastani, F. B., and Fuller, J. W., 1985, "An Experimental Study of the Logical Complexity of Data Structures", Empirical Foundations of Information and Software Science, Agrawal, J. C., and Zunde, P., eds., Plenum Press, New York.

Ledbetter, L., and Cox, G. J., 1985, "Software-ICs", BYTE, June 1985, pp. 307-316.

Love, T., 1977, "An Experimental Investigation on the Effect of Program Structure on Program Understanding", ACM SIGPLAN Notices, 12, pp. 105--113.

MacLennan, B. J., 1982, "Simple Metrics for Programming Languages, Proc. Empirical Foundations of Information and Software Science, Atlanta, GA, November 1982, pp. 209-222.

Mayer, R. E., 1979, "A Psychology of Learning Basic", Communications of the ACM, 22, (11), pp. 589-593.

Mayer, R. E. 1981, "The Psychology of How Novices Learn Computer Programming", Computing Surveys, 13, (1), pp. 121-141.

McCabe, T. J., 1976, "A Complexity Measure", IEEE Transactions on Software Engineering, SE-2, pp. 308-320.

McKeithen, K. B., Reitman, J. S., Rueter, H. H., and Hirtle, S. C., 1981, "Knowledge Organization and Skill Differences in Computer Programming", Cognitive Psychology, 13, pp. 307-325.

Moranda, P. B., 1981, "Is Software Science Hard?", Computing Surveys, Surveyor's Forum, 10, pp. 503-504, December 1981.

Myers, G., 1977, "An Extension to the Cyclomatic Measure of Program Complexity", ACM SIGPLAN Notices, 12, ACM SIGPLAN Notices, 12, (10), pp. 61-64.

Negrini, R. M., and Sami, M., 1983, "Some Properties Derived from Structural Analysis of Program Graph Models", IEEE Transactions on Software Engineering, SE-9, (2), pp. 172-178.

Newell, A., and Simon, H. A., 1972, Human Problem Solving, Prentice-Hall, Englewood Cliffs, New Jersey.

Olsen, D. R., 1983, "Automatic Generation of Interactive Systems", Computer Graphics, 17, (1), January 1983, pp. 53-57.

Olsen, D. R., and Dempsey, E. P., 1983, "SYNGRAPH: A Graphic User Interface Generator", Computer Graphics, 17, (3), July 1983, pp. 43-50.

Oviedo, E., 1980, "Control Flow, Data Flow and Program Complexity", Proceedings of COMPSAC '80, Chicago, IL, pp. 146-152.

Parameswaran, N., and Iyengar, S. S., 1983, "Logical Complexity of Programs",

Proceedings of the IEEE-SMC Conference, Bombay, India.

Parameswaran, N., Iyengar, S. S., and Ramesh, S., 1983, <u>A Complexity Measure That Takes Into Account the Complete Program Semantics</u>, Technical Report TR 83-022, Department of Computer Science, Louisiana State University.

Piwowarski, P., 1982, "A Nesting Level Complexity Measure", <u>ACM SIGPLAN Notices</u>, <u>17</u>, pp. 44-50.

Rama Rao, K. V. S., and Iyengar, S., 1984, "A General Measure for Program Complexity", <u>Software Engineering Workshop</u>, Nice, France, June 1984.

Ramsey, H. R., Atwood, M. E., and Van Doren, J. R., 1978, <u>A Comparative Study of Flowcharts and Program Design Languages for the Detailed Procedural Specification of Computer Programs</u>, ARI Technical Report TR-78-A22, Science Applications, Inc.

Reisner, P., 1981, "Formal Grammar and Human Factors Design of an Interactive Graphics System", <u>IEEE Transactions on Software Engineering</u>, SE-7, (2), March 1981, pp. 229-240.

Rosenthal, D., and Yen, A., 1983, "User Interface Models Summary", <u>Computer Graphics</u>, <u>17</u>, (1), January 1983, pp. 38-45.

Shannon, C. E., 1948, "A Mathematical Theory of Communication", <u>Bell Systems Journal</u>, reprinted in <u>Key Paper in the Development of Information Theory</u>, Slepian, D., ed., IEEE Press, New York, 1974.

Shen, V., Conte, S. D., and Dunsmore, H., "Software Science Revisited: A Critical Analysis of the Theory and Its Empirical Support", <u>IEEE Transactions on Software Engineering</u>, SE-9, (2), pp. 155-165.

Sheppard, S. B., Kruesi, E., and Curtis, B., 1981, "The Effect of Symbology and Spatial Arrangement on the Comprehension of Software Specifications", <u>Proceedings of the 5th International Conference on Software Engineering</u>, San Diego, CA, pp. 207-214.

Shneiderman, B., 1976, "Exploratory Experiments in Programmer Behavior", <u>International Journal of Computer and Information Sciences</u>, <u>5</u>, (2), pp. 123-143, April 1976.

Shneiderman, B., 1977, "Measuring Computer Program Quality and Comprehension", <u>International Journal of Man-Machine Studies</u>, <u>9</u>, pp. 737-751.

Shneiderman, B., Mayer, R., McKay, D., and Heller, P., 1977, "Experimental Investigations of the Utility of Detailed Flowcharts in Programming, <u>Communications of the ACM</u>, <u>20</u>, pp. 373-381.

Shneiderman, B., 1979, "Human Factors Experiments in Designing Interactive Systems", <u>IEEE Computer</u>, <u>12</u>, (12).

Shneiderman, B., and Mayer, R., 1979, "Syntactic/Semantic Interactions in Programmer Behavior", <u>International Journal of Computer and Information Sciences</u>, <u>7</u>, pp. 219-239.

Shneiderman, B., 1980, <u>Software Psychology</u>, Winthrop, Reading, MA.

Shneiderman, B., 1982, "Control Flow and Data Structure Documentation: Two Experiments", <u>Communications of the ACM</u>, <u>25</u>, (1), pp. 55-63.

Soloway, E., Ehrilich, K., and Bonar, J., 1982, "Tapping into Tacit

Programming Knowledge", <u>Proceedings of the Conference on Human Factors in Computer Systems</u>, ACM, New York, pp. 52-57.

Weiser, M., 1981, "Program Slicing", <u>Proceedings of the Fifth International Conference on System Science</u>, Honolulu, HI, March 1981.

Weiser, M., 1982, "Programmer Use Slices When Debugging", <u>Communications of the ACM</u>, <u>25</u>, (7), pp. 446-452.

Woodfield, S. N., 1979, "An Experiment in Unit Increase in Problem Complexity", <u>IEEE Transactions on Software Engineering</u>, <u>SE-5</u>, pp. 76-79, March 1979.

Woodfield, S. N., Dunsmore, H. E., and Shen, V. Y., 1981, "The Effect of Modularization and Comments on Program Comprehension", <u>Proceedings of the 5th International Conference on Software Engineering</u>, San Diego, CA, March, 1981, pp. 215-223.

Woodfield, S. N., Shen, V. Y., and Dunsmore, H. E., "A Study of Several Metrics for Programming Effort", <u>Journal of Systems Software</u>, <u>2</u>, December 1981, pp. 97-103.

Woodward, M. R., Hennell, M. A., and Hedley, D., 1979, "A Measure of Control Flow Complexity in Program Text", <u>IEEE Transactions on Software Engineering</u>, <u>SE-5</u>, pp. 45-50.

Zeigler, B. P., and Rada, R., 1982, "Abstraction in Methodology: A Framework for Computer Support", <u>Proc. Empirical Foundations of Information and Software Science</u>, Atlanta, GA, November 1982, pp. 63-80.

Zunde, P., 1982, "Empirical Laws and Theories of Information and Software Sciences", <u>Proc. Empirical Foundations of Information and Software Science</u>, Atlanta, GA, November 1982, pp. 5-18.

Zweben, S. H., 1977, "A Study of the Physical Structure of Algorithms", <u>IEEE Transactions on Software Engineering</u>, <u>SE-3</u>, (3), pp. 250-258.

4. USER-SYSTEM INTERACTION

A COMPARISON OF THE USABILITY OF SQL VS. A MENU-DRIVEN INTERFACE

J. Steve Davis

Department of Management
Clemson University
Clemson, SC   29631

Abstract: This paper presents results of an experiment which compares the usability of a menu-driven system to that of an alternate version with a query language. Subjects performed better with the query language version and considered it easier to use. With both versions they had more difficulty accomplishing queries which required associating more than one screen or table (relation) of data.

INTRODUCTION

Users want information systems which are easy to use. Though vendors often stress the friendliness of their systems, there is little empirical evidence to support vendor claims, to serve as a sound basis for user evaluation, or to guide system developers.

Most current information systems employ either a menu-driven interface or a database query language. Studies of user-friendliness (usability) have compared alternative query languages, but still unresolved is the relative friendliness of menus vs. query languages (Leitheiser, 1986).

In the remainder of this paper we discuss results of an experiment which compares the usability of a particular MIS with a menu-driven interface to an alternate version with a query language. We focus on one of the most common activities of information system users, database query, and do not consider updating.

We selected the Manufacturing and Production Information Control System (MAPICS) as the basis for the investigation. This IBM product is the most popular material resource planning (MRP) system. Advertised as user-friendly, MAPICS has a menu-driven interface and is intended for installation and use by people without special training.

The interface of the alternate version was SQL (Chamberlin et al., 1976) as implemented in Knowledgeman (Micro Data Base Systems, Inc., 1984). Since SQL is widely used on minicomputer and mainframe DBMS, it can be considered representative of current query languages. Our alternate version of MAPICS consisted specifically of the Knowledgeman DBMS loaded with data similar to that in the MAPICS system.

The task of the subjects was to answer 7 questions about the data in each system. They were allowed 15 minutes for each set of 7 questions.

EXPERIMENTAL PROCEDURE

Subjects

The subjects were 115 undergraduate students enrolled in an MIS course. Students received a 30 minute introduction to MRP and a 2 hour introduction to database management systems (but no hands-on work) during the course.

Materials

The students were provided:

1. A cover sheet which described the two part exercise.

2. A one page guide to the data in the MAPICS system. The guide provided a list of data items associated with each of the 4 main menu options relevant to this exercise.

3. A one page guide to the data in the SQL system. This included names of relations (tables)and their attributes (fields).

4. For the MAPICS exercise, an IBM System 36 with MAPICS on-line, and data concerning an office products company installed.

5. For the SQL exercise, an IBM PC with Knowledgeman on-line, and data concerning a garden equipment company installed.

6. A list of 7 questions for each exercise. The questions for each exercise were equivalent in the sense that only the items and order numbers were different, for example:

   SQL question: Reference order number M000050 for the 12" industrial bucket, what is the due date of this order?

   MAPICS question: Reference order number M000036 for the 2-drawer work desk, what is the due date of this order?

Table 1. SQL vs. MAPICS, Performance and Preference (N-115).

	SQL	MAPICS
Mean number of correct answers	4.84	2.71
Choice as easier to use*	85	26

*Four subjects indicated no preference.

Table 2. Performance on Selected Questions.

	MEAN SCORES	
	SQL	MAPICS
The 2 questions requiring references to more than 1 table or screen.	.21	.18
The other 5 questions	.88	.47

Orientation

Immediately prior to each part of the exercise, the subjects were given a 15 minute introduction to the system they would use. All subjects successfully completed a sample query during the orientation on each system.

Scoring

Responses to the questions were scored as correct or incorrect.

RESULTS

Subjects performed better with SQL ($p < .0001$) and considered SQL easier to use than menu-driven MAPICS (see Table 1).

The order in which subjects used the systems was insignificant with respect to performance.

With both systems, subjects scored fewer correct answers on the questions which required reference to more than one table or screen (see Table 2).

A comparison of scores for subjects with varying typing skills and DBMS experience is shown in Table 3. There is no indication that typing skill was a significant advantage in composing queries in SQL, and DBMS experience shows little effect on performance.

The number of computer courses had a significant positive correlation with performance on SQL ($r = .34$, $p < .0002$), but no significant correlation with MAPICS performance ($r = .16$).

Four sources provided information on subject difficulties: the number of incorrect answers; student remarks after each exercise; comments written on answer sheets; and direct observation by the experimenter.

The following were common problems in using MAPICS:

1. Avoiding the "blind alley", a screen of data which lacks the desired information and is at the end of a chain of menu choices. This situation requires "backtracking" to previous menus in the chain.

Table 3. Typing Skill and DBMS Experience vs. Performance.

| | MEAN NUMBER OF CORRECT ANSWERS | |
	SQL	MAPICS
Typing Skill		
Low (n=27)	4.6	2.0
High (n=47)*	5.1	3.1
DBMS Experience		
No (n=44)	4.6	2.5
Yes (n=72)	5.0	2.8

*Subjects were grouped as follows, depending on their
self-evaluation: High - good touch typist; Med -
poor touch typist; Low - hunt and peck. There were
42 in the Med group.

Many subjects complained that the menu labels did not provide enough information to make the proper choice.

2. Finding the desired item on a MAPICS screen which is crowded. For example, the "Order Status Inquiry" screen contains 47 labels and 47 data items. Some participants were confused by inconsistent screen formats, which group some related data items in a horizontal arrangement and others vertically.

3. Determining how to proceed when the terminal locks (does not respond to any keystrokes) and the system provides no clue on how to continue. Most subjects encountered this situation at least once and were unable to continue until aided by the experimenter.

4. Determining that the HELP key was necessary to access data associated with a given screen. For example, many subjects failed to find the status description of a certain order. 18 subjects wrote the correct status code on the answer sheet, but were apparently unable to find the associated status description.* The only way to determine the status description is to first find the status code on a MAPICS screen and then press the HELP key to find a table of status codes together with their descriptions. This problem occurred in spite of an introduction to the HELP key during the orientation.

5. Finding data associated with a screen which is accessible only by pointers from that screen. This problem is similar to that discussed in item 4. Some information is found only by first finding a screen which provides data "close" to what is needed, and then selecting an option associated with that screen, such as "command key 5 - detailed data".

The following were common problems in using SQL:

---

*Probably there were more subjects who also found the status code but did not write it because they were not sure it was the right answer.

1. Composing a syntactically correct query. Some subjects had to retype a command many times. The most common problems were simple mistakes like omitting a closing quotation mark. The Knowledgeman version of SQL does not allow editing of a command once it is entered.

2. Choosing an appropriate table or criteria for selection from a table. This problem was particularly evident in attempting to answer the questions which required reference to more than one table. Some subjects assumed that a single table would suffice. For example, subjects were asked to determine the status description of a particular order for item number 933. There was no single table associating item number with status of an order. There was a table, ST, which associated status codes with status descriptions, but did not contain item numbers. Yet over 25% of the students attempted this query:

   SELECT STATUS FROM ST FOR ITEM#="933".

   23 subjects found the status code from a single table reference, but were unable to find the associated status description.

DISCUSSION AND CONCLUSIONS

In addition to the interface, there were some other system differences, such as the keyboard and display, which could have influenced the results.

The questions, selected from introductory materials for a production and operations management course, were rather simple. Only two required references to more than one table in SQL or more than one screen of data in MAPICS. We cannot be sure that results would be the same for more complicated queries.

The strong preference for SQL over MAPICS suggests that information system designers should consider alternatives to menu-driven interfaces, even when the system is intended for users without special training. It may be that the computer literacy of the typical office worker has increased to the point that query languages are not difficult to learn.

Results confirm that it is more difficult, using SQL, to retrieve information which requires the association of more than one table. The difficulty in formulating multi-table queries may be addressed by on-line aids. Some new systems, such as FRED include an "intelligent assistant" to aid in query formulation (Jakobson, Lafond, Nyberg, and Piatetsky-Shapiro, 1986).

The association of related screen displays in MAPICS must be accomplished in some cases by using the HELP key and in other cases by entering a selection from a menu embedded within a screen of data. This inconsistency confuses some users. Our conjecture is that most people expect to find assistance but not actual data through a help facility. The tendency of users to overlook menus built into data screens might be overcome by highlighting or flashing the menu portion.

ACKNOWLEDGEMENTS

Dr. R. Lawrence LaForge provided the MAPICS database from his course in Production and Operations Management and assisted in development of experimental materials. Dr. Charles McNichols assisted in experimental design.

REFERENCES

Chamberlin, D. D., Astrahan, M. M., Eswaran, K. P., Griffiths, P. P., Lorie, R. A., Mehl, J. W., Reisner, P., and Wade, B. W., 1976, "SEQUEL2: A Unified Approach to Data Definition, Manipulation and Control", IBM Journal of Research and Development, 20, November 1976, pp. 560-575. (A subset of SEQUEL is now called SQL.)

Gray, C., 1986, "MRP II Software", Computerworld, January 27, 1986, p. 37.

Jakobson, G., Lafond, C., Nyberg, E., and Piatetsky-Shapiro, G., 1986, "An Intelligent Database Assistant", IEEE Expert, 1, (2), Summer 1986, pp. 65-79.

Leitheiser, R. L., 1986, "Computer Support for Knowledge Workers: A Review of Laboratory Experiments", Data Base, Spring 1986, pp. 17-45.

Micro Data Base Systems, Inc., 1984, The Knowledge Manager (Knowledgeman) Reference Manual.

USE OF QUERY LANGUAGE BOOLEAN OPERATORS BY PROFESSIONALS

Bill Ferns and B. Loerinc Helft

Baruch College, City University of New York
Department of Statistics and Computer Information Systems
Box 513
17 Lexington Avenue
New York, New York 10010

Abstract: This study looks at the use of Boolean operators in query languages as a specific aspect of the human/machine interface. The difficulties
casual users have with Boolean operators are often explained by the assumption that those users simply do not understand Boolean logic, and the difficulties would not be so prevalent if users applied themselves to understanding this logical system. We investigate the possibility that the
issue is not simply misunderstanding on the user's part, but perhaps a
deeper, fundamental difference caused by the contextual and structural
semantics of the user's logic, which Boolean operators, functioning basically
as keywords, fail to address.

We present the results of a study of professional programmers, who do
have training and experience in the use of Boolean operators, comparing their
use of natural language vs. formal logic in the phrasing of database queries.
These programmers displayed significantly different uses of the words AND,
OR, and NOT in a natural language setting as opposed to a more formal Boolean
setting. And, despite concerns about natural language's ambiguities, there
exist more consistencies in the English use of AND, OR, and NOT than we might
have believed.

These consistencies, and their contradictions with formal logic,
strongly suggest that people have 'deep structure' groupings which are not
adequately or easily supported by Boolean operators. By studying professional programmers and database users, we look at the question of whether
these deeper logical structures in natural language maintain a stronger
hold than Boolean operators, and whether or not use of Boolean operators is
an external and 'unnatural' task.

We recommend that further studies in defining these natural language
logical structures will contribute in the long run to a more effective
human/computer interface than will maintaining the use of Boolean logic.

INTRODUCTION: MOTIVATION AND GOALS

There has been much work in making the human/computer interface more

211

SAMPLE EMPLOYEE DATABASE USED IN STUDY

LASTNAME	FIRSTNAME	SEX	DEPT	GRADE	STATUS	DEPENDENTS
Chin	Philip	M	Sales	2	Full	1
Clark	Judith	F	Administration	5	Full	0
Giordano	Judy	F	Accounting	4	Full	3
Jackson	Elvira	F	Sales	3	Full	2
O'Malley	Patrick	M	Accounting	1	Part	1
Santiago	David	M	Administration	4	Full	2
Stein	Gilda	F	DP	3	Part	0

Figure 1.   Sample Employee Database.

amenable to human productivity (Badre and Shneiderman, 1983; Schneider, 1982; Shackle, 1981). In particular, we are interested in the study of query languages to enhance problem-solving and database use. With the proliferation of database management systems available, especially for microcomputer users, and with the migration towards natural-like language interfaces for these systems, we noticed a number of interesting phenomena among our students.

- Students have difficulty constructing compound conditions when learning programming languages, even if they have encountered Boolean operators in other contexts - symbolic logic courses, for example.

- Students learning the use of database packages had difficulty formulating queries according to the rules specified by the query language, often somewhere between a Boolean logic system and a query language designer's view of what was 'natural'.

- Students who used on-line bibliographic search languages, including those students who studied programming and database querying, often confused intersection with union. This resulted either in obtaining many references that were not relevant, or in no reference on the subject of interest.

We address the issue of correct formulation of queries for two reasons. First, query problems are generally simpler than the typical applications program, and could be tested more easily with, hopefully, less statistical 'noise' from other variables. Also, specifically because of the greater likelihood that more casual, or non-professional, users will be database queriers and not programmers, optimization of this interface would have a wider impact.

CONFLICTS OF BOOLEAN OPERATORS WITH NATURAL LANGUAGE SEMANTICS

Boolean operators are logical connectors, such as AND, OR, and NOT, used to join several criteria for selecting records from a database. Although other operators exist, these three enjoy usage in natural language; we test the influence natural language has upon their use in a formal setting by first requiring that the subject formulate the query in natural language and then, after instruction in the use of Boolean operators, requiring that the subject formulate similar queries using these operators. We provided

EXAMPLE OF WITHIN-FIELD PRIORITY

Given the following query:

List the employees who are male and are in Administration or Sales

There are two ways to evaluate it - **Boolean** hierarchy would first find the intersection of employees who meet both criteria of being male and in Administration, and joining the result with **all** the employees who are in Sales. **Within-Field Priority**, however, first evaluates the union of the employees who are either in Accounting or in Sales, since these are elements of the same field, and then intersects that subset with employees who are male. Using the sample database in figure 2 (this database was also used in the study), these two approaches yield the following results:

BOOLEAN	**WITHIN-FIELD PRIORITY**
O'Malley	O'Malley
Chin	Chin
Jackson	

Figure 2. Within-Field Priority.

no training in natural language; we wanted to allow free-form expression without restraint. Any coaching would produce a restricted subset of English, thus an 'unnatural' language (Palme, 1981).

We address the semantic conflicts between Booleans and natural language in the query language context. Padin (1979) urged the use of nonsense words in place of the Boolean AND, OR, and NOT, to be able to better compare their use formally and in English. Our approach was to isolate the use of these words, first by allowing the subject to express queries in a natural language manner, and then to focus attention on the Boolean operators, reformulating the queries. The sample data base, which was used in this study, is shown in Figure 1.

As opposed to formal logic, natural language may not utilize the hierarchy for evaluating Booleans (i.e., NOT, AND, OR, and left-to-right precedence). We also found an implicit within-field priority in the way natural language thought processes evaluate queries. Our term within-field priority (see Figure 2) is used whenever a single field is tested for several potential values, and the Boolean operators used in combining these values receive a higher priority of evaluation than they would under hierarchy conventions. For example, in the testing that took place, the implicit within-field priority was repeatedly evidenced both in the query-formulating and query-analysis efforts of the subjects.

It was also noted that if two criteria in a query are different values for the same field, the natural language tendency is to select records where either condition is met, regardless of the operator used to connect the two criteria; we term this condition within-field union (see Figure 3).

Within-field priority and within-field union are not merely natural language operations on two (or more) values for the same field in a database, but also on two elements of the same entity in a real world application. While our examples are pertinent to relational database models, the implementation should be transparent to the user, who ideally only needs to know the actual application, not how that application is presented.

In English, the word OR has several different uses, as an inclusive OR, exclusive OR, or total set. Meaning may depend upon whether the criteria being joined are between-fields criteria (criteria to select a record based on several different fields, inclusive OR) or within-field criteria (criteria

Given the following query:

List the employees who are in Accounting and Sales

There are two ways to evaluate it - **Boolean** evaluation of AND would find the set of employees who meet the condition of being <u>both</u> in Accounting <u>and</u> Sales. Since each employee can only be in one department, the boolean interpretation yields the null set. However, since both criteria are values for the department field, **within-field union** finds the set of employees who are in either department. The AND is relegated to being merely a connective between the two criteria; it has no external logical function. Using the sample database in Figure 2, these two approaches yield the following results:

BOOLEAN	WITHIN-FIELD UNION
nil	Chin
	Giordano
	Jackson
	O'Malley

When **within-field union** is used to evaluate a query, it does not matter whether the connective is an OR or an AND.

Figure 3.   Within-Field Union.

to select a record based on several different values for the same field, exclusive OR). The usage of OR to describe the total set, as in "Get me a list of employees, male or female, who have dependents", was not included in our study, since the gender values requested include the entire range of values for that field; database users rarely create queries with this meaning of OR.

There are times when AND may be used in natural language to represent the union of entities that meet any of the specified criteria. There are two contexts in which AND is used to express a sense of union:

1)   As a connective used between two different values of the same entity, discussed in Figure 3 as <u>within-field union</u>.

2)   To join separately formed constructs, such as "List the employees who are part-time and those who have no dependents".

Besides the inconsistencies between Boolean operators in formal logic and their usage in natural language, there are other ways in which logical subsetting operations are expressed in natural language without using these operators explicitly.

1)   Adjectives and qualifiers ("with") are used to express selection criteria for intersecting operations without the operator AND, such as 'Select the full-time females with grade 2'. Lochovski and Tsichritsis (1982) suggest that between-fields intersection may be just as natural and implicit a semantic interpretation as within-field union subsetting.

2)   Commas may be interpreted as reiterations of the operators, acting as ANDs for connecting between-fields criteria, as in "List any employee who is female, in administration, and has no dependents", and acting as ORs for connecting within-field criteria, such as "List any employee in Sales, Accounting, or Finance".

OVERVIEW OF QUESTIONNAIRE CONSTRUCTION AND SAMPLE QUESTIONS

The final version of the questionnaire had the following construction:

Frontpiece – how to fill out the study
Demographic questions
Introduction to query languages
Sample Database
Natural Language Format
    Query Analysis – Part One
    Query Construction – Part Two
Review of Boolean Operators
Formal Boolean Format
    Query Analysis – Part Three
    Query Construction – Part Four

Sample Query Analysis Questions (For Parts One and Three)
Testing Within-Field Union:
    Select the employees who are in Sales and DP
Testing Within-Field Priority:
    List the employees who are men and are in Administration and Sales.

Sample Query Construction Questions (for Parts Two and Four)
Testing Between-Fields Intersection:
    Construct a query that selects any record that meets the following criteria:
      a) The employee is male
      b) The employee is a full-time worker.
Testing Within-Field Priority:
    Construct a query which accomplishes the following goals:
      a) Finds the employees in DP
      b) Finds the employees in Administration
      c) Finds, from the records selected above, the employees with
        grade > 2

Figure 4. Questionnaire Used in The Study.

3) Parentheses are not used in natural language except to express an aside; in formal grammar, they are used to change or enforce priority of execution. However, natural language does provide a means of 'implicit parenthesization' of logical combinations, by the use of such word pairs as 'Both...and', 'Either...or', and 'Neither...nor' (Sager, 1981). These pairs are rarely seen in query languages, and indeed, if required by a natural-like query language, would make that query language a 'restricted' one; some studies have found that restricted natural languages may be just as problematic and difficult to learn as formal grammars (Palme, 1981).

The assumption that Boolean conventions are adequate and comprehensive have led to the proliferation of their use in implementing many query languages. Two problems arise. First, there exist logical structures in English which do not easily fit into a Boolean environment, as demonstrated by the descriptions of <u>within-field priority</u> and <u>within-field union</u>. This causes difficulty in the conversion of informally worded retrieval tasks into formal queries. Second, software designers have different approaches to implementing Boolean operators, especially when implementing a pseudo-natural language environment, thus forcing users to adapt to each designer's decision.

While there has been work on the contradictions between Boolean logic and natural reasoning, it is in the area of propositional logic (Rips, 1983;

Braine, 1978) and not directly relevant to the study of query languages.

WORK EXPERIENCE OF SUBJECTS

	Query Language Only	Programming Language Only	Both
Number of Subjects	1	3	27

Experience of Subjects (in years)	Query Languages	Programming Language
AVERAGE (experienced only)	3.3	6.0
MEDIAN	3.0	4.0
LOW	0.5	0.5
HIGH	10.0	22.0

Figure 5. Relevant Data About Subjects.

DESCRIPTION OF THE QUESTIONNAIRE

We constructed a questionnaire, described in Figure 4, to address these issues. There were basically two parts to the questionnaire - one for testing responses in a natural language format, and the second, following a brief description of Boolean operators, which required the subject to answer questions using formal Boolean constructions. Each of these parts was further broken up into two more sections - a query analysis section, in which the subject's task was to list the records which would be selected by pre-constructed queries, and a query construction section, in which the respondent would construct queries that asked for specific criteria. The purpose of the query analysis section was to reveal how the subjects themselves interpreted and evaluated Boolean operators, and thus shed some light on how they would actually process these tasks, as opposed to how they constructed commands which would instruct the computer to perform these same tasks. We hoped that reviewing how subjects answered queries would contribute to our understanding of why they constructed queries in the manner they did.

An earlier pre-test and test was administered to students who had no expertise with programming or database querying. These tests were designed along the same lines previously described; however, they tested a wider range of issues concerning contradictions between English semantics and Boolean conventions. The results of these tests provided early indications of the power of within-field priority and within-field unions (Ferns, 1985). This led to the re-design of the present testing instrument in order to bring these issues to the forefront.

Several questions arose from these earlier results. How strongly held is the logic of these natural structural groupings (within-field priority and within-field union)? Can training in a different logical system, namely Boolean logic, override and replace these natural tendencies?

We initially held the view that novices could easily learn Boolean logic, and after exposure, none of these problems would exist. After the pretests, however, we hypothesized that even experienced users would, in a natural language setting, use non-Boolean logical structures, and that Boolean operators which contradicted these natural language structures would be used only when externally reinforced.

With this purpose in mind, we conducted the present version of the questionnaire with computer professionals as participants. There were 31 subjects used in this study. They were all programmers and/or users of query languages on the job, and all indicated that they had previous experience with Boolean operators. They were chosen from several different businesses; the subjects used a wide variety of programming and query languages. This diversity assured us that no one language's orientation had an overwhelming influence on the study group's responses. Figure 5 illustrates our subjects' work experience.

Each question in the natural language section was designed to have a matching one requiring parallel tasks in the formal Boolean section, so that the responses to the same kind of logical operation could be compared. Each section was comprised of six questions, and the first few questions in each section had simple combinations of only two criteria logically combined in order to test issues such as between-fields intersection and within-field union. The remaining questions dealt specifically with the problems of within-field priority. Even though the subjects in this study were programmers and/or professional database users, a review of Boolean operators was included to reinforce the usage of Booleans for the second section (see Figure 4 for the construction of the questionnaire and sample questions).

There was some discussion as to whether the test should also be administered with different sequencing, putting the formal Boolean section first. This was rejected, however, because of the concern that the more alert subjects would be tipped off as to the purpose of the study, and may later, consciously or unconsciously, bias their answers in the natural language section. In an earlier test, for example, a student subject told one of the authors that, had he been told that the focus of the test was Boolean operators, he would have answered the natural language section much differently!

DATA COLLECTION

We chose to administer the study as a pencil-and-paper questionnaire in order to conduct the test in as neutral a manner as possible, keeping biasing and unmeasured variables to a minimum. Since one half of the test measured full natural language use, no computer interface was available. We did not want to introduce variables related to the use of a particular computer system - no one computer was common to all our subjects' experience. Furthermore, subjects worked by themselves, without the interaction of a proctor to influence the outcome.

We also allowed freedom in how specific criteria were expressed in the Boolean section. In other words, the query

List the employees with sex = male and dept = Accounting

was considered equivalent to

Select the employees who are male and in Accounting.

Since we wanted to focus on Boolean operations, we felt that by placing a minimum of restrictions in other areas of a query's formulation, we could better isolate the effect of the review of Boolean operators and the charge to the subjects to use formal logic in the Boolean section.

For each question, responses were classified as either Boolean, natural language (either within-field priority or within-field union, depending

Questions testing AND in Between-Fields and Within-Field Contexts

The following query tested how subjects evaluated two criteria representing values from different fields connected by the word AND:

List the employees who are female and have dependents

Juxtaposed to this was the following query which examined how participants evaluated two criteria representing different values of the **same** field connected by the word AND:

Select the employees in Sales and DP.

Figure 6.   Test Queries for AND.

upon the question's context), and unclassifiable. An extremely small percentage of the responses were unclassifiable; most fell clearly in one of the two other categories. Whichever category each response fell into was assigned a value of 1, the other categories 0. The data for each subject could then be summed to find the total of Boolean, natural language, and unclassifiable responses for each section, and then compared between the natural language and Boolean sections. This also allowed for the results of questions testing similar constructs (Within-field priority, within-field union, and between-fields intersection) to be examined together.

We tested the results of individual questions and groups of questions using paired t-tests; the before and after results were obviously not independent, and the skewness of the observations was not extreme enough to warrant the use of non-parametric procedures.

RESULTS

Repeatedly throughout the natural language section, the manner in which subjects processed queries depended much more upon the criteria's relationship to one another than on what kind of operator joined them; the behavior of the logic processing was dictated more by whether the criteria were within-field or between-field values. In situations where Boolean conventions contradicted these tendencies, the conventions were often ignored. When the Boolean conventions reinforced a natural trend, users were quick to adopt the operator. These characteristics came out in the following ways:

1)   Between-fields intersection: The consistency with which subjects both analyzed and constructed queries utilizing intersection of between-fields values indicates the naturalness of this process for the subjects; AND was typically adopted for this use. There was no significant difference in the respondent's approach in between-fields intersection in the natural language and the Boolean sections.

2)   Within-field union: Questions 1 and 2 (see Figure 6) in the query analysis sections illustrate the power of within-field union. Fifty-four percent of the subjects interpreted AND as an intersection operator for the between-fields values and as a union operator for the within-field values in the natural language section.

This dropped to only 19% analyzing AND as within-field union in the Boolean section; this difference is significant (p < .0002).

218

Overall Responses Grouped by Structure Category

	Natural Language Section			Boolean Section		
			RESPONSES			
	Boolean	Natural Lang.	Unclassifiable	Boolean	Natural Lang.	Unclassifiable
Between-Fields Intersection	90 %	8 %	2 %	97 %	1.5 %	1.5 %
	change between sections not significant					
Within-Field Union	42 %	54 %	4 %	77 %	19 %	4 %
	change between sections significant with $p < .0002$					
Within-Field Priority	30 %	63 %	7 %	67 %	27 %	6 %
	change between sections significant with $p = .0001$					

Figure 7. Experimental Results.

3) <u>Within-field priority</u>: In the natural language section, subjects processed within-field components of the query together, regardless of the operator involved and regardless of their order. This is perhaps the most important break from the Boolean tradition. The preponderance of its use by subjects, especially the more experienced professional, would indicate that even skilled professionals maintain separate bodies of knowledge for logic processing, and that the Boolean model is not internalized. This is buttressed by the change in subjects' rate of Boolean responses for within-field priority questions, from 30% in the natural language section to 67% in the Boolean section, with $p = .0001$. If there is a natural processing priority, we must find a way to integrate it into the database interface.

The overall results broken down by category of question are illustrated in Figure 7.

4) <u>Other Observations</u>: There are some indications that the power of within-field priority may also affect the priority may also affect the priority of evaluation when the NOT operator is used. Though still untested in a controlled environment, our observations point to the possibility that criteria connected structurally as within-field values may be evaluated before a NOT operator, contrary to Boolean hierarchy of evaluation; operators joining between-fields values would still be evaluated after NOT (see Figure 8).

The greatest incidence of unclassifiable answers occurred when subjects had to use the NOT operator, especially in situations requiring an understanding of DeMorgan's Law; further study in these contradictions using the NOT operator are needed.

Application of NOT in Different Structural Contexts

In the following query,

List the employees not in Accounting and full-time

AND joins between-fields values; NOT is evaluated first with 'in Accounting', and then intersected with the employees who are full-time, consistent with boolean hierarchy. Using the employee database in Figure 2, this query returns the records for Chin, Clark, Jackson, and Santiago.

On the other hand, in the query

List the employees not in Sales or in Administration

the natural tendency may be to select the set of employees in either Sales or Administration, <u>then</u> applying the NOT to derive the inverse of this set; this version of within-field priority is in conflict with boolean conventions:

BOOLEAN	**WITHIN-FIELD PRIORITY OVER NOT**
Clark	Giordano
Giordano	O'Malley
O'Malley	Stein
Stein	

Figure 8. Test Queries for NOT.

We purposely omitted any discussion of the use of parentheses to enforce priority of evaluation. However, we were still surprised at how few of the respondents used them, even for the more complex tasks (at most, only 4 out of 31 or 13%, used them on any one question). Possibly the subjects felt the use of parentheses was 'against the rules', but it also suggests that users may not naturally use parentheses. We are currently involved in testing the ease of use of parentheses.

CONCLUDING REMARKS

The tendency to emphasize within-field priority of processing on the part of the subjects cannot be explained by a relative lack of experience by the sample group, who had been programming professionally for over 10 years each. One subject, who had several years experience as a PL/1 and Assembler programmer, noted on his questionnaire concerning hierarchy of Boolean operators that "PL/1 works this way and it's worthless. No one remembers the order and it causes more trouble than it's worth." He solved the ambiguity problems with parentheses; but if an experienced programmer feels this way, what about the casual user who is working on a software system that may not even provide parentheses (which quite a few don't) to enforce priority of execution?

Even in the Boolean section, there was a 32% rate of non-Boolean responses by these professional users in questions using within-field priority. If software designers are trying to make systems easier for the casual user, how many years can we reasonably expect those users to take priority. If software designers are trying to make systems easier for the casual user, how many years can we reasonably expect those users to take to learn Boolean conventions (besides which, how long do people stay programmers before moving on to be analysts and team leaders, leaving those less experienced to do the programming?).

Our position is not to tout natural language over formal language, or vice-versa. What we are trying to emphasize is that correct use of Boolean operators and conventions cannot be taken for granted; they have several levels of context to them. Software developers building natural language

220

environments need to become more aware of the ambiguities involved in the words AND, OR, and NOT, and how the relationship of the various criteria to one another affects the actual meaning of these words. Formal language components, however comforting it may be to have linguistic absolutes, must see that the Boolean operators are <u>not absolute</u>, because we bring so much outside connotation to them.

One can argue that formal Boolean usage is not less ambiguous than natural language. If those conventions provide different rules than the subject were accustomed to, due to the influence of natural language, users have more difficulty in segregating the formal use from their common understanding, thus creating the ambiguity.

Boolean operators are <u>surface-level</u> operators, with no awareness of the deeper structural bindings of the values being operated on. Often, Boolean operations conflict with these structures. Just as we try to create data structures to accurately model the real world, we need to discern what kind of logical operators appropriately reflect querying reality.

The contradictions between Boolean operators and their natural language semantics are too powerful and pervasive to allow their implementation to be approached as an after-thought. It may be necessary to explore the use of very different types of logic processing in the human-computer interface.

We suggest several avenues for further investigation. One is to narrow the focus of the study, concentrating on within-field priority and union. This caused the most difficulty and led to the most inconsistency in expression. We would attempt to extend natural language to convey complicated ideas unambiguously. It may indeed be possible to construct correct queries more easily with such combinations.

ACKNOWLEDGEMENT

The authors would like to thank William Dillon of the Department of Marketing, and Edward Wolf, Mark Berenson, and Mabel Yu of the Department of Statistics and Computer Information Systems, all of Baruch College, for their assistance and support.

REFERENCES

Badre, A., and Shneiderman, B., 1983, <u>Directions in Human/Computer Interactions</u>, Ablex Publ. Co., Norwood, NJ.

Bayman, P. and Mayer, R. E., 1983, "A Diagnosis of Beginning Programmers' Misconceptions of BASIC Programming Statements", <u>Communications of the ACM</u>, <u>26</u>, (9), September 1983.

Braine, M. D., 1978, "On the Relation Between the Natural Logic of Reasoning and Standard Logic", <u>Psychological Review</u>, <u>85</u>, (1), January 1978.

Ferns, B., 1985, <u>Boolean Operators in Query Languages - A Study of the Contradictions Between Formal Logic and Natural Language</u>, Master's Thesis, Baruch College, City University of New York, May 1985.

Harris, L. R., 1983, "The Advantages of Natural Language Processing, <u>Designing for Human-Computer Communication</u>, Sime, M. E., and Coombs, M. J., eds., Academic Press, New York, NY.

Hill, I. D., 1983, "Natural Language vs. Computer Language, Designing for Human-Computer Communication, Sime, M. E., and Coombs, M. J., eds., Academic Press, New York, NY.

Lochovski, F. H., and Tsichritsis, D. C., 1982, "Querying External Databases", Human Factors and Interactive Computer Systems, Vassiliou, Y., ed., Ablex Publ. Co., Norwood, NJ.

Padin, M. E., 1979, "At Ease With Boolean Operators in Online Searching", Online, 3, (2), April 1979.

Palme, J., 1981, "Interactive Software for Humans", Man-Computer Interaction: Human Aspects of Computers and People, Shackle, B., ed., Sijthoff & Noordhoff, Rockville, MD.

Reisner, P., 1977, "Use of Psychological Experimentation as an Aid to Development of a Query Language", IEEE Transactions on Software Engineering, SE-3.

Reisner, P., 1984, "Formal Grammar as a Tool for Analyzing Ease of Use: Some Fundamental Concepts", Human Factors in Computer Systems, Thomas, J. C., and Schneider, M. L., eds., Ablex Publ. Co., Norwood, NJ.

Rips, L. J., 1983, "Cognitive Processes in Propositional Reasoning", Psychological Review, 90, (1), January 1983,

Sager, N., 1981, Natural Language Information Processing, Addison-Wesley Publ. Co., Inc., Reading, MA.

Schneider, L. M., 1982, "Ergonomic Considerations in the Design of Command Languages", Human Factors and Interactive Computer Systems, Vassiliou, Y., ed., Ablex Publ. Co., Norwood, NJ.

Shackle, B., 1981, Man-Computer Interaction: Human Aspects of Computers and People, Sijthoff and Noordhoff, Rockville, MD.

Shneiderman, B., 1976, "Applying the Results of Human Factors Experimentation: Programming Languages and Data Base Query Languages", The Role of Human Factors in Computers, Proceedings of a Symposium co-sponsored by the Metropolitan Chapter of the Human Factors Society and Baruch College, Cuny, NY, November 18, 1976.

Sime, M. E., and Coombs, M. J., 1983, Designing for Human-Computer Communication, Academic Press, New York, NY.

Spohrer, J. C., and Soloway, E., 1986, "Novice Mistakes Are Folk Wisdoms Correct?", Communications of the ACM, 29, (7), July 1986.

Thomas, J. C., and Schneider, M. L., eds., 1984, Human Factors in Computer Systems, Ablex Publ. Co., Norwood, NJ.

Vassiliou, Y., 1982, Human Factors and Interactive Computer Systems, Ablex Publ. Co., Norwood, NJ.

MAN-COMPUTER INTERACTION IN COMPUTER-AIDED SYSTEM ANALYSIS AND DESIGN:

APPLICATION OF PSL/PSA

Zbigniew J. Gackowski

California State University, Stanislaus
School of Business Administration
Department of Business Computer Information Systems
Turlock, California

Abstract: Analysts and designers of information systems are in the business of recommending new or improved applications of computers to their employers and/or clients. However, they rarely use computers as a tool of their trade. Before long students of this subject will face the challenge of computer-aided tools in their profession. This paper presents an experience in teaching system analysis and design with the aid of computers using the Problem Statement Language and the Problem Statement Analyzer (PSL/PSA) developed by the ISDOS Project.

INTRODUCTION - THE "SHOEMAKER'S CHILDREN" SYNDROME

System analysis and design of information systems is the process of studying and examining the business situation and the interactions within an organization in order to improve them by developing better methods and procedures for performing necessary functions. Since computers have pervaded nearly every aspect of business organizations, this means more and more developing of new computer-based information systems.

System analysts and designers of information systems are trained professionals who can assist an organization in conducting systems studies, determining information and processing requirements, designing the new system and supervising the preparation for and conversion to the new system. Thus, today, they are inevitably in the business of recommending new or improved computer applications to their employers or clients. While being busy doing so, they rarely use computers as a tool of their trade. As some shoemakers of the past, who did not have enough time to make shoes for their own children, system analyst and designers have not found time to master the use of computers in the process of analysis and design, not only for conventional, but also for computer-based information systems. Manual efforts are still state-of-the-art in this profession.

According to Couger (Couger, Colter, and Knapp, 1982), the "fifth generation development techniques for computer-based systems" will be "a linked set of techniques to be available to automate all phases of the system development cycle". He could refer only to "one multidisciplinary research activity underway, the ISDOS project, coordinated by Professor

Daniel Teichroew at the University of Michigan. ISDOS is the acronym for Information System Design and Optimization System".

In July 1983, the ISDOS Project was reorganized into two separate, but cooperating, units: the ISDOS, Inc. (presently Meta Systems), and the PRISE Project at the Department of Industrial & Operations Engineering of the University of Michigan. PSL/PSA is one of the first commercial products of the ISDOS Project used by several major corporations and U.S. government agencies. Since July 1984, PSL/PSA has become an IBM program product offering (IBM, 1984). Those currently studying system analysis and design can expect that computer-aided analysis will become wide spread, when supported by the "Big Blue". Before long students of this subject will face the challenge and opportunity of using computer-aided tools in their prospective profession.

This paper presents an experience in man-computer interaction, while teaching system analysis and design with the aid of computers and the Problem Statement Language/Problem Statement Analyzer (PSL/PSA) developed by the ISDOS Project.

PSL/PSA

The Problem Statement Language/Problem Statement Analyzer (PSL/PSA) is a computer-based tool (ISDOS, 1984(a)). PSL is a language for describing information systems in computer analyzable form. PSA is a system of computer programs for checking, storing, retrieving, and analyzing the description of information systems in PSL with the capability to generate reports based on the data stored.

PSL/PSA enables users to express the collected facts and design ideas about information systems in an easy to understand format. After a number of programmed checks, it stores them in a self-contained data base, for the most part in syntactically analyzable form. The data base contents can be presented to users in various ways and forms. However, PSL/PSA is not a new methodology in system analysis and design. It is a concept and a tool which puts the enormous power of computers into the analysts' service, whatever methodology they use.

BENEFITS OF USING PSL/PSA

At its origin PSL/PSA was intended for the analysis and documentation of requirements and functional specifications of information systems. Soon it found use in subsequent phases of the system life cycle, such as detailed design, program development, testing, system documentation, and also in project management and maintenance.

It enables unambiguous communication among all project personnel including: project managers, end users, analysts, designers, programmers, coders, testers, data base administrators, documentation librarians, etc. throughout the system life cycle.

PSL/PSA can be used particularly effectively for very large projects; however, with growing volume of development and maintenance tasks its use can also be justified for medium sized organizations.

These are some of the more important benefits derived from using PSL/PSA in information system development projects.

Once a few initial statements have been entered into the PSA data base, it may be used as a base for task assignment and subsequent monitoring of the cumulative progress, periodical progress, and individual performance of project team members.

PSL/PSA enables establishment of system boundaries at the onset of the development cycle. Management can record and track resources to specific personnel, activities and functional units of the system under development. PSL/PSA, properly used, can facilitate budget adherence.

Effective and unambiguous communication can be maintained between teams and individuals performing consecutive steps of system development and between subgroups responsible for the development of different subsystems and their functional modules within large scale projects by enforcing the use of established standards.

A large number of end users may incidentally produce multiple requirements for the same data under different names and in different forms. Presentation of information in matrix form provides powerful tools for analysis. Overlapping, redundant, incomplete, and inconsistent data may be detected early.

Elaborate checking facilities (automated, built-in, or only on demand) enable a thorough checking of the description of the existing system or any designed alternative, and an early detection of design conflicts.

Via interactive queries or selective reports, PSL/PSA assists in locating requirements and design details. Information can be extracted from the data base without shuffling through piles of paper documentation. The tremendous effort required to document all phases and aspects of the project throughout the development cycle can be significantly reduced. Entries to the PSA data base documenting all development activities accounting for the project progress are made as they are taking place. These PSL statements are the only source for any further formal communications. Having current documentation throughout the life of the project is guaranteed.

The extensive report capability of PSL/PSA enables generation automatically of a complete set of system documentation, or any user or purpose-oriented subset of its current version at a minimal cost.

There exist, also, more advanced, generalized, or custom tailored versions of this language and software. They were successfully used to:

- reverse engineering and document existing systems,

- develop microcode,

- model business enterprises with respect to their organizational units, functions, data creation and usage characteristics.

- support most analysis and design methodologies currently in use,

- document existing operations and procedures in the form of PSA reports and pictures for reference purposes, and

- training aids for new personnel.

THE BARUCH EXPERIENCE

In January 1984, the PSL/PSA software was installed on the IBM 3030 computer at CUNY under VM/CMS (SP2) using the standard ISDOS installation documentation (ISDOS, 1982). It took 17,865 blocks of 1024 bytes of disk space assigned to a 1 Mbyte virtual machine (VM). In addition, each student taking a course using PSL/PSA was assigned a virtual machine (VM account) with a minidisk of 200 blocks of storage linked with multiple, read-only access right to the PSA virtual machine and to the VMs of all project team members. They could acquire a temporary disk space of at least 960 blocks or multiples thereof.

The three hour, three credit course available to teach Analysis and Design of Business Information Systems (STA 4360) at the Department of Statistics and Computer Information Systems, Baruch College, NY, deals with "the development of information systems within business organizations and the analysis and design of systems to fill the total needs of organizations. Traditional and structured analysis and design techniques are covered, including information gathering, definition of objectives, input and output design, file design, real-time and batch processing. Students are actually required to design one or more complex business applications in the areas of accounting and management information systems" (1983/84 Baruch College Catalog).

The paper refers to the courses offered during the spring and summer sessions in 1984. The task was a very challenging one because of the following factors:

- SA&D is taught only as one three-hour course in defiance of the current curriculum recommendations (ACM, DPMA) which suggest a sequence of two courses,

- for the first time students were, indeed, required to work in teams and actually do a limited project which covers a substantial part of the system development life cycle,

- students had never worked previously in the VM/CMS environment, and

- in addition to a new subject, new Problem Statement Language terminology and syntax, and new Problem Statement Analyzer Commands were required.

The most feasible solution seemed to be to teach the students all the necessary technicalities by example alongside the main subject - system analysis and design of information systems.

With this objective in mind, at the beginning of the course students were provided with an itemized description of the term project in the form of a SCHEMA file (table of contents) as required by the Automated Documentation Generator (DOCGEN) which is part of the PSA software. The required components of the term project were: project request, sample investigation report, sample problem analysis report, general description of the proposed system, output design, file design, input design, process design, sample program specifications, sample instructions for manual operations, cost-benefit analysis, implementation schedule, and summary of impact.

Every week or every other week, depending on whether it was a summer course or a regular semester course, students were provided with a written assignment accompanied by a terminal log of a sample terminal session with all the CMS commands, formatting commands, PSL statements, and PSA commands necessary to accomplish the task. Students were required to use the CMS, PSL, and PSA reference manuals only to modify certain commands or to change some of their parameters. Thus, they were introduced step-by-step to the more and more advanced technicalities as needed. Still they had to use their brains in order to formulate within the context of the case study a solution to the problems stated in the consecutive assignments by following the guidelines presented in the classroom. The difference was that it had to be done with the aid of the computer.

ASSIGNMENT 1: PROJECT REQUEST

After an introductory presentation about the system life cycle and the role of system analysts, students were required to read the ABC Company Case Study written by Thierauf (Thierauf and Reynolds, 1980) which indicates the need for a new finished product inventory system. This time, besides the written assignment to prepare a sample project request for the new system by following a set of rules aimed at constraining the designers' freedom in search for solutions at least, the students received the following handouts:

- The log of a sample terminal session which contained: the PROFILE EXEC file which configures the student's virtual machine as required for the use of PSL/PSA; the structure of the SCHEMA (table of contents) and SOURCE (assignment contents) files as required by the Automated Documentation Generator; the PSA command required to run it together with the embedded CMS commands in unabbreviated formats, and some explanatory comments.

- An Introduction to the Problem Statement Language and (PSL) and the Problem Statement Analyzer (PSA) (Teichroew and Chikofsky, 1983).

- Excerpts from "PSL/PSA: A Computer-Aided Technique for Structured Documentation and Analysis of Information Processing Systems" (Teichroew and Hershey, 1977).

After doing their first assignment, the students had learned how to:

- formulate a sample project request,

- set up their virtual machine for the use of PSL/PSA,

- create, edit and store the necessary SCHEMA and SOURCE files,

- run the Automated Documentation Generator in the simplest mode,

- display the results and make the necessary corrections, if necessary, and

- print the assignment in a format exactly as required.

Thus, during the first terminal session the students got accustomed to preparing their assignments, and in the future also their job assignments, with the aid of the computer. Actually they used only one PSA command, did not enter the interactive PSA environment, and did not yet write any statements in PSL. Hence, they were not overwhelmed by technicalities which were rather secondary to the main subject, although crucial to their future performance on the job. Still, they had to formulate the project request statements according to the specified rules within the context of the case study.

ASSIGNMENT 2 & 3: INVESTIGATION AND PROBLEM ANALYSIS REPORTS

Students were required to write short samples of:

- an investigation report with: an introductory statement of
  who conducted the investigation, where and when it was done;
  the indication of investigation methods and the information
  sources to which the methods were applied; a sample list of
  findings with unambiguous references to the information
  sources they were obtained from for traceability of all factual
  statements.

- a problem definition report with three examples of: problem
  or opportunity identification with respect to the objects
  stated in the project request; sample definitions of problems
  and opportunities previously identified (definition of cause/
  effect relationships); methodological and procedural, as opposed to technical, and design recommendations aimed at the
  before identified causes.

No new technical details were introduced. To consolidate their previous
experience and gain some confidence, now, students were required to apply
the Automated Documentation Generator entirely on their own.

ASSIGNMENT 4: OUTPUT DESIGN

The task was to design a Projected Inventory Report which helps to
meet the business objectives stated for the project. This time, in addition
to the written assignment, the students received the following handouts:

- the Miniguide for Using PSA on CMS Machines by Sayani and
  Svoboda (1981).

- "An Example of How to Use PSL/PSA" by Gackowski,

- a list of all possible types of PSL statements which can
  be made about an OUTPUT (a separate type of objects in
  PSL),

- a log of a sample terminal session which contained all the
  commands necessary to: initialize a new PSA database, to
  enter the PSA environment, to set-up the PSA environment,
  to check the syntax of the input file with PSL statements
  which describe the designed report, to correct errors in
  the input file from within the PSA environment, to populate
  the initialized database with the corrected PSL statements,
  to print a Formatted Problem Statement Report about the designed report, to produce a PSA Database Summary Report, to
  orderly exist in the PSA environment; to query the CMS for
  the utilization parameters of the disk space and for the
  list of files stored by student's virtual machine,

- a sample layout of the SCHEMA and SOURCE files required by
  the Automated Documentation Generator. (This time, the
  SOURCE file must contain a few PSA commands which invoke
  the selected database and format the output reports so that
  they can be directly incorporated into the report printed by
  DOCGEN with removed standard headings, suppressed the printing of PSA report command parameters, etc.).

Now, the students had the opportunity to learn how to:

- design a main output (report) in response to business
  objectives specified in the project request by following
  the set of rules explained to them in the classroom.

- describe the report under design directly in PSL and
  to create an INPUTPSL file under VM/CMS.

- initialize a PSA database, enter the PSA environment,
  check the INPUT-PSL file for syntactical correctness,
  correct possible errors, populate the database, read
  its contents with two different PSA report commands,
  and monitor the disk space available under VM/CMS.

- run the Automated Documentation Generator with
  references to an available PSA database with respect
  to a specific object of interest.

Again, the emphasis was put on the main subject - the design of main
outputs, however, the students learned how to do this with the aid of the
computer.

ASSIGNMENT 5: FILE DESIGN

Students were required to define in COBOL convention the inventory
master file which can store inventory data for each product in up to 15
different storage locations and provide all the necessary parameters for
projecting inventory over several lead times. The Automated Documentation
Generator was to be used only.

This far going simplification enabled us to avoid the explanation of
the vast facilities available under PSL/PSA for structured description and
analysis of complex data structures (ISDOS, 1984(b)). Taking into account
that students take a separate course in database organization, this part of
system design has been reduced to an absolute minimum.

ASSIGNMENT 6 & 7: INPUT AND PROCESS DESIGN

For input design a generalized screen layout was required for interactive data entry about transactions which change the level of physical inventory. The teaching procedure is very similar to one described under Output
Design, since the description of inputs in PSL resembles the one of outputs.
Hence, for the sake of brevity only the differences are described. This
time the emphasis was put on a more sophisticated use of the PSL LAYOUT
text-entry and the PSA LAYOUT report commands. The handouts contained an
example of how to describe the layouts in PSL, the width of which exceeds
80 character positions, despite the fact that PSL statement lines cannot
exceed that limit, and how to print those layouts with the LAYOUT report
command using the maximum line length allowed by the printer. Not until
now had the students received the complete set of reference manuals:

- Using PSA under IBM VM/CMS (ISDOS, Ref. #81A52-0346-1),

- PSL Language Reference Summary (ISDOS, Ref. #81A52-0514-6), and

- PSA Command Reference Summary (ISDOS, Ref. #81A52-0315-2).

Only after doing the previous assignments, they had become reasonably prepared for using these materials.

The general description of the inventory control procedure (Process
Design) was limited mainly to using the PSL PROCEDURE text-entry, synonyms
of object names, and printing a PROCESS-SUMMARY report, thus bypassing the
vast capabilities of PSL/PSA to analyze thoroughly the DATA-PROCESS and
PROCESS-DATA interactions and the system dynamics. With both assignments the
students also learned how to incorporate the PSA LAYOUT and PROCESS-SUMMARY
report commands into the SOURCE file and the respective reports into an
embedding document produced by the Automated Documentation Generator.

Exactly the same principles were applied to Assignment 8 - Program
Specifications and Assignment 9 - Manual Procedures which were concerned
with writing sample instructions in support of two types of manual operations: data entry and report handling.

PROJECT RECAPITULATION - TERM PROJECT

At the end of the semester all student teams were required to consolidate all their assignments (No. 1-9) into a complete set of documentation
called Project Recapitulation. This way, it had become a small term project,
a mandatory one for the successful completion of the course. In order to
make that difficult assignment easier, the students could access and copy
from the instructor's master VM:

- the complete SCHEMA file (table of contents) as required for
  the term project (Appendix A).

- the outline of the required SOURCE file for the Automated
  Documentation Generator with inserted narrative comments
  about what is required in each chapter, section, or paragraph; technical hints for obtaining temporary disk space
  capable of accommodating all the consolidated files during
  a terminal session; new PSA commands to be invoked; suggestions on how to change parameters of some of the
  already known commands.

- a sample database file (DBF) with a high-level, general
  outline of the inventory system structure as it could
  have been provided by a senior analyst or a project leader
  for junior analysts in a real world environment.

- the respective INPUTPSL DATA file (DBF) with a high-level,
  general outline of the inventory system structure as it
  could have been provided by a senior analyst or a project
  leader for junior analysts in a real world environment.

- the respective INPUTPSL DATA file for the IPSL command
  which can populate the aforementioned DBF file (Appendix B).

In a printed form they received a copy of the skeleton REPORT LISTING
produced by the Automated Documentation Generator run with the SCHEMA and
SOURCE files made available in the master VM.

Every project team was required:

- to agree upon, and substitute real text for the comments
  found in the master SOURCE file outline,

230

- to extend and complement the sections of PSL statements
  about the objects, defined partially or only listed in
  the skeleton INPUTPSL DATA file, and incorporate into this
  file all PSL statements made by each team member for the
  previous assignments,

- consolidate the master INPUTPSL DATA file and respective
  student files into one PROJECT DATA file, check it for
  correctness, consistency and completeness, and create
  in the temporary disk space the PROJECT DBF (database)
  file,

- insert into the master SOURCE file the necessary formatting commands and PSA report commands in order to
  obtain a relatively complete project documentation with
  all the assignments done during the entire semester
  plus the additional items required now,

- run the Automated Document Generator with the PROJECT
  SCHEMA and PROJECT Source files and print the final
  version of the REPORT LISTING as the term project.

Students were encouraged to correct or redo those previous assignments
in which they made many errors in return for regaining some points they lost
before. This enabled them not only to reinforce what they learned before but
also appreciate the ease with which corrections and modifications, inevitable
with all development projects, can be done with a computer-aided tool.

CONCLUDING OBSERVATIONS

Throughout the course the students were encouraged to focus their
attention more on the subject matter of the project than on how to use
PSL/PSA. However, one can claim that they were exposed to the use of a
computer-aided tool in system analysis and design, and, thereby, learned by
example about 10-20% of the features the PSL/PSA can offer. In a one semester course on analysis and design of information systems this is probably
close to the maximum that can be done without compromising the main substance
of the course.

Despite the demanding requirements imposed by the curriculum and the
course syllabus, those students who worked systematically and took serious
interest in acquiring basic professional skills in this area were able to
absorb the necessary minimum of the "know how" about PSL/PSA. That minimum
seems to be sufficient in order to make them relatively confident about the
future use of any computer-aided tool in their profession. It resulted in:

- more term projects turned in on time than without using
  PSL/PSA,

- much improved form of the submitted documentation,

- incomparably more consistent content.

More students took the opportunity to redo some assignments in order
to improve their grades and the quality of their term project. With the
VM/CMS editor, the PSL/PSA, and the DOCGEN it has become incomparably easier
to modify part of their assignments and resubmit them again.

In addition, they acquired hands-on experience in cooperating within
project teams in the VM/CMS environment, e.g., how to develop separate

sections of their assignments in individually maintained VMs and PSA databases and, later, how to combine them into a complete set of the final
system documentation. This required the use of temporary disk space. The
individual VMs enabled mutual, multiple, read-only access to respective
minidisks belonging to other students within the same project team.

Several students who took the course, later on their own initiative,
shared their experience from job interviews. They reported enthusiastically
that the Analysis and Design of Business Information Systems with PSL/PSA
gave them a substantial advantage over other candidates. They felt that
the course taught this way considerably enriched their curriculum vitae
by enabling them:

- to refer to a sample system project they actively partici-
  pated in and present it in a neatly printed form,

- to make a point that they are capable of using an advanced
  interactive software package in their profession for computer-
  aided design and documenting of their projects, even when
  the prospective employer is only thinking about making the
  first step in that direction.

- to demonstrate that they gained some experience in working
  and cooperating with other team members in the VM/CMS environment which is more popular and more meaningful for
  prospective employers than the academic WYLBUR used with
  other courses.

Of course, this was only the beginning. The man-computer interaction
in system analysis and design with computer-aided tools might and certainly
will undergo many additional, far going improvements.

REFERENCES

Couger, D., Colter, M., and Knapp, R., 1982, Advanced System Development-
    Feasibility Techniques, John Wiley & Sons, 1982.

Gackowski, A., An Example of How to Use PSL/PSA, ISDOS Working Papers (ISDOS
    Ref. #82A52-387-0), ISDOS Project, Department of Industrial and Oper-
    ations Engineering, The University of Michigan, Ann Arbor, Michigan.

IBM, 1984, "Program Offering - Problem Statement Language/Problem Statement
    Analyzer (PSL/PSA)", 1984, General Information Manual, Program Number
    5796-BDX, G320-9171, July 1984.

ISDOS, Using PSA under IBM VM/CMS, Ref. #81A52-0346-1, ISDOS, Inc.

ISDOS, PSL Language Reference Summary, Ref. #81A52-0514-6, ISDOS, Inc.

ISDOS, PSA Command Reference Summary, Ref. #81A52-0315-2, ISDOS, Inc.

ISDOS, 1982, Installation of PSA A5.2R1 Object Form under IBM VM/CMS,
    Technical Memorandum 431, ISDOS Project, The University of Michigan,
    Ann Arbor, Michigan, April 1982.

ISDOS, 1984(a), "PSL/PSA Problem Statement Language/Problem Statement Anal-
    yzer", PSL/PSA Overview, S104-0, ISDOS, Inc., June 1984.

ISDOS, 1984(b), "PSL/PSA Support Environment - Structured Analysis (PSA-
    SA)", Overview, S103-1, ISDOS, Inc., June 1984.

Teichroew, D., and Chikofsky, E., 1983, <u>An Introduction to the Problem Statement Language (PSL) and the Problem Statement Analyzer (PSA)</u>, ISDOS Project, Department of Industrial and Operations Engineering, The University of Michigan, Ann Arbor, Michigan.

Teichroew, D., and Hershey, E., 1977, "PSL/PSA: A Computer-Aided Technique for Structured Documentation and Analysis of Information Processing Systems", <u>IEEE Transactions on Software Engineering</u>, <u>1</u>, January 1977.

Thierauf, R., and Reynolds, G., 1980, <u>Systems Analysis and Design - A Case Study Approach</u>, Charles E. Merrill Publishing Company.

Sayani, H., and Svoboda, C, 1981, <u>Mini-Guide for Using PSA on CMS Machines</u>, Advanced Systems Technology Corp., Greenbelt, MD, September 1981, (ISDOS Ref. #82A52-0387-0).

FILE: MASTER SCHEMA C   06/14/84 12:18:59   CUNY

```
&       TERM PROJECT DOCUMENTATION SCHEMA
&
*TITLE Inventory Control System
#ATP (Academic Title Page designed with Assignment.1)
#CTP (Company Title Page  designed with Assignment.7)
#1.   INTRODUCTION
#2.   PROJECT REQUEST (incorporate Assignment.1)
#2.1 APPLICATION AREA
#2.2 MAIN BUSINESS OBJECTIVES
#2.3 REQUIREMENTS AND CONSTRAINTS
#2.3.1  MANDATORY
#2.3.2  OPTIONAL
#2.4 SYSTEM'S BOUNDARIES
#2.4.1 TIME
#2.4.2 DATA FLOW
#2.4.2.1 INPUTS
#2.4.2.2 OUTPUTS
#2.5 EVALUATION GUIDE-LINES
#2.5.1 COMMON SCALAR VALUE
#2.5.2 CONVERSION OF OBJECTIVES
#2.5.3 CONVERSION OF REQUIREMENTS
#3.   INVESTIGATION (incorporate Assignment.2)
#3.1 METHODS AND SOURCES OF INFORMATION
#3.2 FINDINGS (with references to information sources)
#4.   ANALYSIS (incorporate Assignment.3)
#4.1 IDENTIFICATION OF PROBLEMS AND OPPORTUNITIES
#4.2 DEFINITION OF PROBLEMS AND OPPORTUNITIES
#4.3 DESIGN RECOMMENDATIONS
#5.   SYSTEM DESIGN
#5.1 GENERAL OUTLINE
#5.2 GENERAL PROCEDURE (incorporate Assignment.7)
#5.3 OUTPUT DESIGN (incorporate Assignment.4)
#5.4 FILE DESIGN (incorporate Assignment.5)
#5.5 INPUT DESIGN (incorporate Assignment.6)
#5.6 PROGRAM SPECIFICATIONS (incorporate Assignment.8)
#5.7 MANUAL PROCEDURES (incorporate Assignment.9)
#5.7.1 DATA PREPARATION AND ENTRY INSTRUCTIONS
#5.7.2 REPORT HANDLING INSTRUCTIONS
#5.8 IMPLEMENTATION PLAN (new additional item)
#5.9 COST/BENEFIT ANALYSIS (new additional item)
#6.   SUMMARY OF IMPACT (new additional item)
```

FILE: MASTER DATA A 06/14/84 13:00:21 CUNY

DEFINE PROCESS: Inventory-Control;
SYNONYMS ARE: Main-Process, MP, IC;
DESCRIPTION;
This system covers:
  - data entry for shipping and receiving transactions,
  - update of the inventory master file,
  - printing of inventory reports,
  - generation of stock replenishment documents;
RECEIVES Inventory-Control-Inputs;
GENERATES Inventory-Control-Outputs;
EMPLOYS Inventory-Control-Files;
SUBPARTS ARE: Inventory-Manual-Operations,
               Inventory-Computer-Operations;
HAPPENS 1 TIMES-PER work-day;
PERFORMED BY: Inventory-Department, Computer-Center;
TRIGGERED BY Inventory-Control-Inputs;
TRIGGERS: Purchasing, Manufacturing, Accounting;
RESPONSIBLE-PROBLEM-DEFINE 'students last, first name';
PROCEDURE;
  Incorporate the procedure plan developed in Assignment.7; ... and so on.

Students were required to continued the structured decomposition of the
highest-level system components mentioned above and to insert appropriate
parts of their assignments where necessary in order to create a quasi complete documentation.

LAYOUT AND HIGHLIGHTING IN ON-LINE INFORMATION

Robert Krull and Philip Rubens

Communication Research Laboratory
Rensselaer Polytechnic Institute
Troy, NY

Abstract: Sixty subjects were shown online information similar to commercially marketed microcomputer software. Information content was held constant across experimental groups, while the following layout features ere manipulated: multicolor and monochrome highlighting; single and two-column arrangement of text; and short, medium and long text lines. Eye movement of some subjects was monitored by an eyecamera system; and keystroke errors were monitored for other subjects. Response speed was monitored for all subjects.

Results show negligible performance gain for monochrome highlighting and response speed decrements for some kinds of multicolor highlighting. For example, multicolor highlighting disrupted eye movements characteristics of normal reading patterns. Columnar arrangement and line length had minimal effect on performance.

Subject input errors were evenly balanced between syntactic errors and major logical errors.

The factor most consistently producing gains in user performance was practice on successive trials. When repeated trials were combined with feedback to subjects about their errors, results show substantial reduction in syntactic input errors.

The paper discusses implications of the findings for computer interface design.

1. INTRODUCTION

On-line information is argued to be more effective than printed information, because it saves users from hunting through masses of documentation when they simply want to complete the task on which they are working. However, as on-line information grows in scope, users must perform several tasks with on-line information as well. For example, they must determine when and how to access it, must read it and retrieve what is relevant to their problem. Finally, they must act on what they retrieve. Users might get just as lost in on-line as in printed information.

One solution is to lay out on-line information so that users rapidly can find what they need. In this paper we report findings about three features of on-line layout: length of text lines, arrangement of text into columns, and color highlighting. We tested these layout features for their effects on speed of user performance and on their eye motion.

1.1 Line Length

Research on the line lengths of printed material indicates that a range of 3 1/2 to 5 1/2 inches is optimal (Burt, 1959; Poulton, 1970). Much shorter lines retard reading rates because the eye must frequently sweep from the end of one line to the beginning of the next. Much longer lines cause readers to lose their place.

The relationship of CRT line lengths to printed text is not direct. First of all, most CRTs provide 25 or fewer lines of text depth rather than the 50 or more available on printed pages. Typical display screens provide 40, 60, 80, and 132 characters per line. Second, most CRT alphanumeric characters are sans serif and mono-skeletal strokes. Finally, most CRT characters are large (typically 12-14 points in height, compared to 10 point for print) and are set on closely spaced lines (Arps, Erdmann, Neal, and Schlaipper, 1969). The CRT, then, provides a smaller text window, of different general shape, and covered with lower definition characters than printed text. These differences suggest that recommendations for line lengths be applied only with caution to CRT displays.

For example, Muter and his co-workers (Kruk and Muter, 1984; Muter, Latremouille, Treuniet, and Beam, 1982) have found that CRTs produce 24-28% reading speed decrement due in part to format differences between CRTs and print. Tullis (1983) argues that CRT images should fill 30% or less of the available characters, as opposed to 50% for printed pages. Thus, it is obvious that even basic screen format conventions influence legibility and readability. These reading problems in turn influence task performance.

In this study we collected data about 40, 60, and 80 character lines. We did not examine longer lines because they fell so far outside the expected optimal range. We hypothesized that reading rates for 40 and 60 character lines would be fairly equal and 80 character lines would show slower reading rates and evidence of more eye regressions.

1.2 One and Two-Column Formats

Printed computer documentation has been produced in both one and two column formats. One reason for using two-column formats is that they allow broader pages without requiring users to read very long lines of text. Another reason is that they help segment text and graphics into manageable chunks.

Chunking -- separation of text into coherent blocks -- seems effective for on-line information as well (Frase and Schwartz, 1979; Tullis, 1983) and both column formats can be displayed with line lengths in the optimum range specified in the preceding section. However, display screens limit two-column formats. For example, with an 80 character line CRT a two-column format leaves less than 40 characters per column. A minimum of 5 or 6 characters would have to be allowed between columns for them to be discriminated as separate blocks of text (Tinker, 1963). In addition, the CRT provides fewer rows of text to demarcate the vertical boundaries of text columns. As a result, users are not likely to get as strong an impression of text columns from a CRT as from the printed page.

We tested one and two column layouts. Two column formats were designed for two line lengths -- 25 and 35 characters. We hypothesized the longer line lengths would be more swiftly read and produce fewer eye regressions.

Although a few studies show that users can handle quite complex on-line images (Tullis, 1985), most argue that users do best with a smaller, optimal number of text chunks (Tullis, 1983; Landauer and Nachbar, 1985). We limited screen complexity by showing 5 choice blocks per screen image with both one and two column layouts. Since some studies show little inherent preference for horizontal vs. vertical on-line information arrangements (Coffey, 1961), we hypothesized that users might have difficulty in discerning the reading order intended for two column layouts. They might read across columns rather than down them.

1.3 Highlighting

Printed documentation offers several highlighting systems: underlining, typographic variation, and color. Given limitations of typical display screens, underlining and typographical variation have been used less for highlighting than color and character brightness. Existing research on color cueing indicates that it can be effective for retrieval tasks (Cahill and Carter, 1976; Chute, 1980; Christner and Horace, 1961; Hitt, 1961; Smith and Thomas, 1964). However, research also indicates that using many colors (more than 6 or 7) or complicated coding systems confuses users and is counter-productive (Carter, 1977; Durrett and Trezona, 1982), drawing attention from central to incidental information (Christ, 1975; Chute, 1980; Dwyer, 1970; Katzman and Nyenhuis, 1972). Research also indicates color may be more effective for locating an item than identifying what it is (Luder and Barber, 1985).

To complement our other layout variations we analyzed three color highlighting variations: unhighlighted, single color, and multiple (5) color highlighting. Color highlights were selected from the least saturated color options available on an IBM-PC monitor. Highly saturated colors were found to be illegible during pre-testing.

Given findings about the advantages of color highlighting for retrieval, we hypothesized single color highlighting would produce swifter reading rates than unhighlighted screens. We also expected readers would pay more attention to highlighted parts than the rest of a screen. Finally, we expected considerable attention would be paid to multi-color highlighting at the expense of retrieval tasks and the other text on screens.

2. METHODOLOGY

2.1 Screen Types

We presented subjects with four kinds of on-line information: introduction, menu, data entry, and text search screens. These were arranged in sequences of three with the same layout features. We did this to better estimate how users would respond with practice. Content was held constant across experimental groups while highlighting and layout were varied. We produced 16 discrete screens:

> General Introduction
>
> Menu Introduction 1
>
> 3 Menus
> Menu Introduction 2

3 Menus

Data Entry/Text Search Introduction

3 Data Entry

3 Text Search

   2.1.1 Introductions. Introductions appeared on single screens and
varied in highlighting and line length.

   2.1.2 Menus. Three menus asked subjects to choose their favorite
item and three asked them to choose the item that seemed most logical to
them. Each menu involved a different topic. Menus varied in line length,
column layout, and highlighting.

   2.1.3 Data Entry and Text Search Screens. Data entry and text search
screens asked subjects to find specific words. Target words were displayed
in short instructions at the top of each screen. This allowed subjects to
consult instructions if they forgot target words. The same data entry
screen was used for each trial, but the target word to be found varied.
This was also the case for the text search screens. Data entry and text
entry forms were all full screen width and depth.

   Data entry screens were designed to be similar to typical form filling
screens. They were a mixture of text and graphics characters giving the
appearance of ruled lines. The latter were used to represent locations where
users normally would enter characters from a keyboard. These screens were
either unhighlighted or single-color highlighted.

   The text search screens were designed to get at how users try to locate
items in displays full of text. The search tasks involved a library database. These screens were either unhighlighted or multi-color highlighted.

2.2 Demography

   Our 22 subjects ranged in age from 20 to over 40. About 60% had at
least a Bachelor's degree, the lowest level of education being a high school
diploma. The typical form of computer instruction was short-courses, but no
one reported having no computer experience. Our subjects were somewhat
better educated and more computer experienced than is typical of business
workers. It is likely that our subjects performed a little better than
would be expected of most office workers. Subjects were systematically
assigned to treatment groups.

2.3 Subject Response Times

   To assess how long subjects took to read through screens we asked them
to press a single key on a computer keyboard when they completed reading
each screen. The microcomputer displaying the screens also recorded these
elapsed times. To eliminate users' familiarity with keyboards and to maintain calibration of the eye motion equipment, we masked off the single key
users were to push.

2.4 Eye Motion

   The eye motion collection system consisted of a viewing hood, a 19
inch monitor driven by a microcomputer, and an eye camera. The subjects
looked at the monitor through the viewing hood. The large monitor was used
to assure legible images through the eye camera equipment.

Subjects had 20/20-20/30 (or better) vision and did not wear or need corrective lenses.

3.   RESULTS

3.1 Speed of Response

3.1.1 Short versus Long Lines. Results show no statistically significant differences due simply to line lengths.

3.1.2 One Versus Two-Column Layout. Results show no statistically significant differences due simply to columnar layout.

3.1.3 Key-Pressing and Layout Combinations. Although there may not be simple effects of columnar layout and line lengths, it is possible that combinations of these features would affect subjects. Comparison of the combination of line lengths and column layouts for the first set of menus shows a mixed pattern that is difficult to interpret.

3.1.4 Highlight vs. Unhighlighted Screens. We had expected highlighting to make it easier for subjects to identify important screen features. Contrary to expectations, the subjects looking at highlighted screens were slower to respond - 26.4% overall. The pattern of differences between the two groups was statistically significant (t = 3.37; p < .01).

These results are surprising. They suggest that, instead of increasing the ease of reading screens, highlighting may produce an additional burden on viewers. Our eye motion data support that interpretation.

3.1.5 Key-Pressing and Experience. We expected that subjects would gain from experience and would become quicker in responding as the test went on. Since tasks and content differed among menus, data entry and text search screens, the effect of experience would be more likely to appear within each set of screens rather than between sets. In other words, users might be slow to respond to the first screen in a set and then move more quickly through the remaining screens. In addition, we expected the practice effect to be less marked with the menus, where layout was constant from screen to screen while content varied somewhat. The effect should be more marked with the same data entry and text search screens, where layout and content were constant for three trials while subjects repeatedly searched the same screen for different target words.

The practice effect was found consistently. For three of the four sets of screens, subjects responded progressively more quickly. For only one screen out of 16 did subjects respond slower than expected. The practice effect did not produce statistically significant differences for menus, but were significantly stronger for the data entry and text search screens. Overall these data seem to show a small practice effect for layout and a larger one where layout and content are both consistent.

3.2 Due Motion

3.2.1 Line Length and Due Motion. Line length did not appear to affect the total amount of eye motion or eye regression. The second finding is surprising. We had expected subjects to lose their place in 80 column layouts. Perhaps our maintaining optimal text densities of approximately 30% allowed subjects to overcome the long lines.

Line length slightly affected the average location of gaze. Subjects looking at long-line text looked, on average, a few characters to the right of other subjects. This is strange since all text was centered on the screen.

   3.2.2 Columnar Layout and Due Motion. Columnar layout did not affect the total amount of eye motion. However, it did affect the pattern of eye motion. Repeated viewing of the eye tracks in slow motion showed that for the first lines of text subjects often read across the column blocks rather than down the blocks. In other words, subjects looking at the first line of two-column text continued to read horizontally across the five blank spaces separating the blocks. After the first line subjects corrected their eye motion to follow the designed reading patterns. This pattern was subtle and did not affect the total amount of eye motion or eye regression patterns, our two statistical eye motion measures.

   3.2.3 Highlighting and Due Motion. Subjects shown highlighted screens looked about 5 characters further right than other subjects (t - 3.49; p < .01). This may be due to placement of much of the highlighted text somewhat to the right of the left-hand margin. Subjects seemed to concentrate more on the highlighting than on the numbers that accompanied items in menus and other screens.

   Additional support for this interpretation comes from the amount of eye motion in vertical and horizontal directions. Subjects shown highlighted screens moved their eyes about the same amount in the horizontal direction but much more in the vertical direction (t = 4.27; p < .01), particularly upwards (t = 3.62; p < .01). Slow motion viewing of the eye tracks showed that subjects often first moved their eyes up and down the highlighting and only then read horizontally along the lines of text. This probably accounts for part of the amount of vertical motion.

   Another cause of vertical motion seemed to be subjects' forgetting what they were to do. For multicolor screens in particular, subjects often read through all of the text and then returned to re-read instructions appearing at the top of the screen. Statistically, this appeared as an average location of gaze higher on the screen than for other subjects. For example, subjects shown multicolor screens that covered some part of all 24 lines looked on average at the level of the fourth line. Subject debriefing interviews also supported this interpretation -- subjects reported that multicolor screens left them confused about what they were supposed to do.

   Color highlighting so regularly disrupted what one would expect of eye motion during reading that we looked for some analog activity for it. The pattern we found is similar to that of viewers of paintings and so we now call it the "painting mode". Subjects looking at colorful screens first seem to respond to them as graphic designs and then as text.

4. CONCLUSIONS

   Our study examined the effects of user eye motion and performance speed of three common on-line layout features: color highlighting, line length, and column arrangement. Our findings seem consistent, although they did not often confirm our hypotheses.

   Color highlighting seems to disrupt normal reading patterns resulting in slower performance. Subjects certainly looked at highlighted areas, sometimes nearly to the exclusion of other areas of the screen. These findings argue for great care and lowered expectations in using color highlighting. Subjects say they like it, but it doesn't seem to speed them up and may be confusing.

Neither of our other layout features, line length and column arrangement, seemed to affect user performance appreciably. This may be due in part to our providing optimal screen densities. Denser screens, typical of those in commercial computer products, may show stronger effects. For example, one motivation for using all 80 columns of an 80 column display is to cram onto the screen as many characters as possible. Several studies have shown the detrimental effects of high screen densities (Tullis, 1983), part of which may be due to long line lengths.

Two serendipitous findings are provocative. The consistent improvement in subjects' performance through practice seems to argue that people can gradually adapt to many on-line information designs. How much product designers can abuse user adaptability remains undetermined. Poor visual design seems to have hurt marketability of some computer products, at least according to anecdotal reports.

Most provocative is the user eye motion pattern we call painting mode. Users seemed easily to slip into this non-reading scanning of the screen. It would be interesting to see if the same pattern is also found with other graphic features such as the electronic desktop metaphor.

ACKNOWLEDGEMENT

This project was supported by the IBM Corporation.

REFERENCES

Arps, R. B., Erdmann, R. L., Neal, A. S., and Schlaipper, C. E., 1969, "Character Legibility Versus Resolution in Image Processing of Printed Matter", IEEE Transactions on Man-Machine Systems, 10, (3), pp. 66-71.

Burt, C., 1959, A Psychological Study of Typography, Cambridge University Press, Cambridge.

Cahill, M., and Carter, R. C., 1976, "Color Code Size for Searching Displays of Different Density", Human Factors, 18, (3), pp. 273-280.

Carter, R. C., 1977, "Visual Search with Large Color Codes", Proceedings of the IEEE International Conference on Displays for Man-Machine Systems.

Christ, R. E., 1975, "Review and Analysis of Color Coding Research for Visual Displays", Human Factors, 17, (6), pp. 542-570.

Christner, C. A., and Horace, W. R., 1961, "An Evaluation of the Effect of Selected Combinations of Target and Background Coding on Map-Reading Performance -- Experiment V", Human Factors, 3, pp. 86-92.

Chute, A. G., 1980, "Effect of Color and Monochrome Versions of a Film on Incidental and Task-Relevant Learning", Educational Communication and Technology Journal, 28, (1), pp. 10-18.

Coffey, J. L., 1961, "A Comparison of Vertical and Horizontal Arrangements of Alpha-Numeric Material -- Experiment 1", Human Factors, 3, pp. 93-98.

Durrett, J., and Trezona, J., 1982, "How to Use Color Displays Effectively", Byte, 7, (4), pp. 50-53.

Dwyer, F. M., 1970, "Exploratory Studies in the Effectiveness of Visual Illustrations", Audio-Visual Communication Review, 18, (3), pp. 235-248.

Frase, L. T., and Schwartz, B. J., 1979, "Typographical Cues That Facilitate Comprehension", <u>Journal of Educational Psychology</u>, <u>71</u>, (2), pp. 197-206.

Hitt, W. D., 1961, "An Evaluation of Five Different Abstract Coding Methods -- Experiment IV", <u>Human Factors</u>, <u>3</u>, pp. 120-130.

Katzman, H., and Nyenhuis, J., 1972, "Color vs. Black-and-White Effects on Learning, Opinion, and Attention", <u>Audio-Visual Communication Review</u>, <u>20</u>, (1), pp. 16-28.

Kruk, R. S., and Muter, P., 1984, "Reading of Continuous Text on Video Screens", <u>Human Factors</u>, <u>26</u>, (3), pp. 339-345.

Landauer, T. K., and Nachbar, D. W., 1985, "Selection from Alphabetic and Numeric Menu Trees Using a Touch Screen: Breadth, Depth and Width", <u>Human Factors in Computing Systems</u>, San Francisco.

Luder, A., and Barber, P. J., 1985, "Redundant Color Coding in Airborne CRT Displays", <u>Human Factors in Computing Systems</u>, San Francisco.

Muter, P., Latremouille, S. A., Treuniet, W. C., and Beam, P., 1982, "Extended Reading of Continuous Text on Television Screens", <u>Human Factors</u>, <u>24</u>, pp. 501-508.

Poulton, E. C., 1970, "Ergonomics in Journal Design", <u>Applied Ergonomics</u>, <u>1</u>, pp. 207-209.

Smith, S. L., and Thomas, D. W., 1964, "Color Versus Shape Coding in Information Displays", <u>Journal of Applied Psychology</u>, <u>48</u>, (3), pp. 137-146.

Tinker, M. A., 1963, <u>Legibility of Print</u>, Iowa State University Press, Ames, Iowa.

Tullis, T. S., 1983, "The Formatting of Alphanumeric Displays: A Review and Analysis", <u>Human Factors</u>, <u>25</u>, (6), pp. 657-682.

Tullis, T. S., 1985, "Designing a Menu-Based Interface to an Operating System", <u>Human Factors in Computing Systems</u>, San Francisco.

5. INFORMATION SYSTEM DESIGN AND DEVELOPMENT

PERFORMANCE MEASUREMENT AND TUNING OF INTERACTIVE INFORMATION SYSTEMS

I. Mistrik* and D. A. Nelson**

*Gesellschaft für Information und Dokumentation mbH (GID)
Tiergartenstr. 17
D-6900 Heidelberg 1, F. R. Germany
**Information Engineering
P. O. Box 91413
Santa Barbara, California 93190

Abstract: We describe a strategy for instrumenting an Interactive Information System (IIS) and performing performance measurement and tuning. A
hierarchy of measuring nodes is superimposed on a multi-layer IIS under
this approach. Each instrumentation node accumulates and records the changes
in parameter values of all instrumentation nodes subordinate to it. Adhering
to this technique of selective accumulation assures that the performance
behavior of the system can be understood, and the necessary data obtained
for construction of event frequency profiles and process frequency and
duration profiles. Data is collected only when it is needed as input for
analysis. Frequency and duration profiles of system services functions
provide the principal information needed for selecting system components
and processing paths for performance tuning.

A side-effect of installing performance measurement instrumentation in
a software-based system is that it significantly enhances the error detection
and fault isolation facilities available to the systems developers. It also
provides the means for measuring and evaluating software maintenance performed on the system. This enhanced capability for process-oriented handling
of errors, faults and maintenance forms the foundation for an engineering
approach to attaining high-quality software systems.

1.   INTRODUCTION

1.1 Rationale

There are several reasons why performance (Anderson, 1984; Bernstein
and Yuhas, 1984; Bucci and Maio, 1982; Penniman, 1985; Polson and Kieras,
1985; Stonebraker et al., 1983; Tolle, 1985; Whiteside et al., 1985) is a
central issue in the design, development and deployment of Interactive
Information Systems (IISs). The most important of these are:

a)   Performance is inextricably intertwined with quality.
     Good performance is one of the accepted measures of
     system quality.

b)   Performance constraints are extremely helpful during system design. They actually help the designers make better choices.

c)   User acceptance of an IIS is strongly influenced by user perception of how well the systems performs.

d)   Performance is a determinant of system capacity, particularly in multi-user systems. The number of users who can obtain acceptable service in a given period of time is directly related to systems performance.

e)   Poor performance makes an IIS needlessly expensive to use and to maintain.

1.2 Definition

Performance is a measure of the efficiency with which a given set of resources are used over time. Hardware, software, and people are resources.

Hardware resources include: processors, main storage (RAM), bulk storage (DASD, Disk), display screens and printing devices (Boehm, 1981).

Software resources include: databases, application programs, operating systems, and system directories.

People resources include: system users, system support staff, system development and redevelopment staff, and system management.

Performance of an information system is largely determined by its design. Performance can often be improved after the fact, but only within the limits imposed by the design (Penniman, 1985).

System response time (SRT) is one often cited measure of system performance for interactive information systems (Bernstein and Yuhas, 1984). However, minimizing SRT is _not_ equivalent to minimizing the time taken by a user to perform a task. Instead, minimizing user task time requires that system designers reflect, in the system design, a thorough understanding of:

a)   how the system will be used,

b)   system workload characteristics, and

c)   the relationships between workload characteristics and resource utilization.

Good system design for IISs requires that _user_ performance is emphasized. There are sound economic reasons for this emphasis: user costs are usually greater than the costs of all of the remaining system resources combined. Thus, user performance is an overriding consideration in system performance, and good overall performance is one of the requirements that must be met by a high-quality IIS (Polson and Kieras, 1985).

2. DETERMINANTS OF INTERNAL SYSTEM PERFORMANCE

Internal system performance (exclusive of user interaction) is determined by several factors, each of which is an aspect of its design. These factors are, in order of their impact on performance:

a)   architecture,

b)   configuration of resources,

c)   data structures (and/or object structures), and

d)   algorithms.

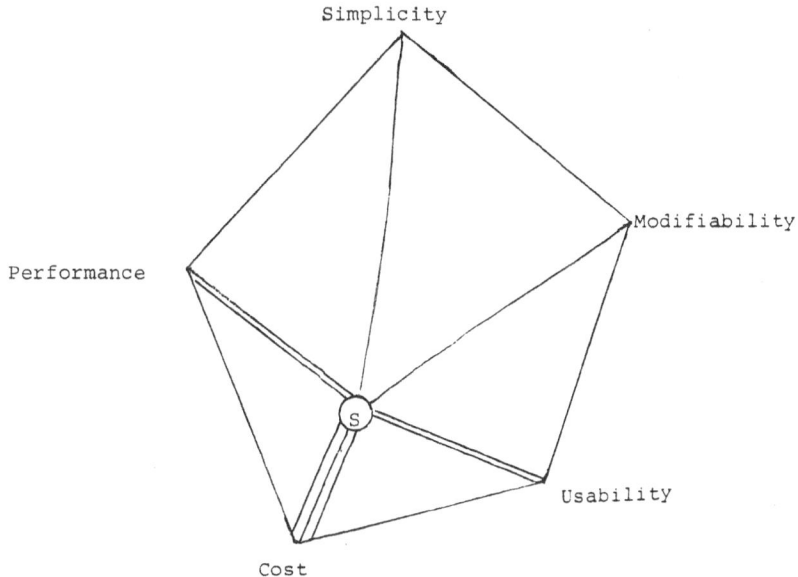

S = System

The radial line segments have width proportional to the relative weight assigned to the
constraint. Tangential line segments show
the interconstraint tension.

Figure 1. A Constraint Diagram for Design Tradeoffs.

In system design, performance requirements are traded-off against
other system requirements to obtain "best fit" design choices. Figure 1
illustrates the fundamental relationship between the requirements (i.e.,
constraints) and their combined influence on the design of a system. A
good design satisfies each single requirement only to the extent of its
relative weight in the statement of requirements.

Architecture influences performance more than any other dimension of
design. Architecture is, in turn, influenced by the User Services Model for
the system and the available hardware software and firmware technologies.
Figure 2 describes architectural trade-off issues in the design of interactive systems.

Configuration deals primarily with the replication of software, firmware, or hardware components within a given layer. Configuration is also
concerned with migration (reassignment) of remappable resources (e.g.,
files, programs) between system components that exhibit significant differences in performance characteristics. An example is the frequent substitu-
tion of hard magnetic disk devices for flexible (floppy) disks. Figure 3
describes the principal trade-off issues associated with configuration
(Stockenberg and van Dam, 1978).

Architecture

Architectural Tradeoffs (Interactive Information Systems)

Example of
Vertical Layering

1) <u>Vertical Decomposition</u> (Layering)

5	User Interface Services
	$\updownarrow$
4	Application Functions
	$\updownarrow$
3	Data(base) Services
	$\updownarrow$
2	Operating System
	$\updownarrow$
1	Hardware

2) <u>Horizontal Decomposition</u> (into <u>components</u> within a layer)

functional decomposition (e.g., 1 subroutine per user
command/request)

<u>vs</u>   <u>vs</u>

execution-path decomposition (e.g., 1 subroutine per unique
processing sequence)

3) <u>Interfaces (or Interconnections)</u>

a) <u>User</u>:   1. bit-mapped display <u>vs</u> character generator
display.

2. menu <u>vs</u> command language.

b) <u>Software</u>: 1. procedure call <u>vs</u> object messaging.

2. call-by-value <u>vs</u> call-by-reference.

c) <u>Hardware</u>: 1. bus <u>vs</u> cross-bar switch

2. Direct Memory Access <u>vs</u> synchronized data
transfer.

3. bus <u>vs</u> local area network.

Figure 2. Determinants of Performance: Architecture.

Configuration Tradeoffs (Interactive Information Systems)

1. Replication

    a. parallelism
        e.g., degree of multi-processing
        e.g., degree of multi-tasking (multiprogramming)

    b. capacity increase/decrease
        e.g., number of bytes of main storage (RAM)
        e.g., number of bytes of bulk storage (e.g., disk)
        e.g., number of active users

2. Migration Between Components

    e.g., main storage vs bulk storage
    e.g., cache in main storage for files
    e.g., buffer in main storage for printer images

Figure 3. Determinants of Performance: Configuration of Resources.

Data structures and/or objects represent the entities (and relationships between them) of the User Services Model. Figure 4 illustrates data (object) structure trade-offs using the automated telephone directory as an example.

Algorithms are selected to support the operations on the data (and object) structures that are required to fulfill the User Services Model.

Figure 5 illustrates algorithm trade-offs for the automated telephone directory example.

Data (Object) Structure Selection (Telephone Directory Example)

Structure Category	Relative Amount of Storage per Entry	Relative Cost of to Search
Objectbase	10	4
Linked List	2	3
Relation	1	2
Array	1	1
Segmented Text*	3	6
Unsegmented Text	4	10

*Directory entries separated by pointers.

Figure 4. Determinants of Performance: Data (Object) Structures

Algorithm Selection (Telephone Directory Example)

Algorithm	No. of Entries Accessed for Each Request	Cost of Accessing 1 Entry
Indexing (e.g., B-Tree)	1	$10 \log_2 d + 6$
Hashing	1+	15
Binary Search	$\log_2 n$	7
Fibonacci Search	$\log_2 n$	5
Linear Search	$n/2$	3
Text Search	$n/2$	3c

---

n = number of entries in Directory
c = average number of characters per entry
d = depth of B-Tree

In instruction executions (approximate) and exclusive of any secondary storage accesses required.

Figure 5. Determinants of Performance: Algorithms

3. METHODOLOGIES

The principal methodologies for dealing with performance are discussed here in the approximate order of their earliest applicability in a software system development project (Anderson, 1984):

a)020User Interface Modeling

Simulation based on User Services Model (Nelson, 1984).

b) Workload Modeling

Ranges _and_ design points are derived from the User Services Model (Anderson, 1984).

c) Resource Usage Modeling

Based on workload modeling and estimates of resources required (over time) to process those workloads (Gifford and Spector, 1984).

d) Experimental Prototyping

Used for design verification (Floyd, 1984).

e) Queuing Network Modeling

Formal modeling to determine effects of resource contention, replication (parallelism) and duration of processing steps on performance (Anderson, 1984).

f) <u>System Simulation</u>

A model based on events, processing intervals, delays, and control flow. Used during design <u>and</u> redesign to guide trade-offs (Anderson, 1984).

g) <u>Evolutionary Prototyping</u>

Deployment of partially developed system to assure that functions and performance meet the (evolving) needs of the systems users. Also called "rapid prototyping" (Floyd, 1984). It provides early indication of system performance characteristics while there is still time and money available to change them.

h) <u>User Task Performance Evaluation</u>

Determination of effectiveness of system support of actual user tasks. Especially appropriate when comparison can be made with other (manual and/or automated) systems for performing the same tasks (Bucci and Maio, 1982; Kosmatka, 1984).

<u>Data Acquisition Results</u>

      events: occurrences (i.e., frequencies)

    processes: occurrences <u>and</u> durations

<u>Data Analysis Results</u>

      events: even occurrences/process

               sub-event occurrences/event

    processes: sub-process occurrences/process

               minimum, average, and maximum duration of a process

     profiles: function invocation frequency profiles for events and processes.

               resource usage profiles for events and processes.

Figure 6. Overview of Relationship Between Data Acquisition and Data Acquisition.

4. PERFORMANCE MEASUREMENT AND TUNING STRATEGY

4.1 <u>Measurement That Supports Tuning</u>

Each instrumentation node (or point) must accumulate and record the changes in parameter values at <u>all</u> instrumentation nodes subordinate to it. Only by adhering to this technique of selective accumulation can the performance behavior of the system be understood in terms of system structure and the necessary data obtained for constructing the event frequency profiles and the process frequency and duration profiles (Tolle, 1984).

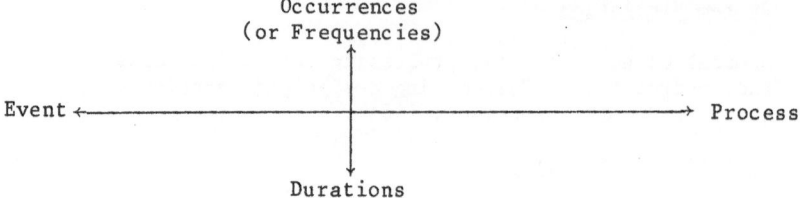

Occurrences
(or Frequencies)

Event ←————————————————————————→ Process

Durations

the cost of handling an event is given as $C_E = \Sigma_O \, D$

C_E is to be minimized

Each event occurrence triggers $p \geq 1$: processes.

Each process has a duration.

Each process consumes/occupies resources over its duration.

Figure 7. Event Handling Cost.

Figure 6 illustrates the strategic relationship between data acquisition and data analysis: data is acquired (collected) only when it is needed as input for data analysis. Figure 7 illustrates the relationship between data analysis results and performance tuning. Frequency and/or cost profiles of system service functions provide the principal information needed for selecting system modules and processes for performance tuning (Tolle, 1985).

4.2 Using Profiles to Focus Performance Tuning Efforts

Figure 8 illustrates the way in which system functions and/or modules are selected for modification in order to improve their performance. This figure illustrates the use of frequency of occurrence as an objective selection parameter. However, it assumes that the costs of handing these events are of approximately the same magnitude.

By refining the procedure of Figure 8 to use Cost instead of Frequency, the selection process can be made even more objective. Figure 7 defines cost as a component of total processing cost over the set of events of interest.

Figure 8 is an example of an invocation frequency profile (or event frequency profile).

Function invocation frequency profiles are also used to evaluate the results of doing performance tuning. Expected frequency of invocation can be used temporarily as an approximation to actual frequency of invocation. The Frequency/Cost profiles provide a means of evaluating the results of actually doing performance tuning. This requires that performance measurement workloads are repeatable. (See Stonebraker et al., (1983), and Tolle (1984) for illustrations of applying these techniques to performance tuning of IISs.)

4.3 Strategic Applications of Measurement Capabilities

A side-effect of installing performance measurement instrumentation in a software-based system is that it significantly enhances the error detection and fault isolation facilities available to the systems developers (Gohsman, 1985). Some new, or at least improved, detection and isolation capabilities

Selection of User Service Requests to be Tuned

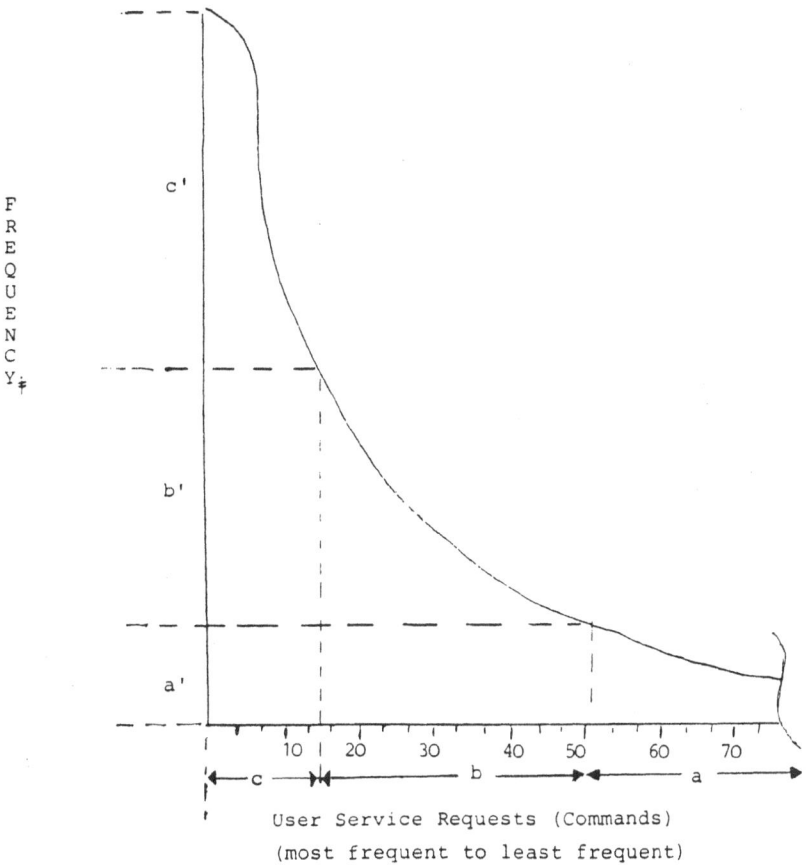

‡ frequency of occurrence in operational use

Indicated   a =consider for removal
action: b =no action until group c has been tuned
             c =candidates for intensive tuning

Figure 8. Application of Methodologies.

are:

a)   Detection of transient errors (e.g., failure to log up-
      dated data record in the special case where a write-
      to-database error occurs),

b)   Detection of omitted processing steps (e.g., failure to
      rewrite an updated data record to a database), and

c)   Isolation of loop count errors (e.g., erroneous setting
      of loop control variables, erroneous testing of loop
      control variables).

The facilities installed in a software system for performance measurement and tuning facilitate system maintenance in still another way: they

provide the means for measuring, and evaluating software maintenance performed on the system. Adding new features and repairing faults are frequent
causes of reduced system performance.

Thus, performance measurement instrumentation can make a substantial
contribution to system quality by increasing system reliability and by decreasing system (re)development costs (Gohsman, 1985).

This enhanced capability for process-oriented error detection fault
isolation and maintenance forms the foundation for an engineering approach
to attaining high-quality software systems (Bernstein and Yuhas, 1984).
This engineering paradigm can largely supplant "trial-and-error", ad-hoc
methods of error detection, fault isolation, and evaluation of maintenance
efforts.

This alternative paradigm also provides a basis for unifying the two
concepts of performance and reliability under the broader concept of quality
(Bernstein and Yuhas, 1984). Note that usability (ease of use) by intended
user population (not by developers of the system) is also a component of
system quality, when "the system" is defined to include its users.

4.4   Selection of Parameters to be Measured

   a)   Type of Parameters to be Measured

        The two basic measurement parameter categories are occurrences
        (of events) and durations (of processes). (See Figure 7.)

        There are four semantic levels of events:

        1.   User tasks (e.g., describing screen formats for end-
             user application);

        2.   Dialog segments (e.g., formulating and executing a
             database query or update);

        3.   Database commands (e.g., perform a restrict or a
             project on a single relation; and

        4.   Low-level operating systems restrictions (e.g., Disk
             I/O's).

        Obtaining the measurements needed to do effective performance
        tuning requires that measurements be taken at each of the 4
        levels (Plattner and Nievergelt, 1981).

        At each level the selection of parameters to be measured must
        be guided by a knowledge of system behavior. For example, the
        selection of an error processing module as a measurement node
        usually cannot be justified on the basis of either frequency of
        invocation or duration with regard to system resource costs.
        However, if the error condition which causes that module to
        be invoked is a user error that occurs relatively often then
        measurement of its frequency is of great importance.

        A user error that occurs with (relatively) high frequency is
        an indication of poor UI/F design (Norman, 1983). Correct-
        ing such design errors makes a major contribution to system
        performance when "system" is defined as "Users + IIS".

256

b) Types of Parameters Not to be Measured

The following types of parameters should not be measured, even if it is convenient to do so:

1) a parameter whose value is functionally dependent on the value of another measured parameter in a known way, and

2) parameters that do not provide values that are needed for constructing either frequency or cost profiles.

c) Guidelines for Selection of Measurement Points

The actual placement of measurement parameters and their acquisition procedures should be guided by:

1) program structures (modules, entry points, exit points), and

2) data structures (e.g., arrays, entries, pointers, linked lists, files).

Placement of duration (of event handling) counters requires that the appropriate program steps be inserted into the execution path whose duration is to be measured.

However, the placement of the accumulator(s) for collecting the values of process durations should not be embedded in the execution path being measured. Instead, these accumulators should be inserted into a data structure that is superior to that execution path. (E.g., the parameters of the procedure call that invoke the execution path.)

The use of existing data structures to provide support for measurement parameters is encouraged. For example, it is appropriate to extend an operation vectoring table to incorporate a set of accumulators for measuring the frequency of invocation and the duration of processing for each operation represented in the table. The Operation Vectoring (Transfer) Table of a UCSD p-code processor is just such a structure.

4.5 Procedures of Installation of Measurement Probes

The program steps and the data structures for accumulating measurement values should be installed permanently in the IIS using normal system maintenance procedures (Tolle, 1984).

Both the program steps and the data structures are to be documented to describe both their functions and their relationship to other system structures.

a) Assignment of Measurement Probes to Software Layers

Probes should be assigned to layers in the following manner:

1) parameters are placed one layer higher than the program steps that reference them, and

2) links to higher level parameters are passed via the pro-

cedure calls that invoke the modules or paths being
measured.

b) Supporting Data Structures

Data Structures that support collection of measurement data
should be installed in the same execution path hierarchy as
the modules and/or paths being monitored.

5. APPLICATION OF METHODOLOGIES AND MEASUREMENTS

The methodologies and measurements described above are employed to aid
in performance prediction, measurement, evaluation, and tuning.

These steps are repeated, in the order shown, over the development and
deployment life of the system.

Predicting performance requires a performance model. This can be
either a formal model, a simulation model, or an operational system.

In the case of an operational system, prediction applies to the effect
of contemplated changes.

Performance evaluation should be based on quantitative data acquired
by measurement of either the actual system or a model of that system. This
evaluation should be based on relevant criteria. These criteria are derived
from the mission of the system and the User Services Model (Bucci and Maio,
1982; Gifford and Spector, 1984; Nelson, 1984).

Performance tuning involves modifying either a model or the actual
system to attempt to obtain a predicted change in system performance. (Note
that "system" includes user interactions with system software, firmware,
and hardware (Stonebraker et al., 1983).

Selection of workloads to serve as benchmarks for performance measurement should be derived from actual usage sessions in realistic operational
environments. Use of development center workloads violates this rule. Use
of artificial workloads based on a priori assumptions of the development
staff must also be avoided. All artificial, contrived benchmarks should be
based on cumulative workload profiles in at least two operational installations (Bernstein and Yuhas, 1984).

Poor performance on realistic benchmarks can be an indication of poor
design (Roberts and Moran, 1981). There are two related causes:

a) there was a mismatch between the expected modes of system
    use (as predicted by the system's designers) and the ac-
    tual modes of use (as determined by the behavior of real
    users), and

b) inadequate consideration to performance was given by the
    system's designers.

Performance tuning is no cure-all for either of these design deficiencies. In many cases of bad design, the performance of the system can be
made acceptable only by (partial) redesign and redevelopment. Performance
tuning can often improve performance, but it cannot always raise it to an
acceptable level.

6. CONCLUDING REMARKS

The performance measurement and tuning strategies described in this report are being applied to an existing IIS (Mistrik et al., 1985). This IIS (known as IV+V) is also the target of a new, visually oriented, user interface (Mistrik and Nelson, 1985). Thus the development of the measurement facilities will proceed in parallel with the development of the new user interface.

ACKNOWLEDGEMENT

The authors acknowledge the support and encouragement of the Gesellschaft für Information und Dokumentation mbH (Heidelberg, FRG) and Information Engineering (Santa Barbara, CA).

REFERENCES

Anderson, G. E., 1984, "The Coordinated Use of Five Performance Evaluation Methodologies", Communications of the ACM, 27, (2), February 1984, pp. 119-125.

Bernstein, L., and Yuhas, C. M., 1984, "Taking the Right Measure of System Performance", Computerworld, CW Comm, XVIII, (7), ID/1-ID/4, 30 July 1984.

Boehm, B. W., 1981, Software Engineering Economics, Prentice-Hall.

Bucci, G., and Maio, D., 1982, "Margining Performance and Cost-Benefit Analysis in Computer System Evaluation", Computer, 18, (9), IEEE, September 1982, pp. 23-31.

Floyd, C., 1984, "A Systematic Look at Prototyping", Approaches to Prototyping, Budde, R., et al., eds., Springer Verlag.

Gifford, D., and Spector, A., 1984, "The TWA Reservation System", Communications of the ACM, 27, (7), July 1984, pp. 649-665.

Gohsman, G., 1985, "Performance Analysis Aids Software Development", Computer Design, 24, (10), 15 August 1985, p. 92.

Kosmatka, L. J., 1984, "A User Challenges Value of Subsecond Response Time", Computerworld, CW Comm., XVIII, (23) ID/1-ID/18, 11 June 1984.

Mistrik, I., et al., 1985, The (IV+V) System Software Package: System Description, GID, Heidelberg, FRG, November 1985.

Mistrik, I., and Nelson, D. A., 1985, "A Technique That Supports Both Evaluation and Design of User Interfaces", 3rd Symp. Empirical Foundations Infor. & Software Sci., Denmark, 21 October 1985.

Nelson, D. A., 1984, "A Software Development Environment Emphasizing Rapid Prototyping", Approaches to Prototyping, Budde, R. et al., eds., Springer Verlag.

Norman, D. A., 1983, "Design Rules Based on Analyses of Human Errors", Communications of the ACM, 26, (4), April 1983, pp. 254-258.

Penniman, W. D., 1985, "Information System Performance Measurement Revisited", Proc. Com. Sci. Conf., ACM, 12 March 1985, pp. 29-32.

Plattner, B., and Nievergelt, I., 1981, "Monitoring Program Execution: A Survey", <u>Computer</u>, <u>14</u>, (11), IEEE, November 1981, pp. 76-93.

Polson, P., and Kieras, D., 1985, "A Quantitative Model of Learning and Performance of Text Editing Knowledge", <u>Proc. CHI'85</u>, ACM SIGCHI, 14 April 1985, pp. 207-212.

Roberts, T., and Moran, T., 1981, "The Evaluation of Text Editors: A Methodology and Empirical Results", <u>Communications of the ACM</u>, <u>26</u>, (4), April 1981, pp. 265-283.

Stockenberg, J., and van Dam, A., 1978, "Vertical Migration for Performance Enhancement in Layered Hardware/-Firmware/Software Systems", <u>Computer</u>, <u>16</u> (5), May 1978, pp. 35-50.

Stonebraker, M., et al., 1983, "Performance Enhancements to a Relational Database System", <u>ACM Trans. Database Syst.</u>, <u>8</u>, (2), ACM, June 1983, pp. 167-185.

Tolle, I. E., 1984, "Monitoring and Evaluation of Information Systems Via Transaction Log Analysis", <u>Research & Development in Information Retrieval</u>, van Rijsbergen, ed., Cambridge Univ. Press, pp. 247-258.

Tolle, I. E., 1985, "Performance Measurement and Evaluation of Online Information Systems", <u>Proc. Comp. Sci. Conf.</u>, ACM, 12 March 1985, pp. 196-203.

Whiteside, J., et al., 1985, "User Performance with Command, Menu, and Iconic Interfaces", <u>Proc. CHI'85</u>, ACM SIGCHI, 14 April 1985, pp. 185-191.

A METHOD FOR DESIGNING TOOLS FOR INFORMATION RETRIEVAL FROM DOCUMENTS

Airi Salminen

University of Jyväskylä
Department of Computer Science
SF-40100 Jyväskylä
Finland

Abstract: The paper describes an experimental document database language. It consists of document database extensions to Prolog. An extended Prolog is suitable for specifying, prototyping, and in some cases also for implementing information retrieval tools.

1. INTRODUCTION

Computer-based documents can be regarded as data in a database. Editing of documents can then be regarded as updating of the database and showing a part of a document on a display screen can be regarded as information retrieval from the database. We call these kind of databases "document databases". The basic problem of information retrieval from a database, in general, is to find those data items that contain the useful information. In information retrieval from documents we have basically two problems: first, we have to find the documents and the "parts containing the needed information" and, second, we have to "present the retrieved information" in an appropriate way. In many environments a great deal of work consists of document editing. Therefore, editors, or at least some basic features of them, are familiar to the persons working in these environments. These familiar tools could be used even more for information storage, if the facilities for information retrieval from documents were better.

Current document processing systems contain powerful facilities for the construction and manipulation of documents (Clocksin and Mellish, 1984). However, information retrieval is much more application oriented than information storage and manipulation. In storing and maintaining information using an editor, the user sees the document on the display screen and can use some extra structures for seeing the information better. For example, in writing a letter a user does not need a special letter writing facility. Letters are written in a form from which the receiver, the day of writing, and so on, can quickly be seen. When retrieving information from the letters, the user sees them only by using some kind of browsing technique. In cases where the amount of documents is large or the information has to be collected from several places, the browsing is not a suitable method for retrieval.

Retrieval capabilities of document processing systems can be extended by combining the document processing system with a database management system (Bancilhon and Richard, 1984; Biller, 1983; Ceri and Crespi-Reghizzi, 1983; Gibbs, 1984; Horwitz and Teitelbaum, 1985; Kowarski and Lopez, 1982; Sacco, 1984; Schek and Pistor, 1982; Stonebraker, Stettner, Lynn, Kalash, and Guttman, 1983). Our approach is to extend a programming language by a document database language. A document database contains, in addition to the documents, also information about different parts of documents. We have designed and implemented an experimental document database language called EDLA (Experimental Document Database LAnguage). The language is implemented using Prolog and is intended to be used as an extension of Prolog (Clocksin and Mellish, 1984). EDLA can be used in two ways in designing retrieval tools. First, it can be used as a method for specifying and prototyping the tool or the interface of the tool. The final tool is implemented according to the specification. Second, it can be used for specifying, prototyping, and implementing the final tool. The latter is possibly only in environments where an efficient Prolog is available.

The design of information retrieval capabilities, to the satisfaction of the users, may be a very difficult task. The designer of the retrieval capabilities from documents should find answers to a number of questions, such as:

a) What kind of parts contain the needed information and not too much extra information?

b) What kind of criteria do the users want to use for retrieving information?

c) In which form should the answers to the queries be presented to the users?

One method for studying the requirements of users is the construction of a series of prototypes (Gomaa and Scott, 1981; Lee and Lochovsky, 1985; Mason and Carey, 1983). When the user requirements are specified using Prolog, then the specification is executable and, therefore, serves as a prototype (Davis, 1982; Komorowski and Maluszynski, 1986; Venken and Bruynooghe, 1984). Prolog extended by EDLA is suited for prototyping retrieval capabilities from documents.

EDLA is implemented in Edinburgh Prolog and can be used for extending different Prolog systems. The first version of EDLA was used with C-Prolog running on a VAX/750 machine (Pereira, 1984). Currently we use EDLA as an extension of LPA MacPROLOG running on a MacIntosh computer (Clark and McCabe, 1985). Later, we are going to use EDLA as an extension of a Prolog running on a graphical work station.

The examples in the following chapters concern two different sample cases. In the first case, we consider a Pascal programming environment. The environment contains a collection of large (several thousands of lines) Pascal programs. The programs have to be updated now and then. The maintainers are usually not the same persons as those who have initially written the programs. The environment will be extended by a tool designed for the maintainers. The purpose of the tool is to help the maintainers find information from programs and to understand programs. The tool can be used either alone or together with the editor of the environment. When used with the editor, the screen contains two windows: an editing window and a retrieval window. Using EDLA we construct a series of prototypes for studying the user requirements for information retrieval from programs.

In the other sample case, we are designing an information retrieval tool for some researchers. The tool is used for storing and retrieving information about books and papers concerning their research interests. The researchers store to the database, in addition to the reference entries, also information about the content of the references, e.g. table of contents, definitions given in the reference, references from one paper to another. However, in the beginning of the design the designer does not know for sure what kind of information the users want to store, what kind of criteria they want to use for retrieval and in which form they want to see the answers. The designer constructs a series of prototypes for helping both the users and him- or herself to find the requirements for the tool.

2. OVERVIEW OF EDLA DOCUMENT DATABASES

EDLA originates from a generic document model presented in set theoretic notions (Salimen and Back, 1985). The model was designed for specifying information retrieval tools (Salimen, 1986). The description of the full syntax and semantics of EDLA is under preparation.

Documents

In EDLA a "document" is presented as a binary relation. Any subset of the relation is called a "part" of the document. A tuple in the document is called an "elementary part". The attributes of the document are called EPID (Elementary Part IDentifier) and CONTEL (CONTent ELement). EPID is the primary key of the relation. In a document, the EPID column describes the "structure" of the document and the CONTEL column describes the "content" of the document. There is always an order defined both in the structure and in the content. The "structural order" is an order defined among the elements of the domain of EPID. The "contential order" is, in spite of its name, defined for the tuples of a document. The contential order may be determined by the content elements or by structural elements or by both of them together. For a given part, the "location" of the part is the set of EPID components in the tuples of the part. On the other hand, the set of CONTEL components in the tuples of the part, in the contential order, is the "content" of the part.

Figure 1 shows a document. It contains some references of this paper. In the document, the EPID values are positive integers and the CONTEL values are pieces of text. The structural order is the order defined among integers. The contential order is the alphabetic order of content elements. In the figure the tuples of the document are presented according to the contential order.

In our sample documents, the EPID values are integers and the CONTEL values are pieces of text. However, in EDLA no predefined structure (e.g., sequential or tree) is postulated for documents. Neither is postulated the kind of data the documents can contain. The domains of relations need not be atomic values. For example, if the domain of CONTEL is the set of words, then the domain of EPID may be a set of pairs (i,j). In a pair (i,j) i denotes the i'th sentence in the document and j denotes the j'th word in the i'th sentence. If the structure of a document is a tree, then the EPID values are tuples $(i_1,...,j_n)$ expressing a position in the tree. For the elements of domains we can define comparators and operators which can be used in queries.

Document Databases

For each document of EDLA we associate a collection of relations called "property relations". A property relation describes a property of some parts of the document. The names of the property relations and the relation

EPID	CONTEL
20	Bancilhon, F. and Richard, P., Managing texts and facts in a mixed data base environment, in New Applications of Data Bases, Academic Press, 1984, 89-107.
8	Davis, R.E., Runnable specification as a design tool, in Logic Programming, ed. by K.L. Clark and S.-A. Tärnlund, Academic Press, 1982, 141-149.
3	Kowarski, I. and Lopez, M., The document concept in a data base, Proc. ACM SIGMOD, 1982, 276-283.
15	Stonebraker, M., Stettner, H., Lynn, N., Kalash, J., Guttman, A., Document processing in a relational database system, ACM Trans.Off.Inf.Syst. 1,2 (April 1983), 143-158.

Figure 1.   An EDLA Document.

schemes of the property relations are determined by the "type" of the document.   An EDLA document database consists of a collection of document type
definitions and a collection of documents with their property relations.
One of the documents is always the "current document" (with the current
document type).   Therefore, we need not use names of documents in other
database statements except in statements for creating a document of a specific type and for selecting the current document.   Suppose we have defined

    'DOCUMENT_TYPE'(entry).
    ...
    'DOCUMENT_TYPE'(paper).

Then we create documents by writing:

    'CREATE'(reference.entry).
    'CREATE'(atlanta_paper.paper).

The EDLA statements are written using Edinburgh Prolog where variable
names begin either with an upper case letter or with an underscore.   The
reserved words of EDLA are written in upper case letters.   They are written
with single quotes for over-riding the variable name conventions.   In the
examples of this paper, the names selected by the designer are written in
lower case letters.

3.   DEFINING DOCUMENT TYPES

A document type defines for the documents of the type the relation
schemes, the domains, and the structural and contential order.   In property
relations, parts are denoted by "part identifiers".   The document type
defines what is the location of a part denoted by a part identifier.

Example 3.1

Suppose we are designing the researcher's retrieval tool discussed in
Section 1.   We propose storing reference entries to a document like the
document in Figure 1.   In the document each reference entry appears as a
content element.   Positive integers are used for identifying entries.   New
entries are always added to the end of the structure.   The contential order
is the alphabetic order of references.   In the query answers, the entries
are always displayed in this order.   In the document type definition for
the first prototype we define property relations "author", "keyword", "refers", "table_of_contents", "my_comments", "in_window", and "selected_entry".

author	
EPID	author_name
3	Kowarski
3	Lopez
8	Davis
15	Stonebraker
15	Stettner
15	Lynn
15	Kalash
15	Guttman
20	Bancilhon
20	Richard

keyword	
EPID	kword
3	documents in databases
8	logic programming
8	prototyping
15	documents in databases
20	documents in databases
20	text in databases
20	Take a copy in Helsinki!

refers	
from	to
20	15

in_window
EPID
3
15
20

selected_entry
EPID
3
20

table_of_contents	
EPID	table_text

15	1. Introduction
	2. Variable-length strings
	3. Ordered relations
	   3.1. Simple ordered relatios
	   3.2. Ordered relations in two dimensions
	   ...

my_comments	
EPID	some_text
3	Text as a tree structure.
8	Phases in the development of "correct" software. Construction and testing of specifications. Horn Clause specifications. An example about combining pictures.
15	Documents as ordered relations. Supported by a special storage structure.
20	Text as a tree structure.

Figure 2. Property Relations for the Document Shown In Figure 1.

Figure 2 shows these property relations for the document of Figure 1.

The properties are always defined for single entries. Therefore, parts can be identified in property relations by elementary part identifiers. The relation "author" contains the authors of the references and the relation "keyword" their keywords. For keywords the user can store any text he or she wants (for example: 'documents in databases', 'Take a copy in Helsinki!'). For each reference the researcher can store the table of contents which is stored to the relation "table_of_contents" and a text part which may contain any text whatsoever. This text is stored in the relation "my-comments". The relation "refers" is used for storing information about references from one paper to another. In the following we outline the way the tool will be used.

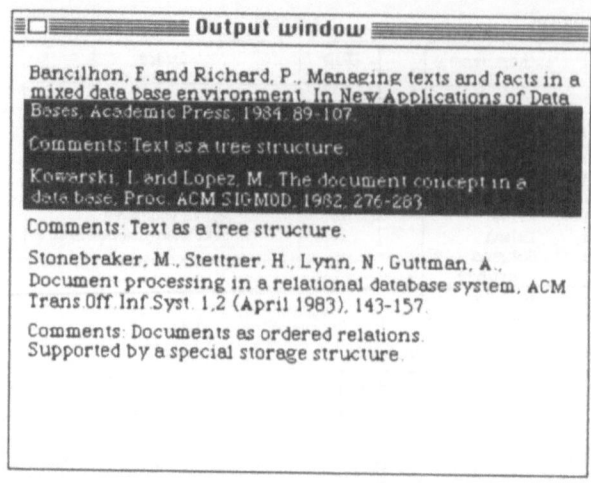

Figure 3. The Output Window.

We propose that the answers to queries are either displayed in the
Output window or, in some cases, in a temporary small window. The Output
window shows the reference entries in alphabetic order and after each entry
possibly the table of contents and/or user comments concerning the reference.
The relation 'in_window' is used for storing the numbers of those entries
which appear in the Output window. After retrieving some information, the
user can select from the Output window some part and use it as an operand
in the following operation. (For example: "Remove the selected entries",
"Find the entries from which the selected entries are referred.") The
relation "selected_part" contains the numbers of the entries which are
selected in the window. Figure 3 shows the content of the Output window in
the database state described in Figure 2. The user has retrieved to the
Output window three references such that the comments of the user are also
displayed. After this the user has selected a part of the Output
window text (the first two references).

Larger pieces of new information, e.g., new references of the tables
of contents, are written in the Input window using the text processing
system. Text can also be cut from a file and pasted to the Input window.
Any number of new references can be written in any order. However, there
is some convention about the separation of references, for example, two
carriage returns. The changes to the entries are also made in the Input
window. After writing text to the Input window, the updated references are
shown in the Output window in alphabetic order. The correctness of the
updates can be checked by the user at this stage.

The information concerning entries is given by the user. For example,
for telling the author of a reference, the user first selects the name of
the author from the entry text in the Output window, and then selects from
the pull down menu titled "New Information" the menu item "author". For
retrieval there may be different types of queries, e.g., queries accessing
entries only, queries accessing entries and user comments, queries which
add the retrieved information to the previous information in the Output
window, or queries which select a subset of the information in the Output
window. In any case, the Output window always shows the reference entry
which the retrieved information concerns.

The domain of the attributes CONTEL, "author_name", "kword", "table_
text" and "some_text" is defined to be text:

```
'DOMAIN'(text,X):-atomic(X).
```

For making character string comparisons and for combining character
strings we define in the document type definition the comparator "subtext"
and the operator "combine_text":

```
'COMPARATOR'(subtext,[text,text]).
   ...
'OPERATOR'(combine_text, [text,text,text]).
   ...
```

After the described proposition for the document type has been tested
together with the users, the needed changes are made. For example, new
relations and new comparators and operators are easy to append to the document type.

```
'DOCUMENT_TYPE'(piece_of_pascal_text).

'DOMAIN'(posint, X) :- integer(X), X>0.
'DOMAIN'(text, X) :- atomic(X).

'DOMAIN'('PID', X) :- 'LOCATION'(X, _).
'DOMAIN'(declaration_type, const).
'DOMAIN'(declaration_type, var).
'DOMAIN'(declaration_type, type).
'DOMAIN'(declaration_type, subr).

'ATTRIBUTE'('EPID', posint).
'ATTRIBUTE'('CONTEL', text).

'ATTRIBUTE'(declaration_lines, 'PID').
'ATTRIBUTE'(identifier, text).
'ATTRIBUTE'(decl_type, declaration_type).
'ATTRIBUTE'(uses, 'PID').
'ATTRIBUTE'(subroutine_lines, 'PID').
'ATTRIBUTE'(subroutine_brackets, 'PID').
'ATTRIBUTE'(declaration_part, 'PID').
'ATTRIBUTE'(statement_part, 'PID').

'STRUCT_ORDER'(X1,X2) :- X1<X2.
'CONT_ORDER'(piece_of_pascal_text(X1,Y1),piece_of_pascal_text(X2,Y2)) :- X1<X2.

'COMPARATOR'(subtext, [text, text]).
   ...
'OPERATOR'(combine_text, [text, text, text]).
   ...

'LOCATION'([X,-,X],[X]) :- !.
'LOCATION'([X,_,Y],[X|R]) :- !, X1 is X+1, 'LOCATION'(X1,Y,R).
'LOCATION'(X,[X]) :- integer(X), !.
'LOCATION'(L,L).

'RELATION'(declaration, [declaration_lines, identifier, decl_type, uses],
                primary_key([declaration_lines]) ).
'RELATION'(subroutine, [subroutine_lines, subroutine_brackets,
                declaration_part, statement_part],
                primary_key([subroutine_lines]) ).
```

Figure 4. Part of a Document Type Defined for Pascal Programs.

Example 3.2

Figure 4 shows a part of a proposal for a document type definition for
Pascal programs. In the type "piece_of_pascal_text" the attributes EPID and
CONTEL are defined in the same way as in the preceding example. However, in
this case the EPID values are used, not only for identifying content elements, but, also for specifying the order of the content elements. A content
element is a program line (or a sequence of lines) and an EPID value is a
line number. The structural order is defined using a special comparator
STRUCT_ORDER. It is defined by CONT_ORDER.

The domain name PID is used in all document type definitions for the domain which contains all part identifiers of the type. The locations of the parts denoted by part identifiers are defined in the procedure LOCATION. For documents of type "piece_of_pascal_text" we define properties for parts which consist of one or more lines. A part consisting of one line is denoted by the line number. A part consisting of a sequence, I,...,J of lines is denoted by the list [I,-J]. We constrain that in all documents of this type the line numbers are sequential 1,2,3,.... Finally, a part consisting of an arbitrary set of lines is denoted by the list of the line numbers. The elements of the domain "declaration_type" are used for denoting different types of declarations in Pascal programs.

The relation "declaration" contains information about the declarations of the program. For each declaration the following information is given: the location of the declaration in the program text, the declared identifier, the type of declaration and the lines where the declared entity is referred to in the program. The relation "subroutine" contains information about the procedures and functions of the program: the location of the declaration, the location of the beginning and ending lines, the location of the declaration part, and the location of the statement part.

4. INFORMATION RETRIEVAL FROM DOCUMENT DATABASES

In EDLA, queries to a document are made using statements FIND_LOC and FIND_CONT. Queries to property relations are made using FIND statements. The statement FIND_LOC finds all parts which have some given properties. The result of the operation is the location of the part which consists of the found parts. For example, the following statement finds from the bibliographic database the location of the part containing the entries for such papers where some paper of Stonebraker is referred:

'FIND_LOC'(X,(author(Y,'Stonebraker').refers (S,Y)),L).

The first variable in the statement is a domain variable whose domain is PID (Part IDentifier). The resulted location, a unary relation of EPID, is the value of the last variable of the statement. The statement

'FIND_LOC'(X(entry(X,Y),subtext('SIGMOD',Y)),L)

finds all references which contain the string "SIGMOD". The location is directly selected from the document, not on the ground of property relations. The following statement finds from a Pascal program the statement part of the procedure "factor":

'FIND_LOC'(X,(declaration(Y,factor,subr_),subroutine(Y,B,D,X)), L).

The beginning and ending lines of all procedures and functions of a Pascal program are found by:

'FIND_LOC'(X,subroutine(_,X,_,_), L).

The statement FIND_CONT retrieves the content of a given part. The content elements of the given part are retrieved according to the content order. The statement specifies what is done to each content element. When writing content elements to the screen, the layout for the elements can be given in the FIND_CONT statement. In the statements

```
'FIND_LOC'(D1,(declaration(D1,tokentype,type,_),
               declaration(D2,scanner,subr,_),
               'CONTAINING'(D2,D1)),L),
```

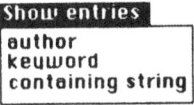

Figure 5. Pull Down Menu.

        'FIND_CONT'(L,_,Y,(nl,write(Y)))

the first statement finds the part of the Pascal program where the type
"tokentype" is declared inside the subroutine "scanner". The comparator
CONTAINING is defined in EDLA for the part identifiers of any document
type. The second statement writes the lines of the declaration of the type
in the ascending order of line numbers.

        The following statements write from the bibliographic database all
references concerning "documents in databases". Each reference is followed
by the comment part of the reference, if there is any. Before the comment,
the text "Comments:" is written

        'FIND_LOC'(E,keyword(E,'documents in databases'),L),
        'FIND_CONT'(L,X,Y,(nl,write(y),nl,
                    my_comments(X,Y1),
                    combine_text('Comments:',Y1,Y2),write(Y2),nl)).

        In the case of the document of Figure 1, the result of this query can
be seen in Figure 3 (without the black color produced by a selection of the
user).

        The statement FIND is used for accessing from property relations some
other information than part identifiers. The statement

        'FIND'(X,(keyword(Y,'logic programming'),
                author(Y,X)),Authors)

finds all separate authors of papers whose keyword is "logic programming".
The resulting unary relation will be the value of the last variable of
the statement and is presented as a list.

        The above statements are not intended for the end-users. Instead,
they are used for testing and possibly implementing the final interface.
Suppose we are designing the bibliographic database to a MacIntosh computer
using LPA MacPROLOG . We have defined the pull down menu in Figure 5.

        The first line contains the name of the menu, the following three
lines the menu items. A selection of the second menu item is a call for
the following procedure:

        'Show entries'(keyword):-'FIND'(K,keyword(_,K),Keywords),
                        'SCROLL-MENU'(['Select a keyword'],
                                    [Keywords],[],[Selected]),
                        'FIND_LOC'(X,keyword(X,Selected),L),
                        'FIND_CONT'(L,_,Y,(nl,write(Y),nl)).

        The FIND statement finds all separate keywords used in the database.
The MacPROLOG statement SCROLL-MENU displays the text "Select a Keyword"
and a scrolling menu where the keywords are in alphabetic order. After the
user has selected a keyword from the scrolling menu, the selected keyword
appears as the value of the variable Selected. The statement FIND_LOC
finds all references which have the selected keyword, and the statement

FIND_CONT writes the found references in alphabetic order such that there is an empty line between two references.

5. UPDATES IN DOCUMENT DATABASES

EDLA contains statements for appending and deleting tuples both in the document and in the property relations. The statement DELETE deletes from the current document the tuples of a given position and APPEND appends a tuple to the current document. The following statements remove from the bibliographic database those references which are selected by the user from the text in the Output window.

```
'FIND_LOC'(X,selected_entry(X),P),
'DELETE'(P).
```

The DELETE statement deletes, not only tuples in the document, but also those tuples in the property relations which express some property of a deleted entry.

The statement APPEND_PROPERTY appends a tuple to a property relation and the statement DELETE_PROPERTY deletes one or more tuples from a property relation. The following statements remove a selected keyword totally from the bibliographic database:

```
'FIND'(K,keyword(_,K),Keywords),
'SCROLL-MENU'(['Select the keyword you want totally delete:'],
               [Keywords],[],[Selected]),
'REMOVE_PROPERTY'(keyword(_,Selected)).
```

For making changes in a document there are two commands: SHIFT and CHANGE. SHIFT is used for changing the structure of a document and CHANGE is used for changing the content of a document. For example, the structure (Ceri and Crespi-Reghizzi, 1983; Gibbs, 1984; Meyrowitz and van Dam, 1982; Stonebraker, Stettner, Lynn, Kalash, and Guttman, 1983) of the document in Figure 1 can be changed (Banchilhon and Richard, 1984; Biller, 1983; Ceri and Crespi-Reghizzi, 1983; Clark and McCabe, 1985) by SHIFT command. In the reference document, this operation may be needed after a large amount of updates. The new entries are always added to the end of the document structure. If a lot of deletions have been made, the structure of the document may be very sparse.

6. CONCLUSIONS

We have described some features of a new experimental database language EDLA which is designed for document databases. In these databases information appears either as a part of a document or as a property of some part of a document. A document is presented as a binary relation and the properties of parts are stored in relations called property relations. The experimental language is used as an extension of Prolog. In the language no predefined structure is postulated for documents and the documents can contain any data which can be presented in Prolog. The document types of a specific document database are defined using the data definition language of EDLA.

The query language of EDLA is a domain calculus-like language which contains statements for retrieving information from a document database and statements for updating the relations of a document database. In this paper, we have primarily treated the retrieval capabilities of EDLA. The updating of document databases is discussed only slightly. A Prolog extended by EDLA is suitable for specifying document databases and tools for handling information in document databases. These specifications are executable and, therefore, serve as prototypes of the tools. Using these prototypes, a tool designer and the users of the tool can make experiments for finding the requirements for the tool, for example, answers to the questions (a)-(d) in Section 1. In an environment where an efficient Prolog is available the last prototype may also serve as the implementation of the tool.

ACKNOWLEDGEMENTS

This research was supported by the Academy of Finland. The author wishes to thank Ralph-Johan Back, Pertti Järvinen and Kari-Jouko Räihä for their comments on an earlier version of this paper.

REFERENCES

Bancilhon, F., and Richard, P., 1984, "Managing Texts and Facts in a Mixed Data Base Environment", New Applications of Data Bases, Academic Press, pp. 89-107.

Biller, H., 1983, "On the Architecture of a System Integrating Database Management and Information Retrieval", Proc. of the Int. Conf. on Research and Development in Information Retrieval, Springer-Verlag, pp. 80-97.

Ceri, S., and Crespi-Reghizzi, S., 1983, "Relational Data Bases in the Design of Program Construction System", ACM SIGSOFT Software Eng. Notes, 8, (3), July 1983, pp. 17-29.

Clark, K. L., and McCabe, F. G., 1985, LPA MacPROLOG Reference Manual, Logic Programming Association.

Clocksin, W. F., and Mellish, C. S., 1984, Programming in Prolog, Second Edition, Springer-Verlag.

Davis, R. E., 1982, "Runnable Specification as a Design Tool", Logic Programming, Clark, K. L., and Tärnlund, S.-A., eds., Academic Press, pp. 141-149.

Gibbs, S. J., 1984, An Object Oriented Office Data Model, Computer Systems Research Group, University of Toronto.

Gomaa, H., and Scott, D. G. H., 1981, "Prototyping as a Tool in the Specification of User Requirements", Proc. of the 5th Int. Conf. on Software Engineering, IEEE, pp. 333-339.

Horwitz, S., and Teitelbaum, T., 1985, "Relations and Attributes: A Symbiotic Basis for Editing Environments", ACM SIGPLAN Notes, 20, (7), July 1985, pp. 93-106.

Komorowski, H. J., and Maluszynski, J., 1986, Logic Programming and Rapid Prototyping, Technical Report, Department of Computer and Information Science, Linköping University.

Kowarski, I., and Lopez, M., 1982, "The Document Concept in a Data Base", Proc. ACM SIGMOD, pp. 276-283.

Lee, A., and Lochovsky, F. H., 1985, "User Interface Design", Office Automation, Tsichritzis, D. C., ed., Springer-Verlag, pp. 3-20.

Mason, R. E. A., and Carey, T. T., 1983, "Prototyping Interactive Information Systems", <u>Communications of the ACM</u>, <u>26</u>, pp. 347-354.

Meyrowitz, N., and van Dam, A., 1982, "Interactive Editing Systems", <u>ACM Computing Surveys</u>, <u>14</u>, (3), pp. 321-415.

Pereira, F., ed., 1984, <u>C-Prolog User's Manual Version 1.5</u>, EdCAAD, Univ. of Edinburgh.

Sacco, G. M., 1984, "OTTER - An Information Retrieval System for Office Automation", <u>Proc. of the 2nd ACM-SIGOA Conf. on Office Information Systems</u>, pp. 104-112.

Salminen, A., 1986, "A Specification of a Tool for Viewing Program Text", <u>Proc. of the Europian Symp. on Programming, Lecture Notes in Computer Science 213</u>, Springer-Verlag, pp. 250-261.

Salminen, A., and Back, R. J. R., 1985, "A Relational Model for Documents", <u>Proc. of the Int. Symposium on New Directions in Computing</u>, IEEE Computer Society, pp. 50-59.

Schek, H. -J., and Pistor, P., 1982, "Data Structures for an Integrated Data Base Management and Information Retrieval System", <u>Proc. of the Eighth Int. Conf. on Very Large Data Bases</u>, pp. 197-207.

Stonebraker, M., Stettner, H., Lynn, N., Kalash, J., and Guttman, A., 1983, "Document Processing in a Relational Database System", <u>ACM Trans. Off. Inf. Syst.</u>, <u>1</u>, (2), April 1983, pp. 143-158.

Venken, R. and Bruynooghe, M., 1984, "Prolog as a Language for Prototyping of Information Systems", <u>Approaches to Prototyping</u>, Budde, R., et al., eds., Springer-Verlag, pp. 447-458.

IMPLEMENTING MODIFICATIONS OF INFORMATION SYSTEMS WHILE USING THEM:

AN INTENTIONALLY INTERVENING APPROACH

Gunhild Sandström

University of Lund
Information and Computer Sciences
LUND, Sweden

Abstract: Great importance is attached to seeing the possibilities of
developing information systems while they are being used. It then becomes
significant to break unwanted habits. One way of doing this is to permit
the end users to make system changes while using the system, i.e., to develop
the system 'in the small'. To fetch the users' ideas of improving their
information systems may also be effective for the organization as a whole,
even if the system is a local one. In this report I propose and discuss
attempts to break what looks like invariances and an inquiry method of
why/how-type in order to make it easier for such a development to occur.

1. INTRODUCTION: INTEGRATION OF SYSTEMS DEVELOPMENT AND SYSTEMS USE

There are two main activities within information and computer science
where it is urgent to make more research efforts:

- to use information systems

- to develop information systems

In both activities the users of the information systems should be
involved, and the two can be related to each other in two ways (Figure 1):

The development of an information system and the use of that system
should be bound up thoroughly with each other, not only in the way that the
use is a result of the development. It is also necessary to tie both the
development and the use of an information system very tightly together,
that is to develop the system while using it. This latter connection is
the one I am most concerned about in this article.

Most information systems development can no longer successfully be
divided strictly into a number of prescriptive or standardized phrases
after a model, which consists of mainly 'before'-, 'during'- and 'after'-
phases in continuing top-down analyses to bottom-up syntheses (Sandström
and Wormell, 1980). Examples of such traditional models is the Systems
Life Cycle Model (Rubin, 1972) and its successors with their phases of conception, analysis, design, programming, installation, operation, and cessa-
tion, one at a time in the named order.

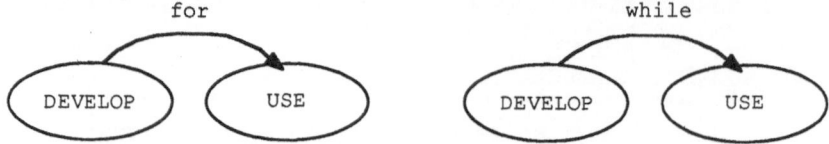

Figure 1.   Interesting Fields and Their Connections -
            Realms for Research.

        More promising approaches to systems development nowadays are the
adaptive design model and the prototyping model (Keen, 1980; Jenkins, 1983).
I call this kind of approach an iterative design (Sandström, 1985) (Figure
2). The various moments of the traditional phases named above are mixed,
more inseparable, and invisible in such a design, through a learning and
integrating process. The iterative design implies that the end users participate as users of the system on trial on a number of occasions. Hereby,
they will have possibilities to propose improvements and requirements on
the system before they get a new version to test. By this way of working
they also learn about how an information system works and how to use it.
In iterative design the end users themselves make the trial systems and
meet their own needs in a direct way. The designers of the information
system also learn from the potential users through their actual use and
evaluation of the trial system.

        However, the completed information system must not be looked upon as
an invariable product. Someone will act upon messages mediated by a system
or someone will act upon the system. During such use of the system, the
user should either be able to make important changes or be permitted to get
changes made according to his/her ideas and requirements. These requirements
are seldom delivered at the request of a designer to the full extent in the
beginning of a system's development (Flensburg, 1984), when the designer
wishes to have them. Instead, the users will not become aware of many of
these desires and needs until they start to use a system. I do not mean
that it is possible to change a system unlimitedly at any time. It is
impossible to meet every requirement that can be thought of, but more flexibility can be built into an information system for administrative work,
even if it is computerized (Sandström, 1986).

        After some time the users know their system and they require more from
it. Their needs may then have risen so high or their information system
may have become worn out to justify a new larger systems development. The
used and modified system becomes too old. We may start <u>a new iterative
design process</u>. (Figure 2.)

        The tight binding of the two activities together can fruitfully be
accentuated as the types:

    1) When mainly developing, it is necessary to test and learn,
        and a good way of doing this is to make a prototype or a
        similar product in order <u>to use the system on trial</u>.

    2) Mainly when using the system, it is necessary to absorb
        the users' ideas of improvements of the system and a
        good way of doing this is to permit the users' to make
        alterations when using the system, that is <u>to develop
        the system in the small</u>.

        One main research goal of mine is to make it easier for the users to
develop the systems in the small while using them. I believe it is an

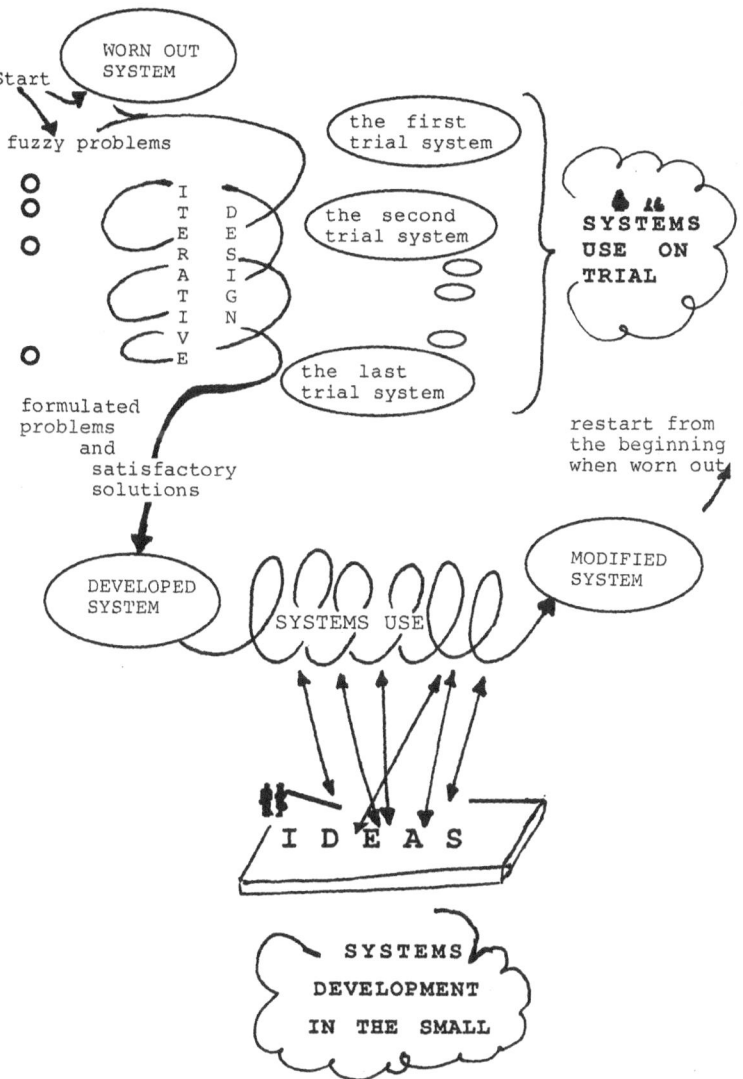

Figure 2. Systems Use on Trial and Systems
Development in The Small.

ethical and effective way of obtaining better information systems, as the
users themselves know best what they want and, after some use, also the
best realistic needs for their actions in administrative and librarian
work. I acquire knowledge for the consumers of the information support,
for example the administrative workers and the clients of a hospital, a
library, and a manufacturing company. The knowledge could, of course, be
very useful for the suppliers of data systems and data technology too. But,
if there is a contradiction here, I am on the user side of the information
system and I am mostly interested in the individual human being and the
groups around a limited task or work situation, as I believe very much in
these, not too big or not too small, information systems.

2. WHY STUDIES OF INFORMATION SYSTEMS USE ARE IMPORTANT

Compared to technological research very little has been done in user-oriented research concerning information systems and even less has been done for the use of such systems. The importance of studying this field might be illustrated by the following quotations, which also support my intention to gain knowledge for the information consumers in the first place.

> "Computerized parts of information systems can be developed applying very simplifying assumptions about the users and their organizational settings." (DeMaio, 1980.)

> "When a system is implemented this is always done in a real organization with real life users." (Nissen, et al., 1981.)

Such information systems are often designed to the designer's ideal of a user and of an organization. This is reported by Gingras and McLean (Gingras and McLean, 1982) in a study measuring users' and designers' profiles and characteristics within the context of the design of information systems. They found that

> "The designers' 'ideal user' differs significantly from the actual user's self profile, but there was found to be no difference between this 'ideal user' and the designers' self image." (Gingras and McLean, 1982, p. 169.)

If this is the case, it does not help the real users very much even if the designer's purport is to be user-oriented. And there is a lot of other empirical findings and reasonings about the designer, his opinions of himself as a designer, and his role in the development process (Churchman, 1971; Hedberg and Mumford, 1979).

Furthermore, the user representations in the development process may have been merely some kind of hostage (Bjørn-Andersen, 1976; Hedberg, 1974). Also, the information need is changing and as the users have learned the system and how to use it, their requirements are extended.

For these reasons:

● the oversimplified settings,

● the differing profiles,

● the user hostage, and

● the changing need,

it is important to study the use of information systems and to acquire knowledge primarily for the end users of information systems.

3. USER AND DESIGNER PARTICIPATION

Within the realms of information systems, there are people with quite different educational backgrounds and practical experience. Two main groups are the Electronic Data Processing specialists, 'the EDP-specialists' and the professionals in administrative and librarian work, 'the end users'. The EDP-specialists are well trained in systematic ordering and in setting up formal rules. Today many designers, especially those from the information technology industry, choose their perspectives mostly to facilitate mechanization and computerization. When studying a computerized information system in use, their systemizing already exists. Maybe the users want it redone after having detected, by themselves or supported by other people, a better way of using the system. This belongs to an active part of a learning and adaptive process.

The competence of an average end user of a computer is based on working life experience. The perspective is on various work tasks. The end users also have their individual knowledge and their priorities and ways of solving problems.

The users' experienced knowledge and skill and the EDP-experts' knowledge about data systems may together form new ways of problem finding and problem solving during the use of the system.

A researcher, as a change agent in studying information systems use, could also contribute to the problem finding and problem solving processes with her/his scientific knowledge. My own experience is much of this kind (Sandström, 1985).

Presuppositions and theoretical frames and guesses about the practice, along with a 'plan of intervention' are ingredients in the framework presented in Figure 3, which illustrates participation when studying and modifying information systems. The different parts, the "developed system", the "USE OF SYSTEM" and the "modified system" in Figure 3, are the same as those in Figure 2. The results are changes in real use and modifications in system design, and also scientifically interesting questions or contributions to an information systems theory based on empirical work.

In the empirical part of the research job, the end users should be met as professionals in their own professions. They never look upon themselves as users of information systems. They are doctors, secretaries, forwarding agents, librarians, and so on. They do not even imagine the information systems that support them.

4.   THE POSSIBILITY OF INVARIANCE BREAKING

When studying the use of existing information systems, invariances could be found, which either should be maintained as good ones or broken as unwanted habits according to the users' ideas. In order to acquire knowledge for the users to apply as a basis for meaningful emancipatory actions in practice, invariance-breaking has to be adopted as a design and scientific activity. Much knowledge will be of a kind that intend to aid people to alter habits in their way of interacting with information systems and computer experts. I have to look for patterns worth saving and patterns necessary to break. In order to get such general traces and patterns in the social realms, I also have to do research on some kind of invariance-seeking.

The two expressions 'invariance-seeking' and 'invariance-breaking', I have borrowed from Galtung (1977, p. 73). He says that:

"A generalization is a production that is not completely singularistic.

An invariance (law) is a generalization with a condition-set that permits variation in space, time subject, and object....

A prediction is an invariance applied to future situations specified in space and time."

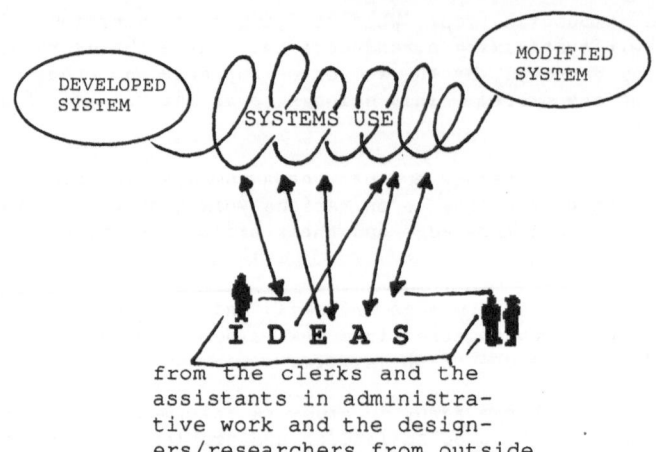

from the clerks and the
assistants in administra-
tive work and the design-
ers/researchers from outside

THE DESIGNER´s RESEARCHER´s FRAMEWORK OF CONCEPTIONS ANI THEORIES

THE REAL RESULTS AND
THE SCIENTIFIC RESULTS
BASED ON EMPIRICAL WORK
including
THE DESIGNER´S/
RESEARCHER´S REVISED
FRAMEWORK

Figure 3. User and Designer/Research Participation When
Modifying and Studying the Use of Information
System.

And further in a dialogue between an invariance seeker and an invariance
breaker he - as the latter person - points out:

> "I see Man and Society as more equal" (than Man and Nature)
> "they shape each other - and social science should reflect
> this."

> "... any invariance is only a stepping stone, the test of
> which is not whether it is confirmed by the empirical state
> of the world that happens to come around, but whether it
> shows the way to a better empirical state of the world."
> (Galtung, 1977, pp. 93-94.) (Text in parentheses is my
> interpretation.)

Sometimes we enjoy invariances and sometimes we create them. I propose
that invariances should be accepted only as long as they serve us and then
one may look for ways of breaking them. The invariance should be seen as a
culturally/socially produced phenomenon in work, and it should be broken if
it constitutes an obstacle for people willing to pay the price of breaking
it.

Thus, both in invariance-seeking and in invariance-breaking scientific
activities are important in development and research. Designers, users, and
other involved persons need to know when it is worth taking advantages of a

constraint. In my empirical studies, I have looked for such constraints as expressed prescriptions and restrictions or as tacit taboos and I have found rather many (Sandström, 1986).

In one department, there were people who wrote down by hand information extracted from sheets produced by the data system. Well-founded or not, they could not even think of using a terminal to extract and process this type of work. "Never" they say. This kind of self-inflicted restriction is hard to break. But, very often, the opposite is the case, especially through group discussions. It is rather easy, in departments where the members feel secure in their work, to help the users to see something in a new light. "This display layout might be better, if we change it in this way" or "For what do I do this, after all?" and similar statements are very common in my studies. For instance, I observed, at the end of one of the studies, the users' willingness to adopt pictures in their information system. They have made sketches and from that it is not far away to use pictures in the computerized part. They discussed it and they claimed equipment to this use possible.

5. PLANNED INTERVENING PROCESSES FOR DEVELOPMENT AND RESEARCH PURPOSES

The users are supported to acquire knowledge of new ways of action when using information systems. A learning and trying out strategy has been used several times with success, and, therefore, I have planned interventions for the empirical work. This is in a way a necessity, in order to aid the users of the information system to get new ideas and to dare to take chances to alter their use of the information system, or to develop and realize a new idea of their own about system performance.

I had to decide whether there were parts of my study that might be tackled in different ways with respect to the aim of my research. A great part of my studies had methodological problems of a non-deterministic and non-stochastic character.

Both quantitative and qualitative methods are needed for designers and researchers. The quantitative methods are needed as preliminaries for qualitative methods and vice versa. I needed both qualitative insight into the users' real problem and quantitative overviews of general conditions. Qualitative insight and quantitative overview could be achieved both in parallel and interleaved. These kinds of integrated perspectives I share with other researchers and they have good arguments for their use (Grönmo and Tschudi, 1984).

Interventions can be regarded as experiments that are not repeatable. In such experiments real important differences are apparent. Repeated experiments may be looked upon as special cases of interventions. They are characterized by:

(1) a high degree of control over the situation by the experimenter; and

(2) a decision to disregard as unimportant all remaining differences.

I have made planned interventions in my empirical research in two organizations in order to get material which cannot be gathered by traditional means.

The very first time it just happened. A great deal of my research work became fuel for discussing important things among the users about their work. As a researcher I became, without then knowing it, a very strong intervening factor as a result of earlier and/or hidden conflicts within one of the organizations.

Thanks to Dennett (1983), I have found out that what I have done methodologically is that I have used similar tools to those of a detective. This method, therefore, is call "the Sherlock Holmes' method", which by the intentional stance is a tool for generating or designing anecdotal circumstances (Dennett, 1983, pp. 348-350).

Sherlock Holmes usually arranged for traps and analogously I arranged for interventions. Sometimes I did it when I was not quite consciously aware of my intentions. Afterwards, I observed the striking effects and, therefore, I tried a new similar intervention. Now it was more planned, based on earlier experience. The key of the method is to shape 'a climate for anecdotee telling'. The method is, of course, especially effective in such situations, where the anecdotees could be generated several times under similar conditions.

From these interventions and often planned situations, I strove to secure permanent traces. In these I tried to find a pattern, useful for the users of the systems studied, for other users, for systems designers, myself, and my contemporaries in research and education.

The research process contains conscious interventions and its six main steps, DIAGNOSE, PLAN, ACT, STUDY and EVALUATE, LEARN AND SPECIFY can be repeated several times, hopefully, improving and understanding the knowledge of the information and the information system use (Susman and Evered, 1978; Nissen, et al., 1982).

My work should be seen as a learning process in order to gain further insight into information and information systems, from their use and practice. The learning process has similar features to the hermeneutic helix (Radnitzky, 1970), which is essentially a very general model of the development of knowledge through a tacking procedure or dialectics. The perspectives are the same as those in the two important processes 'systems development' and 'systems use' I told you about in the beginning.

This is not exact science. The main interest is about functions in, intentions with, and importance of an information system for people and these are not predictable items.

This so called action research process is recommended (Järvinen, 1984) for application and problem-solving tasks, which both exist in this work.

Researchers and designers should be in on the users' problematic situations and act for better solutions. It is not enough just to study it. From the users' problematic situations (Checkland, 1981), or the bad symptom of the information system in a rather fuzzy description, maybe an anecdote, a possible solution can be suggested that may not be a satisfactory one. However, from this solution it may be possible to clarify the basic problem and reach a new solution that is more satisfactory than the first one, and so on, until sufficient remedies are achieved for the problem. Not before this point has the problem been satisfactorily defined. During this spiral process, more and more knowledge is accumulated about the context and the history of the problem and the users' purposes in using the information system.

From several learning processes, as the one described in Figure 4, on the same theme, it is then possible to see general features, after the

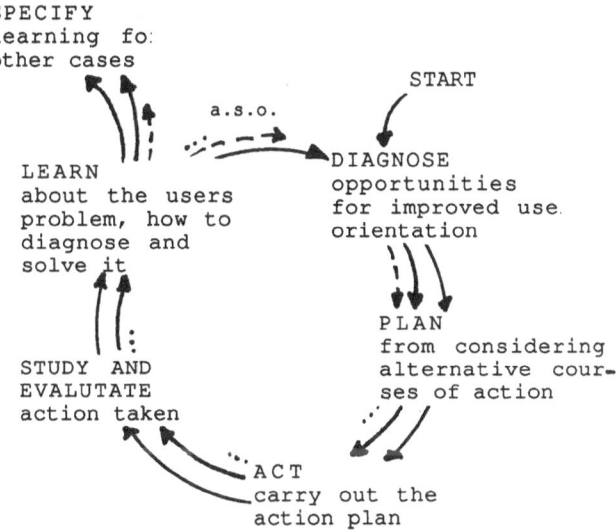

SPECIFY
learning fo:
other cases

START

a.s.o.

DIAGNOSE
opportunities
for improved use
orientation

LEARN
about the users
problem, how to
diagnose and
solve it

PLAN
from considering
alternative cour-
ses of action

STUDY AND
EVALUTATE
action taken

ACT
carry out the
action plan

Figure 4. Conscious Intervention Steps In
A Learning Process.

study and evaluation phase. When using a planned intervening research
process, there is a fully realistic possibility of accumulating knowledge
to achieve a higher degree of generalization. In empirical work, it is a
very useful way of saving traces and patterns that could be seen, in some
aspects, as being generally useful in other cases. Generalization, however,
always means consciously ignoring differences between the cases. Therefore,
it seems important to state explicitly for each theory which differences
have been ignored.

Permanent traces of the processes, I studied and tried to learn about,
were saved - for people in the field of study, for me, and for other researchers - in order to reflect upon and interpret and re-interpret later
on. These interpretations may result in identifying patterns of some kind.
For these patterns it makes sense of asking if they are to be continued or
broken.

6.   A METHOD OF INQUIRY

As a method to question a person about things that I do not know much
about in advance, I utilized an idea (Postman and Weingartner, 1971) used
for teaching purposes in my investigations.

Instead of starting to ask about figures, labels, and values, I asked
for functions, intentions, and importance. Instead of trying to cover the
contents of what is going on, I wanted the users to talk about their fresh
ideas, their problems and opinions. The questions must open the ability
to think both for the users and the designer(s)/researcher. The hermeneutic
helix (Figure 4) should not be rigidly planned in the same sense as the
planned sequence of a formal education. The helix is not an instrument to
follow slavishly.

The quantitative material I gathered in another way. Much of the
quantitative material was documented already and was rather easily gathered
in the users' own report on statistics, which they had been told to make
by law and superiors.

An example concerning the inquiry method:

I did not start asking for "How many transactions...?	I was asking for "How does the information system take care of transactions?"
"Of what parts does the system consist?"	"How does this system work?"
"Is this system good or...?" • •	"Why is this system important?" • . among others (Sandström, 1984; Sandström, 1985)

I have tried to find questions which activate the users' minds and get them to the point of emancipating: "Maybe this could be changed...." I think they told me much about their problems and ideas, but the real point was that they - maybe I can say - 'spontaneously' came to think about them at all.

The aim of this method of inquiry is to support a person:

● to raise his ability to learn and act,

● to get rid of the distrust of originality,

● to believe in his ability to improve, and

● to realize that problem solving is something to enjoy.

The method helped both the users and me. When people were allowed by management to do something about their work situation, i.e., to really change, if they feel a need, is of course of the greatest importance here. Whether this was the case in the situations in question was not always easy to get a clear opinion of.

The material in this kind of investigation should be developed for research and systems use, on the basis of the users' reaction and not so much on the logical structure that had been made beforehand. Success was measured with the help of the actions and/or expressed wishes of the users of the information system.

Similar discoveries has been made by other researchers:

"In many respects the logic of intervention differs from the logic of analysis. It limelights and focuses on the situations as they are experienced by the actors: systems, functions, procedures, and technical equipment are not just wiped out as irrelevant, on the contrary they are necessary elements of the actors' situation contributing to shape it, but they lay - so to speak - in the background of the situation". (Lanzara and Mathiassen, 1984.)

7.   CONTINUOUS SYSTEMS DEVELOPMENT 'IN THE SMALL'

The basic idea with this work is to make it possible for the users to develop their information system, when new needs appear. There need not always be a lot of analyzing work and financial investment to motivate a necessary change - to 'see' a problem and to 'see' a solution and to apply them. The main thing is to let users acquire knowledge and self-confidence to be able to more and more judge by themselves which kind of computer information system really supported them in their work and which did not. The increased self-confidence should make them secure enough to convey their judgement both to their bosses and to any experts who care to listen. It is not at all impossible to let the users themselves take responsibility for these kinds of changes. They know best whether changes are needed or not. This must not be a business for a system designer or a machine supplier to the same extent as it has been before. Personnel outside the work situation must be involved only when they are influenced by it or have a special interest in it. Systems development 'in the small' costs little effort when carried out and much self-esteem is gained, through 'knowing how' (Ryle, 1949) and when in work as a whole, and in adequate information support, through making alterations if and when needed.

When speaking of the responsibility above, I would like to refer to Nurminen, who argues that man should be responsible for both job and information.

Responsibility does not appear only as accountability:

"Responsibility means being responsible. Beyond the usual meaning related with accountability we will try to find another connotation from the root 'respond'. In the context of informal systems, the receiver is able to respond to a message, if he can use it correctly at his work. This naturally requires a genuine understanding of the message, not only stimulus-response type of behavior. So we understand that a responsible user of information understands the pragmatic meaning .... It will be argued that this pragmatic understanding creates a good prerequisite for accountability." (Nurimen, 1982.)

It is also very important to care about the employee resources within an enterprise. The employees must have varying work and be trusted to handle their own information systems. They are also the people who best know their own information requirements and how it should be presented, and it is a waste of resources not to take advantage of their knowledge when they utilize the information system. It may also be possible to get rid of most of the unnecessary sediment (Sandström, 1986 (regarding the phenomenon of sedimentation in information systems)) that nobody normally questions in daily work. People do not feel responsible or they do not even realize its existence.

There are no clearly defined obstacles for greater investment of people, users, and EDP-persons, and time, in systems development initiated by new technology, or radical changes in the work and organization, due to the fact that the old computer is ready for the scrap-heap. However, there seem to be tacit obstacles of social kinds of smaller efforts concerning better use of the existing information systems.

ACKNOWLEDGEMENT

This research has been done with financial support from the Swedish Work Environment Fund, the Swedish National Board of Technical Development and the University of Lund.

REFERENCES

Bjørn-Andersen, N., 1976, "Organizational Aspects of Information Systems

Design", <u>DATA</u>, <u>12</u>, R & D, pp. 75-80.

Checkland, P., 1981, <u>Systems Thinking, Systems Practice</u>, John Wiley and
Sons Ltd., Chichester, U.K.

Churchman, C. W., 1971, <u>The Design of Inquiring Systems - Basic Concepts of
Systems and Organizations</u>, Basic Books, New York.

DeMaio, A., 1980, "Socio-Technical Methods for Information Systems Design",
<u>The Information Systems Environment</u>, Proceedings from the IFIP TC 8.2
Working Conference, Bonn.

Dennett, D. C., 1983, "Intentional Systems in Cognitive Ethology: The
Panglossian Paradigm Defended", <u>The Behavioural and Brain Sciences</u>, <u>6</u>,
Cambridge University Press, U.S.A., pp. 343-355.

Flensburg, P., 1984, <u>Lägesrapport frän ett aktionsorienterat forskningsproj-
ekt</u>, Rapport Informationsbehandling-AdmDB, Lunds Universitet, Lund,
Sweden, (in Swedish).

Galtung, J., 1977, <u>Methodology and Ideology, Volume One</u>, Christian Eljers,
Copenhagen.

Gingras, L., and McLean, E. R., 1982, "Designers and Users of Information
Systems: A Study in Differing Profiles", <u>Proceedings of the Third International Conference on Information Systems</u>, Ginzberg and Ross, eds.

Grönmo, S., 1982, "Forholdet mellom kvalitative og kvantitative metoder i
samfunnsforskningen", <u>Kvalitative metoder i samfunnsforskning</u>, Holter, H.,
and Kalleberg, R., eds., Universitetsforlaget, Drammem, Norway (in Norwegian).

Hedberg, B., 1974, "Computer Systems to Support Industrial Democracy",
<u>Human Choice and Computers</u>, Mumford, E., and Sackman, H., eds., North-Hol-
land, Amsterdam.

Hedberg, B., and Mumford, E., 1979, "Some Theoretical Ideas of Relevance
to Systems Design", <u>The Impact of Systems Change in Organizations</u>, Bj∮rn-
Andersen, N., Hedberg, B., Mercer, D., Mumford, E., and Solé, A., eds.,
Sijthoff and Noordhoff, Netherlands.

Järvinen, P., 1984, "On Selection of Methods for Studying Interactive
Systems - Analysis of the Topic as Structured by Keystroke-level Model",
<u>Seventh Scandinavian Seminar on Systemeering, Part I</u>, Sääksjärvi, M., ed.,
Helsinki School of Economics, Helsinki.

Keen, P., 1980, "Adaptive Design for Decision Support Systems", <u>Data Base</u>,
<u>12</u>, (1-2), pp. 15-25.

Lanzara, G. F., and Mathiassen, L., 1984, <u>Mapping Situations Within a System
Development Project - An Intervening Perspective on Organizational Change</u>,
University of Aarhus, Aarhus, Denmark.

Nissen, H-E, Carlsson, S., and Nadel, D., 1981, <u>Why is User Orientation a
Must in Information Systems Development</u>, Report, Information and Computer
Sciences, University of Lund, Lund, Sweden.

Nissen, H-E, Carlsson, S., and Flensburg, P., Holmberg, K-A, Sandström, G.,
and Wormell, I., 1982, <u>User Oriented Information Systems - A Research Pro-
gram</u>, Department of Information and Computer Sciences, University of
Lund, Lund, Sweden.

Nurimen, M. I., 1982, Human-Scale Information System, Institutt for Informationsvitenskap, University of Bergen, Bergen, Norway.

Postman, N., and Weingartner, C., 1971, Teaching as a Subversive Activity, Penguin Education Specials.

Radnitzky, G., 1970, Contemporary School of Metascience, Volume II, Scandinavian University Books, Gothenburg, Sweden.

Rubin, M. L., 1972, Introduction to the Systems Life Cycle, Brandon System Press, London.

Ryle, G., 1949, The Concept of Mind, Penguin Books Ltd., Harmondsworth, G. B., 1963.

Sandström, G., 1984, An Intervening Method to Facilitate Systems Development 'In the Small', Report LU-ADB-R:85-06, Information & Computer Sciences, University of Lund, Lund, Sweden.

Sandström, G., 1985, Towards Transparent Data Bases – How to Interpret and Act on Expressions Mediated by Computerized Information Systems, Dissertation, Studentlitteratur-Chartwell Bratt, Lund, Sweden.

Sandström, G., 1986, "Historical Sediment of Formalizing in Administrative Work", Quality of Work versus Quality of Information Systems, Flensburg, P., Nissen, H-E., and Sandström, G., eds, Proceedings from 9th Scandinavian Seminar on Systemeering, in print at University of Lund, Lund, Sweden.

Sandström, G., 1986, "Augmented Thesaurus for Multicontextual Descriptions", Intelligent Information Systems for the Information Society, Brookes, B. C., Proceedings of the Sixth International Research Forum in Information Science, North-Holland, Amsterdam.

Sandström, G., and Wormell, I., 1980, Studier av modeller för systemutveckling hos Lantbrukskooperationen, rapport Lunds Universitet, Informationsbehandling-ADB, Lund, Sweden, (in Swedish).

Susman, G. I., and Evered, R. D., 1978, "An Assessment of the Scientific Merits of Action Research, Administrative Science Quarterly, December 1978, pp. 582-603.

Tschudi, F., 1982, "Om nödvändigheten av syntese mellom kvantitative og kvalitative metoder", Kvalitative metoder i samfunnsforskning, Holter, H., and Kalleberg, R., eds., Universitetsforlaget, Drammen, Norway, (in Norwegian).

THE SEMANTIC MODEL IN INFORMATION RETRIEVAL

Jean Tague

School of Library and Information Science
University of Western Ontario
London, Ontario Canada N6G 1H1

Abstract: Infological models of information systems represent a user's conception of the real-world environment which is to be captured by the system. As such, they provide a basis for the design of the human-system interface. A number of models have been proposed for information retrieval systems: the Boolean model, the vector space model, and the relational model. In this paper, another model, the semantic model comes from database theory and is, in fact, an extension of that model. However, it provides a number of features which make it more powerful and expressive than these earlier models of retrieval systems. The implementation of the semantic model in an experimental information retrieval system which permits users to build their own interface is described.

INTRODUCTION

Tsichritzis (Tsichritzis and Lochovsky, 1982) has distinguished two realms of data modeling: the infological realm, in which the real world application is mapped into a human conceptualization, and the datalogical realm, in which these concepts are mapped into a computer representation. Infological models, thus, should logically precede datalogical models in the development of an information system and serve as the basis for both the datalogical model and the user interface.

INFOLOGICAL MODEL

Infological model is based on work in database theory on what is called the semantic data model. In the presentation, information retrieval systems are not meant to be defined exclusively as bibliographic retrieval systems. Retrieval objects, in commercial systems, may, of course, be descriptions of items other than books -- companies, associations, substances, geographical areas, etc. However, since bibliographic retrieval systems predominate, examples will be drawn from this environment.

A complete infological model for an information retrieval system must represent both the structures and the processes of the application, i.e., both its static and dynamic aspects. Static components include:

1. Objects or tokens, i.e., physical or mental constructs in the real world. In an information retrieval system, some examples of objects are documents, books, articles, queries, keywords, classification codes, descriptors, titles, authors, publishers, publication dates, journals, citations, thesauri, and users.

2. Relationships among the objects. In an information retrieval system, a book <u>is a kind of</u> document, an author <u>is an attribute of</u> a document, a title <u>consists of a sequence of</u> keywords, a query <u>specifies a disjunction of</u> keywords.

3. Structures. These are complexes involving two or more objects and the relationship among them, for example, a database of document descriptions, the attributes of a document description, and the descriptors and relationships in a thesaurus. An object which cannot be expressed as a structure involving other objects is called an atomic object. Entities are atomic objects or structures which form a part of the model.

4. Names or labels of entities, for example, attribute names and database names.

5. Numeric or logic value functions defined on the objects and entities of the system, for example, the number of documents retrieved by a Boolean query, the ranks of documents in the output for a vector query, the truth value of a Boolean query with respect to a single document, and the weight assigned to a descriptor.

Models differ with respect to one or more of these aspects, and are appropriate or inappropriate to the extent that they permit a system developer or a system user to describe the important objects, relationships, and functions of the application. The most significant distinctions, however, relate to the atoms and the relationships of the model.

In conventional data modeling (hierarchical, network, and relational models), atoms are, for the most part, assumed to be values from a limited domain, with no further characterization or analysis beyond the fact that they are numbers or strings. In information retrieval, it is important to make distinctions at the character level. Hence, a complete model for information retrieval will incorporate characters as atoms and define other objects in terms of relationships among characters.

In theory, the number of relationships among a set of n objects is $2^{[n(n-1)/2]}$. In fact, however, only a few relationships are semantically meaningful in information retrieval system design. The following are suggested as meaningful relationships for this purpose. This set was suggested by the work of Warnier (1979), but is an extension and reclassification of the original.

1. Concurrency of x and y (denoted x,y): x and y taken together in either order. For example, x and y might be two subject headings assigned to a document.

2. Sequence of x and y (denoted xy): x followed by y. For example, x and y might be two words in the title of a document.

   2.1 Repetition of x (denoted [x]): a special kind of

sequence in which x is followed by itself. For example, a document description might consist of a sequence of up to three author attributes.

3. Hierarchy. Three kinds may be distinguished:

    3.1 Classification (denoted x⊂y): x is a kind of y. For
    example, a book is a kind of document.

    3.2 Membership (denoted xεy): x is an instance of y. For
    example, Jane Eyre is a book.

    3.3 Characterization (denoted x:y): x is characterized by
    y, or y is an attribute of x. For example, a title is
    an attribute of a book.

    3.4 Recursion. This is a special kind of hierarchy, in which
    an entity has a hierarchical relationship with itself
    (denoted x⊂x, xεx, or x:x). For example, a query may be
    characterized as a (previous) query, followed by a
    keyword.

4. Alternation (denoted x/y): x or y. For example, a query
specifies United States or Canada.

5. Implication (denoted x→y): x implies or causes y. For
example, if the author is Charlotte Bronte, output the document description.

6. Difference (denoted x-y): that part of a structure x which
is not y. Negation (-y) is a special case of difference
where the parent entity x is implicit. For example, a query
specifies not Canada -- i.e., the set of descriptors omitting
Canada.

Models, for the most part, involve the definition of and assignment of
names to structures, i.e., non-atomic entities. Structures which involve
relationships among names, rather than terminal text values, are called
schemas. In a fixed format data base, instances of a schema will contain
text values whose arrangement is described by the schema. Structures whose
arrangement cannot be totally described by a schema are called text. In
information retrieval, some structures, for example, MARC records or other
records with variable format, are partly formatted (described by a schema)
and partly text. These structures typically include both names and text
values, rather than separating the two.

The dynamic components of a model are expressed as procedures, i.e.,
structures involving relationships of atomic actions such as input, output,
compare, store, add, etc. Such structures accomplish the operations of
structure creation, modification, searching, transformation, deletion, and
sorting. Because of the dynamic aspects, all structures have, at least
implicitly, an associated time aspect. Some structures, such as queries
may be relatively transient; others, such as schemas, relatively permanent.

A number of infological models have been proposed for the information
retrieval field, including the Boolean model, the vector space model, and
the relational model. Commercial on-line retrieval systems are said to be
based on the Boolean model. In its pure form, this model implies that item
or document descriptions are unordered sets of keywords and queries are
Boolean expressions (entities consisting of keywords and the relational
indicators of concurrency [and], alternation [or], and negation [not]).

The retrieval procedure determines the document descriptions for which the Boolean expression of the query is true. Such a model ignores some of the common features of present-day systems, such as string searches, truncated searches and proximity searches.

In the vector space model, document descriptions are regarded as ordered sets or n-tuples of numbers, where the ith number is the weight of the ith keyword in the document. Queries are similarly represented. Retrieval involves the evaluation of a document-query weight based on some function of the two vectors such as the cosine function and a ranking of document descriptions for output based on the values of this function.

The relational model, originally developed for database systems, has been applied to information retrieval by a number of writers, for example, Crawford (1981). A bibliographic item is represented by a set of relations (sequences of attribute names). The relations include author, keyword, bibliographic item, publisher, etc. The information about a document is distributed among the relation, rather than being united in a single entity, chiefly because of normalization requirements. Another disadvantage, as Crawford has pointed out, is that queries which specify more than one of a non-unique attribute (for example, "information" and "retrieval" both as keywords) cannot be expressed directly in the relational model. In terms of the relationship listed above, the relational model permits only sequence to be expressed, and, as a result of normalization, forbids even repetition.

The problem with the earlier models is that they are incomplete. They are not sufficiently expressive to permit a system designer or user to describe fully all the information items and queries which many information retrieval systems are required to handle. In particular, they do not provide facilities for describing:

1. Information sets in which the retrieval objects have a hierarchical structure.

2. Information sets in which objects are a mixture of formatted and textual elements.

3. String searches, i.e., searches for a sequence of text within an entity.

4. Proximity searches, i.e., searches requesting two strings within a specified number of words or sentences of each other.

5. Truncated searches, i.e., searches on keywords truncated to the right or left.

6. In the relational model, searches on repeating fields.

SEMANTIC MODEL

Semantic model is a rather loose term which has been applied to a number of database and artificial intelligence models which incorporate a greater number of the total set of components of an infological model, as described earlier, than do the standard database hierarchical, network, and relational models. A number of semantic models are reviewed by King and McLeod (1985). The present work has been guided by these previous realizations, particularly that of Zaniolo (1983). However, a number of features needed in the generalization from database systems to information retrieval systems have

Table I. Operators Defining Relationships.

Relationship	Operator	Example
sequence	(no operator)	xy
repetition (0 or more)	[]	[x]
(0 or 1)	$[]_1$	
(0 or n times)	$[]_n$	
concurrency		x,y
classification	⊂	x⊂y
membership	ε	xεy
characterization	:	x:y
alternation	/	x/y
implication	→	x→y
difference	−	x−y
negation		−y

been added in the present work, and a new notation introduced.

It has already been pointed out that information retrieval systems describe objects by means of unformatted text as well as values from a limited domain of numbers or strings, the norm for database systems. This limitation of data models has been addressed by Desai, Goyal, and Sadri (1986), who present a text data model, which attempts to formalize the key concepts of text and define a set of text objects and operations. This work has also been extremely useful in the development of a semantic model for information retrieval systems described herein.

The semantic model begins with atomic objects, operators which create structures from atomic objects or other structures and functions. The atomic objects are characters which, for most purposes, can be the characters in the extended ASCII set. Named subsets of the total character set are the alphabetic, the numeric, and the special characters. The wildcard character used in truncated searches is a special kind of character, as is the null character. Following the usual practice, the name of a structure is enclosed in angle brackets, e.g., <characters>. Names of operators are not enclosed in angle brackets; however, when the character itself is meant, it is enclosed in quotation marks.

The operators defining relationships are indicated in Table I.

Parentheses may be used, in the usual fashion, for indicating the order of operations.

The basic structures to be found in any information set are as follows:

```
<characters>   :  a,b,c ...z,A,B...Z,0,1, ...9,...
<numerics>     :  0,1,2,3,4,5,6,7,8,9
<alphabetics>  :  a,b,.....
<special>      :  <characters> - <alphabetics> - <numerics>
<char>         ε  <characters>
<text>         :  <char> [<text>]
<num>          ε  <numerics>
<alpha>        ε  <alphabetics>
<word>         :  <alpha> [<alpha>]
```

```
<operator>        :   ","," "," "," ":",""/","" "," "_"
<structure>       :   <text>[operator ][<structure>]
```

An example of the structures in a particular bibliographic database
might be as follows:

```
<bibliog-item>    <bibliog-db>
<bibliog-item>  : <book> / <paper> / <chapter>
<book>          : <callnumber> [<author>]₃<title> [<subjects>]₄
<publisher> <date>
    <paper>     : [<author>]₃ <title> [<subject>]₄ <journal> <volume>
<pages> <date>
    <chapter>   : [<author>] <title> [<subject>]₄ <date> <pages>
<book>
    <title>     : [<word>]
    <publisher> : <name> <address>
<journal>                 : <name> <publisher> <callnumber>
```

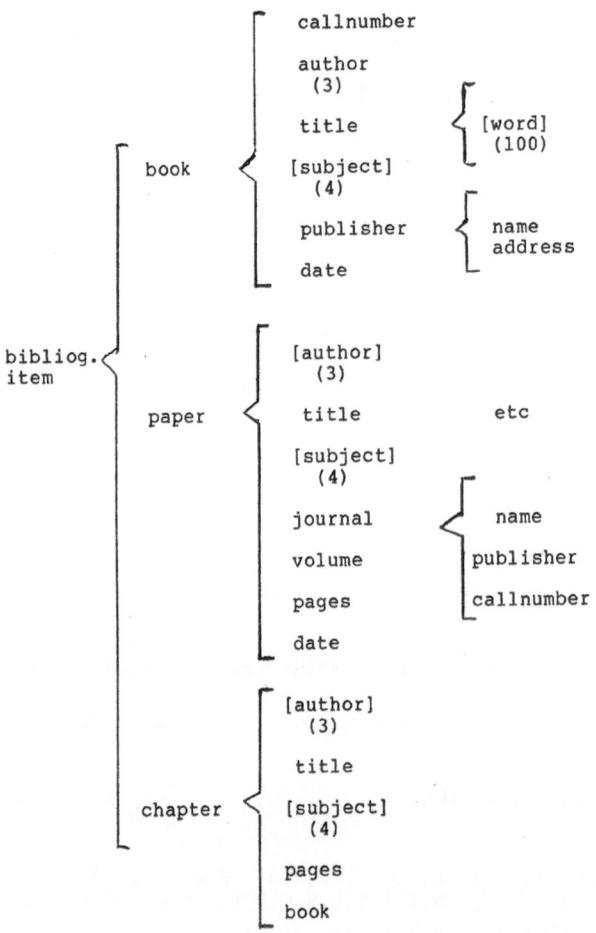

Figure 1.   Warnier/Orr Diagram of a Model
            of the Bibliographic Database.

An alternative presentation is given, using a Warnier/Orr diagram, in
Figure 1.

Note that names may be terminal values, in which case they are also put in quotation marks. For example, a variable format record, in which field names are followed by field values, might be described as:

```
<marc-item>     : ["<tag>"<tag>]
<tag>           : <author> / <editor> / <translator> / <title> /
<subtitle> / ...
```

Queries may be defined in a similar manner:

```
<boolean-query>: ["<tag>"] word ["/" / "," <Boolean-query>]
<vector-query> : <w(1)> <w(2)> ... <w(n)>
```

where n is the number of keywords in the database and <w(i)> is a real number, for i=1 to n. A search is a function defined on the product set of the queries and the bibliographic items, which assigns a numeric or logical value to each pair. A search procedure will consist of one or more search statements.

IMPLEMENTATION

WIRES (Western Information Retrieval System) is an experimental information retrieval system based on the semantic model. It is written in the C programming language and has been implemented in both a UNIX and MS-DOS environment.

Records in WIRES may be pure text or formatted; they may be described by a schema in whole or in part. Attributes or field names are defined independently of records. The records may be bibliographic records and the attributes title, author, etc., but there is nothing in the system itself that requires these particular attributes. A record can, thus, contain any combination of fields in any order. All fields can be repeated in a record an arbitrary number of times. A field and, thus, a record can be of any length (limited by disk space). For pure text records or parts of records, paragraphs are considered to be repeating fields.

Each field name and instance is indexed. This index defines sorted orders for the instances of all the fields, thus allowing a user to browse the database in order on a particular field. For example, the user could view records in order on title. Each word in each field is indexed also, i.e., the words are considered values of a repeating subfield. Each instance of a field value or a word is uniquely identified by giving the number of the record, the field name, and the field occurrence number within the record. The index is used in doing Boolean and proximity searches on the database.

WIRES is thus based on a generalization of the inverted file model. The over-all structure consists of three datasets -- the records file, the postings file, and the index file -- and five procedures -- the screen handler, the data entry module, the searching module, the output module, and the updating module.

The records file contains all information structures in the form of variable length records, whether they are schemas, schema instances text without schemas, or mixtures. The index file consists of fixed length records containing keys, which may be terminal values, attribute names, or other entity names. Each index record points to a linked list, in the postings file, of the locations of records containing these keys. The index record for an entity name points to a linked list in the postings file of all instances of the entity.

The use of the semantic model as a basis for interface design is currently being explored. The next stage in the development of WIRES will be the design of an interface builder, which will permit users to design their own interface to an information retrieval system. It is expected that the interface builder will be implemented in a trial mode during the next year.

REFERENCES

Crawford, R., 1981, "The Relational Model in Information Retrieval", Journal of the American Society for Information Science, 32, pp. 51-64.

Desai, B. C., Goyal, P., and Sadri, F., 1986, "A Data Model for Use with Formatted and Textual Data", Journal of the American Society for Information Science, 37, pp. 158-165.

King, R., and McLeod, D., 1985, "Semantic Data Models", Principles of Database Design, 1, Logical Organization, Prentice-Hall, pp. 115-150.

Tague, J., 1984, "A Semantic Model and Schema Notation for Bibliographic Retrieval Systems", Research and Development in Information Retrieval: Proceedings of the 3rd BCS ACM Symposium, Cambridge University Press, pp. 71-93.

Tsichritzis, D. C., and Lochovsky, F. H., 1982, Data Models, Prentice-Hall, Chapter 11, pp. 226-241.

Zaniolo, C., 1983, "The Database Language GEM", ACM SIGMOD Record, 13, (4), pp. 207-217.

6. SOFTWARE ENGINEERING

COUNTING LEAVES -- AN EVALUATION OF ADA*, LISP, AND PROLOG

Jagdish C. Agrawal+ and Shan Manickam++

+Department of Computer Science
 Embry Riddle Aeronautical University
 Daytona Beach, Florida 32014
++Department of Mathematics and Computer Science
 Western Carolina University
 Cullowhee, North Carolina 28723

Abstract: There are three kinds of man-machine interfaces for programming
and packaging design problems -- not readily portable, highly portable, and
intelligent and portable. Examples are: Not readily portable -- FORTRAN,
COBOL, BASIC, etc.; Highly portable -- Ada; Intelligent and portable --
LISP and PROLOG. Because of their difficulty to port, we are not considering
not readily portable language interfaces.

We wrote programs for a specially selected design problem in these
three languages and compared implementation of the principles, processes,
and goals of the PPG Model -- Modularity, Abstraction, Localization, Hiding,
Uniformity, Completeness, Confirmability; Purpose, Concept, Mechanism,
Notation, Usage; Understandability, Reliability, Efficiency, and Modifi-
ability.

INTRODUCTION

We looked at a special design problem to compare the language features
of Ada, LISP and PROLOG from the point of view of the well known PPG (Process, Principles, and Goals) Software Engineering Model presented by Ross,
Goodenough, and Irvine (1975). This design problem is one of counting
leaves in a tree. It was first used in the context of Ada packages by
Grady Booch (1983). We wrote solutions for this design problem in Ada, LISP
and PROLOG and used the problem and its solutions as a focal point in our
comparisons.

The problem selected was favorable to LISP and to PROLOG, in that
built-in data structures are available in these languages to handle trees.
However, Ada provides for a high degree of portability and reusability
while, not withstanding the ease of programming, the other two languages do
not. In fact, Ada offers a multi-layered portability:

_____

*Ada is a registered trademark of the U.S. Government, AJPO.

- Portability across environments through KAPSE

- Portability through language standardization
  (ANSI MIL-STD 1815A)

- Portability through explicit implementation of software engineering principles via generics.

The last feature fully exploits data abstraction, data encapsulation, and
information hiding through private types.

Information visibility offered by LISP and PROLOG, lack of uniform
language standards, and lack of KAPSE type interface for these languages
restrict portability and maintainability of LISP and PROLOG software. On
the other hand, the intelligence feature of LISP and PROLOG makes them
ideal for creative applications in a rich environment, e.g., automation of
human intelligence as it would apply to Expert Systems, Knowledge Based
Systems, Rule Based Systems, etc.

During the process of this research work, we came to a realization
that the PPG model, when proposed more than ten years ago, was very insightful. However, now with the proliferation of computer architectures, operating systems, and programming languages, a new dimension -- environment --
needs to be added to the PPG model in order to enhance it to reflect the
current state of computer technology. This suggested that adding a new
dimension to the original three-dimensional PPG model would provide the
capability of addressing issues such as:

- Portability

- Reusability

- Configuration Management

in an explicit manner.

THE DESIGN PROBLEM

The problem is to count the leaves of a binary tree. Of course one
could start at one node and traverse the tree until all of the leaves have
been visited. However, such a technique would require an implementation
detail in the form of an intimate knowledge of how the elements of the tree
are physically connected. One of the requirements of the problem is that
if the representation of the tree changes physically then the logical structure of the solution should remain invariant (Booch, 1983).

An Ada Solution

We formalized the informal strategy outlined by Booch (1983) by providing an algorithm, complete with all packages in Ada.

```
with COUNTER_PACKAGE, PILE_PACKAGE, TREE_PACKAGE;
use  COUNTER_PACKAGE, PILE_PACKAGE, TREE_PACKAGE;
with TEXT_IO;
use  TEXT_IO;

procedure COUNT_LEAVES is
    LEAF_COUNT     :  COUNTER_TYPE;
    LEFT_SUBTREE   :  TREE_TYPE;
    RIGHT-SUBTREE  :  TREE_TYPE;
```

```
      PILE           :  PILE_TYPE;
      TREE           :  TREE_TYPE;
begin
   GET_INITIAL (TREE);
   NEW_LINE;
   PUT_INITIAL (TREE, ON => PILE);
   ZERO (LEAF_count);
   while IS_NOT_EMPTY (PILE)
      loop
         TAKE (TREE, OFF => PILE);
         if IS_SINGLE_LEAF (TREE)
         THEN
            INCREMENT (LEAF_COUNT);
            THROW_AWAY (TREE);
            NEW_LINE;
          else
        SPLIT (TREE,
               LEFT_INTO => LEFT_SUBTREE,
                RIGHT_INTO => RIGHT_SUBTREE);
        PUT ( LEFT_SUBTREE, ON => PILE);
            PUT (RIGHT_SUBTREE, ON => PILE);
       end if;
      end loop;
   NEW_LINE;
   PUT ("Number of leaves in the tree is:");
    DISPLAY (LEAF_COUNT);
  exception
  when CONSTRAINT_ERROR =>
      PUT_LINE ("Constraint error!!");
    when other =>
      PUT_LINE ("Undetermined exception.");
end COUNT_LEAVES;


package COUNTER_PACKAGE is
   type COUNTER_TYPE is limited private;
   procedure DISPLAY    (COUNTER: in     COUNTER_TYPE);

   procedure INCREMENT (COUNTER:  in out COUNTER_TYPE);

   procedure ZERO       (COUNTER:     out COUNTER_TYPE);

private
   type COUNTER_TYPE is new NATURAL;
end COUNTER_PACKAGE;
with TEXT_IO; use TEXT_IO;


package body COUNTER_PACKAGE is
   procedure DISPLAY   (COUNTER: in     COUNTER_TYPE) is
      package COUNTER_IO is new INTEGER_IO (COUNTER_TYPE);
      use COUNTER_IO;
   begin
    NEW_LINE;
      put (COUNTER);
      NEW_LINE;
   end DISPLAY;

   procedure INCREMENT (COUNTER: in out COUNTER_TYPE) is
   begin
      COUNTER := COUNTER + 1;
```

```
            end INCREMENT;

            procedure ZERO  (COUNTER:      out COUNTER_TYPE) is
            begin
                COUNTER := 0
            end ZERO;
      end COUNTER_PACKAGE;


      with TEXT_IO; use TEXT_IO;
      with COUNTER_PACKAGE; use COUNTER_PACKAGE;
      package TREE_PACKAGE is
            X : CHARACTER;
            type TREE_TYPE is private;
            procedure GET_INITIAL    (TREE      :     out TREE_TYPE);

            procedure SPLIT             (TREE      : in out TREE_TYPE;
                                         LEFT_INTO :    out TREE_TYPE;
                                         RIGHT_INTO :   out TREE_TYPE);

            procedure THROW_AWAY     (TREE      : in out TREE_TYPE);
            function IS_SINGLE_LEAF  (TREE      : in     TREE_TYPE)
                                                     return BOOLEAN;
            function MAKETREE  (X : in CHARACTER) return TREE_TYPE;
            function MAKE_TREE (X : in CHARACTER; TREE : in
                                                       TREE_TYPE)
                                               return TREE_TYPE;

      private
            type TREE_NODE;
            type TREE_TYPE is access TREE_NODE;
            type TREE_NODE is
               record
                   INFO : CHARACTER;
                   LEFT : TREE_TYPE;
                  RIGHT : TREE_TYPE;
                end record;
               TREE      : TREE_TYPE;
               NEW_TREE : TREE_TYPE;
               TREES     : array (1...32) of TREE_TYPE;
      end TREE_PACKAGE;


      package body TREE_PACKAGE is
      function MAKETREE (X : in CHARACTER) return TREE_TYPE is
      begin
         if X =
         then
            TREE := null;
         else
            TREE.INFO  := X;
            TREE.LEFT  := null;
            TREE.RIGHT := null;
         end if;
      return TREE;
      end MAKETREE;

      function MAKE_TREE (X : in CHARACTER; TREE : in TREE_TYPE)
                                          return TREE_TYPE is

         begin
```

```
      if TREE = null
      then
          return new TREE_NODE (X, null, null);
      elseif TREE.ALL.INFO = X
          then
              TREE.ALL.LEFT  := MAKE_TREE (X, TREE.ALL.LEFT);
          else
              TREE.ALL.RIGHT := MAKE_TREE (X, TREE.ALL.RIGHT);
      end if;
return TREE;
end MAKE_TREE;

procedure GET_INITIAL (TREE : out TREE_TYPE) is
begin
NEW_LINE;
PUT_LINE ("INITIALIZING THE PROCESS OF MAKING A TREE");
NEW_TREE := MAKETREE (' ');
NEW_LINE;
PUT_LINE ("TYPE A LETTER REPRESENTING A NODE");
NEW_LINE
GET (X);
while X /= 'Z' loop
    NEW_TREE := MAKE_TREE (X, NEW_TREE);
    NEW_LINE;
    PUT_LINE ("TYPE A LETTER REPRESENTING A NODE; Z TO END");
    GET (X);
end loop;
TREE := NEW_TREE;
end GET_INITIAL;

function IS_SINGLE-LEAF (TREE : in TREE_TYPE) return BOOLEAN
    is
begin
if TREE = null
    then
        IT_IS_SINGLE_LEAF := TRUE;
    else
        IT_IS_SINGLE_LEAF := FALSE;
    end if;
return IT_IS_SINGLE_LEAF;
end IS_SINGLE_LEAF;

procedure SPLIT (TREE        : in out TREE_TYPE;
                 LEFT_INTO  :     out TREE_TYPE;
                 RIGHT_INTO :     out TREE_TYPE) is
Y : CHARACTER;
Z : CHARACTER;
begin
LEFT_INTO  := TREE.LEFT;
RIGHT-INTO := TREE.RIGHT;
X          := TREE.INFO;
if TREE.LEFT = null
    then
        Y := ' ';
    else
        Y := TREE LEFT INFO;
end if;

if TREE.RIGHT = null
    then
        Z := ' ';
```

```
            else
                Z := TREE.RIGHT.INFO;
        end if;
    end SPLIT;

    procedure THROW_AWAY (TREE : in out TREE_TYPE) is
    begin
    TREE := null;
    end THROW_AWAY;
    end TREE_PACKAGE;


    with TREE_PACKAGE; use TREE-PACKAGE;
    with COUNTER_PACKAGE; use COUNTER_PACKAGE;
    package PILE_PACKAGE is
        TREE : TREE_TYPE;
        type PILE_TYPE is limited private;
        function IS_NOT_EMPTY (PILE : in     PILE_TYPE)
                                              return BOOLEAN
        procedure PUT            (TREE : in out TREE_TYPE;
                                   ON : in out PILE_TYPE);


        procedure PUT_INITIAL  (TREE : in out TREE_TYPE;
                                   ON : in out PILE_TYPE);


        procedure TAKE         (TREE :    out TREE_TYPE;
                                  OFF : in out PILE-TYPE);

    private
        type PILE_OF_TREES is array (1..32) of TREE_TYPE;
        type PILE_TYPE is record
            NUMBER_OF_TREES : INTEGER;
            TREES           : PILE_OF_TREES;
        end record;
        ON  : PILE_TYPE
        OFF : PILE_TYPE
    end PILE_PACKAGE;


    package body PILE_PACKAGE is
    function IS_NOT_EMPTY (PILE : in     PILE_TYPE)
                                    return BOOLEAN is
        IS_NOT_EMPTY : BOOLEAN;
        begin
        if PILE.NUMBER_OF_TREES /= 0
            then
                IS_IT_NOT_EMPTY := TRUE;
            else
                IS_IT_NOT_EMPTY := FALSE;
        end if;
        return IS_IT_NOT EMPTY;
        end IS_NOT_EMPTY;

    procedure PUT            (TREE : in out TREE_TYPE;
                               ON : in out PILE_TYPE) is
        begin
        ON.NUMBER_OF_TREES                := ON.NUMBER_OF_TREES + 1;
        ON.TREES (ON.NUMBER_OF_TREES) := TREE;
        OFF
        end PUT;
```

```
      procedure PUT_INITIAL  (TREE : in out TREE_TYPE;
                              ON : in out PILE_TYPE) is
          begin
          ON.NUMBER_OF_TREES    := 1;
          ON.TREES(1)           := TREE;
          OFF                   := ON;
          end PUT_INITIAL;

      procedure TAKE          (TREE :    out TREE_TYPE;
                              OFF : in out PILE_TYPE) is
          begin
          TREE                  := OFF.TREES(OFF.NUMBER_OF_TREES);
          OFF.NUMBER_OF_TREES   := OFF.NUMBER_OF_TREES - 1;
          ON                    := OFF;
          end TAKE;
      end PILE_PACKAGE;
```

A LISP SOLUTION

```
(SETQ COUNT '0)
(DEFUN  (CNTLEAVES (L)
        (COND
        ((NULL L) COUNT)
        ((ATOM (CAR L)) (ADD 1 COUNT)
                        (CNTLEAVES (CDR L)))
        (T  (CNTLEAVES  (CAR L))
            (CNTLEAVES  (CDR L)) ) ) ) )
```

A PROLOG SOLUTION

```
countleaves ([ ],0).
countleaves (X,1):- atom(X).
countleaves ([X|Y],C):- countleaves (X,A), countleaves
        (Y,B), sum (A,B,C).
sum (X,Y,Z):- Z is X + Y.
```

DISCUSSION OF THE PROGRAMS

The COUNT_LEAVES procedure of the Ada program contains the logic of
the counting process. The LISP and PROLOG programs use essentially the
same logic, except that these are written with recursion, for convenience
and brevity. The brevity of the LISP and PROLOG programs is primarily due
to the fact that these languages have a built-in list data structure and
inherent operations and functions/notations to manipulate lists.

While all three programs implement the principles of software engineering as prescribed by the PPG model to varying degrees, there is a significant
difference between the Ada implementation and the LISP and PROLOG implementation. The latter two are not nearly as portable, reusable, and flexible
as the Ada program across different hardware and environments. We feel
that such distinctions be used as motivation to enhance the PPG model by
adding a new dimension to it that would provide the capability of addressing
issues such as portability, reusability and flexibility. In fact, flexibility could perhaps be imbedded in a much wider consideration of configuration management.

The Ada code derives its portability, reusability, and flexibility
from, among other features, packaging, language standardization and Ada

Programming Support Environment, including KAPSE. Ada's strong-typing, although a low level concern, is a trade-off for gaining flexibility and security when used in conjunction with private and limited types. The LISP and PROLOG codes, while truly high level, lack such features, since data abstraction, and information hiding are not the forte of these languages. The bulk of the Ada code beyond the COUNT_LEAVES procedure thus serves a purpose which is somewhat foreign to the other two languages.

It is precisely the truly high level nature of LISP and PROLOG that provide powerful tools such as the built-in data structures, control structures, separability of logic and control, rather than an emphasis on such low level details as data abstraction, information hiding through private and limited private types, separate compilations of subprogram units, etc.; that make them ideal for creative applications where the user can easily afford to trade-off portability and flexibility for a rapid and high level implementation of his creative ideas.

ADA, LISP, PROLOG -- A COMPARISON

The foregoing programs and discussion motivated us to attempt a comparative overview of the three languages based on the following criteria.

1. Evolution versus design by standards.

2. Lack or proliferation of dialects.

3. Strong data typing through formal specifications versus primary and inherent data types.

4. Information hiding versus visibility.

5. Dependence versus independence of logic and control.

6. Special strengths and weaknesses.

Our findings are summarized in the paragraphs below.

ADA

1. The common high order language program initiated by the U.S. Department of Defense (DoD) culminated into the STEELMAN (1978) specification document of requirements for high order programming languages. Ada was designed in accordance with the requirements specified in STEELMAN in the form now known as ANSI/MIL-STD-1815 A (1983).

2. The language standards as defined in the ANSI/MIL-STD- 1815 A leave little room for subsets and supersets being called Ada.

3. Data types and data structures are formally specified, created, and maintained via abstract data types. Thus, strong typing is enforced.

4. Ada provides the system designer a choice and means for implementing information hiding or visibility.

5. By design, logic and control are highly dependent.

6. Packages, generic units, tasks, and control over information via

private and limited private types are special strengths. Environmental features, e.g., ASPE and CAIS are additional strengths. However, complexity and a high degree of formality may be looked upon as a weakness. On the other hand, as pointed out by Rude (1985), Ada has capabilities to deal with problems typically solved in LISP, although not recommended for use in artificial intelligence research.

LISP

1. LISP evolved for over two decades without the benefits of prior established standards.

2. There is an abundance of dialects, some of which are even incompatible with each other.

3. LISP is heavily oriented towards the primary type, namely list. This precludes strong typing through formal specifications to a considerable extent.

4. Information visibility is encouraged.

5. Control and logic are dependent to a large degree.

6. LISP is a simple language with a conceptually and creatively rich environment. It is symbolic, as opposed to formal and emphasizes heuristic approaches as opposed to algorithmic approaches emphasized by languages like Ada. LISP's ability to represent and manipulate complex relationships among data makes it extremely suitable for creative applications and to ill-specified problems (MacLennan, 1983).

PROLOG

1. PROLOG was designed for logic programming.

2. There are many dialects and versions.

3. It has very few primitives and a small number of built-in data types and associated operations.

4. Information visibility is encouraged.

5. It is a truly nonprocedural language. Also, the procedure calls can be executed in any order, even concurrently. This makes PROLOG a potential language for multiprocessing and parallel computers.

REFERENCES

Booch, G., 1983, Software Engineering with Ada, The Benjamin/Cummings Publishing Company, Menlo Park, CA.

Department of Defense, 1978, "Requirements for High Order Programming Languages", STEELMAN, Department of Defense, June 1978.

Department of Defense, 1983, "ANSI/MIL-STD-1815 A", Reference Manual for the Ada Programming Language, U. S. Department of Defense, June 1983.

MacLennan, Bruce J., 1983, Principles of Programming Languages: Design

<u>Evaluation and Implementation</u>, Holt, Rinehart, and Winston, New York.

Ross, Douglas T., Goodenough, John B., and Irvine, C. A., 1975, "Software Engineering: Process, Principles and Goals", <u>Computer</u>, May 1975.

Rude, Allen, 1985, "Translating a Research LISP Prototype to a Formal Ada Design Prototype", <u>Proceedings of the Annual Washington Ada Symposium</u>, March 24-26, 1985, Copyright -- Association for Computing Machinery, Inc.

DIFFUSION OF SOFTWARE ENGINEERING METHODS

Sridhar A. Raghavan* and Donald R. Chand**

*Wang Institute of Graduate Studies
Tyngsboro, MA 01879
**Bentley College
Waltham, MA 02254

Abstract: The success of software engineering as a discipline depends not only on our ability to come up with creative and innovation methods for addressing the problems of software development, but, also on our ability to effectively diffuse these innovations into practice. In order to succeed well in the latter role, we need to have a good understanding of the process of diffusing innovations in general, and how they apply in the context of diffusion of software engineering methods. This paper attempts to provide that understanding using Rogers' framework for diffusion of innovations.

Roger's framework is used to show that even though diffusion is a complex process it can be studied systematically, and successful diffusion can be facilitated by consciously planning a diffusion process that takes into account the underlying factors and issues. The attributes of innovations and communication aspects of innovations are identified as factors of special importance as they have significant impact on diffusion, and are, also, within the purview of the software engineering community. These ideas are developed and illustrated in the context of diffusion of program design methodologies. Using the understanding gained through these, a set of guidelines and recommendations are developed for successfully diffusing software engineering innovations.

INTRODUCTION

Diffusion is the process of transferring technology from those who develop it to those who apply it. Though diffusion is important in all disciplines, it assumes critical importance in applied disciplines such as Software Engineering, which are committed to the advancement of the state of practice. This can be made more explicit by recognizing that the success of software engineering as a discipline depends not only on our ability to come up with creative and innovative methods for addressing the problems of software development, but, also on our ability to diffuse these innovations into practice and advance the state of practice of software development. As a result, we as members of the software engineering community are, also, responsible for ensuring successful diffusion of our innovations. The general concern that software engineering methods have not been diffusing to the desired and anticipated levels, further adds to this burden.

In this paper, we take a position that the less than desirable diffusion of software engineering innovations is partially a consequence of our community's general lack of understanding of the principles and issues associated with the diffusion of innovations, and the limited view the community has of its role in the diffusion of software engineering technology.

The software technology transfer literature (Bolognani and Corti, 1983; Freeman, 1983; U.S. General Accounting Office, 1980; Hayen, 1977; Holton, 1977; IEEE Computer Society Press, 1983; McGill, 1980; Thayer and Lehman, 1979) endorses our position that software engineering innovations have not diffused well and that the problems of diffusing software engineering technology are not well understood. It suggests that this difficulty may be due to the unique nature of innovations in software engineering where technology transfer involves both a transfer of knowledge and a change in the way people think.

However, we feel that the issues of transferring knowledge from the innovators to the adopters is not unique to software engineering innovations. The areas of technology transfer and diffusion of innovations have been studied extensively by both social scientists and management scientists for many years. There exists a sound body of literature on these areas (Rogers, 1983). The objective of this paper is to explore how this existing body of knowledge on diffusion of innovations can be adapted to the diffusion of software engineering innovations, both to explain the issues involved in their adoption by the practitioners and to develop a set of guidelines and strategies for facilitating their successful diffusion and adoption.

To achieve these goals this paper presents and analyzes the framework for diffusion of innovation which was first developed by Rogers (1962) as an explanatory device for adoption-diffusion in agricultural technology. Rogers' framework has been used successfully in the analysis of innovations and has proved to have good explanatory power (Beal and Meehan, 1978; Berelson et al., 1964; Fliegel and Kivlin, 1966(a); Fliegel and Kivlin, 1966(b); Kiehl, 1970; Rogers and Kincaid, 1981; Singh, 1966; Wharton, 1977). The framework, as presented here, shows that even though diffusion of innovations is a complex process it can be studied systematically, and that successful diffusion can be facilitated by consciously planning a diffusion process which takes into account the underlying factors and issues. The attributes of innovations and communication aspects of innovations are identified as factors of special importance as they have significant impact on diffusion, and are, also, within the purview of the software engineering community. These ideas are developed and illustrated in the context of diffusion of program design methodologies. Using the understanding gained through these, a set of guidelines and recommendations are developed for successfully diffusing software engineering innovations.

The rest of the paper is organized as follows. The next section contains a detailed description of Rogers' framework. This is followed by the illustrative application of the framework to the diffusion of program design methodologies. The section that follows it presents the set of recommendations and guidelines that can help us play an effective role in the diffusion of our innovations. The last section summarizes the key aspects of this paper.

ROGERS' FRAMEWORK FOR DIFFUSION OF INNOVATIONS

Rogers (1983) has developed a theoretical framework for diffusion of innovations based on his extensive study of agricultural innovations. It is a comprehensive framework which can be used in a normative or descriptive manner. The framework has been validated through a large number of empirical studies (Beal and Meehan, 1978; Berelson et al., 1964; Fliegel and Kivlin, 1966(a); Fliegel and Kivlin, 1966(b); Kiehl, 1970; Rogers and Kincaid, 1981; Singh, 1966; Wharton, 1977). This framework is described in this section. The description begins with formal definitions of the terms, then moves through an explanation of the main elements in the diffusion process, and ends with a summary of the framework.

Definitions of Terms

Diffusion. Diffusion is formally defined as a process by which an innovation is communicated through certain channels, over time, among the members of a social system.

The four main elements in this definition are: innovation, communication channels, time, and the social system. The key members of the social system are innovators, diffusers, and adopters. These are creators of innovations, intermediaries who assist in diffusing innovations, and target users of innovations, respectively. Rogers' framework identifies the characteristics of these elements and provides an understanding of the role they play in the diffusion of innovations.

Innovation. Innovation is defined as an idea, a practice or an object which is perceived to be new by the persons who are targets for its adoption.

Communication Channel. Diffusion uses a communication process that results in the transmission of new ideas. In a diffusion context, this involves diffusers, adopters, and communication channels that connect them.

Time. Time is an important dimension in the study of diffusion for at least two reasons. First, diffusion is a continuous process which takes place over a period of time with a predictable life cycle of distinct stages. Second, the level of adoption of any innovation as a function of time turns out to be a S-shaped curve, which has interesting implications.

Social System. The fourth element in Rogers' framework is the social system. It is the environment in which diffusion processes take place and it includes aspects such as social structures, cultural norms, and value systems.

Characteristics of Innovations

Rogers identifies five key characteristics of innovations that directly affect the rate of diffusion of an innovation. These characteristics are:

- Relative Advantage

- Compatibility

- Complexity

- Trialability

- Observability

Relative Advantage. Relative advantage is a measure of the degree to which an innovation is perceived as better than the idea it supersedes. Innovations that enjoy high levels of perceived relative advantages usually tend to diffuse very rapidly. The degree of relative advantage may be measured in economic terms, but social factors such as prestige, convenience, and satisfaction are also often important components.

Compatibility. Compatibility is a measure of the degree to which an innovation is perceived as being consistent with the existing values, past experiences, and the needs of the potential adopters. Adoption of an incompatible innovation may require the prior adoption of a new value system.

Complexity. Complexity is a measure of the degree to which an innovation is perceived as difficult to learn and use. In general, new ideas that are easy to understand will be adopted more rapidly than innovations that require the adopters to develop new knowledge and skills.

Trialability. Trialability is a measure of the degree to which an innovation can be experimented with on a limited basis. New ideas that can be tried on installment plans will generally be adopted more quickly than innovations that cannot be tried in an incremental and progressive fashion. Furthermore, it is possible to learn a trialable innovation by doing. Generally, if an innovation is trialable, then there is less uncertainty to the individual who is considering it for adoption.

Observability. Observability is a measure of the degree to which the results of an innovation are visible to others. The easier it is for individuals to see the results of an innovation, the more likely they are to adopt the innovation.

Conclusion. Thus, an innovation that enjoys relative advantage, is compatible with the present environment and past experiences, is easily comprehensible, is trialable on small scale applications, and whose performance is easy to observe and evaluate, has greater potential for rapid and widespread adoption than an innovation which lacks one or more of these properties.

Characteristics of Communications

Communication Channels. There are two types of communication channels available for communications between the innovators and the adopters. They are:

- Mass media channels, and

- Inter-personal channels.

Mass media channels are all those means of transmitting messages that allows a source of one or few individuals to reach an audience of many. This includes media such as radio, newspapers, and trade publications. The inter-personal channels represents direct communications that involve face-to-face exchange between two or more individuals. Generally, mass media channels are rapid and efficient as a means for creating awareness knowledge of innovations. On the other hand, inter-personal channels are more effective in persuading an individual to adopt a new idea. Successful diffusion requires a proper balance between the use of mass-media channels and inter-personal channels depending on the characteristics of the innovation and the social grouping of the adopters.

Nature of Participants: Homophily vs. Heterophily. Another important factor that affects communication is the nature of fit between the participants. The fit could be homophilous or heterophilous. Homophily is the degree to which pairs of individuals who interact are similar in certain attributes such as beliefs, education, social status etc. Heterophilous refers to the lack of such similarity. More effective communication occurs when two parties are homophilous. However, if the diffuser and diffusee are similar in terms of their technical grasp of an innovation, no diffusion can occur. Therefore, the very nature of diffusion demands that at least some degree of heterophily be present between the participants. Ideally,

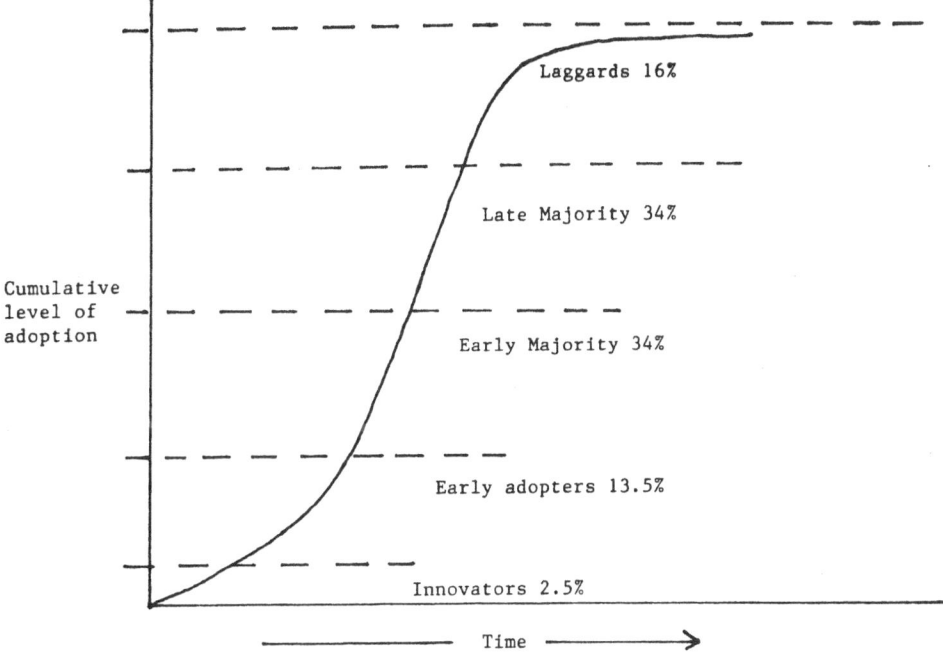

Figure 1.   The Innovation-Adoption S-Curve.

they would be homophilous along most other variables, but heterophilous
with respect to their knowledge of the particular innovation.

Time

Diffusion usually proceeds through a series of phases. It starts with
the creation of an innovation and it is followed by the phase where the
innovation is communicated to the potential adopters. This triggers the
innovation-decision process in the minds of adopters and concludes with the
adopter either rejecting the innovation or accepting and committing to it.

Innovation-Decision Process. The innovation-decision process can be
partitioned into five steps. These steps are: Knowledge, Persuasion,
Decision, Implementation, and Confirmation. In the knowledge step, the
(potential) adopter seeks and obtains information about what the innovation
is, and how it works. During the persuasion stage the diffuser tries to
influence the potential adopter into accepting the innovation. In the
decision phase, the adopter seeks various kinds of evaluation information
in order to reduce his uncertainty about the consequences of the innovation.
The decision stage leads to an adoption or rejection decision. If the
adopter decides to accept the innovation, he proceeds to implement it in
his environment. During the implementation stage the innovation is tested
in the local environment of the adopter. This may lead to a commitment to
the innovation or its rejection.

Characteristics of Adopters. There is another important aspect of the
time element in the diffusion of innovations that needs to be recognized.
This relates to the level of adoption by the social system over time.
Studies have shown that the adoption of innovation follows an S-curve as
depicted in Figure 1. This occurs because individuals differ in their
propensity to adopt innovations. Based on this propensity, individuals can

be grouped into categories such as Innovators, Early adopters, Early majority, Late majority, Late adopters, and Laggards. These categories also reflect the relative order in which these individuals will adopt innovations. Therefore, diffusion is necessarily drawn out over a period of time and the slope of the S-curve represents the rate of adoption of an innovation at the corresponding point in time.

Social System

The social system constitutes a region within which diffusion occurs. Rogers identifies five issues in the social system which affect the diffusion process that occurs within it. These issues are social structure, social norms, roles of opinion leaders and change agents, types of innovation decisions, and the consequences of innovation.

Social Structure. Social structure refers to the arrangement of the members of a social system for communication purposes. Two types of communication structures exist in any social system. They are formal communications structures and informal communications structures. A formal structure is consciously designed to promote goal attainment, process control, and predictability. This structure gives regularity and stability to the system and aims to reduce the uncertainty of human behavior within the social system. On the other hand, informal structures refer to the collection of other mechanisms by which the members of the social system communicate with each other. Unlike formal structures, these are not designed consciously and explicitly. They usually come into existence due to the social needs of the members.

The structure of a social system can facilitate or impede the diffusion of innovation in the system. Furthermore, an individual's propensity to adopt innovations is affected both by his individual characteristics, and by the nature of the social system in which he resides.

Social Norms. Social norms are established behavior patterns for the members of a social system. They define a range of tolerable behavior and serve as a guide or standard for the members. Rigid social norms can be a serious barrier for diffusion of innovations.

Change Agents & Opinion Leaders. Change agents and Opinion leaders are key individuals in any social system. Opinion leaders are influential members of the social system whose opinions are highly valued. They are usually technical leaders with proven track records and enjoy a very high level of credibility. Endowed with these abilities, they are often capable of greatly influencing the attitudes and behavior of the other individuals in the system. Change agents are individuals who are formally authorized and empowered to change parts of the social system. Unlike Opinion leaders, Change agents may not be technical leaders. They derive their strengths from their privileged formal positions within the social system, rather than from their technical knowledge and past performance.

Opinion leaders and Change agents play critical roles during the diffusion process. Their attitude towards the innovation largely determines the outcome of the diffusion process. If they favor the innovation, they may serve as effective catalysts, thereby promoting rapid diffusion and adoption. However, if they are critical about the innovation they may become strong barriers against its diffusion.

Types of Innovation Decisions. Decision to adopt an innovation may take place at the individual, group, or authority level within a social system. The social system itself may or may not influence the level at which the adoption decisions are made.

Individual level innovation decisions are called Optional-Innovation decisions. Here an individual adopts or rejects an innovation independent of the decisions of the other members of the social system. However, the individual's decision may be influenced by the social norms, and/or by the members of his interpersonal network. Collective innovative-decisions are choices that are made by consensus among the members of the system. These are very efficient from the viewpoint of diffusion, as they represent the situation where the majority of the social system has agreed to adopt the innovation voluntarily. Authority innovation-decisions are usually made by a few key individuals of the social system who possess power, status, or technical knowledge. Once they make the decision, it becomes binding on the rest of the members of the social system.

The level at which innovation decisions are made has many implications for the diffusion process. The rate of diffusion associated with optional innovation-decisions follows a S-curve. The flatness of the S-curve partially depends on the level at which the innovation decision are made. Collective decision processes may take longer to make the innovation decision. However, since they are made by consensus, they may diffuse rapidly once the adoption decision is made. Authority decisions may or may not diffuse rapidly depending on the attitude of the members of the social system towards authority. If the members submit to authority, the rate of adoption is accelerated. However, if the members resist authority they may undermine the adoption of the innovation.

Consequences of Innovation. A social system is affected in a number of ways by adoption of an innovation. These consequences may be classified under one or more of the following categories:

- Desirable Consequences

- Undesirable Consequences

- Direct Consequences

- Indirect Consequences

- Anticipated Consequences

- Unanticipated Consequences

Social systems will generally accept and commit to innovations which produce direct, desirable, and anticipated consequences. If an innovation has many undesirable consequences, it will be rejected by the social system even if it is accepted initially.

SUMMARY OF ROGERS' FRAMEWORK

The key points made by Rogers' framework are as follows:

1. The perceived attributes of an innovation have strong implications for its diffusion.

2. Diffusion is accompanied by change. Therefore, effectively managing the change process is critical for successful diffusion.

3. Diffusion requires effective communication. Therefore, the selection of communication channels and the match between the participants are important factors in promoting diffusion.

4. Change agents and Opinion leaders act as catalysts during the diffusion process. Their attitudes towards the innovation can largely determine the success or failure of the diffusion.

5. Innovation adoption decisions are influenced by both rational and perceptual factors.

6. Innovation adoption decision processes may be carried out individually, collectively, or by authorities. The level at which the adoption decisions are made have significant implications for the diffusion process.

7. Diffusion occurs in a social context. Hence, social factors such as social structure, culture, and norms can facilitate or impede diffusion of innovations.

8. Individuals differ in their propensity to adopt innovations. Based on this propensity, individuals can be grouped into categories such as early majority, late majority, and laggards. These categories also reflect the relative order in which these individuals will adopt innovations. Therefore, diffusion is necessarily drawn out over a period of time.

ROGERS' FRAMEWORK AND SOFTWARE ENGINEERING DIFFUSION

In this section we will first address some basic questions that deal with the applicability of Rogers' framework to software engineering diffusion. We will then illustrate how Rogers' framework may be applied to explain the current status of the diffusion of some software engineering innovations, namely program design methodologies.

Applicability of Rogers' Framework

The fundamental issue is whether Rogers' framework is applicable to the diffusion of software engineering technology? Our literature search suggests that, apparently, this framework has not been empirically validated for software engineering innovations. At the same time it showed that Rogers' framework has been successfully utilized as an explanatory and predictive device in a wide variety of disciplines (Beal and Meehan, 1978; Berelson et al., 1964; Carlson, 1965; Linton, 1973; Fliegel and Kivlin, 1966(a); Fliegel and Kivlin, 1966(b); Holloway, 1977; Kiehl, 1970; Rogers and Kincaid, 1981; Singh, 1966; Wharton, 1977). These include diffusion of educational innovations such as programmed instruction and modern math (Carlson, 1965; Clinton, 1973; Holloway, 1977) which are similar to software to software engineering innovations in the sense that their diffusion involves both transfer of knowledge and changes in value system. Furthermore, the framework is comprehensive, general, and intuitively valid. Therefore, we maintain that this is a very valuable framework for understanding and explaining the diffusion of software engineering innovations.

A secondary question that arises is: how can this framework be effectively applied to software engineering diffusion? Rogers' framework suggests that diffusion of innovations is a complex process which can be systematically analyzed, and that successful diffusion of any type of diffusion can be ensured by a consciously planned process which takes into account the underlying factors and issues. From the software engineering community's point of view, the strategy to use is to identify the key issues in Rogers' framework that provide the maximum leverage. That is, these issues must be

Table 1. A Partial List of Program Design Methodologies.

- Structured Programming a la Dijkstra & Wirth

- Integrated Top-Down Design Method of Baker and Mills

- Stepwise Refinement Using Abstract Data Types based on Liskov's Ideas

- Warnier's Approach for Logical Construction of Programs

- Jackson's Design Method

- Structured Design Methodology ala Constantine & Yourdon

recognized as critical issues of the framework, and they must be within the control of the software engineering community. The two issues that come under this category are the characteristics of innovations and communication of innovations. The other issues, such as those related to the social system, become significant only after the innovations are validated to be sound and are objectively and effectively communicated to the adopters. Further, interacting with the social system characteristics, such as culture, norms and value systems, for facilitating the diffusion of innovations are outside the normal scope of activities of the software engineering community. Therefore, analyzing the characteristics of innovations and communication of innovations appears to be the most effective way of utilizing the framework for evaluating software engineering innovations, for effectively diffusing them, and for clarifying the role of the software engineering community in the diffusion of software engineering technology. These ideas will be illustrated in the context of diffusion of program design methodologies in the next section.

Diffusion of Program Design Methodologies

Program design methodologies have been active research topics in software engineering for the past fifteen years. A host of methodologies have been developed to facilitate the development of quality programs. During the same period we have also witnessed the rapid growth of a satellite industry involved in offering professional development seminars, in-house training programs, consulting services and developing support tools for these design methodologies. Despite these elaborate efforts of the satellite industry and the strong commitment and the enthusiasm of the software engineering community, the adoption of some of the well-known methodologies (Chand, 1984) listed in Table 1, are far below the desirable levels.* In this section we will illustrate how Rogers' framework can be used to explain this less than desirable level of diffusion of program design methodologies.

To use Rogers' framework as an explanatory device we need a clear understanding of the software engineering community's view of program design methodologies, the practitioners' view of these design methodologies, and

---

*The question of what is a satisfactory rate of diffusion for software engineering technology is a controversial issue. Redwine & Riddle (1985) conclude that it takes on the order of 15 to 20 years to mature a technology to the point that it can be popularized and disseminated to the technical community at large. Their conclusion is actually an observation based on their analysis of several software technology case studies. This cannot be used to justify the current state of software engineering diffusion as it will amount to a circular argument. Also see Willis (1983) who concludes that technology transfer takes six plus or minus two years in most of the cases.

also the process of communication of these design methodologies by the developers to the practitioners. Although a comprehensive and consolidated view of program design methodologies by these different constituencies is not available, the literature provides several case studies, well thought-out opinions, anecdotes, and a few empirical studies from which one can sketch a reasonably accurate picture of the reality. The viewpoints presented here are based on authors' experience in the field. Even though they have not been validated formally, we feel they capture the perceptions of the software engineering community and the practitioners quite accurately.

The application of Rogers' framework to the diffusion of program design methodologies is illustrated as follows. We first present a summary of the innovators'/missionaries' view of the characteristics of program design methodologies. This is followed by a summary of the how these methodologies are communicated to the practitioners. After this the perceptions of the practitioners are outlined. These perceptions are then used as a model of the reality to analyze the innovation characteristics of program design methodologies along the five dimensions of Rogers' framework and to evaluate the diffusion process from the viewpoint of communication of innovation.

Innovators'/Missionaries' View

The perspective of the innovators, missionaries, and diffusers of program design methodologies can be summarized as follows:

- They provide a systematic and uniform way of attacking programming problems.

- They provide frameworks for checking the internal consistencies of program designs.

- They promote standardization of both the program development processes and program products.

- They facilitate a lucid and precise documentation of the thought processes underlying a program design.

- They provide a common framework, which promotes effective communications between the members of a programming team.

- They assist in developing correct and reliable programs.

- They assist in developing understandable programs.

- They assist in developing modifiable programs.

- They extend the repertoire of programming techniques of programmers.

- They assist in increasing the overall productivity of programmers.

- They help in identifying automation opportunities related to program development.

Communication of Program Design Methodologies

The key aspects of how the program design methodologies are often communicated to practitioners can be summarized as follows:

- Methodologies are complete in the sense that following

the prescribed steps will produce a good program design.

- Methodologies are general in the sense that they are applicable to broad classes of problems.

- Methodologies are illustrated through small scale problems.

- Logical arguments are used to establish and justify the soundness of these methodologies.

- Logical reasoning is used to establish the merits of these methodologies.

- Methodologies may not be useful when applied to small problems due to the overheads, but they will definitely payoff in the context of large problems. Logic and rhetoric is used to communicate this message.

- Methodologies can be easily learned and used by any programmer.

- Methodologies increase program development productivity.

- Methodologies enhance the visibility of program development activities.

- The constraints imposed by the methodologies produce valuable benefits.

Perceptions of the Practitioners

The perceptions of the practitioners' community can be summarized as follows:

- Methodologies are not complete. They need creative jumps while applying them.

- They have large overheads. These overheads tend to explode rapidly as programs increase in size.

- They cannot be easily applied to large problems.

- They require lots of peripheral work which may nor may not be useful in the long run.

- They generally slow down the programmers.

- They are not robust and can be easily misapplied.

- It is very difficult to determine their applicability to a given problem.

- They are too general and do not provide clear guidance for their proper application.

- No information is available regarding the risks involved in adopting these methodologies.

- They constrain the programmer to apply some form of top-down design approach.

- They do not indicate how the methodology can be combined
  with other methods.

- They have to be applied in their entirety to derive benefits.

- They take away the challenge and enjoyment associated with
  the program design activities.

- There is a lack of experimental results that conclusively
  prove that these methodologies work in practice.

- The learning acquired by applying these methodologies on
  small problems does not prepare a programmer to attack
  large problems with these methodologies.

- It is difficult to establish that the success of a design
  is due to the methodology and not due to the ingenuity of
  the designer.

Analysis of This Worldview of Program Design Methodologies

Rogers' framework points out that a prerequisite for the successful
diffusion of an innovation is that the innovation measures well along the
following characteristic dimensions:

- Relative Advantage

- Complexity

- Compatibility

- Trialability

- Observability

Let us analyze how well the program design methodologies measure along
these characteristics dimensions.

From the practitioner's viewpoint, there does not seem to be any clear
advantages in adopting these methodologies. This is based on the following
perceptions of the practitioners. Methodologies are not complete and they
need creative jumps while applying them. They are too general and do not
provide clear guidance for their proper application. They are not robust
and can be easily misapplied. They have large overheads and these overheads
explode rapidly as the problem size increases and, therefore, they cannot
be easily applied to large problems. They require lots of peripheral work
which may or may not be useful in the long run. This generally slows down
the programmers. It is also very difficult to determine their applicability
to a given problem.

They seem to be poor in trialability, due to the following perceptions
of the practitioners. They have to be applied in their entirety to derive
benefits. The learning acquired by applying these methodologies on small
problems does not prepare a programmer to attack large problems with these
methodologies. They cannot be easily applied to large problems. They have
large overhead and these overheads explode rapidly as the problem size
increases.

They have some problems along the complexity dimension as supported by
the following perceptions of the practitioners. It is very difficult to
determine their applicability to a given problem. They are too general and

318

do not provide clear guidance for their proper application.

As far as observability is concerned, it is very difficult to establish the benefits accrued by the use of the methodologies. There is a general lack of empirical results that establish the benefits of these methodologies in a conclusive manner. Furthermore, it is very difficult to observe and/or ensure that a chosen methodology is being followed properly. These are supported by the following perceptions. Methodologies are not complete and they need creative jumps while applying them. They are not robust and can be easily misapplied. It is not possible to establish that the success of a design is due to the methodology and not due to the ingenuity of the designer.

Since these methodologies require a different way of thinking about design problems, they are generally incompatible with the design processes that are in use. Further, these methodologies do not concern themselves with the transitions. These are supported by the following perceptions. They do not indicate how the methodology can be combined with other methods. They constrain the programmer to apply some form of top down design approach. They take away the challenge and enjoyment associated with the program design activities.

The preceding analysis makes the case that from the point of view of the potential adopters these methodologies, as innovations, do not seem to measure up well along the key characteristics identified by the framework. Let us now analyze how these methodologies are being communicated.

There are several problems associated with the communication of these methodologies. A review of the details provided under communication will reveal that these methodologies are oversold and empirical evidence for the strengths of the methodologies are not communicated. Furthermore, information regarding the risks associated with the methodologies and other evaluation information for innovation decision processes are not communicated.

Thus, in the context of program design methodologies, there are problems with innovation characteristics, and problems with the way innovations are communicated. Under these circumstances, Rogers' framework suggests these innovations will be very difficult to diffuse and that they will diffuse very slowly. This is consistent with our observations of the diffusion of program design methodologies in practice.

GUIDELINES AND RECOMMENDATIONS

In this section we will present guidelines and recommendations that will be useful in the context of diffusing software engineering technology. In software technology transfer literature (Bolognani, 1983; Ehrlich, 1985; Freeman, 1983; IEEE Computer Society Press, 1983; McGill, 1980; Rogers, 1962) there are other guidelines outlined.

Guidelines for Diffusing Innovations

Rogers' framework provides a clear understanding of the factors and issues that affect diffusion of innovations. These ideas can be consolidated into the following set of guidelines for successfully diffusing innovations:

● Ensure that innovations measure well along the following dimensions:

  - Relative Advantage

  - Complexity

319

- Compatibility

- Trialability

- Observability

- Understand the social structure and norms of the potential adopters.

- Select appropriate communications strategy.

- Pay attention to communication aspects: Homophily and Heterophily issues.

- Develop diffusers.

- Manage change. Develop change agents.

- Work through Opinion leaders.

- Seek collective acceptance of innovations.

- Seek commitment.

- Document the consequences of adopting innovations.

- Develop objective measures/evidences for establishing the relative advantages and consequences of adopting innovations.

Role of Software Engineering Community

In the illustration of program design methodologies we showed how the two key areas of innovation characteristics and communication of innovations were major sources of problems. We maintain that this is representative of the general state of diffusion processes in software engineering. To remedy this situation, we have to play an active role in ensuring that our innovations measure up well along the innovation characteristics, and that our innovations are effectively communicated to the practitioners. Since software innovations are generally abstract in nature, these roles cannot be played effectively by people outside the software engineering community. Some of these additional roles and responsibilities we have to fulfill are summarized below:

- The diffusion literature, which exists within the management discipline, needs to be studied and adapted to software engineering. This paper is an initial step in that direction.

- We should strengthen our innovations along the characteristic dimensions of relative advantage, trialability, complexity, observability, and compatibility. This requires:

  - A clear articulation of the trade-offs of adopting these innovations backed by strong empirical and experimental results.

  - Imaginative schemes that enable these innovations to be learnt and experienced in real, small-scale, reduced-risk situations.

  - Studying and documenting the problems and risks of scaling-up.

320

- Development of measurement techniques so that the consequences of adopting an innovation can be clearly identified and measured.

- Developing ways to overcome the transition problems when an innovation is intrinsically complex and/or incompatible with current ways.

• The software engineering community generally feels that its responsibility in the diffusion process is over once it has published its innovations in professional journals and/or given professional seminars. Rogers' framework has shown that these innovations have to be communicated objectively to the potential adopters. In order to facilitate effective communication, the community needs to develop Opinion leaders and diffusers, and widen the scope of its research and publication activities.

• Software engineering students can play an effective role as diffusers. In this regard, they should learn how to manage change, become effective communicators, and learn to deal with incorrect perceptions. They should be taught measurement techniques by which they can evaluate the performance of tools they diffuse into their parent organizations. They should be provided comprehensive information about available empirical results.

• Software engineering education should address techniques for justifying and diffusing software engineering technology in addition to teaching tools, techniques and methodologies.

SUMMARY AND CONCLUSIONS

Rogers' framework, as discussed in this paper, provides a good understanding of the various factors that affect the diffusion of innovations. One important aspect of Rogers' framework is its recognition and articulation of innovation characteristics that determine the potential of an innovation for its successful diffusion. In other words, the characteristics of innovations, as defined in Rogers' framework, may be viewed as a yardstick to evaluate its potential diffusion or adoption by the practitioners. We illustrated how these ideas can be operationalized in the context of diffusion of software diffusions. The implication of this is that to promote successful diffusion of our innovations, we should ensure that the technology we create measures well along these characteristic dimensions.

The second key area for promoting diffusion is communication of innovations. Since software innovations are generally abstract in nature, communication roles cannot be played effectively by people outside the community. Therefore, we have to play an active role in ensuring that our innovations are properly communicated to the practitioners.

At the outset we took a position that the success of our discipline, as an applied discipline committed to advancing the state of practice of software development, depends not only on our ability to come up with creative and innovation methods, but also on our ability to diffuse them effectively into practice. In this latter regard, this paper has outlined a set of guidelines and strategies that can provide concrete directions for action.

REFERENCES

Beal, G. M., Meehan, P., 1978, "The Role of Communication in Knowledge

Production, Dissemination, and Utilization", <u>Research Committee on Mass Communications, 9th World Congress of Sociology</u>, International Sociological Association, Uppsala, Sweden, September 1978.

Berelson et al., 1964, "A Study in Fertility Control", <u>Scientific American</u>, <u>210</u>, pp. 29-37.

Bolognani, M., and Corti, E., 1983, "Technology Transfer Processes in Software Development", <u>Proceedings of MELECON '83</u>, Mediterranean Electrotechnical Conference, May 1983.

Carlson, R. L., 1965, <u>Adoption of Educational Innovations</u>, Center for Educational Administration, University of Oregon, Eugene, Oregon.

Chand, D. R., 1984, "Tutorial Notes on Program Design Methodologies", <u>ACM Professional Development Seminars</u>, December 1984.

Clinton, A., 1973, <u>A Study of the Attributes of Educational Innovations as Factors in Diffusion</u>, Ph.D. Thesis, University of Toronto, 1973.

Ehrlich, K., 1985, "Factors Influencing Technology Transfer", <u>SIGCHI Bulletin</u>, <u>17</u>, (2), October 1985, pp. 20-24.

Fliegel, F. C., and Kivlin, J. E., 1966(a), "Attributes of Innovations as Factors in Diffusion", <u>American Journal of Sociology</u>, <u>72</u>, pp. 235-248.

Fliegel, F. C., and Kivlin, J. E., 1966(b), "Farmers' Perceptions of Farm Practice Attributes", <u>Rural Sociology</u>, <u>31</u>, pp. 197-206.

Freeman, P., 1983, "Software Engineering: Strategies for Technology Transfer", <u>Proceedings of International Computing Symposium on Applications Systems Development</u>, Stutgartt, FDR, March 1983, pp. 333-351.

U.S. General Accounting Office, 1980, <u>Wider Use of Better Computer Software Technology Can Improve Management Control and Reduce Costs</u>, FGMSD-80-38, U. S. General Accounting Office, Washington, D.C.

Hayen, F. L., 1977, "An Investigation of the Application of Top-Down Design and Programming in Organizations", <u>Proceedings of AIDS National Meeting</u>, Abstract, Chicago, Illinois, November 1977, p. 617.

Holloway, R. E., 1977, <u>Perceptions of an Innovation: Syracuse University Project Advance</u>, Ph.D. Thesis, Syracuse University, Syracuse, New York.

Holton, J. B., 1977, "Are New Programming Techniques Used?", <u>Datamation</u>, <u>23</u>, (7), December 1977, pp. 97-103.

IEEE Computer Society Press, 1983, <u>IEEE Computer Society Workshop on Software Engineering Technology Transfer, April 25-27, 1983</u>, IEEE Computer Society Press.

Kiehl, E. R., 1970, "An Information Network for the Agricultural Sciences", <u>Agricultural Science Review</u>, <u>8</u>, December 1970, pp. 11-15.

McGill, M. J., 1980, "Considerations in the Transfer of Software Engineering Technology", <u>AFIPS Conference Proceedings: 1980 National Computer Conference</u>, Arlington, VA, pp. 683-686.

Redwine, S. T., 1983, "Some Suggested Policies to Aid Technology Transfer for the DoD Software Initiative", <u>IEEE Computer Society Workshop on</u>

Software Engineering Technology Transfer, April 25-27, 1983, pp. 90-93.

Redwine, S. T., and Riddle, W. E., 1985, "Software Technology Maturation", *The Proceedings of the Eighth International Conference on Software Engineering, August 28-30, 1985*, pp. 189-200.

Rogers, E. M., 1962, *Diffusion of Innovations*, The Free Press, New York.

Rogers, E. M., and Kincaid, L., 1981, *Communication Networks: Toward a New Paradigm for Research*, The Free Press, New York.

Rogers, E. M., 1983, "Bibliography of Diffusion Literature", *Diffusions of Innovations*, The Free Press, New York.

Singh, R. M., 1966, *Characteristics of Farm Innovations Associated With the Rate of Adoption*, Agricultural Extension Education Report 14, Guelph, Ontario, 1966.

Thayer, J. H., and Lehman, J. H., 1979, *The Results of a Survey on Management Techniques and Procedures Used in Software Development Projects in U.S. Aerospace Industry, Volume II*, TR 79-54, Sacramento Air Logistics Center, McClelland AFB, California (Paper presented to the Research Committee on Mass Communication, 9th World Congress of Sociology).

Wharton, C. R., Jr., 1977, "The Role of the Professional in Feeding Mankind", *The Proceedings of The 1976 World Food Conference*.

Willis, R. R., "Technology Transfer Takes 6+/-2 Years", *IEEE Computer Society Workshop on Software Engineering Technology Transfer, April 25-27, 1983*, pp. 108-117.

HOW DO SOFTWARE PRACTITIONERS WRITE PROGRAMS? AN EMPIRICAL STUDY

Jawed Siddiqi

School of Computing and Information Technology
The Polytechnic
Wulfruna St.
Wolverhampton, WV1 1LY
United Kingdom

Abstract: Findings of a research investigation into problem decomposition
strategies employed by software practitioners during program design are
introduced. A cognitive model of designer behavior advances the view that
program design is a problem solving task involving repeated application of
decomposition and elaboration. The former activity is viewed as goal generation, while the latter activity is considered to consist of the allocation
of known 'clusters' or plans to the existing decomposition structure. The
paper argues that problem decomposition is not performed in an idealized
top-down manner, but is influenced by availability effects caused by problem
specification characteristics and subject familiarity with component parts
of the problem. In addition, it argues that the elaboration of a decomposition involves either the retrieval of known process action clusters or
the transformation and re-categorization of information into new clusters.
These characteristics of the model provide specific experimental hypotheses.
Results from an observational experiment evaluating these hypotheses provide
empirical support for the model. The results obtained are discussed in
relation to other empirical investigations into program design and directions
for further experimentation are presented.

1.   INTRODUCTION

Structured programming advocates such as Dijkstra (Dahl, Dijkstra, and
Hoare, 1972) and Wirth (1971) advanced a programming philosophy recommending
that design should be documented through successive levels of problem refinement using a restricted set of sequencing structures. The main arguments in favor of these guidelines, which were based on intuitive reasoning
and personal experience, were that it would facilitate the handling of
complexity due to program size and, thereby, increasing the likelihood of
achieving program correctness. The response to this has been that many
human factors researchers have felt it desirable to investigate the validity
of these claims, via the scientific method (i.e., by conducting experiments
and gathering empirical evidence).

Without doubt, the recommendations made by the structured programming
school provide guidelines as to how program development should proceed,

however, this still begs the question as to "How do practitioners actually write programs?".

It is our view, that appropriate investigations attempting to answer this question can increase our understanding of the software development process and, thereby, add to the significant contribution made by the structured programming school.

Section 2 presents a conceptual model of designer behavior that proposes a problem-solving framework for the program design process involving decomposition and elaboration where the former is viewed as a goal generation activity, while the latter activity consists of 'clustering' components and the allocation of these clusters to the skeletal decomposition structure produced. In Section 3, experimental hypotheses based on the proposed model are advanced and empirical evidence that supports these hypotheses is also presented. Finally, in Section 4, the conclusions reached are briefly discussed in relation to other empirical work in the area of the program design.

2. COGNITIVE MODEL OF DESIGNER BEHAVIOR

In general terms, program design can be viewed as a repeated process of
problem understanding, problem decomposition, and solution elaboration. More specifically, the model views program design as a problem-solving activity that transforms an initial state via a solution sequence into a final state by the application of a given set of operators. The correspondence between program design (in structured programming terms) and problem-solving can be specified as:

- initial state: problem specification

- operators: decomposition strategies and synthetic techniques using both composite (i.e., concatenation, selection, and repetition) and elementary operators

- solution sequence: levels of refinement

- final state: the program in an executable notation.

In structured programming terms there is no specific and well-defined decomposition strategy or composite technique. However, since the two main ingredients in the description of most programming problems are the data specification and the stated processing requirements, it is our view that either can act as a primary focus for problem decomposition. Therefore, two distinct approaches can be hypothesized. They are termed as "data-driven" and "process-driven", respectively, corresponding to the situations when the designer refines the problem based on the data specification or the processing requirements. Two problem decomposition strategies of general applicability, namely Process Next Item and Incremental Design are also hypothesized. The first strategy, which is strongly associated with the data driven approach, bears some similarity to findings of Hoc (1977), that strategies for program construction are influenced by the role of "mental execution of the program". It is reasonable to assume that the most likely self-elaboration of the task is that subjects would visualize, having contemplated the data, dealing with the list an item at a time. The second strategy, which is associated with a requirements driven approach, is one in which familiar and immediately achievable sub-goals are isolated to formulate a partial solution and the remainder of the design subsequently made to conform. Its somewhat bottom-up character can be summed by the phrase "Do what you can and make the rest fit around it".

The problem solver is viewed as an information processor, whose structure is hypothesized to consist of a set of knowledge structures relevant to program design, memory for storing and processing information and a facility for planning. The former, as Shneiderman (1979) and others have pointed out, is a complex multi-leveled body of concepts and techniques that is often referred to as 'semantic knowledge'. In general terms, this knowledge includes general methods for constructing programs (e.g., Process Next Item and Incremental Design), specific strategies for producing specific programs or program segments (e.g., summing a list of numbers), and the effects of various program statements.

The memory structure adopted is based on the works of Greeno (1973) on problem-solving and Shneiderman (Shneiderman and Mayer, 1979) on programmer behavior. The structure consists of three components: short term memory, long-term memory, and working memory. The latter component is due to Feigenbaum (1979). Of particular interest in the present context is the knowledge acquired through experience by the problem solver, which is permanent and resides in semantic form in the long-term memory, whose capacity is essentially unlimited and retrieval from which is systematic. The stored information is assumed to be hierarchically structured in the form of a semantic network, in terms of generic categories where each node represents a category and is related to its sub-nodes by an 'ISA' (i.e., is an instance of) relationship (Lindsay and Norman, 1977).

Problem understanding produces in the working memory an internal representation that captures the relationship among elements of the problem to be solved.

Problem decomposition is characterized as a goal generation activity that defines the current state, the desired state and a set of possible strategies to transform the former into the latter. It is further hypothesized that goal generation is due to cognitive processes that are a function of an "availability heuristic". The rationale for this characterization is influenced by Pollard's (1982) application to logical reasoning tasks of Tversky and Kahneman's (1973) theory of non-rational intuitive judgement. This theory proposes that a subject's judgements are mediated by an availability heuristic which Pollard suggests is responsible for two different types of availability effects, both types having the essential common feature that they directly "cue" the subject's response. One type being the availability derived from the subjects experience and the other from salient characteristics of the problem wording.

The elaboration of a decomposition is a process of composition that involves categorizing components into appropriate clusters and allocating these clusters to the existing decomposition structure. During this process action, clusters are retrieved from long-term memory and are allocated in either their retrieved form or with certain components re-categorized. These action clusters are either retrieved from long-term memory or are generated in the working memory, respectively, corresponding to the cases when the solution to the sub-problem is "known" or "not known". In the former case the method for solving the problem is immediately remembered as soon as the problem is understood. The method may not be remembered all at once and, generally, retrieval of known clusters may involve several steps. In the latter case since the problem solver does not have a method for solving the problem and, therefore, a solution plan has to be constructed. This construction is analogous to a child building a structure out of toy components of an erector set by choosing the appropriate ones from those available. The task is non-trivial and may often require considerable ingenuity.

327

An operational overview of the model is as follows:

(i)   A representation of the problem to be solved obtained
      by reading the problem specification (i.e., the stimulus)
      is entered into short-term memory;

(ii) The designer's response is a function of available cues
      derived essentially from the data specification/pro-
      cessing requirements (i.e., stimulus activated) and/or
      from designer experience (i.e., knowledge activated).
      These cues activate cognitive processes that generate
      goals in working memory;

(iii) The appropriate representation of the problem description
      and the goal are transferred into working memory and the
      appropriate decomposition strategy applied;

(iv) Subsequently, a decomposition that accommodates the goals
      generated is derived; and

(v)   Appropriate action clusters are either retrieved from
      long-term memory or generated in working memory and are
      then allocated to 'slots' in the decomposition.

3.   EXPERIMENTAL REPORT

The model developed in the previous section formed an explanatory
framework for an experimental study into decomposition and elaboration
processes in which a number of hypotheses were advanced and tested. The
study, which investigated the strategies used in program design, involved
six experiments that were performed over a period of 18 months in academic
environments. The subjects used in the experiments were mainly computer
science undergraduates. Each experiment involved groups of subjects, all
of whom had been previously taught to program in a 'structured manner',
undertaking various program design tasks. Complete details of this study
are reported in Siddiqi (1984), from which two hypotheses; one concerning the
decomposition process, and the other concerning the elaboration process are
as follows:

(i)   During the decomposition process, a response will generally
      be both stimulus and knowledge activated, hence, availability
      strength will depend on the degree of cue emphasis in the
      presentation of the specification and the extent to which
      a goal matches a subject's experience. It, therefore,
      seems reasonable to predict that the proportion of different
      decomposition types should be dependent on the number of
      available cues of varying strengths.

(ii) Provided the 'slots' in the skeletal decomposition structure
      are such that they can accommodate "known" action clusters
      (i.e., in their retrieved form) then the process is relatively
      error free. If, however, the process involves generating
      clusters or re-categorizing components of clusters then it
      will be relatively error prone.

An observational experiment to gather evidence concerning these hypotheses was carried out. It involved 36 third- year computer science undergraduates trained in structured programming and Algol 68, each supplied

with a problem specification derived from Naur's (1969) line-edit problem, for which they had to design a program during a 50-minute class period. Subjects' solutions underwent the following analysis:

(a) Decomposition Process

Each solution to the problem was classified into one of three possible decomposition types. The problem specification with representations corresponding to each decomposition, hereafter referred to as L1, L2, and L3 are given in the appendix. They, respectively, correspond to three possible sources of available cues in the data description, namely the keywords: 'line', 'character', and 'word'. Though none of these is particularly emphasized, the availability effects for each is further reinforced by the subject associating with each the familiar strategy of Process Next Item. Of the processing requirements, the second is considered to be the dominant source of availability given that it captures a large slice of the overall problem and is fulfilled by the familiar goal of building a sequence of m characters. Note that the other requirements do not effect the decomposition type produced. On the basis of this analysis and interpreting cue availability strength as a count of the number of possible sources, the division of frequencies of L1, L2, and L3 should, respectively, be in the ratio of 1/2, 1/4 and 1/4. The division of observed frequencies, respectively, corresponding to L1, L2, and L3 were 48%, 20%, and 32%. Chi-squared was used to test the consistency of the observed data. Since we wish to test whether the data is consistent with our predictions (i.e., we have a vested interest in the null hypothesis). Choosing a significance level of 0.2, the test revealed that the data is consistent with the predictions advanced.

(b) Elaboration Process

To make predictions for the line-edit problem, we apply the principle that the error likelihood of the elaboration process depends upon whether the required clusters can be simply retrieved or will require re-categorization/re-generation. This means that the elaboration of L1-type decompositions (see appendix) is likely to be relatively error prone. This is because the required clusters "build a line" and "adjust a line and then output" are highly unlikely to be known and, therefore, need to be generated. Whereas, the elaboration of L3-type decompositions (see appendix) is likely to be relatively error free because the required clusters "build a word" and "output a word" are more likely to be familiar problems and, therefore, can be retrieved rather than to generated. In the case of L2-type decompositions (see appendix) the required clusters consist of the same components as an L3-type, but they need to be re-categorized into different clusters. The error analysis carried out consisted of accumulating subject's errors associated with fulfilling the following problem requirements:

(1) removing successive spaces;

(2) inserting a single space between words;

(3) preventing a space being output before the first word; and

(4) preventing a space being output before the
end of a line.

The results of error percentages for L1, L2, and L3-type
decompositions were 78%, 45%, and 30%, respectively.
The rank order of these percentages provides supporting
evidence for the predicted hypothesis.

Since the factors being investigated were attributes of the participants
in the experiment, causal inferences cannot be made; although, a controlled
experiment in which problem decomposition was a treatment is reported in
Siddiqi and Ratcliff (1987). However, from the results obtained concerning
the frequency of decompositions and the error percentages, the following two
propositions can be advanced:

(i) for the decomposition process, there is an association between the proportion of distinct decomposition types and
number of available cues.

(ii) the presence of familiar action clusters is indicative of
an error-free elaboration process and vice-versa.

4.   CONCLUSION

The view that program design is performed in an idealized top-down
manner is rejected in favor of the alternative view that it is a repeated
process of forming a partial solution (i.e., an initial decomposition)
accompanied by fitting collections of program segments (i.e., action clusters) piece by piece into a partially developed program structure. The
model advances the view that such aspects as keywords in the problem wording,
subjects familiarity with component parts of the problem and level of abstraction skills developed are major contributory factors by which the
decomposition process is effected. In addition, the accompanying process
of "tying loose ends together" is influenced by whether the action clusters
required by the designer are familiar or unfamiliar sub-problems.

It is considered that the proposed model provides a richer description
and captures more of the flavor of "how program design might actually proceed" than the traditional top-down exposition of "how program design should
proceed". Although further confirmatory evidence for this viewpoint is
provided in Siddiqi (1984), there is still a continuing need to, not only,
carry out experimentation to further characterize the identified factors, but
also to determine additional factors that are responsible for "shaping" this
complex task of program design. One such attempt in order to provide a more
detailed description of designer behavior is the development of an experimental framework that explains the results obtained as well as providing a
means of investigating the sequence of decisions made is reported in a
companion paper (Siddiqi and Sumiga, 1986).

In conclusion, the research findings in general suggest the need to
look for richer models that characterize this complex activity. Recent
works (Soloway and Ehrlich, 1984) provide a number of different yet complementary models. In particular, our idea of Incremental Design of "do
what you can and fit the rest around it" bears close similarity with that
of Rist's (1986) notion of a "focal segment" and Kant's (1985) concept of a
"kernel idea".

REFERENCES

Dahl, O., Dijkstra, E. W., and Hoare, C. A. R., 1972, <u>Notes on Structured Programming</u>, Academic Press.

Feigenbaum, E. A., 1970, "Models of Memory", <u>Information Processing and Memory</u>, Norman, D. A., Academic Press, pp. 451-469.

Greeno, J. G., 1973, "The Structure of Memory and the Process of Solving Problems", <u>Contemporary Issues in Cognitive Psychology: The Loyola Symposium</u>, Solso, R. L., V. H. Winston & Sons, pp. 103-131.

Hoc, J. M., 1982, "Analysis of Beginners Problem Solving Strategies in Programming", <u>Proceedings of a Conference on the Psychology of Problem Solving with Computers</u>, Vrijie University, Amsterdam, pp. 85-93.

Kant, E., 1985, "Understanding and Automating Algorithm Design", <u>IEEE Transactions on Software Engineering</u>, pp. 1361-1374.

Lindsay, P. H., and Norman, D. A., 1977, <u>Human Information Processing</u>, Academic Press, pp. 381-417.

Naur, P., 1969, "Programming by Action Clusters", <u>Bit</u>, <u>9</u>, (3), pp. 250-258.

Pollard, P., 1982, "Human Reasoning: Some Possible Effects of Availability", <u>Cognition</u>, <u>12</u>, pp. 65-96.

Rist, R. S., 1986, "Plans in Programming: Definition, Demonstration, and Development", <u>Empirical Studies of Programmers</u>, Soloway, E., and Iyengar, S. S., eds., Ablex, New York.

Siddiqi, J. I. A., 1984, <u>An Empirical Investigation into Problem Decomposition Strategies Used in Program Design</u>, Ph.D. Thesis, University of Aston in Birmingham.

Siddiqi, J. I. A., and Ratcliff, B. R., 1987, "The Influence of Problem Specification on Problem Decomposition", <u>International Journal of Man-Machine Studies</u>, to appear.

Siddiqi, J. I. A., and Sumiga, J. H., 1986, "Empirical Evaluation of a Proposed Model of the Program Design Process", <u>The Symposium on Empirical Foundations of Information and Software Sciences</u>, Georgia Institute of Technology, Atlanta, Georgia.

Shneiderman, B., and Mayer, R., 1979, "Syntactic/Semantic Interactions in Programmer Behavior: A Model and Experimental Results", <u>International Journal of Computer and Information Sciences</u>, <u>8</u>, pp. 219-235.

Soloway, E., and Ehrlich, K., 1984, <u>Empirical Studies of Programmers</u>, Ablex.

Wirth, N., 1971, "Program Development by Step-Wise Refinement", <u>Communications of the ACM</u>, <u>14</u>, (4), pp. 221-226.

APPENDIX: THE LINE-EDIT PROBLEM

A piece of text consisting of words separated by one or more characters is terminated by an *. It is required to convert it in line by line form in accordance with the following rules.

(a) Redundant spaces between words are to be removed;

(b) No line will contain more than m characters and each line is filled as far as possible;

(c) Line-breaks must not occur in the middle of a word.

(You may ignore the presence of line-feed characters and the possibility of a word being greater than m characters.)

Design a program to read the text and output it in accordance with the above rules.

Decompositions are shown in Figure 1 (Note: In the diagrams the super-scripts "o" and "*" denote unordered alternation and unbounded repetition, respectively; the prefix "P" to component names stands for "Process".)

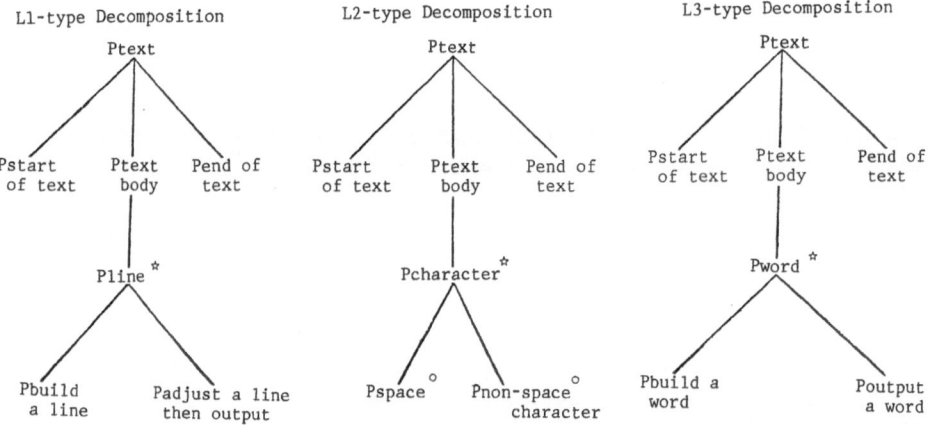

Figure 1. Decompositions.

EMPIRICAL EVALUATION OF A PROPOSED MODEL OF THE PROGRAM DESIGN PROCESS

J. I. A. Siddiqi and J. H. Sumiga

School of Computing and Information Technology
The Polytechnic
Wulfruna Street
Wolverhampton
West Midlands, U.K.

Abstract: Program design methodologies can be considered to be based on implicit cognitive theories. Therefore, studies evaluating the effectiveness of methodologies from a human factors perspective need to be conducted so that the results of these studies can be used in the design of IPSE's. Structured programming, the most widely used methodology, has a very simple underlying cognitive theory. Because this theory has been shown to have limitations, the paper presents a richer theory of program design with emphasis on problem decomposition, based on the blackboard model, together with some supporting experimental evidence. A model of program designer behavior, based on the proposed theory, incorporates specific forms of sequential planning and island driving, which are steered by data and process oriented approaches. The model is expressed in terms of cognitive processes operating on long-term memory and communicating via information posted on a specific blackboard structure. The operational model, when applied to a particular programming problem, resulted in certain predictions; the most significant being that solutions based on primitive as opposed to abstract perceptions of problem structure are preferred. An immediate implication is that either of the preferred solutions require less effort to produce, or that they are the only perceived possibility. Supporting empirical evidence is advanced, from attempting the same programming problem. The implications for the man-machine interface of IPSE's are considered, limitations of the experimental approach adopted are discussed and suggestions are made for further work.

1. INTRODUCTION

One way of attacking the difficulties involved in the production of software, is to use program design methodologies, most of which have one or more claimed benefits associated with them. Most methodologies attempt to steer the designer towards a particular perspective and suggest the use of a restricted set of techniques. When such methodologies are embedded within IPSE's, the question is raised as to whether this constraint becomes a help or hindrance.

Program design can be considered to be a planning exercise and,

333

therefore, a particular type of problem-solving activity. Consequently, it is possible to view a methodology as being based on an implicit cognitive theory incorporating specific problem-solving and planning methods. These form the basis of the techniques associated with a particular methodology. For instance, the most widely used methodology, Structured Programming, is based on an extremely simplistic cognitive theory, i.e., the use of the 'divide and conquer' approach. However, program design in general, is an extremely complex activity and there is much evidence to suggest that the techniques and approaches required to effectively tackle real problems are more varied and complex than current methodologies allow. Our view is that for an environment to be successful, it must be based on a realistic and appropriate cognitive theory, i.e., one which is relevant and appropriate cognitive theory, i.e., one which is relevant to the design process and which reflects the capabilities of the typical designer.

In order to develop appropriate design methodologies and adaptive program support environments, it is necessary to consider which techniques and approaches are actually used by designers, and to take account of these in the provision of tool kits. The strategy we adopt is a two-stage process: firstly, to carry out empirical work as a means of determining what is actually going on in the design process; secondly, to propose a model of the design process that provides an explanatory framework for the observations.

Section 2 proposes such a model that provides both an explanatory and predictive framework from an empirical study. The model, based on specialists acting on a blackboard model, is computational and, therefore, has a potential implementation. It can also be used for the specification of human-factors requirements for adaptive environments. In Section 3, the model is applied to a particular problem to provide two animations (i.e., two plausible decision chains corresponding to differing approaches). These are used to explain the results of an observational experiment. The conclusions drawn from this work are presented in Section 4.

2. THE MODEL

Our initial premise is that programming and, in particular, program design can be viewed as a planning activity. Many accord with this view; indeed as has been pointed out:

> "The task of design involves a complex set of processes.
> Starting from a global statement of the problem, a designer
> must develop a precise plan for a solution that will be
> realized in some concrete way..." (Jeffries et al., 1981).

The proposed model is based on the Blackboard Model (Hayes-Roth and Hayes-Roth, 1979) in which the planning process is simulated using many distinct cognitive specialists whose actions result in decisions being recorded on a blackboard structure. This structure enables specialists to interact and communicate by allowing them access to previously made decisions, irrespective of which specialist made them.

The function of specialists is to make tentative decisions to be incorporated into a proposed plan. Different specialists influence different aspects of a plan, ranging from high-level issues such as the approach taken to detailed ordering of specific operations. Specialists under which it can be activated, while the latter describes the effect it has on the blackboard.

The blackboard structure, as suggested by Hayes-Roth and Hayes-Roth (1979), consists of five planes reflecting different conceptual categories of decisions. In addition, each plane is partitioned into hierarchically organized 'levels of abstraction', such that decisions recorded at each level are potential refinements of those recorded on the level above.

In order to model the program design process, we propose the following characterization:

- An executive plane consisting of a three level hierarchy.

  The first level (priorities) is where specialists record decisions about the priorities associated with the allocation of resources (e.g., where to apply one's efforts first). The second (focus) holds decisions about where the designer has chosen to focus his/her attention at specific points in the process. The third level (schedule) which is used for control purposes is not relevant to the present discussion.

- A meta-design plane consisting of four levels: problem definition, design approach, policies and evaluation criteria.

  These levels are not hierarchical but reflect different aspects of the designer's approach to designing a program. The problem definition level contains decisions about understanding the problem specification and formulating the task to be performed. The design approach level represents decisions about how the designer intends to generate solutions. For instance, should the designer 'rigidly' follow a specific methodology e.g., structured programming, then the decision recorded would be to use stepwise refinement, whereas if no particular discipline is followed then ad hoc and intuitively based approaches would be chosen. The policy level indicates the global aims, constraints, and desirable features of an acceptable solution. These can often reflect the designer's intentions, for example 'Do the bits I can do and then worry about the rest', but they can also be derived from specified constraints on the problem, such as efficiency. The final level, evaluation criteria, is the refinement of the above level and corresponds to decisions made about how a potential design is to be judged.

- A design abstraction plane and a design plane, each containing four hierarchically organized levels. There is a strong interaction between corresponding levels on these two planes, such that decisions recorded on a level of the former plane usually characterize types of decisions to be incorporated on the corresponding level of the latter plane.

  On the design abstraction plane, the four levels are: intentions, schemes, strategies, and tactics. The corresponding levels on the design plane are: outcomes, algorithms, procedures, and operations.

  The intentions level is where specialists record decisions about low-level aims such as satisfying problem requirements. A decision made at this level could result in a corresponding decision on the outcomes level, refining the recorded intention(s), for example, naming the particular problem requirements to be satisfied.

The schemes level contains decisions as to how the intentions and outcomes are to be achieved and the algorithms level records decisions about the specific way the scheme is to be implemented.

The strategies level is where specialists record decisions which refine those made at the schemes and algorithms levels, these being made more specific at the procedures level. A A similar relationship exists between the tactics and operations levels.

- An observations plane which can be seen as a series of slots containing observations, perceived by the designer to be pertinent to the solution of the problem. Among the slots we have found most relevant to the design process are: observations about structures (e.g., problems, data or processes), similarities (e.g., structural similarities), analogies (e.g., similar problems previously solved), and assessment (e.g., perceived difficulty of individual tasks).

It should be clear from the above that when the designer proceeds cautiously, i.e., users 'least commitment' and/or 'divide and conquer' approaches, then the flow of decision-making is from the meta-design plane to the design abstraction and design planes. In program design terms this is known as top-down decomposition or step-wise refinement. In cases involving synthetic techniques or 'most commitment' approaches, the decision-making proceeds in a reverse direction, for instance a decision-making proceeds in a reverse direction, for instance a decision made on the design plane may cause a change in the policy level of the meta-design plane. This corresponds to bottom-up design.

Our choice of specialists for program design, from those identified by Hayes-Roth and Hayes-Roth (1979) for the planning process, are shown in Figure 1. This set of specialists, whose names are intended to suggest their function, constitute a framework for high-level decision-making. Each specialist is shown as linking the level from which it is triggered to where its decision is recorded. Some specialists are triggered immediately by a decision being posted, while others may require the presence of additional configurations of prior decision. For example, the recording of a decision on the policies level will, in general, initiate a chain of decisions involving the priorities and director specialists, thereby forming the necessary configuration for triggering the aim formulator.

The additional specialists required for our characterization can be divided into those that correspond to general problem-solving methods and those relating specifically to the program design task. The former set include:

- A features noter, which records relevant features of the problem specification on the observations plane.

- A comparator that notes similarities in problem features, recording these on the similarities level.

- An analogizer, which identifies previously attempted sub-problems in the problem being solved, records its decisions on the analogies level.

- An assessor, which notes the perceived level of difficulty of sub-problems, on the assessment level.

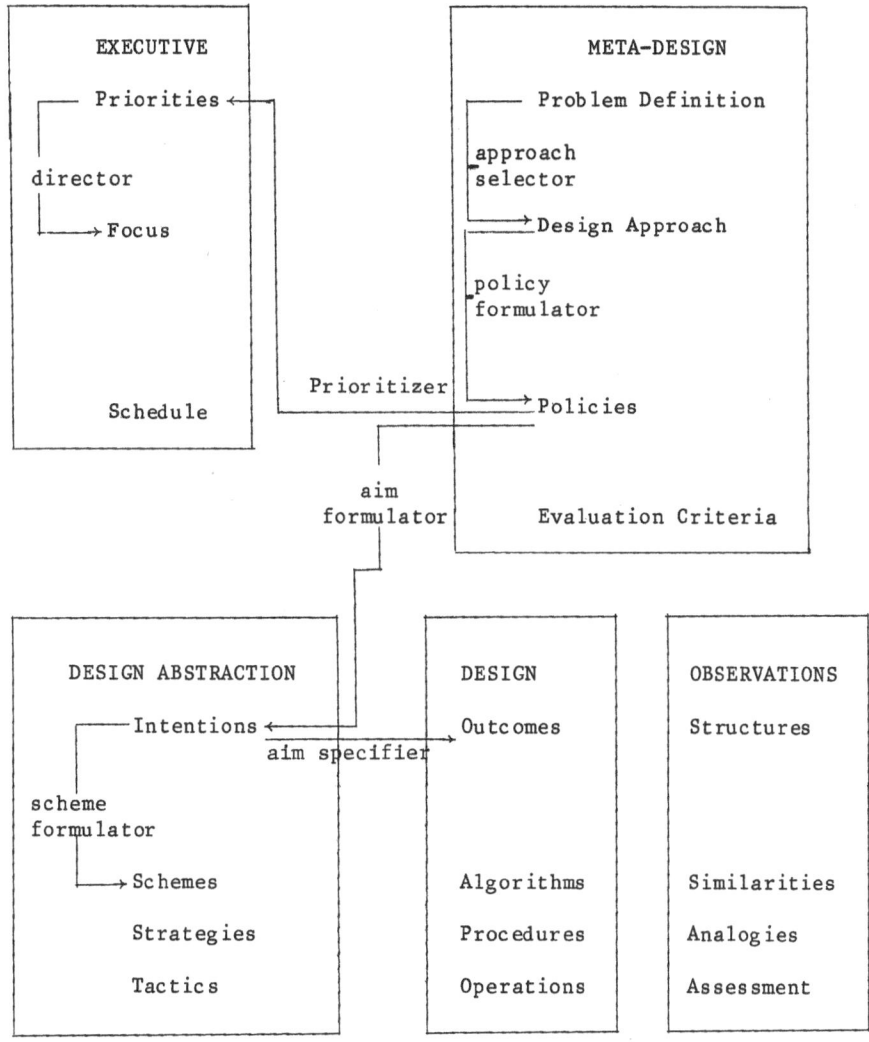

Figure 1. The Blackboard Planes and Some Example Specialists.

- Two closely connected specialists whose combined function can
be described as 'do what you can and fit the rest around it'.
One specialist, the island formulator, identifies achievable
goals and can alter the recorded policy. The other, the
island driver, causes the remaining goals to be fulfilled and
will often also result in a change of policy.

The domain-dependent specialists include algorithm, procedure and
operations retrievers, which perform low-level retrieval from long-term
memory, and a data structure analyzer, which records observations about
structural properties of the data.

Our motivation in presenting this blackboard-based model is to find a
perspective which offers an effective framework for investigating the sequence of levels of abstraction used and the decisions made during the
design process. In the next section this model is applied to a specific

```
┌─────────────────────────┐      ┌─────────────────────────┐
│       EXECUTIVE         │      │       META-DESIGN        │
│                         │      │                          │
│  Priorities            │      │  Problem Definition      │
│                         │      │                          │
│  5.  Find structure    │      │  1.  Specification       │
│      of data, then     │      │                          │
│      decide how to     │      │                          │
│      process it        │      │                          │
│                         │      │  Design Approach         │
│  Focus                 │      │                          │
│                         │      │  3.  Data-driven         │
│  6.  Structures        │      │                          │
│  8.  Intentions and    │      │                          │
│      Outcomes          │      │  Policies                │
│                         │      │                          │
│  Schedule              │      │  4.  Use data stream     │
│                         │      │                          │
│                         │      │  Evaluation Criteria     │
└─────────────────────────┘      └─────────────────────────┘

┌──────────────────────┐ ┌──────────────────┐ ┌──────────────────┐
│ DESIGN ABSTRACTION   │ │    DESIGN        │ │  OBSERVATIONS    │
│                      │ │                  │ │                  │
│ Intentions           │ │ Outcomes         │ │ Structures       │
│                      │ │                  │ │                  │
│ 9.  Satisfy all      │ │ 10. Computation  │ │ 2.  Data stream  │
│     requirements     │ │     of VC, SL,   │ │     is present.  │
│                      │ │     LWP          │ │ 7.  Sequence of  │
│                      │ │                  │ │     signals      │
│ Schemes              │ │                  │ │                  │
│                      │ │ Algorithms       │ │ Similarities     │
│ Strategies           │ │                  │ │                  │
│                      │ │ Procedures       │ │ Analogies        │
│ Tactics              │ │                  │ │                  │
│                      │ │ Operations       │ │ Assessment       │
└──────────────────────┘ └──────────────────┘ └──────────────────┘
```

Figure 2. Data-Driven Approach, Stage 1.

problem, namely the signal problem (see appendix for problem specification and two possible decompositions).

3. DISCUSSION

Our approach differs from the traditional approach, as used by Hayes-Roth and Hayes-Roth (1979), that of demonstrating sufficiency by interpreting subjects' protocols. Our primary aim is to apply the model to the signal problem to produce possible decision chains that can be used to make predictions about designer behavior. The empirical evidence to be presented in this section originates from a study, involving six experiments, which investigated the strategies used in program design (Siddiqi, 1984). A compatible model of wider scope, used to explain the results of that study and from which some of the specialists have been derived, is presented in a companion paper (Siddiqi, 1986).

EXECUTIVE	META-DESIGN
Priorities	Problem Definition
Focus	Design Approach
10. Lower levels	
Schedule	Policies
	16. Do what you know and what is easy
	Evaluation Criteria

DESIGN ABSTRACTION	DESIGN	OBSERVATIONS
Intentions	Outcomes	Structures
17. Do similar requirements	18. Computation of VC & SL	
Schemes	Algorithms	Similarities
12. Process stream a signal at a time	19. Loop to total two types of item	13. Computation of VC & SL
Strategies	Procedures	Analogies
	20. WHILE and IF construct	14. Know how to do it!
Tactics	Operations	Assessment
	21. Detailed code re-trieved	15. Easy!

Figure 3. Data-Driven Approach, Stage 2.

3.1 Application of the Model

It is our conjecture, from previous work (Ratcliff and Siddiqi, 1985)
that designers adopt what may be broadly described as either 'data-driven'
or 'requirement-driven' approaches. We present diagrammatic representations
of two animations of the model reflecting these alternatives, starting from
the point at which the problem specification is presented to the designer.
The decisions are numbered in the sequence in which they occur and they
remain on the blackboard irrespective of subsequent decision-making.

Stage 1 of the data-driven approach, shown in Figure 2, begins with

```
┌─────────────────────────┐        ┌───────────────────────────────┐
│        EXECUTIVE        │        │         META-DESIGN           │
│                         │        │                               │
│      Priorities         │        │     Problem Definition        │
│                         │        │                               │
│       Focus             │        │     Design Approach           │
│                         │        │                               │
│      Schedule           │        │     Policies                  │
│                         │        │                               │
└─────────────────────────┘        │     27.  Fit around what      │
                                    │          has already been     │
                                    │          done                 │
                                    │                               │
                                    │     Evaluation Criteria       │
                                    └───────────────────────────────┘
```

```
┌─────────────────────────┐ ┌─────────────────────┐ ┌──────────────────────┐
│  DESIGN ABSTRACTION     │ │     DESIGN          │ │   OBSERVATIONS       │
│                         │ │                     │ │                      │
│  Intentions             │ │  Outcomes           │ │  Structures          │
│                         │ │                     │ │                      │
│  22. Do remaining       │ │  23. Computation    │ │                      │
│      requirements       │ │      of LWP         │ │                      │
│                         │ │                     │ │                      │
│  Schemes                │ │  Algorithms         │ │  Similarities        │
│                         │ │                     │ │                      │
│  24. Accumulate WP's    │ │                     │ │                      │
│      and find LWP       │ │                     │ │                      │
│                         │ │                     │ │                      │
│  Strategies             │ │  Procedures         │ │  Analogies           │
│                         │ │                     │ │                      │
│                         │ │                     │ │  25. Know how to     │
│                         │ │                     │ │      do it!          │
│                         │ │                     │ │                      │
│                         │ │                     │ │  Assessment          │
│  Tactics                │ │  Operations         │ │                      │
│                         │ │                     │ │  26. Not too         │
│                         │ │                     │ │      difficult       │
└─────────────────────────┘ └─────────────────────┘ └──────────────────────┘
```

Figure 4. Data-Driven Approach, Stage 3.

the recording of decision 1 on the problem definition level. This results
in the invocation of the features noter specialist, which records the observation that the specification contains a data stream. At this point, the
approach selector, the policy formulator, prioritizer and director are
fired recording decisions 3-6 in the sequence shown. Decision 6, to focus
on the structures level, triggers the data structure analyzer which notes
the observation that the data stream can be seen as a sequence of signals.
This changes the focus (decision 8), because the first priority, to find
the structure of the data, has been completed. The chain of decisions that
resulted in the focusing of the intentions level allows the aim formulator
to trigger; this in turn fires the aim specifier, leading to decision 10
being posted. The completion of this stage corresponds to the end of high-
level decision making.

Stage 2, shown in Figure 3, begins by focusing on lower levels of the design abstraction and design planes. The scheme formulator, because the data stream is perceived as a sequence of signals, records decision 12, i.e., to process the stream a signal at a time. This results in the crucial observations that the computations of VC and SL are similar, familiar and easy tasks (decisions 13-15). These opportunistic realizations produce a change in policy, through the invocation of the island formulator, recorded as decision 16. The policy change initiates the intention of doing similar requirements, with the outcome being the computation of VC and SL (decisions 17 and 18). Since these similar tasks were both familiar and considered to be easy, they form an achievable 'island of certainty'. Consequently, the algorithm, procedure and operations retriever are successively fired (decisions 19-21). The completion of this stage corresponds to the designer arriving at the following skeletal structure:

```
read (signal)
DOWHILE signal <> 0
        IF signal = 1
        THEN
              vehiclecount := vehiclecount + 1
              .
              .
        ELSE
              surveylength := surveylength + 1
              .
              .
        ENDIF
        read (signal)
ENDWHILE
```

The next stage, shown in Figure 4, begins with a change in intention of fulfilling the remaining requirements. The essential part of this stage is the designer's observations, via the analogizer and assessor, that this is a known and not too difficult task (decisions 22-26). The result of this is the invocation of the island driver, which changes the policy to one of attempting to fit the remaining part of the design around the skeletal structure given above (decision 27).

From the above, we can see that the design activity is not strictly top-down, but multi-directional. Initially, the high-level decision-making follows a cautious top-down approach with opportunistic interventions, corresponding to designer observations, forcing a goal-oriented approach that alters the original policy.

In contrast to the above animation, Figure 5 presents a sequence of decisions corresponding to a requirements-driven approach to the signal problem. In this case, decisions 1 to 4 result from the invocation of the same specialists as in the data-driven approach, the main difference being that the features noter's action corresponds to the designer's attention being centered on the problem requirements. This is reflected in subsequent decisions. In the data-driven approach, the policy decision triggers the prioritizer, director, etc., whereas in this case, the designer is strongly attracted to fulfill the requirements to find VC and SL because of their perceived simplicity (decisions 5-7). Another important difference is that the observations result in the invocation of the island formulator at this early stage (decision 8). These early observations and this opportunistic intervention characterize the difference between the two approaches. We can see that the requirements-driven animation, which initially used a 'most-commitment' approach rather than a cautious top-down one, is at the same stage as the data-driven approach was after decision 18.

```
┌─────────────────────────────┐        ┌─────────────────────────────┐
│        EXECUTIVE            │        │        META-DESIGN          │
│                             │        │                             │
│  Priorities                │        │  Problem Definition         │
│                             │        │                             │
│  9.  Do VC & SL,           │        │  1. Specification           │
│      then do LWP           │        │                             │
│                             │        │                             │
│  Focus                     │        │  Design Approach            │
│                             │        │                             │
│  10. Intentions and        │        │  3. Requirements-driven     │
│      outcomes              │        │                             │
│                             │        │                             │
│  Schedule                  │        │  Policies                   │
│                             │        │                             │
└─────────────────────────────┘        │  4. Use requirements        │
                                       │  8. Do what you know        │
                                       │     and what is easy        │
                                       │                             │
                                       │  Evaluation Criteria        │
                                       │                             │
                                       └─────────────────────────────┘
```

```
┌──────────────────────┐ ┌──────────────────────┐ ┌──────────────────────┐
│ DESIGN ABSTRACTION   │ │ DESIGN               │ │ OBSERVATIONS         │
│                      │ │                      │ │                      │
│ Intentions           │ │ Outcomes             │ │ Structures           │
│                      │ │                      │ │                      │
│ 11. Do similar       │ │ 12. Computation      │ │ 2. Requirements      │
│     requirements     │ │     of VC & SL       │ │    are present       │
│                      │ │                      │ │                      │
│ Schemes              │ │ Algorithms           │ │ Similarities         │
│                      │ │                      │ │                      │
│                      │ │                      │ │ 5. Computation       │
│                      │ │                      │ │    of VC & SL        │
│                      │ │                      │ │                      │
│ Strategies           │ │ Procedures           │ │ Analogies            │
│                      │ │                      │ │                      │
│                      │ │                      │ │ 6. Know how to       │
│                      │ │                      │ │    do it!            │
│                      │ │                      │ │                      │
│ Tactics              │ │ Operations           │ │ Assessment           │
│                      │ │                      │ │                      │
│                      │ │                      │ │ 7. Easy!             │
│                      │ │                      │ │                      │
└──────────────────────┘ └──────────────────────┘ └──────────────────────┘
```

Figure 5.   Requirements-driven Approach.

The signal problem can be considered to have two different solutions which result from distinct decompositions. The two approaches detailed above both lead to a D1-type decomposition. It is, of course, possible to provide similar animations which would arrive at D2-type decompositions. For the data-driven approach this solution type results from the perception of the data stream as a composite rather than primitive structure, i.e., as a sequence of waiting periods each made up of a sequence of timing signals. This perception corresponds to an abstraction of the observation modelled in the animation. In the requirements-driven approach, the designer needs to concentrate his/her attention on dealing with LWP, in order to derive a D2-type solution.

Our initial premise is that abstractions in problem-solving are inherently more difficult to perceive and grasp. Supporting evidence for this was obtained from a controlled experiment involving subjects designing a solution to the signal problem (Ratcliff and Siddiqi, 1985). From the animation and our premise, it can be argued that the D1 pathway is the more obvious to most designers because it is based upon more simplistic perceptions related to data or processing requirements than the D2 pathway. Another factor which may influence decomposition is the presence, in the problem specification, of certain key words and phrases and other textual features. These may cause attention to be centered on particular problem components, thereby triggering a signal stream emphasis in the problem wording, providing an explanation of the decision posted by the data structure analyzer in the animation of the data-driven approach. Similarly, the presence of two easily achievable goals explains the invocation of the island formulator. These arguments provide a strong justification of the hypothesis that designers are highly likely to produce D1-type decompositions.

3.2 Empirical Considerations

In the previously mentioned study an observational experiment was carried out, in which 129 computer science students from a number of different educational establishments (ranging from pre-university to post-graduate) were each supplied with the specification of the signal problem. They were asked to design a program in any high-level language. Subjects' solutions were classified on the basis of process structure rather than factors such as syntax, notation used or positioning (correct or otherwise) of elementary actions. (For detailed discussion of the experiment see Siddiqi, 1984).

The most significant result of this experiment was that the percentages of D1 and D2-type decompositions were 91.5% and 8.5% respectively. This result clearly supports the arguments presented above.

In addition, the final check for the longest waiting period was absent in 94% of the D1-type solutions. This can be explained because the 'final check' component forms a part of the overall decomposition structure, but its necessity is not perceived until attention is paid to the requirement to find LWP. This is because the designer's focus of attention is on the lower levels of the design abstraction and design planes and, therefore, the designer 'loses sight' of the overall design structure, which results in the omission of this component. Rumelhart has termed this behavior as being 'sensitive to the local context' (Rumelhart, 1977).

4. CONCLUSION

The model advanced in this paper can describe multi-directional decision-making by means of both hierarchical (i.e., top-down and bottom-up) and heterarchical plan structures for the design process. For example, the data-driven animation, in its initial stages, illustrates a cautious, hierarchical approach interrupted by the action of heterarchical and opportunistic specialists that cause the triggering of the island formulator, which focuses the designer's attention on easily achievable sub-goals, thereby altering the top-down flow of decision-making. Another example of this type of interruption, is the invocation of the island driver specialist, which is needed to fulfill the requirement to compute the longest waiting period. Both of these patterns concur with the results of previous work, that suggest that program design is carried out in an incremental rather than top-down manner.

One result from the experimental work is that subjects' attempts to apply the principles of structured programming to a reasonably simple programming problem yielded relatively high percentages of incorrect and incomplete solutions. The approaches postulated that arrive at these solutions are 'do what you know and what is easy' and 'fit around what has already been done'. If these are generally used, then there are obvious implications for methodologies, training, and the design of IPSE's. Specifically, where attempts are being made to provide adaptive environments, attention must be paid to minimizing the effect of factors that promote the ad hoc usage of such approaches, as well as to the provision of a tool-kit of design criteria and guidelines covering a wide range of different classes of problems. It is our view that an effective method of obtaining these specific requirements and human factors requirements, in general, is through empirical studies.

This model provides an investigative framework for gathering evidence about program designer behavior, through protocol analysis and subsequent hypothesis testing. This involves gathering protocols and then developing an animation that attempts to explain the behavior observed. From this animation predictions can be made and used as the basis for designing and carrying out empirical studies. More importantly, this formulation provides a means of obtaining protocols in a more systematic manner. It identifies crucial points in the decision-making that suggest junctures at which it is important to elicit subjects' clarification of their behavior. This can be achieved either by direct experimenter intervention or by the setting of appropriate sub-problems.

The degree to which the model adequately explains the behavior of a typical designer is currently under investigation. We are attempting to both identify additional specialists and to further characterize those already proposed, by manipulating factors such as problem size and complexity.

REFERENCES

Hayes-Roth, B., and Hayes-Roth, F., 1979, "A Cognitive Model of Planning", Cognitive Science, 3, pp. 275-310.

Jefferies, R., Turner, A. A., Polson, P. G., and Atwood, M. E., 1981, "The Processes Involved in Designing Software", Cognitive Skills and Their Acquisition, Anderson, J., and Hillsdale, J., eds., Lawrence Erlbaum, NJ, Chapter 8.

Ratcliff, B., and Siddiqi, J. I. A., 1985, "An Empirical Investigation into Problem Decomposition Strategies used in Program Design", International Journal of Man-Machine Studies, 22, pp. 77-90.

Rumelhart, D. E., 1977, Introduction to Human Information Processing, John Wiley and Sons.

Siddiqi, J. I. A., 1984, An Empirical Investigation into Problem Decomposition Strategies Used in Program Design, Ph.D. Thesis University of Aston in Birmingham.

Siddiqi, J. I. A., 1986, "How do Software Practitioners Write Programs?: An Empirical Study", The Symposium on Empirical Foundations of Information and Software Sciences, Georgia Institute of Technology, Atlanta, GA.

APPENDIX

Problem Specification

A traffic survey is conducted automatically by placing a detector at the roadside, connected by data-links to a computer. Whenever a vehicle passes the detector, it transmit a signal consisting of the number 1. A clock in the detector is started at the beginning of the survey and, at one second intervals thereafter, it transmits a signal consisting of the number 2. At the end of the survey, the detector transmits a 0. Each signal is received by the computer as a single number (i.e., it is impossible for two signals to arrive at the same time). Design a program which reads such a set of signals and outputs the following:

    (a)   the length of the survey period;
    (b)   the number of vehicles recorded;
    (c)   the length of the longest waiting period without a vehicle.

D1-Type Decomposition:

```
surveylength, vehiclecount, waitperiod, longestwaitperiod := 0
read (signal)
DOWHILE signal <> 0
    IF signal = 1
    THEN
        vehiclecount := vehiclecount + 1
        longestwaitperiod := MAX(waitperiod, longestwaitperiod)
        waitperiod := 0
    ELSE
        waitperiod := waitperiod + 1
        surveylength := surveylength + 1
    ENDIF
    read(signal)
ENDWHILE
```


D2-Type Decomposition

```
surveylength, vehiclecount, longestwaitperiod := 0
read(signal)
DOWHILE signal <> 0
    IF signal = 1
    THEN
        vehiclecount := vehiclecount + 1
    ELSE
        waitperiod := 0
        read(signal)
        DOWHILE signal = 2
            waitperiod := waitperiod + 1
            surveylength := surveylength + 1
            read(signal)
        ENDWHILE
        longestwaitperiod := MAX(waitperiod, longestwaitperiod)
    ENDIF
ENDWHILE
```


Note: In the text, vehiclecount, surveylength, waitperiod, and longestwaitperiod are denoted by VC, SL, WP, and LWP, respectively.

7. SOFTWARE AND SYSTEM PERFORMANCE EVALUATION

AN EVALUATION MODEL FOR DISTRIBUTED COMPUTER SYSTEMS

Jagdish C. Agrawal*, Shan Manickam**, and Aboalfazi Salimi*

*Department of Computer Science
 Embry Riddle Aeronautical University
 Daytona Beach, Florida 32014
**Department of Mathematics and Computer Science
 Western Carolina University
 Cullowhee, North Carolina 28723

Abstract: During the design phase of a distributed computer system, the designer needs to have access to a set of attributes, the amount of which can be used as common units of measure for both the characteristics of the distributed system and the requirements. It is important that these attributes are chosen independent of any particular candidate system.

The designer needs to make quantitative decisions on trade-offs on amounts of attributes and how they affect the final measure of any candidate system relative to the requirements. It is desirable that this decision be based on an evaluation process for selecting an individual distributed system from a set of alternatives on the basis of design decision resulting from different combination of attributes. Measures developed by earlier authors for this type of trade-off analysis are a set of weighted differences of unnormalized surpluses and deficits of various attributes selected for the design process. In this paper, we have developed normalized measures for the surpluses and deficits of the attributes, so that the difference of the two is meaningful.

INTRODUCTION

We limit our discussion to distributed computer systems as defined by Jensen (1987). Gonzalez and Jordan (1980) proposed a framework for the quantitative evaluation of distributed computer systems by relating abstractions to the requirements of the actual system. However, the measures developed by them, which are a set of weighted differences, use unnormalized deficits and surpluses for attributes required in the system. These deficits and surpluses are obtained by dividing the amount of an attribute delivered, by the amount of attribute required, and subtracting 1 from the quotient. Even though these deficits and surpluses are non-dimensional quantities, further normalization is required for a meaningful comparison of a deficit in attribute A with a surplus in attribute B. We are proposing a model for normalizing the deficits and surpluses to measure the extent to which a system satisfies the requirements.

PROBLEM DESCRIPTION

Let the set of A of attributes be:

A = {A_1, A_2, ..., A_n},

in terms of which of the problem requirements and the system characteristics are described. Examples of attributes include:

- Fault Tolerance

- Integrity

- Maintainability

- Modularity

- Performance

- Reconfiguration Potential

- Security

One of the concerns in considering attributes such as the ones listed above is the mutual independence of the attributes themselves. Such an orthogonality is beyond the scope of the current model. We are assuming independence of the attributes in the set A above.

The distributed computer system S consists of m components:

S = {S_1, S_2, ..., S_m}.

Let the set r below define the set of attribute requirements of the desired distributed computer system:

$$r = \{r_1, r_2, ..., r_n\}. \tag{1}$$

where r_i represents the amount of attribute A_i required.

However, in the delivered system S described above, the subsystem S possesses an amount q_{ij} of the attribute A_j. Thus, the matrix:

$$Q = (q_{ij}), \; i = 1, 2, ..., m \text{ and } j = 1, 2, ..., n \tag{2}$$

describes the characteristics of the delivered system (extent to which the delivered system possesses given attributes).

The problem here is to determine how the delivered system compares with the requirements. The delivered system S will have more than required amounts of certain attributes and less than the required amounts of others. The problem then is to determine how do the surpluses of certain attributes compare with the deficits of others.

Alternative statement of the problem is as follows. While designing the distributed computer system, the designer needs to make some trade-off decisions. Each decision will lead to a different matrix Q for the characteristics of the candidate system. The designer needs to make a decision as to which best meets the requirements.

THE PROPOSED EVALUATION MEASURE

Assume that empirical or analytical bounds a_j, b_j for the measure of each attribute A_j are available, and, hence,

$$a_j \leq r_j \leq b_j, \text{ and} \tag{3}$$

$$a_j \leq q_{ij} \leq b_j, \quad i = 1, 2, \ldots, m \text{ and } j = 1, 2, \ldots, n. \tag{4}$$

We define normalized delivery matrix D_{ij} and normalized requirement vector R_j of quotients as

$$D_{ij} = \frac{(q_{ij} - a_j)}{(b_j - a_j)}, \text{ and} \tag{5}$$

$$R_j = \frac{(r_j - a_j)}{(b_j - a_j)}. \tag{6}$$

Further, if weights w_j are available or can be assigned to each individual attribute A_j, $j = 1, 2, \ldots, n$, then a measure of the extent to which the subsystem S_i delivers or possesses the attributes is

$$\sum_{j=1}^{n} D_{ij} w_j.$$

whereas the requirements of attributes add up to

$$\sum_{j=1}^{n} R_j w_j.$$

Upon combining delivery and requirement, we propose the normalized tradeoff measure

$$D = \{D_1, D_2, \ldots, D_m\}. \tag{7}$$

where D_i, the trade-off yielded by the subsystem S_i, is given by

$$D_i = \sum_{j=1}^{n} (D_{ij} - R_j) w_j, \quad i = 1, 2, \ldots, m;$$

$$D_i = \sum_{j=1}^{n} \frac{(q_{ij} - r_j)}{(b_j - a_j)} w_j, \quad i = 1, 2, \ldots, m. \tag{8}$$

This (vector) measure, due to appropriate normalization of deficits and surpluses of attributes, has the advantage of accurately reflecting the extent to which a system actually satisfies the requirements. A comparison of this with the unnormalized measure $D = \{D_1, D_2, \ldots, D_m\}$ of Gonzalez and Jordan (1980) where

$$D_i = \sum_{j=1}^{n} \left(\frac{q_{ij}}{r_j} - 1 \right) w_j,$$

is given in an example below.

Table 1. Weighted Differences for the
Evaluation Example.

A_j	q_{ij}	r_j	$\dfrac{q_{ij}}{r_j} - 1$	$D_{ij} - R_j$
A_1	90	10	+8.00	+0.80
A_2	45	90	−0.50	−0.45
A_3	70	80	−0.125	−0.10
A_4	10	90	−0.889	−0.80

AN EXAMPLE

To show the contrast between the weighted differences of Gonzalez and Jordan and ours, we present an example of a subsystem S_i where the attributes are A_1, A_2, A_3, and A_4, $a_j = 0$, $b_j = 100$, $w_j = 1$ for $j = 1, 2, \ldots, 4$, and the q_{ij}'s, the requirement of r_j's and the two weighted differences are given in Tabular form in Table 1 above.

Gonzalez and Jordan's weighted difference for S_i is:

$$D_i = \sum_{j=1}^{4} \left(\frac{q_{ij}}{r_j} - 1 \right) w_j = +6.486.$$

Our weighted difference for S_i is:

$$D_i = \sum_{j=1}^{4} (D_{ij} - R_j) w_j = -0.55$$

It is interesting to note that the delivered system is deficient in three of the four required attributes. The excess is in the attribute A_1, which was almost not required. Yet the Gonzalez-Jordan theory says that the subsystem S_i of the delivered system has an impressive surplus of the attributes over what was required.

REFERENCES

Jensen, E. D., 1987, "The Honeywell Experimental Distributed Processor -- An Overview", Computer, January 1987, pp. 28-37.

Gonzalez, M. J., Jr., and Jordan, B. W., Jr., 1980, "A Framework for the Quantitative Evaluation of Distributed Computer Systems", IEEE Transactions on Computers, C-29, (12), December 1980.

COMPARISON AND EVALUATION OF FLOATING POINT REPRESENTATIONS IN

IBM/370 AND VAX-11/80

Jagdish C. Agrawal* and Paramjit Singh Sehdev**

*Department of Computer Science
Embry Riddle Aeronautical University
Daytona Beach, FL 32014
**Department of Mathematics and Computer Science
Fairleigh Dickinson University
Teaneck, New Jersey 07666

Abstract: Each computer system supports a set of data types which serve as
standard interfaces between the user and the computer, and between the computer and peripheral devices. There are scientific applications where,
from the user's point of view, the numerical accuracy is an important quality
factor. According to Knuth (1981), the concept of floating point representation can be traced back to Babylonian mathematicians (about 1800 B.C.);
the machine use of floating point representation was independently proposed
by Leonardo Torres y Quevedo (Madrid, 1914), Konrad Zuse (Berlin, 1936),
and George Stibitz (New Jersey, 1939).

Floating point computation is inexact and, if not used properly, it is
entirely possible to come up with answers that may consist almost entirely
of "noise". For scientific applications, it is important to understand the
floating point architecture of the machine being used, and make necessary
accommodations in the algorithms for problem solving. This impacts on the
portability of data across machines.

The authors examined the data types supported by IBM/370 and VAX-11/780
for purposes of comparison and evaluation. The floating point representations in the two present some interesting comparisons that are summarized
in the theories derived in the paper. We found the magnitude range of
values on a 4-byte long storage area is better for IBM than for VAX. However, for a certain range of values, VAX has a better precision than IBM on
a 4-byte long floating point representation. Similar results for double
and quad word floating point numbers on the two machines have also been
provided.

We use our analysis to identify steps to be taken towards building a
methodology that offers a high degree of portability and interoperability
of data across different hardware architectures.

1.   INTRODUCTION

Portability and interoperability of large applications programs is dependent on many things and can be helped by providing common standard interfaces like KAPSE or Unix-like environments. However, differences in instruction set architectures and internal data representation of the hardware present challenges to portability and interoperability of programs, especially where micro and macro arithmetic and scientific computations are important. Jean Sammet (1969) in her classic book on programming languages made a similar observation:

> "Two of the machine features which tend to 'ruin' compatibility most are word size and collating sequence; actually both of these could be corrected by the compiler -- but at prohibitive cost. The word size effects the precision and sometimes even the actual results of numeric calculations because numbers are usually stored in one or two machine words."

In this paper we will examine various numeric data representations in the IBM/370 and VAX-11/80 with the intent of examining the portability and interoperability issues with regard to the data; and identifying steps to be taken towards building a methodology that offers a high degree of portability and interoperability of data across different hardware environments.

We begin by first examining some of the numeric data types supported on the IBM/370 and VAX-11/780.

2.   DATA TYPES

A data type is a term that refers to the kind of data. Each computer system supports a set of data types. Some of the widely used data types include: Integer, Real, Character, Packed Decimal, Variable-length bit field, etc. In this paper we shall discuss the data types supported by the IBM/370 machine and the VAX-11/780.

2.1 Data Types Supported by IBM

IBM/370 supports a wide variety of data types. These data types are listed in Table I in alphabetic order.

Table I.
Data Types Supported by IBM/370

SYMBOL	DATA TYPE
A	Address
B	Binary Bit Sequence
C	Character
D	Double Precision Floating Point
E	Single Precision Floating Point
F	Fixed Point
H	Half Word
L	Extended Form Floating Point
P	Packed Decimal
Q	Address
S	Address
V	External Symbol Reference
X	Hexadecimal
Y	Half Word Address
Z	Zoned Decimal

Table II.
Primary Data Types Supported by IBM/370

PRIMARY DATA TYPE	SYMBOLS
INTEGER	F and H
FLOATING POINT	E, D, and L
CHARACTER (OR TEXT)	C
DECIMAL NUMBER	P and Z
BIT STRING	B
HEXADECIMAL STRING	X
ADDRESS	A, V, Y, S, and Q

The listed types in Table I belong to one of the primary data types known as integers, floating points, character, decimals, bit strings, hexadecimal strings and addresses as listed in Table II.

2.2 Data Types Supported by VAX-11/780

VAX-11/780 support six primary data types -- Integer, Floating Point, Character, Packed Decimal, Variable-length bit field, and Queue. Out of these data types, the integer and floating point support a variety of variations. These are shown in Table III.

3. MEMORY TERMINOLOGY OF IBM AND VAX

For clarity of discussion, we will first explain the memory terminology of IBM and VAX machines.

On IBM, the smallest unit of memory is called a bit and can assume the value 0 or 1. The other units of memory are:

Byte   = 8 contiguous bits

Word   = 4 contiguous bytes

Half word   = 2 contiguous bytes

Double word = 8 contiguous bytes

On VAX, the smallest unit of memory is also called a bit. Byte is the next higher unit of memory and consists of 8 contiguous bits. The other

Table III.
Integer and Floating Point Data Types Supported by Vax-11/780

Integer	Byte, Word, Longword Quadword, & Octaword
Floating Point	F-floating, D-floating, G-floating, & H-floating

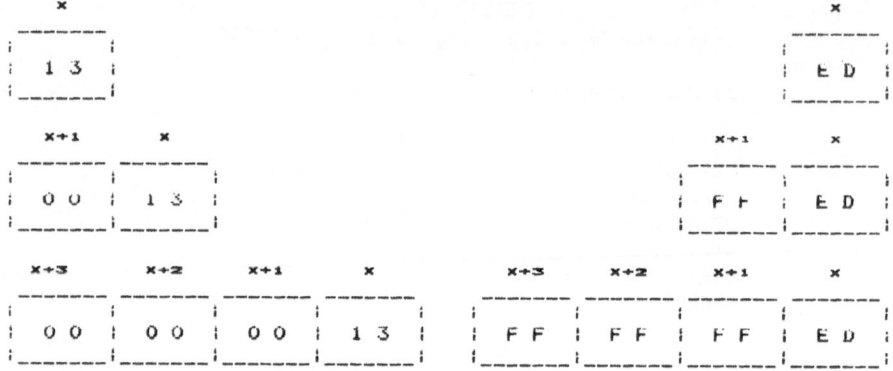

Figure 1. Representation of Integers of Example 3.1.

units of memory are:

Word   =   2 contiguous bytes

Longword   =   4 contiguous bytes

Quadword   =   8 contiguous bytes

Octaword   =   16 contiguous bytes

We shall use the above terminology of the IBM and the VAX and depend on the context for the meaning. If we feel that the context is insufficient to clarify, we shall specifically mention the machine name.

The address of a storage unit for an integer data type is the address of the lowest byte within the storage unit both for the IBM and the VAX. The least significant bits of the binary number are stored in the low addressed byte and the most significant bits of the binary number are stored towards the high addressed bytes. The following example is used to illustrate this point.

Example 3.1

Representation of integers, +19 and -19, in 1, 2, and 4 bytes respectively starting at address X (Figure 1).

4.   INTEGER DATA TYPE

Signed integers are represented according to the rules below on both the IBM and the VAX:

(i)   binary equivalent for non-negative integers, and

(ii) two's complement form explained below for negative integers.

● find binary representation of the absolute value of the integer, then

● complement all the bits, and

● add 1 to the complemented result.

Table IV.
Range of Values for Integer Data Types on IBM/370 and VAX-11/780

Size In Bytes	IBM Data Type	VAX Data Type	Range of Values
1	n.a.	Byte	-128 to +127
2	Half word	Word	-32768 to +32767
4	Full word	Longword	-2 to $+2$ -1
8	n.a.	Quadword	-2 to $+2$ -1
16	n.a.	Octaword	-2 to $+2$ -1

On the VAX, a signed integer could be represented using a byte, word, longword, quadword, or octaword. The IBM supports only two integer representations -- full word and half word. Table IV shows various integer data types for both the IBM and the VAX and the range of values.

From Table IV we observe that the VAX has a larger variety of integer data representations than the IBM. The VAX has instructions that operate upon these data types to optimize the use of memory for small ranges of signed integers.

The quadword and octaword sizes provide an optimal usage of the memory for some large numbers (e.g., $2^{63}-1 = 9,223,772,036,854,775,808$ could be represented in a quadword of storage as compared to 10 bytes of storage for its packed decimal representation -- a 20% storage saving!).

5.   FLOATING POINT DATA TYPE

Floating point numbers are represented in the normalized form on both the IBM and the VAX. The user expressed decimal form is converted by the assembler into the normalized form, which is then coded in the machine form.

The word normalized has different meanings for IBM and VAX machines as described below.

5.1 Normalized Form for IBM

The normalized form of a decimal number is

$$\pm H \times 16^P = \pm 0.h_1 h_2 \ldots \times 16^P$$

where p is a positive or negative integer, $h_1 > 0$, and each h_k is a hexadecimal digit. The following example compares the IBM normalized form to unnormalized form.

Example 5.1

unnormalized form	normalized form
$0.6B2 \times 16^2$	$0.6B2 \times 16^1$
$-0.000C9 \times 16^{10}$	$-0.C9 \times 16^7$

357

A floating point number is represented with a radix of 16 on the IBM/370 which is the reason that these machines are called hexadecimal machines with respect to floating point.

5.2 Normalized Form for VAX

In the case of VAX, the normalized form of a decimal number is

$$\pm 0.1b_2b_3 \ldots \times 2^p$$

where p is a positive or a negative integer and each of b_k is a binary digit. The base or radix of the normalized form of a floating point number in a VAX machine is 2, which makes the VAX a binary machine with respect to floating point.

Both IBM and VAX support 4, 8, and 16 byte representation of floating point numbers. The IBM allows three data types for floating point numbers -- E, D, and L. The VAX permits four different data types for the floating point numbers -- F floating, D floating, G floating, and H floating. For the sake of clarity we shall subscript these types with i for IBM discussion and v for the VAX machine. Therefore, in our discussion E_i, D_i, and L_i would refer to E, D, and L data types of IBM and F_v, D_v, G_v, and H_v would stand for F, D, G, and H floating point data types of VAX respectively.

5.3 Three Fields in a Normalized Form

We have seen above that the normalized form of a floating point number is

$$sf \times r^p = s0.f_1f_2 \ldots f_n \times r^p$$

where s, f, r, and p are the sign, mantissa, radix (base), and signed power respectively. The radix r is assumed by the machine and, therefore, not coded as a part of the representation.

5.3.1 Sign Field s.
The sign s is either + or - and could be represented in a bit of storage. The convention for the representation of the sign is same for both the IBM and the VAX machines and the sign bit is coded as 0 when s is positive, and 1 when s is negative.

5.3.2 Mantissa Field f.
The number of bits used by the mantissa fields for various floating point data types of IBM and VAX are shown in Table V. In IBM, the radix r is 16 and the f_k's are hexadecimal digits. In VAX, the radix r is 2, the f_k's are binary digits, and $f_1 = 1$. VAX does not code f_1, instead the VAX assembler and CPU take care of this implied f_1 = 1 at the time of assembly and execution respectively.

5.3.3 Exponent Field p.
The exponent field usually consists of two subfields -- its sign and its absolute value. However, on both the IBM and the VAX, a special technique of expressing the actual exponent as a biased exponent is used to enhance the efficiency of the internal operations of the floating point fields.

The actual exponent is coded as a biased exponent which is obtained by adding a number, called biased quantity, to the actual exponent to get the biased exponent. The value of this biased quantity depends upon the number of bits used for the exponent field in the representation of a floating number. To be more precise the biased quantity is chosen so that it may almost represent an equal number of negative and positive exponents. This in mathematical terms means that, if t bits are used to represent the exponent field. Then the biased quantity equals 2^{t-1}. Table VI shows the

Table V.
Mantissa Fields for Floating Point Data Types of IBM and VAX

Data Type	Number of Bits For Mantissa
E_i	24
D_i	56
L_i	112
F_v	23
D_v	55
G_v	52
H_v	112

Mantissa field: the number of fractional bits for various floating point data types.

number of bits used by various floating point data types for the IBM and the VAX machines, along with the biased quantities.

5.4 Example of IBM Exponent Field

In the IBM normalized floating point numbers

$+0.C29 \times 16^{19}$ and $+0.C29 \times 16^{-19}$

the true exponents are +19 and −19. Since each of the three data types,

Table VI.
Exponent field: Number Of Bits Used And The Corresponding Biased Quantity.

Data Type	No of bits Used For The Exponent Field t	The Biased Quantity 2^{t-1}
E_i	7	$2^{7-1} = 64$
D_i	7	$2^{7-1} = 64$
L_i	7	$2^{7-1} = 64$
F_v	8	$2^{8-1} = 128$
D_v	8	$2^{8-1} = 128$
G_v	11	$2^{11-1} = 1028$
H_v	15	$2^{15-1} = 16384$

E_i, D_i, and L_i have 7 bit exponent fields, the biased quantity is $2^{7-1} = 64$. After adding this biased quantity 64, the biased exponents of the above two IBM normalized floating point numbers are 83 and 45.

5.5 Example of VAX Exponent Field

In the VAX normalized floating point numbers

$+0.11001 \times 2^{23}$ and $+0.11001 \times 2^{-23}$

the true exponents are +23 and −23. Table VII gives the biased quantity, biased exponent, and binary representation of the biased exponent of the true exponents +23 and −23.

5.6 Four Byte Long Floating Point Data Representation

E_i in IBM and F_v in VAX are four byte long data types for the floating point numbers. Before we can proceed further, we need to explain the IBM and VAX memory representation terminology.

5.7 Memory Diagram

IBM represents a string of bytes of memory with the lowest address on the left, and the highest address on the right. For VAX, the address increases from right to left. Figure 2 illustrates this.

5.8 Bit Reference

Figure 3 clarifies the bit reference for IBM and VAX machines. The A in the picture is the address of a byte.

5.9 Floating Point – E_i

The floating point number s $0.h_1 \ldots h_2 \times 16^P$ is coded for the IBM machine as shown in Figure 4. Bit number 0 represents the sign of the floating point number; bits 1 through 7 represent the characteristic p of the floating point number. Bits 8 through 31 represent the 24 bit long mantissa field.

The range of floating point values that could be represented in the E_i format is as shown in Figure 5.

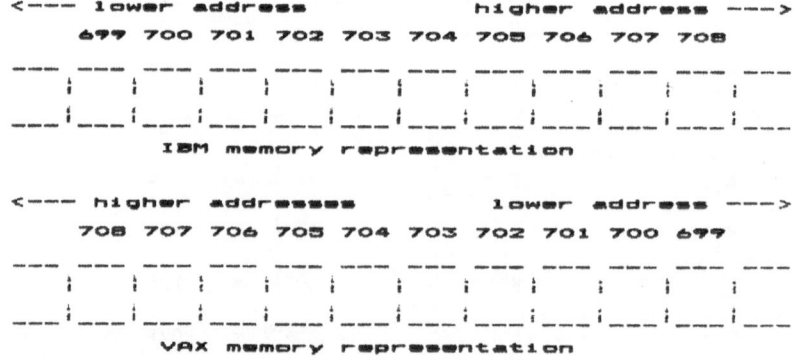

Figure 2. IBM and VAX Memory Representation.

Table VII.
Biased Quantity, Exponent and Binary Representation of Biased Exponent.

True expo nent	Data Type	No of Bits Used For Exponent Field (t)	Biased Quantity	Biased Exponent	Binary Represen- tation of the Biased Exponent
+23	F_V	8	128	23+128 = 151	10010111
+23	D_V	8	128	23+128 = 151	10010111
+23	G_V	11	1024	23+1024 = 1047	10000010111
+23	H_V	15	16384	23+16384 = 16407	100000000010111
-23	F_V	8	128	-23+128 = 105	01101001
-23	D_V	8	128	-23+128 = 105	01101001
-23	G_V	11	1024	-23+1024 = 1001	01111101001
-23	H_V	15	16384	-23+16384 = 16361	011111111101001

5.10 Floating Point - F_v

The normalized floating point number

$$s\ 0.1\ b_1 b_2\ \dots\ b_{24}\ x\ 2^P$$

is coded for the VAX machine, in the F_v format, as shown in Figure 6.

Since the main unit of memory in VAX is a word, Figure 7 better illustrates the configuration of the various fields where s is 1 for +, and 0 for -. The true value p of the exponent is represented as $p + 2^7$. The mantissa is represented in 23 bits. The range of values that could be represented by the F_v data type on the VAX machine is as shown in Figure 8.

Theorem 1

The magnitude range of values on a 4 byte long storage area is better for E_i than F_v.

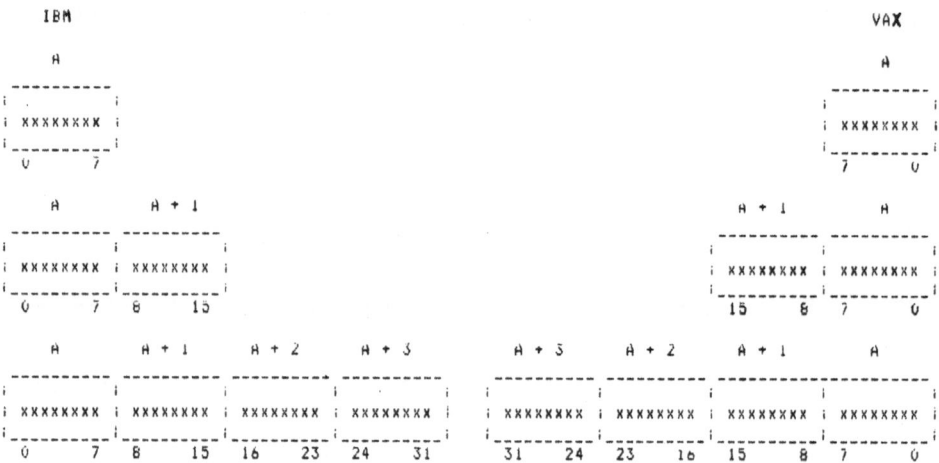

Figure 3. Bit Reference for IBM and VAX Machines.

Proof

The magnitude range of values for E_i format is

$$R\ (E_i) = 5.4\ x\ 10^{-79}\ to\ 7.2\ x\ 10^{75}$$

and the magnitude range of values for F_v format is

$$R\ (F_v) = 2.9387\ x\ 10^{-79}\ to\ 1.7\ x\ 10^{38}$$

It immediately follows that: $R\ (F_v) < R\ (E_i)$

COROLLARY 1

Porting from the VAX-11/780 to the IBM-370, full range of data values on 4 byte long floating point representation being used on the VAX-11/780 will be accommodated on the IBM-370. However, the next theorem will offer results regarding arithmetical precision on such porting.

COROLLARY 2

Porting from the IBM-370 to the VAX-11/780, some steps (to be identified in later theorems) will be necessary so that full range of data values on four byte long floating point representation being used on the IBM-370 can be accommodated on the VAX-11/780.

Theorem 2

In the range of values from

2^{-124} to $0.111111111111111111111111 \times 2^{127}$

Figure 4.   Coding of s $0.h_1 h_2 \ldots h_6 \times 16^P$ for IBM.

the VAX has better precision than IBM on a four byte long floating point representation.

Proof

Part 1.   First we will prove that every IBM normalized number in the range

2^{-124} to $0.111111111111111111111111 \times 2^{127}$

could be represented in VAX normalized form n_v.

Let n_i be such a number and h_1, h_2, $\ldots$ h_6 be hexadecimal digits with $h_1 > 0$ and an appropriate integer p, such that

$n_i = 0.h_1 h_2 \ldots h_6 \times 16^P$

Sign	Range of values
Positive	16^{-65} to $16^{63} \cong 10^{-78.2678}$ to $10^{75.8576}$ $\cong 5.4 \times 10^{-79}$ to 7.2×10^{75}
Negative	-16^{-65} to $-16^{63} \cong -5.4 \times 10^{-79}$ to $-7.2 \times 10^{+75}$

Figure 5. Range of Floating Point Numbers in E_i Format.

We note that $16P = 2^4P$. It immediately follows that $-124 \leq 4p \leq 127$. Further, each of the hexadecimal digits is represented as four contiguous bits of binary digits:

$$h_1 = b_{11}\ b_{12}\ b_{13}\ b_{14}$$

$$h_2 = b_{21}\ b_{22}\ b_{23}\ b_{24}$$

$$h_3 = b_{31}\ b_{32}\ b_{33}\ b_{34}$$

$$h_4 = b_{41}\ b_{42}\ b_{43}\ b_{44}$$

$$h_5 = b_{51}\ b_{52}\ b_{53}\ b_{54}$$

$$h_6 = b_{61}\ b_{62}\ b_{63}\ b_{64}$$

Up to m ($0 \leq m \leq 3$) leading bits in the binary expansion:

$$h_1 = b_{11}\ b_{12}\ b_{13}\ b_{14}$$

may be zero preceding the first non-zero bit. Thus, n_i could be rewritten as

$$n_i = 0.1b_2 \ldots b_{24} \times 2^{4p-m}$$

by dropping the leading m zero bits and adding m bits on the right padded with zeroes to keep it a 24 bit mantissa field. It is now clear that $-128 < 4p - m < 127$. Therefore, the VAX normalized form

$$n_v = 0.1\ b_2 \ldots b_{24} \times 2^{4p-m}$$

could be represented as F floating point number.

Figure 6. Normalized Floating Point Number $s\ 0.1b_1b_2 \ldots b_{24} \times 2^P$ Coded in F_v Format.

<u>Part 2</u>. We will now prove that there is at least one n_v in the range

2^{-124} to $0.11111111111111111111111111 \times 2^{127}$

that can be represented in the n_i form but cannot be coded into the E_i format.

Select an integer p such that: $-124 \le p \le 127$ and $mod(p,4) = 1, 2,$ or 3.

The exponent p could be written as $p = 4q - m$, where $m = 1, 2,$ or 3.

Therefore,

$n_v = 0.1b_2 \ldots b_{24} \times 2^p$

$\quad = 0.1b_2 \ldots b_{24} \times 16^q \times 2^{-m}$

The net effect of 2^{-m} is to insert m leading zero bits following the decimal. Since only 24 bits can be used for the mantissa field in the E_i format, the trailing m bits above can not be coded into the E_i format. Since $m \ge 1$, at least one bit is lost. Therefore, what is coded in E_i format is a different number than the n_v that we started out with.

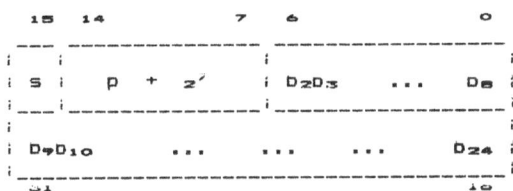

Figure 7. F_v Format Representation for s $0.1b_1b_2 \ldots b_{24} \times 2^p$.

COROLLARY 3

Although in going from the VAX-11/780 to the IBM-370, full range of data values in 4 byte long floating point representation being used on the VAX-11/780 will be accommodated on the IBM-370, loss of precision is more

Sign	Range of values
Positive	2^{-128} to $2^{127} \doteq 2.9387 \times 10^{-39}$ to 1.7×10^{38}
Negative	-2^{-128} to $-2^{127} \doteq -2.9387 \times 10^{-39}$ to -1.7×10^{38}

Figure 8. Range of Values for F_v Data Types on Vax Machine.

```
         ---  --------  -----------------------------
        i    i        i                             i
        i s  i p + 64  i h₁n₂    ...    ...   h₁₃n₁₄ i
        i___ i_____ i_____i
bits --->  0   1      7  8                          63
```

Figure 9. D_i Format Representation for a $0.h_1h_2 \ldots h_{13}h_{14} \times 16^P$.

likely. If precision is important then longer floating point representation on the IBM-370 will have to be considered.

5.11 Eight Byte Long Floating Point Data Representation

Both the IBM and the VAX support 8 byte representation of floating point numbers for a better precision and magnitude range. The IBM has one format in 8 byte representation that we will refer to as D_v. The VAX provides two different formats each using 8 bytes of storage and we shall refer to these as D_v and G_v for our discussion.

5.12 Floating Point - D_i

Using hexadecimal digits h_k and s for the sign,, the normalized number

$n_i = s \ 0.h_1 \ldots h_{14} \times 16^P$

is coded in D_i format as shown in Figure 9.

5.13 Floating Point - D_v

The normalized number $n_v = s.0.1b_2 \ldots b_{56} \times 2^P$, is coded in D_v format as shown in Figure 10.

For better readability, we have redrawn the representation in Figure 10 as four consecutive words as shown in Figure 11.

5.14 Floating Point - G_v

The normalized number $n_v = s \ 0.1b_2 \ldots b_{53} \times 2^P$ is coded in G_v format as shown in Figure 12. Again, as before, in order to improve readability, we have redrawn the above representation as four consecutive words as shown in Figure 13.

Table VIII summarizes the three fields of normalized floating point numbers that are stored in D_i, D_v, and G_v formats.

The IBM machine provides the D_i format for basically a better precision as compared to its E_i format. As a result, there is a slight improvement on the magnitude range also. The number of bits used for the exponent field is again 7, the same as in the case of E_i. However, the number of bits

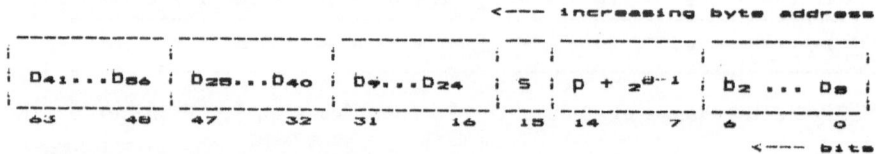

Figure 10. D_v Format Representation for a $0.1b_2b_3 \ldots b_{56} \times 2^P$.

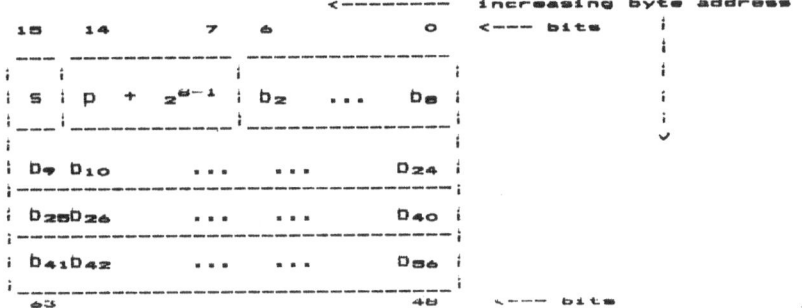

Figure 11. D_v Format Representation for s 0.1 b_2b_3 ... b_{56} x 2^P.

used for the mantissa is considerably higher than as in E_i.

In D_i format the mantissa is coded in 56 bits.

The exponent fields in D_v and G_v formats, respectively, are 8 and 11 bit long. As a result, the magnitude range for G_v is much better than that of D_v. On the other hand, the number of bits for mantissa field is 55 and 52 bits for D_v and G_v, respectively. Therefore, in the magnitude range

$$0.29 \times 10^{-38} \text{ to } 1.7 \times 10^{38} \quad \text{(approximately)}$$

the D_v has a better precision than G_v. And clearly in comparison to the F_v type

- the D_v type provides almost the same magnitude range as F_v type. However, the precision is better by two times of F_v.

- the G_v type offers not only a better magnitude range than F_v type, but also provides a much better (by two times) precision.

The following result gives a relationship between the magnitude range for D_i, D_v, and G_v.

Theorem 3

The magnitude range R (x) for x, where x = D_i, D_v, or G_v, satisfy

R (D_v) < R (D_i) < R (G_v)

Proof

The result follows by observing the following carefully:

R (D_v) = 0.29 x 10-38 to 1.7 x 1038,

R (D_i) = 5.4 x 10-79 to 7.2 x 1078, and

Figure 12. G_v Format Representation for s 0.1b_2b_3 ... b_{53} x 2^P.

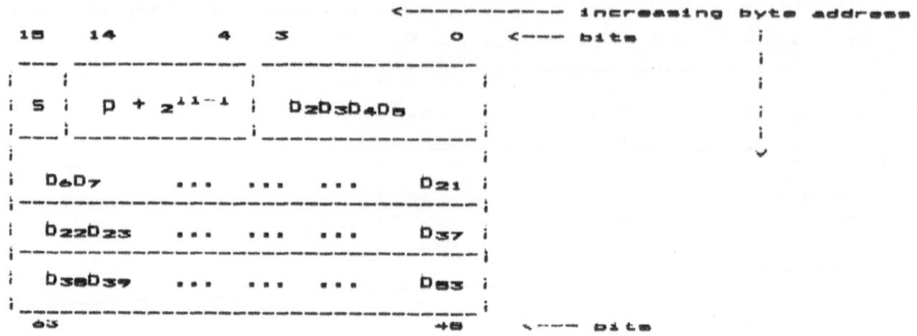

Figure 13. G_V Format Representation for s 0.1 b_2b_{53} ... b_{53} x 2P.

$R(G_V) = 0.56$ x 10^{-308} to 0.9 x 10^{308}.

We have similar results for the precision of floating numbers.

Theorem 4

The range of mantissa values $P(x)$, where $x = D_i$, D_v, G_v, satisfies

$P(G_v) < P(D_i) < P(D_v)$

Proof

Part 1. First we prove that $P(G_v) < P(D_i)$.

Table VIII.
Summary of D_i, D_v, and G_v Representations.

| Data type | Bit field* for | | | | | |
| | sign s | | exponent | | fraction | |
	bit no	no of bits	bit field	no of bits	bit field	no of bits
D_I	0	1	1 – 7	7	8 – 63	56
D_v	15	1	7 – 14	8	0 – 6 and 16 – 63	55
G_v	15	1	4 – 14	11	0 – 3 and 16 – 63	52

*The bit numbers mentioned in the table refers
to the terminology of the machine. That is, bit number
0 of 8 byte storage unit of IBM refers to bit number
63 of the corresponding 8 byte storage of VAX.

Consider the VAX normalized floating point number, n_v, to be coded into G_v format

$$n_v = 0.1b_2\ b_3\ \ldots\ b_{53}\ x\ 2^P$$

This could be rewritten as

$$n_v = 0.f_i\ \ldots\ f_m1b_2\ \ldots\ b_{53}\ x\ 2^P\ x\ 2^m$$

$$= 0.f_i\ \ldots\ f_m1b_2\ \ldots\ b_{53}\ x\ 2^{P+m}$$

where each $f_i = 0$ and $m = 0, 1, 2,$ or 3. The m is chosen so that the exponent $p + m$ is a multiple of 4, say $p + m = 4q$, so that the corresponding form n_i of n_v would be

$$n\ = 0.f_i\ \ldots\ f_m1b_2\ \ldots\ b_{53}\ x\ 2^{4q}$$

$$= 0.f_i\ \ldots\ f_m1b_2\ \ldots\ b_{53}\ x\ 16^q$$

Clearly this could be coded into the D_i format, without losing any precision.

<u>Part 2.</u> Now, we prove that $P\ (D_i) < P\ (D^v)$.

Since both D_i and D_v have equal number of bits in the mantissa field, the above inequality could be proved on similar lines of argument as in Theorem 2.

REFERENCES

Knuth, D. E., 1981, <u>The Art of Computer Programming, Volume 2: Seminumerical Algorithms</u>, Addison-Wesley Publishing Company, Reading, MA.

Sammet, Jean E., 1969, <u>PROGRAMMING LANGUAGES: History and Fundamentals</u>, Prentice Hall, Englewood Cliffs, NJ.

INVESTIGATING DOWNTIME AND TROUBLESHOOTING IN COMPUTER-CONTROLLED PRODUCTION

SYSTEMS

Susan R. Bereiter* and Steven M. Miller**

*Ph.D. Candidate
Department of Engineering and Public Policy
Carnegie Mellon University
Pittsburgh, PA 15213
**Assistant Professor
Graduate School of Industrial Administration
Carnegie Mellon University
Pittsburgh, PA 15213

Abstract: Some manufacturers, who have invested in sophisticated computer-
controlled production equipment, are finding that the technologies do not
perform as well as initially expected. While these new automated systems
hold the potential for a company to regain a competitive edge by increasing
product quality, decreasing production costs, and increasing flexibility,
users of such systems are finding that the new production processes are
difficult to keep operating. Downtime is a major problem and is expensive
in terms of repair costs and lost revenue. The first issue addressed in this
study is the extent to which downtime, in general, and maintainability, in
particular, is a problem in computer-controlled production systems. We
addressed this issue by analyzing failure data in a computer-controlled
production process in the automobile industry. This analysis indicates that
downtime is a problem and that problems with maintainability are a major
contributing factor to the large amounts of downtime. The second issue
addressed is the relative contributions of different kinds of failures to
downtime and maintainability problems. Addressing this issue can help
guide the focus of efforts to reduce downtime. Anecdotal evidence suggests
that difficulty in troubleshooting failures via the computerized process
controllers is driving the maintainability problems. Analysis of the same
failure data mentioned above supports this evidence. The last issue raised
is the question of what can be done to design a system of computer-controlled
machines so that the system is more maintainable. We propose an experimental
design to address this issue. The experiment focuses on two factors which
we hypothesize contribute to troubleshooting difficulty and which are also
design variables under the control of system designers. These two factors
are complexity of the process control logic in the computerized process
controllers in the system design and hierarchical arrangement of display
pages in the design of the user interfaces.

INTRODUCTION

This research is motivated by a critical problem of growing importance in the application of computer-controlled production technologies. Some manufacturers that invested in sophisticated computer-controlled production equipment are finding that the technologies do not perform as well as initially expected. While these new automated systems hold the potential for a company to regain a competitive edge by increasing product quality, decreasing production costs, and increasing flexibility, users of such systems are finding that the new production processes are difficult to keep operating. Downtime is a major problem and is expensive in terms of repair costs and lost revenue. The automobile industry, a leader in the application of computer-controlled production systems, has indicated that it plans to slow down the rate of investments in computer-controlled production systems; partly because downtime is more excessive and production systems are more costly to maintain than expected (Levin, 1986; Nag, 1986; Mitchell, 1986; and Winter, 1986).

This research addresses three questions:

1) To what extent is downtime, in general, and maintainability, in particular, a problem in computer-controlled production systems?

2) Where should efforts to reduce downtime be focused?

3) What can be done to design a system of computer-controlled machines so that the system is more maintainable?

The first and second questions are being addressed by an analysis of plant-based field data on failure frequency and downtime in component and assembly plants in the automotive industry. Newly automated systems in the automobile industry have been chosen for analysis because they represent state-of-the-art applications of computer-controlled production equipment. Their downtime characteristics should be representative of downtime characteristics of computer-controlled production systems that are currently under design. Therefore, the results of this study can help future design efforts to reduce downtime in computer-controlled production systems. These plants have also been chosen because we have access to the types of information required to conduct the analysis.

The first question is motivated by the desire to empirically investigate recent claims about downtime and maintainability difficulty in computer-controlled production systems. The question is also driven by the need to understand more thoroughly the relationship between the degree of sophistication of computer control of a production system and the extent of downtime difficulty in that system. Downtime data are being analyzed in terms of downtime as a percent of production time, number of failures per production hour (i.e., reliability), and downtime per failure (i.e., maintainability). Understanding the extent to which reliability and maintainability are problematic will help guide future efforts to reduce downtime in computer-controlled production systems. The research plan is to collect and analyze downtime data from several plants which vary in terms of extent of computer control, kinds of products and processes, volume, and product mix. So far, collection and preliminary analysis have been performed for data from one part of one plant: the body shop of a vehicle assembly plant that was modernized to include large amounts of computer control. The results of this analysis are presented in this report. These results indicate that downtime is a problem in the system studied, and that the problem is driven more by difficulty in maintainability than by difficulty in reliability.

The purpose of the second question is to investigate the relative effects of different kinds of failures on downtime and maintainability difficulty. If certain kinds of failures can be pinpointed as particularly troublesome, then these failures can be the focus of research attention. One approach used to address this issue is an investigation of whether certain kinds of equipment are more troublesome in terms of downtime as a percent of production time, frequency of failures, or downtime per failure. Another approach used in this study involves investigating whether failures requiring different forms of diagnosis are more troublesome in terms of the same measures. Results of these analyses on the data from the body shop of the vehicle assembly plant are also included in this report. The preliminary results indicate that maintainability is a more severe problem for failures which require diagnosis through the process control logic than for failures which do not require this computer-based diagnosis. No differences in maintainability can be seen from the comparison of failures in different kinds of equipment.

The underlying hypothesis behind the third question is that improving a troubleshooter's ability to locate and diagnose faults in computer-controlled production systems will shorten the mean time to repair failures, and thus help alleviate downtime problems in these systems. The approach used to address this question focuses on the effects of two particular design factors on fault diagnosis. These two factors are the complexity of the process control logic of the process controllers in the design of the system and the hierarchical arrangement of the display pages in the design of the user interfaces. We are interested in investigating how these design factors affect troubleshooting performance, and which aspects of the troubleshooting process are most strongly affected by these two design factors.

The third question will be addressed through an experimental study. Subjects will be presented with representations of a manufacturing system which contains a fault. Each subject will be asked to diagnose the fault. Troubleshooting performance will be measured as the time and the number of tests required to diagnose a fault. The complexity of the process control logic and the hierarchical display of this logic will be varied between tests to investigate how these two factors and their interactions affect troubleshooting performance.

The experimental study is also concerned with why troubleshooting performance depends on the complexity of the system design and the hierarchical arrangement of the display pages. To address this question, we will study closely the troubleshooting process of the experiment subjects. We will analyze the information acquisition behavior of the subjects to look for indications that the subjects had difficulty because of the paging arrangement or because of the complexity of the manufacturing process being diagnosed. Some indications of problems might be frequent page changes or repeated requests for the same information. We are also considering modelling the troubleshooting process using a modified production system model of human problem solving (Newell and Simon, 1972). The production system model describes human problem solving as a list of situation-action rules (productions) with conflict resolution rules used to choose a production when more than one are applicable. Using a production system model, problem-solving difficulties would appear as poor choices of rules.

The design of this experiment is presented in this report. This discussion includes a description of the experiment environment, the measurement of independent and dependent variables, the choice of subjects, the structure of the tests, and steps taken to minimize confounding effects.

INVESTIGATING DOWNTIME IN COMPUTER-CONTROLLED PRODUCTION SYSTEMS

To investigate downtime in computer-controlled production systems, we are analyzing data collected by plant personnel about failure downtimes and frequencies. Data are being collected from several newly built or modernized component manufacturing and final assembly plants in the automobile industry. So far, data from one part of one plant have been collected and analyzed. This section describes conclusions based on this analysis. From our exposure to other such manufacturing facilities, we believe that the results of this field study are generally true. However, we will be able to test the generality of what we report here and make more substantial conclusions when we have completed the analysis of data from all the plants in the study.

The data described here are from the body shop of a vehicle assembly plant which was modernized during the summer of 1984. In the body shop of a vehicle assembly plant, stamped metal components are fit together and welded in place to form the structural body of the vehicle. In this particular body shop, nearly all of the spot welds are performed by computer-controlled automatic press welders and robots. Transfer and positioning of the workpieces between stations is also done automatically via conveyors and shuttles. Most of the loading and fitting of parts, however, is still done manually by operators.

The downtime data collected cover a one-year period between February 28, 1985 and March 1, 1986. The modernized plant began production nearly six months before the start of this data collection period. Downtime data for the first six months of production are not included in this analysis because the plant was still in a "startup and debug" mode of operation, running at only a fraction of its planned rate of output. At the beginning of the period for which data were collected, the plant was approaching "full production" levels, achieving nearly 90 percent of its target output rate during a normally scheduled five-day work week.

Data on downtime at this plant were originally recorded by data processing personnel, production line operators, and production supervisors. The personnel at the plant use these data on a daily and weekly basis to pinpoint particular machines or groups of machines within the plant which need the attention of the maintenance staff. Failures are categorized into about 50 categories, according to the kind of machine that failed and the kind of failure that occurred (e.g., electrical, mechanical, or hydraulic failures.) Each time there is a failure, the cause of the failure is categorically noted and the total downtime associated with that failure is recorded. The data are then aggregated each week into summary reports which describe the total amount of downtime and the frequency of each failure category for each conveyor line of the body shop during that week.

Is Failure Downtime A Problem?

The extent of the downtime problem in this particular computer-controlled production system is analyzed first by estimating the percent of total production time that was lost because of failures. This estimate was calculated for each week and plotted as weekly averages for the year under study (see Figure 1). An exact measure of the fraction of time that the body shop was stopped due to failures is not available from existing data because the automated system is organized into seven major conveyor segments which are separated by accumulators (i.e. storage buffers) which hold work in process. When there is a breakdown within one conveyor segment, machines on conveyors behind the problem can continue producing until their accumulators are full and machines on conveyors after the problem can continue producing until their accumulators are empty. Thus, one cannot simply calculate the total amount of downtime by summing the downtimes for each recorded line stoppage, as one could do if the entire body shop were one single conveyor without storage buffers.

Plant personnel collect downtime data separately for each of the major

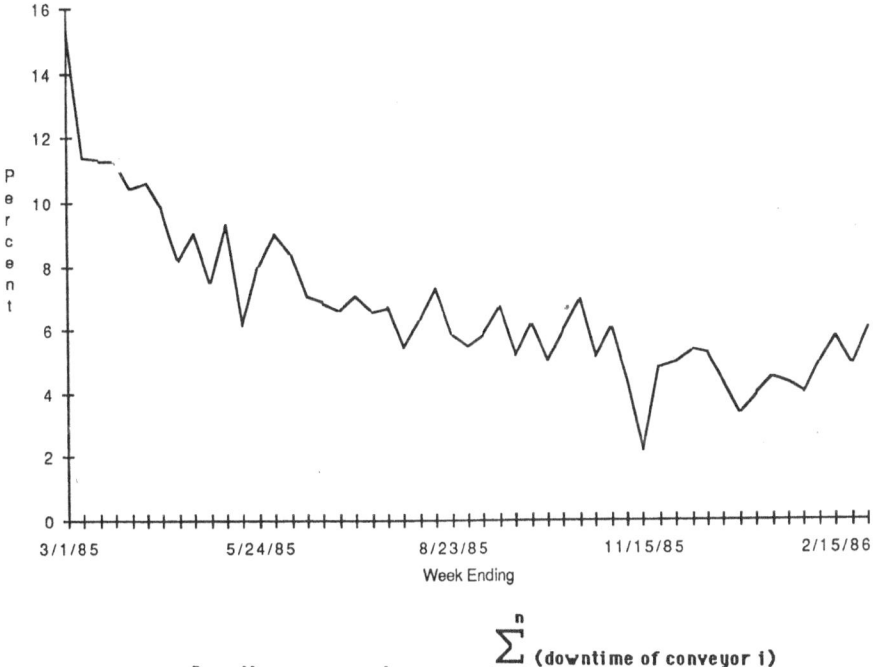

$$\text{Downtime as percent production time} \quad = \quad \frac{\sum_{i=1}^{n} (\text{downtime of conveyor i})}{n * (\text{clock hours of production})}$$

where n = number of conveyors (in this case, 7)

Figure 1. Downtime Expressed as Percent of Production Time.

conveyor segments. If one simply aggregated the downtime across all the major conveyor segments, there could be more hours of downtime than there are scheduled hours of production in a given time period. Given the way the automated system is designed and the failure data are organized, we assume that for each hour of clock time the body shop is operating, there are actually seven hours of machine processing time (one machine processing hour for each of the seven major conveyor segments is divided by the total amount of machine processing time to obtain the system-wide average percent of time that production is stopped due to failures). This measure is only an approximation. The major conveyor segments are of different lengths, hold different amounts of work in process, and operate at different cycle times. Thus, the impact of a minute of downtime depends on which segment of which conveyor is down. However, in this analysis a unit of time on each conveyor segment is equally weighted across all seven major conveyor segments.

Figure 1 shows the resulting graph of body shop downtime expressed as a percent of production time, averaged over the seven conveyor groups of the body shop and over each week. The graph indicates that downtime is indeed a problem at the plant studied. The graph clearly shows that the fraction of production time that the plant was not operating ("down") fell over the year from about 15 percent to about five percent. Such a reduction can be expected, since the number of failures in the plant should fall as the plant matures and the "bugs" worked out. Also, one would expect maintenance personnel to become more adept at tracing and fixing failures as their experience with the new process increases. The slope of the line, as given by a linear ordinary least squares fit to the data, is -.14 (with r^2 =.72).

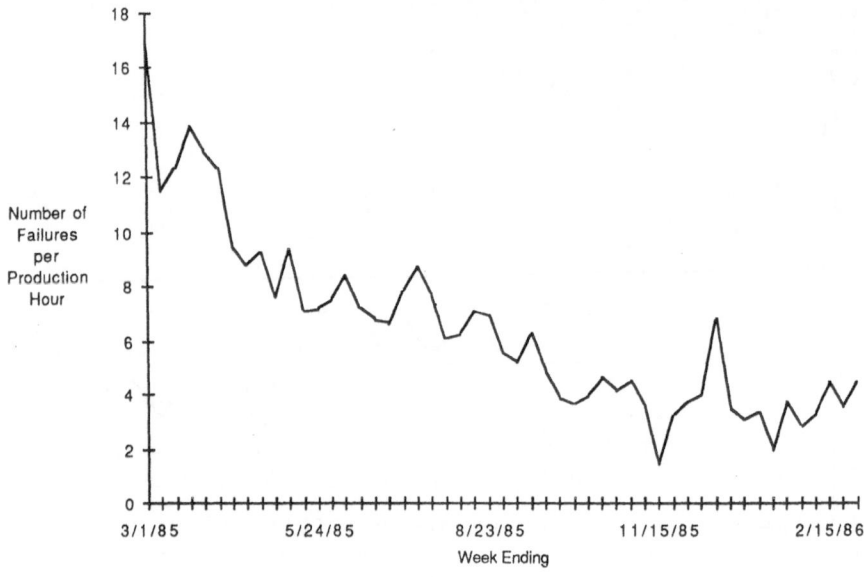

$$\text{Number of failures per production hour} = \frac{\displaystyle\sum_{i=1}^{n} (\text{failures of conveyor } i)}{(\text{clock hours of production})}$$

where n = number of conveyors (in this case, 7)

Figure 2.   Number of Failures per Production Hour.

A t-test indicated that this slope is significantly less than zero.* In a high-volume, high value-added facility such as the one studied here, even five percent downtime can mean significant cost in terms of lost minutes of downtime. With a line rate of 60 vehicles per hour, 48 minutes of downtime means 48 vehicles were not produced. At about $10,000 to $15,000 per vehicle, this amounts to roughly half to three quarters of a million dollars in lost revenue each day.

Is Downtime Principally Due to Reliability or Maintainability Problems?

Total downtime is the product of the number of failures and the average downtime per failure. Reliability refers to the number of failures, and is normally measured as the frequency of failures or the mean time between failures. Maintainability refers to the case with which the system can be fixed once a failure has occurred, and is usually measured as the mean time to repair. Design strategies used to control reliability and maintainability differ widely, and, in fact, are sometimes contradictory. For example, a typical design strategy used to increase the reliability of a system is to add redundancy to those components which are failure-prone. One way of increasing the maintainability of a system is to make it more simple by minimizing the number of parts and the interconnections between parts. Adding redundancy increases both the number of parts and the numbers of interconnections between parts, and might make the system more difficult to

---

*All statistical results reported here are significant at the .999 level, unless reported otherwise.

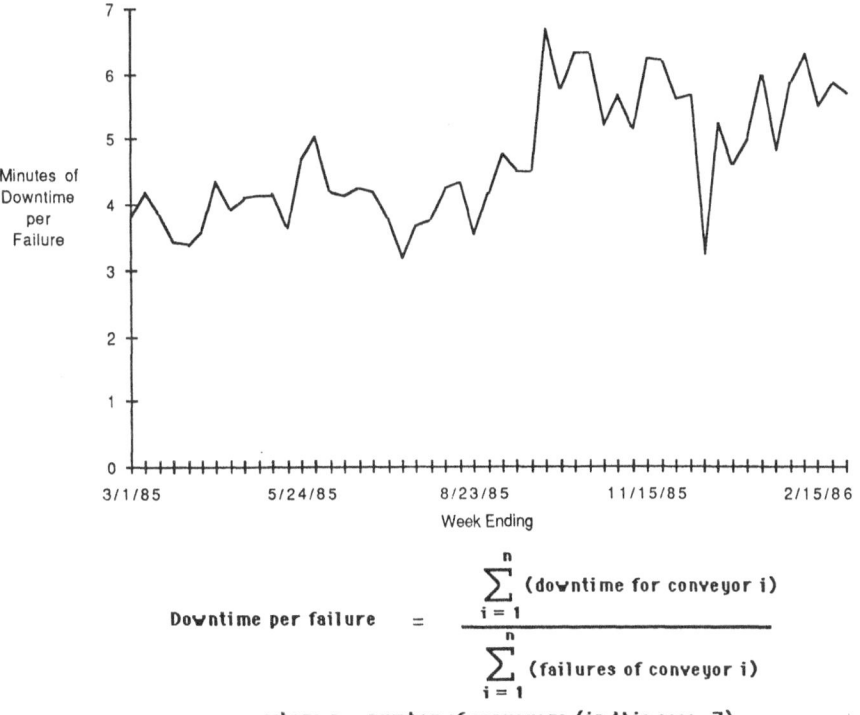

$$\text{Downtime per failure} \quad = \quad \frac{\displaystyle\sum_{i=1}^{n} (\text{downtime for conveyor } i)}{\displaystyle\sum_{i=1}^{n} (\text{failures of conveyor } i)}$$

where n = number of conveyors (in this case, 7)

Figure 3. Downtime per Failure.

maintain. Since the purpose of this research project is to determine ways of designing a system to reduce downtime, a natural starting place is to determine the extent to which reliability and maintainability contribute to downtime problems.

Figure 2 shows the graph of the average number of failures that occur per production hour, summed across all conveyors of the body shop. The values were calculated by dividing the total number of failures that occur each week by the total number of hours the body shop operated that week. The graph clearly shows a decrease in failure frequency over time, from about sixteen failures per hour to about four per hour. A linear ordinary least squares fit to the data shows that failure frequency fell by about .19 failures per hour each week (r^2 = .76). A t-test indicated that this slope is significantly less than zero. Note that failure frequency decreased by about the same proportion as did downtime. Thus, it appears that efforts to improve reliability at the plant are working, but availability (i.e., percent of production time that the plant is actually producing) is still a problem. This leads to the conclusion that the major problem is one of maintainability.

Figure 3, the graph of weekly average downtime per failure (mean time to repair), reinforces the conclusion that maintainability is a problem. The values in the graph were calculated by dividing the total amount of downtime across all conveyors of the body shop each week by the total number of failures during that week. One would expect downtime per failure to decrease over time as the maintenance personnel become more familiar with the new production system and can more quickly associate symptoms with causes. However, this graph shows the surprising result that downtime per failure actually increased over time, with a slope of about .045 minutes per failure each week (r^2 = .48). Results of a t-test indicate that this slope is significantly greater than zero. The number of failures fell considerably during the year studied, yet downtime per failure has not decreased at all. Thus, it appears that downtime problems are driven by the fact that the failures take too long to fix. This seems to indicate that efforts to reduce downtime should focus on improving the maintainabilit of the system.

What Kinds of Failures Are Driving the Maintainability Problem?

The analysis of summary failure data in the body shop indicates that an appropriate focus for reducing downtime is to investigate the causes of maintainability problems in computer-controlled production systems. We further analyzed the failure data to investigate whether certain kinds of failures involve more maintainability problems than others. We performed this analysis by regrouping the approximately 50 failure categories used in recording the data into smaller numbers of groups. We performed these regroupings based on extensive conversations with a maintenance engineer about the nature of each failure category. We regrouped the data twice: according to the kind of equipment that failed and according to the ways the failures are diagnosed.

The most obvious way to regroup the data is to divide them according to the kinds of equipment that fails (e.g., welding equipment or transfer equipment). We tried this regrouping, and it yielded no insight into which kinds of equipment failures are more difficult to maintain. There were no significant differences in the graphs of downtime per failure for the major equipment failure groupings.

To look for a way to recognize downtime data that might lead to insight into why downtime is a problem in computer-controlled production systems, we thought about important differences in maintaining a system that is mechanically or electromechanically controlled versus one that is computer-controlled. According to "expert" maintenance engineers with whom we are working, one key difference is in the ways that failures are diagnosed. In a mechanically controlled production system, troubleshooters diagnose many failures by directly sensing the operation of the machine. For example, a troubleshooter can visually observe that water is squirting out of a water hose, indicating that the hose has a leak. A troubleshooter can also diagnose failures by their sound, for example, when he hears the loud bang when two pallets carrying workpieces have crashed into one another, indicating that a conveyor pallet jam has occurred. Some failures in computer-controlled production systems are still found this way, but many others are found only through looking at the process control logic in the computerized process controllers. This logic is the software that controls the equipment, and the software is viewed through the CRTs of the computerized process controllers. Some of the failures found through the process control logic are caused by problems or "bugs" in the control logic itself. Other failures found only through studying the process control logic are actually mechanical problems that manifest themselves in control problems. For example, a broken clamp which is not visible from the floor does not trigger the appropriate switches that the control logic "reads".

During the discussions with maintenance engineering experts, we obtained anecdotal evidence which suggested that the maintainability problems might have to do with the difficulties of diagnosing failure through the process control logic. The evidence suggested a difference in the amount of time required to diagnose failures mechanically versus the amount of time required to diagnose failures through the process control logic. Many failures which are diagnosed by observing mechanical operations are obvious from visual or auditory events, so they require little diagnosis time. It takes little

Failure	Symptoms	Way of Diagnosis
Broken clamp on welder	The clamp is supposed to trip a limit switch when it closes. The limit switch does not get tripped. The machine stops as it waits for the limit switch to trip. The machine controller does not signal "end of sequence" to its station controller. The station controller does not signal "end of cycle" to the conveyor controller. The conveyor controller thinks the station is not finished with its cycle yet, so it waits indefinitely. Thus, the production system stops.	The troubleshooter reads the control logic of the conveyor controller to find out what went wrong it its logic and which station is responsible. He goes to the station controller to find out what wend wrong in its logic. If the welder is controlled by another process controller, the error will appear as an incorrect signal from the welder controller. He then studies the logic of the welder controller until he sees that the limit switch associated with the broken clamp was not triggered.
Clamp is out of adjustment on welder	The clamp does not close as tightly as it should, so there is a gap between the parts that are welded.	An operator or quality inspector notices a gap between the metal components. A troubleshooter finds out which machine is makes those welds and the clamps on that machine that hold the metal near the gap.

Figure 4. Representative Failures, Symptoms, and Diagnoses.

time to notice water squirting out of a broken water hose or to recognize that the loud crashing noise and the resulting positions of the workpiece pallets indicate that the pallets have been jammed. On the other hand, diagnosing a broken limit switch by tracing through the process control logic of at least one (and often several) computerized process controllers can require a long time.

To investigate the notion that downtime problems are being driven by the maintainability problems of failures diagnosed through the process control logic, we regrouped the data in terms of the ways that failures are diagnosed. The three categories used in the following analysis are: problems requiring analysis of the process control logic; problems which require analysis of the mechanical operations; and miscellaneous problems which result in downtime, but do not require diagnosis (such as quality checks, operator delays, and stock unavailability). Figure 4 describes a representative failure in each of these categories. One important point, noted in the figure, is that the ways that failures are diagnosed are independent of the kind of equipment which has failed. Notice that the kind of equipment is the same in the examples of Figure 4, but the ways the failures are diagnosed differ in the various kinds of failures in this equipment. A maintenance engineering expert at the plant helped define the regrouping of failures according to the way the failures are diagnosed. For each of the

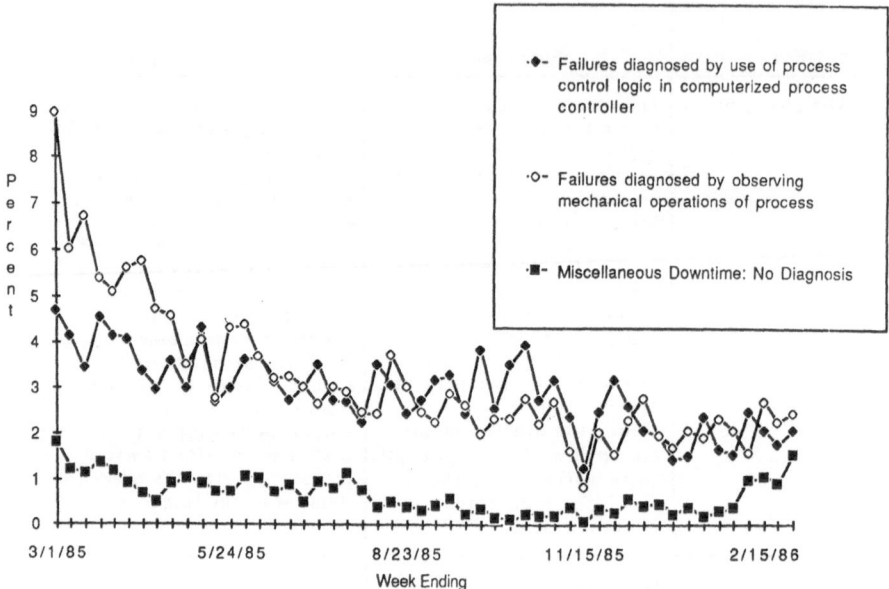

Figure 5. Downtime Expressed as Percent Production
Time Distinguished by Form of Diagnosis.

50 failure categories used to record the failure data at the plant, he
described the cause of the failure, the symptoms, and the way the failure
is detected, diagnosed, and repaired.

Figure 5 shows the downtime associated with these three categories,
expressed as a percent of total production time. As in the previous graphs
of downtime per production hour, the data are averaged across all conveyors
of the body shop, with all conveyors receiving equal weighting. The data
indicate that the amount of downtime caused by failures diagnosed by observing the mechanical operations of the process fell more rapidly than the
amount of downtime caused by failures diagnosed by observing the process
control logic of the computerized process controllers.

At the beginning of the time period studied, mechanically-diagnosed
failures accounted for more than twice the amount of downtime than failures
diagnosed through the process control logic. By the end of the one-year
time period, both categories accounted for roughly the same percent of downtime. Downtime attributed to mechanically diagnosed failures fell by about
a factor of three, while downtime attributed to failures diagnosed through
the process control logic fell only by a factor of two. These observations
are reinforced by an ordinary least squares fit of straight lines to the
data. The slope of the regression line for the mechanically diagnosed failures is $-.083$ ($r^2 = .65$), while that of failures diagnosed through the
process control logic is $-.043$ ($r^2 = .58$). An F-test showed that the differences in the slopes of these two lines is significant.

We infer from these data that maintenance personnel in the body shop
studied are able to reduce downtime due to failures diagnosed mechanically
more easily than they can for failures diagnosed through the process control.
In other words, the effects of learning are stronger for mechanically-diagnosed failures than for failures diagnosed through the process control
logic. Learning might be stronger in mechanically-diagnosed failures because
people at the plant have many years of experience with diagnosis by observing

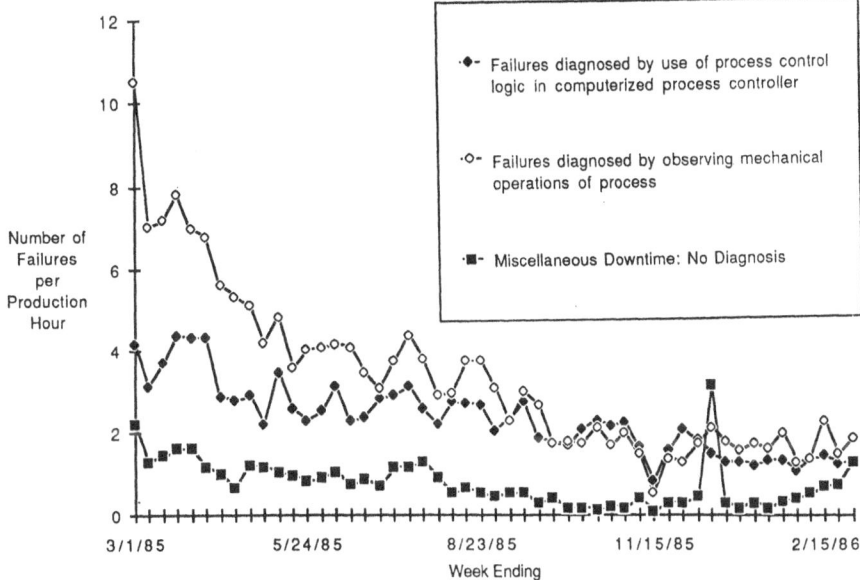

Figure 6. Number of Failures per Production Hour
Distinguished by Form of Diagnosis.

mechanical operations, while they are much less experienced at diagnosis by
analyzing process control logic. Or, the difference might be due to the
fact that failures which are mechanically diagnosed are decreasing in frequency more rapidly than failures diagnosed through analysis of process
control logic.

How much of this improvement is due to reduction in the number of failures and how much is due to improved diagnosis and repairs? Figure 6 shows
the weekly average number of failures per production hour in the body shop
for each of the categories by kind of diagnosis. This figure shows that
the frequency of failures fell over time for all three categories. It
appears from the graph that the frequency of mechanically diagnosed failures
fell more quickly than that of failures diagnosed through the process control
logic. This is reinforced by the results of an ordinary least squares fit
of straight lines to the data. The slope of the regression line for mechanically diagnosed failures has a slope of $-.120$ ($r^2 = .76$), while the line
fit to failures diagnosed through the process control logic is $-.051$ ($r^2 =
.76$). An F-test showed that this difference in slope is significant.

Figure 7 provides strong evidence that maintainability is still a problem, especially for failures which require diagnosis through analyzing the
process control logic of the computerized process controllers. This figure
shows the average downtime per failure each week over time for two of the
three categories of diagnosis.* This figure shows that downtime per failure
actually increased over the time period studied, both for failures requiring
analysis of mechanical operations and for failures requiring analysis of
process control logic. This observation is reinforced by an ordinary least

---

*The graph of downtime per failure for the miscellaneous downtime
category was excluded here, because it does not add insight to the
analysis and its large variability due to the small sample size
clutters the graph.

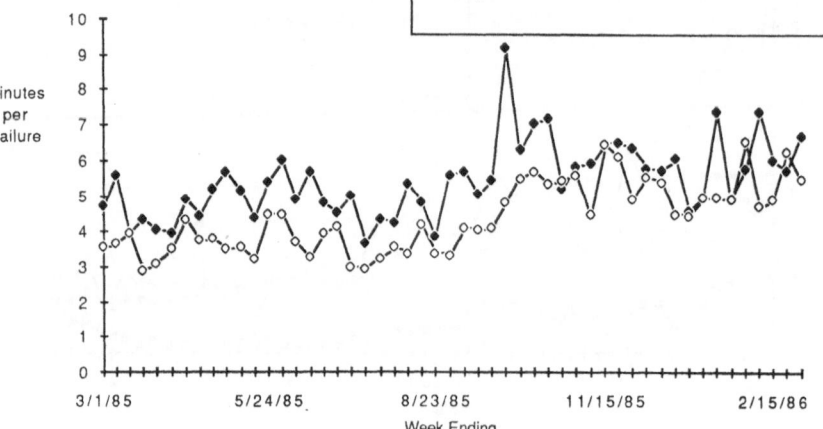

Figure 7. Downtime per Failure Distinguished
by Form of Diagnosis.

squares fit of straight lines to the data. The slope of the line for mechanically diagnosed failures is .049 (r^2 = .54, significantly greater than zero), and that for failures diagnosed through the process control logic is .039 (r^2 = .29, significantly greater than zero). Thus, even though the maintenance personnel at the plant are reducing the frequency of failures, they are not improving the ability to diagnose and repair a failure once it has occurred, despite any learning on the part of troubleshooters. The data in Figure 7 indicate that downtime per failure for failures requiring analysis of process control logic remained consistently higher than that for failures requiring analysis of mechanical operations throughout the year studied. A t-test reinforced this observation by showing statistical significance. Thus, it appears that failures requiring analysis of process control logic take longer to diagnose and fix than mechanically diagnosed failures.

The analysis presented so far indicates that maintainability is a problem in computer-controlled production systems. Thus, this research focuses on investigating ways to improve the maintainability of these systems. Because the maintainability of failures requiring analysis of process control logic appears to be worse than the maintainability of mechanically diagnosed failures, the focus is on the ways to improve the maintainability of failures that require analysis of process control logic. Anecdotal evidence suggests that the reason maintainability is a problem for failures diagnosed by use of process control logic is the amount of time involved in fault diagnosis. If diagnosis time could be factored out of the downtime data, we believe the results would show that diagnosis is a serious problem in the maintenance of computer-controlled production systems. Thus, we believe that one effective way to improve the maintainability of computer-controlled production systems is to improve the ability to perform diagnosis of faults that require analysis of process control logic. We cannot test this hypothesis or other hypotheses related to fault diagnosis in particular by analyzing the plant downtime data, since the downtime measured in the failure data is the total downtime from the time the failure occurred until the time the conveyor resumes operation. This time includes the time involved in detecting and recognizing the fact that there has been a failure, dispatching maintenance personnel to the site of the failure, diagnosing the cause of the failure, and repairing the failure. The effort involved in diagnosis cannot be separated from the other monitoring and maintenance functions. Thus, we have designed an experiment which is meant to investigate in more detail the reasons why maintenance personnel have difficulty in diagnosing equipment problems that require analysis of process control logic. The following chapter describes an experiment under design that is focused on the troubleshooting process.

INVESTIGATING TROUBLESHOOTING IN COMPUTER-CONTROLLED PRODUCTION SYSTEMS

The purpose of the experimental component of this research is to explore ways to design computer-controlled production systems to make them more maintainable. Relevant literature and field experience indicate that design variables can be adjusted to improve troubleshooters' ability to diagnose faults. Two such design variables which affect troubleshooting ability are the design of the user interface and the design of the process control logic in the computerized process controllers. This research investigates the relationships between these two design factors and troubleshooting performance. In particular, the research focuses on the complexity of process control logic design and on the hierarchical arrangement of display pages in the user interface design. We will investigate the effects of these two factors on troubleshooting performance through an experimental study.

A plant-wide system of programmable controllers can be very large and can involve hundreds of processors. The troubleshooter views this system by looking at the process control logic of one programmable controller at a time. Even then, at one time he can only see the portion of this logic that can fit on a single CRT screen. Thus, the design problem is one that Furnas (1986) described as that of providing "small" views of a "large" system. The ideal case is when the troubleshooter has all the information to diagnose the fault (and nothing more) available on the one display page he sees. Fault diagnosis in practice diverges from this ideal case in three ways:

1. The information needed by the troubleshooter is not available on a single page (or a small group of pages), so the troubleshooter must frequently change to a new display page.

2. Even if the troubleshooter requires only a small number of page changes to obtain the information he needs, he has difficulty in changing from one page to another because of. the way the user interface is designed.

3. The troubleshooter does not understand the overall functions of the system because the user interface does not allow him to understand how the individual pages are related to one another at a higher, system-level perspective.

The first issue is controlled primarily by system complexity. A more complex system is one which cannot be divided into small, independent pages or "modules". Thus, any division into smaller modules will result in modules that are highly dependent on one another. For the troubleshooter of a complex system, this means that when he sees a symptom on one display page, it is very likely that the cause of the symptom is shown on another display page. To trace the symptom, the troubleshooter must change his display page.

A less complex system is one that can easily be divided into independent modules, so that the troubleshooter needs to change the display page less frequently in order to obtain the same amount of information.

The second and third issues are principally affected by the design of the user interface and the training in using that interface. The second issue concerns the troubleshooter's ability to select the page he wants to view. An interface which can hinder the changing from one page to another would be a scrolling interface, in which the troubleshooter scrolls from one page to the next with no idea of where each page is in relationship to the rest of the system. In this case, the troubleshooter must move one page at a time until he reaches the desired page. This can be compared with an interface which allows more easy maneuverability, such as one in which the troubleshooter maneuvers from page to page by choosing a page from a "system-level" listing of the display pages.

The third issue concerns the inclusion of the relationships between display pages in the user interface. A simple list of the possible display pages to choose from, such as a single menu, does not show the user the relationships between the display pages. An alternative display design would be a hierarchical display page arrangement, in which the user not only sees a "system-level" view of the display pages, but he also sees how the display pages are related to one another in the hierarchy. If the troubleshooter is able to make use of this additional information, then he can diagnose his diagnosis strategy so that he can make his search very efficient. One diagnosis strategy that can make use of this additional information would be to start at the top level of the hierarchy, so that large portions of the process control logic can be eliminated quickly from the set of possible faults.

These three factors are highly interrelated. Even a system that is divided into independent display pages might be difficult to troubleshoot if the user interface makes maneuvering through the system difficult. Likewise, even with a hierarchical display page arrangement, troubleshooting can be difficult if pages are so interrelated that the troubleshooter must frequently change display pages and cannot rule out portions of the system as the possible source of the fault. The extent to which complexity affects troubleshooting can depend on the way the display pages are arranged in the user interface. Also, the extent to which display page arrangement affects troubleshooting can depend on the complexity of the system being displayed.

A number of studies have investigated the effects of specific components of physical system complexity (e.g. number of components or number of connections between components) on the ability to diagnose faults in that system. A number of other studies have investigated the effects of different display strategies on the ability to comprehend a complex system and solve problems in that system. A number of other studies have investigated the effects of different display strategies on the ability to comprehend a complex system and solve problems in that system. Because complexity of the system design and the design of the display are so interrelated, studies that focus on one factor without the other often suffer from unanticipated confounding effects. This study is intentionally designed to study the interactions between these two design choices, to compare their relative effects, and to investigate the relative merits of improving one or the other in an effort to improve the overall maintainability of a system.

Complexity

As more functions in production systems are converted to computer control, and as these functions become more complex, the complexity of the process control logic needed to synchronize and coordinate the production process increases substantially. More computerized process controllers are involved, the controlled logic within each of the controllers is more complex, and the controllers are coupled into "integrated systems" which require large amounts of inter-processor communication and coordination. A typical computer-controlled production system can involve hundreds of process controllers. The number of controllers that must work together can vary from less than ten at the station level to a hundred or more at the conveyor or plant-wide level. The more inter-processor coordination that is involved, the more complex the system of process control logic is.

Figure 8 shows that the number of process controllers and the number of communication paths between process controllers needed to execute a spot weld at a robotic welding station increased substantially, after modernization from a manual to a computer-controlled production process in the body shop of the vehicle assembly plant described earlier in this report. Each box in Figure 8 represents an information source or an information processor and each arrow represents a communication path through which information flows at least once during operation. The left side of the figure is a description of a typical robotic weld station before modernization, when process control was performed by human operators or by hard-wired "relay-panels". The right side describes a typical robotic weld station after modernization, when the process is controlled by a number of computerized process controllers. One can observe that there are more boxes and more arrows between boxes in the computer-controlled station than in the principally manual and hard-wired station.* Multiply this difference by the hundreds of stations that perform spot welding in the whole production system, and add the inter-station communication and coordination, and the differences are even more distinct.

This complexity is affected by two factors: the nature of the functions being performed and the choices made when information processing tasks are divided between process controllers. As an example to illustrate the first case, two robots working together to assemble a circuit board at a single station require more coordination than two robots working independently on simple pick-and-place operations. We are not concerned with this portion of complexity that is inherent to the functions performed. As an example to illustrate the second case, if two process controllers are controlling two pick-and-place robots, a simple design would be to give each controller responsibility for one robot. A more complex design would be to give each controller partial responsibility for each robot, so that for a single robot to perform its functions, both process controllers must work together to coordinate these functions. This aspect of complexity can change even when the functions remain the same, and it is determined largely by the system designers who, given a functional specification, decide how to divide the information processing functions between programmable controllers.

The effect of this complexity on fault diagnosis ability is that the

---

*The decisions are distributed between several decision-makers in the robotic welding in the old and the new processes. The primary decision-makers in the old process were the relay cabinets for station-level coordination between machines, the robot controller to control robot movement and squeezing of the weld gun, and the weld controller to control the timing of the firing of the weld gun once the robot triggered it. In the new process, the robot controller and a programmable logic controller (the "robot PLC") coordinate the timing of the triggering and the choice of weld parameters and sequences, the weld timer synchronizes the timing of the gun firing, and a set of programmable logic controllers coordinate the timing of the conveyor stops.

386

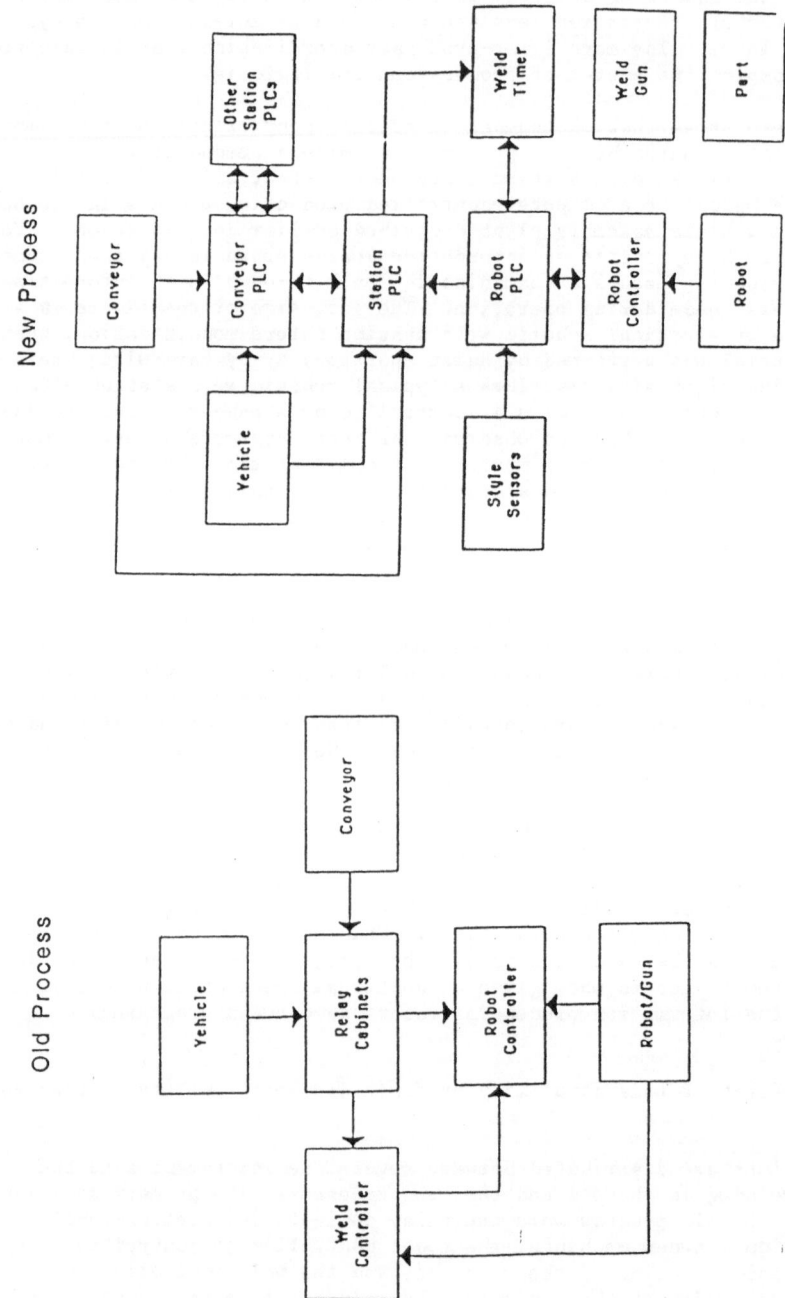

New Process

Old Process

Figure 8. Paths of Information Flow Required to Execute Welding Operations with Robots.

troubleshooter must look at the operations of more controllers in order to diagnose the fault. If he finds a symptom at one controller, he is less likely to be able to find the fault at that controller.

The characteristics of a computer program which make it easy to divide into independent parts or "modules" is termed "modularity" in the software engineering literature. The effects of modularity on the understandability and maintainability of software has been a concern of researchers in software engineering for many years. Few empirical data are available which relate the extent of program modularity to human problem solving performance. However, the existence of such a relationship has come to be a fundamental guideline in the software engineering community, and design techniques have been developed to expressly minimize the number of connections between software modules to increase a program's maintainability (e.g., Stevens et al., 1974; Parnas, 1972). Software design methodologies tend to differ in the definition of a connection between modules, rather than on their philosophy that a "good" design is one which minimizes these connections.

The results of other studies reinforce our notion that the extent of interconnection between components of a system affect fault diagnosis performance. A number of researchers have shown that the number of interconnections between parts of a system strongly affects problem-solving performance in the number of specific applications. Goldbeck, Bernstein, Hillix, and Marx (1957) studied the effects of the number of interconnections between components on fault diagnosis in representations of systems of simple electrical components. In their test systems, faults were manifested as discontinuities in current flow. They found that more tests were required as the number of connections between components increased. Rouse and Rouse (1979) used computer-based schematics of circuits of logical AND and OR gates to measure the effects of number of interconnections on fault diagnosis performance. They found that number of connections was significantly correlated with time required to find a fault. Wohl (1983) tested a predictive theory of maintainability against field data about maintenance of a particular radar computer. According to the theory, systems became substantially more difficult to maintain when their complexity increased. System complexity was measured as the average number of electrical connections between components. He found that the theory closely matched the field data.

Experimenters, who study the relationship between the number of connections in a system and problem-solving in that system, face some experimental difficulties. In some experiments, it is difficult to vary the number of connections between parts without varying the amount of processing performed by the system. For example, changing the number of nodes in a queuing network can drastically change the number of items that can be processed by the network by allowing alternative routes through the system. We do not expect this to be a problem in our experiment. The components of the system being modelled in our experiment are decisions, the interconnections between components are taking the form of information flowing between the decisions. The set of decisions and information will remain constant throughout all tests in our experiment. We will vary the grouping of the individual process control decisions into pages as our measure of complexity.

User Interface

As mentioned earlier, the user interface in computer-controlled production systems provides the troubleshooter with a limited view, via a CRT, of a very large system. The user interface affects the troubleshooter's diagnosis strategy in two ways:

1. It controls the way in which the troubleshooter changes from one page of the display to another.

2. It affects the troubleshooter's ability to understand how
   the small view included in each display page fits into the
   larger system.

A display page arrangement which has been proposed as a way to facilitate a troubleshooter in both of these respects is that of a hierarchy. A
hierarchical display can allow the user to select any page in the system
directly. This is in contrast to a scrolling display, in which the user
must move sequentially through the system until he arrives at the desired
page. A hierarchical display also gives the user a representation of how the
small view included in each page fits into the larger system of pages. This
is in contrast to either a scrolling page arrangement or a simple list of
possible pages to select. In these cases, the relationships between pages
are not shown to the troubleshooter.

Much of the work in hierarchical display arrangement has been confined
to static information retrieval systems (e.g. Snowberry et al., 1983; Miller,
1981). One such system, ZOG (Robertson et al., 1981), consists of a potentially very large database structured as small, interconnected pieces. The
ZOG user maneuvers through the pieces of information via interconnected display pages, presenting one at a time from a computer terminal. Each frame
contains several different items of information which the user may select.
When the user selects an item, the system displays a new display frame. Even
in these static systems, little is understood about design of the display to
facilitate human problem solving. Snowberry (Snowberry et al., 1983, pointed
out that "...decision to use breadth or depth in menu construction have been
based on intuitions about user characteristics rather than on data obtained
from empirical studies".

In a study to determine the effects of hierarchical displays on human
problem solving performance, Brooke and Duncan (1983) tested the effects of
hierarchically paged vs. scrolling displays on fault finding in a computer
simulation of non-time-varying circuits of logical AND and OR gates. They
found that the selection of diagnostic tests was more efficient in the hierarchically paged display than in the scrolling display when the subjects
were less competent at diagnosis. The difference was not as evident in more
competent diagnosticians.

The results of the Brooke and Duncan study highlight the importance of
distinguishing between the two ways in which a hierarchically paged display
can facilitate human problem solving. The experts might have brought into
the experiment a better ability to understand the high-level functions of the
system as a whole, with or without a hierarchical display. This might account for the performance differences between novice and expert troubleshooters. However, this hypothesis cannot be tested with the data because
the effects of system-level understanding cannot be separated from the
effects of ease of maneuverability.

A study by Seppala and Salvendy (1985) investigated the ability to
maneuver through a database in the context of a flexible manufacturing
system. The experiment environment consisted of a computer-based display
of a number of variables for each of a number of machines in a manufacturing
process (e.g. temperature and pressure). The variables were presented in a
number of hierarchical arrangements which differed in terms of depth and
breadth. Each subject could view one page in one level of the hierarchy at
a time. Subjects were asked to search for a list of specific variables, and
the time required to complete the task was associated to the depth and
breadth of the hierarchical arrangement. Though the context of the system
might have been dynamic, the nature of the tasks was simply a search through
a static database.

The results of the Seppala and Salvendy study highlight the importance of studying the combined effects of system design and the design of the user interface. The researchers found that working with hierarchical data organization took more time and resulted in more errors than did working with a parallel data organization, and that increasing the levels in the hierarchy increased acquisition times and errors. After closer study of these unexpected results, the researchers concluded that the information structure was well organized, so that subjects could easily recall from memory the appropriate search codes. The "problem-solving" task was inadvertently reduced to a simple motor task. The parallel information structures required fewer keystrokes, so they took less time to search through. Because the task was driven by motor limitations rather than human problem-solving limitations, the results cannot be used to describe how user interfaces should be designed to aid problem-solving performance.

Recognizing the strong interrelationships between system design and user interface design, Miller (1981) chose to study their combined effects. In his experiment, subjects searched for words in a semantic hierarchy. Search time was the dependent variable, and depth and breadth of hierarchical display page arrangement and the arrangement of words within the display pages were the independent variables. He found that "intermediate" levels of breadth and depth are the best option when search items are randomly arranged (i.e., highly interrelated, complex system design), but that broad structures result in better performance when search items are categorically arranged (i.e., less complex system design).

In summary, studies that focus on the effects of display page arrangement on human problem-solving performance seem to indicate that hierarchical display arrangement affects problem-solving performance. However, the results of these studies suggest refinements in experimental design. First, the studies suggest that an important distinction needs to be drawn between two ways in which a hierarchical display can facilitate troubleshooting performance: facilitating display page changes and providing a representation of the relationship between display pages. We intend to draw this distinction by comparing three display strategies: a scrolling display, a display that provides the same ease of page changes as a hierarchically paged display but does not describe relationships between pages, and a 3-level hierarchically arranged display page design. Second, some studies have shown that problem-solving performance is affected by both the design of the display and the design of the system being displayed. Thus, experiments that focus only on the effects of display design on problem-solving performance are easily confounded by the effects of and complexity of the system being displayed. To alleviate the difficulties involved in isolating the effects of system design, we will study their interactive effects through a two-factor complete factorial design rather than attempt to isolate their effects in a single-factor design.

DESIGN OF AN EXPERIMENT TO STUDY FACTORS AFFECTING TROUBLESHOOTING

The purpose of our proposed experiment is to assess the extent to which complexity of system design and hierarchical arrangement of display pages affect troubleshooting effort in computer-controlled production processes. In particular, we are interested in comparing the relative effects of these two factors and investigating their interactions.

During each test, a subject will be presented with a functional representation of a production system that has failed. The representation will be viewed on a computer terminal. The subject's task will be to diagnose the fault in the system. Through the computer-based experiment environment, the subject will be able to perform "tests" on the system to obtain information about the state of the system when it failed. The performance of each subject will be measured in terms of the time required to diagnose the fault and the number of tests performed on the system. The experiment environment will time-tag and record each of the user inputs, so that the troubleshooting process can be reconstructed for more detailed analysis.

Variables

Independent Variables. There will be four within-subject independent variables: complexity of the system design; hierarchy of the user interface; the specific system fault being diagnosed; and the ordering of the tests. The first two variables will be varied to determine main and interaction effects. The last two variables will be distributed so that their effects are evenly distributed across all combinations of the first two variables when the results are aggregated.

Complexity of system design will take on two possible values: "more complex" and "less complex". In the more complex system, we will arrange the process control information processing and decision-making so that the number of connections between pages of the display is high. In the less complex design, we will arrange the information processing and decisions to minimize the number of connections between pages.

Hierarchical arrangement of display pages will take on three possible configurations: no grouping or hierarchy; grouping but no hierarchy; and a three-level hierarchy. In the "no grouping or hierarchy" condition, subjects will change display pages by scrolling to adjacent pages. In the "grouping but no hierarchy" condition, subjects will be able to choose the page they want to view by selecting from a numbered list of display pages. The "hierarchy" condition differs from the "grouping but no hierarchy" condition in that the pages are named according to the kinds of decisions they include and the hierarchical relationships between pages are displayed.

Six possible faults will be designed into the experiment: one fault for each test on each subject. All subjects will confront the same six faults. The symptom of the faults will be the same: the line stops. A fault will be represented by an incorrect decision by a process controller.

The order of the tests is considered explicitly as an independent variable. We distribute the ordering of the tests so that biases due to learning effects are evenly distributed.

Dependent Variables. Two performance measures will be used as indicators of troubleshooting difficulty: the amount of time and the number of tests required for subjects to diagnose the system faults. The experiment environment will record these results.

The amount of time required to diagnose a fault was chosen because time is a critical element in the diagnosis of failures in computer-controlled production systems. Since each minute of downtime can mean tens of thousands of dollars in lost revenue, the goal in design for maintainability is to design systems so that their faults can be diagnosed quickly. Also, diagnosis time is often used as a performance measure in fault diagnosis experiments. In a survey of fault diagnosis experiments by Henneman and Rouse (1986), they found that fault diagnosis time was used most often as a performance measure.

Brooke and Duncan (1981) presented a strong argument for using number of tests (i.e., number of times a piece of information is requested) as a performance measure. According to their reasoning, in practice each test has a cost associated with it. Thus, efficient diagnostic procedures which

390

lead to diagnosis with fewer tests are better than diagnostic procedures which require many tests. Thus, design for maintainability can also be interpreted as designing systems so that their faults can be diagnosed with few tests.

Task time and number of tests are likely to be correlated. Both variables are being used as performance measures because measuring both requires little more effort than measuring one or the other. Also, using both measures will allow comparison of the results of this experiment with the results of experiments which involve either measure.

Confounding Variables. In each of the tests, the functional specifications of the production system being diagnosed will remain the same. The system will perform the same functions in the same sequence. This is done to reduce the effects of other confounding system-related variables, such as the size of the system or the kinds of functions being performed by the system.

Learning effects will be reduced by using an extensive training session, but to the extent that learning and other order effects still exist, they will be controlled by varying the order of the tests between subjects. Likewise, the variations in difficulty in diagnosing any particular fault will be controlled by varying the fault-treatment combinations between subjects. These methods are described in the following section.

The effects of inherent variations in skill differences between subjects cannot be controlled, but they will be recognized and included in the statistical tests. The response times measured during the training sessions will be used as a covariant to account for some of the variations between subjects.

Structure of Tests

This experiment will incorporate a repeated measure, 2x3x6x6 mixed fractional factorial design. All of the dependent variables are within-subject variables. Viewed separately, the first two factors form a 2x3 factorial design. These factors are the complexity of the system design and the hierarchical display in the user interface design. Each subject will be tested in each of the conditions of this 2x3 factorial design; thus, each subject will undergo six tests. The third and fourth factors are incorporated to evenly distribute biases that are predictable, but unavoidable. The third factor is the particular fault being diagnosed, and is meant to evenly distribute bias due to inherent ease or difficulty in diagnosing particular faults. The fourth factor is the order in which the tests will be administered to the subjects, and is meant to evenly distribute learning effects. According to the experiment design, if an order or learning effect exists, it is controlled in the weak sense that each treatment combination appears equally often in each of the orders. Likewise, if effects of the fault being diagnosed exist, then they are controlled in that each fault appears equally often in each treatment combination.

The 2x3 portion of the design will be collapsed into a single 6x1 dimension, making the experiment a 6x6x6 factorial design. The experiment will incorporate a balanced set of 6x6 Latin squares with a weakly correlated Latin square superimposed on each square of the balanced set.* Each subject

---

*This design was developed for pairs or orthogonal Latin squares. However, there exists no pair of 6x6 orthogonal Latin squares. The best approximation is to choose the pair of Latin squares that are least correlated, to minimizing the confounding effects.

DECISIONS WHICH ARE INCLUDED IN
REPRESENTATION

TIMING AND SEQUENCING CONTROL:

WHEN TO BEGIN DRILLING SEQUENCE?
WHICH HOLE TO DRILL NEXT?
WHEN TO BEGIN DRILLING HOLE?
WHEN TO MOVE DRILL INTO DRILLING
POSITION?
WHEN TO MOVE DRILL OUT OF
DRILLING POSITION?
WHEN TO SIGNAL END OF SEQUENCE?

OPTIONS AND PARAMETER-SETTING:

WHEN TO READ OPTIONS
INFORMATION FOR NEW WORKPIECE?
WHEN TO INDEX OPTIONS
INFORMATION FOR WORKPIECES?
WHAT ARE OPTIONS FOR NEW
WORKPIECE?
WHICH SEQUENCE OF HOLES TO
DRILL?
WHAT DRILL SPEED TO USE FOR
CURRENT DRILL HOLE?

WORKPIECE MOVEMENT:

WHEN TO START NEW WORKPIECE AT
BEGINNING OF PRODUCTION LINE?
WHEN TO INDEX WORKPIECES ON
CONVEYOR?
WHEN TO TRANSFER WORKPIECE TO
NEXT CONVEYOR?
WHEN TO REMOVE COMPLETED
WORKPIECE FROM END OF
PRODUCTION LINE?

REPAIRS:

WHEN TO CHECK COMPLETED
WORKPIECE FOR REPAIR NEEDS?
WHAT ARE WORKPIECE REPAIR NEEDS?
WHERE TO SEND WORKPIECE FOR
REPAIRS?

Figure 9.   Decisions Incorporated in the
Production System Model.

will be assigned to a row of the Latin square. The columns of the Latin
squares will define the order in which the subject will be observed in each
of the test configurations. The superimposed Latin square will represent
the particular fault being diagnosed. The resulting set of Greco-Latin
squares will include a total of 216 observations collected: six observations
on each of 36 subjects. For each combination of the two factors in the
original 2x3 design, there will be 36 observations. (See Winer, 1971, pp.
719-723, Plan II.)

Experiment Environment

Much of the effort in designing this experiment has focused on designing
the experiment environment. The goal was to develop an environment that can
be used in follow-ups to this experiment. The first criterion used to judge
potential designs was its ease of use. We did not want the notation used
in the environment to be difficult to understand or the command entry to be
awkward. The second criterion was the representativeness of the model of
process control to "real-world" process control. We wanted the model to be
a reasonable approximation to the kinds of information processing and decision-making involved in process control, and we wanted the "faults" modelled in the representation to generate symptoms that are like the symptoms
encountered in real applications.

Function Model of Manufacturing System. The model of a manufacturing

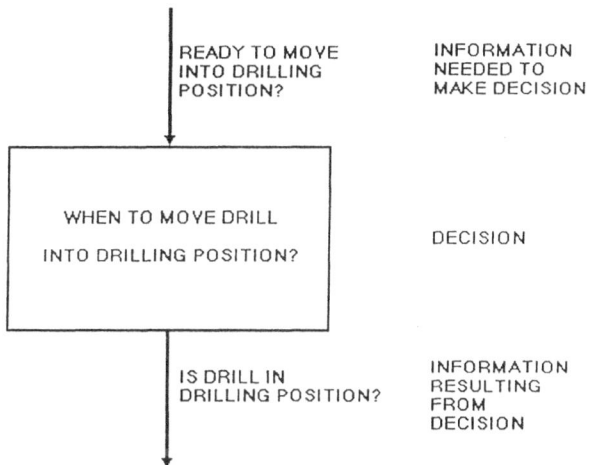

READY TO MOVE
INTO DRILLING
POSITION?

INFORMATION
NEEDED TO
MAKE DECISION

WHEN TO MOVE DRILL

INTO DRILLING POSITION?

DECISION

IS DRILL IN
DRILLING POSITION?

INFORMATION
RESULTING
FROM
DECISION

Figure 10.   Box and Arrow Representation
of a Decision.

system used in this experiment focuses on tasks and functions performed in
the production process, rather than physical layout of the plant. In particular, the model focuses on the process control information processing
and decision-making required to coordinate the sequencing and timing of
operations and to select process parameters for tool operations. In discrete
parts manufacturing systems, such as the system being modelled in the experiment, the production process is principally a sequence of discrete events.
The principal purpose of process control is to sequence and coordinate
these events. With asynchronous, independent control, control of one piece
of equipment often depends on the state of other equipment. Also, the properties of the output are often unique for each individual part produced,
although the degree of variation between parts tends to decrease with increasing production volumes. Thus, another purpose of process control is
to choose appropriate parameters to obtain the desired configuration of
each product. For example, in spot welding for vehicle assembly, process
parameters such as weld parameters must be chosen for each weld spot on
each workpiece.

A process control decision in this function model is a choice between
alternatives. The types of decisions modelled are those made by the system-
level controllers to coordinate the functioning of a manufacturing process
consisting of tools, parts, and material handling devices for a known production process and schedule. Although in practice human operators are an important part of the production process, they are not included in the function
model because the purpose of the model is to describe a production system
so that its equipment failures can be diagnosed. Figure 9 lists some of
the kinds of decisions included in the model. The decisions are written
for the specific example of drilling holes in pieces of metal to give the
representation a more concrete example. However, the decisions are chosen
and written so that they incorporate aspects of process control that are
applicable in many manufacturing processes. Some decisions involve choosing
the timing of operations (such as when to begin a drilling sequence).
Other decisions involve choosing a particular task or option from several
predetermined alternatives (such as which sequence of holes to drill). The
level of decision-making used in this model is at a "higher level" than
basic machine control, since we do not consider details such as how a robot
controls its actuators to move its arm from one position to another. The
level of decision-making modelled is at a "lower level" than strategic

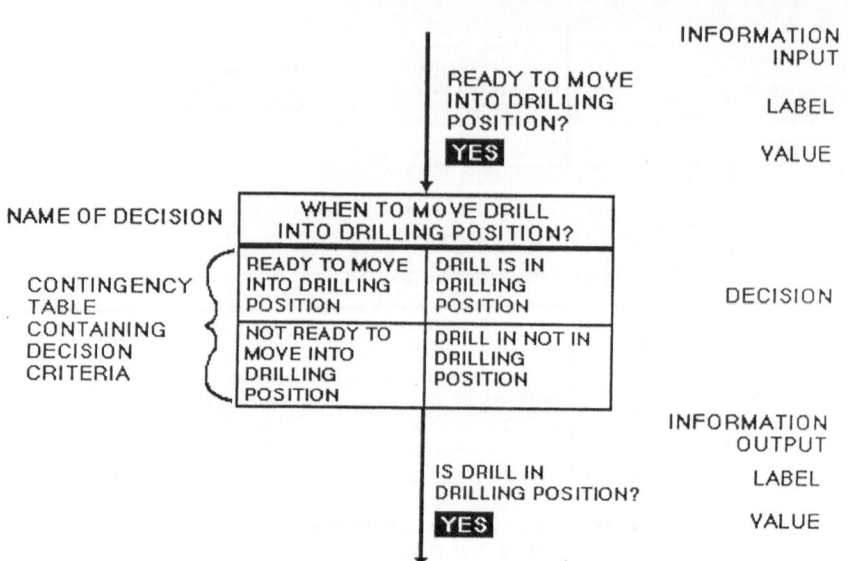

Figure 11.   Example of a Properly Functioning
Decision.

management decisions, such as alterations in the regular schedule of the
amount of output per day.

The notation used to describe a decision is based on a simple box-
and-arrow design, like that shown in Figure 10. A box represents a decision
and the arrows represent the information flowing between decisions. An
incoming arrow represents information used to make a decision, and an outflowing arrow represents the information resulting from the decision.
Figure 11 shows a more detailed view of the functions of the same decision.
The values of the information are shown underneath the labels. In this
case, the value of the information labelled "Ready to move into drilling
position?" is "Yes". Inside the box is the detail of the decision criteria.
The criteria can be read as a contingency table. The values of the incoming
information are matched to one of the boxes on the left side, then the
values of the outflowing information determined by the corresponding box on
the right side. Implicit in the decision is an action that is not seen by
the process controller. In the case of a decision of when to move a machine
into drilling position, this action is the movement of the machine into
drilling position. The actions themselves are not modelled because they
are not actually "seen" by the process controllers in real applications,
but are inferred by the values of the information the process controllers
receive.

Using this notation, a fault is an "incorrect" decision. A fault involves a decision in which, according to the contingency table, the values
of the incoming information should not result in the values of the outflowing
information. An example fault is shown in Figure 12. In this case, a
value of "yes" for the incoming information should result in a value of
"yes" for the outflowing information. Since the value of the outflowing
information is "no", the decision is a fault.

Using this notation, an example display page is shown in Figure 13.
Each display page will represent the decision-making of one process con-
troller. Figure 13 also defines an example of a "less complex design".
This design is less complex because the number of information arrows which

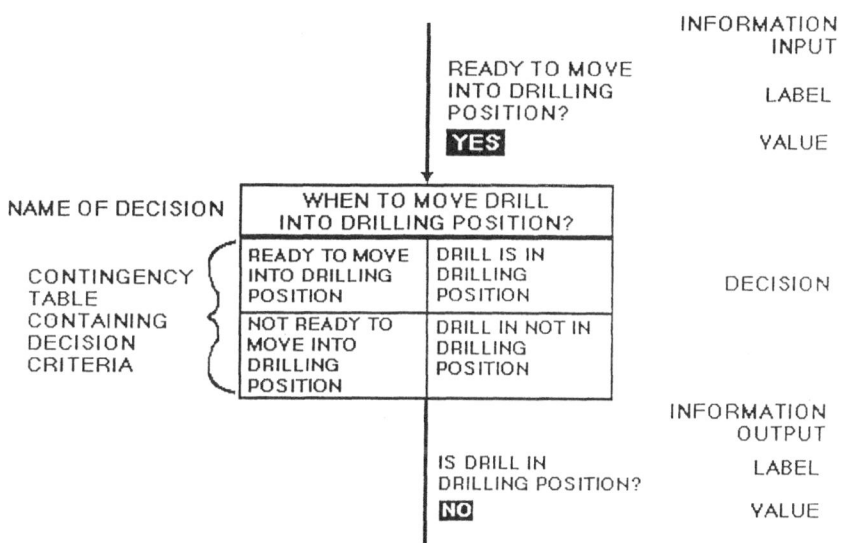

INFORMATION
INPUT

READY TO MOVE
INTO DRILLING
POSITION?   LABEL

YES   VALUE

NAME OF DECISION   WHEN TO MOVE DRILL
                          INTO DRILLING POSITION?

CONTINGENCY   READY TO MOVE   DRILL IS IN
TABLE   INTO DRILLING   DRILLING   DECISION
CONTAINING   POSITION   POSITION
DECISION   NOT READY TO   DRILL IN NOT IN
CRITERIA   MOVE INTO   DRILLING
                 DRILLING   POSITION
                 POSITION

INFORMATION
OUTPUT

IS DRILL IN
DRILLING POSITION?   LABEL

NO   VALUE

Figure 12.   Example of a Fault.

flow off the page is small. The controller receives a small number of pieces
of information telling it to start, operates primarily on its own, and sends
out one piece of information telling the other controllers that it is done.
For illustrative purposes, the arrows which lead to another page (i.e.,
process controller) are emphasized. This can be compared to the page shown
in Figure 14, in which the number of interactions with other controllers is
large.

     The way the subjects will move from page to page depends on the display
arrangement treatment condition. For the case of "no grouping or hierarchy",
each page will have a border on it, like that shown in Figure 15. The arrows
which lead to another controller simply run off the page. If the subject
wants to trace one of those arrows, he clicks the mouse button on the portion
of the border that the arrow crosses. For example, if he wants to see the
page above the current page, he would click on the portion of the border
labelled "ABOVE". For the case of "grouping but no hierarchy", the arrows
which lead to other controllers are labelled with the identity of the controller that it leads to. The controllers will be labelled by number. The
user will have a box on each controller page, which he can click the mouse
button on, to call up a "System Overview" page, such as that shown in Figure
16. He can choose to view any controller by clicking the mouse button on
the appropriate box. For the "hierarchy" condition, the user will change
pages much as in the case of "grouping but no hierarchy". The only difference is that the controllers are labelled according to the kinds of
functions they control (i.e., the functions of a particular station on a
conveyor, the conveyor-level functions between stations on one conveyor, or
the area-level functions between conveyors), and the hierarchical relationships between the conveyors are made explicit. An example of the "System
Overview" page for the hierarchy condition is shown in Figure 17.

     Equipment. The experiment will be implemented on computer workstations
which use the Andrew* distributed computing environment developed and in

─────────────────────
*Andrew was developed by the Information Technology Center (ITC), a joint
 project between Carnegie Mellon University and IBM.

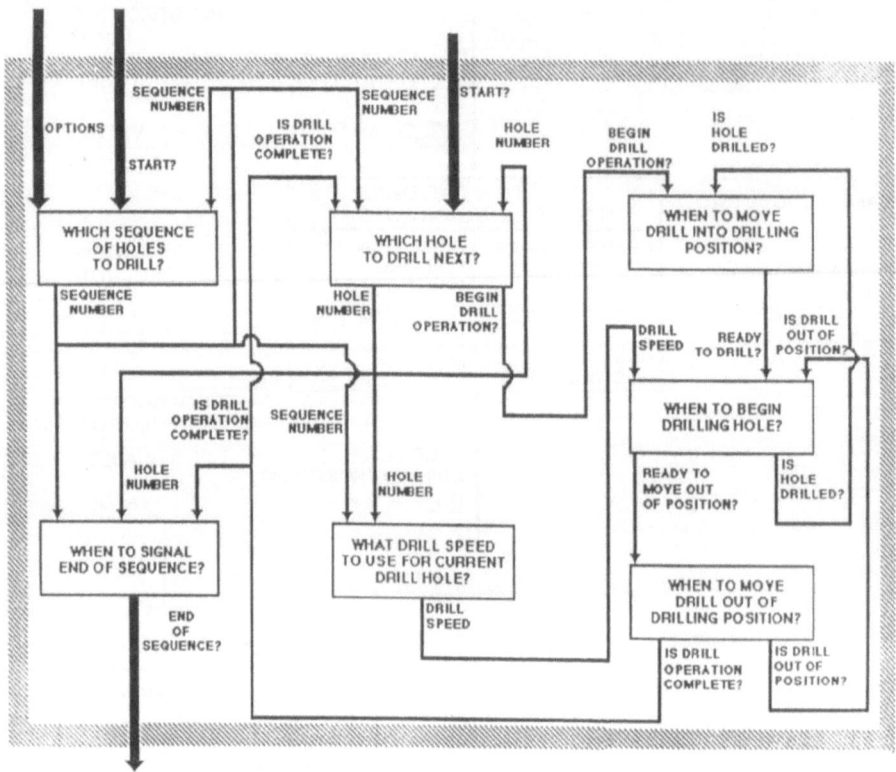

Figure 13.   An Example Display Page Representing the
Decision-Making of One Process Controller.

use at Carnegie Mellon University. Workstations using Andrew can run in a
stand-alone fashion. This is an important feature, since the experiments
will take place at the plants where the subjects are employed. These workstations have the advantage of a larger, higher-resolution screen than
traditional computer terminals and personal computers. For this experiment,
the added size and resolution allows more flexibility in the design of the
display pages. The experiment will be implemented with CMU Tutor*, a screen
display control language written to aid the authoring of computer-aided
instruction programs. This program is useful for this study because it is
a high-level language that will allow us to develop screens that include
text and figures (boxes and arrows), and to condition screen paging upon
user inputs.

A computer-based experiment environment was chosen for a number of
reasons, most of them related to the fact that the troubleshooting process
as well as troubleshooting performance measures should be recorded. The
computer will be able to record the subjects' information acquisition behavior during the decision-making process. Reconstruction of the decision-
making process based on patterns of information acquisition has several
distinct advantages over verbal protocol analysis for this experiment.
First, there is concern that generating verbal reports is a secondary task

---

*CMU Tutor was written by Bruce Arne Sherwood and Judith N. Sherwood
at the Center for Design of Educational Computing (CDEC) at Carnegie
Mellon University.

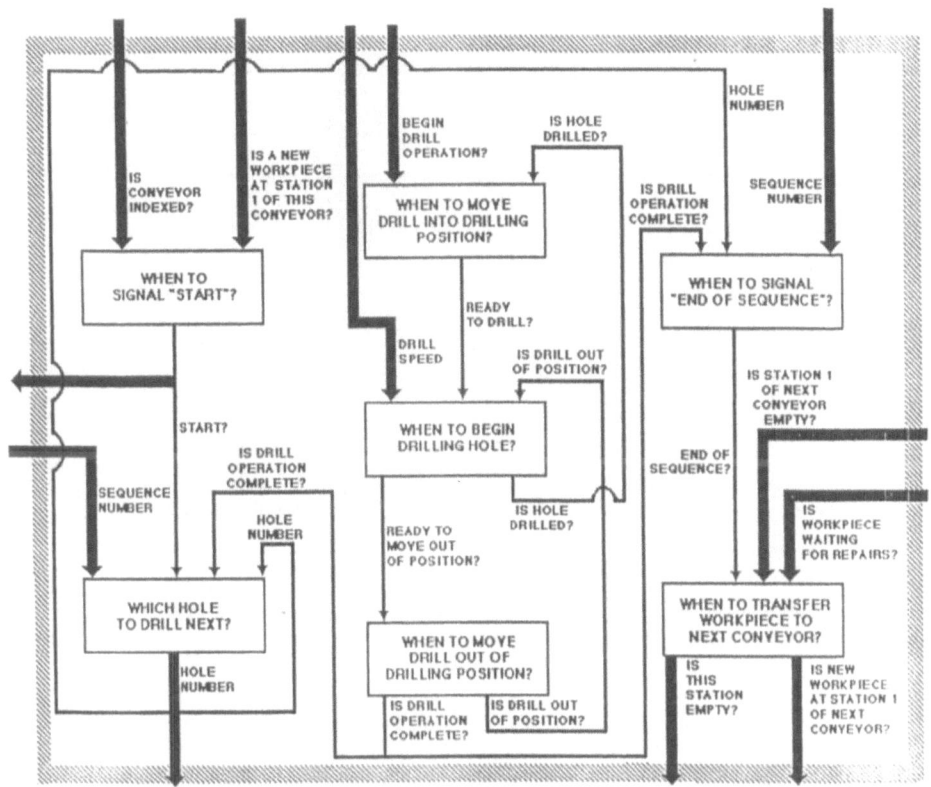

Figure 14. An Example of a More Complex Display of
Decision-Making of One Process Controller.

that must be performed along with the primary decision task (Russo et al., 1985). Such a secondary task might substantially slow down or alter the decision-making process. Also, because verbal reporting is a secondary task, subjects often fail to provide a complete verbal report of all the information acquired. Finally, the coding of information acquisition behavior is generally easier than the coding of verbal reports (Johnson et al., 1986).

The portability of the computer gives it a distinct advantage over eye-tracking equipment as an experiment medium. Eye-tracking, which is an alternative way to collect and record information acquisition behavior, involves using sophisticated equipment to trace and record eye fixations. Eye-tracking equipment is not portable, while the computer workstation used in this experiment is portable. This will allow the experimenters to visit factory environments in order to get "real-life" troubleshooters as subjects. We see this as one of the most important aspects of this experiment.

The mouse was chosen as the computer-based pointing and entry device for three reasons. First, the mouse is easy to learn. Card (Card et al., 1983) compared the mouse, the joystick, and two key operating devices for selecting text on a screen. They found that the mouse and the joystick have a significantly faster rate of learning than using cursor keys. This will minimize subjects' apprehension about the experiment environment and reduce learning effects in the experiment. Second, the mouse allows rapid movement. Card (Card et al., 1983) found that the mouse is significantly

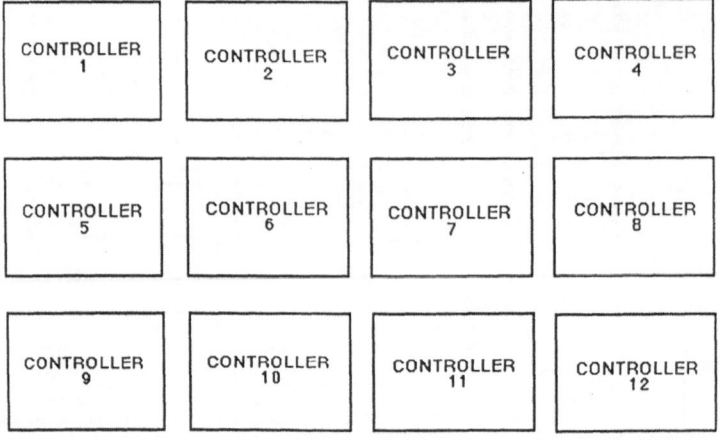

SYSTEM OVERVIEW

Figure 15.   Screen Paging for "Grouping But No Hierarchy".

faster than the other devices they tested. English (English et al., 1967)
found the mouse to be faster than a lightpen and several other devices.
Johnson (Johnson et al., 1986) found that subjects could move between information cells in less than 100 milliseconds. These times are of similar
magnitude to eye movements, or about 160-200 milliseconds per bit of information, Card (Card et al., 1983). Eye-tracking is often the process-tracing
method of choice because eye movements have small information acquisition
times. Since the mouse is comparable in speed to eye movements, the mouse
is nearly as good at information acquisition as eye movements, but com-
puter-mouse set-ups do not have the disadvantages of the eye-tracking equipment. A third advantage of the mouse is its error rate, measured as the
percent of times that the device is used to select an incorrect item. Card
(Card et al., 1983) reported that mice have significantly lower error rate
than other entry devices.

Training

Before the experimental tests, the subjects will undergo training exercises to become acquainted with the experiment environment. The subjects
will be introduced to the experiment environment via written instructions
displayed on the computer terminal used in the experiment. These instructions will contain an explanation of the production system being modelled,
a description of the subject's tasks as troubleshooter in the experiment,
and a summary of the commands available to the subject and the ways the
subject executes the commands during the experiment. Each section of the
instructions will include a set of questions that will be used to assess
the subject's comprehension of the material. Furthermore, by using the
computer for training, the subjects will become familiar with the workings
of the computer. Thus, they will be used to the experiment environment by
the time the experiment tests begin. During the quizzes, the training
program will note incorrect answers and follow-up with more descriptions.

The subjects will practice troubleshooting during a training practice
session which will closely resemble the experiment tests. The system described during the practice session will be same system modelled during the
experiment, but the particular fault in the system will not be repeated
during the experiment. The practice session will allow the subjects to
gain practice in using the experiment environment and in troubleshooting

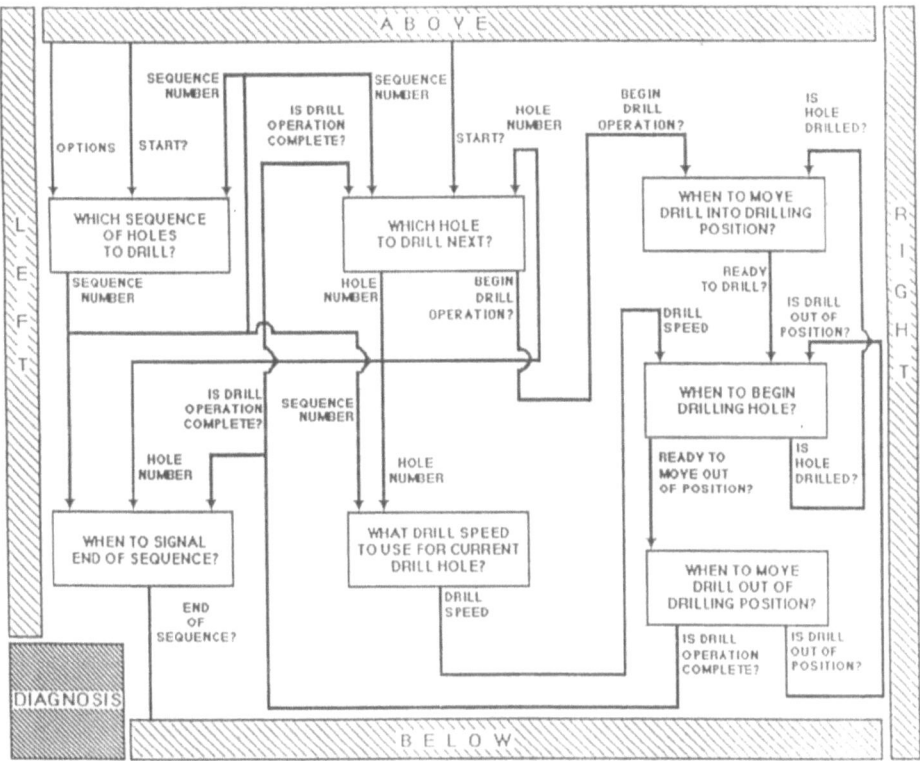

Figure 16.   Screen Paging for "No Grouping or Hierarchy".

the production system being modelled.

Task

At the beginning of each test, the subject is presented with the
highest-level view of the functions of a production system for the particular
treatment combination of the test. For the treatment combinations which
include no hierarchy or grouping of the information on the display pages,
the first view will be the upper left-most screenful. He is told that
there is a fault somewhere in the system which caused the production line
to stop. He is asked to find the fault.

As described earlier, the way a subject chooses a page to view depends
on the display page arrangement condition. When a subject views a new page,
the boxes and arrows are labelled, but the values of the arrows and the decision criteria are not shown. Thus, he can read the flow of information
between decisions, but he cannot see the details of how the information is
used to make each decision or the values of the information at the time of
"failure". He maneuvers through the logic to run "tests" via a mouse. To
read the status of the information (i.e., to run a "test"), he moves the
mouse until it is positioned on an information arrow of interest and clicks
a button on the mouse. This will light up the value of the information.
In a similar way, he can view the decision criteria by moving the mouse
until it is positioned on the box of interest and clicking the mouse. The
value of only one piece of information will be shown at a time. When the
mouse button is clicked on a piece of information, the value of another
piece of information that was displayed will disappear and the value of the

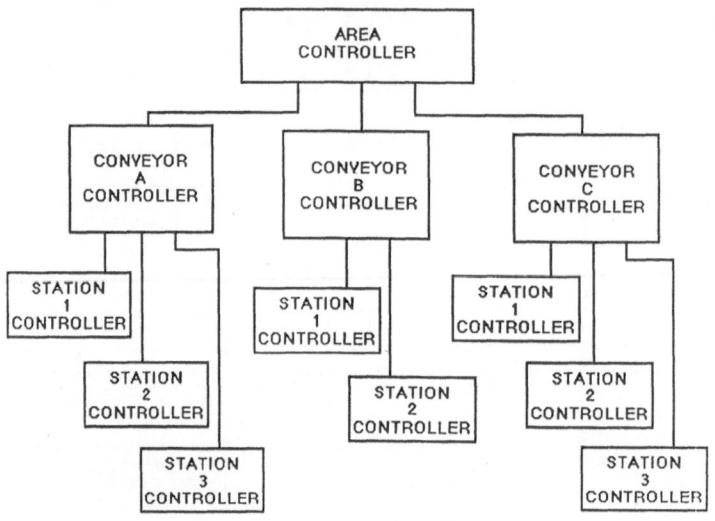

SYSTEM OVERVIEW

Figure 17. Screen Paging for "Hierarchy".

new information will be shown. Similarly, only one detailed description of the criteria of a decision can be seen at one time.

When he finds the incorrect decision (i.e., the fault), he makes sure the decision criteria for that box are shown, then he moves the mouse to the "Diagnose" box at the bottom of the page and clicks the mouse button again. If the diagnosis is correct, the experiment test is completed. If he is incorrect, the computer beeps, the words "Incorrect Diagnosis" appear briefly on the screen, then the screen returns to its status before the incorrect diagnosis. He continues trying until he correctly diagnoses the problem.

Subjects

The subjects will be electricians and maintenance engineers in computer-controlled production systems in the automotive industry. In general, electricians are responsible for maintaining all electrical and microprocessor-based equipment on the plant floor. It is important to note that not all electricians are involved in the troubleshooting of day-to-day failures within the computer-controlled production equipment. Some perform other conventional electrician activities such as "pulling wires" and "changing lightbulbs". Only those who are very knowledgeable about troubleshooting the new production equipment will be used as subjects. Plant personnel will guide us in the selection of electricians with the appropriate levels of expertise. Maintenance engineers are part of the plant's engineering staff. Like electricians, maintenance engineers also perform troubleshooting and failure tracing. The difference is that, theoretically, maintenance engineers tend to work on problems with longer time horizons, such as problems which occur frequently for several weeks in a row. In practice, the work of electricians and maintenance engineers overlaps considerably and there is frequent interaction between these two groups. In fact, many maintenance engineers were formerly electricians. Both groups are familiar with the same kinds of troubleshooting on the same kinds of equipment.

These personnel have been chosen as subjects for two reasons. First, their problems are the focus of this study. Using troubleshooters in an experiment to understand troubleshooting increases the internal validity of the experiment. Second, these maintenance personnel are experts in troubleshooting. The troubleshooting techniques and problems encountered by troubleshooting experts might differ from those of novices. Many experimental studies use novices, such as university undergraduates who participate in paid experiments, so their ability to generalize the results to describe the performance of experts is severely limited.

The subjects are employed at the same automotive component manufacturing and final assembly plants from which we are obtaining the field data on downtime. For example, several of the subjects will come from the body shop discussed earlier. We chose to use the same set of plants for both field data analysis and selection of experiment subjects to maintain the study's internal consistency and validity. Conclusions from the field data analysis can be integrated with conclusions of the experimental study to develop a single set of conclusions that describe the sources of downtime and troubleshooting difficulty in computer-controlled production systems in the automotive industry. Since the auto industry is a leader in the application of computer-controlled production technologies, and because its production technologies are representative of many mass production industries, we believe our findings will be generalizable (with appropriate caution) to other kinds of computer-controlled production systems in other industries.

What Parts of the Troubleshooting Process Are Affected by Complexity of System Design and Hierarchical Arrangement of Display Pages?

The experiment described above will give insight into how complexity of design and hierarchical arrangement of display pages affects troubleshooting performance. A supplementary detailed analysis of the troubleshooting process can give additional insight into why troubleshooting performance is affected. This additional insight would be instrumental in helping determine how to design manufacturing systems and their user interfaces to be maintainable. Possible approaches are being explored for studying the troubleshooting process to find out what parts of the process are strongly affected by the two factors under investigation.

The experiment environment will time-tag and record each of the user inputs. From the recorded data, we can obtain information about the information the subject seeks; the sequence of acquisition; how much information is required; and for what duration information is examined. The fault diagnosis process will be reconstructed from these data. This type of information has been used by other researchers to highlight the role of memory in fault diagnosis decision-making (Einhorn and Hogarth, 1981).

Some indications of problems in troubleshooting performance can be obtained directly from the reconstructed process. For example, frequent requests for page changes would indicate problems with the paging arrangement of the user interface. In a similar way, repeated tests of the output of the same decision would indicate that the subject needed to retrace previous troubleshooting steps. Retracing troubleshooting steps might indicate that the system design is too complex and interrelated to allow efficient troubleshooting strategies.

Also under consideration is modelling the troubleshooting process used by subjects. Studying the model might indicate where complexity of the system design and hierarchical display page arrangement affect the troubleshooting process. One way of formally modelling the troubleshooting process is to use a modification of the production system model proposed by Newell and Simon (1972) as a way to describe human problem solving. A production system model is a list of situation-action rules (called productions). The

401

situation side of a production describes a possible condition of the world. The action side describes an action to be performed if that state of world exists. When the conditions of more than one production are satisfied, conflict resolution rules govern the choice of production to perform. Early production system models used priority ranking as a conflict resolution procedure. More recently, production system models used a set of conflict resolution rules including recency of conditions (productions with conditions that have been satisfied more recently are chosen over productions with conditions that have been satisfied longer), specificity (productions with conditions that are more specific are chosen over productions with conditions that are general in nature), refractoriness (a production cannot be performed twice on the same set of conditions), and recency of production (newer productions are chosen over older productions). We do not know which kinds of conflict resolution rules will be appropriate for this application.

Production system models were originally developed to describe the details of basic information processing tasks, such as reaction time tasks, and explicitly modelled the changes in the contents of short term and long term memory. Finding this level of detail too cumbersome for their application, Rouse, Rouse, and Pellegrino (1980) modified the production system model. Their modification maintained the priority-ranked set of situation-action rules, but at a more aggregate level of detail which focused on tasks rather than on the contents of long-term and short-term memory. Rouse, Rouse, and Pellegrino used the modified production system model to describe the decision-making processes of fault diagnosis. Their work has shown that production system models of troubleshooting performance can be derived from studying a troubleshooting subject's information acquisition behavior. In their study, the rules governed choices of tests to be performed. In this study, the analogous decision would be which decision box or arrow to "click" the mouse on to test.

Given a production system model of the troubleshooting process, problems can be pinpointed by studying the possible rules to determine whether a better rule (i.e., one which would lead to the fault more quickly) could have been invoked at certain points in the process (i.e., if the subject had better information). Comparing the rules actually chosen with the rules that are "better", but were not chosen might lead to insight into why the better rules were not chosen. Understanding why the better rules were not chosen might lead to insight into what could be done in terms of design of the system or design of the user interface to make the better rules more likely to be chosen.

Using the fault diagnosis problem-solving model, the subjects' choices of rules could be compared between different treatment combinations to see whether certain combinations of complexity in system design and hierarchical display page arrangements lead to more frequent choices of "better" rules.

CONCLUDING REMARKS

This study is unique from an industrial perspective because it approaches familiar data from a new perspective. The field data used in the first portion of this study are collected and analyzed by plant management to decide which pieces of equipment to focus maintenance efforts on each week. Plant personnel who are busy keeping their plants operating do not have the time to abstract these data to help in the design of future plants. An academic vantage point allows longer-term analysis such as the analysis described here.

The study is also unique from an academic viewpoint because it involves analysis of data not normally available to researchers. Field data from

computer-controlled production systems are scarce in academia for two
reasons. First, computer-controlled productions are new, so little field
data is available. Second, to gather and interpret the available data
requires close interaction with personnel at manufacturing facilities.

Many other research projects focus on designing systems to prevent
excessive downtime. Most of these studies, focus on reducing the <u>number</u>
of failures by designing the systems to be <u>reliable</u>. Since our preliminary
evidence suggests that personnel in computer-controlled production systems
are having more difficulty in reducing maintainability than reliability, we
have chosen to study design of these systems for maintainability.

For many years, researchers have focused on ways of designing systems
to be maintainable. Much of the work on design for maintainability has
focused on physical aspects of the repair tasks in maintenance, such as
placing screws where they can be easily reached by a screwdriver or designing
electronic modules for ease of replacement. This study focuses on psychological aspects of maintainability, and on diagnosis tasks rather than
repair tasks.

The psychological aspects of fault diagnosis in software have been the
focus of research projects for several decades. In fact, there is a strong
parallel between the development of software and its maintainability and
the development of manufacturing systems and their maintainability. The
problem of maintainability of software developed as computer programs became
larger and more complex. Now the problem of maintainability is becoming a
growing problem in computer-controlled manufacturing systems as these systems
become larger and more complex.

While there is a body of experimental research that addresses the psychological aspects of fault diagnosis and system maintainability, no study
has addressed the problem in the same way as this study. A number of previous studies have investigated the effects of specific components of physical system complexity (e.g. number of components or number of connections
between components) on the ability to diagnose faults in that system.
Other previous studies have investigated the effects of different display
strategies on the ability to comprehend a complex system and solve problems
in that system. This study provides a new contribution because it investigates the interactions between these two factors in the specific context
of computer-controlled manufacturing systems.

ACKNOWLEDGEMENTS

We acknowledge the contribution of the Department of Engineering and
Public Policy and the Engineering Design Research Center, an engineering
research center funded by the National Science Foundation, for providing
graduate student support for this project.

REFERENCES

Brooke, J. B,. and Duncan, K. D., 1981, "Effects of System Display Format
    on Performance in a Fault Location Task", <u>Ergonomics</u>, <u>24</u>, (3), pp. 175-
    189.

Brooke, J. B., and Duncan, K. D., 1983, "A Comparison of Hierarchically
    Paged Scrolling Displays for Fault Finding", <u>Ergonomics</u>, <u>26</u>, (4), pp. 465-
    477.

Card, S. K., Moran, T. P., and Newell, A., 1983, <u>The Psychology of Human-</u>

Computer Interaction, Lawrence Erlbaum Associates, Inc., Hillsdale, NJ.

Dray, S. M., Ogden, W. G., and Vestewig, R. E, 1981, "Measuring Performance with a Menu-Selection Human-Computer Interface", _Proceedings of the Human Factors Society 25th Annual Meeting_, pp. 746-748.

Einhorn, H. J., and Hogarth, R. M., 1981, "Behavioral Decision Theory: Processes of Judgment and Choice", _Annual Review of Psychology_, 32, pp. 53-88.

English, W. K., Engelbart, D. C., and Berman, M. L., 1967, "Display-Selection Techniques for Text Manipulation", _IEEE Transactions on Human Factors in Electronics_, 8, pp. 5-15.

Furnas, G., 1986, "Generalized Fisheye Views", _Human Factors in Computing Systems_, CHI '86 Conference Proceedings, Mantei, M., and Orbeton, P., eds., April, pp. 16-23.

Goldbeck, R. A., Bernstein, B. B., Hillix, W. A., and Marx, M. H., 1957, "Application of the Half-Split Technique to Problem-Solving Tasks", _Journal of Experimental Psychology_, 53, (5).

Henneman, R. L., and Rouse, W. B., 1986, "On Measuring the Complexity of Monitoring and Controlling Large-Scale Systems", _IEEE Transactions on Systems, Man and Cybernetics_, SMC-16, (2), March/April, pp. 193-207.

Johnson, E. J., Payne, J. W., Schkade, D. A., and Bettman, J. R., 1986, _Monitoring Information Processing and Decisions: The Mouselab System_.

Levin, D. P., 1986, "In a High-Tech Drive, GM Falls Below Rivals in Auto Profit Margins", _The Wall Street Journal_, 22 July 1986, p. 1, col. 6.

Miller, D. P., 1981, "The Depth/Breadth Tradeoff in Hierarchical Computer Menus", _Proceedings of the Human Factors Society 25th Annual Meeting_, pp. 296-300.

Miller, S. M., and Bereiter, S. R., 1986, _A Comparison of a Manual and Computer-Integrated Production Process in Terms of Process Control Decision-Making_, Technical Report CMU-RI-TR 86-6, The Robotics Institute, Carnegie Mellon University, Pittsburgh, PA.

Mitchell, R., 1986, "Detroit Stumbles on Its Way to the Future", Business Week, 16 June 1986, pp. 103-104.

Nag, A., 1986, "Tricky Technology: Auto Makers Discover 'Factory of the Future' Is Headache Just Now", _The Wall Street Journal_, 13 May 1986.

Newell, A., and Simon, H., 1972, _Human Problem Solving_, Prentice-Hall, Englewood Cliffs, NJ.,

Parnas, D. L., 1972, "Information Distribution Aspects of Design Methodology", _Information Processing_, 71, North-Holland Publishing Company, pp. 339-344.

Robertson, McCracken, G. D., and Newell, A., 1981, "The ZOG Approach to Man-Machine Communication", _International Journal of Man-Machine Studies_, 14, pp. 461-488.

Rouse, W. B., and Rouse, S. H., 1979, "Measures of Complexity of Fault Diagnosis Tasks", _IEEE Transactions on Systems, Man and Cybernetics_, SMC-9, (11), November 1979, pp. 720-727.

Rouse, W. B., Rouse, S. H., and Pellegrino, S. J., 1980, "A Rule-Based Model of Human Problem Solving Performance in Fault Diagnosis Tasks", _IEEE Transactions of Systems, Man and Cybernetics_, SMC-10, (7), pp. 366-376.

Russo, J. E., Johnson, E. J., and Stephens, D. L., 1985, _When are Verbal Protocols Valid?_, Unpublished working paper, Cornell University.

Seppala, P., and Salvendy, G., 1985, "Impact of Depth of Menu Hierarchy on Performance Effectiveness in a Supervisory Task: Computerized Flexible Manufacturing System", _Human Factors_, 27, (6), pp. 713-722.

Snowberry, K., Parkinson, S. R., and Sisson, N., 1983, "Computer Display Menus", _Ergonomics_, 26, (7), pp. 699-712.

Stevens, W. P., Myers, G. J., and Constantine, L. L., 1974, "Structured Design", _IBM Systems Journal_, 13, (2), pp. 115-139.

Winer, B. J., 1971, _Statistical Principles in Experimental Design_, Second Edition, McGraw-Hill Book Company, NY.

Winter, D., 1986, "High-Tech's Midlife Crisis", _Ward's Auto World_, 22, (6), June 1986, pp. 33-36.

Wohl, J. G., 1983, "Cognitive Capability Versus System Complexity in Electronic Maintenance", _IEEE Transactions on Systems, Man and Cybernetics_, SMC-13, (4), July/August 1983.

SOFTWARE PATTERN CONSTRUCTS

Ross A. Gagliano and G. Scott Owen

Department of Mathematics and Computer Science
Georgia State University
Atlanta, Georgia 30303-3083

Abstract: A software pattern construct is a syntactical structure in a
higher order language which provides examples of correct format for common
programming expressions. Typical applications include: input and output
phrasing and the use of prompts; control structures; conditional and logical
constructs; and secondary data structures as arrays, records, and files.
This paper attempts to describe software patterns, and to provide motivation
and examples for their use with several languages in an evolving on-line
reference system.

INTRODUCTION

Novice programmers, occasional programmers, and programmers who use a
variety of languages frequently have difficulty in remembering the precise
syntax of a particular software construct. An example of this, which is
shown later, is the multiway branch statement; e.g., CASE in Pascal and Ada,
and SWITCH in C. These constructs are all quite similar, but do have slight
variations among them.

Another example might be the use of string versus character delimiters.
Ada and C use " for strings and ' for characters while Pascal uses ' for both
strings and characters. A simple example of the particular software construct is usually sufficient, and it has occurred to us that the computer
system itself could provide such assistance for the more common expressions.

The notion of a software pattern construct is modeled after the so-called
Cloze Procedure (Cook, Bregar, and Foote, 1982; Entin, 1986). This procedure
utilizes a skeleton of a particular fragment of code to test the skill of
the programmer. This use of the Cloze Procedure with programming languages
was derived from its original application, that of measuring the comprehension of a group of readers by requiring them to correctly insert words that
were deleted from a passage of prose.

Another approach to the problem was to provide what is called a "Conversational Programming System" (Sebesta, 1985). These systems consist of:
syntax directed editors, graphics oriented editors, incremental compilers,
and other software tools. Several variations of this approach have been
attempted, and work is continuing in this area (Meyer, 1986; Harrison,

Rosenfeld, Wang, and Westin, 1986). However, these systems are difficult to implement, and, also, cumbersome to modify for new languages.

A much simpler approach, it seems to us, would be to have a set of readily available sample software pattern constructs. This would be both more easily implementable and directly modifiable to incorporate new languages. Thus, our work on the development of a set of software pattern constructs has begun, and a viable means to implement their use has been explored in an on-line system at the Georgia State University.

ORLS SYSTEM

A major goal of this research is to establish an Online Reference for Language Syntax (ORLS) System. The ORLS system would be menu driven, and would include several programming languages. The objective of the ORLS system is to provide examples of many of the necessary Software Pattern Constructs in order that programmers could quickly resolve their own questions regarding language syntax. This paper presents some preliminaries of the design and implementation of the ORLS system. Even though this system is primarily aimed at undergraduate and graduate students, its principles are generally applicable to other programming environments.

Before discussing the design of the ORLS system let us define the constraints and provide a description of our local programming environment. At Georgia State University (GSU), much of the Computer Science (CSc) program is based on IBM PC compatible microcomputers. The students are exposed to a variety of programming languages, all of which run on these machines. These languages include Pascal, Ada, C, FORTRAN, and PROLOG.

The students use Pascal (and some FORTRAN) for their first two courses, and then Ada is used for the third course (Data Structures). They are introduced to the languages C and PROLOG in a course on Programming Languages. In many courses, e.g., Computer Graphics and Numerical Analysis, they can use any language of their choice. More languages will be made available in the near future.

Until recently, the PC's available to the students were stand alone floppy disk based systems. These systems are all hardwired to the GSU mainframe system, thus used primarily as terminals by both the students and many others outside of the CSc program. With this configuration, any kind of general on-line help facility was not feasible. However, the GSU Computer Center now has begun to network all of the PC's together with several hard disk based file servers. With these commonly accessible disks, it is now feasible to implement the ORLS system.

The ORLS system will actually be a part of an overall help system which the Computer Center is in the process of installing. The primary focus of the overall system will not be beginning programmers, but, users who are mainly running canned programs on the mainframe.

This major system is designed in two parts. A small memory resident program will always be available via a set of keystrokes. Having this program resident in memory allows the user to invoke it in the middle of editing text or other mainframe sessions, without exiting. When invoked, this program will display a menu of possible choices. After the user has made a menu selection, the program will then download from the hard disk system the appropriate submenus or help screens.

The ORLS system will be made a part of the main menu. When this choice is made, a second menu will be displayed. This menu will list the available

The CASE statement is a multiway branch statement of the form

```
CASE expression IS
    WHEN alternative1 => DO1;
    WHEN alternative2 => DO2;
    WHEN alternative3 => DO3;
              .
              .
    WHEN OTHERS => DO_SOMETHING;
END CASE;
```

Expression is a discrete type and

the alternatives are possible values of the discrete type or subranges.

For example, assume the user defined type:

```
Type Day is (Mon, Tue, Wed, Thu, Fri, Sat, Sun);
Today: Day;
```

Then we can have a CASE statement:

```
CASE Today is
    WHEN Mon => Do1;
    WHEN Tue|Wed => Do2;    -- Tue or Wed
    WHEN Thu..Sun => Do3;   -- Thu through Sun
END CASE;
```

Remarks:
All possibilities of a CASE expression must be accounted for, using WHEN OTHERS => DoS; if necessary. Each alternative may appear in only one WHEN statement. After the procedure corresponding to a particular choice is executed, execution proceeds to the first statement after the CASE statement.

Figure 1. The CASE Statement for Ada.

languages. The user will then select one of the languages, which will invoke another menu displaying the suboptions. For each language, this menu will be divided into: Control Statements, Data Types, and Utility Programs for that particular language. The Control Statements will be subdivided into the standard classifications of Selection, Repetition, and Sequential. The Data Types will be subdivided into Intrinsic and User Defined Data Types.

EXAMPLE CONSTRUCTS

Some of the more widely needed constructs involve the use of external input formatting (the use of prompts) and the means for continuous execution of a program without additional commands for the particular trace of compile, link, load and execute, etc. Likewise, the formats for parameters, both formal and actual, are a constant source of error and confusion. In Pascal and Ada, for example, it is possible to have: global parameters, value/IN or variable/IN-OUT parameter types.

Similarly, the constructs for secondary data types; i.e., not the simple date types of INTEGER, REAL, CHARACTER, etc., cause great difficulty in correctly specifying their structure. These include the ARRAY, LINKED LIST, RECORD and FILE. None of these have been illustrated here.

However, several examples of help screens are given in Figures 1 and 2. Figure 1 is a Help Screen for the CASE statement in Ada. It contains a

The SWITCH statement is a multiway branch statement of the form

```
switch (expression) {
    case alternative1 : do1; break;
    case alternative2 : do2; break;
    case alternative3 : do3; break;
            .
            .
    default : do_something; break;
}
```

Expression is an integer expression or an expression that can be converted to an integer expression.

The _alternatives_ are constant integer expressions or expressions that can be converted to constant integer expressions.

For example, look at a switch statement using characters:

```
switch (c) {
    case 'a' : doa (); break;
    case 'b' : dob (); break;
    case 'c' : doc (); break;
    default  : do_something (); break;
}
```

Remarks:
Each alternative may appear in only one case statement. After the procedure corresponding to a particular choice is executed, execution proceeds to the next case statement. When a break statement is encountered, the execution proceeds to the first statement after the switch statement. All possible alternatives do not have to be covered; and if no matches to (c) are found, execution proceeds to the first statement after the switch statement.

Figure 2.   SWITCH Statement in C.

brief description of the CASE statement and the language specific constraints or idiosyncrasies. In Ada, for example, all possible choices must be accounted for by using the OTHERS statement, if necessary.

Figure 2 is a similar help screen for the SWITCH statement in C. Here, it should be pointed out that after executing the statement corresponding to one choice, execution does not automatically drop through to the end of the switch statement. Instead the next choice is executed unless a BREAK statement is used.

When appropriate, brief hints as to the use of certain software constructs are also provided. An example of this would be the EXCEPTION data type in Ada. A common way to use EXCEPTIONS is to declare and handle them in a local block. There would then be an example shown of this usage. Also, the scope of an EXCEPTION is frequently confusing, and this too would be discussed in the help screen.

DISCUSSION

Although not in the category of software pattern constructs, part of the ORLS system will provide a description of available utility programs and software tools for the different languages. Also planned for inclusion are libraries of procedures. This will be especially important for Ada since new software tools and packages will be constantly added as the Ada programming environment is improved.

This component of the ORLS system will include a brief description of each software tool or package and an example of its usage. One such example is envisioned for the string handling package in Ada.

The ORLS system will go on-line at GSU during the Fall quarter of 1986. Student usage will be monitored and the system will be modified as necessary, in response to user demand. Because it will continually have new languages added and the entire system upgraded, the ORLS system will be both dynamic and evolving.

SUMMARY

Methods to assist the programming community, particularly those who infrequently maintain or modify code in a variety of languages, are crucial to future software systems. Novel techniques, such as the software pattern constructs as presented here will be invaluable for increasing productivity and bringing computer proficiency to a wider, and, perhaps, less fluent, group of practitioners.

A judicious application of these constructs, and the particular usage in an on-line fashion such as the evolving GSU ORLS system, appears promising in improving both the user-friendly products and the research into man-machine interfacing. In essence, the use of these constructs appear to allow the human to more effectively perform pattern recognition and symbol manipulation, while leaving the tasks of tracking and maintaining large sets of text, strings, tokens, and data to the machines.

REFERENCES

Cook, C., Bregar, W., and Foote, D., 1982, "A Preliminary Investigation of the Use of the Cloze Procedure as a Measure of Program Understanding", Proceedings of the 1st Symposium on Empirical Foundations of Information and Software Science (EFISS), Atlanta, November 1982.

Entin, E. G., 1986, "Using the Cloze Procedure with Computer Programs: A Deeper Look", Proceedings of the 1986 ACM SIGCSE Meeting, Cincinnati, pp. 153-162.

Harrison, W. H., Rosenfeld, J. L., Wang, C. C., and Westin, B. A., 1986, "Structured Editing with RPDE", Computer Language, 3, (9), September 1986, pp. 93-100.

Meyer, B., 1986, "Cepage: A Software Design Tool", Computer Language, 3, (9), September 1986, pp. 43-53.

Sebesta, R. W., 1985, "Conversational Programming Systems", Journal of Pascal, Ada, and Modula-2, May/June 1985, pp. 9-22.

8. SOFTWARE TRANSITION TOOLS AND TECHNIQUES

A TOOL FOR TRANSITIONING COBOL PROGRAMMERS TO ADA*

Arthur Jones, Daniel Hocking, and Jagdish Agrawal

United States Army Information System Engineering Command
Army Institute of Research in Management Information
Communications, and Computer Science
(AIRMICS)

Abstract: Transitioning of large systems from one environment to another involves a large front-end cost of "porting people" to the destination environment. Programmers who have been working in the old environment for several years have gained considerable expertise in using that environment. Capitalizing on that expertise while training these programmers to use the new environment is very useful in increasing productivity in the new environment and in reducing the front-end cost of the transition.

Information System Engineering Command has many experienced COBOL programmers with considerable expertise in using an existing environment that is being transitioned from COBOL to Ada, and from batch oriented file systems to interactive database oriented systems. Ada training of these programmers benefits from capitalizing on the understanding these programmers have of the data structures they deal with, and of the software engineering principles they use in developing their systems. We are developing a Computer Assisted Instruction (CAI) package that uses such a philosophy.

INTRODUCTION

The computer was employed as a tool of instruction as early as 1960. Yet CAI developers have not taken advantage of this early beginning to mature CAI. In academia, for example, CAI has suffered from a lack of institutional incentives. Accordingly, this promising learning medium has been decidedly under-utilized at all levels of education.

The mistaken perception of such developments as mainly programming projects may have discouraged subject-matter specialists from directing more effort to CAI. Consequently, technical as well as educational direction CAI courseware development was dictated more by programmers than by learning theorists and subject-matter experts. Courseware has tended, therefore, to be categorized as clever programs, but uninspired, unimaginative, and ineffective instruments of education. These early disappointments further retarded acceptance of CAI.

Today, as the CAI development process is better understood, high quality courseware is emerging as a more frequent project outcome. An equally

```
.......................................................
    .              .                .              .
    .              .                .              .
    Instructor          Trainee           Self-paced
    .              .                             learner
    .              .
    ...........
    .Edit      .         ...............      ..........
    .course    .         .Follow course .     .Creat    .
    .material  .         .sequence      .     .lesson   .
    ...........          ...............      .sequence.
    .                                         ..........
    .
    ...........                               ..........
    .Edit      .                              .Select   .
    .lesson    .                              .lesson   .
    .sequence  .                              ..........
    ...........
    .
    ...........
    .Edit      .
    .student   .
    .diskette  .
    ...........
    .
    ..............
    .Print       .
    .Examination.
    ..............
```

Figure 1. CAI Service Tracks.

important improvement today has been realized in the area of hardware development. Until the late 1970's access to CAI authoring tools was limited
to expensive mainframes. The erstwhile requirement of high-cost mainframe
computer systems for running CAI applications can now be addressed by low-
cost microcomputers. Thus, currently the hardware and the methodology and
tools needed to implement effective CAI courseware are within the grasp of
the modest budget.

    This project evolved from an appointment of Prof. Arthur Jones of
Morehouse College as a 1986 Summer-Professor at AIRMICS. Dr. Jones' assignment was to port his Apple II based Ada tutorial to an IBM PC compatible
system and to modify the course to reflect a COBOL-literature audience.

IMPLEMENTATION

    The courseware that we are developing was designed with three cate-
gories of users in mind. First, the instructor of a formal course who has
certain administrative needs; second, the trainee in a formal Ada classroom
setting whose lessons may be "programmed" by his/her instructor; and third,
the independent learner in a self-paced mode, who may require more freedom
than the classroom trainee. The self-paced learner is expected to have prior
programming experience with a high-order language. Operational services
provided for the instructor include a facility for creating a course diskette
for trainees, editing or modifying an existing lesson schedule sequence,
and generating exercises or printed examinations. These services are designed to give the instructor as much control as required over the pace of
this out-of-classroom learning activity.

    The Ada CAI provides for the learner expository rules on Ada in a
frame oriented format, illustrative examples of those rules, and exercises.

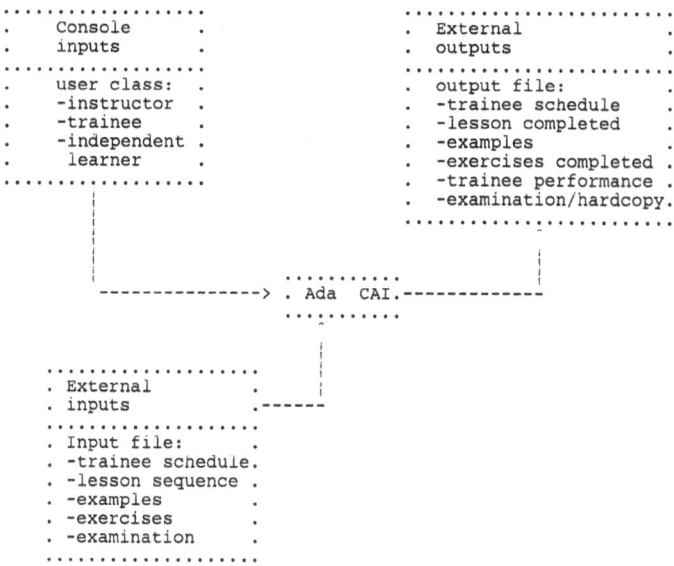

Figure 2.   Data Flow Diagram.

The learner is prompted to answer exercises, mainly of the multiple choice type, and is informed as to the correctness of his/her response. A record of the performance of the trainee is maintained by the CAI system. Following the termination of a training session, the CAI system "remembers" the point of exit as the point of re-entry of the next session. Generally, a trainee's access to course material is limited to a review of previously covered material and the next section of uncovered material; he may not advance beyond his next section. The self-paced learner, on the other hand, may proceed through the course material with complete freedom.

Understanding of the Ada CAI may be enhanced by Figure 1 and Figure 2.

INSTRUCTIONAL DESIGN

The Ada CAI is designed to exploit the learner's knowledge of COBOL as it transitions him/her to Ada programming. It presumes that the COBOL programmer has had some exposure to large system development and maintenance. As a result of this background, the goals and, to some extent, the methodologies of software engineering may be profitable used as a common theme throughout the CAI course.

Software engineering methodologies and goals as well as the concepts of analogy and context form the foundation upon which the Ada CAI learning strategy is based. Analogy will be the primary line of attack: when possible, Ada concepts and techniques will be explained in terms of COBOL analogues. Inherent in this approach is the desire to match an Ada solution to a COBOL situation rather than the converse. That is to say, that by the analogy approach we propose to exercise an "Ada mind-set" against a COBOL foil.

In many instances, of course, Ada-COBOL parallel constructs do not exist. These cases, when appropriate, may be addressed by borrowing a well-known application from the COBOL environment. For example, the Ada concept of overloading may be introduced as a solution to certain variant computer applications across the branches of U.S. military services. Such analogies as these may be helpful, of course, in forging a bridge from COBOL TO Ada concepts, but they have severe limitations in transmitting the Ada style of programming. After all, the batch oriented COBOL environment is a far cry from the interactive, database, parallel processing real-time Ada environment. The package, for example, which is so essential and fundamental to Ada, has no counterpart on COBOL. Yet, when discussed in terms of such software engineering goals as program modularity and information hiding, the package can be easily appreciated by the COBOL programmer.

Finally, the Ada style of programming will be inculcated through the use of program segments as well, as given in the example in the appendix, where the coded complete programs for the solution to "the leaf counting problem" cited by Booth (1983) is listed.

SUMMARY

This approach to "porting" COBOL programmers to an Ada programming environment should be viewed as somewhat experimental. It is offered as a reasonable solution to a very real problem, but with no claims on its perfection. However, its adaptability does not permit improvements through easy modifications.

REFERENCES

Arstrong, Russell, 1973, Modular Programming in COBOL, John Wiley & Sons.

Booth, Grady, 1983, Software Engineering with Ada, Benjamin/Cummings Publishing Co.

Chmura, Lewis J., and Ledgrad, Henry S., 1976, COBOL with Style-Programming Proverbs, Hayden Book Co.

Davis, John S., 1981, Ada - Suitable Replacement for COBOL?, AIRMICS Report, February 1981.

Dennis, J., and Kansky, R., 1984, Instructional Computing, Scott Foresman and Co.

O'Neil, Harold F., 1981, Computer-Based Instruction, A State-of-the-Art Assessment, Academic Press.

Reference Manual for the Ada Programming Language, 1983, Department of Defense.

Spence, J. Wayne, 1985, COBOL For the 80's, 2nd edition, West Publishing Co.

Waldrop, P. B., 1984, "Behavior Reinforcement Strategies for Computer-Assisted Instruction: Programming Success", Education Technology, 24, Summer 1984, pp. 38-42.

Coded solution to the "leaf counting problem" in (3)

```
with TEXT_IO; use TEXT_IO;
package body COUNTER_PACKAGE is

procedure DISPLAY (COUNTER:  in COUNTER_TYPE) is
     package COUNTER_IO is new  INTEGER_IO (COUNTER_TYPE);
     use COUNTER_IO;
begin
     NEW_LINE;
     put (COUNTER);
     NEW_LINE;
end DISPLAY;

procedure INCREMENT (COUNTER:  in out COUNTER_TYPE) is
begin
     COUNTER := COUNTER + 1;
end INCREMENT;

procedure ZERO (COUNTER:  out COUNTER_TYPE) is
begin
     COUNTER   :=0;
end ZERO

end COUNTER_PACKAGE;



   package COUNTER_PACKAGE is
      type COUNTER_TYPE is limited private;
      procedure DISPLAY (COUNTER: IN  COUNTER_TYPE);
      procedure INCREMENT (COUNTER: in out COUNTER_TYPE);
      procedure ZERO  (COUNTER:  out  COUNTER_TYPE);
   private
      type COUNTER_TYPE is new NATURAL;
   end COUNTER_PACKAGE;



   with COUNTER_PACKAGE, PILE_PACKAGE, TREE_PACKAGE;
   use  COUNTER_PACKAGE, PILE_PACKAGE, TREE_PACKAGE;
   with TEXT_IO;
   use  TEXT_IO;
   procedure COUNT_LEAVES is
      LEAF_COUNT     : COUNTER_TYPE
      LEFT_SUBTREE   : TREE_TYPE;
      RIGHT_SUBTREE  : PILE_TREE;
      PILE           : PILE_TYPE;
      TREE:          : TREE_TYPE;
   begin
      GET_INITIAL  (TREE) ;
      NEW_LINE;
      PUT_INITIAL  (TREE, ON =) PILE) ;
      ZERO (LEAF_COUNT) ;
      while is_NOT_EMPTY  (PILE)
        loop
           TAKE (TREE,  OFF =) PILE) ;
           if IS_SINGLE_LEAF  (TREE)
           then
             INCREMENT  (LEAF_COUNT) ;
             THROW_AWAY  (TREE) ;
             NEW_LINE;
           else
             SPLIT  (TREE,
                     LEFT_INTO =)  LEFT_SUBTREE,
                     RIGHT_INTO =)  RIGHT_SUBTREE) ;
             PUT  ( LEFT_SUBTREE,  ON =) PILE) ;
             PUT (RIGHT_SUBTREE,  ON =) PILE);
           end if;
      end loop;
      NEW_LINE;
      PUT ("number of leaves in the tree is : ") ;
      display (leaf_count);
   exception
      when CONSTRAINT_ERROR =)
        PUT_LINE ("Constraint error!!) ;
      when others =)
        PUT_LINE ("undetermined exception.") ;
   end COUNT_LEAVES;
```

```
package  body  PILE_PACKAGE is

    function IS_NOT_EMPTY (PILE  :  in   PILE_TYPE)
                                    return BOOLEAN is

    IS_NOT_EMPTY  :  BOOLEAN;
    begin
    if  PILE.NUMBER_OF_TREES  /= 0
      then
         IS_IT_NOT_EMPTY  := TRUE;
      else
         IS_IT_NOT_EMPTY  := FALSE;
      end if;
      return  IS_IT_NOT_EMPTY;
      end  IS_NOT_EMPTY;

procedure PUT              (TREE  :  in out TREE_TYPE;
                           ON  :  in out PILE_TYPE)  is
    begin
    ON.NUMBER_OF_TREES              := ON.NUMBER__OF_TREE + 1;
    ON.TREES (ON.NUMBER_OF_TREES):= TREE;
    OFF                      := ON;
    end PUT;

procedure PUT_INITIAL   (TREE  :  in  out  TREE_TYPE;
                         ON  :  in  ouy  PILR_TYPE) is

    begin
    ON.NUMBER_OF_TREES  := 1;
    ON. TREES (1)       := TREE;
    OFF

    end  PUT_INITIAL;

    procedure  TAKE         (TREE  :  out  TREE_TYPE;
                            OFF  :in out PILE_TYPE) is
    begin
    tree               := OFF.TREES(OFF.NUMBER_OF_TREES) ;
    OFF.NUMBER_OF_TREES := OFF.NUMBER_OF_TREES - 1;
    ON                 := OFF;
    end TAKE;

end PILE PACKAGE;
```

```
with TREE_PACKAGE;  use  TREE_PACKAGE;
with COUNTER_PACKAGE; use  COUNTER_PACKAGE;
package  PILE_PACKAGE  is
   TREE  :  TREE_TYPE;
type  PILE_TYPE is limited private;

function  IS_NOT_EMPTY (PILE  :  in   PILE_TYPE)
                                    return BOOLEAN;

procedure  PUT          (TREE  :  in out TREE_TYPE;
                         ON  :  in out PILE_TYPE);

procedure PUT_INITIAL   (TREE  :  in out TREE_TYPE;
                         ON  :  in out PILE_TYPE);

procedure TAKE          (TREE  :     out TREE_TYPE;
                         OFF  :  in out PILE_TYPE);

private
    type PILE_OF_TREES is array  (1..32) of TREE_TYPE;
    type PILE_TYPE is record
       NUMBER_OF_TREES  :  INTEGER;
       TREES            :  PILE_OF_TREES'
    end record
    ON  :  PILE_TYPE;
    OFF :  PILE_TYPE;
end PILE_PACKAGE;
```

```
package body TREE_PACKAGE is

function MAKETREE (X : in CHARACTER) return TREE_TYPE is
begin
if x = , ,
then
  TREE  := NULL;
else
  TREE.INFO  := X;
  TREE.LEFT  := null;
  TREE.RIGHT := null;
end if:
return TREE;
END MAKETREE;

function MAKE_TREE (X : in CHARACTER; TREE : in   TREE_TYPE
                                      return TREE_TYPE is

begin
if  TREE = null
then
  return new TREE_MODE' (X, null, null);
else if TREE.ALL.INFO = X
then
TREE.ALL.LEFT  :=MAKE_TREE (X,  TREE.ALL.LEFT);
else
  TREE.ALL.RIGHT  := MAKE_TREE (X, TREE.ALL.RIGHT);
end if;
return TREE;
end MAKE_TREE;

procedure  GET_INITIAL (TREE : out TREE_TYPE) is
begin
NEW_LINE;
PUT_LINE ("INITIALIZING THE PROCESS OF MAKING A TREE");
NEW_TREE := MAKETREE (' ');
NEW_LINE;
PUT_LINE ("TYPE A LETTER REPRESENTING A NODE");
NEW_LINE;
GET (X);
while x /= 'Z' loop
  NEW_TREE := MAKE_TREE (X, nEW TREE);
  NEW_INE;
  PUT_LINE ("TYPE  A LETTER REPRESENTING A NODE; Z TO END");
  GET (X);
end loop;
TREE := NEW_TREE;
end GET_INITIAL;



function IS_SINGLE_LEAF (TRE : in TREE_TYPE)  return BOOLEAN is
IT_IS_SINGLE_LEAF  : BOOLEAN;
begin
if TREE = NULL
  then
    IT_IS_SINGLE_LEAF  := TRUE;
else
    IT_IS_SINGLE_LEAF; := FALSE;
end if;
return  IT_IS_SINGLE_LEAF;
end IS_SINGLE_LEAF;

procedure SPLIT (TREE       : in out TREE_TYPE;
                 LEFT_INTO   :    out TREE_TYPE;
                 RIGHT_INTO  :    out TREE_TYPE) is

Y : CHARACTER;
Z : CHARACTER;
begin
LEFT_INFO  := TREE.LEFT;
RIGHT_INTO := TREE.RIGHT;
    .       := TREE.INFO;
if TREE.LEFT = null
  then
  Y := ' ';
  else
    Y := TREE.LEFT.INFO;
  end if;
```

421

```
                          if TREE.RIGHT = null
                             then
                                Z := ' ';
                             else
                                Z := TREE.RIGHT.INFO;
                          end if;
                          end SPLIT;

                    procedure THROW_AWAY  (TREE  : in out TREE_TYPE) is
                    begin
                    TREE   := null;
                    end THROW_AWAY;
                    end TREE_PACKAGE;




          with TEXT_IO; use TEXT_IO;
          with COUNTER_PACKAGE; use COUNTER_PACKAGE;
          package TREE_PACKAGE is
              X  :  CHARACTER;
              type TREE_TYPE is private;

              procedure GET_INITIAL    (TREE        :    OUT TREE_TYPE);

              procedure SPLIT          (TREE        : in out TREE_TYPE;
                                        LEFT_INTO    :    out TREE_TYPE;
                                        RIGHT_INTO   :    out TREE_TYPE);

              procedure TROW_AWAY      (TREE        : in out TREE_TYPE);

              function IS_SINGLE_LEAF (TREE         : in     TREE_TYPE
                                                       return BOOLEAN;

              function MAKETREE (X : in CHARACTER) return TREE_TYPE;

              function MAKE_TREE (X : in CHARACTER; TREE : in TREE_TYPE)
                                                     return  TREE_TYPE;

              private
                type TREE_NODE;
                type TREE_TYPE is access TREE_NODE;
                TYPE TREE_NODE is
                    record
                    INFO  : CHARACTER;
                    LEFT  : TREE_TYPE;
                    RIGHT : TREE_TYPE;
                  end record;
              TREE        : TREE_TYPE;
              NEW_TREE    : TREE_TYPE;
              TREES       : array (1..32) of TREE_TYPE;
          package COUNTER_PACKAGE is
              type COUNTER_TYPE is limited private;
              procedure DISPLAY (COUNTER: IN  COUNTER_TYPE);
              procedure INCREMENT (COUNTER: in out COUNTER_TYPE);
              procedure ZERO  (COUNTER:  out  COUNTER_TYPE);
          private
              type COUNTER_TYPE is new NATURAL;
          end COUNTER_PACKAGE;
```

422

COMPUTER ASSISTED PASCAL TO ADA PROGRAM TRANSLATION

G. Scott Owen

Dept. of Mathematics and Computer Science
Georgia State University
Atlanta, Georgia 30303

Abstract: This paper discusses the program PasTran, developed and distributed by RR Software, which performs a Pascal to Ada program translation.
This tool is extremely useful as it decreases the translation time by a
factor of about ten. PasTran, which runs on IBM PC's and compatibles, does
both syntactic and semantic checking and translates all standard Pascal
constructs, including those for which no direct Ada analogue exists. PasTran
flags nonstandard Pascal constructs as errors, reports them, and continues
with the translation. PasTran performs the translation at an approximate
rate of 250 lines per minute on an IBM AT, a rate which is somewhat dependent
on the number of errors which PasTran reports.

PasTran has been used to translate many Pascal programs, ranging in
size from trivial 20 line programs to large (4 - 6,000 lines) programs.
While some translated programs can be directly compiled and executed, there
generally is some stylistic cleaning up to perform, plus the remove of some
"errors" due to the presence of nonstandard Pascal constructs. The paper
will discuss how PasTran translates the standard Pascal constructs with no
direct Ada analog, e.g., the Pascal WITH for a record, how it deals with
nonstandard Pascal constructs, and will give some hints as to how to pre-
process the input Pascal program.

INTRODUCTION

The large and growing commitment to Ada by the U.S. Department of
Defense, and several other Federal agencies and large international commer-
cial firms, is well documented. This commitment has been primarily for
embedded computer systems and scientific programming. However, at the 4th
Annual National Conference on Ada Technology held at Atlanta, Georgia,
March 1986, it became apparent that the same sort of commitment is forth-
coming for government data processing activities, particularly for the U.S.
Army standard management information systems.

This commitment to Ada indicates that not only will new applications be
developed in Ada, but, also that previously developed applications will be
translated into Ada. Automated software tools will play an important part
in this transition from a non-Ada to an Ada environment. In this paper, I
will briefly review general work in this area and then discuss one such

tool, PasTran, which translates Pascal programs into Ada.

GENERAL LANGUAGE TRANSLATION TOOLS

The general issues involved in the moving from a Non-Ada environment to an Ada environment, for example, from FORTRAN to Ada or COBOL to Ada, have been briefly discussed in the literature (Martin, 1986; Wallis, 1985). There are several issues to be considered, some of them of a non-technical and more general managerial nature. These include managerial implications and changes in working practices, as well as the actual code conversion process.

One of the first issues to be considered would be the rationale of converting from one language, such as COBOL, to Ada. Positive reasons for such a conversion would include reduced code size. For example, in Schill (Schill, Smeaton, and Jackman, 1985) they report a 10:1 code size reduction in moving from COBOL to Ada. They admit that this is very unusual as there was a large amount of redundant COBOL code and a rewrite in COBOL would have provided a significant reduction. But, in general, it is not known how much of a reduction is to be expected.

The question of improved functionality also has to be considered. Will the Ada code perform better than the old code, in terms of speed and response time? A major issue is maintainability of the old code versus Ada code. For example, Schill (Schill, Smeaton, and Jackman, 1985) claims the Ada code is generally more readable and easily maintained than the old COBOL code, but again, this has not really been studied.

In the area of actual code translation, several issues arise. There have been simple table driven translations of FORTRAN to Ada, for example in Slape (Slape and Wallis, 1983), but these have not been satisfactory. There are problems with specific language constructs, e.g. the COMMON block and DO-LOOP in FORTRAN. Other problems arise from global language issues such as differences in data typing and the scope of variables. The programs need to be looked at from a semantic as well as a syntactic viewpoint. This has been discussed for FORTRAN programs (Santhanam, 1986).

One possible technique is to use Artificial Intelligence methods as well as compiler technology in the translation. Claims have been made for this approach (Electronics, 1985).

Because the design of Ada was based on Pascal, the translation from Pascal to Ada should be easier than would be the case with languages such as FORTRAN or COBOL. After a syntax and semantic translation from Pascal to Ada, the major task would be to give the resultant program more of an Ada flavor. This would include items such as the breaking up of the translated Ada program into Ada packages, and perhaps adding new features such as the use of exceptions and generics.

We have used a software tool, PasTran, to help in the conversion of Pascal programs to Ada. We have used PasTran to translate over fifty small Pascal programs (<1000 lines of code), primarily for Computer Science class programs. We have also used it to translate three moderate sized programs (between 3,000 and 6,000 lines of code) used in research.

DESCRIPTION OF PASTRAN

PasTran is a product of RR Software, Inc. (P. O. Box, 1512, Madison, Wisconsin, 53701), who also market a partial Ada compiler (Janus/Ada) for IBM PCs and compatibles. PasTran requires 180 K bytes of free memory and can be

```
C>pastran fibtst.pas/q/f1/v

P A S T R A N - Version 2.0
  Serial number: AIMP-1260
  Copyright (c) 1984, 1985 - R R Software, Inc.  All rights reserved.
  8086/8088 version (MS-DOS 2.xx)
Pass I
No user prompting after errors.
Use short software floating point.
Generate code for validated Ada compilers.
Input file is FIBTST.PAS
Result file is FIBTST.PKG
#
22 lines found
String space usage: 10% (450 characters out of 4479)
Hash table usage: 12% (82 buckets out of 661)
Pass I completed
Pass II
%
Heap usage: 3% (1803 bytes out of 45242)
Parse stack usage: 14% (22 stack items out of 150)
Report usage: 0% (9 reports out of 1000)
Pass II completed
Pass III
*
Pass III completed
```

Figure 1. Invocation of Pastran and Screen Messages.

run off of a floppy disk system. PasTran comes with a well written manual
of about 150 pages. The current price of PasTran is $2,000 but educational
discounts are available.

PasTran performs both syntactic and semantic checking of the input
Pascal program. It will convert about 95% of the full Pascal language and
it flags untranslatable constructs, either at translate time or in the
output code. PasTran expects a correct Pascal program as input, but it
will sometimes work even with an incorrect program.

PasTran is a three pass translator. The first pass performs the syntax
analysis of the input program. PasTran will attempt to correct any syntax
errors, such as missing semicolons, but if there are severe syntax problems
then PasTran aborts after the first pass. The second pass performs the
semantic analysis of the input program. If there is a semantic error or if
PasTran cannot understand the semantics, then it issues an error message.
After each error message, the user has the option of aborting the translator
or continuing. The third pass of PasTran generates the Ada code. If there
were semantic errors found in the second pass, then these may be carried
over to the generated Ada code.

PasTran is fairly robust in the sense that it rarely aborts, even with
nonstandard Pascal constructs. However, it is possible that one error may
give rise to a cascade of errors, and so it is necessary to go back and fix
that error and re-run PasTran.

INVOCATION AND OPTIONS

PasTran is invoked with the command line: PasTran progname.ext/op-
tions. The output file will be named progname.pkg. There are several
options to control the translation process and to tailor the output Ada
code. One option (Q) causes PasTran not to ask for user interaction after
each error message. In my experience, most of my Pascal programs cause some

```
program fibtst (input, output);
const
      max = 21;
var
   n: integer;

function fib (n: integer): integer;
begin
  if (n = 1) or (n = 2) then
    fib := 1
  else
    fib := fib (n-1) + fib (n-2)
end;

begin { main }
  for n := 3 to max do
    writeln ('N = ', n:4, ' The answer = ', fib (n):4);
  write(2.0);   { just to show float io }
end.
```

Figure 2.   Input Pascal Program.

sort of PasTran error message so I always use this option.

Two other important options concern the type of Ada code to be generated. When version 2.0 of PasTran was developed and the then extant version
of Janus/Ada (1.5.2) contained several non-standard Ada constructs. Thus,
there are options to have PasTran generate code for either version 1.5.2 of
Janus/Ada or for regular Ada. The current version of Janus/Ada (1.6.1) is
much closer to Ada, so it is preferable to choose the standard Ada option,
even when generating code for Janus/Ada.

Figure 1 shows the invocation of PasTran to translate a program named
fibtst.pas. There are three options chosen, the meanings of which are given


```
with TEXT_IO;
procedure FIBTST is

    package Q_INT_IO is new TEXT_IO.INTEGER_IO (INTEGER);
    package Q_REAL_IO is new TEXT_IO.FLOAT_IO (FLOAT);
    MAX: constant INTEGER := 21;

    function FIB (N: in INTEGER) return INTEGER is

        Q_RETURN_FIB: INTEGER; -- *+*+* return variable
    begin
        if N = 1 or N = 2 then
            Q_RETURN_FIB := 1;
        else
            Q_RETURN_FIB := FIB (N - 1) + FIB (N - 2);
        end if;
        return Q_RETURN_FIB;
    end FIB;

begin --  main
    for N in INTEGER range 3 .. MAX loop
        TEXT_IO.PUT ("N = ");
        Q_INT_IO.PUT (N, 4);
        TEXT_IO.PUT (" The answer = ");
        Q_INT_IO.PUT (FIB (N), 4);
        TEXT_IO.NEW_LINE;
    end loop;
    Q_REAL_IO.PUT (2.0); --  just to show float io
end FIBTST;
```

Figure 3.   Output Ada Program.

```
program rectst (input, output);
type
    datrec = record
                    n: integer;
                    x: real;
                    c: char;
                end;
var
    dat: datrec;

begin
  with dat do
    begin
      n := 3;
      x := 4.0;
      c := 'm';
      writeln (n, x, c);
    end;
end.
```

Figure 4.   Pascal Program Using a Simple Record.

by PasTran in Pass I, e.g., /q is "No user prompting after errors".   PasTran
prints one "#" for every sixteen lines of code read during the first pass.
During Pass II, PasTran prints one "%" and in Pass III prints one "*" for
every subprogram.   PasTran reports the usage of different internal storage
areas and if these approach 100% then the Pascal program must be broken up
into modules.

Figure 2 shows a short Pascal program to compute the Fibonacci sequence.   Figure 3 shows the Ada code generated for this program.   PasTran
puts reserved words in lower case and other identifiers in all upper case.
When PasTran creates an identifier, the first two letters are Q_.   This is
shown in the instantiations of the integer and float i/o packages.   (There
is one bug we have found in PasTran.   In the instantiation of the float i/o
package PasTran generates a reference to TEXT_IO.REAL_IO, rather than
TEXT_IO.FLOAT_IO, and the resultant Ada program must be changed before it
will compile.   This change has been made in the Ada programs in the figures.)

Another example of PasTran defining new identifiers is in functions.

```
with TEXT_IO;
procedure RECTST is
    package Q_INT_IO is new TEXT_IO.INTEGER_IO (INTEGER);
    package Q_REAL_IO is new TEXT_IO.FLOAT_IO (FLOAT);
    type DATREC is record
        N: INTEGER;
        X: FLOAT;
        C: CHARACTER;
    end record;
    DAT: DATREC;

begin
    DAT.N := 3;
    DAT.X := 4.0;
    DAT.C := 'm';
    Q_INT_IO.PUT (DAT.N);
    Q_REAL_IO.PUT (DAT.X);
    TEXT_IO.PUT (DAT.C);
    TEXT_IO.NEW_LINE;
end RECTST;
```

Figure 5.   Output Ada Program.

```
program rectst2 (input, output);
type
    datrec = record
                    n: integer;
                    x: real;
                    c: char;
                end;
        datarr = array [1..10] of datrec;
    var
        dat: datarr;
        i: integer;

    begin
      for i := 1 to 10 do
      with dat[i] do
        begin
          n := 3;
          x := 4.0;
          c := 'm';
          writeln (n, x, c);
        end;
end.
```

Figure 6.   Pascal Program Using an Array of Records.

Since the result of a function in Ada is not assigned to the function name,
as it is in Pascal, PasTran creates the identifier Q_RETURN_function_name,
e.g., Q_RETURN_FIB in Figure 3, and inserts a special comment, preceded by
-- *+*+*, to let us know what it has done.

An example of a construct that Pascal has, but that is not in Ada, is
the WITH clause for a record. PasTran handles this in two ways. In Figure
4 is a Pascal program with a simple record and in Figure 5 is the resultant
Ada program. For this simple case PasTran just uses the dot notation.
Figure 6 shows a more complex example of an array of records. Just using
the dot notation would be inefficient so PasTran uses the block construct
of Ada (Figure 7). PasTran declares a new identifier Q_WITH_1, of the

```
with TEXT_IO;
procedure RECTST2 is
    package Q_INT_IO is new TEXT_IO.INTEGER_IO (INTEGER);
    package Q_REAL_IO is new TEXT_IO.FLOAT_IO (FLOAT);
    type DATREC is record
        N: INTEGER;
        X: FLOAT;
        C: CHARACTER;
    end record;
    type DATARR is array (INTEGER range 1 .. 10) of DATREC;
    DAT: DATARR;

begin
    for I in INTEGER range 1 .. 10 loop
        declare
            Q_WITH_1: DATREC renames DAT (I);
        begin
            Q_WITH_1.N := 3;
            Q_WITH_1.X := 4.0;
            Q_WITH_1.C := 'm';
            Q_INT_IO.PUT (Q_WITH_1.N);
            Q_REAL_IO.PUT (Q_WITH_1.X);
            TEXT_IO.PUT (Q_WITH_1.C);
            TEXT_IO.NEW_LINE;
        end;
    end loop;
end RECTST2;
```

Figure 7.   Output Ada Program.

appropriate type and then uses the dot notation with this identifier.

After translating a program with PasTran, I usually go back and manually change the Q_ identifiers to better mnemonics. This is not required for the program to compile and execute, but makes it more readable.

PERFORMANCE OF PASTRAN

PasTran translates Pascal programs at a rate of about 250 lines per minute on an IBM AT. This rate is quite sensitive to the number of errors which PasTran reports during pass II and, if the input program is in standard Pascal, then the rate would be much faster. PasTran expects a program written in standard Pascal, but most Pascal compilers have many extensions. PasTran usually flags these extensions as "errors" and continues with the translation. These "errors" then must be handled manually.

In order to translate a large Pascal program it must be broken up into smaller modules. This is easily done by prefacing the module with a dummy program header and adding a BEGIN-END pair at the end. This is not a real problem since you would normally break up a large program into Ada packages. For example, one 3,500 line Pascal program was divided into 10 Ada packages. This was done primarily for logical reasons rather than because of the limits of PasTran.

The only significant problem which we found using PasTran was as a result of breaking up the Pascal program into modules. Sometimes a reference is made in one module to subprograms in other modules. These can usually be commented out and then later uncommented. This did cause a problem in IF-THEN-ELSE clauses. PasTran did not like null statements in these clauses and, so, would sometimes go looking for a non-null statement. Thus, some care is necessary in breaking up the Pascal program. Actually, if the Pascal program were written according to modern programming practices, this is not much of a problem; it only occurred with some old mainframe Pascal programs that were rather poorly designed.

CONCLUSION

PasTran is an inexpensive Pascal to Ada translator which is fast and easy to use. It does a very good translation and usually requires only minor manual revisions of the translated code, mainly for esthetic purposes. We have been quite pleased with its performance in translating both small and medium sized programs.

REFERENCES

Electronics, 1985, "AI Tools Automate Software Translation", Electronics, September 23, 1985, p. 59.

Martin, Donald G., 1986, "Non-Ada to Ada Conversions", Ada Letters, VI, (1), January, February, 1986, pp. 72-81.

Santhanam, V., 1986, "A Practical Approach for Translating FORTRAN Programs to Ada", Proceedings of the 4th Annual National Conference on Ada Technology, March 19/20, 1986, pp. 142-148.

Schill, J., Smeaton, R., and Jackman, R., 1985, "The Conversion of Command and Control Software to Ada: Experiences and Lessons Learned", Ada Letters, IV, (4), January/February 1985, pp. 38-48.

Slape, J. K., and Wallis, P. J. L., 1983, "Conversion of FORTRAN to Ada Using an Intermediate Tree Representation", The Computer Journal, 26, (4), pp. 344-355.

Wallis, P. J. L., 1985, "Automatic Language Conversion and Its Place in the Transition to Ada", Ada Letters, V, (2), September, October 1985, pp. 275-284, (Proceedings of the Ada International Conference, Paris, France, May 14-16, 1985).

AN INFORMATION SYSTEMS SOFTWARE ENGINEERING METHODOLOGY

Bill Schmidt

SofTech, Inc.
460 Totten Pond Road
Waltham, MA   02254-9197

Abstract: This paper describes an Information Systems Software Engineering
Methodology developed by SofTech, Inc. It is for the development and maintenance of large information systems. The methodology is extensive, covering
all technical aspects of software development (and maintenance). The manner
in which the methods are used together is the essence of the methodology.
As it cannot be completely explained here, this paper will give an overview
of the methodology and focus on the integration of the methods in the software life cycle.

The material covered is based primarily on work done for the U.S. Army
Information Systems Engineering Command (ISEC)*. ISEC is making a concerted
effort to modernize many of the large systems it currently supports. Advanced technology in database, distributed, and interactive systems will
play a key role in providing users with state-of-the-art systems.

ISEC is also preparing to transition to the use of the Ada** programming
language. This methodology supports the use of Ada, but, is not dependent
upon it. The methodology is also intended to be implemented with a complete
set of tools such as those of an Ada Programming Support Environment (APSE).
The methodology does not completely cover any one technique. More detailed
information regarding methods, tools, and areas such as database and distributed systems will be necessary depending on the nature of the project.

METHODOLOGY OVERVIEW

A software engineering methodology is an integrated collection of software development procedures used together to obtain some goal. The methodology represents a systematic means of developing software. Its overall
purpose is to enable ISEC Software Engineers to develop and maintain large,
low-cost, high-quality Information Management Systems.

The new software engineering practices employed at ISEC will involve

---

*ISEC Ada Investigations, Contract No. F33600-84-D-0280.
*Ada is a registered trademark of the U.S. Government, Ada Joint
 Program Office.

greater formality and structure needed for large projects. The methodology will be standardized throughout ISEC so that development efforts run smoothly and efficiently, and better tool support can be obtained. Enhanced product uniformity and reduced training requirements are also benefits of standardization of the development procedures.

Much emphasis in the methodology is given to practices employed early in the development cycle (Requirements Analysis and Design Phases). Concentrated early effort is needed to minimize the need for later changes which are most often indicated as high cost drivers.

Quality assurance and configuration management steps play an important role throughout the life cycle. Quality, is thereby, built into software and documentation products and remains there. Project management practices sometimes overlap with technical issues, for example, risk analysis and project reviews. These are given due consideration.

Influence and Distinctive Features

During recent years, important approaches to software development have evolved. Several of these are incorporated in this methodology. They are practical and some have proven effective for previous ISEC projects. Most notable of these are:

- Top-down emphasis;

- Iterative procedures allowing product refinement;

- Co-location and continual review cycles;

- Rapid prototyping;

- Comprehensive database development procedures.

The methodology promotes consistent use of software engineering principles throughout the life cycle. It has been designed for ease of use in that the practices and products are prescribed at a necessary and sufficient level of detail.

The methodology is oriented to take advantage of current technology (relational databases, Ada, etc.), but, is general enough to be independent of specific vendor products. It is well-structured and, therefore, easy to tailor or upgrade in response to future advances in technology and changes within ISEC.

Automated Support Environment

There are many extensive procedures and methods needed to develop quality systems. Some may seem like they would be cumbersome and cause project slow-downs. For this reason, tools must be used to help carry out the methods efficiently, enforce their conventions, and eliminate "drudgery".

A comprehensive, coherent Automated Support Environment allows software engineers to apply the methods correctly and efficiently. The environment consists of tools that pertain to specific methods used in each phase. Tools that are used throughout the life cycle are also included. An Ada Programming Support Environment can be ideal for use with the techniques included in this methodology.

Software Project Library

An underlying feature of the methodology and support environment is the Software Project Library (SPL). The SPL is a repository of all project relevant information. The information pertains to requirements and design specifications, support documents, code, test case data, etc. It is essentially a database with data management capabilities implemented with the Automated Support Environment.

Methodology support tools require automated storage and retrieval of products. The varied information maintained in the SPL is used throughout the life cycle. A data dictionary, problem reports, and, obviously, source code are but a few examples of the input and output of the methods and tools.

The SPL will be used by various members of the development staff and at different points in the life cycle. The information contained in the SPL should thus be partitioned in some way and available to developers in "folder" format. This does not necessarily mean information is output in hardcopies. The folder ideally includes only the collection of specifications needed for, say, a formal review. The information can be off-loaded from the project library to separate files under an engineer's account. A set of tools can then be used to help analyze and maintain information in the "folders".

SOFTWARE LIFE CYCLE

Life Cycle Model

The backbone of this methodology is its life cycle. The life cycle model is a hybrid of that used in DOD-STD-2167 and ISEC's Contemporary Life Cycle. The procedures and methods, hence, support tools and project library, are integrated within the context of the life cycle.

ISEC develops and maintains large software systems which require a more precise degree of control over the development process. A life cycle model with several, clearly defined, separate phases provides a means of introducing greater managerial control, and better documentation into the development process. The life cycle is based on that of DOD-STD-2167. It is segmented into the 6 phases listed on the left:

- Requirements Analysis   <==== Requirements Definition

- Preliminary Design   <=|
                            |<= Design

- Detailed Design   <=|

- Code and Unit Test   <=|
                            |<= Programming

- Integration Test   <=|
                            |<= Test and Validate

- System Test   <=|

Many procedures from the Contemporary Life Cycle phases listed above on the right have been incorporated in this life cycle. The Preliminary Design and Integration Test Phases offer several advantages. Foremost of these are:

- Early (high-level) design and test reviews;

- Enables (preliminary) logical data design
  prior to design of detailed program logic;

- Facilitates structured design and structured
  testing.

Iterations and Overlap of Phases

Adherence to the life cycle model as defined is crucial. However, a flexible approach to doing so is encouraged. Software development does not usually lend itself to a situation where a complete set of requirements is defined followed by the design of the entire system and so on.

A portion of the system (i.e., a primary component) can be developed by following the sequence of phases. Then, another primary component is developed by iterating the same sequence. These iterations to develop separate components can occur one after the other or they can be performed in parallel by separate teams.

Overlapping phases result when, for example, core requirements are defined, preliminary design begins, and more detailed requirements analysis continues. This concept can apply to the non-discrete termination-initiation of the other phases as well.

Project Management

Project management activities are integral parts of a Pre-Software Development Phase (which is external to this methodology). Managers are also key participants in the formal reviews conducted for each phase, and the entire System Test Phase.

In the Pre-Software Development (Planning) Phase the following techniques are used:

- Work Breakdown Structures;

- Scheduling via PERT/CPM and Gantt Time-lines;

- Cost Estimating via COCOMO or similar spreadsheet
  based models;

- Risk Analysis with cost/benefit simulations.

The resulting products form part of the Software Development Plan (SDP), a document which is periodically updated, especially after formal reviews such as the Preliminary Design Review (PDR).

Reviews

Formal reviews are conducted to validate each product of every phase. The intent is to ensure that each product complies with standards and quality criteria before further development continues. High-level problems such as those identified in outstanding Software Problem Reports (SPRs) are addressed and entered in the review minutes as action items whose status is tracked.

A formal review is conducted at the end of each phase. The following reviews correspond directly to the life cycle phases listed above:

- Software Requirements Review (SRR)

- Preliminary Design Review (PDR)

- Critical Design Review (CDR)

- Source Code Review (SCR)

- Test Readiness Review (TRR)

- System Configuration Audit (SCA)

Quality Assurance

A Quality Assurance group involves itself with each project. These independent evaluators are also key participants in all formal reviews and the System Test Phase. They also conduct random design and code audits (among other products). QA responsibilities and IV&V techniques pertain to all aspects of the system and the practices employed in its development and maintenance.

Configuration Management

A configuration management team performs all of the necessary tasks to maintain the developmental and operational integrity of the software and documentation products. The modules of a system must be combined (as part of the Integration Test Phase) and updated correctly. This involves establishing and archiving product baselines, problem report monitoring, version control, and software installation.

Software Products and Documentation Set

All software and documentation products are stored and retrieved under the Software Project Library. This is done using the engineering tools provided in the Automated Support Environment especially the configuration management toolset.

Source and object codes are obvious software products. Falling within this category are reusable components for applications or other systems to be developed in the future.

The database developed as part of the system is also a deliverable product. Schemas, packaged command and query procedures, etc. are included. Test case data must also be produced and maintained. Most of it is stored in the format of the production database.

Scaffolding software is that which will not be included in the deliverable system (as specified by requirements). This includes program stubs and drivers, data converters, etc. This software may or may not be reusable. If it is deemed to be non-reusable it is discarded.

System documentation evolves and is baselined in the same way software is. The SDP and SUM are refined throughout the life cycle. The others are initiated as preliminary documents in one phase and are extended, refined, and baselined one or two phases later. The following list represents the documentation set for most systems:

- Software Development Plan (SDP)

- Software Users Manual (SUM)

- Software Requirements Specification (SRS)

435

- Software Product Specification (SPS)

- Software Test Plan (STP)

- Software Test Report (STR)

Documents consist of text, tables, diagrams, glossaries, etc. Each type of document is developed and maintained in sections, or as a whole in some circumstances (e.g., when global changes must be made). Each section is eventually folded into one master document. The reverse is also true. Each section is separated when isolated changes are needed or when only a portion of the document is to be examined.

Other products such as Software Problem Reports and Version Description Documents are produced as needed. These are generally much less extensive than those documents listed above.

INTEGRATED METHODS

As stated above, the methods described throughout this guide are ordered according to a software life cycle. Several methods are used in each phase of the life cycle. Some of the methods can be used in more than one phase, but, each is prescribed where it is most beneficial.

In the Detailed Design Phase for instance, a highly structured form of PDL (Ada as a design language) is used to express the detailed processing logic of a system. The other procedures are structured development guidelines and general database implementation procedures. It is noted that the structuring guidelines apply to the products of the Preliminary Design Phase, and Code and Unit Test Phase as well.

Each of the methods are based on a unique objective. The objective supports that of the phase in which it is included. Because each method has a different objective, the output of each will be different. The product(s) of one or more methods will be input to another. This input may be feedback from one method to one that was performed previously, but must be used again to revise a preliminary product. For example, requirements may be refined after a high-level design of the system is established. In this case the effect is that instead of saying "the system must provide inventory status", we can say "the status reporting component must provide the current stock level of each item...."

Methods to develop software and related products can be represented as abstract state machines. The methods may be decomposed into a discrete series of steps. They typically have a set of elements associated with them. For example, Data Flow Diagrams deal with "bubbles", arrows, boxes, etc. Various conventions or rules are used to dictate how the steps are carried out. For example, in a data flow diagram, arrows are usually labeled as some data item going from one process to another. However, if the data is to be stored, the arrow is broken and separated by the data name inserted between two parallel lines.

In order to use a method to produce software, design specifications, etc., the engineer must refer to previous information pertaining to the development effort. The information is considered input to a method and must be explicitly defined with regard to the method's unique objective and necessary steps. In this way the methods form an integrated methodology.

The flow of products and the necessary steps to develop them efficiently and effectively is the underlying basis of the methodology.

CONCLUSION

This Information Systems Software Engineering Methodology provides a generic, comprehensive, integrated framework for developing large information systems. However, it should be tailored (slightly modified) wherever necessary to accommodate the particular type of system being developed. Consider an information system where a rich set of decision support functions are needed. SADT* (Structured Analysis and Design Technique) or even a simulation language could be emphasized for use over Data Flow Diagrams in the Requirements Analysis Phase.

Even though clear guidance is given on the use of PDL in the Detailed Design Phase, more detailed procedures may need to be prescribed. That is, the PDL section may need to be supplemented for critical or reusable components. This may hold true for any of the methods.

A software engineering methodology is an indispensable aid when used with good sense. The methodology must be straight forward and it must be enforced at all levels in the development organization. However, there are always exceptional circumstances that arise during software development. No methodology can adequately address all software development alternatives. The idea is not to pointlessly restrict creativity, but to harness it for positive results -- inexpensive, high quality systems.

Methodology Design

The methodology is outlined below in pseudocode format. The life cycle phases, methods, and products flowing in and out of each method are shown. For clarity, products such as Software Development Plan and Software User's Manual which evolve throughout the life cycle are not indicated. Since the phases may be iterated, products developed in one phase can serve as feedback input to an earlier phase that is performed over gain for refinement of earlier products or maintenance. At this level of detail feedback is also "hidden", only the most significant interfaces are specified.

```
        begin Life_Cycle (User_Needs : in;
                     Software,
                     Documentation : out);
          Requirements_Analysis (User_Needs : in;
                           Requirements_Specs : out);
            Requirements_Language (User_Needs : in;
                           Data_Definitions,
                           Business_Rules : out);
            Data_Flow_Diagram (Data_Definitions : in;
                           Corp_Info_Model : out);
            Rapid_Prototyping (Data_Definitions,
                           Corp_Info_Model : in;
                           User_Data_Views : out);
            Preliminary_Design (Core_Reqmts_Specs : in;
                           Prelim_Design_Specs : out);
            S_A_D_T (Corp_Info_Model,
                  Data_Definitions : in;
                  Basic_System_Model : out);

            Database_Design (Requirements_Specs : in);
                     DB_Meta_Schema : out);
```

_____

*SADT is a trademark of SofTech, Inc.

```
          High_Level_P_D_L (Basic_System_Model,
                     DB_Meta_Schema : in;
                     Skeleton_Architecture : out)
         Detailed_Design (Detail_Reqmts_Specs,
                  Prelim_Design_Specs : in;
                  Detail_Design_Specs,
                  Database : out);
        Detailed_P_D_L_etc (Skeleton_Architecture,
                     Basic_System_Model : in;
                     Pseudocode_etc : out);
          Structured_Development (Pseudocode : in;
                          Detail_Design_Specs : out);
          Database_Implementation (DB_Meta_Schema : in;
                           Database : out);
         Code_and_Unit_Test (Detail_Design_Specs,
                     Database : in;
                     Program_Modules,
                     Test_Case_Data : out);
          Coding_Conventions (Detail_Design_Specs : in;
                          Program_Modules : out);
         White_Box_Path_Testing (Program_Modules,
                          Test_Case_Data,
                          Requirements_Specs : in;
                          Verified_Modules : out);
          Integration_Test (Program_Modules,
                     Test_Database : in;
                     Primary_Components,
                     Test_Plan : out);
          Integrate_Components (Verified_Modules : in;
                          Primary_Components : out);
          Black-Box_IO_Testing (Primary_Components,
                          Test_Database : in;
                          Validated_Components : out);
         System_Test (Primary_Components : in;
                  Software,
                  Documentation : out);
          Configuration_Audits (System : in;
                          Validated_System,
                          Validated_Documentation : out);
     end Life_Cycle;
```

REFERENCES

Freeman, P., and Wasserman, A. I., 1982, <u>Software Development Methodologies and Ada</u>.

Rubey, R. J., 1985, Software Development Guide, SofTech Inc., Fairborn, OH, July 1985.

Schmidt, W., 1986, <u>ISEC Methods and Tools Requirements Analysis Interim Report</u>, SofTech Inc., Waltham, MA, July 1986.

Schmidt, W., 1986, <u>ISEC Methods and Tools Recommendation Interim Report</u>, SofTech Inc., Waltham, MA, July 1986.

Schmidt, W., 1986, <u>DRAFT ISEC Software Engineering Guide</u>, SofTech Inc., Waltham, MA, August 1986.

Schmidt, W., 1983, <u>Army Automation Software Design and Development</u>, Technical Bulletin 18-103, U.S. Department of the Army, Washington,

D.C., February 1983.

Schmidt, W., 1983, <u>Defense System Software Development</u>, DOD-STD-2167, U.S. Department of Defense, Washington, D.C., 1983,

Schmidt, W, 1986, <u>DRAFT Generic Tools Requirements for ISEC Ada Transition</u>, Technica' Report MJ86-ISEC-065, Teledyne Brown Engineering, Washington D.C., June 1986.

Schmidt, W., 1986, <u>Procedures for Contemporary Life Cycle Development (Draft)</u>, U.S. Army Information Systems Software Development Center, Fort Lee, VA, May 1986.

CONFIGURATION MANAGEMENT WITH THE ADA* LANGUAGE SYSTEM

Richard M. Thall

SofTech, Inc.
Waltham, Massachusetts

Abstract: Three characteristics of large software projects and five basic configuration management capabilities are identified. The design of the Ada Language System (ALS) is then described in terms of these basic capabilities. The ALS is a computer programming support environment for Ada.

1. INTRODUCTION

The emergence of software engineering as a distinct discipline has fostered examination of the methods used to program computers. This, in turn, has led to the development of a number of unified environments to aid programmers and improve their productivity. Many of these environments have viewed the programmer as an autonomous individual producing self-contained software. However, in most industrial, military, and commercial applications, it is much more reasonable to view the programmer as a member of a team producing software that must be precisely matched to the software produced by other members of the team. This fact has been acknowledged in the Ada programming language, where emphasis has been placed on the production of an entire coordinated software system rather than a collection of loosely coordinated modules. The Ada Language System (ALS) is a programming environment that supports the development of large systems in Ada. The ALS provides the underlying facilities necessary to coordinate programmers working in teams. The ALS was developed by SofTech, Inc. for the U.S. Army using the Stoneman Requirements (Buxton, 1980) as a guideline.

This paper first identifies three major aspects of large team-oriented projects which differentiates them from small one-man efforts. The ALS features which support such projects are described.

2. CHARACTERISTICS OF LARGE SOFTWARE PROJECTS

Large team-oriented software efforts have three characteristics which differentiate them from small individual-oriented projects.

---

*Ada is a registered trademark of the Department of Defense (Ada Joint Program Office) OUSDRE (R&AT).

- Large projects are usually developing a family of similar programs rather than a single program.

- Configuration management is of critical importance.

- Close coordination of many programmers is necessary.

Although the discussion of these issues is separated, they are all heavily interrelated.

2.1 Families of Programs

Software is aptly named. It is the soft part of any computer system; it is the most malleable, easily changed part of the system; it is the part that is expected to adapt to changing requirements and changing hardware. In fact, the software is often specifically designed to be adapted to differing situations. It is the part that can be altered most rapidly at the least expense, provided changes are made in an orderly fashion. Even a perfect piece of software with no errors will still tend to accumulate changes for the following reasons:

- the requirements of the original application have changed,

- the hardware configuration has changed, or

- the software is to be incorporated into a new application.

A change in the original requirements can result from a change in the external world or the identification of a shortcoming in the requirements as originally conceived. Hardware changes occur for many reasons: the correction of hardware problems, improved capacity and performance, reduced cost, production and supply problems, etc. Software is often designed at the outset to run on a variety of hardware to accommodate various sized applications. In general, each hardware configuration requires a different copy of the software even though the difference in the software might be as minor as the adjustment of a compile-time constant. Finally, bits and pieces of software tend to migrate from one application to another, from one computer to another, changing in some way each time a migration occurs.

Every change to a software component that can affect its operation must be regarded as creating a new component with different properties. It is a serious error to assume that the significance of a change is related to the amount of source text altered. A single character alteration can be just as devastating to the final operation of a system as a 10,000 character alteration. However, programs differing textually by only a small amount are related and should be treated as such. It is important to maintain the identity of such families of programs because an error in one member of the family is likely to exist in many members of the family. Members of a family may also be textually unrelated; e.g., they may be coded in different programming languages. However, if they are functionally similar, they may share errors. A program family may be loosely defined as those modules which have evolved from a common source text. The source text is often, but not always, the compilable text of a program; it may be the definition of an algorithm or pseudo-code. In general, the members of a program family will all perform similar functions (Cargil, 1980; Tichy, 1980). The notion of a program family is supported in the ALS by a database feature called a "variation".

Program families inevitably arise wherever there must be ongoing software support for multiple field installations. Unless the field installations are all identical, and never change, there will be differing software for the various hardware configurations. Given the rate of change in the computer industry, it is inconceivable that any product would not undergo design changes for cost reduction alone. Many classes of products can be expected to undergo continuous field upgrades which require software alteration. The ability to control families of software may reduce the need to apply field upgrades to bring hardware into conformance with a standard. With strong support for program families, the software could be custom-generated to adapt to each hardware configuration.

2.2 Configuration Management

Configuration Management (CM) is the "consistent labeling, tracking, and change control of the ... elements of a system" (Bersoff, Henderson, and Siegel, 1979). There are a number of economic and technical forces which mandate increasing emphasis on CM for industrial grade software. Among these are:

- reliability requirements,

- complexity, and

- ongoing support requirements.

A growing number of computer applications have exceedingly high reliability requirements. In such applications as aircraft and spacecraft control, automotive control, weapons control, and medical systems, software failure can result in personal injury or loss of life. In such cases, strong CM is necessary to ensure that all operational software has been fully tested and that unproven alternations do not find their way into delivered systems. In very complex systems, the change control aspect of CM is used during development simply to ensure that the elements of a system are kept stable enough over time to be successfully integrated. In applications where software corrections and improvements are to be provided on an ongoing basis to remote field locations, CM is necessary to assure that delivered software is appropriate to the hardware configuration at that site.

CM is usually achieved by the creation of one or more "baseline" copies of the software. Each baseline has some official status. There can be working baselines updated frequently by the programming team, frozen baselines preserving exact copies of software delivered to field locations, etc. CM is obtained by management review of proposed changes to baselines and monitoring and recording of actual changes. In order to perform CM, one must be able to:

- absolutely identify the elements of a baseline at any point in time,

- absolutely identify the elements of a system placed in revenue service,

- account for and control all changes to a baseline,

- recreate exactly a system that existed in the past or exists at a field site, and

- control the correspondence between tested and delivered systems.

Even though companies and projects have diverse methods for performing CM, there are five capabilities basic to all CM. These are:

- absolute identification,

- change identification,

- change tracking,

- inventory control, and

- access control.

Absolute identification is the ability to reliably associate a name with a component of a system, usually stored in a file. When a component changes, no matter how small the change, a new component with a different name is created. Change identification is the ability to readily recognize when a change has occurred. Change tracking is the ability to record and review the sequence of changes to a component. Inventory control is the ability to record exactly what components constitute a system at any point in time. Finally, access control is the ability to guarantee that all changes to a baseline are authorized and documented.

A capability fundamental to all CM is absolute identification of software components. Most conventional file systems fail to provide the basic underlying support for absolute identification. Typically, the source code for a component, say a sine routine, is stored in a file that may be named SINE.SRC. Another file, SINE.OBJ, usually holds the object code. SINE.OBJ might be bound into any number of executable images with unrelated names. CM problems occur when a change is made. Typically, the change is introduced by in-place editing of the source file. The name of the source file remains unchanged after the alteration. A revision history may be part of the source file, but the person inserting the change may not possess enough self-discipline to note the change, particularly when the change is viewed as minor. The altered source is subsequently recompiled with the new object replacing SINE.OBJ. Since the file name is altered, the change is invisible to programmers incorporating SINE.OBJ in their system.

If the change engenders an unexpected problem, identification of the problem may be very time-consuming. In general, recompilation from source followed by file comparison is necessary to determine if a change in SINE.SRC was ever applied to SINE.OBJ. Determining if a given system has the new or old version of SINE.OBJ involves keeping explicit records of when the change to SINE was applied and when the system in question was last rebuilt. Such records are seldom kept. Partial rebuilds of systems complicate the situation even further. Very often it is easier to correct the present system than reconstruct a clear historical picture of what caused the problem. If an erroneous change finds its way into many systems, there can be many parallel efforts to identify and correct the same error.

A major part of this problem can be alleviated by incorporating a revision number in file names. Every time a file is changed, the revision number is incremented. Identification of changes is then readily accomplished by recording the names of files built into a system. The differences between two builds of a system can then be quickly identified by comparing the revision numbers of the components. Such visibility of changes is fundamental to the notion of absolute identification. Every change or closely related group of changes must be viewed as creating a new object with a distinct name. In short, the name must identify the object absolutely. (A single object may have several names, but one name must refer to a unique object throughout the lifetime of the name.)

A revision numbering capability supplies, at one stroke, both change identification and tracking mechanisms. As long as a new revision is created every time a change is made in a baseline, changes are easily identified by the high visibility of new file revisions. The numbered sequence of

444

revisions for each file provides a change tracking mechanism upon which tracking mechanisms for entire baselines can be readily constructed.

Even with revision numbers, problems arise in absolutely identifying components when names have been changed. Component names should be highly mnemonic. But it is desirable to allow mnemonic names to be changed so they stay mnemonic as software development progresses. This broaches the possibility of renaming or deleting a file and then creating another file with the old name. This can result in two distinct components having the same name and revision number. To avoid any possibility of confusion, it is necessary to have a secondary naming mechanism where renaming and reuse of names is not possible. In the ALS, these secondary names are called unique identifiers. The mnemonic quality of unique identifiers is sacrificed for the uniqueness property. To absolutely identify a component, it is desirable to record both the mnemonic name and the unique identifier. The mnemonic name, while not absolutely necessary, helps human users. The unique identifier is used mostly by configuration control tools, to avoid ambiguity which could otherwise arise if mnemonic names were used to compare configurations.

Inventory control is the ability to create and store a complete list of all the components of a baseline at some point in time. Saved inventory lists can be subsequently compared to determine the changes in a baseline over some interval, or find the differences between an installed system and the current baseline.

Access control is the ability to guarantee that no undocumented or unauthorized changes find their way into a baseline. The term can be more broadly interpreted to encompass examination as well as modification of baselines. Of course, no guarantee can be absolute. Most computer systems can be penetrated by sufficiently clever and malicious users. In addition, hardware or software failure can always compromise access control. It is assumed here, that ALS users are friendly and the hardware and software are sufficiently reliable.

The problem of supporting many installations with slightly differing configurations requires CM for families of programs. The inability to do this effectively usually results in software which must dynamically reconfigure itself or which must be completely rebuilt at each field site. CM mechanisms must be able to deal with conditional compilation or macro expansion techniques used to generate family members. In the ALS, revisions and derivations combine with variations to support CM for families of programs.

2.3 Coordination of Programmers

In multi-person projects, the effective coordination of programmers is vital. Lack of coordination results in costly redesign and retrofits during system integration. In complex projects, the lack of adequate coordination can jeopardize the successful conclusion of the project. An official working copy or baseline of the software is usually used to coordinate the efforts of the programmers. There is a spectrum of scenarios for using such a baseline. At the ends of the spectrum are:

● the total sharing scenario, and

● the private copy scenario.

Under total sharing, all incremental changes are immediately applied to the working baseline. The system is periodically rebuilt from the working baseline. Such a rebuild or relink usually occurs frequently, on the order

445

of once or twice a day. Under the private copy scenario, each programmer
has his own copy of the baseline which he can modify or rebuild at will.

The problem with sharing is that programmers interfere with each other,
each making changes that affect the other. Much time is lost keeping up
with alterations made by other programmers. Changes tend to proliferate,
one change engendering others which engender still more changes. The rate
of change and lack of testing of changes seriously reduces the chances of
obtaining a system that works correctly. Sharing allows for little programmer freedom or the opportunity to apply changes experimentally. Even
in a two-programmer team, total sharing may be unworkable.

The private copy scenario solves the problems of sharing, but does not
provide any coordination. With private copies of the baseline, each programmer works independently. The longer a programmer works in his private
area, the greater is the chance that his software diverges from software
developed by others. On the other hand, the programmer has total freedom
to make changes, even to components which are the purview of others. A
programmer working with an isolated copy of the system does not benefit
from improvements introduced by other team members.

In practice, some combination of the two scenarios is used to prevent
the divergence of the software. Typically, this involves the use of private
work areas for incremental development. When an element is completed and
tested, it is then integrated with the official baseline. The integration
is very often performed in a private area and the new system tested before
it is placed in the project baseline. In addition, there are often administrative procedures for controlling baseline changes and for preventing
changes to components one is not authorized to change. The ALS provides a
general sharing mechanism as well as conventional copying to facilitate
almost any scenario for programmer coordination. In addition, the Program
Library services of the ALS gives programmers a totally isolated work area
for building and modifying systems starting from a baseline copy.

Although the examples in this paper are confined to the source and
object forms of computer programs, the discussion is equally valid with a
more comprehensive interpretation of the word "software". The same problems
occur with all types of documentation, e.g., requirements specifications,
design specifications, user reference manuals, tutorial materials, etc.
All of these should be included under the umbrella of the term "software".
Similarly, although the discussion is illustrated by examples of software
in the development phase, all arguments apply equally well to the maintenance
phase of the software life-cycle. Indeed, there is no qualitative difference
between the development and maintenance phases in relation to the issues
treated here.

3. ALS CAPABILITIES

This section describes the features of the ALS specifically designed to
support large-scale programming projects. The user's view of the ALS database is presented in some detail. The use of these capabilities as they
relate to program families, CM, and programmer coordination is treated in
the next section. Information on ALS features not related to CM can be
found in Wolfe (Wolfe, Babich, Simpson, Thall, and Weissman, 1981) and Thall
(1982).

3.1 Nodes

The ALS provides users with a database capability that can be viewed
as either a sophisticated file system or a rudimentary database management

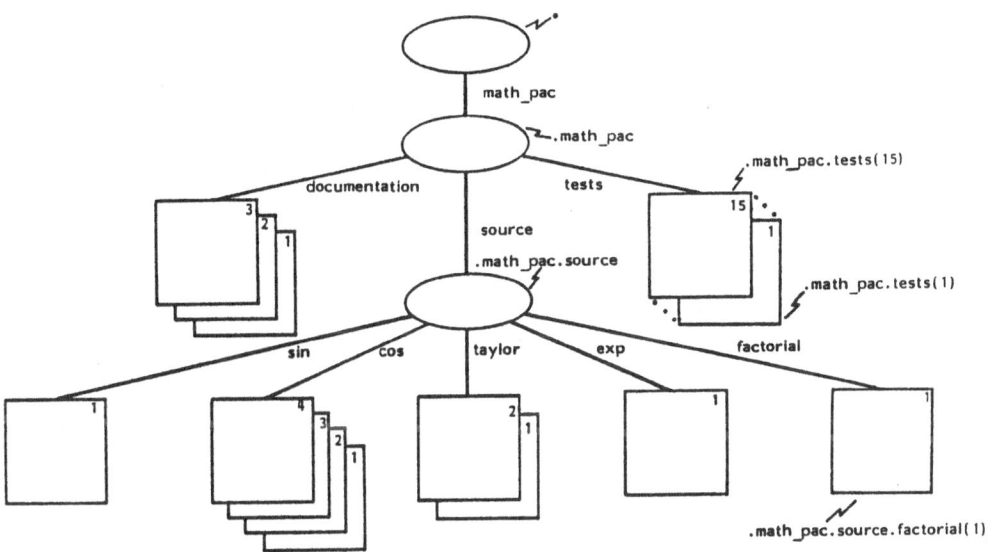

Figure 1. Directories and Revision Sets.

system. The database is a collection of objects called nodes. There are three varieties of nodes:

- files,

- directories, and

- variation headers.

Files correspond to the usual notion of a named data collection. Directories and variation header nodes are used to create groupings of nodes. All nodes in the database possess descriptors called attributes and associations. An attribute describes the node which possesses it. Associations establish relationships between nodes, in addition to the relationships established by virtue of the groupings under directories and variation headers.

3.2 Node Naming and Structuring

Hierarchical data structures are built by using directories to group nodes. Directories are used to group any combination of files, variation headers, and other directories. Figure 1 gives an example. Every ALS has exactly one connected file structure with one root directory. (Strictly speaking, the root node is anonymous; however, it can be referred with the name ".".) The root node of our example possesses a single node named "math_pac". The reader is free to think of node names as being properties of either the node or the link to the node. However, because of node sharing, a single node may acquire aliases. Thus, it is more accurate to think of the names as properties of the links. Putting it another way, the name resides in the parent director, not in the node itself. To avoid any ambiguity, the diagrams show node names on the links. In the example, "math_pac" is the child (or offspring) of "." which is the parent of "math_pac". A parent node is said to contain its offspring.

The "math_pac" directory has three off-spring, the directory "source" and the files "documentation" and "tests". "Source" in turn, has five

447

offspring: the files "sin", "cos", "taylor", "exp", and "factorial". Directories are shown as ellipses; and files are shown as squares. Just as in
Ada, the identity of an object depends upon its position in the whole structure. The full name of an object is known as the pathname and is constructed
by tracing the path to the object from the root and naming the links trans-
versed along that path. The pathname of math_pac is ".math_pac". The name
of the factorial subprogram is ".math_pac.source.factorial". Several pathnames are shown in Figure 1. Users are encouraged to view the data structure
as a tree; however, due to sharing of nodes, the structure is not strictly
a tree, it is a directed acyclic graph. The ALS excludes cycles from the
structure. In other words, a directory may not contain a subtree that contains that same directory.

3.3 Revision Sets

Every file in the ALS database is, in actuality, a member of a revision
set. The revision set tracks the changes made to a file over time. Each
member of a revision set is a snapshot of the file as it existed at some
point in time. The members, called revisions, are ordered in chronological
sequence and are automatically numbered in order starting from one. The most
recent revision supersedes all previous revisions. Although a revision is
most often a modified form of the previous revision, this relationship is not
imposed. In some cases, a revision may come from a revision that predates
the immediate predecessor in the same revision set or from some other source
entirely. Most operations such as opening, reading, writing, and deleting,
apply to individual revisions of a revision set. Sharing, however, can only
be accomplished for the revision set as a whole. If the last revision of a
set is deleted, the number is not reused when the next revision is created.
To provide absolute identification, in-place editing of revisions is restricted. Only the latest member of a revision set may be modified in-place,
and then only under certain conditions. The most recent revision supersedes
all previous revisions. The latest revision can also be explicitly frozen,
after which it may not be modified. A revision can become unmodifiable for
three reasons:

- it was explicitly frozen by the user or a program,

- it is not the latest revision, or

- it has been used to generate another object which is under
  configuration control.

Only in the last case, when the derived object is removed from the database, can an unmodifiable revision again become modifiable. In the other
cases, the action of freezing is irrevocable. In the first two cases, the
revision is said to be frozen. Unmodifiability applies only to the text of
a revision; it does not limit changes to attributes or associations. Each
revision possesses a distinct set of attributes and associations. Revisions
from which files under configuration management have been derived may not
be removed from the database until the derived file has been removed.

Any revision can be named by attaching a parenthesized revision number
subscript to the pathname of the file. If no subscript is given, the latest
revision is assumed. If the subscript "+" is specified, the latest frozen
revision is referenced. The latest frozen revision is either the last revision or the next-to-last revision. The use of subscript notation promotes
the view that the revision set is an array possessing elements that are the
individual revisions. Figure 1 shows the pathnames of three different revisions.

3.4 Unique Qualifiers

The ALS automatically assigns each node an identifier which is temporarily and spatially unique. In other words, once assigned, no other node in any other ALS database will ever have the same identifier, unless it is a copy of the original. Moreover, once assigned, the identifier cannot be changed. These identifiers are called unique identifiers or UIDs. UIDs have three fields:

- object serial number (10 bytes),

- ALS database identifier (7 bytes), and

- organization identifier (10 bytes),

An object serial number is assigned automatically by the ALS each time a node is created. To that is appended the database identifier, which is unique for each database within an organization. Finally, the organization identifier, naming the organization owning the database, is appended. Database identifiers are administratively assigned by a specifically appointed person within each organization to which the ALS has been delivered. Organization identifiers are assigned by the government agency responsible for configuration management and distribution of the ALS. The name space is large enough to allow the creation of 10,000 nodes per second for the next 2.6 million years in each of 8 trillion databases in each of 1400 trillion organizations. With simple compression techniques, only 10 bytes out of the full 27 bytes would have to be stored for each node.

The ALS supplies tools for copying nodes from one ALS database to any other ALS database. When files are copied in this way, the original and the copy are automatically frozen. In the receiving database, copies are created with the same UIDs as the original. It is, therefore, possible to compare baselines on two hosts by comparing only the UIDs of the files in the baselines. Because both the original and copy are frozen, there is a reasonable level of confidence that the files are the same. Without this capability, it would be necessary to transmit the entire contents of all the files in the baseline to one of the hosts where an exhaustive file comparison would have to be run. Recording the UIDs of files from which an installed system is built provides a similar level of control for delivered software which may not reside on a host.

3.5 Variation Sets

To represent families of programs, the ALS provides a construct called the variation set. Members of variation sets are functionally similar software components that differ in their implementation details. Since variation set members do not supersede one another, they are named, not numbered. Nodes called variation set headers are used to represent variations sets in the ALS database. A variation set header can occur anywhere a directory node can occur, except at the root of the database. The members of a variation set appear as off-spring of the variation set header node. The members can be revision sets, other variations sets, ordinary subtrees (i.e., directories), or any combination of these. A default variation can be designated.

Figure 2 shows an example of the use of variation sets. Variation set headers appear as hexagons. In this example, the source for math_pac exists in two variations, one for integer hardware and another for computers with floating point hardware. The floating point variation is further divided into variations for long words and short words. Variation set headers are similar to directories, except that in pathnames, references to their off-spring appear in parentheses rather than being separated by dots from the

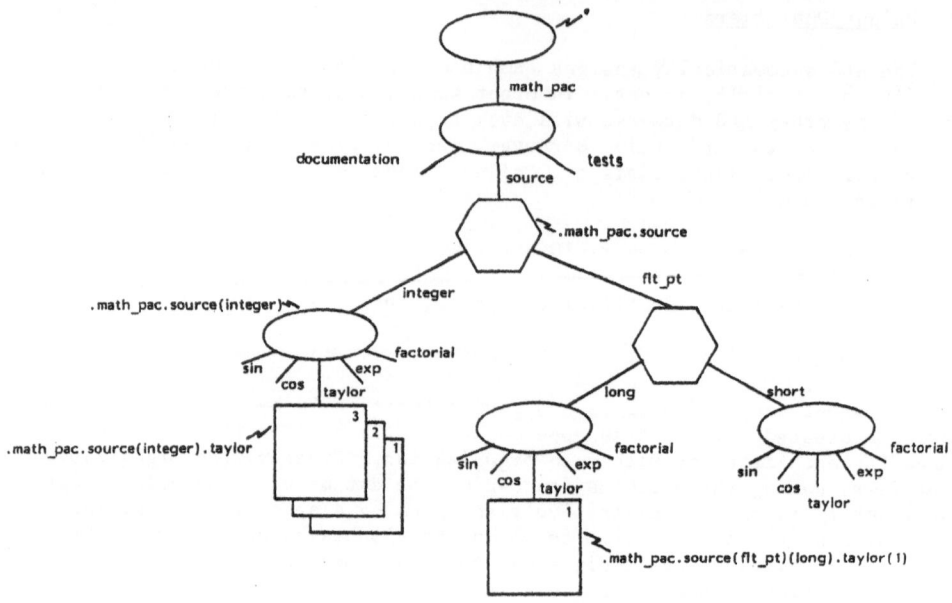

Figure 2.   Variation Sets.

preceding path element. In this respect, the members of a variation set are viewed as array elements, where the elements are named rather than numbered. Figure 2 shows how pathnames with variation references and nested variation references are formed. If empty parentheses are specified and a default variation has been designated, the default variation will be selected.

3.6 Node Sharing

To ensure that the ALS can readily support many scenarios for programmer coordination, there is a sharing mechanism in addition to the usual copying capability. Any node may be shared provided the sharing does not introduce a cycle into the database structure. In essence, sharing a node creates an alias for that node. A node may have two kinds of parents, true parents and foster parents. A true parent is the directory (or variation header) in which the node was originally created. Every node has exactly one true parent. A foster parent is a directory (or variation header) that subsequently shares an existing node. A node may have an arbitrary number of foster parents. Figure 3 shows a node sharing situation. In this case, the short word length variation of math_pac shares the "sin", "cos", and "series" files with the long word length variation. Notice that the taylor series procedure has two names, ".math_pac.source(flt_pt)(long).taylor" and ".math_pac.source(flt_pt)(short).series". It is the same revision set, but shared with a different name on the link. Individual elements of a revision set cannot be shared, only the whole set. Directories and variation headers may also be shared.

3.7 Attributes

An attribute is a named character string used to describe the node which possesses the attribute. A node may have an arbitrary number of attributes. The ALS uses certain attributes to control the database and restricts the use of these attributes. Programs can create, delete, and modify any other attributes, subject to the normal access controls. There is no global list of attributes or registration procedure for attributes. Other

450

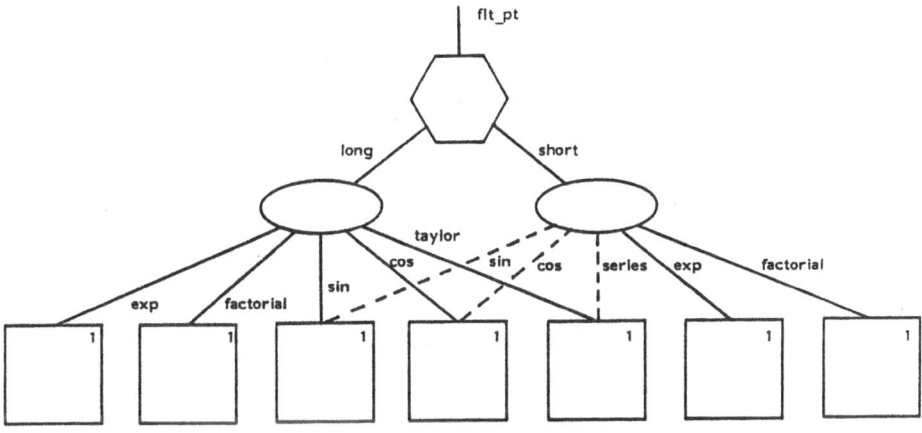

Figure 3. Node Sharing.

than the attributes used for database control, there are no attributes that
every node must possess. The values of attributes are strings which can be
up to 64K characters long.

Attributes can be used to select variations. This is accomplished by
giving a sequence of (name=>value) pairs in place of the variation name.
The pairs are separated by commas. Figure 4 shows an alternate organization
for the example of Figure 2. In this case, instead of nesting variations,
there is only one variation header with variations named "va", "vb", and
"vc". Variation "va" of "source" has an attribute named "mode" with a value
"integer". Variation "vb" has an attribute named "mode" with value "flt_pt"
and another attribute named "size" with value "long". Finally, variation
"vc" has an attribute named "mode" with value "flt_pt" and an attribute
named "size" with value "short". Figure 4 shows two examples of variation
selection with attribute values. Additional variations and selection attributes can be added dynamically as the software configuration evolves.
If attribute selection is used, the specification must select a single variation unambiguously.

3.8 Access Control

ALS access controls are based upon a conventional lock and key mechanism. Users and programs have keys and database objects have locks. The
user and program keys must match the appropriate lock in order to obtain
access. Attributes are used to store the locks and keys.

Each user has two keys: a user name and a team name. The user name
is determined when the user enters the ALS from the host operating system.
The team name may be chosen by the user from a roster of team names and
team members controlled administratively. The key of an executing program
is obtained from an attribute named "access_name" attached to the ALS file
where the executable image of the program resides.

Locks are attached to each database object with attributes named read,
append, write, attr_change, execute, and via. The values of these attributes
are lists of the keys which will satisfy the lock. The lock can be satisfied
by either the team name or the user name. An asterisk can be used to match
a substring of all keys. For example the lock "*Smith" will match all users
with a key ending in "Smith". The key "*" matches all keys. If the read
lock is satisfied, then the user may examine the file or may learn the
offspring of a directory or variation header. If the append lock is

451

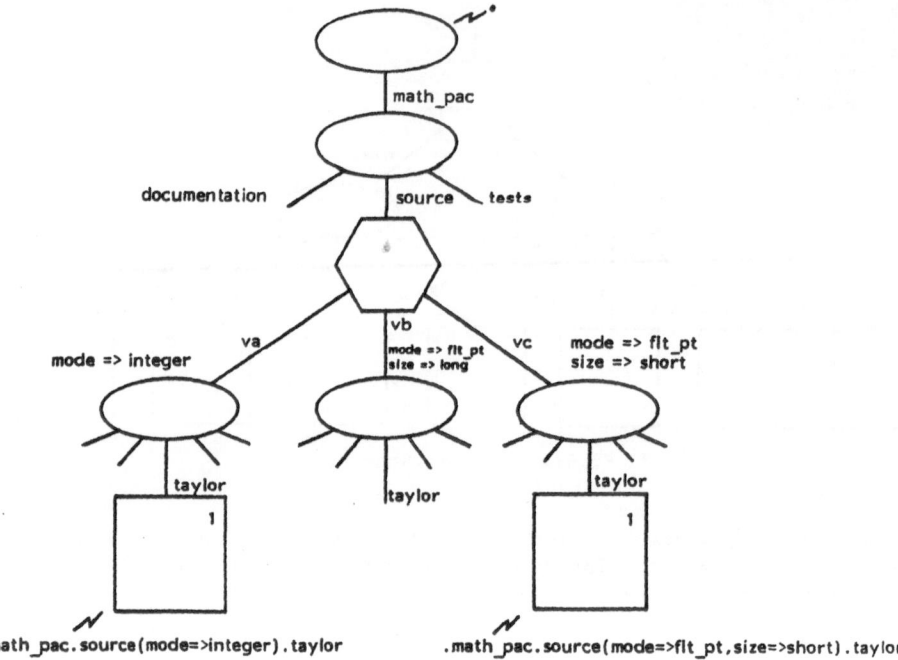

Figure 4.   Attribute Variation Selection.

satisfied, then the user may add to the end of a file, or add entries to a directory or variation header. If the write lock is satisfied, then the user may change a file or add and delete entries of a directory or variation header. If the attr_change lock is satisfied, then the user may alter the values of attributes and associations and add and delete attributes and associations. If the execute lock is satisfied, the user may place the executable image or command script into execution.

The via lock allows the creation of database objects that can be accessed only by programs intended for that purpose. If the via lock is not empty, then the key of the program used to access the object must satisfy the via lock. Even if the via lock is satisfied, either the user name or the team name must still satisfy the lock appropriate to the type of access desired. If the via lock is null, any program may be used, provided access is otherwise granted. This feature is utilized, for example, to prevent the user from altering object code produced by the Ada compiler.

3.9 Associations

Associations are similar to attributes, but used to document the relationships between nodes. The value of an association is a list of pathnames. The ALS ensures that the elements of the list are syntactically valid pathnames, but otherwise performs no validation or maintenance on the list. An example of the use of associations is the Ada compiler which records the names of previously compiled modules referenced during a compilation in an association named "depends_on". This association is subsequently used by the linker to enforce the Ada compilation ordering rules by checking that no module named in a "depends_on" association has been compiled later than the module which possesses the association.

3.10 Derivations

The Stoneman calls for the generation of detailed histories of objects under configuration management. The ALS does this by means of deviations. Any ALS file can, potentially, possess a derivation. A derivation is a combination of attributes and associations that document the circumstances under which a file was created or modified. Comparison of derivations shows why files differ rather than the exact text of the differences. Although derivations are not intended or used for database backup, they contain enough information so that the contents of a file can be exactly recreated from the derivation if the files named in the derivation exist.

Files in the ALS database can only be created or modified during the execution of some program called the creating tool. The derivation is an accounting of the conditions under which the creating tool executed. The name of the program, the parameters passed to the program, and files opened and read by the program are automatically recorded in the derivation. The creating tool can modify the derivation based on specific knowledge that a particular input is insignificant or that some other unrecorded information is significant. The ALS internally maintains the information required for derivations. Whenever an output file is closed, the information is posted, if derivations have been enabled by the creating tool.

A derivation consists of the attributes derivation_text and the associations logged_inputs, derived_from, and other_inputs. These attributes and associations collectively constitute the derivation. Derivations are controlled by the KAPSE and cannot be modified except by the creating tool. The functions of the derivation components are:

derivation_text

  This attribute conveys the name of the tools that created or modified the file, the parameters passed to those tools, and annotations posted by those tools.

logged_inputs

  This association lists the pathnames of files that were opened and read by the creating tool. References in this association engender the incrementation of the derivation_count of the named file.

derived_from

  This is a special association that contains, not pathnames, but the unique identifiers of the files named in the logged_inputs association. By using derived_from, the files named in the derivation can be found, even if they have been renamed. This is used by the ALS when decrementing derivation_counts.

other_inputs

  This association lists the pathnames of files that were open and read by the creating tool, but were not entered in the logged_inputs association, because the citation was explicitly suppressed. References in other_inputs do not engender incrementation of the derivation_count of the name file.

Files, which have been named in the logged_inputs association of the

derivation of one or more other files, possess a cited_by association and a
derivation_count attribute. Cited_by contains the UID's of the files that
name this file in their derivations. These are the back-links of the de-
rived_from associations. In other words, cited_by refers to those files
that have been created from the file possessing the cited_by association.
Derivation_count is, simply, the number of entries in the cited_by association. Cited_by and derivation_count are managed automatically by the ALS
and are not subject to direct alterations by tools or users. Entries in
cited_by are removed when the named file is deleted. A revision cannot be
deleted if it possesses a positive derivation_count. Since this makes deletion very complicated, the use of derivations is recommended only for
baseline objects under configuration management.

4.   USE OF ALS FEATURES

    This section describes how the features of the ALS can be used to over-
come some of the problems faced in large-scale software efforts. For discussion purposes, the use of variations will be illustrated in the context
of providing support for program families; the use of revisions, access
control, and derivations will be outlined in relation to CM; and the use of
sharing will be couched in the discussion of programmer coordination. However, in reality, the partitioning is not as clear. Variations are also
necessary for CM; access control is necessary for programmer coordination;
and all aspects of CM are intimately related to programmer coordination.

4.1 Program Families

    All changes to software components fall into two classes:

● changes that make previous versions of the component
  obsolete, and

● changes that do not cause previous versions to become
  obsolete.

    The first class of change is called revision; the second is termed
variation.

    Examples of changes of the first class are error corrections. Once an
error is discovered and corrected, there is no reason, other than historical
investigation of failures, to use old, erroneous, versions of a component
in any new systems. The latest version supersedes all older versions.
Revision sets are used to represent this type of change in the ALS database.
Revision does not give rise to families of programs. If all components are
changed by superseding the previous revision, then at any given time, there
is only one current copy of the software incorporating all of the latest
revisions of all components.

    Examples of changes of the second class are changes in the function or
implementation of a component. One common source of variation is testing.
A program may have some components used only during testing and other, similar but not identical, components used in production variations of the
system. In this case, the existence of a test variation does not make a
production variation obsolete; the variations legitimately exist simultaneously. An error in one variation may or may not appear in another variation. Variations may also exist because of differences in implementation
of identical functions. Our SINE routine, for example, might be coded in
any number of languages for different computers. There may be a separate
variation for computers that lack floating point hardware, or a separate

double precision variation, etc. ALS variation sets are used to represent changes of this type. It is variation that gives rise to families of programs because multiple systems can be constructed by incorporating the latest revision of one or another variation of a component in each of the systems.

Variation set headers mark the places in the software where evolution of the families diverges. Components above variation headers are shared by all members of the family of programs. Components below variation set headers are specific to some subset of family members. In general, it is best to have the variation set headers as low in the structure as possible so the shared components do not appear below variation headers. In this sense, the example in Figure 3 is less than ideal.

A single functional variation often results in many changes distributed throughout the structure of the baseline. If a single variation header were used, it would have to be placed so high in the structure that many common components would appear in the subtree of the variation header. In such cases, it is better to use multiple variation headers for a single functional change. However, each of the resulting variations should either be given the same name, or should all have common identifying attributes. For example, if a variation is introduced in a system to support double precision arithmetic, then all components that are specific to single precision should be named "single" and components specific to double precision should be named "double". Using the variation notation, this would yield names like sine(single), cosine(single), etc., in one case, and sine(double), cosine(double), etc., in the other case. Alternatively, attribute variation selection could be used, in which case the corresponding component names would be sine(precision=>single), cosine(precision=>double), respectively. Several attributes can be used for selecting a single variation, e.g., sine(precision=>double, target=>8086). In this way, variations with different names can be selected with a common set of attributes.

The ALS supplies these capabilities so that tools for constructing individual members of a program family can be readily developed. Such tools would be given the attribute values or variation names to use in selecting components from a baseline containing many variations. The tools would then collect the necessary components and bind them together to form an executable program. Combinations of many attributes and variation names could be used to generate a very large number of family members closely matched to the requirements of individual applications. Such a "custom tailoring" approach to software is often avoided simply because conventional methods for dealing with program families are cumbersome and expensive.

The proper use of variations can lead to substantial cost savings during maintenance. Conventionally, members of a program family are maintained in entirely separate baselines, often by entirely different staff. This tends to encourage the continued divergence of the family members, even when it is unnecessary. By using variations, a family of programs can be stored in a single baseline. This approach keeps the evolution of the software from diverging to the point where a separate maintenance staff is required. Since all variations are readily visible, grouped under a single header, it is much easier to assess the effect of a software change on all members of a family. It is also much easier to prevent unnecessary divergence and easier to apply error corrections to all appropriate variations.

It is true that the notion of variations could have been supported by using directories. However, it is the author's view that the concept will only work successfully if programmers are continually reminded of the difference between revisions and variations. Every time a change is introduced, the programmer must decide whether the change is a revision or variation and must use the appropriate structure to apply the change to the baseline.

4.2 Configuration Management

A design goal of the ALS was to provide the underlying database mechanisms to perform configuration management. It was recognized that there are many differing scenarios for CM and many tools that can be implemented to support these scenarios. Rather than impose one method, the ALS supplies the fundamental capabilities which make all CM tools easy to implement. Rudimentary CM tools can be implemented directly in the ALS command language without writing a computer program in the conventional sense. An implementor of CM tools is likely to rely upon the following ALS mechanisms:

- revisions,

- unique identifiers,

- variations,

- attributes,

- derivations, and

- access control.

Revisions and unique identifiers give the ALS user the means to absolutely identify software components. The use of variations has been treated in the previous section. Attributes supply a method of attaching descriptive information to an object. Derivations provide a detailed accounting of how an object was created and why it differs from a similar object. Finally, the ALS access control services give the CM tools flexibility in restricting access to baselines.

Revision sets and UIDs are the keys to absolute identification; and absolute identification is the key to configuration management. Changes to baselines are made by appending revisions to revision sets and then freezing the latest revision. From then on, the name of the revision, say sine(6), stands for that object only. Any change to sine would result in a new, highly visible, revision named sine(7), which has a new UID.

Revision sets facilitate the comparison of baselines with other baselines and installed systems, two fundamental CM operations. Suppose that there exists a baseline from which is generated a number of variants of a system. The systems are constructed by a tool such as described in the previous section. As a system is constructed, the tool produces a component list of the revisions incorporated. For each component, the list contains the full file name, including the revision number and any variation name, and the UID. Every system constructed for testing and every system generated for revenue service has its component list attached. The elements of any system can be readily identified by examining its component list. If a programmer needs to examine the source text of the system, he merely displays the contents of the revisions specified in the component list. Since the revisions cited in the component list are frozen, there is no question that the source text is exactly that used to generate the system. Any change between the given system and the current baseline can be rapidly identified by comparing the revision numbers and UIDs in the component list with the latest revision numbers and UIDs in the baseline. The system can be exactly recreated by extracting from the baseline the revisions cited in the component list. Finally, the correspondence between a test system and a production system can be easily verified by comparing the component lists of the system.

In addition to system building tools, CM typically entails the creation of many tools for such tasks as installation and accounting of baseline changes, tracking of error reports, tracking of project status, baseline inventory and audit, error diagnosis, etc. Tools of this nature often require auxiliary information about the objects in the baseline, e.g., installation date, author, pending changes, systems in which the object was used, etc. ALS attributes are used to conveniently store such auxiliary information.

Attributes are a method of attaching descriptive information to an object without modifying the contents of an object. Without attributes, there are three choices: modify the object, build auxiliary files to contain the descriptive information, or use naming conventions. Modification of the object is very inflexible since it affects the programs that manipulate the object. This approach leads to such abberations as highly coded control information embedded in comments in source code. Naming conventions are inadequate for the amount of information necessary for configuration management. If auxiliary files are used, each program that uses them must build and maintain the data structure of the auxiliary file. By providing attributes, much of the data manipulation burden is removed from the configuration management programs. Attribute values can be quite large, up to 64K characters. Attributes are used where the information is to be kept with the object being described. Auxiliary files will still be used where information about many objects is to be collected in one place.

Derivations are required by the Stoneman. In essence, they are a semi-automatic method for incrementally tracking the history of software components. In fact, the Stoneman uses the term "history attribute". The ALS implementation of derivations is similar to the implementation proposed in the Ada Support System Study completed in the UK (Stenning, et al., 1979 and 1980). A common CM operation is the comparison of components to identify the differences between the previous software that functions correctly and the current software that malfunctions. Unfortunately, direct textual comparison is often useless. For example, the textual comparison of object modules will usually establish that a difference exists, but rarely yields a clue about the significance of the difference. Textual comparison of source may not be much more enlightening about the relevance of any differences discovered. However, comparison of the derivatives of two components can reveal that different revisions or variations of source were used to obtain object modules, or that different compiler options, e.g., optimization, were used in each case, etc. CM tools can post any relevant information in the derivation_text attribute. This might include a component list, or a short description of a change entered by a programmer during an edit operation. This type of information is significantly more useful than textual comparison by itself.

Access to baselines must be controlled to ensure that no unauthorized changes are applied. The ALS uses a relatively conventional paradigm for access control, for CM, the via lock is especially useful. With the via lock, it is possible to create subtrees in the ALS database that can only be accessed through the services of a tool or group of tools. In this way, access to baselines can be controlled by CM tools created for the purpose. Such tools are used to ensure that changes are applied in an orderly fashion, that all recording of changes is duly performed, that changes have been authorized, and so forth. This feature is used, for example, by the ALS Ada compilers to deny users direct access to program libraries where object modules are stored. In this way, the user is prevented from circumventing the recompilation ordering rules of the Ada Language.

4.3 Coordination of Programmers

This discussion will be limited to programmer coordination during the manipulation of source and object code. There are many other aspects of programmer coordination not treated here because the ALS currently provides no specific tools for interface control, design coordination, requirements analysis, etc. Some of these problems are addressed by the Ada language; others will be addressed by tools written for the ALS. It is expected that the features of the ALS already outlined will simplify the implementation of such coordination tools. Many of these tools will follow the CM paradigms established for baseline control.

For source code, most coordination will be done by the use of baselines. Source used by more than one programmer will be stored in a controlled baseline. Any modifications to the source will be accomplished by first locking the code to be modified, performing the modifications and testing them in a private area, then installing the modifications in the baseline, after suitable notice has been given to all interested parties. Locking prevents more than one person from modifying a component simultaneously. It also serves to alert other users that a modification may soon be applied.

The baseline can be used in three ways:

- source files can be copied from the baseline,

- any subtree can be shared, or

- the baseline can simply be referenced.

If source is copied, then the programmer is insulated from any changes that occur. He is also cut off from any error corrections or improvements. If the source is shared, new revisions of the source files will automatically appear in the sharer's area, potentially without notice. If the source is referenced, then there are a number of choices, references to explicit revisions and variations, references to the latest revision or latest frozen revision, and/or references to the default variation. Explicit references provide isolation, general references do not.

Sharing prevents unnecessary divergence of software. In more conventional systems, sharing is accomplished by copying. But once copied, the evolution of software components is likely to diverge because the copy will be overlooked during maintenance. With sharing, there is only one copy to maintain. If changes for one sharer are inappropriate for all, then a variation should be introduced to document the divergence. Keeping all the source logically in the baseline and only referring it during compilation is a good compromise. Isolation can be achieved by using explicit revisions and variations, but the divergence of evolution is less likely. However, with referencing, deletion of old revisions must be controlled to avoid deletion of source text that is still in use. In some sense, this is an abrogation of the obsolescence property or revisions, and, therefore, should not be used in place of variations. In other words, explicit revision references should only appear when there is an intent to track the evolution of the source component; otherwise, a variation should be created.

The ALS supplies much stronger support for programmer coordination at the object code level. All Ada object code must be placed in a structure called a Program Library. In general, there is one Program Library (PL) for each variation of an executable program. A PL is a collection of directories and revisions in one subtree. Via locks are used to restrict access to PLs. Programmers are encouraged to think of PLs as buckets into which they place components of a system. When all components are in the PL, they can be linked together to form an executable program. Revisions are used inside PLs so that one PL can be repeatedly used for recompilation and relinking during the system development. Ada recompilation ordering rules are enforced by all tools that operate on PLs.

Components can be placed into a PL by compilation or by acquisition from another PL. Suppose, for example, that an Ada package exists for trigonometry. The package can be initially compiled into a publicly available PL. Programmers who use the package can then acquire the object code directly without recompilation. This is done by using a tool named LIB, short for library. Acquisition is accomplished by reference, so that duplicate storage of the object code is avoided while maintaining isolation of PLs. Changes in the acquired_from PL do not automatically appear in the acquired to PL. The addition of a subscription capability is anticipated. With this mechanism, the owner of an acquired_to PL would be notified if any changes were made in the acquired_from PL. He could then reacquire at his option. PLs provide the isolation of copying without the duplication of storage. Acquisition can be done from a baseline to a private PL to establish a private work area. The acquisition mechanism provides a method for easily sharing while still preserving some isolation. The guiding philosophy behind PLs is that neither a baseline nor a private PL can be altered without explicit action by the owner.

5. CONCLUDING REMARKS

A major technical contribution of the ALS is the support for large-scale software projects. The ALS is one of the first production-quality programming environments to offer native, rather than tacked-on, support for configuration management of program families. Specifically, it is the first environment to offer:

- differentiation of revisions and variations,

- explicit named variations,

- freezing of revisions, and

- derivations.

The notion that there is a qualitative difference between revision and variation has been independently proposed by two other investigators, Cargil and Tichy (Cargil, 1980; Tichy, 1980). The ALS will test the value of this model by exposing the idea to a large number of software engineers in production situations. In the author's opinion, the distinction between revision and variation will prove to be a fundamental notion.

ACKNOWLEDGEMENT

The work described in this paper is being performed under US Army CECOM Contract No. DAAK80-80-C-0507.

This paper is a revision of a paper entitled "Large-Scale Software Development with the Ada Language System" which appeared in the Proceedings of the ACM Computer Science Conference, February 1983.

REFERENCES

Bersoff, E. H., Henderson, V. D., and Siegel, S. G., 1979, "Software Configuration Management: A Tutorial", Computer Magazine, January 1979, IEEE, pp. 6-14.

Buxton, J., 1980, STONEMAN, (Department of Defense Requirements for Ada
   Programming Support Environments), U.S. Department of Defense, February
   1980.

Cargil, T. A., 1980, A View of Source Text for Diversely Configurable Software, University of Waterloo, Dept. of Computer Science, 100p.

Stenning, V., et al., 1979 and 1980, Ada Support System Study, System Designers Limited and Software Sciences Limited.

Tichy, W. F., 1980, Software Development Control Based on System Structure
   Description, Carnegie-Mellon University, Computer Science Department,
   January 1980, 180p.

Thall, R. M., 1982, "The KAPSE for the Ada Language System", Proceedings of
   the AdaTEC Conference on Ada, October 1982, ACM, pp. 31-47.

Wolfe, M., Babich, W., Simpson, R., Thall, R., and Weissman, L., 1981,
   "The Ada Language System", IEEE Computer Magazine, June 1981, pp.
   37-45.

9. INFORMATION, KNOWLEDGE, AND VALUE

EXPERT SYSTEMS FOR KNOWLEDGE ENGINEERING: MODES OF DEVELOPMENT

Glynn Harmon

Graduate School of Library
and Information Science
The University of Texas
Austin, Texas 78712-1276

Abstract: The problems of human-computer interface design will be confronted increasingly by human knowledge engineers--those who acquire and
incorporate the knowledge of domain experts and other users into expert or
knowledge-based systems. Knowledge engineers thus occupy a central role in
integrating friendly use with user-friendly systems. But knowledge engineering expertise itself is already targeted for expert system development.

The work of the knowledge engineer can be described in six phases:
selection of appropriate problem; development of prototype; development of
complete expert system; evaluation; integration of system; and maintenance.
Increasingly, more emphasis is being placed on rigorous, expert-driven
formulations of problems. A knowledge engineer expert system could be
developed in a top-down manner, from scratch, without much initial recourse
to the existing system infrastructure. Here, knowledge engineering would be
mapped upon itself as the key technology. In contrast, the system could be
developed in an evolutionary, bottom-up manner so as to integrate previously
developed tools. Top-down approaches are expected to be used increasingly,
as they have been in structured software design.

This paper contrasts these alternative modes of expert system development, and reports on engineering efforts which use these contrasting approaches. Future designs and evaluations of human-computer interfaces are
expected to be based largely on criteria used to design and evaluate the
performance of knowledge engineering and expert system interfaces.

INTRODUCTION

The objective of this paper is to study the problems of human-computer
interface design via the relatively new technologies of expert or knowledge-
based systems and the ways in which these systems are engineered. Expert
systems are typically described as computer programs which use expert or
expert-like knowledge to attain high levels of performance in a narrow
problem area. The term expert system is often synonymous with the term
knowledge-based system. Knowledge-based systems utilize computer programs
that use inference procedures and knowledge to solve, or assist in solving,
difficult problems. The domain knowledge of these programs is separate from

463

its other sectors of knowledge. These systems are developed by knowledge engineers -- persons who work with users and/or in user environments to assess problems, acquire and analyze relevant knowledge, and build systems for use by experts or their surrogates. Knowledge engineers concentrate on the task of knowledge acquisition -- the process of locating, evaluating, defining, capturing, structuring, and organizing source knowledge so that it can be used in a computer program by expert or semi-expert users (Waterman, 1985, pp. 1-23). Accordingly, the study of expert systems and knowledge engineering tends to focus squarely on many problems of human-computer interface design.

While knowledge systems technology has had a short history, a few empirical lessons about its development and implementation appear to be emerging. Case studies of the knowledge engineering process, and of the successes and limitations of working expert systems occasionally suggest some provocative (if not counter-intuitive) insights about the nature of human-computer interface. The original intent of this study, then, was simply to codify some of these lessons and to extend them to the realm of human-computer interface design. But this turned out to be too simple. It was observed that the knowledge engineering and knowledge systems movements are predicated on assumptions which challenge some key orthodoxies of conventional systems analysis and software engineering, including interface design. It was further observed that the knowledge engineering itself has been targeted for expert system development.

This brought forth a vision of a technology being mapped upon itself to create a sort of "infinite-improvement loop". Knowledge experts could engineer expert systems for better knowledge engineering; improved knowledge engineering could lead to even better expert systems for knowledge engineering, and so on. One might envision the central and side effects of this "infinite-improvement loop" extending to drastically improved human-computer interfaces, inasmuch as this is precisely where knowledge engineering appears to be centered. Next, it was observed that the knowledge engineering process (especially knowledge acquisition) has been formalized sufficiently to become a candidate for wholesale automation, and a few research projects aim in this direction. But a deeper analysis of these formularizations reveal two contrasting approaches, herein referred to as the "bottom-up" and "top-down" approaches to knowledge engineering. The bottom-up approach is characterized by incremental improvement and the better integration of existing knowledge engineering tools (software and hardware packages which simplify expert system development). Top-down knowledge engineering is characterized by holistic problem analysis and the successive decomposition of problems into subproblems until specific tasks or processes are described, in a manner much akin to the hierarchical design protocols and step-wise refinement of structured programming.

Although the circle of inquiry widens in the above ways, the original objective still holds: to study human-computer interface design via the results of empirical studies about expert systems performance and knowledge engineering. The subobjectives are these: (1) to analyze the knowledge engineering process, including knowledge acquisition; (2) to review empirical cases of knowledge engineering which illustrate a bottom-up approach; (3) to illustrate top-down knowledge engineering design; and (4) to summarize a few implications for human-computer interface design.

KNOWLEDGE ENGINEERING AND INCREMENTAL DEVELOPMENT

The term knowledge engineering generally refers to the process of designing and building expert or knowledge systems. More specifically, it refers to the process of knowledge acquisition, which involves extracting knowledge from specialized sources, usually experts, and organizing it for conversion into a (usually symbolic) program. Knowledge acquisition is typically conducted in a highly interactive mode between the knowledge engineer and the one or more experts from whom source knowledge is derived. Because these experts or their surrogates become ultimate users, and their input is a critical baseline for software design, this interaction constitutes a critical human-computer, input-output interface.

This critical interface typically develops from a first approximation effort between the knowledge engineer and the expert source to develop a modest system prototype. Subsequent knowledge acquisition cycles result in incremental prototype adjustments as the system evolves toward greater operational capability. Incremental development typically continues through the life cycle of the system, which includes modification, maintenance, and redevelopment. Some systems evolve from their initial demonstration prototype stage through the stages of research prototype, field prototype, production prototype, and commercial system. Through these various cycles and stages, the incremental development/redevelopment theme is constant. Prototyping and incremental development appear to be the key dynamic of human-computer interfaces in knowledge-engineer systems. Recent studies of the prototyping approach have produced statistically significant results that users who were subjected to prototyping rated their information systems favorably in terms of system output accuracy, helpfulness in problem-solving, and overall user satisfaction. But system designers were required to make more changes to accommodate users and found prototyped systems more difficult to manage (Alavi, 1984).

Consider the case of XCON RI, Digital Equipment Corporation's system which configures VAX-11/780 computer systems. Waterman's summary of this case reveals, first, that the level of knowledge engineering effort needed to develop and extend the system remained relatively constant over the life of the system; the knowledge base of the system also grew at a fairly constant rate. Incremental development thus became a way of life. Second, the developers found that through incremental development the system could be put into operation before it was complete. After all, it took over 800,000 VAX orders to uncover inadequacies in RI's knowledge configuration. Even then, the developers found that the system did not have (and probably never would have) all the knowledge it needed, and that it continued to make mistakes. But the strength of the ongoing knowledge acquisition interface apparently sufficed to keep the system operationally and economically useful. Third, the developers found that building the system is a seemingly unending process, requiring continuous incremental growth:

> "Though much of RI's knowledge was added to correct or
> complement exiting knowledge, a significant part of the
> additions came as a result of RI having to have the
> knowledge to perform new tasks. Some of these were the
> result of Digital introducing new computer system types
> and the result resulted from the users' observations
> that things would be better if RI could do one more
> thing. We believe all expert systems will be hounded
> to continue to grow for both of these reasons. Tasks
> that expert systems are good for are just those whose
> objects change significantly over time. Moreover, in
> such tasks no clear boundaries delimit what should and
> should not be within the province of the expert. Thus,
> whenever an expert system finds itself on a boundary, its
> public encourages it to extend the boundary."
> (Waterman, 1985, quoted from p. 218.)

The flexibility and modular organization of the RI expert system, along with its interface based on incremental development, appear to underlie the success of the system.

The knowledge engineering and incremental development approaches stand in rather stark contrast to conventional software design approaches. Conventional analysts and programmers typically interview users and then retreat to their closets to design and test programs in relative isolation. Initial design dictates much of the programming effort, user-analyst-programmer interaction can be minimal, and the time between the initial interviews and program delivery can be lengthy (Harmon and King, 1985, pp. 7-9). There is some evidence that a "root cause" of behavioral problems which arise when computer systems are implemented in organizations might be the inadequate conceptualizations of users among systems designers. While designers do seem to cognize multiple models of users, these models can be slow to change and are often mismatched with user groups. System designers need to know how better to predict user needs and behaviors, and to assess and use organizational development methods (Dagwell and Webber, 1983). Knowledge engineering is also geared to the specialized domain knowledge of users, and to one or more generic functions which cut across different specialties (interpretation, prediction, diagnosis, design, planning, monitoring, debugging, repair, instruction, control) (Hayes-Roth, Waterman, and Lenat, 1983, p.14). Collectively, these specialized orientations of knowledge engineering appear to enhance the quality of its human-computer interfaces.

In conclusion, the factors of user specialization, intense and continuous levels of user involvement, organizational change, and other situational factors drive prototyping and incremental development. The user-system interface constitutes a relatively tight and continuous feedback loop. Thus, knowledge engineering approaches can avert many of the interface problems associated with the use of conventional software design. Knowledge engineering methodology provides a potentially promising attack on human-user interface problems.

PHASES OF KNOWLEDGE ENGINEERING

Numerous versions of the knowledge engineering process have been presented in the last few years. Waterman offers three alternative views of the process:

(1) Developmental stage view -- develop demonstration, research and field prototypes, and then offer a commercial system;

(2) Knowledge acquisition view -- proceed through knowledge acquisition by on-site observation of expert problem-solving episodes. Secure further expert cooperation through the phases of problem selection, description, and analysis, and then conduct system examination and validation; and

(3) System building phases view -- identify then conceptualize the problem; specify solution requirements; formalize the knowledge in a programming framework; specify the program form; and test the prototype program. (Waterman, 1985, pp. 134-140, 156-161.)

Obviously, the above three views of knowledge engineering stress different aspects of the same general process, but the overall emphasis is on an incremental development and close cooperation between domain experts and knowledge engineers. Knowledge engineering appears to have institutionalized the concepts of tight interface design and elaborate, real-time, human-computer interaction.

Other versions of the stages of knowledge engineering also stress tight interface design and real-time problem solving. Harmon and King portray the six phases of problem selection, prototype development, complete system development, system evaluation, system integration into its operational environment and system maintenance (Harmon and King, 1985, pp. 197-207). In the Second Artificial Intelligence Satellite Symposium, sponsored by Texas Instruments, Tennant recommended the following steps: recognize and identify the problem domain; scope the size of the problem and the system; select knowledge engineering tools; acquire and program the knowledge in prototype form; then incrementally develop the knowledge base; deploy and integrate the system into its operating environment; validate the knowledge base through test cases; maintain the system (which is like the process of development) (Texas Instruments, 1986, pp. 2-1 to 2-47). The Texas Instruments approach to knowledge engineering is based on experience from a relatively large number of commercial and industrial installations, and is somewhat more elaborate and empirically-based than the reader normally encounters in tutorial, prescriptive treatments. But the recent thrust of the Texas Instruments approach appears to be rapid experimental prototyping on the numerous smaller problems which exist within organizations. That is, a larger number of modest but quick expert system payoffs are sought in preference to larger but more rare, difficult-to-identify problems which require large expert systems and yield large but slower payoffs. Because this approach calls for developing larger numbers of expert systems throughout organizations, these systems and their human interfaces could be all the more customized to individual or small group requirements.

A retrospective analysis of three successful knowledge engineering cases conducted by Bobrow, Mittal, and Stefik (1986) reveals a newer version of the phases of knowledge engineering: identification of problem domain; conceptualization and formalization of the knowledge; prototype system development; user interface development; system testing and redefinition; and knowledge base maintenance. These phases are unremarkable, except for their inclusion of the user interface step. The authors indicate a need to develop interfaces which emulate what users of noncomputer systems are accustomed to. These cases also indicate that considerably more "front-end", close work with experts and others has come to be necessary during initial phases -- much more than was earlier thought to be necessary in previous versions of knowledge engineering. The cases also reveal a need to proceed beyond the engineering of "low road" systems, which use direct symbolic programming and incremental development for small, bounded, and relatively static knowledge bases. There is a need to progress to "middle road" systems, which represent knowledge about more general and dynamic problems, and then to "high road" systems, which provide knowledge processing capability that is abstract enough to span domains of expertise and to use general facts and principles.

Freiling (1985) goes even further in emphasizing the necessity of prerequisite and rigorous knowledge definition, organization and representation. These steps constitute a first phase -- about a half of the entire knowledge engineering sequence. The second and final phase is prototype implementation. On the basis of experience with the TRW Defense Systems Group, Taylor (1985) notes that "the most important lesson is that expert systems are best conceived of by the experts themselves". Taylor notes that mastery of significant domain knowledge, which can take years, is required to make good design decisions. The role of knowledge engineers is of secondary importance. In both of these cases, the crucial features of interface design emanate from user-experts, rather than from software-hardware parameters or systems personnel.

The knowledge acquisition phase of knowledge engineering, with its notorious "bottleneck problem", has been approached several ways by Stanford University researchers (Buchanan, 1985): through the improvement of tools (smart editors, debuggers, knowledge-base analyzers); inductive learning from cases of successful problem-solving; analogical construction of new knowledge bases from old ones; apprentice-type observation of experts; the reduction of several small problem-solving steps to one basic operation; extension of discovery concepts from old cases to new ones; and conversion of expert knowledge from written text into knowledge bases via nonexpert readers. Ongoing research at Stanford is directed to tools that can "assist or even supplant the knowledge engineer" (Knowledge Systems Laboratory, 1985). Buchanan and others, however, note that more complete automation of knowledge acquisition is a truly difficult task, but the development of automated learning methods might prompt a breakthrough in resolving the bottleneck problem (Hayes-Roth, Waterman, and Lenat, 1983, pp. 155-157). Nevertheless, the whole process of knowledge acquisition is in a rudimentary stage of development and its formalization has just begun. Knowledge acquisition involves an unprecedented mixture of such areas as personal construct theory, fuzzy logic, structured software design, interview techniques, machine induction, Bayesian statistics, vectors and matrices, etc. (Hart, 1986). Because knowledge acquisition is central to human-computer interfacing, clarification of the tougher problems of interface design might have to await formalization of the knowledge acquisition process.

BOTTOM-UP APPROACH

According to Williams, of Inference Corporation, the knowledge engineering process is "much more one of bottom-up discovery than top-down design" (Texas Instruments, 1986, p. 2-31). Bottom-up development involves specialized problem-solving and the incremental aggregation of rules into larger and larger structures (rule sets, frames, networks). Likewise, knowledge engineering selectively employs specific tools or tool kits to develop systems. Tools consist of symbolic or problem-solving programming languages, skeletal or general purpose knowledge engineering languages, and various design or acquisition aids and support facilities (Waterman, 1985, p. 81). At present, thinking in knowledge engineering trends tend to be heavily dominated by the "tool" approach, whether new applications are being developed, existing systems are being improved, or experimental research is being conducted.

The design and development of expert systems for knowledge engineering, or the automation of knowledge acquisition, has been and will probably continue to be approached most frequently from the bottom-up. In the area of knowledge acquisition, Fu and Buchanan (1985) of Stanford University have demonstrated that automatic acquisition, derived from a set of instances and driven by abstract models embedded in an RL program, works reasonably well to form rules of intermediate-level abstraction. These investigators were also successful in demonstrating that inductive machine learning from an existing rule base can be used to infer meta-rules and to improve the efficiency of rule-based systems. These meta-rules serve as heuristics to select good object rules or reject poor ones for the application task or rule base (Fu and Buchanan, 1984). Likewise, many cases in the Heuristic Programming Project at Stanford have had a strong inductive and empirical orientation, whereby experiments tend to use incrementally improved adaptations of previously developed hardware-software combinations, and with considerable success (Engelmore and Cornelius, 1986).

Three rather striking successes have emerged from the bottom-up approach: (1) the inductive formalization of broad functional classes of expert knowledge; (2) the better delineation of expert domain knowledge; and (3) outlines of the anatomy of expertise itself. Pau (1986) reports on his survey of expert systems for equipment fault detection, testing, and maintenance, and notes that generalized knowledge about classification and diagnosis (two of the several "generic categories" or "consultation paradigms" in expert systems) is already emerging. Buchanan (1986) notes from a 1985 survey of about sixty working expert systems that some generalizations are emerging from such expert domains as chemistry, computers, electronics, education, finance, geology, information management, manufacturing, engineering, medicine, and military areas. Better notions of the components of expertise itself are being empirically formulated . Hayes-Roth (Hayes-Roth, Waterman, and Lenat, 1983, pp. 210-214) characterize "know-how" knowledge as that which enables one to abstract general categories from data, to know where to look for data, to know the necessary and sufficient conditions to achieve a goal, to know about actual or hypothetical causes or effects, to know causes of symptoms, and to eliminate uncertainty. Fikes and Keyler (1985) observe that experts should, with respect to some object, possess specialized vocabulary and be able to specify relations, decision rules, processes, constraints, heuristics, disjunctive facts, behaviors, typical situations, and uncertain facts. The categories in the three areas above (functional knowledge, domain knowledge, and components of expertise) might also serve as human-computer interface design categories.

The incremental development, use, and evolutionary improvement of knowledge engineering tools, as a key thrust of the bottom-up approach, can be discerned by comparing functional descriptions of expert system tools. According to Expert Systems (1986), HERACLES (Heuristic Classification Shell) evolved from several earlier systems, including NEOMYCIN, EMYCIN, and MYCIN to become a tool for building knowledge-based consultation systems. MYCIN, a well-known diagnostic system, was stripped of its domain knowledge, leaving EMYCIN as its shell. EMYCIN's diagnostic and domain-specific rules were separated to form NEOMYCIN, and then its classification rules were abstracted to produce HERACLES, with its metalevel control. TIMM 2.0 provides capability to link together an infrastructure of existing expert systems to form a decision network. AGE is a collection of tools and partial frameworks for knowledge engineering. It combines many inference, control and representation techniques, and numerous other features, from previous expert systems and uses them in reprogrammed, domain-independent forms (Walker and Miller, 1986, pp. 73, 76). These tools are evolving rapidly and the list of added or hybridized functions, features, and support environments is now extremely large. The tools appear to be evolving toward many of the idea features suggested by Waterman and Hayes-Roth (Hayes-Roth, Waterman, and Lenat, 1983, pp. 210-214): greater and more flexible levels of generality; more diverse language features; different database structures; alternative control methods. Built-in explanation and interaction facilities and control methods can be adjusted to requirements for efficiency, learning, or self-modification. Collectively, these systems are becoming more highly integrated and complete.

Last, the bottom-up approach is epitomized by the understandable and reasonable tendency to conduct empirical research and to make incremental improvements against the limitations of existing systems, and to merge newer systems with existing systems (Richer, 1986). However, attempts to deal with limitations one-by-one can lead to a series of ad hoc, patchwork improvements; many of which might be responses to symptoms rather than to fundamental problems. The limitations approach is obviously necessary, but apparently not sufficient over the long run.

The top-down approach to knowledge engineering tends to start with an original formulation or reformation of the overall problem and its constraints, the desired goal state, key criteria to be met, and so on. Ploya (1954) urges us to "work backwards" from a desired solution to the specifics of a mathematical problem. Churchman (1971) in his <u>Design of Inquiring Systems</u>, calls for Decarte's method of a "clearing of the slate and the design of an inquiring system <u>de novo</u>." Samuelson, Borko, and Amey (1977) observe that in designing information networks the effort can start from scratch or build on existing subsystems and their operations:

> "It is tempting to jump to the conclusion that money
> would be saved by developing networks from a few cen-
> tralized growth kernels such as traditional libraries,
> data centers, computers and communications technology.
> This could become a disastrous mistake .... the design
> and development of networks from scratch is .... the
> best way to avoiding .... traditional traps and vicious
> circles." (Samuelson, Borko, and Amey, pp. 90-91).

These authors note that funders will often try to cover existing bureaucratic deficiencies and achieve long depreciation periods for earlier investments. Funders may also be unaware of the latest technologies with their longer systems lifecycles. Systems development from scratch can serve to avoid many interfacing problems and other complexities which result from trying to integrate diverse technologies.

Top-down structured design, with its stepwise refinement, modular decomposition, etc., serve as an inherent method of modeling some artificial intelligence (AI) languages, programs, and automated design processes. Mostow (1985) states that systems that learn to design should address the goal structure of the design process, decompose goals into components, develop and evaluate alternatives to reach goals, order the design, induce from their own experience, and learn from expert designers. Several expert system tools designed to support software development, including tools to augment knowledge engineering, have employed top-down design (Frenkel, 1985). However, structured design methods need to be improved to develop the concurrent task processing modules required in real-time systems (Gomma, 1985).

The top-down approach to knowledge engineering could be applied to programming and prototyping a rule-based system based on existing knowledge engineering rules. Such an effort would be customized to the specialty of knowledge engineering, and would not necessarily need to rely on tools or architectures developed for the more established knowledge domains. Buchanan and others have formulated over forty maxims for the major knowledge engineering tasks: assessing task suitability; building a prototype; extending the prototype; finding and writing rules; maintaining the expert's interest; building the final system; and evaluating the system. A number of these maxims, particularly those which bear on interface design, are quoted below:

1. Focus on a narrow specialty area that does not involve a lot of common-sense knowledge.

2. Define the task very clearly.

3. Record a detailed protocol of the expert solving at least one protypical case.

4. Start building the prototype....as soon as the first example is well understood.

5. Work intensively with a core set of representative problems.

6. Separate domain-specific knowledge from general problem-solving knowledge.

7. Use the terms and methods that the experts use.

8. If a rule looks big, it is.

9. Engage the expert in the challenge of designing a useful tool.

10. Insulate the expert, as well as the user, from technical problems.

11. Make system I/O appear natural to users.

12. The user interface is crucial to the ultimate acceptance of the system. (Hayes-Roth, Waterman, and Lenat, 1983.)

Beyond these general rules, more specialized rules could be incorporated into an expert system for knowledge engineering. Waterman and Hayes-Roth suggest maxims for designing knowledge engineering tools. For example:

1. Provide built-in explanation and interaction facilities.

2. Provide an accessible control mechanism if generality is more important than efficiency.

3. Provide a constrained control mechanism if learning, self-modification, or sophisticated explanation is required. (Hayes-Roth, Waterman, and Lenat, 1983, pp. 212-215.)

Additional rules for different phases of the knowledge engineering task can be gleaned from diverse sources. Waterman lists several rules to avoid common pitfalls in planning an expert system. For example:

"If the expert system will require more than a few thousand medium-sized or large rules, reexamine the problem scope to see if it can be constrained." (Waterman, 1985, pp. 186-191.)

Marca (1983) presents over a hundred software engineering principles, many of which could be adapted to knowledge engineering. Examples:

1. Only some problem-solving behaviors can be aided by the computer.

2. An interactive computer system should support part, massed, and trial-and-error behaviors.

3. People feel satisfied when a clump of activity is completed. As knowledge engineering advances, these various rules could be supplemented with additional rules and eventually integrated and abstracted as meta-rules, examples of which follow:

1. If there are conflicting goals, give them priorities

and achieve the important ones first.

2. If there are subgoals that are part of the several
    major goals, plan to satisfy those subgoals before
    other subgoals. (Hayes-Roth, Waterman, and Lenat,
    1983, p. 81.)

In addition, a few expert system tools which are dedicated primarily
to knowledge engineering have been developed. A few of the tools are
experimental and reflect a trend toward top-down design. EXPERT assists in
the development of consultation programs in several technical knowledge
domains by interrelating hypotheses, findings, and decision rules. GEN-X,
still under development at General Electric, is a generic expert system that
can streamline the development of specific expert systems. LES (Lockheed
Expert System) was designed to assist knowledge engineers to solve diagnostic, planning and controlling functions. ROSIE, a programming system, was
designed at Rand Corporation to support knowledge engineering by translating
natural language into INTERLISP. MRS is a knowledge engineering language
designed to represent how an expert system reasons with its own domain
knowledge. RLL is an expert system designed to assist a knowledge engineer
to build, use and modify domain-dependent expert systems. M.1 serves to
explore practical applications of knowledge engineering and to develop
prototypes or small-scale systems (Walker and Miller, 1986, pp. 54-78).
The CYC project being carried out at Microelectronics and Computer Technology
Corporation in Austin, Texas by Lenat and others involves a long-term
effort to build a large knowledge base which is intended to contain a
one-volume, intelligent encyclopedia. This effort can be characterized in
part as a top-down effort, because it deals potentially with the entire
domain of human knowledge and works down to specialized topics (Lenat,
Prakash, and Shepherd, 1986).

As top-down approaches to design evolve, there will probably be more
and more of a tendency to deal with crucial user and use environmental
variables. Woods (1986) points out the need to design joint human-machine
cognitive systems; such designs should be more problem-driven than tech-
nology-driven. Stefik (Stefik and Conway, 1982) observes that the existence
of clans in various organizations calls for merging knowledge engineering
into the existing cultural infrastructure to achieve appropriate formaliza-
tions of knowledge. Chandrasekhran (1983) extends this thesis by noting
that problem-solving in the medical field is vertically decomposed (top-down)
by specialty, and horizontally decomposed according to diagnosis, treatment
and auxiliary categories. Problem-solving, then, occurs in networks of
crossed hierarchies, and knowledge bases should be engineered to reflect
these hierarchies. Rasdoff and Fisher (1985) observe a similar situation in
the engineering profession, and note the need for the integration of expert
systems. "A major trend now exists towards the integration of individual,
stand-alone engineering analysis and design application programs into comprehensive, user-friendly, multicomponent design systems". Overall, the
design of networks and the integration of diverse systems call for top-down
approaches, which are particularly applicable to mapping the multiple
hardware resources of distributed systems. Top-down software design can
also bring about the optimization of compilers to support data flow and
enhanced parallelism (Oxley, Sauber, and Cornish, 1984).

SUMMARY

The study of knowledge engineering, which stands squarely at the
human-computer interface, should serve to identify and clarify many issues
of interface design. As knowledge engineering matures as an area of expertise, and becomes automated, its implications for interface design could

become more potent, and could either challenge or corroborate many of today's systems design assumptions.

In traditional systems design approaches, initial design specifications drive the programming effort and tend to freeze the overall structure of the system. Designer-user interaction is often minimal and irregular. In knowledge engineering, by contrast, continuous user-engineer interaction has become institutionalized and is fairly constant throughout the life cycles of systems. The user-system interface consists of a tight feedback loop through the phases of problem formulation, prototyping, incremental development, implementation, and maintenance. Maintenance is essentially a continuation of incremental development and refinement. A significant, human-computer "bottleneck" problem, however, has persisted in chronic form throughout the short history of knowledge engineering. The bottleneck problem is being addressed by attempts to automate knowledge acquisition and machine learning. In the meanwhile, the knowledge engineering process appears to be evolving in such a way as to center more and more on domain expert-driven design.

The predominant design philosophy in knowledge engineering today is a bottom-up approach, which targets a narrow area of expertise, builds a knowledge base incrementally, and uses various system-building tools. This approach is characterized by induction, experimental empiricism, and the use of an infrastructure of existing tools to build new systems. The notable successes of the bottom-up approach include, first, the pioneering of several impressive experimental and commercial knowledge-based systems. Second, bottom-up approaches have induced the formalization of three broad classes of expert knowledge: (1) specific domain expert subject knowledge, such as medicine, mathematics, or chemistry; (2) generic classes of functional knowledge which cut through various areas of expertise, such as diagnosis, planning, and testing; (3) component skills of expertise itself, such as vocabulary, recognition of key variables, or specification of cause-effect relations. These successes are somewhat offset by the tendency to use ad hoc, trial-and-error methods and to patchwork system improvements. A few individuals might see this bottom-up approach as reminiscent of the era of "spaghetti bowl" computer programming, prior to structural design.

The top-down approach to knowledge engineering design is characterized by efforts specifically dedicated to a formulation of the knowledge engineering problem itself, and an attempt to develop from scratch expert systems for knowledge engineering. The rules of knowledge engineering have accumulated to a point where it is feasible to build at least a prototypical, rule-based expert system for knowledge engineering. In addition, efforts to automate knowledge acquisition are underway and a few expert systems have been customized to the task of knowledge engineering. but it is too early to judge the success of the top-down approach. Future systems should turn out to be even more highly customized to the total dimensions of knowledge engineering. Their software and hardware should reflect the sociology and overall knowledge organization of their respective domain environments.

CONCLUSIONS

A first conclusion is that knowledge-based systems and knowledge engineering bring a clearer focus to the problems of interface design. In discussing "expert systems for systems experts", Martin (1985) notes that it has been stressed repeatedly in the goals of fifth generation research that "the human interface must make systems easy to use by the mass public, not just by trained professionals." He notes that knowledge-base inference can be used to develop greater user friendliness through natural language communication, and the diagnosis of problems, faults, and operator mistakes. Knowledge-based inference can also increase user friendliness by helping systems experts in several areas: operating complex software; locating knowledge in the machine's library or in networks; creating specifications or graphics for the automatic generation of programs; selecting tools for distributed computing or the physical design of data bases. The human-computer interface is a central feature of the evolution of fifth generation, knowledge-based systems languages. Second, there is some evidence that the focus of design attention in the knowledge engineering process has been moving away from software-hardware specification towards the expert or quasi-expert user. The bottleneck problem focused early design attention on the knowledge acquisition interface. Next, came the recognition that more rigorous, initial problem analysis must front end knowledge acquisition. Then the role of initial problem analysis became critical enough to become the first of two major phases of the knowledge engineering effort. More recently, it has been observed that design parameters come first and foremost from domain experts, and that knowledge engineers might have only a secondary role as interface technicians. This apparent trend (even though it could be a special case or a reversible trend) raises the possibility that the truly critical dimensions of effective human-computer interface design stem from, and must be customized to, narrow domains of expertise or to specialized purposes. The effectiveness of such interfaces might be pretty much a function of appropriate knowledge base categorizations and their robustness. Lanlois (Machlup and Mansfield, 1983, pp. 581-600) argues that information processing is primarily a function of the conditional states of readiness of users to respond to signals in one way or another. Receivers are already "informed" to some extent, because their knowledge content is bound up with their classificatory structures. Thus, it might be empirically or normatively true that the structural predispositions of users allow them to "inform" systems as much as systems inform users.

Third, the findings that better classifications of knowledge and more effective systems are evolving around at least three categories (domain expertise, general functions of expert systems, and abstractions of the components of expertise itself) suggest the need to challenge many prevalent design assumptions based on excessively general notions of user behavior and the corresponding adequacy of general-purpose design approaches. The overall lesson that emerges from knowledge engineering is that general-purpose approaches have not worked well, and that design is best customized to specialized segmentations of the user marketplace. Future research might be directed to developing more precisely segmented and better organized typologies of human expertise for purposes of system design and evaluation.

Fourth, a great deal of past and current design philosophy centers on overall system architecture, and users are often regarded as existing "outside" of systems, or are treated as peripherals. A fundamental change in design philosophy might provide for designing systems around specialized users, in a way akin to building aircraft cockpit instrumentation around pilots and the requirements of instrument flying. This might allow for the coordinated use of clusters of several user-system interfaces at about the same time. Moreover, such a refocused, knowledge engineering design philosophy might automatically serve to integrate the findings of user, use, and human factors research with those of software and hardware engineering research.

Fifth, the methodology of AI has evolved to the point where fundamentally different approaches are being identified. Newell (Machlup and Mansfield, 1983, pp. 187-228) lists some thirty-six fundamental issues in AI which have occupied researchers. About fifteen of these issues are active at any one time. Examples include "power vs. generality" and "epistemology vs. heuristics". Hall and Kibler (1985) identify the AI research perspectives of artificial vs. natural intelligence, system performance vs. uncovering principles, empirical vs. speculative investigation, and constructive (bottom-up) vs. form (top-down) in system design. This paper has centered on the last issue of bottom-up vs. top-down design, with the recognition that this distinction can be overplayed and that the two approaches interact in actual design efforts. Top-down design appears to be better suited than its opposite for the development of expert systems for knowledge engineering. In spite of its faddish nature, knowledge engineering has come to be sufficiently important to study in its own right. It can, for example, be regarded as a new body of knowledge about human-computer interface design. The bottom-up merging of tools developed for purposes other than knowledge engineering has been quite productive, but this inductive approach appears to be limited. Ultimately, the knowledge engineering effort and the corresponding problems of interface design will have to be confronted on their own terms. The jet engine was not invented solely through incremental improvement of piston-driven engines.

REFERENCES

Alavi, M., 1984, "An Assessment of the Prototyping Approach to Information Systems Development", Communications of the ACM, 27, June 1984, pp. 556-563.

Bobrow, D. G., Mittal, S., and Stefik, M. J., 1986, "Expert Systems: Perils and Promise", Communications of the ACM, 9, pp. 880-894.

Buchanan, B. G., 1985, Some Approaches to Knowledge Acquisition, Report No. STAN-CS-85-1076, July 1985, Dept. of Computer Science, Stanford University, Stanford, CA.

Buchanan, B. G., 1986, "Expert Systems: Working Systems and the Research Literature, Expert Systems, 3, January 1986, pp. 32-40.

Chandrasekhran, A. B., 1983, "Towards a Taxonomy of Problem Solving Types, AI Magazine, 4, Winter/Spring 1983, pp. 9-17.

Churchman, C. W., 1971, The Design of Inquiring Systems, Basic Books, NY, p. 18.

Dagwell, R., and Weber, R., 1983, "Systems Designers Users Models: A Comparative Study and Methodological Critique", Communications of the ACM, 26, November 1983, pp. 987-997.

Engelmore, R. S., and Cornelius, C. W., 1986, Heuristic Programming Project: October 1982-September 1985 Final Report, Report No. KSL-86-17, Dept. of Computer Science, Stanford University, Stanford, CA, pp. 1-16.

Fikes, R., and Keyler, T., 1985, "The Role of Frame-Based Representation in Reasoning", Communications of the ACM, 28, September 1985, pp. 904-920.

Freiling, M., 1985, "Starting a Knowledge Engineering Project: A Step by Step Project", AI Magazine, 6, Fall 1985, pp. 150-164.

Frenkel, K. A., 1985, "Toward Automating the Software-Development Cycle", Communications of the ACM, 28, June 1985, pp. 578-589.

Fu, L., and Buchanan, B. G., 1984, Enhancing Performance of Expert Systems by Automated Discovery of Meta-Rules, Report No. HPP-84-38, Dept. of Computer Science, Stanford University, Stanford, CA, pp. 1-9.

Fu, L., and Buchanan, B. G., 1985, <u>Inductive Knowledge Acquisition for Rule-Based Expert Systems</u>, Report No. KSL-85-42, Dept. of Computer Science, Stanford University, Stanford, CA, pp. 1-34.

Gomma, H., 1985, "Software Development of Real-Time Systems", <u>Communications of the ACM</u>, <u>29</u>, July 1985, pp. 657-668.

Hall, R. P., and Kibler, D. F., 1985, "Differing Methodological Perspectives in Artificial Intelligence Research", <u>AI Magazine</u>, <u>6</u>, Fall 1985, pp. 166-178.

Harmon, P., and King, D., 1985, <u>Expert Systems</u>, John Wiley and Sons, NY, pp. 7-9.

Hart, A., 1986, <u>Knowledge Acquisition for Expert Systems</u>, McGraw-Hill, NY.

Hayes-Roth, F., Waterman, D. A., and Lenat, D. B., 1983, <u>Building Expert Systems</u>, Addison-Wesley, Reading, MA, p. 14.

Hayes-Roth, F., 1985, "Rule Based Systems", <u>Communications of the ACM</u>, <u>28</u>, September 1985, pp. 921-932.

Knowledge Systems Laboratory, 1985, <u>Knowledge Systems Laboratory: 1985</u> Dept. of Computer Science, Stanford University, Stanford, CA, p. 172.

Lenat, D., Prakash, M., and Shepherd, M., 1986, "CYC: Using Common Sense Knowledge to Overcome Brittleness and Knowledge Acquisition Bottlenecks", <u>AI Magazine</u>, <u>6</u>, Winter 1986, pp. 65-85.

Machlup, F., and Mansfield, U., 1983, <u>The Study of Information</u>, John Wiley and Sons, NY.

Marca, D., 1983, <u>Applying Software Engineering Principles</u>, Little, Brown, and Co., Boston, pp. 195-198.

Martin, J., 1985, <u>Fourth-Generation Languages</u>, Prentice-Hall, NY, pp. 6, 410-411.

Mostow, J., 1985, "Towards Better Models of the Design Process", <u>AI Magazine</u>, <u>6</u>, Spring 1985, pp. 44-57.

Oxley, D., Sauber, B, and Cornish, M., 1984, "Software Development for Data-Flow," <u>Handbook of Software Engineering</u>, Vick, C. R., and Ramamoorthy, C. V., eds., Van Nostrand Reinhold Co., NY, pp. 640-674.

Pau, L. F., 1986, "Survey of Expert Systems for Fault Detection: Test Generation and Maintenance", <u>Expert Systems</u>, <u>3</u>, April 1986, pp. 100-111.

Ploya, G., 1954, <u>Patterns of Plausible Inference</u>, Princeton University Press, Princeton, NJ.

Rasdoff, W. J., and Fisher, E. L., 1985, "AI Research in Engineering at North Caroline State University", <u>AI Magazine</u>, <u>6</u>, Summer 1985, pp. 80-82.

Richer, M. H., 1986, "An Evaluation of Expert System Development Tools", <u>Expert Systems</u>, <u>3</u>, July 1986, pp. 166-183.

Rychener, M. D., 1985, "Expert Systems for Engineering Design", <u>Expert Systems</u>, <u>2</u>, January 1985, pp. 30-44.

Samuelson, K., Borko, H., and Amey, G. X., 1977, <u>Information Systems and Networks</u>, North-Holland, NY, pp. 90-91.

Stefik, M., and Conway, L., 1982, "Towards the Principled Engineering of Knowledge", <u>AI Magazine</u>, <u>3</u>, Summer 1982, pp. 4-16.

Taylor, E. C., 1985, "Developing a Knowledge Engineering Capability in the TRW Defense Systems Group", <u>AI Magazine</u>, <u>6</u>, Spring 1985, pp. 52-63.

Texas Instruments, 1986, <u>Knowledge-Based Systems - The Second AI Satellite Symposium Proceedings/Sourcebook</u>.

Walker, T. C., and Miller, R. K., 1986, <u>Expert Systems 1986: An Assessment of Technology and Applications</u>, SEAI Technical Publications, Madison, GA, 1986.

Waterman, D. A., 1985, <u>A Guide to Expert Systems</u>, Addison-Wesley, Reading, MA.

Woods, D. D., 1986, "Cognitive Technologies: The Design of Joint Human-Machine Cognitive Systems", <u>AI Magazine</u>, <u>6</u>, Winter 1986, pp. 86-92.

WHAT PRICE THE INFORMATION AGE: A MODEL FOR FAIR PAYMENT FOR THE USE

OF INFORMATION

Pat Molholt and Paul M. Hohenberg

Rensselaer Polytechnic Institute
Troy, NY 12181

Abstract: As the flow of information becomes more intensive as well as more important to production and work in general, its economic properties come under closer scrutiny. Although produced, traded, and used like other commodities, information differs in significant respects from most goods. The development of more flexible man-machine interfaces heightens the relevance of questions such as what is being purchased, how is its value determined, how can it be priced, which are discussed in this paper in some detail.

INTRODUCTION

By now it is a cliche to call this the Information Age or ours an information economy. The common fate of even powerful insights is that they lose meaning as they gain currency. We are far from having faced squarely the implications of a system of production and exchange in which information constitutes a leading input as well as output, where knowledge workers comprise the rule rather than the exception and the processing of information forms the principal work activity. What happens when someone sits at a terminal and interacts with a body of organized information is not an autonomous event. It forms one link in a complex system of use, generation, and communication of information.

In this paper, we argue that the crucial step of valuing and pricing the "transaction" taking place at the interface raises difficulties deeply rooted in the properties of information. These problems are great enough to call into question the effective development and deployment of the full information system that technology is making possible. Subjected to cumbersome or onerous access and use controls, users are caught up in a system designed to support print rather than on-line information systems. The paper draws on concepts in economic theory to underscore the difficulties inherent in information as a commodity and to evaluate existing and potential allocative mechanisms in the age of database searchers, expert systems, desktop publishing, and scholar workstations.

PRICES AND MARKETS: A PRIMER WITHOUT SLOGANS

Economists rightfully admire the market. Unfortunately, this appreciation too often spills over into uncritical worship. Thus a little care is needed. With price as the critical instrument, markets fulfill three functions. First, they ration "scarce" goods -- we use the term "scarce" as economists do to imply limits to availability but not necessarily great value or a shortage at the going price. The rationing function of prices is most clear-cut and dominant in short-run contexts, as when one cuts up an existing pie. The correct market price in this situation causes buyers to demand just the number of pieces that make up the pie we have -- no disappointed buyers, no leftover pie.

The second function of prices in a market system is of particular relevance to our present concerns, since it is an information function. Prices signal the degree of scarcity of a good or service, and so steer individual decision makers to make appropriate action. Since Adam Smith, we have marveled at the fact that each individual household or business, though trying only to further its own objectives and generally unaware of what others are doing, responds to prices in ways that improve the efficiency of the system as a whole. This important property of the market system is often referred to as the "hidden hand". The higher the price, the more encouragement for businesses to produce the good -- in preference to others that might be offered -- and for final users to economize on it by substituting something cheaper. That is really what supply and demand are all about. Likewise, producers and packagers of information need to know what types of information and what modes of access and organization users value most.

Finally, prices transfer something of value from buyers to sellers so as to allow the process of production and exchange to iterate. When you buy something you forgo the wherewithal to buy something else, while the seller is reimbursed (normally) for the costs of production. In other words, the game is for keeps. Not only are buyers and sellers forced to live with their decisions but the game is self-supporting. By contrast, many non-market activities require renewed appropriations or donations from some source other than the direct beneficiary.

If a market pricing system really works so smoothly, why is the real-world economy in fact quite bumpy? The logic of the market model is compelling, but it rests on a number of strong and, thus, unrealistic assumptions. Some of these we will explore in examining information as an economic good. But a look around us, or even casual study of economic history, will make it clear that some markets have always worked better than others. A useful generalization is that markets for final goods and services -- apples, Apples, or audits -- work better than those for the basic inputs of human labor, capital, and natural resources. The latter also constitute the areas in which political and social institutions and cultural forces have put up the strongest fight against market rule. In the past there were guilds,usury laws, and at least theoretical ownership of all land by the sovereign. Today we have OSHA and the NLRB, the FDIC and SEC, and a vast system of public lands, national parks, and environmental impact statements. Now that information has joined traditional "factors of production" as a prime input -- since knowledge workers are the principal users, as well as generators and transmitters, of information -- we should not be surprised to find that market principles run into trouble here too.

The information business now occupies well over half the nation's labor force. However, the traditional centers for distributing information, namely libraries, have not kept pace with this growth industry par excellence. In part, the issue is one of perception. Libraries have rarely recognized, much less exploited, their role in the core productive system. Only very recently have service institutions such as libraries or hospitals seen the need to examine their operations in market terms, including concern with competition, active marketing, and rational pricing. Without technology,

480

libraries, clearly, cannot acquire and process information fast enough to sustain their traditional role in the information industries. Even with technology, libraries risk being trapped on the fringes. Kalba (1977) succinctly described one aspect of the situation by noting that "...the public library has become a residual distribution center for those individuals who cannot afford a bookclub membership or discount bookstore prices". Even libraries serving the research and scholarly communities face stiff competition from the "invisible college" or academic zamisdat of pre-prints and conference presentations. The library is remote in space and lags far behind in time in terms of the laboratory or another information factory. In particular, the already discouraging publishing delays for books and journals are aggravated by ordering, cataloging, and shelving time. The negative perception of libraries is reinforced and partly justified by the lack of resources, both human and financial. Without these, it is hardly worthwhile undertaking the difficult task of coordination that would put libraries in their rightful place at the hub of the information system as productive intermediaries between producers and users of knowledge.

INFORMATION AS A COMMODITY

In some respects, information is quite clearly a commodity or economic good. It must be produced with the use of scarce inputs and it is useful enough that people are prepared to pay for it, in other words to sacrifice something else that is valuable. Information is also like other goods in that its value does not last forever, any more than does a ripe tomato or a concrete building. The rate of decay in the value of information ranges very widely. Arbitrageurs have much less than the life of a ripe tomato to take advantage of inconsistencies in exchange rates, while Homer's Iliad had outlived many cities on the site of Troy. High variance in the rate of depreciation is not, however, the only respect in which information is a unique commodity.

A principal reason, why many real-world markets don't work as smoothly as theory promises, is that the participants are not fully informed. Potential sellers don't know what the demand will be like until they have made a commitment to produce; consumers can't take the time to check every vendor before making their decision, and the package can often be opened only at home. It is simplest to think of such informational imperfections as frictional, which does not make them unimportant, of course. But in the case of information itself, the problem is far more deep-seated. Buyers almost always deal with a pig in a poke. The reason, of course, is that any true description of the informational good amounts to giving it away. The informed consumer is literally a contradiction in terms.

The very concepts of buying and selling are ambiguous when information is the subject of the transaction. Normally we think of a sale as transferring ownership of something in return for some valuable consideration -- say a sum of money. It is understood that the seller gives up the good that the buyer gets. At the same time the seller obtains the money to finance future production and so stays in business, normally with a continued advantage over the buyer, expressed for example in the spread between the wholesale and retail price. In the case of information neither presumption holds. I retain what I have sold you, since your use will not interfere with mine (although it can affect how profitable my further use is, not always in a negative sense). On the other hand, it is much more likely that you will emerge as a rival to me by reselling the information or even giving it away, since you can do so without forgoing its use. A relevant example for the issue at hand is that compilers of data are likely to do better selling it than those who do the original work. The partial monopoly

granted authors by copyright recognizes the difficulties involved with
property rights in information.

The implications of these difficulties are fairly clear. Even when
information that is costly to produce is valuable enough to justify the cost,
it is unlikely that a viable business will emerge as normally will happen
in a market system. First, the seller must convince potential buyers that
the information is indeed valuable without disclosing it. Second, the buyers
can resell it at a discount, having gotten their money's worth in using it.
Finally, even if a price can be charged, it is _socially inefficient_ to limit
access in this way, since letting the additional user share the information
imposes no addition (production) cost. In the terms we used earlier, the
rationing function suggests a zero price and free disclosure.

Yet free access would ignore the two remaining functions of prices.
In most markets, the "dollar votes" of buyers distinguish more and less
valuable goods; only those producers who meet the users' needs are rewarded,
so that efforts are channeled in more, rather than less, productive directions. Moreover, these dollars are needed to finance the production of
information. Its use is indeed free, but only once the costs of production
have been met. There is a conflict between what is efficient in the short
run and what will sustain and guide the important work of producing information in the long run.

INFORMATION PRICING IN PRACTICE AND THEORY

Although the growing role of information is adding urgency to the issues, they are far from new. How do we in fact price information? An immediate observation is that many different mechanisms are used. Just as
many theories suggest little real understanding, many solutions suggest
that the problem in fact persists. One approach is to bundle the valued
information with something else. We finance academic research as a natural
complement of higher education. Scholarly authors are willing to do with
relatively small royalties, since there are other rewards for publishing.
Were it not for this, limited markets and high production costs would mean
that their books would usually not be published at all. (Of course, the
costs are passed on to the educational system in the form of reduced teaching
loads and higher faculty-student ratios, but that is another story.) In
the case of commercial media (magazines, television, etc.), the expensive
programming is transmitted together with advertising, a kind of anti-good
for which suppliers are willing to pay recipients. The program/commercial
package is then "sold" at a net price of zero.

Voters are also generally willing to finance information activities
out of public funds. I will allow my tax dollars to pay for elementary
schooling and public libraries even if I have no children and prefer to buy
books; I also like the idea that my city has a museum, even one I have never
visited. The difficulty with this is that the informational product remains
subordinate and vulnerable. Programming is kept bland so as not to detract
from the commercials which pay the way; teaching loads can be increased
when budgets are tight; "frills" such as cultural resources get the axe
when public spending needs to be cut. In addition, there is no obvious
mechanism to distinguish routine, pedestrian knowledge work from true innovation that increases out knowledge or helps make it more available. Neither
the allocation function nor the signalling function is assured when information is provided free to the user.

In certain cases, information is priced directly. The system of copyrights, trademarks, and patents with royalties, license fees, or exclusive
marketing rights fits this mode. But an ample literature documents the
limitations of direct pricing. For example, patents are infringed or tied

up in court, while the traditional patent rules do not accommodate information inventions such as software. On the other side, strong patents may block a whole area of technological development by fencing off an excessively large domain. Copyrights are also hard to protect, particularly in an age of photocopying, facsimile, and desktop publishing.

Computer software illustrates the issues in direct pricing of information. Like patents and unlike books, programs comprise high-value information in a cheap vehicle. Disks are easy to copy and resell or share. The costs of authorship and marketing are high, the probability of success and the useful life of even successful programs are low. Costs of production as such hardly matter, and the discrepancy has led to all sorts of pricing schemes, including honor systems, registration, self-destructing disks, etc.

Certainly it will prove harder and harder to apply direct pricing to modular information, in other words to the use of individual data (citations, numbers, images) taken from large collections or banks. But with the cooperation of the user, technology is making it feasible to keep track not just of what, but also of how intensely, particular items of information are used. This capability plays an important role in the pricing approach we suggest.

By far the most common pricing schemes involve charging for the medium rather than the message. The price of a newspaper may well cover the costs of newsprint, ink, shipping, and retailing. Editorial expenses are certainly not met. The same is true of most books and periodicals. But our concern here is with electronic access to databases, so let us focus on this key operation in the information system.

Start with the person -- probably a producer of information -- sitting at the computer terminal and searching for relevant materials. She or he has access to a vast array of information resources, citations, data, and text. If this scenario takes place in the near future, we see that these resources are linked so that a citation can be followed into the document or a table complemented with related numbers from another source. After browsing for some time, the user emerges with several sorts of results. Data have been copied, for example into a personal file; documents have been ordered in hard copy; citations have been noted for later perusal. Some results, equally valuable, are negative. No, the time series does not go back to 1890; Bloog's book is not yet translated from Swedish; no one has calculated the stress resistance of this configuration in the way I propose to do. In other words, the knowledge worker derives benefit from browsing as well as from the items that are actually selected. Nor is copying (in whatever form) a reliable guide to the degree of interest. A single crucial datum can be jotted down on paper, while the hard copy of an article has been ordered almost as an afterthought.

What pricing system is relevant to such a session? Typically a subscription fee gives access to the system and to its databases. Actual use is charged on a timed basis, regardless of the activity. Finally, any hard copy or downloading is paid for at copying cost plus any royalty that applies. Each of these methods raises one or another question that we have touched on. High connect charges discourage browsing and put off novices; in other words, they violate the rule that one should not charge for something that is available with no (additional) cost. A nominal connect charge, on the other hand, makes little contribution to financing the information system. Fees related to elapsed time are really a measure of the imperfections in the hardware and software: the more efficient and user-friendly the system, the cheaper the search, while a cumbersome, poorly integrated database set adds insult to injury by tying up the computer and so consuming the user's money along with her or his time. Copying charges are a function of form rather than substance. The important number copied from the screen is free while the when-I-get-around-to-it article earns a royalty. Finally, telecommunications charges compensate the common carrier and are, once again, higher the less sophisticated the search system.

Pricing the medium rather than the message will work less and less well as the information system evolves. To the extent that the producer and packager of information are separate, paying for access and computer time just transfers the dual problem of compensating and directing the production of knowledge to the transaction between the producer of information and the packager. Insofar as the interface between data and user becomes more efficient and its cost lower, it is important to allow the price to fall so as to encourage expanded use. But the lower price will not support an ever growing knowledge production activity. Nor will over-reliance on direct pricing, e.g., copy royalties, work any better, since the temptation to copy the copies increases with their price and the system is unenforceable against individuals.

Can economic theory furnish any help? Curiously, the problem we are dealing with has a long history, and the relevant work was done by people -- beginning with the French engineer Dupuit over a century ago -- trying to calculate the correct toll for a bridge. As with information, so long as the bridge is uncongested it is costless to allow an extra person to cross. Therefore, a toll inefficiently rations the use of the bridge, the more so as it costs something extra to operate the toll barrier. But, if the users do not pay for the bridge someone else has to, taxpayers for example, and they may well vote down a worthwhile project because the majority will not use that particular bridge.

The ideal solution, which is worth pondering despite the fact that it is not practical, is to charge each user the same fraction of the highest price he or she would pay rather than forgoing the crossing (or the piece of information). This means actually charging different people different prices for the same thing, a solution that is strongly counterintuitive because it violates our sense of fairness. However, as it turns out no one can pay for the bridge or the database while charging every user -- even those who pay the most -- less than under any alternative pricing method that raises the same total revenue. This is a surprising and powerful result. Air fares frequently embody an approximation of the ideal solution, in the sense that a plane carries people who pay vastly different fares to the same destination at the same speed. (Airline travel fulfills two important conditions for the model to hold: near-zero incremental cost of an additional passenger and non-transferability of the service.)

How does one get the user to disclose the maximum price he or she would pay rather than do without, when it pays to lie? Clearly, that is why the ideal solution is seldom practical. As the example of air fares shows, one can sometime approximate the distinctions one is looking for by putting people in categories (business travellers, families, seniors) while attaching different prices to small differences in service so as to keep people happy. Advance-purchase requirements, peak and off-peak hours, and variations in service are examples. In the case of information, one can easily cite special subscription rates for educators and students, limited free computer use for students and faculty, and cheaper rates for database searches with partial access and simplified search procedures. It must be understood that such service differences make little economic sense insofar as the price being charged extends beyond the actual vehicle costs to financing the information content. Research contractors have often objected to paying a higher price for computer use than do others. But, if one applies economic rather than accounting logic, it is easy to show that the contractor actually pays less than would be the case if students were excluded by a single price from contributing to the use (and financing) of the system.

In the case of the bridge, finding an approximation to the value different users attach to the good (as shown by the maximum price they would pay rather than do without) is important to resolve the contradiction between the short-term rationing and long-term financing functions of pricing. In the case of information, and, specifically, the use of electronically accessed information, and, specifically, the use of electronically accessed databases, there is an equally important additional reason for knowing what users want and how much they want it. Compared to building a bridge, the production of knowledge, say via research, is an open-ended and murky process. The results of research efforts may be nearly nothing or something very far removed from what the researchers and their sponsors were looking for. This makes it even more important to have some guidance from users, since one can, at least hope to, put resources into promising rather than played-out or fanciful endeavors, to fund people and organizations with a good record rather than a poor one. Yet as we have seen, tying intensity of use or value to the user to the price charged only encourages subterfuge. Clearly the signalling and financing functions will have to be separated.

TOWARD AN ALTERNATIVE PRICING MODEL

One signaling device that receives considerable use in the academic and scientific community is the citation index. Frequency of citation is used to measure the importance of particular publications, and, therefore, helps determine the salary, conditions of employment, and status of practitioners. Everyone familiar with these matters can recite the litany of problems raised by citation indexes, from abusive citation of self and colleagues to the overvaluation of review articles and the like as opposed to original contributions. Yet, as the man who sat glumly at the fixed roulette wheel said, it's the only game in town. The virtue of a citation index is that it does track the action of information users without, for the most part, affecting their behavior.

Taking off the citation index, it is reasonable to suppose that persons who search databases could be led to indicate voluntarily the material that they are using intensively so long as this information did not directly serve to determine the price they pay. The key word is _directly_. The information gathered would go toward making a kind of super citation index aggregating the use of the system by all, with due notice taken of specific information that is used frequently or prized highly. A system such as this, relying both on electronic tracking _and_ on user feedback, can form the basis of the signalling component for a generalized pricing scheme.

If we return to the example of a search session we can now picture how the value signaling mechanism might work. As the searcher retrieves information, the system automatically records the book or journal sources. Retrieving 50 items and quickly perusing five or six before modifying the search indicates that the search question was not on target. On the other hand, dwelling over a paragraph, an abstract, or a graph signals that something of interest has been found. Alternatively, a quick scan of three or four items followed by a download command for all 62 in the sampled set signals usefulness. The power of artificial intelligence to interpret actions such as combinations of commands, time intervals between actions, and the relationship between successive search statements is critical to the model. In fact, rudimentary but remarkably effective passive signalling capacity is already available in a program called _Paperchase,_ which interprets end user searches in the medical database Medline. Finally, there can be interactive exchange between machine and user to elicit more information about the session or to confirm unusual patterns (You lingered ten minutes over this table; were you pondering it or did you fall asleep?).

Signalling user value is one half of the job. It will guide the distribution of revenue to finance the production of knowledge and its packaging in accessible form. Useful, i.e., heavily used and prized information, will be profitable to produce, while irrelevant, unreliable, or mundane information will not. However, the revenue must also be raised. It is legitimate to charge users of information systems, so long as the charge does not appreciably discourage use. For example, a monthly or annual fee proportional to total use can be levied, while knowledge-using organizations can subscribe to large information systems and pay a tax based on their number of knowledge workers. The rate can differ for commercial as opposed to educational users. There is also scope for public funding, as has always been the case for research. A rational system for deciding what knowledge work to support would give added confidence that the public funds were being well spent.

Many issues remain, not all of them relating to the details of practical implementation of what we have merely sketched out. Both on the using and producing end, there must be recognition of what an uncertain adventure the search for information is. Browsing must be encouraged and novices given a chance to see whether there are serendipitous treasures to be found. Sweeny (1980) estimates that 18-20 percent of ideas and information derive from browsing in such systems. Even more important, the training of knowledge workers, the early stages of a research career or new direction, and the pursuit of risky, long-term, but exciting ventures in intellectual exploration must be protected, indeed nurtured. Finally, the system must be patient, in that certain kinds of knowledge reveal their value with a long lag.

In our market-oriented society, it is often hard to convince people that important goods cannot, by their nature be left to the market. Yet information is just as important to our long-term well-being as national security. In order to ensure that the large-scale, complex, long-run enterprise of developing useful knowledge and making it widely available goes forward, financing must be assured and reliable as well as adequate. At the same time, we cannot afford to lose the signals that market prices give in other contexts. Without a mechanism for efficient allocation, the knowledge sector could house boondoggles of enormous appetite, much like Gulliver's Laputa. Equally important, the public perception that much knowledge work is useless can threaten the financing of even the most valid endeavors. What we propose is a combination of market-type signaling mechanisms with the broadly-based financing and general access typical of public services, yet with minimal regulation and bureaucratic control. The progress of technology makes us confident that the practical aspects can be worked out, even as it sharpens the need to move beyond ad hoc, inefficient pricing, and financing mechanisms for information retrieval.

REFERENCES

Kalba, Kas, 1977, "Libraries in the Information Marketplace", Libraries in Post-Industrial Society, Leigh Estabrook, ed., Oryx Press, Phoenix, pp. 306-320.

Sweeny, G. P., 1980, "The Library and Documentation Collection: A Sociological Framework", Seminar for Problem Solving in Socio-Economic Development, Paper given at the Fourth UNISIST Meeting on the Planning and Implementation of National Information Activities in Science and Technology, Reston, VA, pre-print p. 5.

FRAMEWORK FOR EVALUATING LEARNING FROM COMPUTER PROGRAMMING COURSES:

PROBLEM SOLVING IN AN INTRODUCTORY COMPUTER SCIENCE COURSE

Aboalfazi Salimi

Department of Computer Science
Embry-Riddle Aeronautical University
Daytona Beach, Florida 32014

Abstract: Most computer science programs at various universities offer
courses in problem solving which are generally taken by the student in the
first year. The student learns problem solving methodology which includes
problem definition, analysis, design, and documentation. Although a student
is graded/evaluated in each course, it may not reflect the student's success
potential in a real work environment. What is lacking is standards for
various components of problem solving methodology.

Standards will offer a framework for evaluation of students' real learning by setting measurable goals. The standards should be flexible enough
to be updated and modified as technology advances in software and hardware
design methodology and as new philosophies evolve. The flexibility will
keep the methodology dynamic and commensurate with the state-of-the-art
and/or the state-of-the-practice.

This paper presents a model for such standards and framework for a
methodology for problem solving that includes problem definition, analysis,
design and documentation.

INTRODUCTION

This paper describes how problem solving in an introductory computer
science course should be implemented by using the following approach:

1. Problem Analysis

    1.1 Preliminary Problem Statement

    1.2 Thinking, Formulating the Questions, and Making
        Discussions

    1.3 Input/Output Requirements

    1.4 Detailed Problem Statement

2. Design

      2.1   Structure Chart

      2.2   Pseudocode

3.   Verification of Design

4.   Implementation

5.   Program Testing

6.   Documentation

A simplified software engineering approach is chosen in this implementation. The emphasis is on design of small to medium scale classroom projects. The suggested systematic approach to problem solving includes the software development phases suggested by the 1983 task force under the ACM Education Board's Elementary Schools and Secondary Schools Subcommittee ("Computer Science for Second Schools: Course Content", 1985), (i.e., problem definition, design, implementation and testing, plus some intermediate steps simplifying the problem solving process). At the end of the paper, a simple pseudocode (Salimi, 1984) is introduced that can be used during the design phase.

STEPS IN PROBLEM SOLVING

In the computer laboratory and classroom environment it is observed that most students do not follow the software development phases suggested by their textbooks (Orr, 1977; Meek and Heath, 1980; Yourdon and Constantine, 1979) and espoused by their instructors. For example, students often begin a programming project by first coding their program, then later writing the algorithm or drawing the flowchart for the coded program. Worst of all, a student will write a program for a problem that he/she does not fully understand. Of course, most students will eventually succeed in generating a working program by trial and error. As long as further testing and modification of the program is not required, the student is well satisfied!

To solve this problem to some degree, the beginning student should not be given all the tools of problem solving at once; especially coding should not be introduced at an early stage. The student should be forced to develop the habit of using the right tools at the right time. To develop the good habits in problem solving, sufficient time should be devoted to the disclosure and mastery of all the problem solving phases suggested prior to the coding phase (Orr, 1977; Meek and Heath, 1980; Yourdon and Constantine, 1979).

The suggested phases in problem solving are as follows: problem analysis, design, verification of design, implementation, testing, and documentation. It should be noted that the problem solver may have to go through the phases in a 'back and forth' fashion until the solution is completed. For example, while working in the design phase, the problem solver may notice the need for additional input or output entities which were overlooked during the problem analysis phase. In this case these entities must be added to the input/output requirement step of problem analysis phase.

1.   Problem Analysis

Students often pay little attention to this most important phase of the problem solving process. Students should be encouraged/required to complete, and submit this phase for correction before they continue with the remaining phases.

During this phase, the problem must be well understood and all input and output requirements of the problem must be determined by the problem solver. In order to accomplish this important task: the problem should be briefly described; it should be analyzed for clarity of purpose; questions should be formulated and asked; and necessary discussions should be carried out.

1.1 Preliminary Problem Statement. Naturally, the statement of a problem should be known before any attempt is made in solving the problem. The problem statement may be initiated in different forms, such as a conversation or a written document. No matter what the form of initiation is, the problem solver should write down the statement of the problem very briefly in his/her words.

1.2 Thinking, Formulating Questions, and Making Discussions. The IBM's THINK slogan generally states: That, however short your deadlines are or however compressed your time is or any other external activity that might be bothering you; the time you spend thinking of the problem as a whole will definitely be time well spent (Brian and Heath, 1980).

The 'think' phase will lead the problem solver into formulating a list of questions about the problem. The questions should clarify the unknown terms, ambiguous statements, available information, required results, and so on.

The problem solver should consult appropriate reference materials, and discuss the issues with others (such as the instructor and other knowledgeable people) in order to seek their technical knowledge and clarify all ambiguities as discussed by Behforooz and Sharma (1986).

1.3 Input/Output Requirements. This step can be comfortably completed if the previous step is accomplished properly. During this step all the input, output, and the required intermediate data values should be identified and tabulated. Note that the tabulated data values may not be complete at this point. They will be gradually updated during the design phase.

1.4 Detailed Problem Statement. This is the final step in the analysis phase of software development/problem solving. Everything gathered during previous steps must be put together to form the complete skeleton of the problem, which contains the detailed description of the problem along with all terms, formulas, and ambiguities clarified.

2. Design

After the problem is well defined and all input and output requirements of it are determined and analyzed. The problem solver is to decide HOW the problem should be solved.

Through top-down design or stepwise refinement the problem should be divided into smaller, simpler, and more understandable subproblems, and in the end these subproblems should be synthesized to solve the original problem.

In order to depict the subproblems, the flow of information between the subproblems, and the detailed solution to each subproblem, different design methodologies may be used. Two design tools; structure diagrams/charts and pseudocodes, seem appropriate for the stepwise refinement and the detailed solution process respectively. These two design tools seem to be referenced and used most often in textbooks and the classroom environment. Even though different design methodologies may be introduced and used, the emphasis on just one or two tools will be more appropriate and more effective for the beginning student. Other design tools can be introduced in later courses.

As mentioned before, during the design phase, the requirement for more input/output items makes the modification of previous phase necessary.

3. Verification

Prior to the implementation of the design, some time must be devoted to the verification of the solution in order to detect possible design errors. A desk-checking technique is the most common method and probably the most appropriate method of verifying the design for the student. The instructor may even require the students to verify each other's designs. During this phase, all the subproblems must be fully checked for correctness. At this stage, the problem solver may see the need for redoing part of the design, or going back to previous steps of the problem solving process to make required modifications. This phase is the last critical part of the problem solving process. When this phase is successfully completed, the solution to the problem is actually derived.

4. Implementation

This phase is considered to be the easiest of the phases discussed so far. Implementation is the mechanical translation of design (e.g., pseudocode) into a programming language (i.e., coding). The choice of the language depends on the availability of the compiler and the desired features of the language. The closer the control structure and data structure features of the language are to those of the design tools (e.g., pseudocode), the easier the translation and the modification of the code will be. There are even software tools available for automatic translation of designs into the codes.

5. Program Correctness

If the design has been thoroughly checked for correctness, this testing phase corresponds mainly to syntax errors in the program, and, also, to the run time behavior of the design. However, during this phase, most beginning students will still detect logic errors in their design and will be forced to use the 'back and forth' method to correct the errors. To test the code, the appropriate input values must be supplied to the program. The program should work correctly for the valid and expected input values, for the illegal values that the user may put in, and, also, for the input values at the extreme sides of the expected values.

To locate the possible run time errors, different debugging tools may be used. The simplest, but not necessarily the best, way of locating the run time errors is the use of output instructions at different points of the program. The output instructions can display the values of the variables and the locations of the instructions being executed.

The use of a system debugger is not recommended at this time. The idiosyncrasy of the system debugger may distract the student from the other stages of problem solving process. More complicated debugging tools should be introduced in the follow-up course.

6. Documentation

This is another phase of problem solving which is not emphasized enough. Real world cases should be used to demonstrate the significance of documentation. A small completed project should also be prepared and handed out to the students for their reference.

This phase corresponds to the collection and completion of internal and external documentations (Ransom, 1984). The external documentation is the collection of all work done throughout the problem solving process. For example, the detailed problem statement, input/output requirement tables, structure charts, Pseudocodes, program listings, and the program output samples are all part of the external documentation. The internal documentation corresponds to the comment statements in the program listing which describe the purpose of the program, purpose of each variable name used, operation of the individual segments of the program, and any other relevant information.

EVALUATION OF PROBLEM SOLVING PHASES

The following are the suggested points and the lecture/project hours that may be assigned to each phase of problem solving process:

1. Problem Analysis   30%

   1.1 Preliminary Problem Statement

   1.2 Thinking, Formulating the Questions, and Making Discussions

   1.3 Input/Output Requirements

   1.4 Detailed Problem Statement

2. Design   25%

   2.1 Structure Chart

   2.2 Pseudocode

3. Verification of Design   10%

4. Implementation   10%

5. Program Testing   10%

6. Documentation   15%

To assist instruction in the problem solving area, a workbook is being developed that will be available soon directly from the author.

An Algorithmic Language (AL)

INTRODUCTION TO AL:

AL is a simple algorithmic language designed to help the problem solver to create structured, readable and easy to code problem solutions. The attempt is to stay away from language constraints imposed by some programming languages. The AL user may add additional features if necessary.

This paper describes the syntax and semantics of AL briefly.

Notations:

< ... > : Indicates the user suplied identifiers
ident   : Stands for identifier

COMMENTS:

Comments are enclosed in a pair of braces {}. e.g., {A comment}

IDENTIFIER:

An identifier is a sequence of characters that forms the name of a program (or Algorithm), procedure, function, variable or label.

Syntax: A String of letters, digits, and _ (i.e. Underscore) beginning with a letter.

e.g. AMOUNT, CLASS_1, QUIZZ_GRADE, ...

CONSTANT:

Constant is a value which do not change during the execution of algorithm. There are two types of constants:

1. Numeric constant: corresponds to either a whole number (i.e. INTEGER) or a number with fraction (i.e., REAL)

    e.g. integers -23, 45, 0, ...
         reals -23.4, 45., 0.0, 0.6, ...

2. String constant: is a sequence of characters enclosed in apostrophes '...'.

SEMICOLON (;):

If there is more than one statement on a line, then they must be separated by a semicolon.

AL GENERAL STRUCTURE:

```
  ALGORITHM <algorithm_name>

  {Purpose: Brief description of Purpose of algorithm}

  CONSTANT           {Constant section}
    <ident> : value
    <ident> : value
      .
      .
    <ident> : value

  DECLARE_TYPE       {Type definition section}
    <ident> : type
    <ident> : type
      .
      .
    <ident> : type

  DECLARE_VARIABLE   {Variable declaration section}
    <ident> : type
    <ident> : type
      .
      .
    <ident> : type

  SUBPROGRAM         {Subprogram listing section}
    <ident>, <ident>, ...

  BEGIN <algorithm_name>
    statement
    statement
      .
      .
    statement
  END <algorithm_name>
```

All the identifiers must be declared before their use in AL; this enforces the readability of the written algorithm.

Procedures and functions can be written external to the main algorithm.

Identifiers with constant values must be defined in constant section of the AL.

example:

```
  PI      :  3.14159
  MIN_PAY :  3.50


  BLANK   :  ' '
```

SUBPROGRAM SECTION:

The names of the procedures and the fucntions used in AL must be listed in this section.

example:

```
  SUBPROGRAM
    SIZE, COMPUTE_WAGE, SEARCH
```

STANDARD TYPES:

INTEGER, REAL, LOGICAL, STRING, POINTER, ARRAY, RECORD, FILE

```
INTEGER            : whole numbers, -45, 65, ...
REAL               : Numbers with fraction, 65.7, 78., ...
LOGICAL            : logical values true and false
STRING(max_size)   : character string of size max_size
POINTER            : address of a memory location

ARRAY              : An array is a sequence of simple or structures items
                     of same type.
```

Syntax:

```
  <Array_ident> : ARRAY [lb1..ub1, lb2..ub2, ...] OF element_type
```

lb and ub correspond to lower bound and upper bound of each subscript.

Reference to an array element:

```
  <array_ident> [index1, index2, ...]
```

example:

```
  DECLARE
    table : ARRAY [-10..10] OF integer {An array of 21 integer elements}

  table[3] corresponds to the 14th element of the array
```

RECORD:

A record is collection of related data items. for example a student record may contain the student's name, age, grade, etc.

Syntax:

```
  RECORD <record_ident>
    <field_ident>, <field_ident>, ... : type
    <field_ident>, <field_ident>, ... : type


    <field_ident>, <field_ident>, ... : type
  END_RECORD
```

Reference to a record element:

```
  <record_ident>.<field_ident>
```

example:

```
  DECLARE
    RECORD student
      name  : STRING(20)
      grade : STRING(1)
      age   : INTEGER
    END_RECORD
```

493

student.grade refers to the grade field of the student.

FILE:

file is a collection of data items or records. for example a file of integers, a file of student records, etc.

Syntax:

  <file_ident>, <file_ident>, ... : FILE

example:

  Book, students : FILE

Files must be opened by the following statements:

OPEN_INPUT (<file_ident>:<external_name>, <file_ident>:<external_name>,
        ...)

OPEN_OUTPUT (<file_ident>:<external_name>, <file_ident>:<external_name>,
        ...)

<file_ident> is the internal file name, being referenced by the algorithm.

<external_name> is the external file name being referenced by the correspondig file_ident.

The files must be closed after their final use using the close statement:

  CLOSE (<file_ident>, <file_ident>, ...)

example:

  OPEN_INPUT (GRADE_FILE:'GRADES', NAMES:'NAMES')

  OPEN_OUTPUT (RESULT:'STUDENT_RESULT')
            .
            .
  CLOSE (GRADE_FILE, NAMES, RESULT)

Note that the standard input/output devices such as terminal need not be opened or closed using above statements.

POINTER:

A pointer contains the address of a memory location.

Syntax:

  <pointer_ident>, <pointer_ident>, ... : POINTER TO location_type

  location_type may be any type except FILE.

Allocation/Deallocation of dynamic memory locations:

  CREATE (<pointer_ident>, <pointer_ident>, ...)

The above statement creates different memory locations and assigns their addresses to the corresponding pointer_identifiers.

  DISPOSE (<pointer_ident>, <pointer_ident>, ...)

Releases the memory location the address of which is stored in pointer_ident

A pointer identifier may be initialized to a null value NULL which indicates that the pointer does not contain an address.

Reference to a dynamic memory location:

  <pointer_ident>^ refers to the location the address of which is stored in pointer_ident

494

Example:

```
DECLARE
  address : POINTER TO integer
        .
        .
BEGIN
  CREATE (address)
  address^ <-- 80
        .
        .
  DISPOSE (address)
        .
        .
END
```

ASSIGNMENT STATEMENT:

Assignment statement is used to initilize a memory location to a value.

Syntax:
  <ident> <-- expression

<ident> and expression must have the same data type. If the data type is
a string, then the value of expression will be stored in <ident> from
left to right padded with blanks when the length of the expression is
less than the size of <ident>, and the expression will be truncated if
its length is more than the length of <ident>.

e.g. DECLARE name : STRING(5)

```
      name <-- 'TITLE'     {Assigns 'TITLE' to name}
      name <-- 'SAMPLE'    {Assigns 'SAMPL' to name}
      name <-- 'BOB'       {Assigns 'BOB  ' to name}
```

NUMERIC EXPRESSIONS:

Form: Operand Arithmetic_operator Operand

Arithmetic operators:
  + (addition)
  - (subtraction), or (negation)
  * (multiplication)
  / (division)
  ^ (exponentiation)

e.g. 2.5*3+2/4-8.3+2^4

LOGICAL EXPRESSIONS:

Forms: expression relational_operator expression

            and

            logical_expression logical_operator logical_expression

relation operators:
  =   (equal)
  <>   (not equal)
  <   (less than)
  <=   (less than or equal to)
  >   (greater than)
  >=   (greater or equal to)

Logical operators:

  AND, OR, NOT

        Operators' order of evaluation

        1. ()   Inner-most to outter-most order
        2. -   Negation
        3. ^   Right to left order
        4. *, /   Left to right order
        5. +, -   Left to right order
        6. relational operators from left to right order
        7. NOT
        8. logical operatator AND from left to right order
        9. logical operatator OR from left to right order

<u>INPUT:</u>

INPUT statement is used to get the values from an external file.

syntax:

   INPUT (FROM <file_ident> : list of variables)

FROM <file-ident> : is optional if there is no external file. If

deleted the default will be the standard input device. (e.g., keyboard)

<u>OUTPUT:</u>

OUTPUT statement is used to output the result on an external device or
file.

syntax:

   OUTPUT (TO <file_ident> : output list)

TO <file-ident> :   is optional if there is no external file. If deleted
the default will be the standard output device. (e.g. terminal screen)

Note that comma (,) separates the items used in input/output operations.

<u>IF-THEN STATEMENT:</u>

Syntax:

```
  IF logical_expression THEN
    statement
    statement
      .
      .
  END_IF
```

<u>IF-THEN-ELSE STATEMENT:</u>

```
        Syntax:
          IF logical_expression THEN
            statement
            statement
              .
              .
            statement
          ELSE
            statement
            statement
              .
              .
          END_IF
```

<u>CASE STATEMENT:</u>

Form (a):

```
  CASE <expression>
    value, value, ... : statement
                        statement
                          .
                        statement
    value, value, ... : statement
                        statement
                          .
                        statement
                  .
                  .
    otherwise         : statement
                        statement
                          .
                        statement
  END_CASE
```

```
            Form (b):

                CASE
                    logical_expression1 : statement
                                          statement
                                            .
                                          statement
                    logical_expression2 : statement
                                          statement
                                            .
                                          statement
                            .
                            .
                    otherwise           : statement
                                          statement
                                            .
                                          statement

                END_CASE
```


FOR LOOP

Syntax:

```
  FOR <ident> <-- initial_value TO final_value BY increment DO
    statement
    statement
      .
      .
    statement
  END_FOR
```

If BY increment is not specified, it defaults to BY +1.

WHILE LOOP

Syntax:

```
  WHILE logical_expression DO
    statement
    statement
      .
      .
    statement
  END_WHILE
```


REPEAT-UNTIL LOOP

Syntax:

```
  REPEAT
    statement
    statement
      .
      .
    statement
  UNTIL logical_expression
```


PROCEDURE

a procedure is a subprogram which accepts a sequence of Zero or more
inputs and returns Zero or more values as output.

Syntax:

```
  PROCEDURE proc_name ( access_type <ident>, <ident>, ... : type;
                                    <ident>, <ident>, ... : type;
                        access_type <ident>, <ident>, ... : type;
                                    <ident>, <ident>, ... : type )
    {Declare the local types, variables and subprograms here}
```

```
         BEGIN Proc_name
           statement
           statement
              .
              .
           statement
         END Proc_name
```

Access_type is either of following two types:

IN: Used when the parameter is an input parameter. i.e., No values will
be returned to the calling routine through the listed parameters.

OUT: Used when the parameter is an output parameter. i.e., values will
be returned to the calling routine through the listed parameters.   These
parameters can not be used as input parameters.

INOUT: Used when the parameters are output, or input and output parameters.   i.e., a value may be sent or/and returned to the calling routine
through the listed parameters.

example: The following procedure computes and returns the average of two
numbers:

```
    PROCEDURE compute_average (IN first_number, second_number : integer;
                                    OUT average :  real)
      DECLARE_VARIABLE
        sum : integer        {Sum of two input values}

      BEGIN compute_average
        sum      <-- first_number + second_number
        average <-- sum/2
      END compute_average
```

PROCEDURE CALL

Syntax:

```
    CALL proc_name (actual_param, actual_param, ...)
```

example: CALL compute_average (num1, num2, average)

note that the actual argruments which correspond to OUT and INOUT dummy
arguments/parameters must be variables.

FUNCTIONS

A function is a subprogram which accepts a sequence of one or more inputs
and returns one output value. The output will be returned through the
name of the function.

syntax:

```
    FUNCTION func_name ( IN <ident>, <ident>, ... : type;
                            <ident>, <ident>, ... : type;
                         IN <ident>, <ident>, ... : type;
                            <ident>, <ident>, ... : type ) : result_type
      {Declare the local types, variables and subprograms here}

      BEGIN func_name
        statement
        statement
           .
           .
        statement
        func_name <-- result    {assign the final result to the name
                                     of the function}
      END func_name
```

note that the final result of the function must be assgned to the name of
the function before the function is terminated.

to call a function the name of function followed by the list of parameters enclosed in parentheses must be used in expressions.

example:

```
FUNCTION average (IN first_number, second_number: integer) : real

   DECLARE_VARIABLE
     sum : integer    {sum of two input values}

   BEGIN average

     sum      <-- first_number + second_number
     average <-- sum/2

   END average
```

INTRINSIC FUNCTIONS:

```
ABS (x)       Absolute value of x where x is a numeric expression
SIN (x)       sine of x where x is in radians
COS (x)       cos of x where x is in radians
ARCTAN (x)    arctangent x, where x is in radians
LOG (x)       logarithm of x in base 10
```

Sample algorithm

Input a set of names and corresponding scores from an input file and store them on an external file in the reverse order of the input.

```
ALGORITHM reverse

   CONSTANT
     class_size : 20    {maximum number of students in the class}
     string_size: 30    {maximum size of a name}

   DELCARE_TYPE
     RECORD student_record    {student record structure}
       name : string (string_size)
       score : real
     END_RECORD

   DECLARE_VARIABLE
     a_student : student_record    {a student record}
     class     : array [1..clsss_size] of student_record {class array}
     infile,             {input file}
     outfile   : FILE    {output file}
     index     : INTEGER    {loop control variable}
     output_file : STRING(string_size) {variable to hold the name of
                                                 external file.}

   BEGIN reverse

     {open the files}

     output_file <-- 'afile'
     OPEN_INPUT (infile : 'infile')
     OPEN_OUTPUT(outfile : output_file)

     {input the names and grades}

     FOR index <-- 1 to class_size DO
       INPUT (FROM infile: class[index].name, class[index].grade)
     END_FOR

     {store the names and grades in reverse order}

     FOR index <-- class_size TO 1 BY -1 DO
       OUTPUT (TO outfile: class[index])
     END_FOR

     {close the files and end}

     CLOSE (infile, outfile)

   END reverse
```

ACKNOWLEDGEMENTS

I thank Dr. Thomas Hilburn for his comments, suggestions, and for the help he gave me in editing this paper. I thank Mr. Joseph Torch, the Embry-Riddle senior student, for his extensive research and his assistance. Finally, I thank Dr. Jagdish Agrawal for his support and final editing of this paper.

REFERENCES

"Computer Science for Second Schools: Course Context", 1985, <u>Communications of the ACM</u>, <u>28</u>, March 1985.

Behforooz, A., and Sharma, O. P., 1986, <u>An Intro to Computer Science</u>, Prentice-Hall, Inc., Englewood Cliffs, New Jersey.

Meek, B., and Heath, P., 1980, <u>Guide to Good Programming Practice</u>, Ellis Horwood Limited, West Sussex, England.

Orr, K. T., 1977, <u>Structured Systems Development</u>, Yourdon Press, New York.

Ransom, A. W., 1984, <u>Pseudocode</u>, (unpublished report).

Salimi, A., 1984, <u>An Algorithmic Language (AL)</u>, (unpublished report).

Yourdon, E., and Constantine, L. L., 1979, <u>Structured Design</u>, Prentice-Hall, Inc., Englewood Cliffs, New Jersey.

10. WORKSHOPS

WORKSHOP ON RESEARCH DIRECTIONS AND OPPORTUNITIES I:

PROSPECTS AND OPEN PROBLEMS

Chair
Raymond E. Miller, Director
School of Information and Computer Science
Georgia Institute of Technology
Atlanta, Georgia

Panelists

John M. Carroll
IBM Thomas J. Watson Research Center
Yorktown Heights, New York

Annelise Mark Pejtersen
Royal Library School
Kopenhagen, Denmark

Gerhard Fischer
University of Colorado
Colorado

William B. Rouse
Ga Institute of Technology Boulder
Atlanta, Georgia

Ralph M. Weischedel
Bolt, Beranek and Newmann Laboratories
Cambridge, Massachusetts

This brief summary of the panel is intended to provide highlights of the panel presentations, and, hopefully, indicate some challenging areas for further research.

In his opening remarks, Miller noted the difference in the understanding and engineering control between hardware and software design. Whereas hardware can be specified and designed in accord with normal engineering principals, rarely is this the case for software. The elusive nature of information and lack of techniques for precise specification for information processing systems was pointed out as primary to these software problems. Thus, he urged research in the fundamental scientific understanding of software systems and application of this science to systems design.

Next Miller discussed the notion of "transparency" in human-computer interface design. The idea here is to make the computer interface "transparent" to the user, in the sense of the user getting the same or more functionality from a computerized system as from a previous non-computerized system without introducing new complexities to the user in the interface. An example given was the driving of a new car which is computerized to provide more efficient and reliable operation, but for which the driver sees no change in the operation of the car. The challenge then is to make more complex tasks, done by information systems, transparent to the user so that additional functionality can be provided without additional complexity to the user.

John Carroll spoke of two areas requiring considerable work. These are theory and methodology. He stressed the need for more theoretical developments in the human-computer interaction area. The need is for a broader theory that takes more into its scope than now exists.

For methodology, Carroll cited the need to have more and higher quality case studies. He called for approaches that would report results that others could use rather than simply to report on something that was built. He believes we need more qualitative methods like thinking aloud and task analysis. He notes that there is nothing integrative in this area, that is, no cookbook on how to run an experiment. One area he believes is worth considering is the use of user interviews to gain a better understanding of interfaces and the useability problem.

Gerhard Fischer approaches the interface problem from an AI background. He feels that the most interesting aspects of systems designs fall between the fully human systems and the fully automatic system; the overall goal in the user/sender system design being the use of AI technologies for improving human productivity. He noted that progress toward this goal could be made in many different, not necessarily mutually exclusive, ways. He listed the significant advances in technology, the need for more quantitative rules in prediction, the advances made by exploratory work in research laboratories, the study of success models, the specific insights and missions of individuals (like Alan Kay's great influence on modern interfaces), and the need to have academics and other researchers live in a very rich computational environment.

Annelise Pejtersen's discussion of areas of research for interface design was aimed at pointing out the need to allow users to have a free choice for their work in a "multidimensional space" of task performance, rather than having normative prescriptions for proper methods for performing tasks. She called for research in: work content in means-end problem space; a repertoire of problem space operations for decision tasks, as well as various strategies and cognitive levels; and models for work content, decision tasks, and strategies and cognitive style at the semantic level of user-task interaction. For implementation at the next level she saw the need for guidelines and models at the semantic level of the user system interface. She called for empirical studies of actual performance in present systems, both quantitatively and qualitatively. She said that most research deals with user interaction on the system in terms of cognitive information flow, and suggested that it might be a good idea to look into analysis of user interaction at the emotional and aesthetical levels. She thought this should be explored to see whether it has been neglected in current systems, and whether it should be used in future system design.

Bill Rouse raised two main issues, the first being a more careful methodology, and the second the need to deal with "discretionary situations". He was skeptical of approaches that tended to just collect more and more data with the hope that simply the collection of all the data would answer all the questions. Instead, he emphasized that most of the data is not useful, it is what can be learned from the correct data and its analysis that is important. He called for more emphasis on methodology. Where manual activities previously were studied by task analysis, he saw this changing to "ecological task analysis" in real work environments. He called for development of taxonomies or classifications and prototypical task descriptions, since people now seem to think of their work in terms of the tasks that they may must perform to complete a job. Such taxonomies and prototypical task descriptions should provide a basis for developing better methodologies for studying the human-computer interaction that is more ecologically valid. The "discretionary situation" area for research raised by Rouse arises in situations where people make a discretionary choice of when to use or not use certain available information in performing tasks. Here they are making a discretionary evaluation of what value or meaning the information might contain to help them in performing a task, and they may choose to not use some of the information. These approaches might be necessary, for example, in some real-time situations requiring quick decisions or actions. Rouse points to this as an area for fruitful research, where one might attempt to design information systems where the use of the information is discretionary.

Ralph Weischedel limited his discussion in the panel to what further developments might provide more functional capabilities in expert systems, since he was talking later in the conference on issues in evaluating natural language interfaces. He noted that the functional characteristics of current expert systems had narrowly defined capabilities, didn't run in real-time, and had very "compiled knowledge" realized in terms of rule based systems that are very quickly processable by some kind of inference engine. He noted that we need systems that can reason much more broadly, that have graceful degradation characteristics, and that can operate in real time. In addition to expert systems that provide an answer, he would like the system to explain its decisions and provide reasons why the answer is appropriate.

He provided a long list of needs including: a model of the user, for greater knowledge representation capabilities than currently available, for more sophisticated interfaces, for case-based reasoning and reasoning by analogy, methods capable of testing or certifying expert systems, systems in natural language interfaces that have contextual knowledge and recognize intention of the user and deal with ill-formed inputs, and continuous real-time speech input systems that deal with a broad domain and are cost effective.

WORKSHOP ON RESEARCH DIRECTIONS AND OPPORTUNITIES I1:

CURRENT FUNDING PROGRAMS

Chair
John R. Mitchell, Director
Army Institute for Research in Management
Information, Communications, and Computer Sciences
Atlanta, Georgia

Panelists

Harold Bamford
National Science Foundation
Washington, D.C.

Steven Cormier
Army Research Institute
Alexandria, Virginia

Lou Chmura
Naval Research Laboratory
Washington, D.C.

John J. O'Hare
Office of Naval Research
Arlington, Virginia

Vince Siglitto
Air Force Office of Scientific Research
Washington, D.C.

Each of the panelists presented an overview of their respective organizations current programs and near term projected programs. These presentations were followed by a short session of questions and answers.

John R. Mitchell (AIRMICS)

The mission of AIRMICS is to:

"Conduct and sponsor applied research in the areas of telecommunications, automation, audiovisual, record management, and publication systems."

A current major thrust of Army automation is the development of a unified, Army wide corporate data base. This will be accomplished in stages over a number of years and involves many different applications operating in many different physical locations with uncertain communications capabilities and quality, on differing types of automated equipment. The desire is to provide useful, timely, effective information for the use of the commander at all echelons. AIRMICS has near term objectives in Software Engineering, Distributed Systems, and Communications and Networks.

The objectives in the Software Engineering area include:

● Implementation Concepts for Information Centers

- Technical Support of Information Systems Engineering Command Transition to the Use of the Ada Programming Language

- Evaluation of Decision Support System Development Methods

- Identification of Target Artificial Intelligence Applications within the Information Mission Area

- Evaluation of Automated Software Maintenance Tools

The objectives in the Distributed Systems area include:

- Development of Distributed Systems Design Evaluation Criteria

- Development of Dynamically Reconfigurable Data Base Concepts

- Development of Techniques for Adaptable Distributed Systems

- Development of Automated Extraction Techniques for Standard Army Multicommand Management Information Systems

- Development of Advanced Prototypes for the Combat Service Support Control System

The objectives in the Communications and Networks area include:

- Determination of Tactical Communications Traffic Types and Volumes

- Development of Prototype Network Gateways

- Development of a Distributed Electronic Mail Prototype

- Incorporation of Network Security Concepts in Army Automated Systems

Steve Cormier of the Army Research Institute (ARI):

ARI's Research on the Human-Computer Interface includes the topic areas of:

- Computer-based simulations

- Software systems emulation

- Software psychology

- Natural langauge/speech synthesis

- Artificial Intelligence/expert systems

In the area of Computer-based simulations, one of ARI's recent projects has been the Command and Control Performance Assessment System (C2PAS). The C2PAS is a computerized means of assessing command and control military performance. In this simulation, a military situation is presented to a participant as a series of video displays. Situations are designed to evoke specific decision-making behavior on the part of the participant. The participant's information-seeking behavior is recorded by the C2PAS computer system and the participant's decisions are written out in a participant response booklet. A panel of subject-matter experts is employed to evaluate the participant's decisions. The design philosophy includes these guide-lines:

- Provide a user friendly interface including:

  -- Menus

  -- Data Entry Forms

  -- Lists

- Allow simultaneous display of graphics and text:

  -- Text on video screen

  -- Situation map and graphics on video monitor

- Provide realism:

  -- Icons conform to military symbols

  -- Text allows military message, report, plan, order formats

  -- Information windows provide resource data

The software features include:

- Menu driven to select processing options or to request information displays

- Video maps include graphic overlays, pan, and zoom capabilities.

- Text Displays are free form, pageable, and may be edited using a full screen editor.

- Data Entry forms are available to display or modify the data base.

- Selection lists may be used to select scenario or vignette of interest, to resolve conflicts, to modify class or attribute status

Planned Future R&D Efforts:

- HCI Laboratory

- Software Engineering Approach to HCI

- Identify elements of abstract user specification

  - Identify specification technique

  - Implement abstract user module

  - R&D for elements of abstract user specification

  - Large scale experiments as part of R&D

- Workshops

- 2nd Workshop on Navy R&D on HCI

- Workshop on theoretical foundations of HCI

- Technology Transition

    - Development of a demonstration/test facility

    - Identify and implement effective procedures (e.g.,
      early delivery of user manuals)

    - Promulgate technology and improvements

    - Two-week course in HCI technology for Navy
      personnel

    - Papers

    - Probably no guidebooks!

John J. O'Hare, ONR:

Research support on the understanding of human computer interaction by
the Engineering Psychology Program, Office of Naval Research (EP-ONR), has
primarily encouraged the development of theories and models of user behavior at several levels of task complexity including:

- Information handling

- Programmer behaviors

- Task allocation

- Command and control

These research programs are representative of recent work that has focused on the machine parameters for displays, controls, and decision aids,
and the human parameters of motor and perceptual skills, workload reduction,
and problem-solving enhancement. The results of those programs have contributed to theory, knowledge bases, and guideline recommendations on human-
machine designs for varied environmental conditions.

The EP-ONR program recently shifted emphasis so as to focus on the perceptual sciences with special attention to visual, auditory, speech, and
tactile modes of information transfer, as well as integrative processes for
those functions in the performance of complex actions. The current research
objectives of EP-ONR now include the development of a perceptual science
that contributes to the general human-computer interaction issues:

- Theories and models of HCI

- Input/Output designs

- Programming language designs

- Supervisory control systems

- Command-control-communication-information system designs

Another research project is "Novice to Expert implications for

Artificial Intelligence Systems". The research objectives include:

- Determine how the representation of knowledge for a command language changes as an individual gains expertise in using the language.

- Examine the relationship between the current state of knowledge and the current level of performance.

- Assess possible benefits of using methods to map knowledge representation to aid in the design of training for command languages.

A third research project in Human-Machine interaction is "Applications of Automated Speech Technology to Land-Based Army Systems". Opportunities for such applications include tanks and weapons systems, command and control communications, transport vehicles, personnel selection, and training, battle simulation, and tactical engagement field exercises.

Lou Chmura, NRL:

The NRL has projects in the areas of Measurement and Human-Computer Interaction (HCI). In measurement, NRL is currently supporting work in Software Technology Evaluation, principally with a goal directed data collection effort on software cost reduction. They are collecting activity and change/error data. In the area of HCI, NRL had little interest prior to 1986. Prior to 1986, such interest as NRL had was reflected by the recognition that some expert systems needed better interfaces. In 1986, NRL had a growing interest for HCI in application to the Strategic Defense Initiative (SDI) and Artificial Intelligence (AI) systems. NRL established the beginnings of a research project titled "Software Engineering Approach to Human-Computer Interaction". Within that project they sponsored a workshop on R&D in NAVAL HCI Systems and funded the establishment of a "Laboratory for the Study of Human-Computer Interactions". In the workshop, 39 participants from Naval organizations identified:

- A need for more basic research; great deal of engineering

- Duplication of effort (e.g., presentation/layout issues for similar interfaces

- Interfaces to expert systems, a prevalent issue

- No leading Navy laboratory in this subject area

The goals of the Laboratory for HCI include:

- Accomplish basic and applied research

- Emphasize software engineering techniques as they apply to HCI

- Establish facilities for HCI research

- Concentrate on applications of HCI principles

The initial research areas of the Laboratory include:

- Multi-mode communication

- Interface effectiveness metrics

- Adaptive systems

- Multi-dimensional information display

- Specifications and rapid prototyping of interfaces

- Secure workstations

Other ONR groups have interests in HCI research. Human-computer inter-action can be approached from other perspectives and some of those options have been pursued at ONR:

- Instruction and learning

- Computer sciences and AI

- Information technology

In FY '86, EP-ONR sought stronger theory-based programs, but, with modest success and the number of supported programs related to HCI were reduced to:

- Software Interface

    - Formats for software comprehension

    - Plans in software modification

- Hardware Interface

    - Task allocation

Planned (FY '87) R&D directions for HCI research by EP-ONR will be contingent on:

- Proposals that represent excellent examples of theory or model based research

- Experimental tasks or vehicles that emphasize dialogue with an interactive system

A further constraint will be a preference for efforts that examine perceptual processes, and their interaction with higher-level processes. For FY '87 a tentative plan for research support is:

- Theories and models

    - Perceptual integration

- Interactive designs

    - Formats, images, and language

Conclusions and evaluations: The research domain of HCI has rapidly increased in importance, developed a modest conceptual structure to guide its efforts, provided research results that are improving in quality and generality, and attracted a cadre of very able research investigators who are moving the field forward as a distinct discipline. It is evident that Naval requirements of the present day and for the foreseeable future will be dependent on computer-based technology. Its effective use by Naval operators can only be assured by greater attention to the design of the interfaces to those systems, both software and hardware. The EP-ONR programs will continue to support fundamental work on HCI that will contribute to the scientific understanding of user interaction with computer-based systems. However, increased attention to HCI research programs by Naval in-house laboratories is mandatory to assure that operational goals are met by computer-based systems prior to the acquisition of those systems by the fleet.

<u>Vince Siglitto, Air Force Office of Scientific Research (AFOSR) (substituted for by Jim Gantt (AIRMICS):</u>

The Artificial Intelligence program at AFOSR includes:

- Core Research Program -- Mathematics and Information Sciences Directorate

- University Research Instrumentation Program (Computer Equipment)

- Northeast Artificial Intelligence Consortium (Cooperative RADC with 6.1 support from AFOSR)

- Artificial Neural Networks

The AFOSR core research program in artificial intelligence resulted from the combination of two internal AFOSR initiatives: system automation through artificial intelligence and space image understanding. It is a high quality program supporting eighteen projects at fourteen major universities. The main areas of concentration are:

- Computer vision/image understanding

- Expert systems

- Natural language understanding

- Planning and scheduling

- Architectures and algorithms for parallel computations

- Cognitive science and biological foundations of Artificial Intelligence

In each project, fundamental understanding of the subject area is sought so as to provide the intellectual and hardware tools needed by AI technology users at other Air Force System Command laboratories.

Projects in computer vision/image understanding include:

- Research in Image understanding - A. R. Hanson and E. M. Riseman, University of Massachusetts

- Parallel Image Processing and Image Understanding - A. Rosenfeld and L. S. Davis, University of Maryland

- Texture Perception and Shape from Texture - N. Ahuja, University of Illinois

- Structure from Motion - W. B. Thompson and A. Yonas,

University of Minnesota

Projects in expert systems include:

- Memory-based Expert Systems - R. C. Schank and C. K. Riesbeck, Yale University

- Distributed Knowledge Base Systems for Diagnosis and Information Retrieval - B. Chandrasekaran, Ohio State University

- Research on Intelligent Fault Detection and Repair Advisory Systems - J. R. Bourne and A. J. Brodersen, Vanderbilt University (new start in FY '87)

- Structures for the Representation and Manipulation of Knowledge in Intelligent Systems - R. Yager, Iona College (new start in FY '87)

The project in natural language processing is "Knowledge Delivery Research" by W. Mann, University of Southern California.

The projects in Planning and Scheduling include:

- Research on Problem-Solving Systems - D. E. Wilkins, SRI International

- Temporal Knowledge Representation and Reasoning for Project Planning - G. E. Bell, University of Iowa (new start in FY '87)

The projects in Architectures/Algorithms for Parallel Processing include:

- Research in Parallel Hardware, Software, and Parallel Logic - J. Minker, University of Maryland

- Connectionist VLSI Architectures - D. Hammerstrom, Oregon Grad. Center

The projects in Cognitive Science/Biological Foundations include:

- Computer and Mathematical Modeling of Massively Parallel Architectures for Self-Organizing Neural Pattern Matching Machines - S. Grossberg, Boston University

- Visual Representations Subserving Texture Perception - J. Beck and K. A. Stevens, University of Oregon

- Interpreting Image Contours - W. Richards, S. Ullman and B. Dawson, MIT (with NL)

- Adaptive Control of Hand-Eye Coordination in Uncertain Environments - M. Kuperstein, Wellesly College (With National Science Foundation)

Other tasks include:

- Research in Algebraic Manipulation - J. Moses, MIT

- Constructive Negation in Logic Programs - R. Hamlet, Oregon Research Center

Future directions of the program will emphasize those areas of research needed to apply expert system technology to the difficult military applications of battle management, tactical decision aiding, sensor fusion, etc. Specific areas of research to be emphasized are:

- Reasoning with uncertain and/or incomplete data

- Non-monotonic reasoning

- Temporal reasoning and logic

- Integration of systems in which large amounts of both numerical and symbolic computations are needed

- Parallel machines to run AI systems in real time

- Much improved pattern recognition algorithms and hardware for AI system front ends

The Northeast AI Consortium includes:

- Clarkson College of Technology

- Colgate University

- University of Massachusetts

- Renselner Polytechnic Institute

- Rochester University

- Rochester Institute of Technology

- SUNY/Buffalo

- Syracuse

and supports 13 principal investigators and 32 assistants.

Harold Bamford, National Science Foundation

The National Science Foundation supports research in the information and software sciences through the programs of its new Directorate for Computer and Information Science and Engineering (CISE), one of the Foundation's five research branches. These programs are directed to fundamental understanding of information and information processes and to the training of scientists and engineers to enlarge and apply that understanding.

"Information processes" are understood to include the capture, storage, and transmission of information and the transformation of information-bearing structures. They are at once the objects of study and the essential tools of scientific and engineering practice. Characteristically, their investigation combines basic with applied objectives and scientific with engineering approaches. It is inherently interdisciplinary, involving not only computer and information scientists, but also electrical engineers, mathematicians, and cognitive and behavioral scientists.

The CISE programs are organized in four divisions to provide a balanced representation of the current content of research and the new research opportunities which now exist.

- The Division of Computer and Computation Research (CCR) supports scientific and engineering research on computation theory, software systems, software engineering methods, computer systems architecture, and numeric and symbolic computation. This Division also houses the Directorate's instrumentation and institutional infrastructure programs.

- The Division of Microelectronic Information Processing Systems (MIPS) supports scientific and engineering research on VLSI chip design, systems architecture, systems prototyping and fabrication, experimental systems, circuits, and signal processing.

- The Division of Advanced Scientific Computing supports the Supercomputer Research Centers, networking activities, and basic research on networking technologies.

- The Division of Information, Robotics, and Intelligent Systems (IRIS) is the successor of the Division of Information Science and Technology (IST) and has expanded significantly to support research on databases, robots and intelligent systems, and interactive systems. Its programs are described below:

The Information Impact Program supports scientific and engineering research into social and economic consequences of the widespread introduction of information technologies. Representative topics include:

- Theoretical economics of information

- Impact of availability, distribution, and use of information on the structure and performance of economic, political, and social systems

- Impact of information technology on organizations and individuals

- Issues relating to the markets for information and information technologies and to the health of information industries.

The Interactive Systems Program supports scientific and engineering research fundamental to the design of systems which can assist or enable uses to perform information-based work. Representative topics include:

- Logical structure of the user-system dialog and the cognitive and machine processes which underlie it

- Logical relations which must be realized across a user-system interface and interaction modalities through which this can be done

- Methods of systematic dialog and interface design

- Methodological problem of arriving at valid empirical generalizations about user-system interaction.

The Knowledge and Database Systems Program supports scientific and engineering research into the properties of symbolic (information-bearing) structures and the dynamics of their propagation and aggregation. Representative topics include:

- Representation of knowledge and uncertainty

- Knowledge retrieval and systems for data storage and extraction

- Inference, learning, memory, problem solving, decision making, and natural language processing

The Robotics and Machine Intelligence Program supports scientific and engineering research fundamental to the design of systems which can implemen some of the characteristics of human intelligence. Representative topics include:

- Pattern analysis, machine vision, and speech understanding

- Sensor-based control

- Automated reasoning

- The planning of complex tasks involving temporal and spatial relationships

SELECTED BIBLIOGRAPHY ON MAN-MACHINE INTERFACE EVALUATION

Pranas Zunde

Georgia Institute of Technology
Atlanta, Georgia 30332

1. Akin, O., and Rao, D. R., Efficient Computer-User Interface in Electronic Mail Systems, International Journal of Man-Machine Studies, vol. 22 (6), 1985, pp. 589-611.

    Abstract: The question of user-computer interface is investigated using a general purpose method for encoding and measuring efficiency of use in computer systems. Three experts with a given system and 3 Ss with routine knowledge of it participated as Ss and were observed performing several mailing tasks. While experts performed these tasks with fewer errors and in a more complex manner, it was not clear that they achieved this any faster than regular uses. Recommendations for system design are made. (14 ref.)

2. Apperley, M. D., and Field, G. E., A Comparative Evaluation of Menu-Based Interactive Human-Computer Dialogue Techniques, INTERACT '84. First IFIP CONFERENCE ON 'HUMAN-COMPUTER INTERACTION', vol. 1E, 1984, pp. 296-301.

    Abstract: Menu Selection is an often-used type of human-computer dialogue. However, there is little data on the effectiveness, efficiency or merits of this technique. This paper describes an experiment designed to compare the utility of recently published, intuitively derived techniques relating to the syntax of menu interaction with more conventional menu techniques. This experiment is a complete problem-solving task which involves retrieving a number of related items from a database using a menu dialogue. Subjects are presented with a task for which they must access, interpret, and relate information from several different pages of a VIEWDATA-like database. Transversal paths and time taken to achieve the goal are monitored, to provide data with which to assess the effectiveness of the menu syntax. It is anticipated that these results will be of significant interest to the designers of VIEWDATA systems and to all people interested in human-computer interaction. (5 ref.)

3. Bannon, L., and O'Malley, C., Problems in Evaluation of Human-Computer Interfaces: A Case Study, INTERACT '84. FIRST IFIP CONFERENCE ON 'HUMAN-COMPUTER INTERACTION', vol. 2, 1984, pp. 280-284.

Abstract: One of the most difficult aspects of interface design is evaluating new or changed features of an interface. The authors discuss methods of evaluation. Their strengths and weaknesses., in the context of a program they developed to assist users in getting quick access to information contained in the UNIX manual. They outline the problems encountered both in the design and the evaluation of this user interface.

4. Chapanis, A., Anderson, N. S., and Licklider, J. C., Research Needs for Human Factors: User-Computer Interaction, US Army Research Institute for the Behavioral & Social Sciences Technical Report, 1983, 67 p.

Abstract: Discusses research in the areas of computer users, tasks, hardware, software, and documentation, placing major emphasis on new methodologies used to evaluate what is meant by ease of use in human-computer interaction. It is suggested that user characteristics -- which may be classified according to user experience, the nature of the job, or personality characteristics -- are important determinants of successful human-computer interaction. In the area of hardware design, more research is needed to evaluate alternatives to hardware design, more research is needed to evaluate alternatives to keyboard input (including voice input), uses of color in displays, the best sizes of displays, and alternatives to CRT displays. Specific problems occur in the implementation of on-line documentation as a replacement for paper documentation. Research on this topic is discussed in terms of capturing the intent of the creators, dynamic graphics, documentation in the form of knowledge bases, and the use of computer systems to facilitate conventional documentation. (18 ref.)

5. Chi, U. H., Formal Specification of User Interfaces: A Comparison and Evaluation of Four Axiomatic Approaches, IEEE Trans. Software Eng. (USA), vol. SE-11 (8), 1985, pp. 671-685.

Abstract: Few examples of formal specifications of the semantics of user interfaces exist in the literature. The author presents a comparison of four axiomatic approaches which have been applied to the specification of a commercial user interface -the line editor for the Tandy PC-1 Pocket Computer. These techniques are shown to result in complete and relatively concise descriptions. A number of useful and nontrivial properties of the interface are formally deduced from one of the specifications. In addition, a direct implementation of the interface is constructed from a formal specification. Limitations of these specification examples are discussed along with future research work. (20 ref.)

6. Delaney, J. R., Digital Simulation as an Evaluation Aid in the Development of Dynamic Color Graphics Human-Machine Interfaces, Proceedings of the 15th Annual Simulation Symposium, Tampa, FL, 17-19 March 1982, pp. 17-44.

Abstract: As part of a continuing effort in the area of system control of military communications networks, The MITRE Corporation, under the auspices of the Rome Air Development Center, has developed a testbed for the evaluation of graphics human-machine interfaces for communications network control centers. The testbed uses a MITRE-developed communications network simulator, SCAT/G, to drive the candidate network status displays. By duplicating the dynamics of the communications network and its environment, SCAT/G provides a realistic testing ground for the graphics displays.

7. Draper, S. W., and Norman, D. A., Software Engineering for User Interfaces, IEEE Trans. Software Eng. (USA), vol. SE-11 (3), 1985, pp. 252-281.

Abstract: The discipline of software engineering can be extended in a natural way to deal with the issues raised by a systematic approach to the design of human-machine interfaces. Two main points are made: the user should be treated as part of the system being designed, and projects should be organized to take account of the current (small) state of a priori knowledge about how to design interfaces. Because the principles of good user-interface design are not yet well specified (and not yet known), interfaces should be developed through an iterative process. This means that it is essential to develop tools for evaluation and debugging of the interface, much the same way as tools have been developed for the evaluation and debugging of program code. Furthermore, it is necessary to develop methods of detecting bugs in the interface and of diagnosing their cause. The tools for testing interfaces should include measures of interface performance, acceptance tests, and benchmarks. Developing useful measures is a nontrivial task, but a start can, and should, be made. (2 ref.)

8. Dzida, W., The IFIP Model for User Interfaces, Office Management, (Germany, vol. 31, spec. issue, 1983, pp. 6-8.

Abstract: The author describes a model being discussed in the european user group of the IFIP WG 6.5. The model enables addifferentiation to be made between different forms of user interface. One advantage is that it is possible to make separate evaluations of user interfaces which are not simply a discussion of their user-friendliness. The model can show the importance of the interface of the user with his working organization. It is capable of coordinating technical developments which have contributed to applications-independent user interfaces. This is illustrated by a number of examples. (5 ref.)

9. Fineberg, M. L., Quantifying Operator Preference During Human Factors Test and Evaluation, Proc. of the Human Factors Soc. Annual Meeting, 22nd, Detroit, Michigan, October 16-19, 1978, Publ. by Human Factors Soc., Santa Monica, California, 1978, pp. 24-28.

Abstract: The present paper describes the construction and pilot testing of a human factors evaluation instrument. The instrument was constructed using psychometric procedures generally applied to development of attitude scales. The goal of the instrument was the quantification of operator preference in helicopter design within four major areas of human factors consideration: handling qualities, comfort/discomfort, human engineering design, and safety. Each area had a common scale against which 10 specific parameters were evaluated. The ten items within each area were chosen using system operations' expertise, human factors standards, human factors experimental literature, and the experience of the author. The instrument was validated using a sample of 16 aviators during the conduct of an actual operational test. The results of these validation studies indicated a test-retest reliability of .85 (p < .001) and an inter-rater reliability of .93 (p < .001). Use of the instrument did provide statistically significant differences among aircraft candidates under various operational test conditions as measured within each of the four indices within the instrument. (9 ref.)

10. Hammond, N., Hinton, G., Barnard, P., Maclean, A., Long, J., and White-field, A., Evaluating the Interface of a Document Processor: A Comparison of Expert Judgement and User Observation, INTERACT '84. First IFIP Conference on 'Human-Computer Interaction', vol. 2, 1984, pp. 135-139.

Abstract: Efforts to improve the usability of systems have resulted in the development of several techniques for interface evaluation. This paper explores evaluation through (1) assessment by human factors researchers, and (2) analysis of user performance. Three pairs of researchers prepared reports on the interface of a document processor. Separately, five novice users were observed learning the system. The two evaluations generated overlapping but separable classes of information. User testing provided low-level information on procedural and conceptual difficulties, while experts provided a more integrated overview and hypotheses concerning the sources of problems. (9 ref.)

11. Hein, H.-W., The Computer as 'Intelligent' Communication Partner, Office Management, (Germany), vol. 32 (12), 1984, pp. 186-191.

Abstract: The meaning of the term 'intelligent' as applied to computer systems is described with reference to man-machine interfaces. User 'action plans' are considered as part of interactive computer use. Modern 'intelligent' interfaces can offer both active and passive help functions, and use multi-media techniques such as sound, mice, graphics tablets, and touch-screen displays. The AiD system, developed at the West German Applied Information Institute (part of the GMD-association for mathematics and data processing), is described. Base don the SYM-BOLICS 3670/3640 development systems, AiD allows the scientific evaluation of man-computer communication.

12. Johannsen, G., Rijnsdorp, E., and Sage, A. P., Human System Interface concerns in Support System Design, Automatica, vol. 19 (6), 1983, pp. 595-603.

Abstract: Current research needs and future prospects in the area of support to man-machine system analysis, design, and evaluation are described. Prospects for enhanced support to the human operator, in problem solving cognitive tasks that involve planning and design as well as physiological tasks that involve controlling, through use of knowledge based systems and decision support systems, are discussed.

13. Kidd, A. L., and Cooper, M. B., Man-Machine Interface Issues in the Construction and Use of an Expert System, International Journal of Man-Machine Studies, vol. 22 (1), 1985, pp. 91-102.

Abstract: Three issues -- knowledge acquisition, knowledge representation, and the communications interface -- are used as a basis for evaluating a prospector-type expert system shell. The application domain used as an example is a small system for fault finding on radio equipment. Long-term implications for the design of good human-machine interfaces for future expert systems are discussed, and shorter-term guidelines for knowledge engineers ar offered. (25 ref.)

14. Landis, D., and Slivka, R. M., Displays for Decision Making, <u>International Journal of Production Research</u>, vol. 10 (3), 1972, pp. 215-229.

Abstract: Summarizes 6 studies on human factors evaluation of displays. The dependent variable in all studies was decision adequacy rather than acquisition. College age male Ss plays games which required them to assimilate and manipulate visually displayed information. These games varied in fact density, compression, color relevancy, size, reinforcement, perceptual clutter, and noninformative irrelevancy. Several of the relationships previously found using acquisition variables are either modified or reversed. A program of research expanding on these studies is described.

15. Lochovsky, F. H., and Tsichritzis, D. C., On Evaluating Interactive Query Languages, <u>Inf. Sciences (USA)</u>, vol. 29 (2-3), 1983, pp. 93-113.

Abstract: The authors propose some user interaction criteria for describing and evaluating interactive query languages. They divide the querying process into three parts: request, reply, and dynamics. For all three parts, certain desirable characteristics are identified that describe the parameters of the user interaction. These interaction parameters provide a framework within which different interactive query languages can be compared. They then identify six different query language types: keyword, by example, natural langauge, menu, graphic, and multimedia. Each query language type is described in terms of the interaction parameters. Due to trade-offs among the desirable characteristics for the various user interaction parameters. There is a need for human factors evaluation of the parameter to decide on an appropriate choice for a given query language. The purpose of the evaluation framework presented is to help guide the design of these human factors experiments. (43 ref.)

16. Marshall, C. R., System ABC: A Case Study in the Design and Evaluation of a Human-Computer Dialog, <u>INTERACT ;84. First IFIP Conference on 'Human-Computer Interaction'</u>, vol. 1, 1984, pp. 419-423.

Abstract: Human factor specialists concerned with the human-computer interface live in two worlds. In the world of theory we are concerned with the properties of the ideal interface - one that is ready to learn and use, and results in performance that is efficient and error-free. In the world of practice we must design working systems in the presence of many constraints. This paper presents a case study in the design and evaluation of a human computer dialog in a constrained environment. It also discusses the relationship between theory and practice in interface design, with particular emphasis on the role of standards and guidelines. (7 ref.)

17. Neal, A. S., and Simons, R. M., Playback: A Method for Evaluating the Usability of Software and Its Documentation, <u>IBM Systems Journal (USA)</u>, vol. 23 (1), 1984, pp. 82-96.

Abstract: Human factors evaluations of software products and accompanying user publications must be conducted sot hat developers can be certain that the target user population can learn to use the product with a minimum of difficulty and be able to perform the intended tasks efficiently. A methodology is described for obtaining objective measures of product usability by collecting performance data on the user interface without affecting the user or the system being evaluated. The log of stored activity is later played back through the host system for analysis. (5 ref.)

18. Norman, D. A., Stages and Levels in Human-Machine Interaction, _International Journal of Man-Machine Studies_, vol. 21 (4), 1984, pp. 365-375.

Abstract: The interaction between a person and a computer system involves 4 stages of activities -- intention, selection, execution, and evaluation -- each of which may occur at different levels of specification. An analysis of these stages and levels illustrates issues in human-computer interaction, such as knowledge of the user's intentions necessary for the system to provide feedback and guidance, the use of naming and pointing to specify actions to the computer, and the use of interface aids such as menus. Problems related to the existence of numerous levels of intentions are considered in relation to potential mismatches between the level at which the user wishes to express the intentions and the level that the system requires, the possibility that the user's memory may be overloaded even by apparently simple tasks, and difficulties in the evaluation stage. (9 ref.)

19. Rabie, S., Bloedon, R., Dockendorff, D., and Cohn-Sfetcu, S., Experimental Facility for Evaluation of the User Interface in the PBX Environment, _Links for the Future Science, Systems and Services for Communications. Proceedings of the International Conference on Communications-ICC 84_, vol. 2, 1984, pp. 872-877.

Abstract: The authors demonstrate that through modular partitioning of hardware and software, through the use of off-the-shelf components, and through careful definition of the scope of the experiment, a facility for subject-based human factors evaluation can be constructed within reasonable time and cost objectives. Moreover, it is shown that the integrated methodology used, as well as the hardware and software tools developed, are readily adaptable to a wide variety of voice and data communication experiments. (5 ref.)

20. Rasmussen, J., Skills, Rules, and Knowledge; Signals, Signs, and Symbols, and Other Distinctions in Human Performance Models, _IEEE Transactions on Systems, Man, & Cybernetics_, vol. SMC-13 (3), 1983, pp. 257-266.

Abstract: The introduction of information technology based on digital computers for the design of human-machine interface systems has led to a requirement for consistent models of human performance in routine task environments and during unfamiliar task conditions. The requirements for different types of models for representing performance at the skill-, rule-, and knowledge-based levels, together with a review of the different ways in which information is perceived at these levels, in terms of signals, signs, and symbols, are discussed. Focus is on the possible ways of representing system properties that underline knowledge-based performance and that can be characterized at several levels of abstraction -- from the representation in terms of intention or purpose. The role of qualitative and quantitative models in the design and evaluation of interface systems is considered. (33 ref.)

21. Reisner, P., Boyce, R. F., and Chamberlin, D. D., Human Factors Evaluation of Two Data Base Query Languages -- Square and Sequel, _AFIPS Conference Proceedings_, Anaheim, California, May 19-22, 1975, vol. 44, pp. 447-452.

Abstract: A human factors experiment intended to evaluate the languages, and to compare them, and to determine whether the languages could be used by the intended populations is reported with data in tabular and graphical form. (4 ref.)

22. Rissland, E. L., Ingredients of Intelligence User Interfaces, <u>International Journal of Man-Machine Studies</u>, vol. 21 (4), 1984, pp. 377-388.

Abstract: Discusses general features of intelligent user interfaces, such as the source of knowledge needed by an interface to be considered intelligent, and characteristics desirable in an interface. Two examples of interfacing between a user and a system are examined: online HELP and tutoring. Some of the challenges to designers of interfaces are discussed in terms of the issue of control, adaptation and learning, and evaluation. (27 ref.)

23. Shuman, B. A., Who's User-Friendly? A Comparative Appraisal of DIALOG, ORBIT, and BRS, <u>National Online Meeting Proceedings</u>, New York, NY, 1983, pp. 491-498.

Abstract: An attempt is made to device and apply a scale of measurement whereby the comparative user-friendliness of the three major online bibliographic utilities, DIALOG, ORBIT, and BRS, are evaluated. Ranking of ten criteria, followed by recomputation using a weighted scale, reveals ORBIT to be somewhat the friendliest of the three, although all studied may be said to have a long way to go before any of them will afford a comfortable interaction with the new user. (1 ref.)

24. Stevens, G. C., User-Friendly Computer Systems? A Critical Examination of the Concept, <u>Behaviour & Information Technology</u>, vol. 2 (1), 1983, pp. 3-16.

Abstract: Argues that the term "user friendly" is not helpful to system designers. This theory is examined with regard to the hardware interface, the software interface, patterns of usage, and purposes of the system. User motivation and the provision of assistance for motivated uses are discussed. (31 ref.)

25. Tullis, T. S., A Computer-Based Tool for Evaluating Alphanumeric Displays, <u>INTERACT '84. First IFIP Conference on 'Human-Computer Interaction'</u>, vol. 2, 1984, pp. 123-127.

Abstract: A computer program has been developed to measure six characteristics of alphanumeric displays: (1) the overall density of characters on the display; (2) the local density of other characters near each character; (3) the number of distinct groups of characters; (4) the average visual angle subtended by those groups; (5) the number of distinct labels or data items; and (6) the average uncertainty of the positions of the items on the display. A study of 520 crt displays which varied on these measures was conducted. Multiple regressions indicated that search times to locate items on the displays could be fitted using these display measures ($R = .71$), as could subjective ratings of ease of use ($R - .90$). (14 ref.)

26. Williges, R. C., Metrics for Evaluation of Human-Computer Interaction in a Personnel Records Task, <u>Proceedings of the International Conference</u>

on Cybernetics and Society, Boston, MA, USA, 1980, pp. 379-384.

Abstract: Meaningful human factors applications to the design of human/computer tasks require a quantitative data base that describes operator behavior as a function of various independent variables. Three classes of metrics including operator satisfaction ratings, work sampling procedures, and embedded performance measurement are described. Polynomial regression procedure were used to generate functional relationships between each of these metrics and four independent variables representing timing attributes of an interactive computer system including system delay, display rate, keyboard echo rate, and rollover buffer length of the keyboard. Each class of metrics showed different functional relationships among the four system variables, and it was concluded that a composite of all three classes of measures is required to provide an adequate description of factors affecting the human-computer interface. (9 ref.)

27. Williges, R. C., and Williges, B. H., Modeling the Human Operator in Computer-Based Data Entry, Human Factors, vol. 24 (3), 1982, pp. 285-299.

Abstract: Three classes of metrics (operator satisfaction ratings, work-sampling procedures, and embedded performance measurement) are described as important measures in evaluating a human-computer interface used to enter and update personnel records. Polynomial regression procedures were used to generate functional relationships between each of these metrics and four independent variables representing system delay, display rate, keyboard echo rate, and keyboard buffer length. Each of the 22 separate dependent variables showed different functional relationships among the four system variables, but overall system delay and keyboard echo rate were the major determinants of operator behavior. Additionally, the three classes of metrics were combined into three underlying interface dimensions relating to operator production, waiting, and planning activities. (14 ref.)

28. Yoder, E., McCracken, D., and Akscyn, R. I., Instrumenting a Human-Computer Interface for Development and Evaluation, INTERACT '84. First IFIP Conference on 'Human-Computer Interaction', vol. 2, 1984, pp. 390-414.

Abstract: The ZOG Human-Computer interface has been instrumented to collect data about the system's performance and the users' behavior. The authors explain which data are collected and how they are recorded. They then suggest that analyzing the instrumentation data is akin to archaeology, because one must infer behavior patterns from low-level data 'artifacts'. Finally, they provide some guidelines for instrumentation design. (6 ref.)

SUBJECT INDEX TO SELECTED BIBLIOGRAPHY